studies in jazz

Institute of Jazz Studies
Rutgers—The State University of New Jersey
General Editors: Dan Morgenstern and Edward Berger

1. BENNY CARTER: A Life in American Music, *by Morroe Berger, Edward Berger, and James Patrick, 1982*
2. ART TATUM: A Guide to his Recorded Music, *by Arnold Laubich and Ray Spencer, 1982*
3. ERROLL GARNER: The Most Happy Piano, *by James M. Doran, 1995*
4. JAMES P. JOHNSON: A Case of Mistaken Identity, *by Scott E. Brown;* Discography 1917–1950, *by Robert Hilbert, 1986*
5. PEE WEE ERWIN: This Horn for Hire, *as told to Warren W. Vaché, Sr., 1987*
6. BENNY GOODMAN: Listen to His Legacy, *by D. Russell Connor, 1988*
7. ELLINGTONIA: The Recorded Music of Duke Ellington and His Sidemen, *by W. E. Timner, 1988; 4th ed., 1996*
8. THE GLENN MILLER ARMY AIR FORCE BAND: Sustineo Alas / I Sustain the Wings, *by Edward F. Polic;* Foreword *by George T. Simon, 1989*
9. SWING LEGACY, *by Chip Deffaa, 1989*
10. REMINISCING IN TEMPO: The Life and Times of a Jazz Hustler, *by Teddy Reig, with Edward Berger, 1990*
11. IN THE MAINSTREAM: 18 Portraits in Jazz, *by Chip Deffaa, 1992*
12. BUDDY DeFRANCO: A Biographical Portrait and Discography, *by John Kuehn and Arne Astrup, 1993*
13. PEE WEE SPEAKS: A Discography of Pee Wee Russell, *by Robert Hilbert, with David Niven, 1992*
14. SYLVESTER AHOLA: The Gloucester Gabriel, *by Dick Hill, 1993*
15. THE POLICE CARD DISCORD, *by Maxwell T. Cohen, 1993*
16. TRADITIONALISTS AND REVIVALISTS IN JAZZ, *by Chip Deffaa, 1993*
17. BASSICALLY SPEAKING: An Oral History of George Duvivier, *by Edward Berger;* Musical Analysis *by David Chevan, 1993*
18. TRAM: The Frank Trumbauer Story, *by Philip R. Evans and Larry F. Kiner, with William Trumbauer, 1994*
19. TOMMY DORSEY: On the Side, *by Robert L. Stockdale, 1995*
20. JOHN COLTRANE: A Discography and Musical Biography, *by Yasuhiro Fujioka, with Lewis Porter and Yoh-ichi Hamada, 1995*
21. RED HEAD: A Chronological Survey of "Red" Nichols and His Five Pennies, *by Stephen M. Stroff, 1996*
22. THE RED NICHOLS STORY: After Intermission 1942–1965, *by Philip R. Evans, Stanley Hester, Stephen Hester, and Linda Evans, 1997*
23. BENNY GOODMAN: Wrappin' It Up, *by D. Russell Connor, 1996*

24. CHARLIE PARKER AND THEMATIC IMPROVISATION, *by Henry Martin, 1996*
25. BACK BEATS AND RIM SHOTS: The Johnny Blowers Story, *by Warren W. Vaché, 1997*
26. DUKE ELLINGTON: A Listener's Guide, *by Eddie Lambert, 1999*
27. SERGE CHALOFF: A Musical Biography and Discography, *by Vladimir Simosko, 1998*
28. HOT JAZZ: From Harlem to Storyville, *by David Griffiths, 1998*
29. ARTIE SHAW: A Musical Biography and Discography, *by Vladimir Simosko, 1998*
30. JIMMY DORSEY: A Study in Contrasts, *by Robert L. Stockdale, 1998*
31. STRIDE!: Fats, Jimmy, Lion, Lamb and All the Other Ticklers, *by John L. Fell and Terkild Vinding, 1999*
32. GIANT STRIDES: The Legacy of Dick Wellstood, *by Edward N. Meyer, 1998*

Duke Ellington

A Listener's Guide

Eddie Lambert

Studies in Jazz Series, No. 26

The Scarecrow Press, Inc.
Lanham, Maryland, & London
and
Institute of Jazz Studies
Rutgers—The State University of New York
1999

SCARECROW PRESS, INC.

Published in the United States of America
by Scarecrow Press, Inc.
4720 Boston Way
Lanham, Maryland 20706

4 Pleydell Gardens, Folkestone
Kent CT20 2DN, England

Copyright © 1999 by Elaine Norsworthy

Raymond Carver's "Late Fragment," from *A New Path to the Waterfall*. First published in Great Britain by Collins Harvill 1989. © Tess Gallagher 1989. Reproduced by permission of the Harvill Press.

The photographers listed in the credit lines in the photo section have given us permission to reprint their photographs. We were not able to determine a source or the photographer's name for some of the photos; in these cases, no credit line is given.

All rights reserved. No part of this publication may be reproduced, stored in a retrieval system, or transmitted in any form or by any means, electronic, mechanical, photocopying, recording, or otherwise, without the prior permission of the publisher.

British Library Cataloguing in Publication Information Available

Library of Congress Cataloging-in-Publication Data

Lambert, Eddie.
    Duke Ellington : a listener's guide / Eddie Lambert.
      p.   cm. — (Studies in jazz series ; no. 26)
    Includes bibliographical references, discography, and index.
    ISBN 0-8108-3161-9 (cloth : alk. paper)
    1. Ellington, Duke, 1899–1974—Criticism and interpretation.
2. Ellington, Duke, 1899–1974—Discography. I. Title.
II. Series: Studies in jazz ; no. 26.
ML410.E44L28   1999
781.65′092—dc21   98-36431
                                                               CIP
                                                               MN

∞ ™The paper used in this publication meets the minimum requirements of American National Standard for Information Sciences—Permanence of Paper for Printed Library Materials, ANSI Z39.48-1984.Manufactured in the United States of America.

Late Fragment

Raymond Carver

And did you get what
you wanted from this life, even so?
I did.
And what did you want?
To call myself beloved, to feel myself
beloved on the earth.

Contents

Editor's Foreword	ix
Preface: About Eddie	xi
Acknowledgments	xiii
1 Duke Ellington and the Phonograph Record	1
2 The Records—1924 to April 1927	5
3 In the Beginning	13
4 The Records—October 1927 to January 1929	19
5 The Miley Era	27
6 The Records—February 1929 to April 1931	33
7 Cotton Club Days	45
8 The Records—February 1932 to July 1936	51
9 The First Full Flowering	63
10 The Records—December 1936 to February 1940	69
11 Steppin' into Swing Society	83
12 The Records—March to November 1940	87
13 1940—An Artistic Peak	93
14 The Records—November 1940 to December 1942	97
15 Departures and Arrivals	107
16 The Records—January 1943 to September 1946	111
17 New Territories and New Musicians	133
18 The Records—October 1946 to December 1950	141
19 Consolidation	157
20 The Records—January 1951 to Spring 1956	161
21 Revolution and Evolution	181
22 The Records—Summer 1956 to February 1959	189
23 The Ellington Units since 1941	205
24 The Records—March 1959 to October 1962	213
25 Triumphs and Travels	233

Contents

26 The Records—November 1962 to December 1965	239
27 World Tourist	261
28 The Records—1966 to 1967	265
29 Billy Strayhorn	277
30 The Records—1968 to 1974	287
31 The Final Years	309
32 Duke Ellington's Music in Perspective	315
Appendix 1: Bibliography	325
Appendix 2: Discography	329
Appendix 3: French RCA Integrale, Volumes 14 to 17: A Guide	345
Appendix 4: The Ellington Musicians and the Dates They Were with the Band	349
Index	353

Foreword

When the Institute of Jazz Studies cohosted the fourth annual Duke Ellington Conference in 1986, I had the great pleasure of meeting Eddie Lambert for the first time. He was that rare sort of man with whom one immediately feels at ease, but in a sense we'd known each other for a long time. We both began to write professionally about jazz in the latter half of the 1950s, and since my first main outlet was Britain's *Jazz Journal* and Eddie was a regular contributor to its rival, *Jazz Monthly,* we would of course read each other's stuff quite avidly.

We shared a great enthusiasm for the music of Ellington, a subject in which Eddie eventually came to specialize, and by the time we met, he was a noted expert on Ellingtonia and had been one of the prime movers in bringing the Ellington Conference to fruition. The Institute had recently begun its association with Scarecrow Press, and we discussed the possibility of a Lambert title for the Studies in Jazz series, as well as many other things, including cricket, and if I'd been aware of Eddie's interest in the work of the great conductor Wilhelm Furtwängler, we'd have talked about him as well (my maternal grandfather and Furtwängler had been friends).

Alas, we never had a chance to become better acquainted, and by the time that Eddie's massive manuscript came into my hands, that remarkable man was gone. No author ever had a more committed and conscientious legatee than Elaine Norsworthy, and much of the credit for the realization of this work must go to her.

It was our joint decision not to attempt any updating of the manuscript. While many additions to the Ellington canon have come into view during the past decade, and treasures continue to be unearthed, these enhancements do not significantly alter our perception of the core Ellington *oeuvre* as it came into Lambert's purview. Sjef Hoefsmit's excellent addendum to the discography will serve as a guide to this additional material.

No one interested in the music of Duke Ellington (and anyone who is not is to be pitied) will fail to benefit from Eddie Lambert's careful, detailed, and loving (but not uncritical) examination of the vast recorded output he has surveyed in these pages. While Eddie would have been delighted to know that a massive amount of Ellington music has become available for analysis in score form, this would not have altered his opinion that the recorded work is the true Ellington legacy, and the composer himself would doubtless agree.

Expert or novice, all who enter the royal realm of Ellingtonia will find Eddie Lambert an invaluable guide.

Dan Morgenstern
Director
Institute of Jazz Studies
Rutgers University, Newark

Preface: About Eddie

Listening to how a person speaks—like listening to the tone of a jazz musician—can convey a world of meaning. Eddie Lambert's voice was a very clear reflection of his characteristics and qualities—unmistakably Lancastrian, but more significantly, that of someone who was warm, enthusiastic, knowledgeable, and full of a terrific zest for the things that make life good. For Eddie, these included music, cricket, vintage trams, literature, and food, and most of all the company of the many friends that he made through each of these loves. His musical tastes embraced opera and orchestral and chamber music as well as jazz. Like many English jazz enthusiasts—and even a few American ones—he was passionate about the game of cricket. The chilly early weeks of the season would invariably find him watching every available game at Old Trafford, the home of the Lancashire County Cricket Club. And in the middle of winter, the laws governing the game's tea interval would provide him with a guaranteed source of entertainment, as well as evoking the delights to be enjoyed the following summer.

But here we are mainly concerned with Eddie's love of jazz, which started to develop in the later years of the Second World War, when he was in his early teens. He began to collect records and learn the cornet, and soon became the youngest member of the Rhythm Club in his home town of Oldham. As meetings were held in a pub, and as Eddie was well and truly underage, at first he had to be more or less smuggled into meetings. It says much for his personality, interest, and growing knowledge that several of the club's members became his life-long friends. In 1943 or 1944, he also began to compile a scrapbook of reviews, photos, and discographical information, largely culled from the *Melody Maker*. No doubt many other schoolboys were similarly engaged, but Eddie went a stage further and incorporated his own earliest efforts at writing about the music. Undaunted by being unable to attend a concert, but having heard records and broadcasts by the participating musicians, he wrote a review of what he thought it would have been like.

As Eddie himself said at the 1984 Duke Ellington conference, he soon realized that he was "rather better at playing the gramophone than the cornet." His career as a jazz writer began in earnest in 1956 when he joined Albert McCarthy's stable of contributors to *Jazz Monthly*. It was a perceptive review of Ellington's concerts at the 1958 Leeds Music Festival (which Eddie *had* attended) in that magazine, that led "Mac" to commission Eddie's first book on Duke. This was published in 1959 as the first of the *Kings of Jazz* monographs and was followed two years later by a volume on Johnny Dodds in the same series. For the next few years, Eddie ranged widely across pre-bop styles for a number of jazz magazines, until he decided to specialize in Ellingtonia.

For a period that began in 1983, and happily continues as we approach the new century, Ellingtonia has acquired an extra dimension. For a few days each year the Duke Ellington conference has provided a haven where enthusiasts from all over the world speak one language. Those who made Duke's music, who were part of his world, who document his legacy, and even the newest enthusiasts, all contribute their unique perceptions to our collective understanding and knowledge of the music. Our picture of Eddie would not be complete without acknowledging the role he played in helping this to come about. In addition to participating each year, he organized the 1985 conference in Oldham—making the event truly international—and began the preparations for its return there in 1988. That first U.K. conference is still remembered for its unique atmosphere; there seemed to be an enchantment that encouraged everyone to give and to share to their utmost. My own feeling is that this was in no small part due to Eddie's personality and to his understanding of the meaning of Duke's music. It seems entirely fitting that the gavel that has been used to open the conference each year since Eddie's death in 1987, is dedicated to his memory.

This book was largely written between 1976 and 1984. It provides a critical survey of Ellington's entire recorded output that had been issued up to that time. For Eddie this was a labor of love that had two main purposes. One was to provide an overview of Duke Ellington's musical achievement comparable to the similar critical works that are the norm for composers of music in the European idiom. Eddie's second aim, no less significant, was to give back some of the tremendous pleasure that Ellington's music had given him.

As well as being wholly characteristic of Eddie, this uniquely fitted him for the daunting task that he had set himself: to express the appreciation of Duke's unique methods and musical language he gained through a lifetime of listening and being open to Duke's music of all periods. May this book succeed in conveying both his enjoyment and understanding of that great Ellingtonian legacy—not only to all who already love it, but also to those who are about to join our ranks.

Elaine Norsworthy
Budleigh Salterton, Devon

Acknowledgments

Thanks are due to the many friends and Ellington enthusiasts and collectors from all over the world who have provided assistance and encouragement during the writing and gestation of this book:

the late Benny Aasland, Tony Adkins, Les Airey, the late Walter Allen, Leif Anderson, Dick Baaker, Michael Ballie, Ken Bamford, Franco Bellaci, Vic Bellerby, the late Gordon Bowers, Sidney Bromley, the late John Callanan, Dave Carey, Peter Carr, Dave Caughran, Ian Celnik, the late David Chertok, John Chilton, Shirley Christy, John Clement, Michael Coates, Alan Cohen, Derek Coller, Sidney Cook, Mike Cox, Bruce Crowther, Marcel Cumps, Stanley Dance, Georges Debroe, John R.T. Davies, Gordon Davies, Doug Dobell, Frank Dutton, George Ellis, the late Gordon Ewing, John Featherstone, Les and Jutta Greaves, David Griffiths, Carl Hallstrom, Bo Haufman, E.H. Hausmann, Franz Hoffman, Andrew Homzy, John Hornsby, Harry Horton, H.F Huon, the late Trevor Huyton, the late Ray Ibbotson, John Irwin, Irving Jacobs, Roy Jenkins, Norman Jenkinson, the late Max Jones, Liam Keating, Jack Kenny, Wayne Knight, Anton Kop, John Lawrence, Jim Lowe, Jack McNamara, Les Mallows, Donald Miller, Irene and the late Malcolm Mitchell, Dan Morgenstern, Tomas Moony, David Niven, June Oliver, Gerald Parker, Mike Pinfold, Lewis Porter, Liborio Pusateri, Henry Quarles, Ken Rattenbury, John Rothery, Dennis and Ann Rowlinson, Brian Rust, Frank Rutter, Rikaya Shirasu, Tony Shoppee, Johnny Simmen, Sheila Simpson, Paul Spinks, Betty Stewart, the late Klaus Stratemann, John Tarr, Willie Timner, the late Eric Townley, Jack Towers, the late Sinclair Traill, Jerry Valburn, Kath Whale, Bert Whyatt, Patricia Willard, the late Russell Woodward, and Satoshi Yuze.

Particular thanks are due to:
- John Chilton for encouragement at a time when the size of the project was beginning to daunt the author,
- Sjef Hoefsmit for so much helpful material as well as for compiling Part Four of the Discography,
- Peter Kennedy both for his careful listening to early Ellington records, and equally careful and thorough reading of the chaotic formative stages of this book,
- and Peter Whatley, volunteer proof reader extraordinaire.

Conversations with the following musicians who worked with Duke Ellington contributed greatly to the author's understanding of the music: the late William "Cat" Anderson, Alice Babs, Willie Cook, the late Jimmy Hamilton, Herb Jeffries, June Norton, Joya Sherrill, and the late Rex Stewart.

Kind permission was given by:
- Eddie Cook to quote from articles published in *Jazz Journal International*, and to reproduce in full the author's article "Duke Ellington Integrale—A Guide to Volumes 14–17."
- Tess Gallagher and Collins Harvill to reproduce "Late Fragment" from *A New Path to the Waterfall* by Raymond Carver.

Eddie Lambert, Oldham, 1984
Elaine Norsworthy, Budleigh Salterton, 1998

Chapter 1

Duke Ellington and the Phonograph Record

DUKE ELLINGTON WAS ONE OF THE GREATEST musicians of the twentieth century. He was also a popular show-business personality, and for 50 years he worked as a touring bandleader, traveling the length and breadth of the United States as well as visiting most other countries of the world. For all but the first three or four of these years he was internationally famous as both bandleader and songwriter. Yet Duke Ellington never enjoyed the life of leisured affluence that such a position usually brings. This was not because of racial prejudice, although Ellington came up against plenty of that in his time; nor was it because of an inability to handle money, for financially he was very astute. Like most highly creative individuals, Ellington was a driven man, quite literally obsessed with his art. One of his favorite sayings was that he worked in music 52 weeks a year. In answer to inquiries about the money he made from his popular songs he would disclaim any detailed knowledge—"I have no monetary interest," he would say, "I live entirely in the realm of art." Such statements were usually thought to be merely clever ways of putting off overly inquisitive interviewers. But in fact Ellington was speaking the truth. He never took a holiday from music, never showed the slightest sign of wishing to enjoy the fruits of his prodigious labors as most other men would. Behind the mask of the smiling, debonair bandleader was a man whose devotion to the art of music was total and uncompromising.

Duke Ellington's reputation as a successful show-business personality often gave those who take people at face value an impression of a rather shallow individual, a glib and superficial man. His attitude often seemed to encourage such a view; for example, throughout his life he was very conscious of his position as a representative of the African American and a serious advocate of black advance, yet he handled racial questions for the most part with a light touch and wit.

Many people found it difficult to square Ellington's keen interest in his band's finances with his repeated assertion that he was concerned only with artistic ends. He was very much involved with making money and very reluctant to spend it unnecessarily. When musicians approached him about a salary increase, he would invent the most varied and outrageous stratagems to evade the issue.

One of Ellington's recurring conversational themes was to compare his position with that of the academic composer who might have to wait years to hear his work performed, while he, Ellington, could hear a new composition within hours of its conception. This, he said, was the reason he needed his band and was willing to pay the price of living the exhausting life of a touring bandleader. And this was the motive behind his attitude to finance. People often asked why Ellington did not retire to live on his royalties and compose to his heart's content. One reason was that he enjoyed the touring life. This was probably insufficiently understood when, in the late 1950s, it was persistently rumored that Duke was about to disband. He would, so the story went, keep a small number of key musicians on retainer and augment them with irregulars for recording sessions, concerts, and the occasional tour. Prompt performances of new compositions would hardly have been a problem in this situation, as he would have had no trouble in finding musicians keen to play his works. The reason Ellington never took such a course was that he did not write simply for a band of skilled and sympathetic musicians, but for a specific group of outstanding jazzmen which he had welded into a unified and flexible ensemble.

To approach Ellington's music as if it were played by a conventional big band is to invite misunderstanding. The Duke Ellington Orchestra was something different and unique. It was created in the 1920s when its leader was also forging his highly individual composing methods, and its development and refinement runs parallel with that of the compositional techniques. Musicians of the caliber Ellington required for his band commanded high salaries, and this is what made the orchestra so expensive an undertaking. The money Ellington worked so hard to earn and managed so carefully was an absolute essential, a precondition of his continuing to function as an artist. He achieved success in show business not because he sought acclaim and riches but because he needed to keep his band in existence.

In his biography of Ellington, Derek Jewell tells of a time when the band's finances were in a particularly bad way. An old friend of Ellington's, Herb Hendler, a man well versed in band management, was called in to look things over with a view to becoming band manager. Hendler soon found that the major item that was keeping the band in the red was the huge payroll. To meet it, Ellington was using private funds, including income from royalties on his songs. Hendler's advice was to cut the payroll in half by the simple device of hiring less expensive musicians. Duke would have none of it. He told Hendler that the band must satisfy *his* standards and that he had to have his top-class sidemen, no matter what the cost. And that was the last Hendler heard about becoming Duke's manager—rather, one suspects, to his relief.

The real evidence of Ellington's priorities is to be found in the vast quantity of music which he created over the years. No man could have gotten through the amount of work this involved without a devotion far beyond that normally exhibited by jazz musicians and show-business personalities. The bulk of the prodigious output does not lie in sheet music, the medium every previous major composer had used to transmit his contribution to posterity. There is, indeed, a considerable quantity of published Ellington sheet music, mostly in the form of song copies, but this tells us little of its creator's genius, nor does it reflect the size or extent of his output. In Ellington's case we must turn to the phonograph record, for there his work can be found in all its rich profusion.

Duke Ellington was born at a good time to take advantage of the recording industry. His career started as electrical recording was coming into general use and extended into the era of stereophonic sound. It should be realized that, but for the phonograph, the music of jazzmen such as Louis Armstrong and Charlie Parker would have died with them, posterity knowing no more of the true quality and flavor of their work than it knows of those of a seventeenth-century keyboard virtuoso or an eighteenth-century singer. And just as the phonograph provides the only authentic record of the jazz soloist's art, it also offers the only truly valid record of the works of jazz composers like Jelly Roll Morton and Duke Ellington. A written score alone would give a totally inadequate impression.

From a very early point in his career, Ellington was aware of the importance of the phonograph, and recording sessions were always treated as a very serious aspect of the band's work. Much of Ellington's early reputation was based on his recorded output, and when he first visited Britain and continental Europe in the 1930s he found that his work was already well known through this medium. In the later part of his career, he frequently recorded the band at his own expense, thus ensuring the survival of compositions and interpretations that did not interest record companies at the time.

From the 1960s onward, there has been a continuous flow of Ellington LPs containing recordings that were not intended for public issue—film soundtracks, private recordings of concerts and dances, private off-the-air recordings, and official transcriptions made for radio use, these last including both studio and location recordings. How much of this kind of material remains unissued awaits full documentation and indeed even the facts regarding unissued recordings from the major companies are still not fully established. When all the information about the many different kinds of Ellington recordings is known and published, the resultant discography will be the definitive catalog of his work, equivalent to the listing of a composer's published works that fulfills this function in academic music.

A discography, however, gives only the bare bones of the matter and is meaningless to a person not conversant with the music. A more detailed guide is needed, and this is the purpose of the present volume, within the limitations of the Ellington recordings that have been issued on disc to date. It is intended to be useful to the person who is not familiar with Duke Ellington's music, while also being sufficiently critical a commentary to interest the jazz specialist. The journey through Ellington's recorded music from 1924 to 1974 is a long one, albeit a delightful and refreshing one. It is perhaps the greatest listening experience jazz music has to offer. Before we embark on this journey a few further comments on the nature of this highly unusual artist are appropriate.

* * *

Duke Ellington was a musician, wit, raconteur, lyric writer, record producer, poet, creator of musical shows, author, and philosopher. He played some of his roles in a deliberately oblique, elusive manner. He was not a politician in the obvious sense, for all that he once recited the lyrics of his *King Fit The Battle Of Alabam'* at one of the Newport Jazz Festivals. Yet over the years his music said a lot about the nature, the condition, and the history of the African American community with a conscious intent to affect the status of that community in American society. Such statements were, like all Ellington's important activities, centered around his basic function as a creative artist. Logically enough he believed that his contribution could best be made in the medium in which he had the greatest authority.

Ellington's contribution to music was fourfold—as composer, bandleader, pianist, and arranger. This is not to suggest that he was some sort of amalgam of the talents of, say, Count Basie, Earl Hines, and Sy Oliver. Only in the most superficial sense is this true, for in Ellington the four functions are perfectly blended. And because he was so strong an individualist, it would be to court misunderstanding to approach Ellington as a typical performer in any one of these fields. He was a strikingly original man who did things his own way, learning from experience and remaining very wary of the academic path.

In Ellington's work we find a singleness of purpose that fuses the different aspects of his music into a perfectly unified whole. The various aspects of Ellington's musical personality—the composer, bandleader, pianist, and arranger—were integrated at a very deep level. This results in works in which various aspects, for example the orchestration, are integral factors in the conception and not the result of building a melodic/harmonic invention into an orchestral score by the later application of the arranger's art.

Listeners are often confused by the many-sidedness of

Duke Ellington's music. Many of them appreciate and enjoy one aspect of his art, or one period of his recordings, while finding others puzzling and enigmatic. Some people enjoy only early Ellington; others like his later works exclusively. Some admire him as a composer but dislike the results of his unorthodox bandleading methods. Others love the band and its array of fine jazz soloists but find the scores overeccentric or overelaborate. The devotees of the conventional big band find the easygoing discipline of the Ellington band a puzzle. And the man who should act as guide, the jazz critic, often finds himself confronted with challenges totally different from those usually presented by jazz music. For example, such writers rarely have to deal with extended compositions. So, confronted with Duke's longer works, the jazz critic's reaction has often been to pay lip service to Ellington's genius and pass on. Unused to considering orchestration other than the black-and-white kind found in conventional big band jazz, he is unable to perceive what is so brilliant and unique about Ellington's. Such critics often regard a soloist who can put together a handful of new phrases and permutate them for 20 years as a creative genius, which leaves them without a vocabulary with which to deal effectively with Ellington's prodigious creativity. So it is that for many listeners Duke Ellington's music remains a mysterious, unexplored terrain with just a few treasured landmarks and no certain guidebooks. Yet Ellington's art is perfectly coherent and understandable to those who are prepared to learn how to deal with it on its own terms.

Although much of Ellington's music is unconventional, he would frequently work in the fashionable forms of the day. On his recordings there is much conventional big band playing of outstanding quality, and literally hundreds of great jazz solos. Yet in taking delight in these qualities the listener should not blind himself to the fact that to look upon Ellington from a conventional point of view will cause more problems than it solves. Ellington was a creative figure of a kind not otherwise found in jazz. Even Louis Armstrong made his vital contributions in his early years and in a sense spent the rest of his life refining them. A musician like Coleman Hawkins, renowned for his ability to keep up with the rapid changes in jazz development, simply modified the style he had fashioned in the twenties and thirties to the techniques of forties and fifties jazz. Ellington, by contrast, adapted new techniques to *his* purposes rather than adjust his music to fashion. He remained a commanding creative figure to the last, a man whose music was always apart from the conventions of his time, one who refused to allow his art to settle into any fixed pattern.

With Ellington, the music of any given decade is different from that of its predecessor; yet there is never a break in the music's evolution, never a deliberate, conscious move into a new style. There are times when extensive changes of personnel within the band cause the interpretation of the music to alter sharply, yet the ultimate unity of the Ellington style remains undisturbed. Ellington's music continued to evolve from its own roots and traditions, being at once the most daring and creative of all jazz music and the most deeply traditional.

A comparison with two of the great innovators among jazz soloists is instructive. Louis Armstrong spent his formative years in New Orleans, Charlie "Bird" Parker his in Kansas City, each at a time when—indisputably in Louis's case and without much doubt in Bird's—these cities were the vital centers of jazz development. What was to prove to be of the greatest importance in the development of African American music was germinating—was indeed manifest—in New Orleans and in Kansas City when Louis and Bird were young men. Ellington was from Washington, D.C., a pretty stagnant backwater of jazz compared with Armstrong's and Parker's native cities. In other words, Duke did not come from a jazz environment. For this and a variety of other reasons he was a slow starter, or, to put the matter the other way round, a late developer. His very earliest recordings give hardly any indication of what is to follow in terms of either quality or musical style. His first truly distinctive works show a reliance on one individual soloist (the trumpet player Bubber Miley) to a degree not found in the music of Ellington's maturity. But once he had established his highly individual techniques he created his own traditions. The Ellington bandsmen—a brilliant group of creative jazz musicians in their own right—were given a stylistic platform as valid as that forged by environment in New Orleans or Kansas City.

It is necessary to understand Ellington's background and his attitude towards the jazz ensemble in order to understand the nature of his contributions as composer, bandleader, pianist, and arranger. These facets will emerge clearly as we examine the records year by year. But perhaps we should say a word here about the kind of composer Ellington was. He was not an academic either by training or by inclination. Persons hearing of Duke's reputation and expecting to find a musician exhibiting the qualities of a composer in the European tradition are invariably disappointed. Indeed, by the standards of that tradition Ellington was a nonstarter. But many of the considerations that would concern a European academic composer hardly affected Ellington at all. He was a black American musician and at all times remained true to his native tradition. His medium was and remained the jazz ensemble; he found the blues tradition a constant source of inspiration and renewal; even his music for symphony orchestra was done from a jazz perspective.

To understand Ellington's music it is helpful to look upon his compositions—even the extended concert works—as developments of the first tentative steps heard on such early recordings as *East St. Louis Toodle-oo* and *Black And Tan Fantasy*. This approach at once brings us up against the kind of problems that confront and often confound an attempt to understand Ellington's music. For although *East St. Louis Toodle-oo* and *Black And Tan Fantasy* exhibit many Ellingtonian compositional qualities, they are at the same time vehicles for the solo work of Bubber Miley, Tricky Sam Nanton, and other musicians. They can be regarded from two points of view—as interesting but crude compositions, early steps along Ellington's journey toward the creation of a viable kind of jazz composition, or as outstanding jazz records of their period with first-class solos and with scores that are strikingly original. The difficulty is that it is desirable to take both aspects into consideration to truly hear and understand the music. If we do so we will find also that Miley's solo choruses, with their great structural strength, are so vital a part of the music's overall unity and balance that without them Ellington's compositions could not have made their effect. The OKeh recording of *Black And Tan Fantasy*, made during one of Miley's temporary absences and with Jabbo Smith substituting, is a good illustration of this. For while the two OKeh takes are fine jazz music, they fail to achieve the compositional effect of the Brunswick and Victor recordings with Miley.

East St. Louis Toodle-oo and *Black And Tan Fantasy* date from 1927. By 1930 Ellington had developed his mastery sufficiently to create works that, from a compositional point of view, speak with a much more unified voice, for example *Old Man Blues* and *Mood Indigo*. These represent an important stage in the process that led to such masterpieces of the thirties as *Lazy Rhapsody*, *Blue Tune*, *Jive Stomp*, and *Saddest Tale*. Such works are true jazz *compositions,* even though academically they possess hardly any more virtues than *East St. Louis Toodle-oo* or *Black And Tan Fantasy*. The forging of Ellington's compositional technique—a technique wholly of the jazz tradition—can be heard clearly on such records. And the dual quality of the music is retained—each recording has valid jazz solos by the sidemen as well as being a manifestation of the art of Ellington the composer. This was a pattern which remained dominant throughout Ellington's long recording career.

* * *

The chapters in this book follow a chronological sequence, those dealing with Ellington's recorded output covering identifiable stages in that output so far as possible. Each such chapter includes a list of outstanding records, a short list of essential Ellingtonia for the period under review. These chapters alternate with more general ones, for example, covering the environment of Ellington and his band and their contemporaries. Notes on important Ellington sidemen will also be found here. In Appendix 2, a comprehensive guide to Ellington's recorded output on LP will be found. A list of CDs and LPs issued since Eddie Lambert's last revision of this text is also provided here. Readers requiring a full discography of Duke Ellington are referred to the discographical section of the bibliography in Appendix 1. The other appendixes contain a guide to the particularly confusing existence of two versions of certain French RCA Ellington LPs; and a list of Ellington musicians and their dates in the band.

Chapter 2

The Records—1924 to April 1927

IN THE LAST DECADE OF HIS LIFE, Duke Ellington would occasionally indulge himself and his audiences in brief versions of what he claimed were his first two compositions—*Soda Fountain Rag* and *What Are You Going To Do When The Bed Breaks Down?* These were written, Duke told us, during his early youth in Washington, D.C., and his performances in later years were usually incomplete, concluding with a throwaway remark to the effect that he now found them too difficult to play. Apart from unofficial concert recordings from the sixties and seventies neither piece was ever recorded by Ellington.

It is impossible to establish with certainty which is, in fact, the earliest recorded example of Duke Ellington's music. Quite possibly it is a piano roll he cut of his composition *Jig Walk,* but the uncertainties in dating player-piano rolls make it impossible to know whether or not this predates the first Ellington disc recordings. Current research suggests that it was done in 1926, two years after the first records. *Jig Walk* does, however, make a convenient starting point for a discussion of Ellington's early music since it is a typical piece of ragtime-derived stride piano, influenced by James P. Johnson's highly popular *Charleston*. It is also, incidentally, very much in the style of *Soda Fountain Rag*, if Ellington's latter-day performances of that first composition are to be taken as authentic.

The piano roll of *Jig Walk* contains three choruses, with a sixteen-bar verse inserted between the first and second of these. It is played in the stride fashion throughout; there are no variations and the thematic material is devoid of any individual character. *Jig Walk* is in fact a period piece which could have been the work of any one of the scores of competent popular musicians of the day. It certainly does not announce itself as an early work by one of the great artists of the twentieth century. The main distinction of this particular piano roll is that it was designed for a player piano with a percussion attachment, and it has been recorded and transcribed to disc with such a device present and working. The percussion bangs and crashes away for the last eight bars of each of the three choruses in a way which is quite unparalleled by even the worst of recorded jazz drummers. This composition was used as part of Ellington's music for a show called *Chocolate Kiddies*, which dates from 1924. There is a recording of it by a group called the OKeh Syncopators from February 1926, which some authorities believe has Duke himself on piano, but it is a piece which Ellington never revived, the number announced as *Jig Walk* during a Cotton Club broadcast of 1938 being a different composition.

* * *

Duke Ellington's first disc recordings date from November 1924, with seven titles recorded for a couple of small labels, Blu-Disc and Up-To-Date. Only one title was recorded for Up-To-Date, a version of *How Come You Do Me Like You Do?* by singer Florence Bristol accompanied by Otto Hardwick (alto sax) and Duke Ellington (piano). This has long been one of the rarest of all Ellington recordings, but it was reissued in a limited edition on Jerry Valburn's revived Blu-Disc label in 1980. This reveals that the music is of historical interest only. The singing is in pure vaudeville style by a lady whose abilities are strictly limited; Ellington backs the vocal and the alto sax solo in competent but anonymous fashion.

Four of the six titles recorded for the original Blu-Disc company are also vocal accompaniments, but the other two are by the embryonic Duke Ellington Orchestra, a six-piece group known as The Washingtonians, of which Ellington was leader and musical director. Earlier in 1924 Duke had taken over leadership of this band from banjoist Elmer Snowden, and the Blu-Disc sides are by what appears to have been the regular personnel of the time:

Trumpet: Bubber Miley.

Trombone: Charlie Irvis.

Reeds: Otto Hardwick (alto and baritone saxes).

Rhythm: Duke Ellington (piano); George Francis (banjo); Sonny Greer (drums).

In differing ways and to differing degrees, four of Ellington's five companions here were important figures in the early evolution of his music. Indeed, two of them—Hardwick and Greer—were to continue as Ellington sidemen for over a quarter of a century, their service only seriously broken when Hardwick was absent from 1928 to 1932.

The two brass men on this 1924 record date did not stay so long, but they each had an important impact on Ellington's musical thinking, more than any other musicians at this time. As late as 1962, Ellington could recall with pleasure the sound Charlie Irvis used to obtain with his mute, "a great big fat sound at the bottom of the trombone . . . , masculine, full of tremendous authority." Of all the musicians who worked with Ellington in the twenties, however, it was trumpeter Bubber Miley who had the strongest and most crucial effect on his musical development. Miley had taken the wa-wa plunger mute style developed by some of the New Orleans cornet players, notably King Oliver and Tommy Ladnier, and altered and refined the technique to suit his own purposes. He was a fiery, passionate improviser with an unusual melodic conception.

A word is perhaps needed here on the subject of growl and wa-wa brass playing, as these became important techniques within the Ellington Orchestra. It is no exaggeration to say that to many listeners the sound of growling, wa-wa brass is what characterizes Ellington's music most of all. The growl itself is produced by the trumpeter or trombonist growling or humming in his throat at the same time that he produces a note on the instrument with his lips. The use of the growl without a mute is rare, although some New Orleans trumpeters use the technique; it was deployed with some subtlety by Henry "Red" Allen, especially in the later part of his career. In the wa-wa style it is customary to use a rubber plunger (for the trumpet, the kind of plunger used to clear domestic waste pipes; for the trombone a slightly larger one), waving it in front of the bell of the instrument to produce a sound which is reminiscent of the human voice pronouncing the sound "wa wa." Many wa-wa trumpet specialists also use a straight mute in the bell of the instrument. The Ellington plunger trombonists followed Tricky Sam Nanton's practice of using a straight *trumpet* mute in the trombone. The combined use of growl and wa-wa techniques is standard practice, although some players, for example Ray Nance, use the growl very sparingly. A great variety of sounds can be obtained by the careful placing of the rubber plunger and by altering its shape by squeezing, Tricky Sam Nanton being the master of this particular art. It is hardly surprising that the choking of the instrument throws it out of tune, and brass players have varied in their use of tuning slides and strong lips to counteract this effect.

The acknowledged master of plunger mute/growl techniques was trombonist Joe Nanton, known as Tricky Sam, a musician whose melodic concept suited this style perfectly. The general public has always looked upon these techniques as clever novelty effects, and quite serious performances by

Miley, Cootie Williams, Nanton and their successors were often greeted with laughter. Even jazz enthusiasts seem to have reservations about the growl and the wa-wa, and it is not often that Nanton has received his due from the critics. But his fellow musicians, notably the trombonists among them, look upon his achievement with reverence and awe.

According to the reminiscences of Ellington and his early associates, the music of The Washingtonians was of considerable originality, with Duke's arrangements giving the band a harmonic richness and a range of tone colors which belied its modest instrumentation. It is therefore surprising to find that the Blu-Disc recordings, and the slightly later ones by enlarged editions of the band for other labels, contain music which is unoriginal and of modest merit. Neither *Choo Choo* nor *Rainy Nights*, the two instrumental titles recorded for Blu-Disc, is anything but a run-of-the-mill period piece, although both have Ellington's name as co-composer. As to the arrangements, these are virtually nonexistent, providing no more than a framework for ensembles which are "collective improvisations" in a manner based loosely on the style of the New Orleans bands. Apart from Miley's lead in the last eight bars of *Rainy Nights*, these ensembles are undistinguished.

Miley was clearly the outstanding musician in the band, contributing muted solos to both titles which foreshadow the melodic distinction of his later work; his solo on *Rainy Nights* is quite beautiful, despite the rather trite cliché he uses to conclude each of the first two eight-bar sections. This solo also has an expressive quality which no other musician present remotely approaches throughout either performance; it runs directly into the final eight-bar ensemble which Miley leads with plunger mute in the King Oliver fashion. The similarity to Oliver's lead playing on his Creole Jazz Band's Paramount recording of *Mabel's Dream* is striking, and Miley's grasp of the style is clearly much firmer than that of the majority of Oliver disciples.

The other soloists of the two titles are Charlie Irvis, who plays open trombone with some skill and a touch of melodic grace, and Otto Hardwick. Hardwick struck up a close relationship with Sidney Bechet during the latter's brief stay with The Washingtonians, and Bechet's influence on his playing is obvious. For all that, Hardwick's solos and lead alto playing in the opening chorus and verse of *Rainy Nights* have a rather commonplace sound.

Ellington's four other recordings for Blu-Disc in November 1924 are accompaniments to singers Alberta Prime, Jo Trent and Sonny Greer (who would have been well advised to stick to the drums). Ellington's first recorded piano solo occurs during a spoken exchange in the course of a vocal duet by Prime and Greer entitled *Parlor Social De Luxe*. It is a straightforward stride chorus of no great distinction. The session mate to *Parlor Social De Luxe* is a song called *It's Gonna Be A Cold, Cold Winter* and this is of interest only because of Ellington's piano accompaniment. Two vocal accompaniments were recorded on the same date as *Choo Choo* and *Rainy Nights*—*Deacon Jazz* (vocal by Jo Trent) and *Oh!* *How I Love My Darling* (vocal, quite excruciating, by Sonny Greer). Hardwick and George Francis were present, the former contributing sound but rather dated solos on alto and baritone saxes. But on both titles Duke has piano solos which, while lacking any great individuality, are well constructed and executed with a considerable mastery of the stride style.

Another Ellington piano solo can be heard on a curious Gennett test pressing, which was unearthed in the seventies and issued in 1980. This was recorded in June 1925 by The Hotsy Totsy Boys, who turn out to be a duo of Irving Mills, the white impresario who was soon to play an important role in the development of Ellington's career, and Duke himself. Mills plays kazoo and sings a totally forgettable song called *Everything Is Hotsy Totsy Now* with accompaniment from Duke, who also contributes a brief solo.

The next recordings by a band under Ellington's direction were made for the Pathé company in September 1925 and March 1926, two titles being cut at each session. Miley was missing from both dates and on the first his place is taken by Pike Davis. Prince Robinson (clarinet and tenor sax) joined Hardwick to make a two-piece reed section, and by this time the banjoist was Fred Guy. Bass Edwards is generally thought to be the tuba player (although Bob Ysaguirre told Juan Carlos Lopez that he played tuba on an Ellington date which, from his description, sounds like this one). There was no drummer on this session, Greer being absent for some reason. The first title, *I'm Gonna Hang Around My Sugar*, opens (after an ensemble introduction) with a lively Pike Davis solo, but this has little to offer beyond its initial driving impetus and soon becomes dissipated in a welter of jerky period clichés. Irvis has a muted solo and Ellington contributes half a chorus of stride piano, but the number is poor and the main point of interest is Irvis's muted trombone. The arrangement is sketchy and undistinguished with a chaotic "collective improvisation" in the final chorus. *Trombone Blues* is a more promising title, but the number is even poorer than *I'm Gonna Hang Around My Sugar*, being a midtempo novelty piece cast in the twelve-bar format. Irvis is heard playing muted trombone again, and at some length this time, but one can form little or no idea of his jazz ability in such a "novelty" context. Again the last chorus is improvised by the band, leading in this instance to a quite dreadful coda.

The March 1926 session has Harry Cooper and Leroy Rutledge on trumpets (of the three trumpeters on these sessions only Cooper is known to have played regularly with The Washingtonians); Don Redman (at this time a regular member of Fletcher Henderson's band) replacing Robinson; and Greer back on drums to bring the rhythm section up to four pieces. *Georgia Grind* is another twelve-bar blues, also taken at medium tempo and treated in novelty fashion. None of the soloists—Cooper, Redman on clarinet, Hardwick on baritone, or Ellington—has much to offer, and the arrangement is thoroughly conventional. Its session mate, *Parlor Social Stomp*, is an early Ellington composition. The arrangement has the sound of a Harlem stride piano piece, but neither the scoring, nor the soloists, nor the band's performance achieves more than a mediocre effect. The number ends with an untidily played scored ensemble in place of the collective improvisations used on the previous recordings.

When the band returned to the studios on April 1, 1926, they had become Duke Ellington and his Washingtonians. This session was the first of two for the Gennett label, each of which produced two titles. With Miley absent again, the band was that of the preceding session, augmented by trombonist Jimmy Harrison, and by Prince Robinson and George Thomas, both doubling clarinet and tenor sax. Thus say the discographers, but aurally the band sounds smaller, and it seems probable that Harrison and Thomas were used solely as vocalists. *"Wanna Go Back Again" Blues* (with a vocal by Thomas) includes the first instance on record of imaginative scoring by Ellington, albeit briefly and in a novelty mold. After the band introduction, Hardwick's playing of the theme on baritone is skillfully offset by two clarinets and the trumpets. This is in considerable contrast to the conventional saxes-against-brass scoring in the eight-bar verse and in the bridge of Irvis's chorus. *If You Can't Hold The Man You Love* (vocal by Jimmy Harrison) has a passage for plunger-muted trumpets which is a distant precursor of what Ellington called his "pep section" in later years. The style, however, looks back to the King Oliver manner and is reminiscent of Oliver's two-cornet breaks with Louis Armstrong on the Creole Jazz Band recordings of three years earlier. Irvis has a terse eight bars but otherwise the performance is dull, despite an attempt to ginger up the last chorus by having Robinson play a piping clarinet improvisation against a written ensemble. This foreshadows a device used regularly and successfully in later years, but in this instance it fails to counteract the prevailing mediocrity.

The second two Gennett titles, done in June 1926, have Bubber Miley and Charlie Johnson on trumpets and Charlie Irvis's replacement, Joe Nanton, on trombone. The reeds are Robinson and Hardwick and the usual four-piece rhythm section is present, with another brass bass player, probably Mack Shaw, replacing Edwards. Once more the material is pretty dreadful, the first tune being the novelty number *Animal Crackers*, scored in an appropriate manner with the group sounding almost like a military band on the verse. The only point of jazz interest is Miley's solo, but this, like all the playing from this date, suffers from such unsteadiness of tempo that one marvels that the master was ever passed for release. The tempo drags during the ensembles and rushes during the solos, and the effect of Miley's driving phrasing is to throw the rhythm section totally out of gear, with hilarious results. Steadiness of tempo is not the strong suit of any of these early Ellington records, but on this session complete disaster is averted only by the narrowest of margins. The second title, *Li'l Farina*, introduces another characteristic of later Ellingtonia when, after twelve introductory bars of pure novelty music, Nanton's muted trombone, hot and swinging, states the theme and manages to make it sound acceptable. Only when the band plays this melody later do we realize how tawdry it really is. Apart from Nanton, only Miley's solo is of note, although Hardwick has a typical baritone solo and the final chorus is again adorned by a piping clarinet part from Robinson.

The records discussed so far are from what we might call a "prehistoric" period of Ellington's music, one which closes with a date in October 1926, again for Gennett, in which the "Ellington Twins" (Ellington and Hardwick) accompany a very ordinary singer of the period (Alberta Jones) in two very ordinary "blues" songs. Duke does not solo and the only interest is in the long, rather tedious examples they offer of Hardwick's early alto style.

* * *

Taken as a whole, the recordings which Duke Ellington made between 1924 and October 1926 offer no clue to the blossoming of his talents as composer-bandleader-arranger which was to manifest itself during the next two years. Still less do they suggest the development of these talents which was to make him, within four short years of the recording of *Animal Crackers*, a musician of international renown. The touch of imaginative scoring on *"Wanna Go Back Again" Blues* and the trumpet passage on *If You Can't Hold The Man You Love* hint at the future of Ellington's music, but such devices can be found on scores of contemporary records by bands whose leaders did not blossom into musical geniuses. In themselves these moments are of little consequence, although they may indeed be the seeds of what is to come, tentative touches by Ellington from a vein which was soon to erupt in volcanic fashion. But only hindsight suggests such an interpretation.

Ellington's principal contributions to these records are a few choruses of rather average stride piano. The band itself fails to swing consistently, and as an ensemble it displays few jazz characteristics. Only the solos by Miley, Irvis, and Nanton are of real musical interest; and even here Irvis is far from outstanding. Only Ellington's later recollections of his contribution to the band give these modest trombone solos the spice of historical interest. Nanton's solo on *Li'l Farina* is notable because it is the first of the hundreds he recorded in his career with the band—surely a good solo, but a long, long way from his best.

Which leaves us with Bubber Miley. If these "prehistoric" Ellington records have one clear lesson it is that Miley was far and away the outstanding soloist in the band at this period. The Washingtonians may have played superior numbers and more characteristic arrangements outside the studios, but those they recorded were a pretty shabby lot, scored in a commonplace fashion. On them we hear all the band's soloists and of these Miley, though still some way from his maturity, stands head and shoulders above the rest; from the first session his voice alone is that of an individual and imaginative artist. The only time this early Ellington music swings is when Miley's rhythmic accents are caught by the rhythm section during a solo, or fleetingly by the band as in the last eight bars of *Rainy Nights*. If we play these records today for other than historical reasons, it is to hear what they can tell us of the music of the great trumpeter. Of the vast talents soon to be displayed by the pianist/leader there is in truth hardly a trace.

* * *

"Duke Ellington and his Kentucky Club Orchestra" was the band name for six titles recorded for Vocalion between November 1926 and February 1927. The personnel of the orchestra at this time was thought to be established beyond question, but recent research has revived a number of doubts about the reed section and the identity of the brass bass player. On these Vocalion recordings the band consisted of:

Trumpets: Bubber Miley, Louis Metcalf.

Trombone: Tricky Sam Nanton.

Reeds: Otto Hardwick (alto, soprano, baritone and/or bass saxes, clarinet) and two others.

Rhythm: Duke Ellington (piano); Fred Guy (banjo); probably Mack Shaw (tuba); Sonny Greer (drums).

For years the discographies gave the other two reeds as Rudy Jackson (clarinet and tenor) and Harry Carney (alto, baritone, clarinet). It is now known, however, that Jackson was with King Oliver in Chicago in February and March 1927 and did not leave for New York until April of that year, while Carney was employed by other bands in the New York area at this time. More recently it has been suggested that the reed section consists of Prince Robinson and an unknown (both doubling clarinet and tenor) in addition to Hardwick, and there is some aural evidence to suggest that Robinson is present on some of the recordings. He was a known associate of Ellington's in this period, while Carney, too, worked with Duke on an irregular basis and may have been hired for some or all of these sessions. All the alto solos, and possibly the baritone solos too, are by Hardwick, although a few of the latter have the ebullience which the young Carney was soon to bring to the band on a full-time basis.

It is from the first of these Vocalion sessions, recorded on November 29, 1926, that the important part of the early Ellington discography can be said to start. Two titles were recorded, *East St. Louis Toodle-oo* (pronounced "toadle-oh"), composed by Ellington and Miley, and *Birmingham Breakdown*, written by Ellington. Both performances represent a tremendous leap forward in the quality of the ensemble playing when compared with *Animal Crackers* and *Li'l Farina* of five months earlier. But the most important aspect of this music is Ellington's score for *East St. Louis Toodle-oo*. This composition gives, for the first time on records, an indication of Ellington's strong musical personality. The piece was used by the band as a signature tune until the middle of 1940, and it remained in the repertoire right through until the seventies. According to Ellington, "the title meant, for me, the broken walk of a man who had worked all day and was leaving the field at sunset. I had never been to East St. Louis, but I thought the locale sounded right."

East St. Louis Toodle-oo is built on two themes, a principal, highly distinctive 32-bar melody with bridge, and a secondary, much more commonplace theme of the sixteen-bars-plus-two-bar-tag *Sister Kate* variety. The introduction consists of what sounds like a slowed-down fugue subject in minims played by low saxophone and tuba, and this goes on to become the accompaniment for the main theme, which is played by Miley. It is a singular theme, so full of Miley's musical character that it must have either been written by him or built by Ellington from phrases created by Miley during improvised solos (a procedure which soon became a standard Ellington practice). Miley's playing is characteristic with its stuttering, vocalized repeated notes and unexpected melodic and rhythmic stresses, and in its coloration of tone by subtle use of the plunger mute. The second eight-bar unit of the main theme is a variant of the first which hints, both rhythmically and melodically, at the change of atmosphere to be found in the bridge. Here the brooding climate created by the heavy sound of the saxophone/tuba accompaniment gives way to a straightforward rhythmic backing, with very precise playing by the tuba in its rhythmic function; in later recordings the trumpet's melody on the bridge is lightly echoed by Nanton's trombone. The last eight bars return to the harmony, mood and texture of the first eight. This chorus is followed by two solos: an open trombone solo by Nanton which introduces the second theme, and a poorly played clarinet solo based on the first eight bars of the main theme. The brass section then plays the second theme, the reeds (soprano lead) play a rather trite variation for half a chorus followed by the brass on the melody again. The record ends with a recapitulation of the first eight bars of the principal theme by Miley over the saxophone/tuba accompaniment.

East St. Louis Toodle-oo was recorded on many occasions by the Ellington band, and the later versions from the twenties (a further four plus an alternative take) provide some interesting contrasts with the 1926 original. There are differences in Miley's statement of the theme and Nanton's trombone solo becomes notably more vigorous, especially on the Victor recording of December 1927. It was not until Barney Bigard joined the band that a satisfactory clarinet solo was created, although Rudy Jackson's performance on the Victor version is an improvement on that of his predecessors. On two recordings (the Victor and the OKeh) the soprano-clarinet variation (much the weakest part of the arrangement) is replaced by a baritone sax solo on the second theme. This is a great improvement, especially on the

Victor version, where it is inserted between the Miley theme statement and Nanton's chorus.

It will be seen that *East St. Louis Toodle-oo* is an uneven composition. Its real importance lies in its unique world of sound, thoroughly Ellingtonian in its quality, and its successful blending of apparently incompatible elements: the fugue-like figure in the introduction and accompaniment, Miley's blues-impregnated line and the "gay twenties" quality of the second theme. These create an emotional ambiguity which is to be found in much of Ellington's mature music. The use of contrasting thematic material is also characteristic, although later it is brought off with much more musical distinction. The recapitulation of the main melody at the end gives the piece a distinct unity and, as this is far and away the most compelling part of the work, provides a satisfactory conclusion. (Thirty years later, in 1956, the Ellington band was to find a perfect and humorous resolution of the problem of the weak second theme when it recorded the piece for the Bethlehem label, but discussion of that had better be deferred until a later chapter.)

By comparison *Birmingham Breakdown* is a rather uninteresting piece, but it provides a basis for an excellent big band jazz performance, one of the best recorded in 1926. Compositionally it reveals Ellington's reliance at this time on his experience as a pianist, and indeed the number sounds like a piece of Harlem stride piano transcribed for orchestra. The solos are only moderate, that by Ellington being almost drowned out by the saxophone accompaniment owing to poor recording balance; the alto solo by Hardwick, and the baritone solo (probably also by him) are competent period pieces, the touch of color given to the latter by the low-register clarinet accompaniment being quite pleasing. There is also an improvised trumpet duet, with Miley in the lead role, which is perhaps another echo of the King Oliver Creole Jazz Band. When the piece was rerecorded three months later, this passage was played simply as an open trumpet solo by Miley. Rather improbably, this composition was revived and recorded in 1937 as *The New Birmingham Breakdown* and revealed rather more strength than critics and historians have given it credit for, although even the skills of the late thirties Ellington brass section cannot disguise the monotony of the main theme as an orchestral conception.

The remaining four titles recorded by the band by Vocalion are all compositions by Duke. None of these is of the quality of *East St. Louis Toodle-oo*, although *Immigration Blues* has a very distinctive and attractive melody and can be said to be the first composition in which Duke's own melodic style, as opposed to that of Miley, can be clearly heard. The recording balance on these sides tends to favor Guy's banjo at the expense of the tuba player, who was much the steadiest of Ellington's rhythm section players at this time. This rhythm section has a driving, disorganized sound, typical of the black bands of the period; perhaps its most distinguished feature is Greer's use of the cymbals.

Immigration Blues, the best of the four titles, opens with a growl tenor sax solo, presumably the work of Prince Robinson, and also features two good Miley solos; the second uses an ending he was later to employ in his famous *Black and Tan Fantasy* solo. *The Creeper*, of which two takes exist, is an uptempo stomp with very prominent banjo, Nanton's trenchant solo being the highspot. *New Orleans Low Down* finds Duke using an eight-to-the-bar bass in one place and a tango rhythm in another, both designed to justify the title, but these attempts to conjure up some local color are not particularly successful. Otto Hardwick quotes *Jackass Blues* in his solo and Miley is again the outstanding performer, his coda over a pedal point by the reeds being highly effective. Miley's solo is also the high spot of *Song Of The Cotton Field*, although he does overstress the wa-wa effect here, as indeed he does on *New Orleans Low Down*; fortunately he soon restrained this tendency. Nanton has a good solo on *Song Of The Cotton Field* and, toward the end of the record, there is a low-register clarinet solo which sounds to be by Prince Robinson.

In January 1927 Ellington and a small group made a date for Victor as accompanists to singer Evelyn Preer, from which only one title has been issued. *If You Can't Hold The Man You Love* has a long vocal of some vivacity by Preer, a typical vaudeville stylist of the time, plus passages by Ellington, a violinist, and Miley, the last a masterly ten bars. The violin solo is usually said to be by Hardwick, who did indeed play the instrument in the band at this time, but it could equally well be by Edgar Sampson, another known Ellington associate of the period and a specialist on the instrument. (It is also possible that Sampson is one of the reeds on the contemporary full band sessions.)

Ellington's next recordings were for Brunswick, and his first two selections for them, made in February and March 1927, were remakes of *Birmingham Breakdown* and *East St. Louis Toodle-oo*. Recording the same compositions for different companies was a feature of Ellington's policy over the next four years; on many of these the band used a pseudonym. For these two Brunswick sides, however, the labels read "Duke Ellington and his Orchestra." The performances are very similar to the initial Vocalion ones, with Miley's trumpet particularly well recorded on *East St. Louis Toodle-oo*, a performance in which the excessive use of wa-wa on the bridge makes it less satisfactory overall than the Vocalion. The version recorded for Columbia eight days later also has this fault and omits the flash of clarinet obbligato during the band's recapitulation of the second theme, which served as a slight distraction from this drab episode on the Brunswick. At the Columbia session (for which Ellington used the old band name "The Washingtonians") two further titles were cut—*Hop Head* and *Down In Our Alley Blues*. Both are vigorous period performances of themes ascribed to Ellington and Hardwick; Miley, this time on open trumpet, once more provides the musical highlights.

The last two titles the Ellington Orchestra recorded in the early part of 1927 were done for Brunswick. On April 30, with Miley absent and June Clark as his deputy, they recorded *Soliloquy,* a composition by Rube Bloom, a white musician whose work hovered between hot dance music and light music. This particular tune became a big hit for Paul Whiteman. Proficiently played, *Soliloquy* might be pleasant enough, but the Ellington band performs untidily and the recording is a failure. The only soloist is a trumpet player, but no one seems to be sure if he is Louis Metcalf or June Clark.

The other session was done thirteen days earlier. Again it produced only one title, this time a new Ellington-Miley collaboration called *Black And Tan Fantasy. East St. Louis Toodle-oo* had shown Ellington's ability to create a new musical climate, and in *Black And Tan Fantasy* this ability is developed to a stage where the composition is a coherent whole. While it still shows Ellington placing contrasting material side by side rather than welding it together as he does in his later works, the effects of contrast are not achieved at the cost of inserting irrelevant improvisations, as was the case in *East St. Louis Toodle-oo.*

Black And Tan Fantasy consists of a twelve-bar theme played by Miley and Nanton tightly muted, a contrasting sixteen-bar melody played by Hardwick on alto, a string of twelve-bar solos by Miley (two choruses), Ellington and Nanton (one chorus each), and a final chorus featuring Miley playing against the band, with a quotation from Chopin's *Funeral March* at the end. Contrast is created by the very sweet nature of the second theme, played in a characteristically "swooning" manner by Hardwick, which is set against the astringency of the opening statement. Then Miley's tight, concise two choruses are followed by a rambling solo by Duke in the Eastern stride manner and not much in the blues idiom, only for the original mood to be reasserted by Nanton and intensified in the peroration by Miley. The full band is used only behind Hardwick to provide harmonic "cushioning" and in the last chorus to act as antiphonal voice in reply to Miley's ferocious outburst. And importantly too in this first recorded performance of *Black And Tan Fantasy* the playing has a new-found unity of purpose. The work of the tuba player is both solid and imaginative, providing an admirable foundation.

Yet, for all the unity of conception shown by Ellington, the work would have failed had the solos been of a mediocre standard. Hardwick simply plays the contrasting theme, though he plays it well, while Ellington's chorus has the mood and substance of an interlude; but Nanton and Miley provide jazz solos which are of genuine musical substance. Nanton's trombone chorus is played with a great variety of tone colors and in a beautifully expressive blues style. Melodically the solo is not so remarkable, but, as is so often the case with Nanton, what are really rather commonplace musical ideas are given a new richness and expressive quality by the extreme subtlety of the note-placing and by the use of the plunger mute to give an infinite variety to the depth and color of the tone.

With Miley's playing on *Black And Tan Fantasy*, and especially his two-chorus solo, we arrive at the very essence of the piece. The Miley solo starts with a sustained high B♭ over the first four bars, which not only provides a perfect contrast to the preceding Hardwick theme but also has a stillness from which the cascading, melodically concentrated solo which follows is set off to maximum effect. In *Black And Tan Fantasy* Miley creates one of the great solos of jazz, irrespective of period or instrument. Not only are the melodic ideas themselves original and perfectly organized, but the use of the plunger mute and the growl are masterly in their subtle restraint. In the sense that Miley's and Nanton's solos are its most important constituents, *Black And Tan Fantasy* shows that the band's soloists still dominate Duke Ellington's musical thinking. He was soon to develop his composing and arranging powers to a level which equaled and then surpassed the achievement of even his greatest soloists, yet in a way which did not inhibit their creative powers. For the rest of April 1927, however, the band simply recorded *Soliloquy* and prepared to leave New York and the recording studios behind as they set off on their summer tour. Not until October were they to record again, and by then new developments were under way which were to have crucial effects on the future of Duke Ellington and his musicians.

Outstanding Recordings

East St. Louis Toodle-oo (Vocalion version), *Birmingham Breakdown* (Vocalion version), *Immigration Blues, Hop Head, Black And Tan Fantasy* (Brunswick version)

Chapter 3

In the Beginning

DUKE ELLINGTON'S ARRIVAL IN NEW YORK in 1923 as a member of The Washingtonians was his second attempt to establish himself professionally in the city. His previous experience there had been gained twelve months earlier when he had played, along with several of his Washington associates, in a band led by the novelty clarinetist Wilbur Sweatman. After the engagement with Sweatman ended, the musicians had been unable to find further work and had returned to their native city. Their second visit was more fruitful, and by late 1923 The Washingtonians were resident at the Hollywood Café on Broadway, an establishment later to become known as the Club Kentucky. The leader of the band at this time was banjoist Elmer Snowden. When he departed after a disagreement with the other musicians, Ellington took over the leadership of the group.

Many people who knew Duke at this time have said that his main interest was in songwriting and that he took on the role of bandleader with reluctance. Evidence of his contemporary activities as a songwriter includes the numbers he wrote in 1924 for the review *Chocolate Kiddies*, which are among the earliest surviving Ellington compositions. This show was not produced in the United States, but toured Europe with great success for some years with a troupe which included Josephine Baker, Adelaide Hall, and the Sam Wooding Orchestra.

In 1923 New York was a city which offered a multitude of opportunities for the young black musician. The "jazz age" was underway and Prohibition had caused the mushrooming of small clubs where entertainment was a cover for illicit drinking. These clubs employed musicians to play for dancing and as accompanists to cabaret performers, while the dance halls, theaters, and larger clubs featured the better-known bands as star entertainers in their own right. With the right contacts, a musician could make a good living in New York, with the black uptown population spending a good deal of money on entertainment and white show business keen to exploit black talent. This was a period when black entertainers were highly fashionable among well-to-do whites with money to spend, and in both Harlem and downtown New York black artists in the cabarets and theaters gave their audiences what they wanted—noisy, colorful, dynamic entertainment which often portrayed the black man in primitive terms. The "jungle" motif was a popular one in such ventures and this was soon to touch on Duke Ellington's developing art as he and his musicians fought through the jungle of the entertainment profession.

Public demand was one reason for the large number of black musicians and entertainers, but it was also a fact that show business in general and music in particular were among the few avenues open to the talented African American in the 1920s. A musician with talent or with some ability as an entertainer could make his way with a large degree of success in this world, providing that he learned how to accommodate himself to the gangster element which dominated show business, most brutally at the lower end of the social structure. An illustration is provided by the well-known story of the gangster who "persuaded" a Philadelphia theater owner to release the Ellington band from a booking so that they could open at New York's Cotton Club in late 1927. The owner was given the choice of being "big" or being dead. He chose the wiser course, and Duke opened at the Club, the plum residency for a black band in the United States, on time. Here Duke found himself in a Harlem club which featured pseudo-primitive revues for the benefit of visiting whites and which operated what amounted to a color bar against blacks unless they were employees or famous entertainers. Such was the club which was then considered the epitome of prestige among black performers throughout the land.

By the time he was offered the Cotton Club residency, Ellington had become well established in New York. He had been broadcasting regularly from the Kentucky Club since late 1923, and appearing with his band, variously described as his Washingtonians, his Orchestra or his Kentucky Club Orchestra, at dances and in theaters. We have seen in the previous chapter how our two sources of information on the music played by The Washingtonians give contradictory evidence. Musicians who played in the band, and many others who heard and admired it, say that the music was subtle and original. By contrast the earliest Ellington band records are at best mediocre. The evidence of the records need not, of course, be conclusive. It is highly improbable that a little-known band, new to the recording studios, would have been invited to record music of its own choice. It is certainly a strong probability that the kind of music and possibly the actual numbers recorded by The Washingtonians were dictated by the record companies.

To gain an impression of Ellington's musical environment in these vital formative years of the mid-twenties one should consult the recordings of contemporary big bands. The most jazz-like of these were the Chicago bands of Doc Cook and Erskine Tate, while the recordings of King Oliver's Dixie Syncopators (the augmented successor to his Creole Jazz Band) probably reflect best of all the embryonic state of big band jazz. Benny Moten's Kansas City Orchestra provides a good example of a territory band of the period. Even the popular Fletcher Henderson Orchestra—the most popular and the best of the black bands—mixed jazz and popular/novelty music in often unstable blends. The few recordings of Charlie Johnson's Paradise Orchestra reflect the work of another highly regarded black band. Among white bands, that of Jean Goldkette was best, but Paul Whiteman's the more popular and prestigious.

Once Ellington had become established in New York his rise to national and international fame was meteoric. This was clearly due in part to his talent, that talent which is hardly glimpsed on the early records, but also to other factors. The range of Ellington's activities as composer, bandleader, pianist and arranger was unusual; he was an uncommonly likeable young man, as many of his contemporaries have attested; and not least he was starting to show an acute business sense. What lay behind this unusual young man who was soon to make so unique a contribution to the interwoven worlds of jazz and show business in the New York of the middle 1920s?

* * *

Edward Kennedy Ellington was born in Washington, D.C., on April 29, 1899. His family was fairly well-to-do by black standards and his childhood was spent in comfortable if not wildly affluent circumstances. The family seems to have been an unusually happy and stable one. For all their compatibility his parents were of strongly contrasting personalities—the father easygoing, the mother of strict principle. This family background certainly had a strong influence on Ellington: right to the end of his life he ran his orchestra as if it were a large family rather than on the disciplinarian lines of most other big bands. The contrast in character between his parents, allied to his keen appreciation of their qualities, seems to have been the determining factor on which rested Duke's acceptance—his relish—of contrasting character and temperament among his musicians. He also commanded and gave a loyalty from and to associates of all kinds of a totally different nature from that usually found among artists. This loyalty was often extended to the followers of the band, who felt themselves in a vague way members of some huge global family. Ellington's own family was a loving one, and this clearly affected him deeply; there was a lot of love in his relationships with people and there is also a lot in his music.

Ellington's hobbies as a child were characteristic of the young American of his era—baseball, football and the movies. He learned at an early age to play the piano but did not rate it as one of his important activities. His aristocratic manner must have been evident very early on, for Edward Kennedy Ellington had the nickname "Duke" bestowed upon him at the age of eight. He spent some three years at one of the leading black schools in Washington, Armstrong High School, where his main interest seems to have been drawing. But he also took regular music lessons, and these were later supplemented by private harmony lessons from Henry Grant of Dunbar High School, a teacher who also numbered Arthur Whetsol and Otto Hardwick among his pupils. After Ellington had won a contest sponsored by the National Association for the Advancement of Colored People, he was offered a scholarship to the Pratt Institute of Applied Arts. It is not in any way fanciful to draw a parallel with these early successes in the visual arts and the later detailed, sometimes fastidious, concern with color in the orchestrations of the mature Ellington. He didn't take up the art scholarship, for by this time he had become totally fascinated with music, with the characters associated with it, and with the poolroom environment they enjoyed in their leisure hours.

The first well-known musical influence in Duke Ellington's life seems to have been James P. Johnson—he has described how he obtained a piano roll of Johnson's famous *Carolina Shout* and played it on the pianola very slowly so that he could follow the fingering and study the intricacies of Johnson's style. Later, when he got to New York, Duke became a friend and disciple of another member of that flourishing school of Harlem stride pianists, Willie "The Lion" Smith, absorbing in particular the subtle harmonic flavoring of Smith's slower compositions. A primary influence away from the piano was the New Orleans clarinet and soprano saxophone player Sidney Bechet, whom he heard in Washington in 1921. Forty-one years later Ellington still considered Bechet "the foundation," his playing "the greatest thing I ever heard!" Another aspect of the complex Ellington personality can be discerned from these Washington days: he noted that the most successful local bandleaders were those with large advertisements in the telephone directory. So he bought one of the largest himself and was soon handling more dates than one band could manage.

Three of Duke Ellington's Washington friends, Arthur Whetsol, Otto Hardwick and Sonny Greer—Greer was in fact a New York musician who had struck up a friendship with Duke while playing at a Washington theater—were in the first New York edition of The Washingtonians, but Whetsol soon returned home to resume his medical studies. He was replaced by Bubber Miley who became, as we have seen, a major influence on Ellington's musical development. Duke has said of Miley: "Our band changed its character when Bubber came in. He used to growl all night long, playing gut-bucket on his horn. That was when we decided to forget all about the sweet music." The remaining *basic* personnel of The Washingtonians was Charlie Irvis on trombone, Otto Hardwick on saxes and violin, Ellington on piano, George Francis (Elmer Snowden's replacement) on banjo, and Greer on drums. The group was frequently augmented and often had to use deputy trumpet players as Miley was not very reliable. Musicians who played with Ellington during this period include John Anderson, Sidney Bechet, Harvey Boone, Benny Carter, Harry Cooper, Bass Edwards, Percy Glascoe, Prince Robinson, Edgar Sampson, and Roland Smith.

The Washingtonians had been featured at the Kentucky Club for five years, enjoying tours of New England dance halls in the summer months, when one evening in 1927 the impresario Irving Mills walked into the Club to hear what was billed as "probably the hottest band this side of the equator." According to Ellington the band was playing *St. Louis Blues*, according to Mills they were playing *Black And Tan Fantasy*, and according to some of the musicians Mills wouldn't have been able to tell one from the other. Mills decided that he "had encountered a great creative artist and the first American composer to catch in his music the true jazz spirit." These are the accepted versions of the encounter which tradition has handed down to us. The discovery in recent years of a Gennett test pressing of a duet by Ellington and Mills recorded in 1925 seems to suggest that these are mythical. What is clear is that by early 1927 Irving Mills had assumed management of the band, and it was he who secured for them the plum location at the Cotton Club. Mills is also said to have helped out financially in augmenting the band for this engagement, an engagement which was to bring Duke Ellington international fame within a couple of years.

Sidemen

Sidney Bechet

Sidney Bechet was one of the greatest of all jazz musicians, and it is indeed unfortunate that his stay with Ellington came in the summer of 1926, when Duke was not making records. Sometime around May 1932, Bechet was again employed by Ellington, not in a playing capacity but as band "coach." This stay is reflected on records only by the fact that Johnny Hodges plays Bechet's standard variations on *The Sheik Of Araby* in the course of the Ellington band's May 1932 recording. It has also been claimed by several Ellington band members, including Barney Bigard and Sonny Greer, that Bechet was responsible for the famous saxophone section passage on *Daybreak Express*. The fact that the saxophones begin with a phrase taken from their chorus on Ellington's 1929 *High Life* may make this seem unlikely, but what seems to have happened is that Ellington wrote a few bars before asking Bechet for his advice. What Bechet provided proved to be a test piece for the reeds and their interpretation of it became famous. These early thirties Bechet episodes are shrouded in mystery, but there is no mystery at all about the profound influence that Bechet's music had earlier on the young Duke Ellington.

Representative Recordings: Sidney Bechet did not record with Ellington. Among his recordings of Ellington compositions are *Old Man Blues* (Victor, 1940), *The Mooche* (Victor, 1941), *Mood Indigo* (Victor, 1941), *Never No Lament* (Jazz Archives and Fat Cat Jazz, 1945), and *It Don't Mean A Thing* (French Vogue, 1957)

Bass Edwards and Mack Shaw

The Ellington Orchestra was always noted for the excellent quality of its bassists. The New Orleans string bass player Wellman Braud, who joined in 1927, is usually cited as being the first of these. However, Ellington always recalled with keen pleasure the work on brass bass of Braud's predecessors Bass Edwards and Mack Shaw. For many years it was assumed that the brass bass playing on all the pre-Braud Ellington records was by Edwards, but recent research has shown that this is unlikely. The man responsible for the tuba work on the Vocalion recordings of 1926/1927 is now thought to be Mack Shaw. Whoever the musician really was, he certainly makes a valuable contribution, notably on the first recording of *Black And Tan Fantasy*.

Sonny Greer

Sonny Greer first met Ellington in 1919, and they at once struck up an enduring friendship. The following year they worked together for the first time, and a professional association began which lasted until March 1951. For over a quarter of a century Sonny Greer was the drummer with the Ellington Orchestra through all its many changes. In the recordings of the 1920s and early 1930s Greer's contribution is often one of color and rhythmic decoration; he was outstanding at this time for his subtle use of cymbals. Unlike most jazz drummers of his generation he does not seem to have been influenced by the New Orleans drummers but rather to have drawn upon his experience as a theater percussionist. Although his work is usually in excellent taste, there are some recordings on which Greer's theatrical effects are overly obtrusive and these, added to his inconsistency in swinging, have caused some jazz writers to underestimate his contribution. The records on which he is rhythmically pedestrian are few, and on the majority Greer shows himself to be a swinging jazz drummer with an exhilarating, exciting beat. In the Ellington band of 1940, he established an outstanding partnership with bassist Jimmy Blanton, and it is from 1940 that one of the best examples of Greer's drumming comes—the recording of a complete dance date at Fargo, North Dakota, on which the drumming is consistently swinging, and powerfully so.

Representative Recordings: Blue Bubbles (Victor, 1927), *Flaming Youth* (Victor, 1929), *Jive Stomp* (Brunswick, 1933), *Me And You* (Victor, 1940), *At A Dixie Roadside Diner* (Victor, 1940), *Jumpin' Punkins* (Victor, 1941)

Fred Guy

From the spring of 1925 until his retirement from full-time music in May 1949 Fred Guy played banjo and, as fashion changed, guitar with Ellington. He was never replaced. Guy was very rarely heard in solo and his part in the rhythm section became less important in the years after the arrival in 1939 of Jimmy Blanton, with his revolutionary conception of the role of the string bass. Perhaps Guy's most valuable contribution was in the late twenties when he had become the best timekeeper in a team which was otherwise on the unsteady side.

Otto Hardwick

A Washingtonian five years Ellington's junior, Otto Hardwick played string bass with Duke in Washington before switching to saxophones. In The Washingtonians he played at various times soprano, alto, baritone, and bass saxophones as well as clarinet and violin, but as the Ellington band developed he specialized more on alto. He was lead alto in the three-man section up to 1929, when he was replaced by Johnny Hodges. Hardwick rejoined Ellington in the spring of 1932, making the section four pieces, and that remained standard until Ben Webster was added in 1940. Hardwick left the Ellington band in May 1946 and soon afterward retired from the music profession.

Although heard on his other instruments on the early Ellington records, Hardwick's most characteristic solos are on alto saxophone. On the records from the twenties Hardwick is the main alto soloist, his choruses having a light, airy, but rather dated manner. At slower tempos the influence of Sidney Bechet can be detected, especially Bechet's melodramatic way of phrasing in ballads. After his return to the Ellington band in 1932, Hardwick was used mostly as a section man, and his solos were confined to occasional rather swooning passages on the more sentimental ballads. A rare opportunity to hear the latter-day Hardwick soloing in a "hot" fashion is offered on a session under Sonny Greer's name for Capitol in 1945. Although Ellington voiced his saxophones more according to personality and style than to conventional methods, the usual lead voice in his saxophone section was that of Hardwick. It was in this capacity that Hardwick excelled, for he had an outstanding melodic sense and a creamy, singing tone which contributed a distinctive quality to the sound of the Ellington band. The light and airy sound of the Ellington reeds in the thirties and early forties was never quite recaptured after Hardwick's departure.

Representative Recordings: Jubilee Stomp (Victor, 1928), *Got Everything But You* (Victor, 1928), *Take It Easy* (OKeh, 1928), *In A Sentimental Mood* (Victor, 1945), *The Mooche* (Sonny Greer, Capitol, 1945), *Come Sunday* (own name, Wax, 1947)

Charlie Irvis

Charlie Irvis was the trombonist with The Washingtonians from the autumn of 1923 to September 1926. He was remembered by Ellington many years later as a player with a unique sound on muted trombone, one which was never captured again by any other Ellington musician, to the leader's considerable regret. Those listening to the records of The Washingtonians for evidence of this will find their search largely fruitless. Perhaps the records which best indicate the range of Irvis's style are those by Thomas (Fats) Waller with Morris's Hot Babies recorded for Victor on May 20, 1927. This session produced three titles: *Fats Waller Stomp, Savannah Blues* (two takes), and *Won't You Take Me Home* (two takes). Charlie Irvis has solos on all five takes and his muted work is well represented.

Rudy Jackson

There are conflicting accounts of the duration of Jackson's stay with Ellington, some authorities saying he was with the band from the autumn of 1926 while others claim that he did not join until June of the following year. On balance, the latter seems to be the more likely. Jackson was a Chicago musician whose engagement immediately prior to joining Ellington had been with the King Oliver band and whose clarinet playing was strongly influenced by the New Orleans style. Although a competent musician by the standards of his time, Jackson's contribution has been overshadowed by that of his successor, Barney Bigard, who replaced him on January 1, 1928. Nonetheless it was Jackson who developed the tradition of a New Orleans style clarinetist in the Ellington band, a tradition first established by Sidney Bechet in 1925.

Representative Recordings: Washington Wobble (Victor, 1927), *Creole Love Call* (Victor, 1927), *Chicago Stomp Down* (OKeh, 1927)

Louis Metcalf

During the two years trumpeter Louis Metcalf spent in the Ellington Orchestra he was generally overshadowed by his section mate Bubber Miley. At this time Metcalf was a young follower of the King Oliver school, content to play in the manner of his mentor rather than to advance the style into unknown territory as Miley was doing. His solos are much less distinguished than Miley's; although his playing is pleasant and relaxed, it lacks the spirit and personality of Bubber's work. There are a few characteristic Metcalf solos on the Ellington records, but he was in the band too early for Ellington to have been able to utilize fully the potential of a rather modest and limited stylist.

Representative Recordings: Jubilee Stomp (Brunswick, 1928), *Yellow Dog Blues* (Brunswick, 1928—second trumpet solo)

Bubber Miley

Saxophonist Garvin Bushell has recalled the enormous impact which the music of King Oliver's Creole Jazz Band made on Bubber Miley and himself when they first heard it in Chicago in 1921. The use of mutes with brass instruments, especially trumpets, was all the rage in jazz and dance band circles at this time. Novelty wa-wa effects were commonplace, but King Oliver had developed the technique of playing with the plunger mute into an art, with a carefully controlled use of tonal variety and a sober, expressive blues style which was the antithesis of the cheap novelty effects with which the technique was then associated. Oliver's disciples included several of the finest New Orleans trumpeters, but no one developed the plunger style in so fresh and creative a manner as Bubber Miley. The pitfalls of mere novelty playing are always close at hand in this style, but on Miley's records with Ellington purely musical considerations are paramount. What Bubber did was to increase the vocalized effect of Oliver's style by use of the growl and of flutter-tonguing, while at the same time fashioning a melodic language very different in its strutting, stuttering manner from Oliver's rolling New Orleans style. But Miley retained the strong blues element from the playing of his mentor and his use of blues phrases played with great feeling in among the growls, wa-was, and stutterings creates an unusual emotional effect. It is as if, behind the surface clowning, there lies at a deeper level a profoundly poignant art. Miley's use of tone color was very sensitive, and this is an aspect of his playing which only one of his disciples, trombonist Tricky Sam Nanton, was able to utilize with Miley's brilliance. Although most critics emphasize Miley's use of the mute, Miley also created an original and fastidious melodic style. His playing was also outstanding for its immense drive and rhythmic energy.

Miley was the leading musical personality of the early Ellington band. Duke himself was greatly affected by the talents of this remarkable musician and obviously studied Miley's music closely, for most of his early musical successes were built around Bubber's playing, with the trumpeter frequently sharing composer credits. The use of plunger mutes by trumpets and trombone, in solo or in section, remained one of the most obvious characteristics of Ellington's music from this time onwards, for under the inspiration of Miley's playing Duke became a keen student of the coloristic potential of muted brass. Miley left the Ellington band in 1929 and he recorded with various groups prior to his death in May 1932. Although they have their moments, the solos Miley recorded away from the Ellington band cannot be compared in quality with those done with Duke.

Because Miley was a heavy drinker and an unreliable character, Ellington ensured that his other trumpet players were adept in the growl style and able to play Miley's solos when the star trumpeter failed to turn up. Thus was established another long-enduring tradition within the Ellington band, that of versatility and flexibility among the sidemen. According to Mercer Ellington, Bubber was a mild, generous, and pleasant man, similar in personality to Paul Gonsalves.

Representative Recordings: Black And Tan Fantasy (Brunswick and Victor, 1927), *Creole Love Call* (Victor, 1927), *Jubilee Stomp* (Victor, 1928), *The Blues With A Feeling* (OKeh, 1928), *Diga Diga Do* (Victor, 1928), *Flaming Youth* (Victor, 1929)

Joe "Tricky Sam" Nanton

"Tricky Sam" was unique. Entering the band rather reluctantly, he graced the Ellington Orchestra from 1926 until his death twenty years later, becoming one of the most devoted Ellingtonians, so loyal that he refused to play on record dates led by other musicians. All his friends agree that he was highly intelligent, very likeable, and a strongly individual man. And they agree, too, that he was a remarkable musician. In his early days with Ellington, Nanton took open trombone solos, but his characteristic sound was that of the plunger-muted horn, of which he was *the* master. None of the other players who have used the technique on either trumpet or trombone has employed it so effectively. His vocalized wa-wa effects are often amazing, but the real core of his art lies in the combination of a highly developed melodic sense with a perfect judgment of shading and density of sound applied to each note in a phrase. The range of sound he could conjure from the trombone was more on the scale of a full orchestra than a single instrument. He was a great blues player and would often seemingly speak to the audience more directly than Ellington's other soloists. On up-tempo numbers Nanton could play with a blistering intensity and drive that would inspire the other musicians. In a conventional sense he was a trombonist with a limited range of melodic patterns who achieved greatness without virtuosity, but the brilliance of his mastery of muted and growl techniques more than made up for this apparent limitation. Tricky Sam was greatly respected by his fellow trombonists—Dickie Wells considered that it would have been fatal to take him on in a cutting contest, while Trummy Young simply asserted that for him Nanton was "the greatest thing that ever walked."

During his years with the Ellington band Tricky Sam Nanton's work remained constant in style and in quality. He adapted his phrasing rhythmically to the changes in the band's style, but in all other respects he was the one unchanging factor in the music, the custodian of the band's soul, as it so often seemed.

Representative Recordings: The Blues With A Feeling (OKeh, 1928), *Harlem Flat Blues* (Brunswick, 1929), *Hot Feet* (Victor, 1929), *Dear Old Southland* (Victor, 1933), *Sidewalks Of New York* (Victor and Fargo Dance Date, 1940), *In The Shade Of The Old Apple Tree* (World Transcriptions, 1945)

Prince Robinson

The reputation of Prince Robinson has never been particularly great among jazz critics and writers, but he was held in very high regard by his fellow professionals. Ellington had to compete fiercely with other bands for his services in the twenties, while Coleman Hawkins regarded Robinson as among the keenest of his early rivals. Doubling tenor sax and clarinet, he worked with The Washingtonians for about a year from the spring of 1925 and was probably used as an "extra" for recording purposes up to April 1927.

Chapter 4

The Records—October 1927 to January 1929

DUKE ELLINGTON AND HIS ORCHESTRA OPENED at the Cotton Club in Harlem on December 4, 1927. Earlier they had recorded three sessions which heralded a great increase in their recording activities. Soon Ellington was to start using pseudonyms extensively on his record issues, but the discs from these three dates came out as by "Duke Ellington and his Orchestra." Of these sessions, two were for Victor and one for OKeh. The Victor dates were on October 6 and 26, 1927, the two titles recorded on the first session being remade along with two new ones at the second. On October 6, *Black And Tan Fantasy* and *Washington Wobble* were recorded, but only two takes of the second title have ever been issued from this date. On October 26, in addition to the remakes, *Creole Love Call* and *The Blues I Love To Sing* were recorded. The total issues from these sessions are three takes of *Washington Wobble*, two of *The Blues I Love To Sing*, and one each of *Black And Tan Fantasy* and *Creole Love Call*. By this time Rudy Jackson and Wellman Braud had joined the band and the full personnel was:

Trumpets: Bubber Miley, Louis Metcalf.

Trombone: Tricky Sam Nanton.

Reeds: Otto Hardwick (alto, soprano, bari-

Rhythm: tone, and bass saxes, clarinet); Rudy Jackson (clarinet, tenor sax); Harry Carney (alto and baritone saxes, clarinet).

Rhythm: Duke Ellington (piano); Fred Guy (banjo); Wellman Braud (bass); Sonny Greer (drums).

In later years Harry Carney recalled his first record session with Ellington as being the OKeh date of November 3, 1927. The third reed on these Victors, however, certainly sounds like him.

The Victor recording of *Black And Tan Fantasy* is a more aggressive and less tidy affair than the Brunswick discussed in the last chapter; the band intonation is mediocre and Braud's string bass less steady than the earlier tuba. On the other hand the sound quality is more vivid, with Nanton and Miley heard to great advantage. So far as Miley's two-chorus solo is concerned, the differences are of detail in phrasing and accentuation only, and it is really a matter of temperament or even of mood whether one prefers the somber, thoughtful Brunswick solo or the more exuberant, extroverted one on the Victor record. But for the realization of the composition as a whole, there can be little doubt that the Brunswick performance is superior.

Creole Love Call is another enduring Ellington classic, and this is the only recording of it from the Miley period. In some ways *Creole Love Call* is less of a musical success than either *East St. Louis Toodle-oo* or *Black And Tan Fantasy*. The piece is basically a twelve-bar blues, its themes derived from King Oliver's *Camp Meeting Blues*. These melodies were presumably introduced to Ellington by Rudy Jackson, who was fresh from working with Oliver and whose name is included in the composer credit of *Creole Love Call* along with those of Ellington and Miley. The Victor recording of *Creole Love Call* introduces a device which Ellington was to use at intervals throughout his career—the blending of a wordless female voice with the instrumental textures. The singer here is Adelaide Hall, and the first chorus presents the main theme sung by her over three low-register clarinets, a delicious tonal combination; in sharp contrast the second chorus is an astringent solo improvisation by Miley, and the third, again contrasting, presents a second theme played by Jackson on clarinet in a singing New Orleans style. From this point the music deteriorates abruptly in quality, the performance ending with two very ordinary antiphonal choruses of reeds against brass and one of solo singing by Adelaide Hall. Although her ethereal voice had been effective in the theme statement, a chorus of wordless singing by Miss Hall to end the piece is less satisfying and not sufficiently substantial to give the work the formal balance of *Black And Tan Fantasy* or even *East St. Louis Toodle-oo*. But the first three choruses constitute a superb sequence, with Miley's great solo the high spot. The maturing of Bubber's art is evident on the first two versions of *Black And Tan Fantasy* but here he brings his style to perfection in arguably his finest solo, one of the greatest in the whole of recorded jazz. Although Miley's successors who recorded this solo on later versions of *Creole Love Call*—for example Cootie Williams and Ray Nance—play it with a great deal of vehemence, Miley himself is restrained and poised, almost statuesque in style. The melodic construction of the solo is a perfect example of formal unity within a slow twelve-bar blues chorus, while the subtle use of timbre and inflection via the plunger mute, added to a sparing use of the growl, give a superb coloring to the structure. This chorus is a perfect example of musical architecture in miniature.

Neither *Washington Wobble* nor *The Blues I Love To Sing* is of comparable stature. The former is one of those early Ellington orchestral stomps which sound like straightforward transcriptions of stride piano pieces. Jackson (on clarinet), Ellington, Hardwick (a characteristic alto solo), and Nanton are heard, but the most interesting soloist is again Miley, starting the performance with a driving passage of open trumpet. *The Blues I Love To Sing* has more good Miley and a passage of Nanton on open trombone which emphasizes the fact that his expressive strength was based on melody as well as on his manipulation of mutes. The record is dominated by the singing, humming, and chanting of Adelaide Hall in an unsuccessful experiment in vocal styling. The only other soloist is a soprano saxophonist (either Hardwick or Carney) who makes an undistinguished contribution.

The OKeh session of November 3, 1927, finds Miley out of the band temporarily. His replacement for this date is Jabbo Smith, who solos effectively on both takes of a third recording of *Black And Tan Fantasy*; on the second of these takes the chorus after the subsidiary theme, normally the first of two by the trumpet soloist, is given to Nanton's muted trombone. Although admirable in themselves, Smith's solos lack the astringency to offset the sweetness of Hardwick's playing of the second theme, and the recordings fail to approach the stature of the versions with Miley, although Braud is more effective here than on the Victor. The other two recordings from this session are of non-Ellington compositions—*What Can A Poor Fellow Do?* with Jabbo Smith on muted trumpet, sounding very much like his namesake Joe Smith, and a Charleston-styled *Chicago Stomp Down*, a not particularly distinguished performance with a not very effective wordless vocal by Adelaide Hall.

* * *

For the first of two sessions made in December 1927 the band was back in the Victor studios. This was the first of many occasions when the repertoire at an Ellington recording session included material by Dorothy Fields and Jimmy McHugh, a songwriting team who wrote much of the material for the Cotton Club reviews. They were the composers of *Harlem River Quiver*, sometimes known as *Brown Berries*, and three takes of the Ellington recording have been issued;

the high spot is Nanton's theme statement. The Victor version of *East St. Louis Toodle-oo* finds the number rearranged to exclude the reed section variation and played at a considerably slower tempo. Both these changes suit the piece well, but some poor ensemble intonation and some heavy bowed bass by Braud do not. Nonetheless, Miley gives his best interpretation of his part here and Nanton has a very robust-sounding chorus. The final number from this date is an Ellington-Miley piece called *Blue Bubbles*, which suffers, as do many of their collaborations, from the fact that nothing that follows can avoid anticlimax after the trumpeter's initial statement. But Ellington had obviously taken a great deal of care over this arrangement with its balanced alternation of chorus and verse and use of a saxophone motif as a binding agent. The wailing, blue note riff of the last chorus is a typical Ellington use of a period device; the dated brass effects in that chorus's middle eight are fortunately less characteristic. The last Ellington session of 1927 was for Vocalion, and it produced recordings of two Fields-McHugh numbers, *Red Hot Band* and *Doin' The Frog*, the former being the better performance with good solo work from Miley.

In 1927 Ellington had taken a leading place among creative jazz artists, although of course few outside the closed circle of jazz musicians thought in such terms then. In 1928 he consolidated this position while continuing to expand his compositional art into new fields. His first session of the new year, however, sounds like a backward slide in more ways than one. Recording as The Washingtonians, the band cut three titles—none of them by Ellington—for Harmony, a Columbia subsidiary label. This was a cheap label, and, remarkably, Columbia had continued to use their old pre-electric machinery for Harmony recordings. This Ellington session marks Barney Bigard's entrance into the band, and he soloed on clarinet on *Stack O'Lee Blues* and on tenor sax on *Bugle Call Rag*. Although the clarinet work on the latter title is usually said to be by Harry Carney, it sounds very like Rudy Jackson in both style and execution, and it is probable that there are four reeds present here: Hardwick, Bigard, Jackson and Carney, with Hardwick playing more bass sax than usual owing to the absence of the string bass.

Bigard's first important solos with Ellington are on the two versions of *East St. Louis Toodle-oo* recorded in 1928, which are considerably enhanced by his presence, although in other respects they are inferior to the 1927 Victor. These new versions were done for OKeh and Cameo (two takes), the OKeh version being retitled *Harlem Twist*.

* * *

The first new Ellington piece to be recorded in 1928 was *Take It Easy*, the first of a group of new compositions recorded between January and November, with the usual summer gap when the band was on tour. Almost all of these were recorded in different versions for different companies, and there are also several alternative takes. It will be advantageous, therefore, if we consider each composition in its various recordings before discussing the non-Ellington pieces recorded in 1928. We can then return to a chronological pattern for the first sessions of the following year.

Take It Easy was recorded initially for OKeh and later for Cameo and Brunswick, with two takes of the Cameo version being issued. The best performance is on the OKeh, although Miley's statement of the first theme again gives all that follows a faint air of anticlimax. Much use is made of Bigard's fast arpeggios, while the second theme is played first by Nanton and then by Hardwick over a tango rhythm. Metcalf has a brief solo here and Greer is outstanding throughout. The Cameo performance is not much inferior but the recording quality is not of comparable quality; the only changes in the scoring are the reintroduction of Miley for four superfluous bars in the final chorus and a new coda based on the second theme and featuring Hardwick.

Bubber Miley was absent from the Brunswick session which produced the third version of *Take It Easy*, and his part is taken by Arthur Whetsol, who was making his recording debut with the band. Whetsol's return (he had been a member of The Washingtonians up to 1924) added a voice of considerable musical distinction to the band; although not a great jazz soloist, he was a first-class musician with a very personal sound. Although Whetsol initially and later Louis Metcalf play acceptable trumpet on *Take It Easy*, there is really no comparison between their interpretations and that of Miley. Whetsol sounds somewhat out of character playing growl trumpet here; although technically he is quite adept at the art, he fails to characterize the piece with Miley's power.

Although not one of Ellington's major compositions, *Take It Easy* is a distinctive number, well structured apart from the imbalance caused by Miley's opening solo. The work of the soloist is notably well integrated with the written parts. (Although most discographies show a second issued take of the Brunswick recording it is quite impossible to find anyone who has heard this, still less anyone who actually owns a copy. It seems probable that this second take is one of the myths of jazz discography.)

Jubilee Stomp is, by contrast, a straightforward piece with the emphasis on solo improvisation. There are one or two Ellington tricks, such as the way in which Bigard's solo is suddenly interrupted by Nanton's trombone, but on the whole *Jubilee Stomp* represents the start of a tradition of Ellington recordings designed to allow the band members to improvise in uncluttered surroundings. There are four versions of *Jubilee Stomp*—on OKeh, Cameo (two takes), Brunswick (without Miley), and Victor. For both recording and musical quality, the Victor is best: Miley's solo here is outstanding with a strutting, assured drive and a brilliantly taken break. The other soloists—Hardwick, Bigard, Nanton on open trombone, Carney on alto, and Ellington—are good on all versions. On the Brunswick, Louis Metcalf takes Miley's chorus, and the contrast shows the difference between talent and greatness.

Although the records from this period have only two trumpets, Ellington had three players on his payroll at this time and seems to have permutated them on the recordings. Any two from Miley, Metcalf, or Whetsol seems to have been the rule in the Ellington trumpet section at this time whenever the band entered the recording studio. Ellington was not slow to utilize the sound of Whetsol's trumpet, and in March 1928 he recorded a composition built around this musician's melodic style—*Black Beauty*. This was dedicated to Florence Mills, a celebrated musical theater star who had died tragically at the height of her fame the previous year. *Black Beauty* is significant above all in that it is the first important Ellington recording which does not rely upon the playing of Miley. On both the Brunswick version (two issued takes) and the Victor, Whetsol presents the melody at the outset in a characteristically clear-cut manner, and he returns for the last eight bars of the fourth and final chorus after Bigard's lyrical clarinet solo. On the Brunswick version, incidentally, Metcalf takes over for the first chorus bridge which is played by Nanton on the Victor. The trombonist is also heard on the second theme, but the most interesting passage is Ellington's piano chorus, his first really important solo contribution on records. This is not simply a piano solo but a trio in which bass (Braud) and drums (Greer) have quite distinct roles in a nonaccompanying fashion. This is hardly evident on the Brunswick as the bass and drums are very backward in the recording balance, but on the superbly recorded Victor the full impact of the trio chorus can be gauged. Both Ellington's conception of an equal-voiced trio for piano, bass, and drums and the way in which Braud and Greer were able to respond are equally unusual in the jazz of this period.

The OKeh *Black Beauty* was recorded seven months later as an Ellington piano solo; this gives us an opportunity to hear Duke's keyboard conception of one of his early orchestral works, and comparison with the band versions is fascinating. Its companion piece is a solo in the stride piano style called *Swampy River*, more clearly pianistic than *Black Beauty* and again displaying that highly distinctive musical character which was lending so special a flavor to Ellington's band recordings. These two 1928 piano solos have received rather less than their due from the critics over the years. There are recordings by other jazz pianists from this period which have more of a virtuoso air, but few which are so consistently interesting in their musical development and so well organized formally over the three minutes of the then standard 10-inch 78-rpm record.

After the two piano solos the band went on to record four more titles, only three of which have been issued. There is an important change in the saxophone section: Johnny Hodges had replaced Otto Hardwick. The Hodges alto style was much "hotter" than Hardwick's and, as befitted a disciple and pupil of Sidney Bechet's, he doubled soprano saxophone to great effect. The first of the band titles from this OKeh session is the initial recording of *The Mooche*, another of those perennials which always retained a place in the Ellington repertoire. Although the middle section is a sequence of blues solos, *The Mooche* sounds very much an entity. Its somber minor-key theme is cast as a dialog between three clarinets and Miley's muted trumpet, and it catches a mood unique in Ellington's music. This theme is used at the beginning and end; the middle part introduces a new melody which the soloists then proceed to ignore. There are four Miley period versions of *The Mooche*—on OKeh, Cameo (two takes), Brunswick, and Victor. Of these the Brunswick is the best, followed by the OKeh. On the Brunswick Ellington (theme), Bigard, Miley and Hodges (duet), and Hodges (solo) take up the five second-theme choruses in a magnificent sequence. Miley is in superb form both in the duet and in his work on the first theme, while the Hodges chorus (included only in this and the Victor versions) is equally outstanding. Note the almost barrelhouse backing given to this solo by Ellington and Braud. There were two guests present on the OKeh session—blues guitarist Lonnie Johnson and scat singer Baby Cox. In *The Mooche* they have a duet chorus which sounds strangely out of context, but Johnson's accompaniment to Bigard's solo adds a fresh dimension to the passage. The band plays particularly well on the two poorly recorded Cameo takes which also find Miley in peak form. Ellington was still permutating his trumpet section, and Miley is absent from the Victor recording of *The Mooche*. This is a rather theatrical reading with temple block effects from Greer; Whetsol takes Miley's part and although he plays well, a good deal is lost in terms of the characterization of the piece. This recording comes from a session on which a brass bass player (probably Billy Taylor) substituted for Braud. It is interesting to note that when Braud bows away in imitations of the tuba style on the other versions of *The Mooche* he brings off the brass bass effect with more fire and character than does his temporary replacement who actually uses that instrument.

From the same richly productive OKeh session as the two piano solos and *The Mooche* come two more new Ellington band pieces—*Move Over* and *Hot And Bothered*. There are two recordings from this period of each number, these intitial OKehs and "cover versions" on Cameo recorded under the pseudonym of The Washingtonians. *Move Over* is a medium tempo number with several interesting features. Its introductory motif anticipates that of Ellington's first concert work, *Creole Rhapsody*, and it has a full chorus of scored saxophone section variations. In an attempt to counteract the unbalancing effect of Miley's opening statement, Ellington also reintroduced him as the final soloist. Both versions of *Move Over* have rough-hewn yet gentle readings of the second theme by Nanton, while the OKeh also has solos by Lonnie Johnson and Barney Bigard. Although the slower tempo of the Cameo suits the piece fractionally better, the OKeh is the preferable version because of the brighter and more vivid recording quality.

Hot And Bothered is one of Duke's excursions on the *Tiger Rag* chords and the Cameo version is again slower than the better-known OKeh. This makes for better saxophone section playing and for a firmer solo from Johnny Hodges, but the hair-raising tempo and the "edge of disaster" excitement of the OKeh are missed. Writing of this OKeh recording in his 1934 book *Music Ho!*, the British composer Constant Lambert stated that "there is nothing in Ravel so dexterous in treatment as the varied solos in the middle of the ebullient *Hot And Bothered* and nothing in Stravinsky more dynamic than the final section." One can only assume that Lambert thought that each solo and each break in *Hot And Bothered* was as carefully calculated as those effects of color and rhythm in the orchestral works of Ravel and Stravinsky. As a judgment on the artistry involved in the production of this exciting but often untidy performance, he could hardly have been more wrong. But as an aesthetic judgment, perhaps Lambert was not so far out after all, for the impact of the incessant drive, the youthful enthusiasm, and the tumbling colors of *Hot And Bothered* are still dazzling. The soloists on the OKeh are Bigard, Hodges, and Lonnie Johnson, but the high spot is the chase chorus between Miley's growl trumpet and Baby Cox's scat singing. This is accompanied by four-to-the-bar bass from Braud, and the excitement is heightened by the false starts, the headlong drive, and the feeling of reckless abandon. Miley's solo on the Cameo is very good but cannot equal this unique passage.

Two numbers in which Whetsol is the main soloist derive much of their character from the trumpeter's delicate, finely edged style. *Awful Sad* is the prototype of the Ellington ballad for orchestra, and its distinctive melody begat many close relations in later years, not all of them in the Ellington family. Whetsol has the prime responsibility here; the other soloists are Carney on alto and Bigard on tenor and clarinet. On the second piece, *Misty Mornin'*, Whetsol is simply one of the soloists, but his personality nonetheless dominates the musical climate. This is one of Ellington's early tone paintings. After the band's theme statement and a variation chorus for the saxophone section, Whetsol and Bigard (on tenor) are heard before the closing ensemble, which is scored for brass and high reeds. The Pathé version of *Misty Mornin'* is probably the best overall realization of the piece and is taken at an ideal tempo; Whetsol and Bigard are the only soloists. The OKeh version has a chorus by Lonnie Johnson's guitar between the trumpet and the tenor, while the Victor has an Ellington piano solo at this point.

Two new and contrasting Ellington compositions were recorded at an OKeh session in November 1928—*Goin' To Town* and *Blues With A Feeling*. The first, a collaboration with Miley, is one of those Ellington pieces which succeeds in satirizing contemporary musical styles. Here is the "jazz age" in all its headless, syncopated naivety goin' to town with a vengeance. Miley opens proceedings with a deliciously zany solo and for once the others are able to keep up the standard with little loss of momentum—Hodges, Nanton, and Carney are heard as soloists while Braud has a crucial role on bass. *Blues With A Feeling* is one of the great Ellington records, a simple but unique arrangement. Over the somber sound of Braud's close-miked bowed bass, Nanton's trombone sings a beautiful twelve-bar melody backed by a choir of low-register clarinets. Hodges solos on soprano over a hushed trumpet section before Miley introduces a second, thirty-two bar theme. This is a great solo, but it does not overshadow the other soloists in the way Miley had previously done, and with this performance both Hodges and Nanton proclaim their stature as jazz musicians of the first rank. On *Blues With A Feeling* the Ellington soloists play the blues with an eloquence unsurpassed in the annals of recorded jazz.

* * *

Turning to the arrangements of non-Ellington compositions recorded by the band in 1928, two of the best are W. C. Handy's *Yellow Dog Blues* and Spencer Williams's *Tishomingo Blues*. These were done at a June 1928 date, the first on which Hodges replaced Hardwick. Hodges is heard on soprano sax on *Yellow Dog Blues* and on alto on *Tishomingo Blues*—both excellent solos—while Miley, Nanton, and Metcalf solo on the first title and these three plus Bigard on the second. The Miley solo on *Yellow Dog Blues* is particularly noteworthy. Both performances are weakened by the inconsistent quality of Ellington's arrangements. Excellent ideas, such as the clarinets with walking bass introduction and coda to *Yellow Dog Blues*, rub shoulders with second-rate and second-hand period devices. Certainly neither of these performances is of the stature of *Blues With A Feeling*, which was recorded only five months later.

Another famous Handy blues which the Ellington band recorded in 1928 was *St. Louis Blues*, but on the record—a 12-inch Victor in the days when 12-inch popular discs were rare—the Ellington band is simply one element in an amalgam also including a fourteen-piece studio band, a nine-piece choir, and an assortment of vocal soloists. This rather fantastic mélange was labeled as "Warren Mills and his Blues Serenaders" and was directed by violinist Matty Malneck. Against all probability there is some good jazz to be heard, including a full chorus of vintage Bubber Miley.

A much lesser known blues is Victoria Spivey's *No Papa No*, recorded by the Ellington band at the Victor session with the brass bass. An unknown trumpet player replaces Miley and can be heard on the first (nonvocal) take along with Bigard, Carney on alto, Ellington, and a superlative Nanton. On the second take, the trumpet solo is by Whetsol, Ozzie Ware gives a fair imitation of a blues singer, and Nanton is again supreme. In his solos on *No Papa No*, Nanton used the variety of tone colors available on plunger-muted trombone to great effect. Two further vocal blues recordings by Miss Ware, also from this session, were issued as by "Ozzie Ware accompanied by Duke Ellington's Hot Five." This quintet consists of the unknown trumpet player, Bigard, Ellington, the brass bass player and Greer. The outstanding feature of these recordings is Bigard's clarinet playing behind the vocals.

The members of the Ellington band, unlike those of

Fletcher Henderson's, were only rarely recorded as blues accompanists, and among the very few examples not already mentioned are two further titles with Ozzie Ware, also recorded in 1928 but on this occasion for the Cameo label. On one side—*It's All Coming Home To You*—the only accompanist is Ellington on piano, but the other—*Hit Me In The Nose Blues*—has a small unit and features obbligatos to Miss Ware's choruses by Whetsol, Bigard, Nanton, and Ellington; Bigard is again very fine, and Nanton plays so well that one regrets that he did not record more in this role, for he would clearly have rivaled Charlie Green as a blues accompanist on trombone.

By late 1928 Freddie Jenkins had joined the trumpet section making it up to three pieces and the full lineup was:

Trumpets: Bubber Miley, Arthur Whetsol, Freddie Jenkins.

Trombone: Tricky Sam Nanton.

Reeds: Johnny Hodges (alto and soprano saxes, clarinet); Barney Bigard (clarinet and tenor sax); Harry Carney (baritone and alto saxes, clarinet).

Rhythm: Duke Ellington (piano); Fred Guy (banjo); Wellman Braud (bass); Sonny Greer (drums).

Of the popular songs recorded by the band at this time the majority were by Dorothy Fields and Jimmy McHugh. Exceptions include *Got Everything But You*, an early example of the "string of solos" treatment of a pop song, and *Louisiana*, which has fine work by Miley, Nanton, Hodges, and Bigard. The Fields-McHugh songs are a mixed bunch, and they inspired some rather varied performances by the Ellington band. The Victor version of *Diga Diga Do* is outstanding because it contains one of Miley's finest choruses. This solo follows a period vocal by Irving Mills and is played very quietly, tightly muted and with sparing use of the growl. The most impressive things about this chorus, less distinguished melodically than Miley's other solo masterpieces, are the use of harmony and above all the precision of the note placing. The mood is of an inward-looking stillness which is accentuated by the fact that it is played over Braud's explosive, extroverted string bass. Here Miley enhances the swing by placing his notes against the beat in a manner which could only be equaled by Louis Armstrong at this time. Indeed, when one considers Miley's work with Ellington in 1928 and early 1929, its rhythmic awareness is one of its outstanding qualities. On the OKeh recording of *Diga Diga Do*, Miley again has a full chorus solo, this time before Mills's vocal, but it is a lesser creation.

Miley was in particularly good form at the Victor session at which *Diga Diga Do* was recorded, and on the other two titles from this date he supplies the first chorus theme statements—driving, urgent, and extroverted on *Bandana Babies* and tightly muted and poised on *I Must Have That Man*, an astringent reading of a sentimental theme which ranks with Billie Holiday's equally un-cloying treatment of a few years later. The weakest of the Ellington band's recordings of 1928 are also from the Fields-McHugh repertoire: *Hottentot*, which sounds like a Cotton Club production number and which introduces the new solo voice of trumpeter Freddie Jenkins; *Doin' The New Low Down*, arranged in conventional fashion and with vocal by Irving Mills; and *I Can't Give You Anything But Love*, a rather disappointing arrangement in which the highlights are Whetsol's almost Beiderbecke-style solo at the beginning and Nanton's trombone backing to the vocals by Baby Cox and Irving Mills.

* * *

Bubber Miley's final recording sessions with the Duke Ellington Orchestra were from January 1929—one for the Brunswick label, which produced *Doin' The Voom Voom* and a two-part *Tiger Rag*, and one for Victor which yielded *Flaming Youth*, *Saturday Night Function*, *High Life*, and a second *Doin' The Voom Voom*. The Brunswick version of this last title lacks the tremendous drive of the Victor and comes out distinctly second best. This composition is at one and the same time a straightforward jazz stomp and a production number used to accompany the Cotton Club chorus line. Using contrasting themes and instrumental combinations, it demonstrates that at this early stage of his career Ellington had already to a degree escaped from his earlier dependence on improvised solos. On the Victor *Doin' The Voom Voom*, Jenkins, Hodges, Whetsol, Miley, Carney, Nanton, Ellington, and Bigard are used (in that order) without any of them having a jazz solo in the accepted sense—even the robust, bubbling duet between Carney and Nanton is a prearranged routine. In its rather modest way the Victor *Doin' The Voom Voom*, a wholly enjoyable, extroverted performance, is a milestone in the Ellington discography.

No such claim could be made for *Tiger Rag*, although this is a fine record in a more conventional sense. It is a free-blowing exercise for the soloists with Bigard's New Orleans style clarinet in a primary role. He is heard playing vigorous counterpoint against the opening ensemble, taking the traditional *Tiger Rag* clarinet breaks, and indulging in two long solos. The other soloists in this two-part double-sided recording are Jenkins, Carney, Hodges, Miley, and Nanton, all of whom are on good form. The chorus by Jenkins was a famous one, and much of the trumpeter's brilliant, high-stepping vigor which appealed to contemporary musicians has survived the years. It is also famous among jazz collectors because Jenkins played it at every opportunity and several other Ellington records of this period are graced by the presence of this solo. There are two takes of the first part of *Tiger Rag*; the only important differences are in Bigard's solo, which is perhaps fractionally more effective on the first take.

Ellington's contribution to *Tiger Rag* is to provide a conventional framework for the solos, which he does well enough. The final chorus features brass against high clarinet in an orchestral version of the old New Orleans small band manner. Duke's most audacious stroke is his scoring of the famous riff ("Hold that tiger!") chorus, which still sounds quite startling in its originality half a century later.

One of the titles from the January 1929 Victor session, *High Life*, is based on *Tiger Rag*, and Bigard and Jenkins simply carry their solos forward from that number. Nanton is also heard to advantage, and *High Life* closes with a dialogue between the band and Sonny Greer, playing what Ellington liked to call "hot chimes." Greer's set of chimes were often prominent in photographs of the Ellington band in ensuing years, but on record they were fortunately used sparingly. Greer probably exhausted their potential on this record and on the later *Ring Dem Bells*.

The other two numbers from the Victor session are masterpieces. *Saturday Night Function* is a blues with a melody based on the spiritual *Were You There When They Crucified My Lord?* On the Victor recording, this melody is played by the trumpet section in the growl style. The solos are by Bigard (two superb choruses), Whetsol in an unusually vigorous mood, and Nanton in a typically expressive chorus. The sober decorations of the theme by Hodges in the opening and closing choruses are simply perfect.

Flaming Youth is the last major Miley recording with Ellington, and he once again takes the first chorus in a manner which makes what follows sound anticlimactic. He only just brings it off here, not because of any shortcomings in his own playing, which is magnificent, but because Ellington's scoring and the solos of Nanton and Hodges are not the stuff out of which anticlimaxes are normally made. But Miley's drive and authority make *Flaming Youth* sound a far finer composition than it really is (compare the later Pathé recording, which has a Johnny Hodges theme statement), and, as so often happened on the Ellington records which start with a Miley solo, the first chorus is the best. (A fascinating alternative take of this recording has been issued on the Up-To-Date label.)

Bubber Miley lived another three and a quarter years after leaving Ellington, but he was never again in his finest form on records. One reason for this was that the context for his work on later records is inadequate, often grossly so. In a very real sense, *Flaming Youth* was therefore Miley's swan song. The maturity of his style compared with his playing of only two years previously is astonishing, the mastery of the plunger mute and the growl is complete, and his rhythmic flexibility is far greater than before. On *Flaming Youth*, Bubber Miley sounds a great jazz musician at the very peak of his powers. His star was to fade quickly, and only in the Ellington orchestra would the imprint of his contribution to music endure. For Duke himself, however, even the loss of his most important soloist could not now hinder the development of the talent which had flowered so wonderfully in the past eighteen months.

Outstanding Recordings

Creole Love Call, *Black And Tan Fantasy* (Victor and OKeh versions, both takes of the latter), *East St. Louis Toodle-oo* (Victor version), *Blue Bubbles*, *Black Beauty* (Brunswick and Victor band versions, both takes of former, and OKeh piano solo), *Swampy River* (piano solo), *The Mooche* (Brunswick version), *Hot And Bothered* (OKeh version), *Awful Sad*, *Misty Mornin'* (Pathé version), *The Blues With A Feeling*, *Tiger Rag*, *Flaming Youth* (Victor version), *Saturday Night Function* (Victor version), and *Doin' The Voom Voom* (Victor version)

Chapter 5

The Miley Era

ONE OF THE PHOTOGRAPHS IN DUKE ELLINGTON'S autobiography *Music Is My Mistress* is of what is described as "the first Cotton Club band." The musicians pictured are:

Trumpet: Bubber Miley.

Trombone: Tricky Sam Nanton.

Reeds: Nelson Kincaid, Rudy Jackson, Harry Carney.

Violin: Ellsworth Reynolds.

Rhythm: Duke Ellington (piano); Fred Guy (banjo); Wellman Braud (bass); Sonny Greer (drums).

The photograph was taken in late 1927 or early 1928. Ellsworth Reynolds was hired as a "front man" at the start of the new and prestigious Cotton Club engagement, but did not stay long, not even long enough to make a single record with the band. Nelson Kincaid's name has not otherwise been associated with Ellington; one must assume that he was deputizing for Otto Hardwick on the day the photograph was taken. The second trumpet, which the records show to have been a regular feature of the Ellington band, is not in evidence—either he too was absent temporarily or he had been dropped in favor of the violinist. The fact that the latter was hired as "front man" shows that Ellington was still a somewhat reluctant bandleader, clearly not relishing the spotlight in the way he came to do in later years. Whatever the reasons for their absence in the photograph of this "first Cotton Club band," Louis Metcalf and Otto Hardwick soon returned to replace Reynolds and Kincaid. There were, as we have seen, further changes in 1928. Most of these were straightforward, but the situation in the trumpets at the time of Arthur Whetsol's return was not. Although employing three trumpet players, Ellington continued to record with two, seeming to permutate two from his stock of three as each recording session came round. The following table shows the pattern:

Recording Date	**Company**	**Trumpet Section**
January 18, 1928	OKeh	Miley, Metcalf
March ?, 1928	Cameo	Miley, Metcalf
March 21, 1928	Brunswick	Whetsol, Metcalf
March 26, 1928	Victor	Whetsol, Miley
June 5, 1928	Brunswick	Miley, Metcalf
July 10, 1928	OKeh	Whetsol, Miley

Miley was notoriously unreliable, but there is clearly some factor other than his occasional and unpredictable absence operating here.

By 1929 the band had assumed that permanence of personnel which was to become an Ellington hallmark. In October 1928 Freddie Jenkins had come in as permanent third trumpet, joining Miley and Whetsol in the section; in February 1929 Cootie Williams replaced Bubber Miley; and in September of that year Ellington added a second trombone in the person of Juan Tizol. These were the only personnel changes until early 1931, when Ivie Anderson joined as vocalist, and the spring of 1932, when Lawrence Brown came in to make the trombones a three-piece section.

* * *

After Miley had left Ellington, he played around New York, visited Paris for a couple of weeks with Noble Sissle, and then worked in New York again with various bands. From early 1930, he was featured with the white orchestra of Leo Reisman as novelty soloist, often joining the band from the audience dressed as an usher. On other occasions, to avoid offending the audience with the color of his skin, he would be hidden behind a screen. Then, after working in the *Sweet And Low* revue for a while, Miley formed his own band in late 1931. It was sponsored by Irving Mills and played in the show *Harlem Scandals*. Bubber had been warned previously that he was tubercular, and in February 1932, he was forced to give up playing because of his condition. His health deteriorated rapidly and he died on May 20, 1932, at the age of 29. It is said that not one musician attended the funeral of this remarkable artist and that the only mark of his contribution to music was a large wreath from Ellington.

None of the records Miley made after leaving Duke approaches the quality of his work with the Ellington band during the later part of his stay. Although some of the solos he

27

recorded with Reisman are good, they lack the melodic distinction of his Ellington work. The records with Jelly Roll Morton are only moderate, and those with his own band greatly disappointing. Deteriorating health may well have been the principal cause of this falling off.

The records made in the period covered by the last chapter show a continuing improvement in the Ellington Orchestra as an ensemble. It was not yet the subtle instrument which would reflect every intended nuance of its fastidious director, but the seeds were clearly germinating. Wellman Braud, especially, and Ellington himself were still inclined to rush the tempo, but overall the band was steadier. The intonation would have been intolerable by the standards of later years, but this was true of all contemporary big bands, and certainly Ellington's late twenties orchestra was a considerable improvement on The Washingtonians in this respect. The solo strength was greatly enhanced by the maturing of Tricky Sam Nanton's elusive art and by the arrival of two great reed stylists in Barney Bigard and Johnny Hodges. While by no means the master he later became, Hodges was already a fine jazz soloist and a considerable advance on Hardwick in this respect, although Hardwick was to remind listeners on his return some four years hence what a superb band musician he was.

* * *

Comparing the best of Ellington's records of this period with those of contemporary bandleaders is interesting. Fletcher Henderson's was a band which rivaled Ellington in solo strength and both the Henderson Orchestra and McKinney's Cotton Pickers were superior to the Ellington band in terms of intonation and precision. But Ellington's musical purpose was deeper and stronger than Henderson's or those of the various leaders of McKinney's, and the music reflects this. The greatest recorded achievements in ensemble jazz during the mid-twenties were Jelly Roll Morton's Victor recordings. It is instructive to compare Ellington's writing for a band at this period with Morton's—that is, with Morton's work with his 1926-1928 small bands, not that with the later big bands, which was below his best standards. On the blues, Ellington was already a master, and his *The Blues With A Feeling* is as successful as any of Morton's simple blues, even that masterpiece by his quartet, *Mournful Serenade*. Duke could not at this stage produce works of the complexity of Morton's *Original Jelly Roll Blues*, but many of his two-theme compositions suggest that his mind was working hard at solving that problem of diversity within overall unity which makes *Original Jelly Roll Blues* such a triumph. For all its excellence the wild *Hot And Bothered* cannot be compared with such Morton stomps as *Black Bottom Stomp* or *Grandpa's Spells* as a composition, although in its rather modest way it foreshadows (as does *Creole Love Call* in a different mood) Ellington's masterly deployment of solo talent and instrumental color in his later records. And it would still be a few years before Ellington could produce arrangements of other people's compositions comparable to Morton's masterly version of King Oliver's *Doctor Jazz* or his transformation of Oliver's *Chimes Blues* into *Mournful Serenade*. Looking at the matter from the point of view of the band rather than the composer, the most interesting comparison with early Ellington is the Luis Russell Orchestra in 1929-1930, but discussion of that remarkable group must wait until we have examined Ellington's own output during these years.

* * *

The most obvious advances in Ellington's work as a composer in the late 1920s are the lessening of his reliance on Bubber Miley and the widening range of his art. If we take the lists of records cited at the end of Chapters 2 and 4 as a sequence, and ignore the intervening performances, we can hear the steady development of Ellington's compositional technique. The primitive handling of the two themes in *East St. Louis Toodle-oo* compared with the use of the same pattern on *The Blues With A Feeling* shows a characteristic advance. The early method of building his compositions round Miley's solos had been developed to a point where a work could now be centered upon a sequence of soloists (*The Blues With A Feeling*) or manage without any improvised solos at all (*Doin' The Voom Voom*). Another player could now take over the dominant role previously allotted to Miley (Whetsol in *Black Beauty* and *Awful Sad*), or a soloist could be used as a main voice without taking an improvised chorus (Miley in some versions of *The Mooche*). Less formal pieces like *Saturday Night Function* could allow the soloists full rein while retaining the full Ellington flavor.

That Ellington was already using his own methods is apparent from both the records and from the later recollections of his musicians. Barney Bigard recalled that "at first, just after I joined Duke, I used to think everything was wrong, because he wrote so weird. It took me some time to get used to hearing all those things. He would make the chords all the wrong way, giving to someone else the part he should have given to the clarinet player" (quoted in *The World Of Duke Ellington* by Stanley Dance, p. 84). Freddie Jenkins had much the same initial reaction: "the Ellington music sounded odd to me, third class discords and all that . . ." (quoted in *Reminiscing In Tempo With Freddie Jenkins* by Roger Ringo, in *Storyville* 46, April–May 1973, p. 129). It is significant that even musicians who were later to become vital parts of the Ellington ensemble took a little time to catch on to what he was doing. Jenkins also tells how Ellington used to pay for band rehearsals at which he would experiment with different voicings within a chord. It seems that Ellington's youthful disinclination toward formal musical tuition was paying off, in that he now had to create his own academy for study, one which would be far more precisely tuned to his needs than any formal institution.

Many Ellington compositions of this period were concocted in the recording studio, an original melody by Duke or one of the sidemen being expanded into a whole by verbal and musical suggestions and improvised solos. Duke would have the final say on the routine and would only later transcribe the piece from the record to sheet music. He even wrote out his scores in a unique way. Although the parts were written as chords on one stave, to understand them they had to be read as separate strands with the accidentals only changed when they affected a particular part. For example, if a C was sharpened in the tenor sax part, Ellington would only use a natural sign to indicate that a later C was natural if this also occurred in the tenor sax part. With all the parts on a single stave, the accidentals had to be read according to the Ellington method or the music would not make sense. Thus, if any of Ellington's scores should fall into the hands of would-be imitators, they would be useless.

It was common practice in the twenties for arrangers to make the rounds of different clubs and shows in order to "steal" music from the more original bands. But they soon found that they could not do this with Ellington. Paul Whiteman wanted to feature some Ellingtonian effects within his band, so he took Ferde Grofé, a very considerable musician who had orchestrated *Rhapsody In Blue* for George Gershwin, to hear the sound. They returned night after night but in the end were compelled to admit that it was impossible to steal this music.

* * *

The skills of the Ellington musicians relative to each other were most varied at this time. Arthur Whetsol's consistency, reliability, and good taste made him a tower of strength. Although the more jazz-inclined soloists would take the lead if the music were being worked out in an impromptu manner, if it were presented to the band via a written score, then Whetsol, whose reading ability was first class, would take the initiative while the other musicians learned their parts. But no matter whether they were outstanding as readers or as improvisors, all the Ellington musicians had to have sharp ears and sharp imaginations in order to interpret their leader's highly original creations.

The directions in which Ellington's art as a composer/arranger were expanding were to some extent due to the stimulus of having to write backgrounds for the various acts which the band accompanied as part of its duties at the Cotton Club. Even though it was located in Harlem the club was a strictly segregated place for a clientele of whites looking for exotic entertainment. The floor shows were lavishly produced, often with an emphasis on primitive "jungle" themes. Soon Ellington was not only using existing material behind the "jungle" tableaux, but also writing new compositions for them, compositions whose titles clearly indicate their origins—*Jungle Jamboree*, *Jungle Nights In Harlem*, *Jungle Blues*, and *Echoes Of The Jungle*. Such was the status of black American culture that its most sophisticated musician was employed producing works which were considered by their audiences to be "jungle music."

This term "jungle music" is often used as a description of Ellington's overall musical style, in particular of his use of growl and wa-wa muted brass during the Cotton Club years. Contemporary publicity exploited this description, of course, but it has also been used by serious jazz writers and historians for years. It is essential for the listener to realize that pseudo-primitivism was only one small element in Ellington's music, but at the same time an influence which he turned very much to his advantage in his development as an artist. Furthermore, the growl styles perfected by Miley and Nanton were a logical development of that "vocalization" of instrumental tone and inflection which is a primary characteristic of black American instrumental music. In origin this has nothing to do with "jungle music," Cotton Club, or otherwise, and indeed some of the supposed definitive examples of Ellington's "jungle style"—numbers like *East St. Louis Toodle-oo* and *Black And Tan Fantasy*—were written before the band went into the Cotton Club. The growl brass style is in fact one of the most traditional elements in Ellington's music.

During the Cotton Club years the Ellington band also played many theater and dance engagements outside the Club, sometimes during brief periods of absence, sometimes as the result of such circumstances as the long 1930 trip across the country to Hollywood to appear in the film *Check And Double Check*. Ellington was also a keen participant in band battles, including some in that famous home of the battling bands, Harlem's Savoy Ballroom. Thus he made the most of all the opportunities open to the black jazzman of the twenties and thirties. His music developed not only in the exotic atmosphere of the Cotton Club shows and in prestigious ballrooms, but also in catering for black demands for robust rhythmic dance music and in competing with the bands which specialized in this field.

At first, this variety of engagements was due to Ellington's own efforts to promote the band. He could hardly have continued to act as band manager as well as being leader, composer, arranger, and pianist. In late 1927 he signed with the Irving Mills agency, with Mills personally handling all but the routine aspects of the Ellington band's management. The part played by Mills in Ellington's career is a controversial one. In having his business matters attended to by Mills, Ellington was able to devote the maximum amount of time to musical matters. It is generally known that Mills made a small fortune—or maybe a not-so-small fortune—out of the Ellington band: for example, he was not a musician but his name appears on countless Ellington compositions for which he would draw regular royalties as cocomposer. He was resented in some sectors of the black community as an exploiter of black talent, but there can be no real doubt that the arrival of Mills to take up the business side of the Ellington Orchestra was an unqualified blessing in the social context of the time. No black manager could have done the work performed by Mills on Ellington's behalf in the social milieu of the twenties and thirties, still less could any of the white aesthetes of fastidious taste who condemned the show-business aspects of the band's work. Mills was a prodigiously energetic man who worked as a song publisher, band manager, publicity agent, sometime vocalist, and, in later years, record company executive. Ellington was served by Mills in all these capacities and throughout their association the Ellington Orchestra was the Mills Agency's number one band, with Mills's personal attendance certain if a crisis blew up.

At the start of their association, the two men formed a company known as Ellington Inc., and Mills then set about making Ellington an internationally known show-business figure. He arranged hundreds of recording sessions many of which were for major record companies in contrast to the comparatively obscure labels—Blu-Disc, Up-To-Date, etc.—for which Ellington had previously recorded. And of course Mills was responsible for the Cotton Club engagement. It is also worth noting that Mills encouraged all Ellington's musical ambitions, including the presentation of concert pieces such as *Creole Rhapsody* and *Reminiscing In Tempo*. The average manager of the day would probably have looked askance at such uncommercial ventures and their probable effect on Ellington's public image at a time when to be branded "highbrow" could be the kiss of death in American show business. In addition to making a good deal of money out of the association, Mills clearly had a great liking and respect for both Ellington and his music. It is hard to believe that anyone could have done a better job in those times and in those circumstances.

Pseudonyms

During the early years of the Mills management, the Ellington Orchestra recorded for Victor under its own name, but under a pseudonym for records issued by other companies. The number of such names used on records by the Ellington band in the late twenties and early thirties is rather bewildering, and the modern collector can be grateful that all reissues are put out under Ellington's name. In addition to being known as Duke Ellington and his Orchestra or Duke Ellington and his Cotton Club Orchestra on Victor, the following band names are known to have been used on Ellington records:

The Broadway Revellers (Australian Bellbird)
Frank Brown and his Tooters (American Parlophone)
The Dixie Jazz Band (Oriole, Regal)
Duke Ellington and his Memphis Men (Columbia)
The Georgia Syncopators (Melotone, Perfect)
Sonny Greer and his Memphis Men (Columbia)
The Harlem Footwarmers (OKeh)
Harlem Hot Chocolates (Hit Of The Week)
The Harlem Music Makers (OKeh)
Earl Jackson and his Musical Champions (Melotone)
The Jungle Band (Brunswick)
Louisiana Rhythm Makers (Banner)
Memphis Hot Shots (Harmony)
Mills' Ten Blackberries (Velvet Tone)

New York Syncopators (Odeon)
The Philadelphia Melodians (Parlophone)
The Ten Blackberries (Perfect, Banner, etc.)
Joe Turner And His Memphis Men (Columbia)
The Washingtonians (Cameo, Romeo, etc.)
The Whoopee Makers (Romeo, Oriole, Pathé, etc.)

Recording quality varied enormously on these labels. The Victors were on the whole the best, although the discs recorded in Camden suffer from the echo associated with the Victor studio there. OKeh, Columbia, Brunswick, and Velvet Tone also produced good recordings, but some of the small companies had very low standards. The Cameos, Romeos, Perfects, etc., are not too bad as recordings, but these companies often used poor quality shellac for their discs; as the masters were destroyed many years ago, a good deal depends on the state of the best available 78s when reissues are engineered. Taking all factors into consideration, it is remarkable that so many reissues sound as good as they do.

A further matter of some interest so far as the Ellington recordings of the late twenties and early thirties are concerned is studio balance. This varies a lot, to such an extent in the case of the rhythm section that one wonders if this factor was used at times to try to disguise the identity of the band.

Sidemen

Barney Bigard

Although his technique is typical of the Creole clarinet school of New Orleans, owing a good deal to the example of Jimmie Noone, Barney Bigard has a unique place in the annals of jazz for the way in which he used the clarinet as an important instrument within a big band. No other player can be compared with him in this respect, and his brilliant counterpoint against the Ellington ensemble creates a unique sound. The understanding between Bigard and Ellington seems to have been perfect, and his contribution was equally valuable as soloist and as bandsman. Bigard was perhaps the most technically gifted of the New Orleans clarinet school and he obviously enjoyed virtuoso performances. As a soloist he covered a considerable range, excelling in slow blues, of which he was one of the masters. Although he had gained a reputation in Chicago as a tenor saxophonist in the days before he joined Ellington he was not an outstanding soloist on that instrument.

Representative Recordings: Tiger Rag (Brunswick, 1929), *Saturday Night Function* (Victor, Columbia, and Romeo, 1929), *Rose Room* (Brunswick, 1932), *Clarinet Lament* (Brunswick, 1936), *Jack The Bear* (Victor, 1940), *Across The Track Blues* (Victor, 1940)

Wellman Braud

When he first joined the Ellington band, Wellman Braud frequently played bowed bass in imitation of the sound of the then fashionable tuba; indeed he was also proficient on tuba although he does not seem to have used it on any Ellington records. He soon started to concentrate on the increasingly popular pizzicato string bass style of which he was one of the early masters. He would still change to bowed bass on occasion and in a big band context, he used this technique better than any other jazz bass player. In essence Braud was a typical New Orleans musician, with more concern for the spirit of the music than for academic accuracy. He never went in for spectacular effects, concentrating wholly on providing a solid foundation for the band. Braud was a very distinctive musical personality whose playing could vary according to the mood of a piece from a roaring, stomping four-to-the-bar style to a gentle slapping on the offbeat which sets up many of Ellington's more relaxed recordings from the middle thirties.

Representative Recordings: The Blues With A Feeling (OKeh, 1929), *Doin' The Voom Voom* (Victor, 1929), *Saratoga Swing* (Victor, 1929), *Double Check Stomp* (Victor, 1930), *Rose Room* (Brunswick, 1932), *Harlem Speaks* (Brunswick, 1933)

Harry Carney

For almost the whole lifetime of the Duke Ellington Orchestra Harry Carney was one of its most distinguished voices. He joined sometime between late 1926 and early 1927—accounts differ—and he stayed on after Ellington's death in May 1974, playing under the direction of Duke's son Mercer, before succumbing to cancer on October 8 of that year. In many ways Carney was, after Duke himself, the key member of the orchestra. It was he, more than anyone, who was responsible for the rich sonority and the rhythmic zest of the Ellington ensemble. His playing was amazingly consistent, and his tone on baritone sax was of incredible depth and resonance. He was able to vary his sound through a remarkably wide range of tone colors. Allied to this he had a wonderful rhythmic sense and was often the main agent of swing in the band. His early solos are not particularly distinguished, but from the early thirties onwards, his style matured rapidly and he soon became the leading jazz soloist on baritone sax, a position he maintained for the rest of his life. He was not always a particularly brilliant improvisor in a conventional jazz solo context, but his contributions in the form of short solos and dialogues in the Ellington Orchestra were of the highest order.

Harry Carney was an unassuming man, but the unassuming air of his playing could be misleading, for he was a saxophonist of the first rank. His playing combined complete mastery of his instrument and highly flexible technique with the judgment and imagination needed to deal with the widely varied musical situations he found in the Ellington band. He was a musician of perfect taste with an emotional range which varied from a gentle, wistful kind of playing to a driving, bouncing, ebullient style which was quite inimitable. His strong tone and great musical sensitivity were factors which caused Ellington to give important harmony parts to Carney's baritone. Harry also played alto sax, clarinet, and bass clarinet in the Ellington band. In later years he became something of a specialist on bass clarinet as well as baritone sax, and the Ellington records contain a number of vital contributions by him on this instrument.

Representative Recordings: Old Man Blues (Victor, 1930), *Jive Stomp* (Brunswick, 1933), *Jumpin' Punkins* (Victor, 1941), *I Like The Sunrise* (from *The Liberian Suite*, Columbia, 1947), *Serious Serenade* (Capitol, 1955), *La Plus Belle Africaine* (Verve, 1966). All the above on baritone sax; a good example of Carney's solo work on bass clarinet is *Intimate Interlude* (Pablo, 1971)

Johnny Hodges

Johnny Hodges is one of the greatest jazz soloists, and along with Benny Carter and Charlie Parker one of the leading alto saxophonists in the history of the music. He was originally inspired by the great New Orleans musician Sidney Bechet, from whom he took lessons in the early 1920s. He retained a great enthusiasm for Bechet's music for the rest of his life. In a dressing room conversation with the author during the Ellington band's 1958 tour of England, his warm, eager enthusiasm for Bechet's music was unexpected in a man noted for a reserved and taciturn manner. Musically, Hodges was his own man, and he developed his personal and forthright manner of playing at an early age. This in turn developed over the years into a unique alto saxophone style with a tone which was utterly inimitable. On the early Ellington records Hodges favors a direct, rather laconic manner, but later he developed a more sinuous, sensuous way of playing. In his later years he would sometimes contrast delicate, sensuous playing with blues phrasing of the most elemental kind. In all situations he was a supreme melodist. It can be said that from the late forties a certain blandness was sometimes evident in his music, but this was a rather deceptive quality since examination of his solos always reveals an alert musical thinker behind the facade of easy virtuosity.

His mastery of the alto saxophone was beyond compare. Ellington noted with wonder that Hodges was the only musician he knew who could "pick up a cold horn and play in tune without tuning up," while John Coltrane considered his playing the epitome of saxophone technique. Alternating with Otto Hardwick (and later Russell Procope), Hodges would often lead the Ellington saxophone section in masterly fashion; in every situation he was a section man of formidable power and skill. Clark Terry, who played in the Ellington trumpet section from 1951 to 1959, said that "even when he is playing a harmony part in the section, you can feel him through the whole band." Hodges led his own band for a spell in the early fifties but otherwise remained a regular member of the Ellington Orchestra. Up to the early forties he doubled on soprano saxophone as both soloist and section leader to great effect. In May 1970 Duke Ellington was pondering the problem of persuading Hodges to take up the instrument again for a piece he had written as a portrait of Sidney Bechet when he received a phone call informing him that Johnny had died suddenly of a heart attack while sitting in his dentist's waiting room.

Representative Recordings: The Mooche (Brunswick, 1928), *That's The Blues, Old Man* (Hodges plays soprano sax; Hodges Orchestra, Bluebird, 1941), *Squatty Roo* (Hodges Orchestra, Bluebird, 1941), *Things Ain't What They Used To Be* (Hodges Orchestra, Bluebird, 1941), *Jeep's Blues* (Columbia, 1956), *Rose Room* (Billy Strayhorn Septet, Felsted, 1959)

Freddie Jenkins

Trumpeter Freddie Jenkins was an erratic soloist and some of his choruses now have a jerky, dated sound. At best, however, his playing reflects an ebullient and attractive personality. Jenkins was the comedy man in the Ellington band of the late twenties and early thirties, but little of this is reflected on the records. Yet his solos often have a humorous twinkle and an unusual, high-stepping bounce. While not a great soloist, Jenkins had the strong personality associated with all Ellington sidemen, and this quality, allied to his sound musicianship, made him a valuable member of the Ellington trumpet team.

Representative Recordings: Tiger Rag (Brunswick, 1929), *High Life* (Brunswick, 1929), *Harlemania* (Victor, 1929), *Harlem Speaks* (Brunswick, 1933), *In The Shade Of The Old Apple Tree* (Brunswick, 1933), *Sump'n 'Bout Rhythm* (Brunswick, 1934)

Arthur Whetsol

Like Otto Hardwick and Juan Tizol, Arthur Whetsol is the kind of musician who might have remained an anonymous section player under any leader other than Duke Ellington. But Ellington made full use of this trumpeter of rare delicacy and taste. Whetsol's characteristic solo style was one of quiet restraint and gentle melancholy, yet on occasion he would play with considerable power and drive. His main forte was not improvisation, although he was capable of interesting thematic elaboration. His main functions were as melodic soloist and as trumpet section leader; in this latter role he was one of the very best of his generation. On many of Ellington's more restrained arrangements, a perfect atmosphere is established at the outset by Whetsol's trumpet stating the theme in its gentle, wistful manner. In the 1929 film *Black And Tan*, it is Whetsol who is shown running through a new Ellington composition with Duke, and this is not without significance. People associated with the Ellington band in the early thirties have said that Whetsol was Duke's anchor man, rather in the way that Harry Carney later played this role.

Representative Recordings: Black Beauty (Victor, 1928), *The Dicty Glide* (Victor, 1929), *Stevedore Stomp* (Victor, 1929), *Jungle Jamboree* (OKeh, 1929), *Rocky Mountain Blues* (OKeh, 1930), *Mood Indigo* (OKeh, Brunswick and Victor, 1930)

Chapter 6

The Records—February 1929 to April 1931

THE FIRST RECORDING BY THE ELLINGTON Orchestra after the departure of Bubber Miley is the soundtrack of a short film entitled *Black And Tan*. The story line is banal, the normal state of affairs in "shorts" of this period. Although a great deal of pleasure can be derived from the visual aspects of such a film, the musical rewards are perhaps more considerable. The duet versions of *Black And Tan Fantasy* are interesting, particularly for the sensitive way in which Whetsol handles the different parts. *Black Beauty* has some modifications in the arrangement compared with the studio recordings, as have *Cotton Club Stomp* and *Hot Feet*. The segment of *The Duke Steps Out* is a very crude forerunner of the arrangement used on the Victor recording of September 1929. The full-length *Black And Tan Fantasy* with which the soundtrack ends has Whetsol playing the trumpet solo—cut down to one chorus—and an additional chorus by Barney Bigard placed between Nanton's solo and the final climax. Although the solos are very rewarding, the presence of the choir makes this version of *Black And Tan Fantasy* uncomfortable listening. (An interesting light on Ellington's views on the roles of his musicians is afforded by the fact that with Hardwick absent, the alto solo on the second theme is taken by Carney rather than Hodges.)

***

The personnel of the band after Bubber Miley left in February 1929 was:

Trumpets: Arthur Whetsol, Cootie Williams, Freddie Jenkins.

Trombone: Tricky Sam Nanton.

Reeds: Johnny Hodges (alto and soprano saxes, clarinet); Barney Bigard (clarinet and tenor sax); Harry Carney (baritone and alto saxes, clarinet).

Rhythm: Duke Ellington (piano); Fred Guy (banjo); Wellman Braud (bass); Sonny Greer (drums).

The replacement for Miley was Cootie Williams, an unknown quantity at this time. Rather than hire one of the several growl specialists who were available, Ellington recruited a young and highly promising jazz musician. Cootie had no reputation as a growl player and indeed did not begin to practice the art until he had been in the Ellington band for some time; his first growl solo on record did not appear until he had been in the band for over six months. Claims that he played in this style with Fletcher Henderson before joining Duke and was responsible for the growl solo on Henderson's recording of *Raisin' The Roof* have been found to be false; Cootie did not record at all during his short stay with the Henderson band. During Cootie's first six months with Ellington, the growl trumpet solos were taken by Jenkins or Whetsol, both of whom had become proficient in the art in order to cover for the rather unreliable Miley. Williams at first played his solos in the Louis Armstrong-inspired manner which remained his style on open trumpet throughout his career. Another trumpeter whom Ellington tried to engage as Miley's replacement was Henry "Red" Allen. After thinking the matter over, Allen decided to join the Luis Russell Orchestra, but he kept the telegram from Ellington as a memento for the rest of his life.

In the years which followed Miley's departure the Ellington band's output was prolific, but also uneven. On some recordings it seems welded already into an ensemble of the quality and style associated with later Ellington bands, only to slip back on the next session into sloppy playing, and routine rather than inspired solo work. On a handful of records, the band is unrecognizable as Ellington's and sounds like any anonymous dance band of the period; the most notable of these are *March Of The Hoodlums*, *Ragamuffin Romeo*, and *Is That Religion?* By contrast, on recordings like *The Dicty Glide*, *Hot Feet*, *The Duke Steps Out*, *Breakfast Dance*, *Jazz Lips*, *Old Man Blues*, and *Rockin' In Rhythm*, they produce jazz performances of the highest quality.

There are a good many popular songs among Ellington's output at this time, featuring a succession of vocalists, all white, brought in specially for the sessions. If a sufficiently banal singer was not immediately available, Irving Mills himself would step forward and faithfully maintain the established standard. Did anyone, one wonders, buy Ellington records for their vocals in those days? An example of the type of popular song Duke was invited to record is an epic entitled *Nine Little Miles From Ten-Ten-Tennessee*, a combination of doggerel verse and mediocre melody. Yet the record contains one of Cootie Williams's best growl solos, a superb piece of work which is all the more surprising as it is cast in the form of a theme statement. Indeed Cootie's playing is so fine on this otherwise dire performance that both issued takes are worthy of attention.

***

The first studio session by the band without Miley was for Victor in February 1929, a session at which two Fields-McHugh songs were recorded. *Japanese Dream* is largely forgettable, but *Harlemania* is transformed into a rough, vigorous stomp. The theme statement, definitive of its kind, is by Tricky Sam Nanton, and the growl trumpet solo is by Jenkins. An exciting sequence of solos is continued by Hodges and Bigard before the final ensemble rather ploddingly reminds us that we are still in the world of Cotton Club show music.

The next session, for Brunswick and recorded on March 1, 1929, produced more interesting material, two compositions by Ellington and one by Don Redman. *Rent Party Blues* is a feature for Hodges on soprano sax, playing very much in the style of Bechet; the other soloists are Whetsol and Nanton and there is a scored variation for the saxophone section. *Harlem Flat Blues* consists of plunger-muted brass section riffs which frame superb solos by Nanton and Bigard. Nanton uses his plunger technique in a remarkably expressive manner even by his own standards, while Bigard demonstrates in a poised fashion the use of the riff in a blues solo.

The most remarkable of these three recordings is that of Don Redman's twelve-bar blues *Paducah*. The previous October, Redman himself had recorded this piece with McKinney's Cotton Pickers plus guitarist Lonnie Johnson under the pseudonym "The Chocolate Dandies." Although Redman's score is of a high standard it does not compare with Ellington's imaginative adaptation. Cootie Williams (making his debut on records as an Ellington soloist) states the theme on open trumpet with a spiky clarinet obbligato from Bigard. Then, after an Ellington piano bridge, the reed section, playing clarinets in the low register over very strong bass playing from Braud, chants the riff Redman had used as his climax. The contrast between the tension of the trumpet-clarinet duet and the lazy yet swinging clarinet trio chorus is enhanced by a third change of color and mood when, after another bridge by the band, Nanton's open trombone sings a melancholy theme with superbly apt saxophone backing. A recapitulation of the first theme by the band is followed by a coda which recalls the introduction by Williams and Bigard. This is a performance in which a great deal of variety is packed into the duration of a three-minute record, all perfectly organized and imaginatively played. This arrangement, as much as any of those Ellington made of his own compositions, shows the great advances he was making at this time.

Six days later, the band was back in the Victor studios for a session at which three Ellington originals and one Fields-McHugh number were recorded. First was *The Dicty Glide*, an unusual theme with a jaunty yet melancholy air which is given a perfect exposition by Arthur Whetsol, with Cootie putting in a couple of bars to adjust the flavoring. Whetsol handles the theme better than the later soloists, Hodges and Nanton, but the overall performance is a fine one. The use of Bigard's clarinet during Hodges's solo turns it into a duet between alto and clarinet in a manner reminiscent of the Jimmie Noone Apex Club Orchestra.

The Fields-McHugh number is *Hot Feet*, which Ellington transforms into a vigorous, no-nonsense stomp. His scoring is very effective in the first and last choruses, the former using Bigard's tenor in dialog with the band (Carney handling the clarinet part at this point) and the latter employing some very original devices without hindering the momentum of the performance. The middle section is given over to the soloists, first Williams's scat singing against Jenkins's muted trumpet, then choruses by Hodges and Nanton. Bigard embellishes the final chorus's middle eight with his New Orleans style clarinet. The most effective part of *Hot Feet* is Nanton's solo, played tightly muted and with great urgency and intensity over driving bass by Braud and excited stride piano from Ellington. This is one of the many moments in early jazz when the music leaps into the immediate present by the sheer power and exuberance of the performance.

Barney Bigard shares composer credit with Ellington for *Sloppy Joe*, a blues played by a small unit of trumpet, alto, and clarinet with wordless vocalizing by Sonny Greer. This kind of vocal by Greer was featured at the band's theater and dance engagements a good deal at this time, Sonny using a megaphone to project his voice. His singing, perhaps fortunately, is not heard very often on records. In more senses than one, the musical core of *Sloppy Joe* lies in the three solo choruses taken by Ellington, Bigard and Williams. Two takes have been issued of this performance and the better solos are heard on the second: a musing, introspective, in-and-out-of-tempo passage by Duke; a superb tightening as Bigard enters over effective work by Braud and Greer; and a very expressive solo by Williams. *Stevedore Stomp* contrasts an ensemble riff figure with a series of driving solos, Wellman Braud again invigorating the rhythm section. Whetsol, Carney and Bigard are heard, and Nanton contributes one of his best open trombone choruses. As if to remind himself that all last chorus middle eights on stomps need not be given to Bigard, Duke here hands the job to Hodges, who is equally effective in the direct, forthright alto style he favored at this time.

On a March 1929 Cameo date, Braud is replaced by a brass bass for a small-group session. The identity of the bass player has never been confirmed, but he is thought to be Billy Taylor. The rest of the unit consists of Williams, Bigard, Hodges, Ellington and Fred Guy. In addition to accompanying Ozzie Ware on one wholly forgettable title, the band recorded two numbers — *Who Said "It's Tight Like That"?*, with a vocal by Williams, and the first of two recordings of a blues by Bigard, *Saratoga Swing*. This last is taken at a very slow tempo with effective solos from Hodges, Williams, and Bigard, but is less memorable than the later Victor version.

The following month the band cut three sides for Columbia. The remake of *I Must Have That Man* uses an arrangement very different from the Victor of November 1928 and features some very adventurous "modern" piano work by Ellington. Another Fields-McHugh number, *Freeze And Melt*, has stomping bass by Braud, a driving Jenkins chorus, and Greer manipulating the chimes. The third title is an Ellington composition, *Mississippi Moan*, with Bigard, Nanton and Williams as soloists in a slow 32-bar-with-bridge number of a rather melancholy cast.

A unique recording followed, made for Victor and intended for a 12-inch disc but never issued on 78. *A Night At The Cotton Club* features the band with Irving Mills acting as MC and purports to take place at the Cotton Club, although in fact it was made in Victor's New York studios. The band acts as audience and Mills rhapsodizes about "Dukey" and his "jungle music" between numbers. The pieces performed are shortened versions of *Cotton Club Stomp, Misty Mornin', Goin' To Town* and *Freeze And Melt*, and there is an interlude by one "Harmonica Charlie," whose playing makes his anonymity wholly understandable. The performances themselves are interesting but the intrinsic value of the disc is the insight it gives into attitudes towards Ellington and his music at this time as typified by Mills's announcements. Whether the Cotton Club atmosphere is captured successfully we cannot know, but one suspects that the approximation is close. In the years before this item was finally issued on microgroove taped copies used to circulate among collectors, and the less scrupulous of these used to offer the recording as an authentic "live" broadcast from the Cotton Club in 1929!

The full version of *Cotton Club Stomp* was recorded at the band's next Victor session on May 3, 1939. Like *Doin' The Voom Voom*, this piece is both a "bring on the dancing girls" type of show number and a vigorous stomp for big band. Carney is used very effectively at the start and the main soloists are Jenkins, Hodges, and Bigard. A good deal of the spirit of this performance stems from Braud's driving bass. The Victor recording of *Misty Mornin'* also has effective work from Braud, and he and Greer are again heard at their best in the small band *Saratoga Swing*. Here Cootie, Barney and Hodges make up the front line and, along with Duke, the solo roster. This excellent sequence of solos, framed by Bigard's attractive melody, must be rated among Ellington's most successful records of the period. The music has perfect poise and a lazy relaxation which is very appealing. A most extraordinary Ellington recording is that of the Fields-McHugh song *Arabian Lover*. The title suggests the mock-eastern paraphernalia of twenties show business, and this is just the treatment which Ellington gives the piece in an unusual and highly imaginative arrangement. The band responds with a first-class performance, not least Hodges and Nanton in the solo roles. One would hardly expect Tricky Sam's to be a primary voice in this context, but it is indeed he who is given the theme statement.

The Columbia session which follows was recorded under Sonny Greer's name and is remarkable for the outstanding recording of Braud's string bass. Made by a reduced ensemble of three brass, three reeds, and rhythm, its most notable product is a version of *Saturday Night Function*. The arrangement is the same as the Victor, but here Bigard adapts his *Harlem Flat Blues* riff as the basis of another outstanding solo. Whetsol's and Nanton's choruses are typically fine in their differing ways and the melody gains from the trumpets dropping the growl used on the Victor, while Hodges's obbligato parts again bind the piece together. Neither *That Rhythm Man* nor *Beggar's Blues* is of the same stature, although the latter is an interesting Ellington orchestral essay in the twelve-bar form.

The next session was for Brunswick and featured a version of a Fats Waller-Andy Razaf number, *Jungle Jamboree*, which has a driving Cootie Williams solo. The small band OKeh recording of this is the superior one, with sprightly open trumpet by Whetsol and a classic low-register clarinet solo by Bigard, full of New Orleans flavor. The session mate to this OKeh version is another Waller-Razaf piece, *Snake Hip Dance*, which features a solo chorus on tenor sax from Bigard.

Around this time—August 1929—the band recorded a third version of *Saturday Night Function*, this time for the Cameo label. All the reissues of this recording have a lot of surface noise but this is well worth tolerating, for Bigard fashions a third classic solo, Whetsol gives a superior version of his chorus, and Nanton, Hodges, and the band are again excellent. At the same session, remakes of *Doin' The Voom Voom* and *Flaming Youth* were recorded, but neither is up to the standard of the original. Some recasting of the solo roles in *Voom Voom* results in Cootie playing the responses in the first and last choruses on open horn, Jenkins doing the growl trumpet, and Carney playing his duet with Nanton on alto sax. The arrangement of *Flaming Youth* is also reorganized, Hodges taking the first chorus and Jenkins playing the solo trumpet. This is a faster and much inferior version to the Miley-inspired Victor.

The next session, recorded for Brunswick on September 13, 1929, is notable for two things. First, Juan Tizol joins the band on valve trombone; the previous October Ellington had employed Harry White as a temporary second trombonist, but now Tizol came in on a regular basis. Second, Cootie Williams is heard playing growl trumpet for the first time on record. On joining Ellington, Williams had at first thought the style a mere novelty, but, reflecting that Ellington had hired him to replace Bubber Miley, he started to study its skills with Nanton. He learned quickly and well, as the records show, and within a few years he was to become the most famous of all growl trumpet players. This first Cootie growl solo is on *Jazz Convulsions*, a stomping number which also has a Cootie solo on open horn. Its session mate, *Jolly Wog*, has an attractive and unusual theme plus good solos, but the banjo rolls and temple blocks introduce rather too much of the Cotton Club climate into the recording studio.

Cootie Williams also plays growl solos on three titles from the Victor session of three days later—*Mississippi Dry*, *The Duke Steps Out*, and *Haunted Nights*. Cootie's solos here are of a quality which shows him to be already a master of growl trumpet. Teddy Bunn is added on guitar for this session, and is heard to best advantage on *Haunted Nights* and *Swannee Shuffle*—particularly effectively over Bigard's low-register clarinet on the former title, an orchestral essay in Ellingtonian blues of rather monotonous character. *Swannee Shuffle* has a chorus by the muted trumpets which looks forward to many later Ellington triumphs in brass scoring. Also looking ahead, while being a wholly satisfactory entity in itself, is *The Duke Steps Out*, a skillfully written stomp with several fine solos integrated into its texture, those by Williams again being outstanding.

***

Throughout his recording career Ellington was constantly involving himself in new musical situations. The next two sessions, issued as by the Six Jolly Jesters, must be among the most unusual he ever played on. The first features a small group from the Ellington Orchestra playing an arrangement of *Six Or Seven Times*, which Don Redman had recorded with The Little Chocolate Dandies the previous month. The vocal talents of Sonny Greer and Freddie Jenkins are featured. Four days later, under the same band name, Jenkins, Williams, Nanton, Hodges, and the four-piece rhythm section joined three members of The Washboard Serenaders—Teddy Bunn (guitar), Bruce Johnson (washboard), and Harold "Blinky" Randolph (kazoo and scat singing)—for a couple of titles. *Goin' Nuts* is largely a showcase for Randolph's talents, but *Oklahoma Stomp* is a driving two-beat band number with enthusiastic solos, including a notably chaotic contribution from the pianist. These two pieces of abandoned, washboard-driven music inhabit a different world from that of the Ellington Orchestra's contemporary output.

The great variety of musical standards and styles within the Ellington band of this period can hardly be better illustrated than by the session of November 14, 1929, recorded for Victor. *March Of The Hoodlums*, a number by Hoagy Carmichael, is arranged and performed in an anonymous manner and is hardly recognizable as an Ellington recording, despite the fact that it features Juan Tizol's first solo with the band. Yet its two session mates are Ellington originals of the most characteristic kind, perfectly realized in the band's interpretations. *Breakfast Dance* is a good example of the band's technical advance over the preceding year. Note the beautifully articulated section playing behind Nanton's first chorus and the improved, more secure sound of the high clarinets. Jenkins and Carney have good solos here, Hodges indulges in a dialogue with the band, and there is effective use of Bigard's clarinet at the end. The performance of *Jazz Lips*, a superb score, is even better. This is a typical Ducal mixture of sixteen and twelve-bar choruses, highly melodic and with a very distinctive blues flavor. The clarinet trio, much in evidence, is used as effective contrast to the muted brass. Williams, Nanton, Bigard and Ellington are the soloists and there is brilliant use of Tizol in the ensemble texture in the last chorus. There is some doubt about the trumpet soloist here; although Williams is usually cited—and the vehement accents do indeed suggest his style—the actual phrasing of the trumpet solo is very close to Arthur Whetsol's growl manner.

The three titles recorded as by The Harlem Footwarmers for OKeh six days later were all Ellington originals. The best is *Lazy Duke*, scored for two brass (Jenkins and Nanton), two clarinets (Bigard and Carney), and the rhythm section. The use of Nanton's trombone is very imaginative here. The two titles by the full band seem to suffer because of Braud's absence—there is no bass present on this date—and the performances are rather stiff, at some remove from the fine band playing of the previous session. *Blues Of The Vagabond* had a nice melody but the banjo is overly prominent in the recording balance, while the highlight of *Syncopated Shuffle* is the excellent solo work by Johnny Hodges, although Jenkins's trumpet and Ellington's stride piano also contribute pleasantly.

On the final Ellington session of 1929 for Brunswick, *Sweet Mama*, *Wall Street Wail* and *Cincinnati Daddy* were recorded. For many years *Cincinnati Daddy* was one of the rarest of Ellington records with only a single test-pressing known to exist, but it is now common enough, thanks to reissues. The soloists featured are Hodges, Nanton and, to rather better effect, Williams, and Bigard. The otherwise ordinary *Wall Street Wail* has more outstanding work by Williams, Bigard, and Nanton. *Sweet Mama*, an Ellington composition, should not be confused with the number of the same name that the band had recorded for Harmony in 1928. This Brunswick recording is less effective than the Velvet Tone version of six months later.

* * *

The recordings by the Ellington Orchestra in the first three months of 1930 are mostly of popular material. Probably because of boredom with the songs and the rather ordinary scores which most of them inspired, the standard of band playing falls back from the peak reached on *Breakfast Dance* and *Jazz Lips*. *St. James Infirmary Blues*, recorded for Perfect and Banner in January 1930, is all too typical. There are three takes, all equally poor, of a performance which features what sounds like a stock arrangement, a dire Irving Mills vocal (nice Bigard behind him, though), and a final ensemble in which the lead trumpet is by Williams. *When You're Smiling* has another miserable Mills vocal, another dull arrangement, and a trumpet solo based on Louis Armstrong's celebrated high-note chorus, played none too securely by Freddie Jenkins. There are two issued takes of this recording.

This session also produced a new recording of *Rent Party Blues* with a performance similar to the 1929 Brunswick (three takes, but the differences are minor), and a new and rather slight composition called *Jungle Blues*. This recording features a growl trumpet solo which has puzzled Ellington collectors down the years. Majority opinion has it that either Jenkins or an unknown player is responsible, largely on the grounds that the melodic structure is untypical of Cootie Williams. The only playing similar to this in the Ellington output of the period is on the Velvet Tone version of *The Mooche*, recorded in April 1930. This has the trumpet in dialogue with the clarinet trio but lacks a trumpet solo. The trumpet tone on *Jungle Blues* sounds too broad and the expression too vehement for Jenkins. Whetsol would be out of the question, for the solo lacks the air of precise musicianship always associated with his playing. This leaves Williams, and indeed it seems quite likely that Cootie might have been experimenting in style, or maybe trying out some ideas suggested by Duke. The other solos on *Jungle Blues* are by Bigard and Nanton. This Ellington piece is a less interesting composition than Jelly Roll Morton's *Jungle Blues*, recorded in 1927. This is of particular interest in that it is one of Morton's rare monothematic pieces and because it was deliberately aimed at the market for pseudoprimitive music which was to be so successfully exploited by Ellington in his "jungle" pieces.

Whetsol's theme statement in *Maori* stands out for its melodic grace and clean-cut lines against the rather dull background of a batch of popular tune recordings done by the Ellington band in February and March 1930. Another version of *St. James Infirmary Blues*, featuring a long vocal by Irving Mills, was recorded for Brunswick, and this has superior solos compared with the earlier Perfect recording. The Brunswick *When You're Smiling* has a lively chase chorus between Williams and Hodges and improved takeoff of the Armstrong trumpet solo by Jenkins—but Irving Mills is still the vocalist.

The April session for the Velvet Tone label produced three titles of varied merit. *Ragamuffin Romeo* is perhaps the most anonymous record ever put out by Duke Ellington, a thoroughly mediocre performance which could have been the work of any competent dance band of the day. Duke is the only soloist, but no one could possibly recognize either him or his band from this recording. On the other discs from this session, Duke offered remakes of two of his earlier successes—*East St. Louis Toodle-oo* and *The Mooche*. In the former piece, the basic format—a highly original principal melody over a low walking accompaniment alternating with a commonplace second theme—is retained, but the superstructure is revised. The first theme is stated by Whetsol and Jenkins in duet, and they are also prominent in the ensemble passage in the first chorus. The solos are on the second sixteen-bar-plus-tag theme and are by Ellington, Carney and Whetsol in duet, Jenkins, and Bigard. The trumpet duet then returns to recapitulate the first theme. With Miley no longer present, Ellington had obviously taken some pains to remove the dominance of one musician from this composition, but in so doing he clearly diluted its flavor, and it was not long before *East St. Louis Toodle-oo* again became a feature for a growl trumpet soloist, Cootie Williams. In the new version of *The Mooche*, the growl trumpet is probably by Cootie, the principal soloists being Bigard accompanied by the band and Nanton accompanied by Bigard—both highly effective.

It is reported that at this time Duke Ellington and his musicians were keen listeners to the Luis Russell Orchestra, which was enjoying a brief but exhilarating period of greatness. The Russell band featured soloists like Red Allen, J. C. Higginbotham, Charlie Holmes, and Albert Nicholas in a framework of unpretentious head arrangements perfectly designed for rugged, swinging jazz. The band's rhythm section was magnificent, powered by the great New Orleans bass player Pops Foster. The Ellington band was able to play in a similar style with considerable success, perhaps as a result of listening. Ellington had an even stronger solo roster than Russell, and the presence of Wellman Braud, another powerful, stomping New Orleans bassist, made for a similar effect in the rhythm section. The February 1929 recording of *Harlemania* had already shown the Ellington band working in a Russell-like style for most of the way, with vigorous solos over a Braud-led rhythm section, only for the concluding ensemble chorus to introduce the comparatively cheap sound of a late twenties show band.

In 1930 Ellington produced *Double Check Stomp*, perhaps the most Russell-like of all his records; here the Russell band style is thoroughly absorbed and transformed into Ellingtonian terms. The Victor of April 1930 is the best of the three recorded versions, with driving band work on the riff ensembles and superb solos by Braud, Williams (a magnificent open chorus), Hodges, and Nanton. The later Brunswick and Velvet Tone recordings are more relaxed, but the urgency of the Victor is to be preferred. A piano accordion wielded by guest artist Joe Cornell (correct name: Cornell Smelser) dilutes the Brunswick, while the Velvet Tone is cluttered by additional brass figurations which add nothing to the piece. This version has further outstanding solos by Williams and Nanton and suffers only in comparison with the classic performance on the Victor. *Double Check Stomp* is a supreme example of the Ellington band working in the conventional big band style of the period and reveals that it was an ensemble unsurpassed in this field.

A further batch of popular song recordings includes a rather painful pair with prehistoric country and western vocals by Frank Marvin and a song featuring Joe Cornell, *Accordion Joe*. This has astonishingly banal lyrics sung in a wholly apposite style by Dick Robertson, but a chorus split between Cootie Williams and Harry Carney guarantees an immortality which the composition does not deserve and which its composers probably did not expect.

The Ellington originals recorded in the first half of 1930 include a number issued on Brunswick as *Cotton Club Stomp* but totally different from the composition of that name recorded for Victor. This number has sometimes been confused with Willie "The Lion" Smith's composition, *Keep Your Temper*, which is very similar melodically but built on a different harmonic base. This was put out on the reverse side of a number called *Wall Street Wail* in the 78 era, and the identity of the piece has been further confused by the fact that this disc had its labels reversed. Compilers of LP reissues have not always been aware of this, and to this day records are issued with *Cotton Club Stomp* labeled as *Wall Street Wail* and vice versa. (Both numbers are taken at a fast-medium tempo, but can be easily identified, as *Cotton Club Stomp* is ensemble throughout apart from a Jenkins solo in the fourth chorus, while *Wall Street Wail* has a Bigard clarinet obbligato in the first chorus and a Williams trumpet solo in the second).

After this Brunswick session Ellington moved over to Victor to record *Sweet Dreams Of Love*, an Ellington ballad for orchestra with rich scoring (note the use of Tizol's trombone in the first chorus), a trombone duet, and plenty of Whetsol's plaintive trumpet. From the same session comes *Jungle Nights In Harlem*, which captures to perfection the quasi-primitive flavor of so much black show music of this period. It is this piece, which could well have been titled *A Portrait Of The Cotton Club*, rather than *Black And Tan Fantasy* or *The Mooche*, which should properly be considered the epitome of Ellington's "jungle style." There is quite a lot of Jenkins's trumpet in *Jungle Nights In Harlem*, but this is an orchestral tone painting rather than a vehicle for jazz solos.

Another Ellington original from this session is *Sweet Jazz O'Mine*, with both Williams's theme statement and Bigard's solo much superior to the arrangement, indicating that Ellington's mastery was not yet wholly consistent. That he could reach the heights of jazz achievement is shown by the final and best recording from this date, *Shout 'Em Aunt Tillie*. Although some jazz followers imagine that evocations of revivalist prayer meetings were brought into jazz by Charles Mingus, the practice is an old one, and indeed inevitable, considering the close relationship between jazz and black show business, where such portrayals were commonplace. Very few early jazz evocations of prayer meetings have the musical substance of Mingus's pieces of the fifties, but one of these few is *Shout 'Em Aunt Tillie*. The hysteria of revival meetings and of Mingus's tone paintings is absent here. The combination of two low-register clarinets and Nanton's muted trombone is a feature of an orchestration which makes good use of Bigard's clarinet and includes excellent solos by

Williams and Hodges. According to some sources *Shout 'Em Aunt Tillie* was composed by Freddie Jenkins. In fact, Jenkins's contribution was to offer some sketchy melodic ideas and to provide the title, the actual composition being the work of Ellington (this information from the late Harry Carney via Johnny Simmen).

A June 1930 session for the Velvet Tone label produced a version of a rather ordinary Ellington tune, *Sweet Mama*, which had been recorded for Brunswick the previous December. Of more interest are remakes of *Double Check Stomp* and *Black And Tan Fantasy*. This last has Carney taking Hardwick's part and, more interestingly, Whetsol taking Miley's, although the trumpet solo proper is reduced to one chorus.

* * *

In July 1930 the Ellington band was in Hollywood to take part in the RKO film *Check And Double Check*. The portions of the sound track of this film which have been released on record are of poor fidelity and modest musical interest, apart from a full length performance of *Old Man Blues* which is worthy of more than passing note. Much more rewarding are the products of two Victor sessions in Hollywood on August 20 and 26, 1930. The three numbers from the first date were remade on the second, and the value of the first session is purely as a source of additional takes. The titles were *Ring Dem Bells*, *Old Man Blues* (both Ellington numbers, each running to six takes with three of each issued) and *Three Little Words* (a popular song of the day of which only the fifth and final take has ever been released).

According to most discographies, the chimes on *Ring Dem Bells* were played by future bandleader Charlie Barnet, a lifelong Ellington fanatic, but Barnet himself has denied that he was responsible. The piece is a simple sixteen-bar with bridge uptempo stomp and it was to become one of Ellington's most successful numbers, being recorded by many other artists. It remained in the Ellington band repertoire for over twenty years in this same arrangement. The three issued takes of *Ring Dem Bells* from the 1930 sessions differ only in the solos. The first part of the piece, omitting the various passages by the band, with and without chimes, consists of a sequence of short solos by Bigard, Hodges, Carney, and Nanton. These are followed by a chase chorus between Hodges's alto and Williams's scat singing, before a four-bar bridge leads into Cootie's two-chorus growl trumpet solo; Bigard is heard again playing against the band in the final ensemble. The differences between the takes are quite amusing in the chase chorus, where Hodges seems determined to play a phrase which will defeat Williams's limited vocal resources in the responses which echo the alto phrases. It would be difficult to find a finer illustration of Cootie Williams's trumpet style than that afforded by the three different solos he fashions here. That on take six is a famous classic, but the others are scarcely inferior in invention, structure, or authority; Ellington provides this solo with a most suitable accompaniment scored for the saxophone section.

Old Man Blues is an important landmark in Ellington's career as a composer, for here the written parts and the contributions of the soloists are in perfect accord and perfectly integrated. This is not to say that overall *Old Man Blues* is superior to any previous Ellington record: some which preceded it may be considered to have better solos or more imaginative scoring; what makes this piece so important is Ellington's achievement of perfect balance between form and content, between improvising soloists and scored ensemble. Despite its title, *Old Man Blues* is an uptempo stomp with a 32-bar-with-release chorus and a second theme of a march-like character. The performance opens with a "vamp 'til ready" eight-bar orchestral introduction, over which Hodges's Bechet-inspired, blues-impregnated soprano saxophone sings briefly. The main theme is not introduced directly, but in the form of a variation by Nanton, muted and driving, with a strong and effective obbligato by Bigard. After an interlude of twenty bars on the second theme, the main subject is repeated by the ensemble with Nanton's open trombone having the middle eight. The next chorus is a solo by Carney, a bouncing, ebullient affair with Ellington's very telling piano in the accompaniment. The fourth chorus is split most effectively between Hodges on soprano and Jenkins, who plays with an increasing drive which seems to be leading to the climax of the piece, only for the second theme to return on saxophones in a brief passage which concludes with a syncopated and harmonically suspended break for the trumpet section. This does in fact herald the final climactic chorus, played by the full band with soaring Bigard clarinet. The middle eight is played by Nanton and Bigard, except on the third take where Bigard alone manages to be even more effective. The variety inherent in *Old Man Blues* is obvious from a summary, but the unity which fuses that variety, and the sheer exuberance of the performance can be savored only by listening.

After two such masterpieces, one might expect that an arrangement of *Three Little Words* with a vocal by Paul Whiteman's Rhythm Boys (Bing Crosby, Al Rinker, and Harry Barris) would be a severe anticlimax. This is not the case, for the number is excellently arranged and superbly played, while the vocal trio reveals an easy rhythmic delivery of a most attractive kind. No doubt the presence of Bing Crosby had a lot to do with this. The alert work of the Ellington band here is in contrast to the stodgy playing found on most of its popular song recordings of these years.

* * *

The Ellington band's very next session, done for Victor, finds a reversion to the unimaginative arrangements and poor vocals of so many previous Ellington popular song recordings. Four non-Ellington songs were recorded, and all have period vocals by Dick Robertson. The band was back in New York, and the change of studio may in part account for the poorer overall sound of the ensemble. The second chorus of *Memories Of You*, recorded at this session, has an odd bit of experimental scoring involving Whetsol, Tizol, Hodges's soprano, and the band over bowed bass, but the rest of the performance is easily forgotten. Of the other titles, *Hittin' The Bottle* (two takes) has interesting Bigard in the coda and some singularly unswinging drumming from Greer, while *That Lindy Hop* has a chorus of stride piano and a distant echo of the Jimmie Noone Apex Club Orchestra in the baritone-clarinet duet in the final chorus. *You're Lucky To Me* has nothing much to recommend it, and the vocal, as on the other four sides, is hopelessly and hilariously dated.

Returning to the OKeh studios as The Harlem Footwarmers, the Ellington band was reduced to a seven-piece unit for a session at which the first recording of *Mood Indigo* was made, only to be rejected by the company. The group consisted of Whetsol (trumpet), Nanton (trombone), Bigard (clarinet), Ellington (piano), Guy (banjo), Braud (bass), and Greer (drums)—the same group which had recorded the two Waller-Razaf tunes for OKeh in August 1929, except that here Bigard does not double tenor sax. Two titles from this October 1930 session were issued: *Big House Blues* and *Rocky Mountain Blues*. The first is a two-theme Ellington composition with a solo by Whetsol which has often been wrongly taken for the work of Williams. On record labels, the composer credit for *Rocky Mountain Blues* reads "Simmons," but the title is included in the list of Ellington compositions in *Music Is My Mistress* and certainly fits the band in a way which would be unusual for an "outside" composition. This recording is outstanding for the fine blues solos by Bigard, Whetsol, and Nanton as well as a couple of Ellington bridge passages which show an Earl Hines influence. Whetsol, muted here, plays a wholly characteristic solo, gentle and reflective in mood. It is surprising that this little-appreciated trumpeter could play Bix-like variations on *I Can't Give You Anything But Love*, passages with a Cootie Williams-like intonation on *Big House Blues,* or plaintive blues choruses as on *Rocky Mountain Blues* or *Mood Indigo* while retaining complete integrity of style. These facts indicate a resourcefulness and variety which is not usually ascribed to Arthur Whetsol's music making.

At the very next Brunswick session, *Mood Indigo* was rerecorded and on this occasion the disc was released, early copies having the original title, *Dreamy Blues*, on the label. This is a definitive reading of an Ellington classic. The band is the same as on the *Big House Blues* session. The theme statement is a classic in itself, with Ellington's subtle voicings creating a unique effect. This version is very well recorded for the period and taken at a lazy tempo at which the relaxed solos of Bigard and Whetsol make their best effect. The melodic grace, the original use of the instrumentation, and the novel harmonization are blended into a concise and integrated whole. None of the later Ellington recordings of *Mood Indigo*—and they are legion—quite capture the quiet perfection of this version, nor its unique emotional climate.

Three popular songs recorded by the full band at this and a subsequent Brunswick date are of much less interest. *Runnin' Wild* is notable for a good open Cootie solo incorporating a quotation from the clarinet solo from *High Society* and for some deftly played saxophone variations. *Home Again Blues* is hardly worth a mention, though it is interesting to note that here Ellington scores for the whole saxophone section in the manner of Barney Bigard's clarinet style. *Wang Wang Blues* is a song which seems to inspire trombonists to imitate motor horns: Kid Ory does it in his 1956 version and Nanton, who also plays a bit of tailgate trombone, does it here. Like the more famous versions by King Oliver and Kid Ory this arrangement is copied from Paul Whiteman's 1921 recording. The vocals on these Ducal pops are by Dick Robertson on the first title, Irving Mills on the second, and a duo of Mills and Benny Payne on the third. (Payne is a very moderate Louis Armstrong imitator, whose singing has dated a good deal less than that of the other two.)

On October 30, 1930, the band recorded a session for OKeh which comprised remakes of *Mood Indigo* and of the three titles recorded for Victor in Hollywood plus a new blues. The OKeh *Ring Dem Bells*, *Three Little Words*, and *Old Man Blues* are inferior to the Victor recordings, although the first and last are well worth study owing to the changes in format. In *Ring Dem Bells*, a number of changes weaken the effect of the arrangement, but the performance is a good one with Bigard in excellent form. The solos by Hodges and Nanton are replaced by a duet between Ellington's piano and Greer on bells, and Cootie's two-chorus masterpiece gives way to a competent but comparatively ordinary solo by Jenkins. The changes in the arrangement of *Three Little Words* again fail to improve the piece, and the vocal by Irving Mills sounds grotesque beside that of The Rhythm Boys on Victor. *Old Man Blues* is perhaps the best of these three remakes and again the arrangement is altered: the Carney solo is reduced to a middle eight in the Nanton-Bigard chorus, which itself is moved from its introductory position and replaced by a band theme statement. The rearrangement of choruses weakens the effect of the piece, while the band does not play with quite the same vigor and enthusiasm as on the Victor. On this version Cootie Williams takes over from Freddie Jenkins as trumpet soloist. These OKeh versions of *Ring Dem Bells* and *Old Man Blues* remind us that Duke Ellington was rarely content to rest on his laurels. Throughout his career, we find him altering and reworking pieces in a way which kept his music in a state of creative flux. With performances which have achieved a classic stature (as in the case of the two we have just been discussing), this can result in a deterioration, and one of the surprising features of the Ellington output is the rarity with which this happened. More often, new ways of looking at a composition were found which were just as valid as the original and in some cases even more apposite. In the case of *Ring Dem Bells*, however, he reverted to the Victor arrangement and kept this in the book until 1951.

The new blues from this October 1939 OKeh session is *Sweet Chariot*, a classic recording. The first chorus is a dialogue between Hodges on alto and Williams singing in an

Armstrong-inspired manner, the weight of emotion seeming to change the words into wordless musical phrases. This provides a superb introduction to the four choruses which follow. These are played alternately by Cootie on open trumpet and Tricky Sam on plunger-muted trombone. The vocal character of the latter seems to echo the despair of Cootie's singing. Cootie's trumpet is supremely eloquent, and his broad tone lends an extra quality to his expressive blues phrasing. Nanton offers a magnificent contrast in tone quality while "singing" the blues in his own equally impressive fashion. Although *Sweet Chariot* is the outstanding title from the session, the recording of *Mood Indigo* (by the same septet which had made the Brunswick version) is a close second. The format of the piece is unchanged, but perhaps the mood is not captured quite so finely here as on the Brunswick, the performance being fractionally less relaxed despite a slightly slower tempo.

Another Ellington classic received its first recording at the next session—*Rockin' In Rhythm*, a composition which, like *Mood Indigo*, remained a regular standby for the Ellington band for the rest of its career. The pace of *Rockin' In Rhythm* increased as the years went by, and this initial 1930 OKeh recording is slowest of all, taken at a sober medium tempo. The main theme is a typically jaunty Ellington melody with a very distinctive flavor. On the early recordings the second theme is played by Williams on open trumpet, and his playing of this melody was the inspiration for a swing era number entitled *Peckin'*, which originally did not include either Ellington or Williams among its composer credits. The solos on *Rockin' In Rhythm* are by Bigard, in a quasi-oriental bridge passage, and Nanton. Bigard's passage, which was taken over by Carney after Barney left the band, seems to bear no relation to the main theme but is a typical example of Ellington's genius in injecting just the right degree of contrast. This is followed by a reprise of the original piano introduction and a forthright Nanton solo, the number concluding with a repeat of the original melodic sequence. *Rockin' In Rhythm* is a superb jazz composition in so many ways—to instance just a few, there are its happy, positive air; its nice balance of themes and solos; and, not least, the way it allows the musicians to relax and swing just as if they were playing for their own pleasure at some after-hours jam session.

The session mates of this original *Rockin' In Rhythm* are both pop tunes with vocals by Sid Garry, who is arguably the most dated of the occasional Ellington singers of this period. After some stilted band playing and an excruciating vocal, *I Can't Realize You Love Me* comes to life for a couple of choruses, one a Nanton solo and the other a chase between Hodges and Williams. There are no such compensations on *I'm So In Love With You*, which stays in a thirties dance music vein throughout, even Carney's alto solo being played "straight."

Three Victor sessions followed, and the only nonpop recording produced is a third version of *Mood Indigo*. This is given a new arrangement for the full band, although the Whetsol-Nanton-Bigard trio is featured extensively. The solos are different from those on the earlier versions and are reversed in sequence, Whetsol introducing a chorus which became the standard for later Ellington trumpeters. It cannot be said that this new *Mood Indigo* is as successful as the older versions, but it does throw new and interesting light on the piece and serves as a perfect complement to the original recordings. It is the first of a long sequence of arrangements of *Mood Indigo*, a sequence astonishing for the variety Ellington managed to draw from this one apparently simple piece.

Of the popular songs recorded at these sessions perhaps *Nine Little Miles From Ten-Ten-Tennessee* and *When A Black Man's Blue* are best by virtue of the excellent Williams theme statements. As has been observed earlier, Cootie is in particularly fine form on the two takes of the first title. It is generally recognized that Cootie's open trumpet reflects his great admiration for Louis Armstrong, but a study of the phrasing and the rhythmic subtleties on muted choruses like that on *Nine Little Miles* reveals that this is equally the case when he is playing growl horn. A half-chorus of Cootie's growling is a high spot of a second recording of *I'm So In Love With You*, which has a new arrangement but an equally wretched vocal, on this occasion by Billy Smith (an alias for Smith Ballew, who also does the honors on *Nine Little Miles*). *What Good Am I Without You?* has an introduction by Hodges which shows just how much he was influenced by Bigard's style at this period, followed by lots of trite banjo playing and a vocal from Dick Robertson. Sid Garry returns to sing *Blue Again*, while the two takes of *When A Black Man's Blue* offer a choice between Robertson and Benny Payne as vocalists.

The Ellington sessions from January 1931 continue the pattern of the previous months, with forgettable pop songs outnumbering original compositions. The latter consist of two new versions of *Rockin' In Rhythm* and the initial recording of Duke's first concert work, *Creole Rhapsody*. The month's first session was for the Banner label and featured three titles with vocals by Chick Bullock. *Them There Eyes* (three takes) has clarinets on the theme statement at the start and probably the most stilted solo Williams ever recorded; *Rockin' Chair* (four takes) has just two choruses plus intro and coda, the first being taken up by Bullock (but note Bigard and Braud in the background) and the second by a superb Nanton passage with first Hodges and then Bigard in an obbligato role, a piece of really first-class jazz making in a rather unexpected place; and finally, a third arrangement of *I'm So In Love With You* which has some superb baritone by Carney in a setting of thoroughgoing mediocrity. The slightly later Melotone recording of *Rockin' Chair* is not as good, mainly because Nanton's role is reduced to a mere six bars, although the vocal by Benny Payne is a considerable improvement on Bullock. But Bullock is also featured on three pops done at a Victor session, from which Bigard's theme statement on *The River And Me* (note the altos scored above the clarinet) and the rather conventional arrangement of *Keep A Song In Your Soul* are the most noteworthy features. The Melotone *Is That Religion?* (vocal by Sonny Nichols) is one of the least characteristic Ellington records in the catalog, in terms of both style and quality.

The new versions of *Rockin' In Rhythm* for Brunswick and Victor (two takes) are excellent, although only on the latter is there a new feature—a passage for muted brass replacing Cootie's statement of the second theme. The tempo of *Rockin' In Rhythm* is already slightly faster with each version but the distinctive flavor of the piece is fully retained. The Nanton solo varies only in detail but always sounds perfectly fresh; his solos on the first four recorded versions of *Rockin' In Rhythm* repay close study. The Ellington recording of *The Peanut Vendor* is no more than a pleasant period trifle, and much the same could be said of *Twelfth Street Rag*. The latter contains a rarity in the form of an improvised jazz solo by Juan Tizol, but the piano duet between Ellington and Benny Payne and a good chorus by Nanton and the saxophone section are of greater musical substance.

* * *

It is ironic that the first piece of concert music by a major jazz musician was issued initially as by The Jungle Band, the Ellington Orchestra's standard pseudonym when recording for Brunswick. It is even more ironic that the idea for such a piece came from Irving Mills. Noting Paul Whiteman's success with concert pieces, he talked Brunswick into recording one by Ellington and then gave Duke twenty-four hours to produce the piece.

Creole Rhapsody should be kept in perspective: it is not the finest composition which Duke Ellington wrote during the period we are discussing; it is not even his best from 1931. But it is the most ambitious and in many ways the most forward-looking. It is the first work Ellington wrote specifically for the concert stage, his first piece of abstract as opposed to functional music. Unlike the concert works written by George Gershwin or Ferde Grofé for the Whiteman Orchestra, *Creole Rhapsody* is cast in the jazz idiom of the day with no borrowings from the world of academic concert music, at least in its first version. Both recordings of *Creole Rhapsody* occupy two sides of a 78, the Brunswick of January 1931 a conventional 10-inch disc, the Victor of June of that year a 12-inch record. Two takes have been issued of the second side of the Brunswick version. There are considerable differences between the Brunswick and Victor performances, each having its own qualities and defects.

In its original format on Brunswick, *Creole Rhapsody* is a composition in which three themes are arranged in rondo fashion—A B A B C B A. The first section (A) is a rather slight affair relying on three chords given out by the band and improvised embellishments around them, rather than on any strongly melodic theme. The second part (B) is a beautiful twelve-bar blues melody, in many ways the choice section of this Brunswick recording. The third part (C) is an academic-sounding exercise in phrases of odd bar lengths, played by the two-piece trombone section. The first theme (A) is presented with embellishments by Bigard and in variations for solo piano before the clarinetist returns with a beautiful, sweeping statement of the blues theme (B). This then undergoes some variation in a second statement by Williams. The main theme (A) is eight bars in length, and on its first return it is heard three times (alto decorations by Hodges) with an eight-bar bridge passage between the second and third statements making it into a conventional 32-bar-with-bridge chorus. The first side of the record ends at this point.

Side two opens with a piano solo by Ellington covering both themes in a loose rhapsodic manner. It is here that the only significant difference between the two Brunswick takes is found, with Duke more reflective on the second of them, though his presentation of the blues theme is perhaps slightly more effective on the first take. Following the piano solo, the band plays a four-bar bridge which heralds the trombone section's presentation of the third section (C). The blues theme (B), returns in a brilliant version which leads to the final 32 bars. Here the main theme has decorative obbligatos by Jenkins and Carney, but the middle eight is a new passage featuring Jenkins and Bigard. The coda, with Greer playing a marching rhythm with brushes, is an anticlimax. The band performance leaves a good deal to be desired, sounding stilted and stiff compared with the best recordings of the period. Only on the second theme does the warmth of the Ellington ensemble come through, though Bigard and Hodges play in characteristic fashion in their embellishments of the first theme. Jenkins sounds all at sea, rhythmically, in the final section, which is most strange for an Ellington musician.

Writers have traditionally ascribed the stiffness of the performance of the Brunswick *Creole Rhapsody* to the fact that the musicians were not used to playing such material. But a pattern virtually identical with the first theme can be found in Ellington's 1928 *Move Over*, while the blues melody is a wholly characteristic piece of Ellington writing. Throughout his career, Ellington liked to produce his scores at the last minute and this fact, allied to the story of Irving Mills's 24-hour deadline, leads one to suspect that the deficiencies in the performance are due to lack of preparation. It is difficult to account for the really dreadful playing of Jenkins in any other way. Certainly, this seems a more likely explanation than the usual suggestion that the musicians were inhibited by the larger framework of the piece.

This first recording of *Creole Rhapsody* is an important landmark in the development of Ellington's music. For the whole of the six-minute performance, his is the dominant voice, with the soloists quite subsidiary to the composition. The only important improvisation is Ellington's own at the start of the second side. Despite the uneven nature of the material, *Creole Rhapsody* does hang together formally, although the middle section for the trombones seems a good deal more unusual when described as a division of the sixteen bars into 5 + 5 + 4 + 2 than it does when listened to. Nonetheless, this section does provide a contrast and in this sense it succeeds within the context of the overall structure.

On February 3, 1931, the Ellington band left the Harlem Cotton Club after its final residency there. They spent a good deal of the year on tour, including a number of vaudeville theater engagements. There is a temptation to look upon the second recording of *Creole Rhapsody*, done in June 1931, as a tarted up version of the original with Gershwinesque passages inserted for the benefit of theater audiences. It is a temptation which should be resisted, for this version is in some respects superior to the first. One disadvantage is that it was recorded in Victor's Camden studio with its notorious echo. Ellington uses different tempos for the different sections here and the trombone passage (C) is replaced by a totally new melody of a gentle, melancholy cast. The first part of the performance corresponds exactly with the first side of the Brunswick, except for the tempo changes, but after the 32-bar variant of the first theme with which the first Brunswick side ended, Ellington plays a brief bridge which leads to the new third theme, introduced by Whetsol over the saxophone section. This third theme is of the 32-bar-without-bridge variety, and after the chorus by Whetsol, the first side of the Victor ends (this is a 12-inch recording, remember). The second side is taken up, for the most part, with this new third theme, the variation played by the three saxophones and Tizol's muted valve trombone at the start being particularly memorable. This is followed by an out-of-tempo duet between piano and clarinet, and the music becomes increasingly diffuse and less coherent as the side progresses. The first theme is given a rather arbitrary recapitulation, but the blues theme is forgotten, and though there are some nice touches here and there, the piece loses its cohesion and purpose and ends in a rather pompous manner reminiscent of Whiteman's concert music.

Despite its failures, the Victor *Creole Rhapsody* rewards study in many ways. It must be said that its failures—lack of form and reliance on show music clichés—are typical of much jazz concert music. The most positive gain is the new third theme, which is a great improvement on the original and is beautifully scored and played. Indeed the entire performance is much more assured than the Brunswick interpretation. The tempo changes are well done and do not detract from the homogeneity of the first part as much as one might expect. But for all that, and allowing for its own weak points, the Brunswick recording gives a clearer idea of *Creole Rhapsody* than the rambling Victor version, although no student of Ellington's music could fail to enjoy both.

* * *

Two further Victor sessions in June 1931 were all the band was to record during the rest of this year. Of the four numbers produced, three are Ellington compositions, the odd piece being a version of *Limehouse Blues* which features a high-quality Ellington arrangement—note the use of saxes led by clarinet in conjunction with Nanton's muted trombone. *It's A Glory* is a score which looks forward to the swing era, and the performance is powered along by Braud's driving bass. Hodges has a rather odd middle eight in the last chorus as well as an earlier solo, but the highlight is an impassioned open chorus by Williams in which he uses the lower register of the trumpet to excellent effect. Perhaps the greatest of these records—arguably Ellington's masterpiece to date—is *Echoes Of The Jungle*. Although the title might suggest Cotton Club music of the *Jungle Nights In Harlem* variety, this is a sixteen-bar blues with a beautiful singing, melancholy melody. Hodges has a roving ensemble role and plays superbly, but the main soloist is again Williams. The first half of his solo is played open in his most majestic style, the second half with mute in a vehement, passionate manner. After Cootie's solo a twelve-bar chorus is interpolated; the first four bars are taken from *Blues Of The Vagabond* and feature Guy's guitar with a whiff of vaudeville greasepaint, while the last eight have Bigard's low-register clarinet over syncopated piano chords. This leads into a chorus of wa-wa brass and Nanton's trombone, cemented by Hodges's embellishments. The last two choruses have the brass singing the melody—first against the Hodges alto, and then against a section of high reeds.

The last title the Ellington band recorded in 1931 was *The Mystery Song*, the opening of which is a moment of pure Ellington magic. After a deliberately prosaic piano introduction the brass section enters muted and pianissimo, playing suspended harmonies in a strangely shifting pattern. This passage is unique in Ellington's music, and the rest of the record, suffering somewhat from the Camden echo, fails to maintain this level of music making, although the immediately succeeding saxophone passage is excellent in its indolent ease and relaxation. A second take was issued in the late seventies; this has a better performance of the later parts of the score, but the first chorus is not improved by touches of clarinet and baritone saxophone.

Outstanding Recordings

Paducah, Harlem Flat Blues, The Dicty Glide, Hot Feet, Cotton Club Stomp (Victor version), *Misty Mornin'* (Victor version), *Saratoga Swing* (Victor version), *Saturday Night Function* (Columbia and Cameo versions), *Breakfast Dance, Jazz Lips, Lazy Duke, Double Check Stomp* (Victor version), *Shout 'em Aunt Tillie, Ring Dem Bells* (Victor version, all takes), *Old Man Blues* (Victor version, all takes), *Rocky Mountain Blues, Mood Indigo* (Brunswick and Victor versions), *Echoes Of The Jungle*, and *The Mystery Song* (first take)

Chapter 7

Cotton Club Days

IN EVALUATING THE RECORDS BY JAZZ ARTISTS of the 1920s and early 1930s it is important to consider the nature of the audience which demanded the music and bought the records when they were first issued. This is not to say that we should adopt that audience's values, but rather that we need to be aware of them in order to understand the music itself. There was no specific jazz audience in those days, and only the more serious of the participating musicians and a handful of unconventional persons in the literary and musical worlds thought of jazz as an art. For the overwhelming majority, jazz music was entertainment pure and simple, of no more artistic importance in the world in which it functioned than a radio commercial, a picture postcard, or a dime novelette. The great innovations of Louis Armstrong were made during this period, but, apart from the recollections of his fellow musicians, there are no accounts of what Armstrong's playing sounded like away from the confines of the recording studio. Armstrong's work is now accepted as being of great artistic importance, yet his most creative years were spent pouring out his genius to an audience which, however positively they may have reacted to his personality, was totally ignorant of the musical importance of what it was hearing. In the twenties and early thirties, the jazz concert was totally unknown and the dance hall, theater and night club clientele were the people the jazz musician had to satisfy if he wished to succeed.

Duke Ellington knew that to realize his musical aims he must succeed commercially to keep his orchestra of expensive virtuosi in existence. Again one should stress the importance of Irving Mills in this period of Duke Ellington's career. Whatever Mills's conception of Ellington's music was and however inadequate it may seem from the vantage point of later years, he certainly recognized its importance and devoted a considerable part of his formidable energies to its promotion—while, of course, ensuring that he made a healthy profit. The Ellington band was Mills's prime concern, and its unconventional music was sold to theater and club owners, to dance halls, and to record companies, and through these intermediaries to the public. The Ellington Orchestra got the very best jobs open to a black band, including, as we have seen, the top job of all, the residency at the Cotton Club. When the Ellington band left the Cotton Club to go on tour, they had their own Pullman car to take them around the United States. Mills is reputed to have made a fortune out of Ellington, but he was also a prime agent in building a secure financial basis on which Duke's musical development could blossom.

Ellington's own attitude to entertainment and show business became clear only in later years when statements of artistic policy by jazz musicians were considered worthy of attention. Basically, it was that when he and his musicians approached a task, they aimed for the very highest quality, irrespective of whether they were dealing with an arrangement of someone else's pop tune or with the interpretation of one of Ellington's own concert works. This attitude, his wish to make his music "sound good now," insured his art against the pretentiousness of so much "serious" jazz endeavor, from Paul Whiteman to Stan Kenton and beyond. Some of the recordings of popular tunes noted in the previous chapter are of considerable musical substance, while behind others a purely commercial intent can be discerned. By the mid-thirties, the quality of Ellington's popular song recordings had acquired much greater consistency. Perhaps the very "commercial" recordings of the early thirties are an indication that in the years before income from royalties became a basic part of the Ellington financial structure, Duke could not always afford the luxury of an independent musical policy.

* * *

The most obvious features of the Ellington output of the post-Miley period are its range and variety, qualities which already made Duke's music stand out from that of his contemporaries. Range and variety were also important attributes of the mature Ellington, and it is interesting to see them emerging as his art was struggling to assume its fully developed form. Included in the recorded repertoire are arrangements of popular songs by other writers, blues with the emphasis on the soloist, blues built into compositional structures, unique Ellington melodic creations such as *The Dicty Glide*, and show numbers for the Cotton Club. There are also jazz stomps in the Luis Russell style and tone paintings on a variety of subjects. Another Ellington characteristic which is already evident is the importance of the individual voices of the performing musicians within a compositional structure, a vital aspect of all Ellington works of this period other than *Creole Rhapsody*. The voices of the individual musicians can of course be heard in *Creole Rhapsody*, but they are not central to the musical development as they are in the more typical shorter works such as *Old Man Blues* and *Mood Indigo*. This reduction in the importance of the individual soloist is a feature of a small number of Ellington's later compositions, including some of his concert works, but it never became a major feature of his music. In this period we can see the germs of many facets of Ellington's development, including, in *Creole Rhapsody*, his highly individual concept of jazz as concert music. Other important Ellington traits established at this time were a total emphasis on the black American tradition of music making as developed by the jazz musician, and a remarkable freedom of expression for the individual musicians within the orchestra.

During the last years of the 1920s and the first years of the 1930s, Ellington seems to be in the final stages of building an ideal ensemble for his musical purposes. At times the band could still sound clumsy, not only on careless pop tune performances, but also in important scores such as the first version of *Creole Rhapsody*. On the other hand, it was already capable of a very wide range of tone color and mood while retaining the feeling of spontaneity essential to any successful jazz performance. An instance of his widening and increasing subtlety is the use of the ensemble clarinets in *Breakfast Dance* and *Jazz Lips* which is worlds away from the simple clarinet trios found on the earliest Ellington records. From this time, too, the use of a small ensemble from within the band had become an established practice and had produced recordings as varied and as successful as *Saratoga Swing*, *Lazy Duke*, and *Mood Indigo*. The integration of the musicians' individual styles into the ensemble was being handled with increasing skill over a widening range. Ellington's employment of his sidemen's skills varied from the use of an individual as a dominant soloist in a composition, such as Cootie Williams in *Echoes Of The Jungle*, to the blending of a musician's voice in various ensemble situations, such as Juan Tizol's strong but curiously unassertive tone in the second part of the Victor *Creole Rhapsody*.

From the records of this period we can begin to see that Ellington chose certain *types* of musician to work in the band. Of course a high standard of professional skill was essential, and with a few exceptions his men were all outstanding jazz improvisers. There are no exceptions to the rule that all Ellington musicians were outstanding ensemble players, although they were all strong musical personalities. Once used to Ellington's eccentric musical ways, they seemed able to interpret his music with almost uncanny insight. This allowed Duke to leave individual parts within his compositions in the hands of the interpreter, certain that the musician concerned would arrive at a suitable conception with regard to the overall musical context. Men like Arthur Whetsol, Juan Tizol, and Otto Hardwick were just as skilled at this kind of thing as the more jazz-oriented musicians such as Cootie Williams, Tricky Sam Nanton and Johnny Hodges. Another factor in Ellington's choice of musicians was his need for diversity of style. He chose men of very strong presence and distinctive musical sound, who not only offered dramatic contrasts in the solo routines but also a reservoir of potential blends and juxtapositions of musical personalities in the ensemble.

The methods which Ellington used to manage his band of highly temperamental individualists were also unusual. The norms of big band discipline were unsuitable, indeed would have been ruinous for the kind of uninhibited expression which he required. So Ellington ran his orchestra on a basis of mutual respect which grew into a kind of family relationship between the musicians as the years went by. We have seen that in the beginning Ellington was a reluctant bandleader, his main ambition being to make a career for himself as a songwriter. When he took over The Washingtonians it was at the request of his fellow bandsmen, and he was careful to retain the collective musical spirit of those early days. This diminished somewhat as the band expanded and musicians more used to the discipline of other large orchestras came into the fold. But throughout its long career, the Ellington orchestra was always involved in collective creation to a vastly greater degree than any other big band.

Ellington always chose the kind of musician who would respond in a fresh and inventive way to the musical demands he made on them, men with whom he could feel wholly confident. Discussion, suggestion, modification were very strong parts of the Ellington way of running a band. That Ellington was able to maintain this tradition with a group of highly talented and temperamental jazz musicians was fundamentally because of his own great musical abilities. No matter how great some of the Ellington soloists were, they all knew that Ellington was the leader for *musical* reasons, that he was the finest musician of them all. His abilities commanded their respect and his approach encouraged their loyalty. He gave them a great deal, placing his genius at their disposal by providing them with ideal platforms for their playing and by creating pliable compositions which could and would be molded to suit the needs of the performer. In the early years especially, Ellington socialized extensively with his musicians, and he certainly worked hard to keep their spirits high at times when morale might be shaken. In return, they gave him a kind of loyalty which could seem overcasual but was in essence deep and enduring.

* * *

For a listener whose experiences in recorded sound are mainly with stereophonic high fidelity, a good deal is demanded in the way of imaginative listening if he or she is to hear the musical qualities of the jazz of the 1920s and early 1930s in a correct perspective. In the case of Duke Ellington, we are fortunate to be dealing with a musician who was often given the best recording facilities of the time, especially on many of his OKeh and Victor recordings, although even on these the sound is a long way from present-day standards. The music itself also poses problems to those not familiar with (or in sympathy with) early jazz styles. Almost without exception, the jazz groups of this era used popular devices which have become dated and their style can indeed sound quaint and crude in the context of the constant and rapid changes in jazz fashion. Here again the demands on the listener are considerable; he or she is required to cultivate what we might call a "historical ear," an ability to listen to the music of the past *on its own terms*. By far the most difficult of such recordings are those made in the early and middle twenties by the pre-electric (or acoustic) method of recording. In Ellington's case such recordings are few and confined to his pre-Vocalion output, apart from three titles on the Harmony label. None of these contains music of great importance, but in the case of many other important early jazz groups—for example the vitally important King Oliver Creole Jazz Band—it is essential to accustom the ear to the sound of acoustic recording before any approach can be made to the music. Heard after high fidelity recordings of the long-playing era, the acoustic sound seems unbearably thin and inaccurate. Yet if one plays a series of acoustic records in succession, the ear will begin to translate their puny sounds into trumpets, trombones, and other instruments until one becomes hardly aware of the restricted sound quality. This procedure will also be found effective so far as musical style is concerned.

It should be stressed that for the person familiar only with later styles in jazz who wishes to enjoy early Ellington—or Armstrong, or Morton, or Oliver, or Henderson—it is no use just listening to an odd track from the twenties in the middle of a program of sixties or seventies jazz. One must listen at length until the true values of the music begin to assert themselves over the period style, over the technical limitations of the recording, and, in some cases, those of the musicians. The real qualities of the music should then become apparent and the best of it will sound just as fresh and spontaneous as it did on the day it was recorded. And freshness and spontaneity are perhaps to be found more in the music of the twenties than in that of any other era of jazz. From the mid-thirties onwards, Duke Ellington's musicians blended into a highly skilled musical ensemble, and the crudities which can be heard in their earlier playing were eradicated. But the best of the early records have an attractive rough-hewn quality which had gone from jazz by the middle thirties, an inevitable casualty of the music's development. For those with what we have called the "historical ear," the freshness and delight of this music can still be fully savored. Without developing this capacity, the listener will not only be denied the pleasures of early jazz but will also be unaware of the essential roots of Ellington's art.

Many listeners find that the most disturbing feature of early Ellington records (and of most other jazz records of this period) is the standard of musicianship, which is undeniably low when measured by the academic yardstick. One should always be aware that this is not an academic music, and that such criteria are not at all apposite. That musical crudities do exist on early jazz records cannot be denied, and these are most common on the records by black orchestras. The reason for this is that in the America of that day high-quality musical training was much more readily available to a white musician than a black one. Yet it would be foolish to regard this lack of academic background in twenties jazz musicians as a wholly negative factor. The cultural forces which made the academy what it was were different from those shaping the jazz tradition. Indeed the introduction of increasing numbers of highly trained musicians into the jazz field from the forties onwards served as a diluting agent in the music so far as character and individuality were concerned, producing in its turn a reaction which was often grotesque in its search for individual musical identity. In the twenties each musician has an immediately recognizable style, one which was often based on an exploitation of his strengths and a covering up of his weaknesses. Under these circumstances a musician could turn an academically unacceptable trait into a major stylistic device. This is a vital factor which must be understood by those seeking the delights of early jazz. Duke Ellington certainly knew all about the matter and clearly relished the distinctive styles of the musicians in his band, going to great lengths to exploit their individual characteristics in his music.

The instrumental virtuosity of the big bands of the sixties and seventies stands in stark contrast to the often sloppy playing of the first large jazz orchestras to record. A strong movement to improve the standard of musicianship in the big black bands was obvious right from the start. The first of these orchestras to achieve a precision comparable to that of the best white dance bands of the day was that led by Fletcher Henderson. By this time, the novelty approach of Henderson's earliest band recordings had largely disappeared, and his band was much admired by Duke Ellington. "My big ambition was to sound like Fletcher," Duke once said. "He had such a wonderful band. But his was basically an ensemble group and in our band the solos—you know, all the various stars we have had—always dominated everything" (quoted in *The Big Bands* by George T. Simon [New York: Macmillan, 1967], p.187). Which is rather an odd statement when one considers that Henderson's band was at all times packed with distinguished soloists. According to all who played with Henderson or heard his band in the flesh this was a stomping, swinging, soloist-dominated group. But for some reason which has never been satisfactorily explained these qualities were never demonstrated on record. On the records made in the twenties and thirties, the Henderson band sounds a neater, better-balanced unit than Duke's, but by comparison the scores played by Henderson are commonplace. And for all the complexity of its music, the Ellington band delivers performances with a much stronger jazz feeling.

Much the same overall impression is created by comparing Ellington's recordings of this period with those of McKinney's Cotton Pickers. With the ex-Henderson alto saxophonist and arranger Don Redman as musical director, McKinney's was the most precise of all the black bands of the twenties, although its roster of soloists never approached Ellington's or Henderson's in quality. Even so, the neat playing by the band of its well laid out scores can still give a wholly musical pleasure half a century later, no mean feat for what was basically a commercial dance band. One session by McKinney's Cotton Pickers is of particular interest to the Ellington student. This is a date done for OKeh in October 1928 under the pseudonym of The Chocolate Dandies (McKinney's was under contract to Victor). Here John Nesbitt's arrangement of Ellington's *Birmingham Breakdown* is both more varied than Duke's and the performance better than that on Duke's own recording. By contrast, Redman's recording of his own composition *Paducah* from this date sounds quite commonplace compared with the Ellington Brunswick of March 1929.

The big band of this period which comes closest to Ellington's in musical quality is the Luis Russell Orchestra of 1929–1930. Some jazz historians have chosen to ignore the contribution of this band, but it has always been held in high esteem by musicians and discerning collectors. This particular group of Russell's foreshadowed in many ways the Count Basie Band of the late thirties, as it was a soloist-dominated big band which played with all the fire and spontaneity of a small improvising group. Indeed the Russell Orchestra is the big band which comes closest to capturing the flavor of New Orleans jazz. As with the later Basie band, Russell's had a powerful rhythm section. This was led by the New Orleans bass player Pops Foster, who was well supported by another New Orleans musician, drummer Paul Barbarin, by Will Johnson on guitar, and by the competent but unexciting piano of Russell himself. The soloists included some of the leading innovators of the day, led by the fiery and inventive New Orleans trumpeter Henry "Red" Allen and the shouting trombone playing of Georgia-born J. C. Higginbotham. The reeds included another New Orleans player, clarinetist Albert Nicholas, and an alto saxophonist from Boston, Charlie Holmes, who played with an attractive directness of style and outstanding swing. The Russell band was, unlike Basie's, a "two year wonder," a comet which shone with unusual brilliance for a short period. As soon as the Russell band started to record conventional big band arrangements its aesthetic magnitude diminished and though it continued to employ outstanding jazz musicians for many years it was never again to be numbered among the best big bands. But the records made by the group for OKeh and for Victor (the latter under Henry Allen's nominal leadership) during 1929 and 1930 remain among the finest and most exciting of all big band jazz recordings. Ellington was affected by the music of both Henderson and Russell, and he and his musicians were frequently among the audience at the Nest Club when Russell was resident there. While admiring the ensemble precision of the Henderson band, Ellington seems to have been more impressed by the New Orleans spirit of Russell's group, as can be gauged from such Ellington recordings as *Hot Feet*, *Stevedore Stomp*, and, above all, *Double Check Stomp*.

Among other outstanding bands of the late twenties were those led by Earl Hines and Andy Kirk, and a study of their recordings, along with those of Fletcher Henderson, McKinney's Cotton Pickers, The Missourians, and Luis Russell, gives a clear idea of the musical standards of the best black bands of this period.

* * *

One of the features of the Ellington records of the twenties and early thirties is the inconsistency of the rhythm section. On some records it swings with the vigor of the Luis Russell section while on others it plods along in pedestrian fashion, its playing hardly distinguishable from that of some mediocre dance band. To some extent this is due to recording balance, for when Wellman Braud is near the microphone, the great vitality of his playing seems to permeate the music.

Braud is a musician whose contribution has been unjustly denigrated by some Ellington commentators. He was one of that school of New Orleans musicians who demonstrated to this and succeeding generations that the string bass had more to offer in the jazz rhythm section than the previously fashionable brass bass. The greatest rhythm section of the swing era, and without doubt the most lauded of all time, was the Count Basie section, and Basie's bassist Walter Page stated that his style was crucially affected by Braud's work with Ellington. The reason that Braud's contribution has been underestimated by the critics is that his accuracy and intonation were of a lower standard than those of later jazz bass players. Braud was certainly no virtuoso, as his vigorous but essentially simple bass solos attest (e.g., *Double Check Stomp* and the 1932 *Blue Harlem*). But he was a good deal more than a slap-happy player with rhythmic drive his only virtue. He adapted well to the many changes of mood in the Ellington band. His work on bowed bass (e.g., *The Blues With A Feeling* and the OKeh *Misty Mornin'*) is comparable with any in jazz history and superior to most; certainly no player ever used the bowed bass so effectively in a big band context. Above all, Braud was a swinger who added to the band the distinct sound of an individual musical personality. Ellington once recalled, admiringly, that Braud's playing had "lots of flavor." One wonders if, from the viewpoint of his musical requirements, he ever paid a greater tribute to one of his bandsmen.

Sonny Greer's work on cymbals was probably the most widely imitated aspect of the early Ellington rhythm section, for not only was he a master of judging exactly the right amount and kind of tone color required, but his cymbal work was also outstanding for its rhythmic placing. At this time, Greer's work on snares, tom-toms, and bass drum was less impressive, although his press roll was much admired by his fellow drummers. Through the years Ellington's rhythm section was more often led from the bass than from the drums, a pattern which originated with this particular section. Fred Guy would sometimes create colorful effects, but he rather tagged along so far as swinging was concerned. Duke's own piano playing seemed happiest at this time the nearer the music was to his favorite two-beat stride style. His best band piano on the records we have been discussing is probably behind Carney's baritone on *Old Man Blues*, a perfect adaptation of stride style to ensemble use. But on *Rocky Mountain Blues* we find a new kind of rhythmic thrust in the two piano interludes, and this was soon to become a feature of Duke's work behind the soloists and when he was providing piano countermelodies against the ensemble.

A frequent criticism of the Ellington rhythm section of this period made by later writers is that it failed to blend consistently. This is valid insofar as it accurately identifies a feature of the section's playing, but overall this lack of blending was probably a good thing, for if all four voices had been equal, the pedestrians might have outbalanced Braud. Indeed, such was the value of the vitality the bassist brought to the band that, far from being one of its minor assets, as some commentators have asserted, Braud is probably better described as the spark plug of the band in the period after Miley's departure. Without the rhythmic vitality generated by Braud's bass the band would surely have been considerably hindered in its development as a jazz unit.

Sidemen

Juan Tizol

Juan Tizol is one of the Ellington musicians whose contribution is greater than is obvious at first glance. He rarely took a jazz solo and is most famous as the composer of such exotic pieces as *Caravan* and *Moonlight Fiesta*. But Tizol, a Puerto Rican who played valve trombone, was an exceptional asset to the Ellington ensemble. Owing to the greater mobility of the valve trombone, Tizol was able to blend with either the saxophones or the trumpets as well as playing as a member of the trombone section. Like Williams and Carney, he was a musician with a strong distinctive tone. This meant that important harmony parts could be assigned to him in the sure knowledge that they would make their full impact within the thick textures of Ellington's scoring.

Representative Recordings: Twelfth Street Rag (Brunswick, 1931), *Caravan* (Master, 1937), *Lost In Meditation* (Brunswick, 1938), *Battle Of Swing* (Brunswick, 1938), *Bakiff* (Victor, 1941), *Moonlight Fiesta* (Mercer, 1951)

Cootie Williams

A native of Mobile, Alabama, Cootie Williams had absorbed a good deal of the New Orleans influence in his formative years. He was a fanatical Louis Armstrong disciple and had gained some experience in New York playing for brief spells in the bands of Chick Webb and Fletcher Henderson. It is said that Coleman Hawkins regarded Henderson's failure to keep Cootie in the band as a grave error. With Ellington, the trumpeter's potential soon blossomed, and he became one of the major voices in the orchestra. After a few weeks in the band he started to study the plunger style and soon achieved such mastery that he became more famous than either Miley or Nanton as a practitioner of the art. Within the growl style, Cootie created a wholly individual and personal means of expression. Williams's work is always recognizably that of a wholly committed musician, and he plays with immense drive and emphatic accents. He is the master of endless sonorities and many moods. No Ellington composition ever demanded a response from Cootie without stimulating a perfect emotional and imaginative realization. He remained just as remarkable a player on open trumpet as on muted, and his big, powerful, majestic tone represents the nearest anyone other than Armstrong has come to projecting the ideal jazz trumpet sound. Ellington took full account of this big sound in his brass scoring, often using Cootie in the lead role or in one of the crucial harmony parts. Williams left the Ellington band in 1940 to play for a year with Benny Goodman. He was a great admirer of Goodman's musicianship and enjoyed his stay with Benny, especially his work with the sextet. After leaving Goodman he led his own big band for many years, scaling down to octet size at the end of the big band era. After almost two decades as a leader and later as a solo attraction, Cootie returned to the Ellington band in 1962. His style had become a good deal simpler during his twenty-two years out of the band but he was still a trumpeter of great majesty and power, and he brought to the Ellington Orchestra in its last years a kind of swing which was rapidly becoming a lost art.

Representative Recordings: Ring Dem Bells (Victor, 1930), *Sweet Chariot* (OKeh, 1930), *Echoes Of Harlem* (Brunswick, 1936), *Ridin' On A Blue Note* (Brunswick, 1938), *Harlem Air Shaft* (Victor, 1940), *Concerto For Cootie* (Victor, 1940), *The Shepherd* (Fantasy, 1968)

Chapter 8

The Records—February 1932 to July 1936

WHEN THE DUKE ELLINGTON ORCHESTRA entered the recording studio on February 2, 1932, after a six-month break caused by its absence from New York on tour, there were two new additions to the personnel. The band now had a regular vocalist, Ivie Anderson, and Lawrence Brown had joined to bring the trombone section up to three pieces. (From this time onward, all the records were issued under Ellington's name, and the days of "The Jungle Band," "The Harlem Hot Chocolates," and the other colorful pseudonyms were at an end.)

The full personnel of the band in February 1932 was:

Trumpets: Arthur Whetsol, Cootie Williams, Freddie Jenkins.

Trombones: Lawrence Brown; Juan Tizol (valve trombone); Tricky Sam Nanton.

Reeds: Johnny Hodges (alto and soprano saxes, clarinet); Barney Bigard (clarinet and tenor sax); Harry Carney (baritone and alto saxes, clarinet). From April 1932 Otto Hardwick (alto and bass saxes, clarinet) was added.

Rhythm: Duke Ellington (piano); Fred Guy (banjo and guitar); Wellman Braud (bass); Sonny Greer (drums).

Vocal: Ivie Anderson.

On the first title from the February 2, 1932, session, *Moon Over Dixie*, Lawrence Brown takes a few bars to make his solo debut, and Sonny Greer sings a chorus, a rare event on records, though Greer was still featured as vocalist on the band's engagements at this time. The other recordings from this Brunswick date are of classic stature: *It Don't Mean A Thing* and *Lazy Rhapsody*. From these two performances it is obvious that the band has gained in polish and refinement while losing nothing in vitality. The title of *It Don't Mean A Thing (If It Ain't Got That Swing)* is derived from a saying of Bubber Miley's. Nanton's driving muted trombone introduces the theme, then Ivie Anderson's sparkling vocal is accompanied by bouncing ad lib parts for Carney and Bigard. This is followed by an alto solo from Johnny Hodges, beautifully integrated with the orchestral part. The improvement in the band's playing is even more marked in the contrasting *Lazy Rhapsody* (a composition entitled *Swannee River Rhapsody* on some early releases). The beautiful main theme is played pianissimo by muted trumpets with Bigard taking the middle eight, the atmosphere enhanced by Braud's easy, relaxed bass playing. A variant theme is given to the saxophones with clarinet lead and played in the most casual manner in dialogue with a Cootie Williams scat vocal. A brilliant orchestral variation on the main theme, in which are heard the solo voices of Carney and Hodges, leads via an Ellington piano passage to the final recapitulation of the melody by muted brass, this time embellished by Bigard's low-register clarinet. *Lazy Rhapsody* is a supreme example of Ellington's "pastoral" manner and succeeds as a composition, in a much shorter span, in a way which the outwardly more ambitious *Creole Rhapsody* does not. In its way, *Lazy Rhapsody* is just as unusual an essay for jazz orchestra as *Creole Rhapsody*, and its concise formal aspect makes for total success. The resemblance of the theme and the harmonic structure to the later popular song *Moonglow* is pretty clear.

The day after this Brunswick session the band was in the Victor studio to record a medley for a series of experimental 33⅓ rpm long-playing records. The discs were not a commercial success, and this medley and a second one recorded on February 9 were among the rarest Ellington collector's items until their reissue in the microgroove era. The first medley consists of *Mood Indigo*, in an arrangement not recorded elsewhere; *Hot And Bothered*, in a cut-down version of just over three choruses; and *Creole Love Call*. The saxes plus Tizol's valve trombone state the theme of *Mood Indigo* with Williams playing the release, while Whetsol (with a new variation) and Ellington provide the main solos. This *Hot And Bothered* adds nothing to our understanding of the piece, and Cootie's growl trumpet is the only solo voice, apart from brief functional appearances by Nanton and Hodges. *Creole Love Call* appears in a full version just one chorus shorter than the later 12-inch Brunswick recording. This performance is superior on almost every count compared with the original Victor, lacking only the pure genius of Miley's own playing of his classic solo. Whetsol provides the responses to the clarinet trio in the first chorus, while in the second, Tizol plays the alternative theme over the clarinets. Cootie then growls his version of Miley's solo before two clarinet soloists present contrasting choruses—a typical Ellington device. Harry Carney is heard first, playing the second theme in a manner established by Rudy Jackson in 1927; he is followed in the most dramatic manner possible by a loose-limbed Bigard blues solo superbly framed by the orchestra. After an Ellington bridge, the main theme is recalled over a walking bass from Braud and with the trumpets building up a pyramid chord over the first six bars. As was the case with *Lazy Rhapsody*, two takes of this medley have been released and both are worth hearing.

The record companies were obviously keen to make up for the gap in the band's recordings, for the Ellingtonians were back in the Brunswick studio on February 4 for the third consecutive day. Two further masterpieces were committed to wax. In *Blue Tune* Ellington creates a composition of rich diversity in the AABA popular song form. Bigard's tenor provides the introduction against the band in a passage which is repeated after Whetsol's statement of the melodic material in the first chorus. This passage, with Hodges's alto in place of the tenor, also provides the coda. The solos of Hodges and Williams are both characteristic examples of their art and, at the same time, parts of Ellington's compositional whole. Indeed, the way in which Ellington achieves this aesthetic conjuring trick, one which he repeated on hundreds of pieces, is one of the greatest triumphs of his art. The playing of the band is admirable, realizing the finer nuances of Ellington's scoring in all their richness of detail. Note the blending of Tizol's valve trombone with the saxophone section and the use of Carney's baritone in the saxophone writing. *Blue Tune* is remarkable for the way Ellington creates so much variety within the time limits imposed by the 10-inch 78 record.

The session mate to *Blue Tune* illustrates an aspect of Ellington which sets him apart from other jazz innovators and was a great source of strength over his long career. This was his ability to return refreshed and with unjaded spirit to that most basic of jazz forms, the twelve-bar blues. *Baby When You Ain't There* has four twelve-bar choruses framed by a passage of twenty bars for Hodges and the muted brass, which is used as introduction and ending. In between, we hear choruses by Bigard, Nanton playing tightly muted (a great solo, this), Williams in the guise of blues singer, and finally the band. This ensemble chorus is played just as freshly and spontaneously as the improvised solo choruses. As on some other Ellington records of the period a few notes are heard from a vibraphone, presumably played by Greer.

In the Victor studios five days later the band recorded the

second of their LP medleys. It starts with a short, one-chorus version of *East St. Louis Toodle-oo* in which Ellington uses the same format as in the first chorus of the Velvet Tone version. This is followed by a number here called *Lots O' Fingers* but better known under the title used on a slightly later Brunswick recording, *Fast And Furious*. Either title gives a clear impression of what the piece is about—a flashy feature for Ellington's piano, very much in the Harlem stride tradition. The Victor LP and Brunswick 78 versions are similar and of identical duration. The Victor medley concludes with a full-length *Black And Tan Fantasy*. Although Williams was in the band, the trumpet work at the start is by Whetsol, very effective in a softer, more lyrical style than usual in the *Black And Tan Fantasy* trumpet solo. Harry Carney plays the alto passage, and Ellington's piano solo is reduced to a four-bar bridge passage, allowing a chorus by Bigard's clarinet to be inserted, as in the version which concluded the 1929 film *Black And Tan*.

Two further titles, of conventional 78 format, were recorded at this session, both standards which were very popular at this time. The Ellington recording of *Dinah* is an example of his ability to lightly satirize the popular styles of the day. After a blown-up concert-type introduction, the band proceeds to play the first chorus in straightforward dance band fashion which persistently falls away into typical Ellington stylings. Cootie is heard briefly on growl trumpet. The second chorus is a hilarious Greer vocal, which outrageously exaggerates the singing style of the day and is sung against racing saxophone figures. Williams then does a vocal takeoff of the Louis Armstrong scat style, widely imitated at this time. The performance ends with some mock-frantic double timing. By contrast, *Bugle Call Rag* is a serious, forward-looking score which had considerable influence on the arrangers of the swing era. The performance is of a highly extroverted nature and the riff figures are played with great enthusiasm and swing. There is superb solo work by Bigard and Nanton, but Williams, playing open, is the main soloist. The drive of his playing is quite remarkable, especially in the penultimate chorus. The intense swing of the string bass break reminds us just how much Braud is contributing to the performance. It should be noted that *Bugle Call Rag*, as well as being a highly influential score, is an uninhibited stomp which does not rely on the string-of-solos routine for its effect.

The recordings discussed so far in this chapter were made within a spell of eight days at the beginning of February 1932. A final recording session from this month featured two items for a 12-inch 78 disc—the previously mentioned version of *Creole Love Call* and a recording of *St. Louis Blues* with Bing Crosby. During his long career, Crosby learned a great deal from the jazz musicians with whom he worked, a debt he never failed to acknowledge. He had no pretentions as a jazz artist, still less as a blues singer, yet his easy, relaxed manner is highly compatible with the music of the Ellington band and his *St. Louis Blues* a pleasant interlude in the Ellington discography. Williams, Nanton, Bigard (behind the vocal), and Hodges are heard to good effect. There are two takes, easily distinguishable as Williams's first chorus is played muted and in the growl style on the first and on open horn on the second. *Creole Love Call* is identical in arrangement to the Victor medley version, except that an extra chorus of dialogue between the clarinet trio and Cootie Williams is added. A further recording from this session (of conventional 10-inch disc duration) is of the popular standard *Rose Room*. This features Bigard in the theme statement and against the ensemble at the end. Ellington contrives to make the melody sound as if it had been written with Bigard in mind, and the scoring throughout is as exquisite as the performance. The other soloists here are Hodges (briefly) and Ellington, while Braud is again the principal agent in establishing a mood of quiet, relaxed swing.

* * *

After this furious February outburst of recording activity the band was out of the studios until May 1932, by which time Hardwick had rejoined to bring the reeds up to four pieces. On three consecutive days in May, they recorded eight titles for Brunswick, the best being two done on the third session of the 18th—*Blue Ramble* and *Slippery Horn*. *Blue Ramble* is a series of variations of the 32-bar-with-bridge song construction, and it reveals the same kind of invention as was found on *Blue Tune*. There are no solos in the normal jazz sense, although the voices of Lawrence Brown, Hodges, Whetsol and Williams are used effectively. Again the rigorous economy of musical thought is impressive. The *Slippery Horn* from this date is the less common recording and two takes have been issued. The tempo is slower than on the better-known 1933 version and Williams's solo is omitted. This number makes effective use of the trombone trio, then still a very unusual feature in a big band, and is another masterpiece of easy-swinging music. Ellington's individual harmonic sensibility is given some play here in a version where the solos are taken by Bigard and Brown, the latter in dialogue with the saxophone section. *Slippery Horn* is another of those early thirties Ellington compositions which uses the chords of the principal theme of *Tiger Rag*.

On the first of these May 1932 sessions Brown recorded his first important solo with the band on *The Sheik Of Araby*, a well constructed, easily paced chorus. Hardwick's return is signaled by a duet with Nanton, an unusual pairing which works remarkably well. Sidney Bechet, employed as "band coach" around this time, had a standard, worked-out solo routine for *The Sheik Of Araby*. We have to wait until the forties before it appears on a Bechet record, but here in 1932, it is performed in its entirety by Johnny Hodges on soprano sax. The piece is given a neat arrangement which concludes with the not altogether successful experiment of having the brass function as part of the rhythm section. *Blue Harlem* from the same session is a medium-tempo Ellington tune on the sixteen-bar-with-tag pattern. It features some meaty writing for the band and solos by Williams, Nanton, Bigard, and, rather unusually, Wellman Braud.

From the second of these May 1932 sessions came two Ellington piano features, the previously mentioned stride extravaganza *Fast And Furious* and a remake of *Swampy River*, which receives a livelier performance than on the 1928 solo recording. Of the two takes of *Best Wishes*, the second is probably the better, though Greer's press rolls are pedestrian on both; Hardwick again duets with a trombonist, on this occasion Lawrence Brown. *Clouds In My Heart* is a Bigard-Ellington song (it was recorded again by the Bigard contingent in 1936) featuring Bigard's clarinet, some nice brass scoring in the *Lazy Rhapsody* manner, and a passage in which Tizol's valve trombone leads the saxophone section.

The masterpiece from the later part of 1932 is *Ducky Wucky*. The unusual melody is played over a jaunty dotted rhythm, which creates one of those ambiguous Ellington emotional effects. Brown is given the responsibility of announcing the theme, Bigard has a good solo, and the ensemble maintains the rather delicate emotional flavor of the piece. Williams has four short solo passages scattered through the score; these are played in a direct manner and provide effective moments of contrast.

Ducky Wucky was recorded at a September 1932 session along with a number called *Blue Mood*—one of the curiosities in the Ellington discography. It lay in the record company's vaults for over ten years, and when it did come out, it bore the composer credit "Mills-Hays" (sic). It was assumed that "Hays" referred to Edgar *Hayes*, pianist and arranger with the Mills Blue Rhythm Band at this time. The MRBR did not record *Blue Mood* until 1935, and their version remained unissued for even longer than Ellington's. When it was finally released on a Jazz Panorama LP (with composer credits said to be unknown), it proved to be a totally different composition. The true relationship between Ellington, Hayes, and the two compositions called *Blue Mood* will probably never be known. It seems probable that the two are unrelated and that when the Ellington record was issued in the forties the wrong composition was checked in the Mills archives for composer credit. The fact that Ellington did not copyright the tune until 1962 (with composer credit shared with Johnny Hodges) tends to support this theory. In itself the late copyright date is not significant—*Lazy Rhapsody* also waited until 1962 to be registered.

As if to make up for its previous neglect, the record companies have issued no less than three takes of *Blue Mood* on microgroove. These differ but little, and the piece itself turns out to be a minor Ellington mood number which just conceivably could have been written as an Ellington pastiche by an arranger as skilled as Edgar Hayes. Bigard has a pleasant solo, but the most notable feature is a passage for the saxophone section which was later used in the more famous *Echoes Of Harlem*.

Two days later, the Ellington band recorded Benny Carter's *Jazz Cocktail*, a characteristic Carter score with no attempt to adopt the Ellington style. It has never been made clear how Ellington came to record this piece. Carter told Dave Caughran many years later that he had written the score when he was with McKinney's Cotton Pickers (1931–32) and submitted it to Irving Mills, who had previously agreed to publish his music. Carter thinks that Mills probably gave it to Ellington to record for promotional purposes (letter from Dave Caughran to the author, March 26, 1982). Mills must have been pushing this particular score; *Jazz Cocktail* was recorded by the Mills Blue Rhythm Band just two days after the Ellington version. A comparison between the two performances finds Ellington's superior on every count—better tempo, greater swing, more relaxation, and finer solos. There are some differences in the arrangement, the variants on the Ellington version being in all cases the more effective. The comparison is instructive as the Mills Blue Rhythm was one of the best bands of the period, and their performance is good by any normal standard. The inclusion of *Jazz Cocktail* in the Ellington repertoire reminds us of Duke's great admiration for Benny Carter's writing. There are two takes of the Ellington *Jazz Cocktail*, with brilliant passages for the saxophone section (a Carter speciality), as well as solos from Bigard, Williams, Brown, Carney, and Hodges. The Ellington band obviously enjoys this essay in more conventional jazz making, Brown going so far as to play a solo in the manner of the up-and-coming Dickie Wells.

The session mate to *Jazz Cocktail* is *Lightnin'*, the first of Ellington's celebrated series of train pieces (disregarding the early *Choo-Choo*). Here the band goes for an easy Pullman ride. The train effects are well integrated into an Ellington medium-tempo stomp, with solos by Carney, Nanton, Bigard, and the leader, the last in his early stride style.

A remake of *Maori* for Victor, from a session which otherwise remains unissued, and an inane popular song called *Stars*, recorded for Brunswick with guest vocalist Ray Mitchell, are among the more forgettable segments of this year's output. *Stars* does at least have the distinction of marking the end of the policy of using guest vocalists—usually of an abysmal quality—for the band's popular recordings, and Mitchell rounds off the series in wholly appropriate fashion. A more substantial item from the same session is *Swing Low*, a Jenkins-Ellington collaboration which captures a good deal of the trumpeter's bounce and vivacity. Jenkins himself, Brown, Carney, and Hodges (on soprano sax) are the soloists, and the saxophone section has the Hodges soprano in the lead role throughout.

So great had been the success of the musical *Blackbirds of 1928* that in late 1932 and early 1933 American Brunswick was busily recording leading black performers in hits from the show for issue in album form. It was indeed remarkable that the highlights of a five-year-old show should be celebrated in this way. The Don Redman Orchestra is used on a couple of the titles, but the bulk of the songs are accompanied by the Ellington Orchestra. The main singers featured are Ethel Waters and Adelaide Hall. The orchestral backgrounds are simple and functional most of the way—tasteful and subdued, only recognizable as by Ellington because none of the other bands of the day could have sounded quite so "classy" in this discreet fashion. The outstanding title is Adelaide Hall's recording of *Baby* (four takes) which has a magnificent accompaniment by Brown. The musical tapestry woven by the trombonist forms a perfect backdrop to the vocal. *Diga Diga Do*, recorded with the Mills Brothers, has brief solo spots for Cootie, Carney, Nanton, and Hodges plus a remarkably good vocal "take-off" on Brown's trombone style by one of the Mills Brothers. One of the most interesting items from the album is the two-part *Blackbirds Medley*, played by the band alone. All the songs were by Fields and McHugh, and some of them had been recorded earlier by Ellington during his Cotton Club association with these writers. Outstanding in the *Medley* are *I Must Have That Man*, with a splendid half-chorus from Brown, and *Porgy*, with equally memorable work from Nanton. A curio is Otto Hardwick's old-style alto on *Dixie*. It is hard to imagine any other group making an interesting record of a show-business medley with all the soloists playing melody; but one of the gifts of all the major Ellington soloists (and most of the minor ones too) is that they were superb melody players. And of course Duke would always provide the ideal musical setting.

Two popular songs—singer Lee Wiley and musical director Victor Young are cocomposers in each case—were recorded at the same time, and these are also very well played and given good arrangements. Hodges has a nice soprano solo on *Any Time, Any Day, Anywhere*, while *Eerie Moan* has excellent Whetsol on the theme and good solos by Bigard, Carney, and Brown. In each case the -A takes are to be preferred, the issues of the -B takes being dubbed from test pressings in very poor condition.

Much has been written about the aptness of Ellington's titles, yet many appearing on records from this period were second or third choices. Sometimes the names Ellington had given to his compositions were replaced by titles concocted by Irving Mills. In February 1933 the band recorded a stomp for which Ellington had devised three provisional titles—*Ace Of Spades*, *Cotton Club Shim Sham*, and *142nd Street and Lenox Avenue*—only for each to be rejected in turn. The fourth and final title was *Merry-Go-Round*, and this is the name by which this driving piece will be known to posterity, if posterity be wise enough to take note of such happy art. The trumpet, trombone, and saxophone sections are featured, as well as solos by Williams, Bigard, Brown, Hodges, Jenkins, and Carney. As with many of Ellington's compositions, there is no apparent symmetry in the arrangement, but one passage follows another with a sure inevitability. From the same session comes the first recording of one of Duke's most famous songs, *Sophisticated Lady*. Brown states the melody in the first chorus with Bigard on the release, while the second is split between Ellington and Hardwick, who have sixteen bars each. Hardwick turns more than one phrase in a felicitous manner during his solo, but his trills are hard to take. The final title from this session is a non-Ellington song, *I've Got The World On A String*, with a casual arrangement and an easy Ivie Anderson vocal. Another pop tune, *Down A Carolina Lane*, was recorded the following day; this is nonvocal and has an arrangement which features typical Ellington voicings in which Brown, Williams, and Bigard can be discerned.

The best-known version of *Slippery Horn* shares a session with the aforementioned *Blackbirds Medley* and the new *Drop Me Off At Harlem*. Ellington's use of the band in *Slippery Horn* is masterly; note, for example, how in the introduction baritone sax and high muted trumpets are used to give contrast to the trombone section as it starts its first chorus. The solos are by Bigard, Williams, and Brown, and each solo, to a different degree, is a kind of dialogue with the orchestra. Cootie's tightly muted solo is played against the saxophone section, and the strong melodic line played by Carney's baritone under the soloist at the conclusion of this chorus is worthy of special note. Ellington's use of the trombone trio in this composition is justly celebrated, but his handling of the entire orchestra is that of a master. *Drop Me Off At Harlem* is given an arrangement which places a good deal of justified emphasis on its melodic charms—this is a delightful number with Brown, Whetsol, and a laconic saxophone section heard in melodic statements. Later in the piece Williams (growl) and Bigard are featured in improvised dialogues with the band, which continues to find fresh ways to play the main melody. Take -A is the standard one here but -B is well worth hearing—the faster tempo alters the flavor of the piece. Take -B is the one with the prominent guitar fill-ins by Fred Guy in the second chorus.

The soundtrack of the film *Bundle Of Blues* has been issued on LP; this was a short musical made in March 1933 featuring the Ellington band. Brief excerpts from *Lightnin'* are heard at the beginning and end, while *Rockin' In Rhythm*, *Stormy Weather*, and *Bugle Call Rag* are also featured. *Rockin' In Rhythm* is a different arrangement from that usually used, with Nanton the only soloist; *Stormy Weather* features a fine vocal by Ivie Anderson along with solos by Whetsol and Brown; *Bugle Call Rag* is a shortened version of the arrangement used on the Victor recording. Sonny Greer is recorded prominently in this film and was clearly using his full kit, including timpani and chimes.

Ellington's next three studio recordings were of popular songs with Ivie Anderson vocals. Neither *Happy As The Day Is Long* nor *Get Yourself A New Broom* is particularly memorable, although the former has no less than three short Freddie Jenkins solos plus a tenor solo from Joe Garland (who was substituting for Barney Bigard). The third title, *Raising The Rent*, has first-class solos and an excellent arrangement. Nanton states the theme, with assistance from Whetsol and the saxophone section in the middle eight, then Anderson's excellent vocal is followed by solos from Carney and Williams.

Bundle Of Blues has nothing to do with the film of that

name, but is a number Ellington had originally titled *Dragon's Blues*. This is one of those Ellington blues pieces which consist of a sequence of solos with appropriate orchestral backing, in this instance framed by an introduction and coda featuring Williams and Duke himself. The soloists, all in excellent form, are Brown, Bigard, Ellington, Williams, and Hodges. Two takes have been issued and there are sufficient differences in details of the solos to make them both worth hearing. The second version of *Sophisticated Lady* was made at the same session—it differs from the first in that half of the second chorus is now taken up by a rich orchestral passage, the solos by Ellington and Hardwick being reduced to eight bars each as a consequence. The version of *Stormy Weather* which concludes the date is another magnificent Ellington arrangement in which the soloists play melody all the way through. The way in which Ellington uses the contrast in styles between the different soloists while providing them with apt and contrasting backgrounds is highly imaginative and in perfect taste. The soloists are Whetsol, Williams, Brown, Ellington, Carney, and Bigard.

The next session was recorded in London during the band's visit to Britain in the summer of 1933. Two Ellington originals and two standards were recorded. *Hyde Park* (alternative title, for transatlantic use, *Every Tub*) is a fairly conventional Ellington stomp which was not recorded in any other version. The other Ellington composition, *Harlem Speaks*, was done again for Brunswick when the band had returned to America. The English Decca version is notable for the superb Nanton solo played very tightly muted and for the splendor of the final, stomping-out chorus by Nanton, Bigard, and the brass section. *Ain't Misbehavin'* and *Chicago* are obviously head arrangements designed to give the soloists maximum space and contain some notable playing. All the horns (except Tizol) solo at one point or another during this very well recorded session. Alternative takes have been issued of *Harlem Speaks* and *Chicago*, both differing sufficiently from the standard versions to make for interesting listening. The day after this session Ellington recorded an interview with Percy Mattheson Brooks, then editor of the *Melody Maker*, with incidental piano. This was pressed on a single-sided disc given away by Levy's record store in London to any customer who bought five or more Ellington records. The interview is a period piece, very stilted in style, although the views expressed by Ellington are of some interest. He indicates that his favorite creations were his unpublished ones, but adds that of his published works he likes *Mood Indigo* best. (Assiduous collectors have discovered an alternative take of this interview; the differences are minimal and the item is of curiosity value only.)

Duke Ellington always maintained that the British tour of 1933 was a great boost for his morale; certainly the band sound in fine fettle on their first recording date back home in America, that for Brunswick at which the second and generally more exciting version of *Harlem Speaks* was recorded. One pop tune, an Ellington number called *I'm Satisfied*, was done at this date. It features some imaginative scoring and solo work, a casually attractive Ivie Anderson vocal, and some rather pedestrian drumming from Greer. The thrusting, ebullient *Jive Stomp* features beautiful interplay between the soloists—Carney, Williams, and Bigard—and the band in a masterly Ellington score. Greer's drumming, especially his cymbal work, is a major factor in this performance's complete success. Regarding the title, Ellington remarked many years later that the word "jive" originally had a better meaning "in the sense that something swung, had spice or tonal zest. . . ." *Jive Stomp* has both. As if two masterpieces were not sufficient for one day, the band went on to record its version of *In The Shade Of The Old Apple Tree*, an affectionate and humorous reading which remained in the repertoire for many years. The trumpet solo in the opening chorus, played against indolent phrasing of the melody by the saxophone section, was copied from this Freddie Jenkins original by later Ellington trumpeters such as Rex Stewart and Ray Nance, for it is a conception which simply could not be improved upon. The second chorus features a droll and lugubrious Nanton and a succinct Hodges, while Bigard floats his counterpoint against the very relaxed and swinging final ensemble.

When the band was in London, Mrs. Constant Lambert, the wife of the composer, persisted in calling Ellington's most popular composition *Rude Indigo*. Duke responded by writing a piece dedicated to her. By the time of the interview for the souvenir record, he had everything ready except the second word of the title. He finally decided to call the piece *Rude Interlude*, and it was recorded at the band's first Victor session for some twelve months in September 1933. Ellington's harmonic usage of this period is perfectly demonstrated in this piece. At the start, the hints of melody are almost lost in a thick cushion of nebulous harmony; Tizol's is the most prominent voice, and the whole is accompanied by irregular piano punctuations. Brief contributions by Cootie's angry growl trumpet and Louis Bacon's wordless voice add to the oppressive mood, only slightly lightened in the more melodic final chorus scored for brass and reed choirs. A second take of this masterpiece has been issued recently, almost as good as the famous version but with a less satisfactory balance in the first chorus. The session mate to *Rude Interlude* is a stomp based on the second theme of *Rockin' In Rhythm* titled *Dallas Doings*. The soloists are Ellington and Brown, while Greer demonstrates that he can still play press rolls in an unswinging fashion.

The band remained with Victor for the next year, and in December 1933 recorded a session for the label which produced two titles. *Dear Old Southland* is a further example—following *Rose Room* and *In The Shade Of The Old Apple Tree*—of Ellington translating outside material into his own musical language. The voice-leading is a trifle confused at the beginning of *Dear Old Southland*; this may be due to the absence of Tizol, for the passage seems to call for his precise musicianship in the trombone part. Greer is using a march rhythm on the snares, and it is noticeable how the performance seems to move into a fresh gear as Carney enters backed by punching brass, at which point the rhythm section lead is assumed by Braud. Dickie Wells has described the tightly muted tone produced by Tricky Sam Nanton as sounding like tissue paper being torn, and one can hear exactly what he means at the start of this solo. Later, Nanton plays in the wa-wa fashion in duet with Louis Bacon, whose wordless chanting over the articulate trombone creates a surrealistic effect. In the closing stages, Williams plays very strong lead over a multivoiced orchestral texture to which Hodges responds with a dancing soprano sax part. The recently issued take two is not quite so good as the standard take one; despite the take numbering, this sounds like an earlier and less assured runthrough.

It would be difficult to imagine a greater contrast between *Dear Old Southland* and its session mate *Daybreak Express*. The latter is the second of Duke's train pieces and possibly the most famous—in the thirties it was one of his most admired recordings. The reason for this lay in its rather obvious brilliance and its portrayal of the latest and fastest of express trains, circa 1933. The saxophone passage was considered to be one of Ellington's most modern conceptions, although part of it, at least, was the creation of Sidney Bechet, whom Duke approached for advice. *Daybreak Express* is much more concerned with train noises than was *Lightnin'* but it remains highly musical, one of the most effective train portraits in music and a remarkably avant-garde piece for a 1933 jazz orchestra. There are no jazz solos as such but Jenkins's trumpet has an important role, and Hodges and Williams are heard briefly during the long introduction. This is a virtuoso performance by the band and the execution of the saxophone section is particularly noteworthy. There is little to choose from between the two takes.

Further contrasts are presented between *Rude Interlude* and *Daybreak Express* and the two titles from the session of January 9, 1934—the gentle, pastoral *Delta Serenade* and the bustling, exuberant *Stompy Jones*. The range of Ellington's art in 1934 can be seen when we consider four such diverse pieces. The two takes of *Delta Serenade* differ only slightly and feature a theme statement by Whetsol in duet with Bigard, plus ultrarelaxed Brown and a solo from Carney in the baritone's high register. *Stompy Jones* is one of the happiest and most vital performances in the whole of recorded jazz. Proceedings burst upon us in the form of a bouncing introduction by Brown's trombone; then the theme is sketched by Bigard's low-register clarinet with poised brass phrasing behind him. A mellow open Cootie, a boisterous Carney, and a driving Brown take solos leading to a long, gradually building climax of ensemble riffs. Duke adds some spicy piano before Bigard joins in with an improvised clarinet part; then Nanton's plunger-muted trombone adds yet another voice, and *Stompy Jones* surges to a mighty climax, Greer's cymbals adding to the color of an intensely driving performance.

In further contrast, the next session features a ballad and a blues. The ballad is the first recording of *Solitude*—one of Ellington's most popular songs—and here the theme statement features the *Mood Indigo* voicing of muted trumpet, low-register clarinet and muted trombone with Carney taking the middle eight. The meat of the performance is a solo by Williams at his most majestic on open trumpet, parts of which are in the form of a dialogue with the saxophone section. Cootie's playing is the main reason why this first version of *Solitude* must always be numbered among the very best of the many which Duke recorded. *Blue Feeling* is a slow blues, played first by trombones, then by saxes, muted trumpets, and finally by the whole band. This alternates with twelve-bar solos from Williams, Brown, and Bigard. The quality of the solo and ensemble work make *Blue Feeling* another Ellington masterpiece, in this case one achieved by the simplest of means.

Ebony Rhapsody is a popular song by Arthur Johnson and Sam Coslow based on a theme from Liszt's *Second Hungarian Rhapsody*. It was performed by the Ellington Orchestra in the film *Murder At The Vanities*, but the soundtrack recording has not been released on disc. The Victor version, recorded while the band was in Hollywood making the film, must be one of the richest and most diverse scores ever created for conventional big band instrumentation. The performance of this immensely influential score is a beautiful one which realizes perfectly the varied writing, while remaining relaxed and swinging. Note the excellent scoring for and playing by the saxophone section as well as the variety of brass techniques employed. The short functional solos are well integrated into the fabric as is the cool, detached vocal by Ivie Anderson. The high standard of the band's playing is all the more remarkable for the fact that two of its members—Tizol and Hardwick—were missing from the session. The other two numbers played by the band in the film—*Cocktails For Two* and *Live And Love Tonight*—were also recorded on this date, but feature comparatively commonplace arrangements and lack particularly notable solos. Four days later, the band recorded a fourth Johnson-Coslow song, *I Met My Waterloo*. It is, like the two previous titles, rather surprisingly, a nonvocal performance and again of little musical distinction.

It is unusual to hear the Ellington band of this period with a female singer other than Ivie Anderson, but the soundtrack of the film *Belle Of The Nineties* features no less a personality than Mae West. Indeed, Miss West is heard in the roles of both blues and ballad singer. There is a full-length version of Handy's *Memphis Blues*, a thinly disguised *St. Louis Blues*, and a short snippet of *Hesitating Blues*. For her ballads, Miss West offers *My Old Flame* and *Troubled Waters*. There is little in the film to excite the Ellington enthusiast, while Mae West hardly qualifies for any jazz hall of fame in either of her vocal roles. A Victor recording of *My Old Flame* by Miss West and the Ellington band is often said to be from the film soundtrack, but comparison reveals that it is a different performance, if every bit as dull. The band also recorded *My Old Flame* and *Troubled Waters* with Ivie Anderson vocals, and these are much better both vocally and instrumentally. *Troubled Waters* is one of the most celebrated of Ellington's popular song recordings, with some of Williams's greatest playing—both in solo and behind Ivie's excellent vocal.

In May 1934 Duke Ellington made a short film, *Symphony In Black*, which offers one of the earliest recorded examples of Billie Holiday's voice. After viewing this film in 1961, Dan Morgenstern wrote:

> *Symphony In Black* . . . is a rather pretentious effort, in typical period style, but interesting as an early example of "extended composition" by Duke. Actually, the music, divided into four movements, contains familiar material along with original passages. Section one, *The Laborers*, has a mordant blues-theme, reminiscent of the first movement of *Black, Brown and Beige*. After introductory shots of Duke composing in his garret, and the band in black tie on a concert-hall set, we see *Ol' Man River*-type black laborers hoisting sacks of coal and stoking blast furnaces. The second movement, *The Triangle*, is a *Porgy And Bess*-type love story, featuring Billie Holiday as the loser. Billie, typecast from the start, appears in a brief scene. She waits on her lover's doorstep, encounters him and his new woman, pleads with him to return and is rewarded with a brutal shove which drops her on the sidewalk. Billie, barely twenty then, is beautiful, vulnerable, and tragic, even in this setting of phony pathos. She sings a few stanzas of blues, going from Duke's *Saddest Tale* to lyrics of her own. It leaves one aching for more. Section three is set in a church and smacks of *Green Pastures* and *Halleluja*: bearded old minister, weeping women and all. Duke's music is hardly more than underscoring to the wordless humming of the congregation. The final segment, *Harlem Rhythm*, is a night club sequence with, among others, Snakehips Tucker; the music is *Merry Go Round* in a somewhat more fully scored version than either the earlier or the later record. In the band, an augmented percussion section features Sonny Greer with even more equipment than usual [and] O'Neil Spencer at the kettledrums. (*Dr. Stearns' Jazz Classes* by Dan Morgenstern, *Jazz Journal*, February 1961, p. 7)

On neither of the LP issues of the soundtrack of *Symphony In Black* can one hear any humming, and *A Hymn Of Sorrow* is a straightforward piece of quiet, quasi-religious Ellington band scoring with Whetsol's trumpet well to the fore. The opening of *The Triangle* is a shortened version of *Ducky Wucky*, while the Billie Holiday vocal blues—*Big City Blues*—is framed by a shortened version of *Saddest Tale*, in which the extended coda by Johnny Hodges is a feature not encountered on the later studio recording.

Saddest Tale was recorded in the Brunswick studios on September 12, 1934, at a session which also produced two nonvocal popular songs and a second instrumental. The songs were Ellington's *Solitude* and the Hudson-de Lange *Moonglow*, based on Ellington's *Lazy Rhapsody*. This second recording of *Solitude* again has two choruses, the first being split between the trio and Carney, as on the Victor, but in the second a totally new band passage replaces the Williams solo—this is a typically colorful Ellington mixture of section scoring and writing for individual voices. The arrangement of *Moonglow* is more commonplace but no less effective; the soloists are Williams on the theme and Hodges in solo variations on soprano sax.

In 1934 Ellington, a strong family man, was greatly distressed at his mother's deteriorating health. His composition *Saddest Tale* is a reflection of his gloom. This is one of the greatest blues ever recorded, and a perfect work of art in several ways. The piece opens with an ascending unaccompanied clarinet solo by Bigard followed by a two-bar fortissimo brass outburst. Ellington himself then chants the mournful couplet:

> Saddest tale told on land or sea
> Is the tale they told when they told the truth on me.

Nanton, Hodges, Williams, and Carney each play highly personal blues choruses before the brass, now muted and pianissimo, repeat their fanfare from the introduction, and Duke closes the performance with a repeat of his sad couplet. The harmonic usage is unconventional although both effective and a development of the traditional harmonic climate of the blues. The intense expressionism of the individual solos which make up the main body of *Saddest Tale* enhances the emotional power of Duke's composition, while the orchestral backing given to each solo heightens its potency.

The fourth title from this session, *Sump'n 'Bout Rhythm*, is pitched in a very different emotional key. Like many of Ellington's earlier stomps, it is derived from stride piano practice, but there is a world of difference between the compositional skills behind this piece and, say, the 1926 *Birmingham Breakdown*. Duke plays one of his mock-primitive stride passages as an introduction and then the theme is presented by Jenkins and Hodges—a brilliant stroke. Jenkins is the dominant partner, and the melody sounds as if it were designed for his perky, assertive trumpet. After a stride piano solo by Ellington, there are two choruses of variations on the theme scored for the band. The use of Nanton's trombone and what was known in later years as the "pep section" (two trumpets and one trombone with plungers) is masterly. This is another beautifully balanced composition.

* * *

Towards the end of 1934, the previously stable Ellington personnel underwent a number of changes. In the latter part of 1933 Ivie Anderson's husband, Louis Bacon, had joined the trumpet section briefly, his main contribution to the recorded output being a couple of vocals. In the following year, ill health forced both Freddie Jenkins (permanently) and Arthur Whetsol (temporarily) out of the trumpet section. Jenkins's replacement was cornetist Rex Stewart, while Charlie Allen joined on lead trumpet until Whetsol was fit to return. In January 1935 Billy Taylor came in as second bassist—this being the first of several spells when Duke used two string basses. Initially, Taylor doubled brass bass, but he is not heard on this instrument on record. Sometime in the spring of 1935 Wellman Braud left and was replaced by Hayes Alvis; it was only when Alvis departed in February 1938 that Ellington reverted to the conventional pattern of using one bass player—in this case Billy Taylor.

The full personnel in January 1935 was:

Trumpets: Cootie Williams, Charlie Allen, Rex Stewart (cornet).

Trombones: Lawrence Brown; Juan Tizol (valve trombone); Tricky Sam Nanton.

Reeds: Otto Hardwick (alto and bass saxes, clarinet); Johnny Hodges (alto and soprano saxes); Barney Bigard (clarinet and tenor sax); Harry Carney (baritone and alto saxes, clarinet, bass clarinet).

Rhythm: Duke Ellington (piano); Fred Guy (guitar); Wellman Braud and Billy Taylor (basses—Braud soon replaced by Hayes Alvis); Sonny Greer (drums).

Vocal: Ivie Anderson.

The first session on which these replacements can be heard is that for Brunswick on January 9, 1935. This was not a very successful recording date, and all four titles were rejected, although they have appeared on LP in recent years. *Admiration* is a new and rather undistinguished Ellington composition which should not be confused with the Juan Tizol piece recorded by the band in 1930. This one has brief solos from all three trumpeters—with Charlie Allen taking over Whetsol's mantle—but is not otherwise notable. An overly busy arrangement of *Farewell Blues* has moderate solos by Stewart and Bigard, while *Let's Have A Jubilee* has excellent Nanton, more Stewart and an Ivie Anderson vocal. *Porto Rican Chaos* is the original title of the Tizol-Ellington *Moonlight Fiesta*, and it appears here in the same arrangement as when the band recorded it a few months later under the better-known second title. Rex is heard here in his highly individual plunger style; the only other soloist is cocomposer Tizol, playing the melody.

It will be noted that newcomer Stewart has solos on all four titles from his first recording session with the Ellington Orchestra. This is most unusual, as Duke's normal practice was to allow a musician a period to settle in and to get used to the ways of the band before featuring him to any large extent as a soloist. But Rex was treated as a major soloist right from the outset, which is an indication of Ellington's assessment of his abilities. Of course Stewart was already an established soloist, famous for his work with Fletcher Henderson, but it seems likely that Ellington's assessment of his abilities and knowledge of his personality were based on their youthful friendship in Washington some twenty years earlier.

Four titles were recorded at the band's next session in March 1935, and again Stewart plays an important part in all four. The first is *Margie*, another of Duke's beautiful adaptations of a standard popular song. In this instance the theme is given out by muted wa-wa brass over a shifting pattern for the two double basses, with Rex providing some sparkling cornet responses. Later there is a soprano—baritone saxophone chase by Hodges and Carney, framed in a marvellously apt orchestral setting. The rerecording of *Moonlight Fiesta* is pleasant enough, but the 1937 Bigard version and (especially) the 1951 revival by the Coronets contingent are both superior. The band is reduced to a sextet for the final two numbers, both rather melancholy minor-key blues, the eight-bar *Tough Truckin'* and the twelve-bar *Indigo Echoes*. Two takes have been issued of each title. The sextet consists of Stewart, Hodges (on soprano), Carney, Ellington, and the two bassists. Stewart is the outstanding soloist and makes full use of his famous half-valve technique.

The next month, the band did a further four titles for Brunswick, starting with Ellington's latest popular song, *In A Sentimental Mood*. In this number Ellington probably reaches the peak of his songwriting achievement, but it is not so popular as some of his other songs, possibly because of its unusual harmonic pattern. The 1935 recording of *In A Sentimental Mood* starts with a theme statement by Hardwick, making one of his increasingly rare appearances as a soloist. His beautiful tone and fine musicianship are as evident here as they are in his more usual role as leader of the saxophone section. Stewart and Brown are the other soloists in this richly scored ballad performance. *Showboat Shuffle* uses a figure similar to those on *Daybreak Express* to simulate the sound of the showboat's paddles, but basically this is an easy swinger featuring Hodges in dialogue with the band and (seemingly inevitably) Stewart. The Chicago drummer Fred Avendorf replaces Greer for this session and does nothing to impair the swing on *Showboat Shuffle* or on the remake of the 1933 *Merry-Go-Round*. This is a fine version, with the arrangement and solo routine as before, except that Freddie Jenkins's chorus is taken over by Stewart. The final title is *Admiration*, superior to the January recording but an anticlimax after its session mates.

After this date the band was out of the recording studios for four months. In August 1935, it resumed recording for Brunswick in a session made up of three popular songs of the day. *Accent On Youth* is the nonvocal title, and after Whetsol has stated the theme, the main soloist is Hodges, his manner spare and concise and quite without the sensuality of tone and phrasing which was to characterize his later ballad playing. Despite the banal lyrics, Ivie Anderson does well on *Cotton*, which also has Hodges, Bigard, and Carney on the theme and some good work by the two bassists, offset to a degree by Greer's press rolls. *Truckin'* is an uptempo number with driving, exciting Cootie, another fine Ivie vocal, and a characteristic Tricky Sam contribution. Ben Webster sat in with the band on this session and contributes a good tenor saxophone solo to *Truckin'* in his early Benny Carter-inspired manner. The arrangement of *Truckin'* is outstanding in its integration of soloists and orchestra and in the way it inspires the band to give such a driving, urgent performance.

* * *

At his next session, held on September 12, 1935, again for Brunswick, Ellington recorded his second major concert work, *Reminiscing In Tempo*. This was the sole product of the session and covers four 10-inch 78 sides. *Reminiscing In Tempo* is in a single movement and is based on the material heard in the opening bars—a motif outlined in the brief piano introduction and the melody played with such clean articulation by Whetsol's muted trumpet. The first 44 bars can be regarded as a form of exposition, a 32-bar chorus with an extended introduction and a two-bar tag. Here Ellington breaks away from conventional phrase lengths and chorus structures to a much more radical extent than in *Creole Rhapsody*. The resolution of the material back to the familiar 32-bar-with-release pattern in the last part of *Reminiscing In Tempo* is a major aspect of the structure of the work, and one which had been prefigured in *Creole Rhapsody*. In the new work, the harmonic usage is more elaborate than on Ellington's contemporary three-minute recordings. The design of the piece is based on constant variation and development of the main material and of supplementary motifs—for example, in the passage based on widening intervals first heard in one of the solo piano interludes. Emotionally, the music gradually clouds over, sinking deeper into darkness and despair and then works through to a final section which allows a brighter, more optimistic conclusion.

Reminiscing In Tempo was written shortly after the death of Ellington's mother, which accounts for its generally elegiac mood. Only in the final part do we find the confident emotional aura usually characteristic of Ellington's art. Duke was very close to his mother, and her death was a severe blow to him, affecting him both personally and as an artist. The ambitious length of *Reminiscing In Tempo* is also a reflection of the confidence engendered by the European tour of two years earlier. The performance by the band is a fine one, quite without the blemishes which affect *Creole Rhapsody*. The dynamics of this 1935 recording of *Reminiscing In Tempo* are clearly restricted by the limitations of the recording techniques of the day, especially those used for popular artists. The habit of the recording companies was to record popular and jazz artists loudly to keep the ratio of surface noise to music as low as possible and the dynamic range was very restricted, even compared with contemporary classical recordings. In a piece which lasts over twelve minutes dynamics are very important, but are largely left to the imagination here.

Ellington's use of the band is tightly controlled and the soloists are used solely for contrasts of color, texture, and phrasing, the main solo voices being those of Whetsol and Tizol. It is impossible to find in all Ellington's vast output a work where he more consciously uses the orchestra as a medium of his own personal expression. *Reminiscing In Tempo* is not the usual kind of cooperative creation by Ellington and his sidemen, but a composition by the leader which is played as written with the minimum of intrusion by the musicians' personalities. For example, Bigard's clarinet part is beautifully played but with hardly a trace of his strong musical character. *Reminiscing In Tempo* would lend itself more favorably to performance by another band than any other work of Ellington's maturity. Duke never returned to this kind of orchestral writing, the more intimate and direct Ellington compositions of later years being in the form of either piano solos or miniature piano concertos where the orchestra is used in a background role, for example, the 1943 *New World A-Comin'*.

There are two later recordings of *Reminiscing In Tempo*, one from a broadcast in July 1945, which has been issued as part of the D.E.T.S. series (D.E.T.S. 15), the other from a December 1948 concert (issued on DESOR Disc 448-1). Both make fascinating contrast with the 1935 original, but the 1945 version is the better of the two. The soloists include Stewart playing Whetsol's original role and Claude Jones in Tizol's part. The band performance is excellent and the greater dynamic range of the recording gives a more vivid impression of some sections. The 1948 recording is shorter and may not be complete, a change of acetates being noticeable at the point where the omission occurs. The 1935 recording runs for twelve and a half minutes and the 1945 for just under twelve, but this 1948 version lasts for just under eight minutes. Harold Baker, Quentin Jackson, and Russell Procope take over from Whetsol, Tizol, and Hardwick. The performance is less convincing than the others, although it is full of interesting detail and rewarding to those wishing to study this work in depth. It is unfortunate that the Ellington band of the fifties or sixties did not record a well-prepared *Reminiscing In Tempo* in good stereophonic sound.

* * *

The Brunswick records of the four parts of *Reminiscing In Tempo* were the last sides the band made in 1935. During the first seven months of 1936, they cut four sessions for this label in which jazz instrumentals and popular songs were fairly evenly mixed. *I Don't Know Why I Love You So* is a little-known Ellington tune, nicely played by Bigard and with a good solo from Hodges and a characteristic one from Stewart. *Dinah Lou* is an uptempo song with vocal by Ivie Anderson and eight excellent bars from Nanton. Lawrence Brown is featured in solo and behind Ivie's vocal on *Isn't Love The Strangest Thing*, in which Bigard and Stewart are also heard. At the opening of *No Greater Love*, the band starts off like a common or garden dance orchestra, but Brown is in good form, and Hodges and Williams split a chorus. Arthur Whetsol's last recorded solo can be heard on *Love Is Like A Cigarette*, which also has an Ivie vocal superbly backed by Rex. These last two titles both have excellent bass playing by Hayes Alvis. *Shoe Shine Boy* and *It Was A Sad Night In Harlem* again have Anderson vocals, with good work by Brown, Bigard, and Stewart on the former and Hodges and Williams on the latter. The pick of the 1936 popular song recordings, however, are *Kissin' My Baby Good Night* and *Oh Babe! Maybe Some Day*. The first has excellent solos, a poised chorus by Rex Stewart outstanding, while the second, an Ellington song, features Anderson along with contributions from Hodges and Williams. The Stewart solo on *Kissin' My Baby Good Night* is famous and notable for a strong Bix Beiderbecke influence; indeed, this superbly relaxed chorus is one of Rex's best. Both this title and *Oh Babe! Maybe Some Day* are taken at swinging medium tempos, and on the latter the brass scoring behind Hodges is a superior development of the idea of having the brass function as a rhythm section, first tried out on the 1932 *Sheik Of Araby*.

One of the features of the Ellington records of the previous six or seven years had been the superb way in which Duke *presented* his soloists, setting off their contributions with the most appropriate (although rarely the most obvious) backings. In 1936, he developed this talent a stage further and introduced four "concertos" for members of the orchestra. The first two are among Ellington's most successful works. *Clarinet Lament* (or *Barney's Concerto*, as it was originally titled) is a blues which features many aspects of Bigard's style, including his superb melodic sense, his command of the resources of the clarinet, and, not least, his mastery of timing in breaks. *Echoes Of Harlem* (or *Cootie's Concerto*) is a brooding, almost sinister piece which features Williams both muted and open in a way which is almost uncanny in its perception of the essentials of the trumpeter's musical personality. In both these pieces, the orchestral scoring is just as rich and as important as the playing of the soloist. The slightly later concertos for Lawrence Brown, *Yearning For Love*, and Rex Stewart, *Trumpet In Spades*, are less successful. *Yearning For Love* is a pleasant sentimental trifle without the musical substance of the first two concertos, while the feature for Rex shows off his fast technique on the horn to the exclusion of almost every other facet of his wide-ranging style. Rex had to wait a couple of years before Duke wrote the perfect "concerto" for him in *Boy Meets Horn*, but it was not until he produced *Golden Cress* in 1947 that Duke finally wrote a showpiece worthy of Brown's talents.

On the session of July 29, 1936, which marked the end of Ellington's association with the old Brunswick company, Ben Webster again joined the saxophone section as guest artist. Three numbers were recorded, of which *Exposition Swing* is available in two takes, the second being the superior. This is an uptempo exercise in the big band style of the day, with a solo roster consisting of Carney, Williams, Bigard, Hodges, Nanton, Ellington, and Stewart. The 32-bar blues *Uptown Downbeat* (or *Blackout*) is one of Ellington's dark, ominous-sounding scores, with Cootie on growl trumpet and Hodges on soprano sax the main soloists. Much use is made of Hodges's soprano as lead voice in the reeds here. This is a great performance, but the masterpiece from the session is without much doubt the medium fast *In A Jam*, one of Duke's happiest creations. An eight-bar bridge passage of solo piano and orchestrated stride frames the soloists' superb sequence—first Nanton and Bigard in duet, then Hodges and Williams in a chase chorus, then Webster, and finally the mercurial Stewart. Perhaps the chase chorus by Hodges and Williams should be singled out for the way it preserves the continuity of melodic line normally associated with a single soloist. But all parts of *In A Jam* are excellent; it is a piece in which Ellington's overall conception is perfectly realized by both soloists and orchestra.

Outstanding Recordings

It Don't Mean A Thing, Lazy Rhapsody, Blue Tune, Baby When You Ain't There, Bugle Call Rag, Creole Love Call (Columbia version), *Rose Room, Blue Ramble, Ducky Wucky, Slippery Horn* (version of February 17, 1933), *Drop Me Off At Harlem, Raisin' The Rent, Bundle Of Blues, Jive Stomp, Harlem Speaks* (Brunswick version), *In The Shade Of The Old Apple Tree, Rude Interlude, Dear Old Southland, Stompy Jones, Solitude* (Victor version), *Blue Feelin', Ebony Rhapsody, Troubled Waters, Saddest Tale, Sump'n 'bout Rhythm, Margie, In A Sentimental Mood, Showboat Shuffle, Merry-Go-Round* (version of April 30, 1935), *Truckin', Reminiscing In Tempo, Clarinet Lament, Echoes Of Harlem, Kissin' My Baby Good Night, Oh Babe! Maybe Some Day, In A Jam*, and *Blackout* (or *Uptown Downbeat*)

Chapter 9

The First Full Flowering

THE LIST OF OUTSTANDING RECORDS at the end of the previous chapter is longer than those for any comparable period covered so far and reflects the flourishing of Ellington's art. As well as becoming a more precise and subtle instrument, the Ellington Orchestra had improved still further in solo strength, and Duke had acquired a new mastery over his self-created compositional techniques. By this time, the Ellington Orchestra was far removed from the conventional big band concept with its mechanical discipline, contracted arrangers, and designated star soloists. Here discipline was based on respect, the arranger was a composer of genius who directed his own works from the keyboard, and every man was a vital part of the band, both as soloist and ensemble player.

By the early thirties there were sufficient connoisseurs of Ellington's music for the hiring of Lawrence Brown in 1932 and Rex Stewart in 1934 to be regarded by the popular music press as controversial events. Neither Brown nor Stewart was thought to be suitable in style for Ellington by either the American critics or those in Britain and continental Europe whose opinions were based largely on records. John Hammond and Spike Hughes were among the most notable of the first generation of jazz critics, and they both condemned the addition of Brown. It was not that they considered him a poor musician, but rather that they felt his personality to be too "sophisticated" (for Ellington!), his style too "virtuoso" for the "essentially direct and simple music" of this band. "It is not that his individuality is too strong," wrote Hughes, "just misplaced." Similar protests followed down the years whenever a new soloist joined the band. The critics were always proved wrong in the fullness of time but never seemed to learn from the lessons of the past. The Ellington orchestra always had a strong collective personality, and this made it difficult to envisage a musician from another environment fitting in. One can well imagine the jazz collectors of the day playing the Lawrence Brown solos from his records with Armstrong and trying to imagine them in a contemporary Ellington context. In the event, Brown adapted to the band and it to him without the slightest difficulty. It is an aspect of Ellington's greatness as a bandleader that he rarely erred in his selection of sidemen, even though so many of his new musicians at first seemed highly improbable choices to contemporary onlookers.

Although the distinguished composer Percy Grainger had arranged the first-ever Duke Ellington concert at Columbia University during 1932, in the early thirties Ellington was becoming disillusioned with the commercialism of his world. In his brilliant study of Ellington's personality, "The Hot Bach," Richard O. Boyer quotes Duke's recollections of this period:

> I'd bring something I thought was good to the music publishers and they'd ask "Can an eight-year-old child sing it?" I'd bring something new to them and they'd say, "This ain't what we're looking for. We want something like Gazookus wrote last week." I'd see guys writing little pop numbers that were going over big. I didn't see why I should try to do something good. I thought I'd stop writing. . . . If something bad was plugged it would go over better than something good that wasn't. I felt it was all a racket. I was on the point of giving up. (Richard O. Boyer, "The Hot Bach," *The New Yorker*, July 1944; reprinted in *Duke Ellington: His Life And Music*, edited by Peter Gammond).

Ellington's friends recommended a tour of Britain and Europe, but they had first to overcome Duke's fear of sailing. Even though he finally agreed to the trip he was worried about icebergs. "I couldn't understand how an automatic pilot could see an iceberg." Aboard ship, he was careful: "I decided I wasn't gonna take any chances by sleeping at night. I slept in the day and stayed up all night. But it was very lonesome." When he disembarked, it was to commence a tour which was a success in every way. Above all, Ellington derived renewed confidence from the way in which his music was received.

In England Ellington's reputation rested solely on his records, and the audience for these included not only devotees of the latest dance music craze but also many dance band and jazz musicians, a growing band of jazz record collectors, and a number of figures of eminence in the world of academic concert music. Such jazz writers as Leonard Hibbs and Spike Hughes continually stressed the importance of Ellington's music, while the distinguished composer Constant Lambert had also enthused in print about his works. Percy Grainger had compared Ellington with Bach and Delius, and much was made of the latter comparison in England. The names of Debussy and Ravel were also bandied about somewhat freely in connection with Duke's music at this time. In addition to this, there was the expected barrage of press publicity of a less esoteric nature promoted by Irving Mills and by the British bandleader/impresario Jack Hylton, who was organizing the band's European trip.

The Ellington Orchestra played variety theaters and occasional dances in various large towns and cities in Britain, including a residency at the London Palladium, and two concerts in London sponsored by the *Melody Maker*. Recollections of those who saw the Ellington band in Britain in 1933 indicate that its approach was just as casual as in later years. At Bolton Palais, where they played a late-night dance after a theater appearance in Liverpool, Barney Bigard took a long spell off during the course of the Ellington set in order to change a reed. The first *Melody Maker* concert of June 25, 1933, provoked bitter controversy. It was designed to show Ellington as a composer and was described as a "Musicians Concert." The first half consisted of *Echoes Of The Jungle*, *The Duke Steps Out*, *Blue Tune*, *Jive Stomp*, *Creole Rhapsody*, *Lightnin'*, *Ducky Wucky*, *Bugle Call Rag*, and *Black And Tan Fantasy*. The audience reaction to the muted work of Cootie Williams and Tricky Sam Nanton was that of people hearing a clever piece of instrumental trickery or some weird novelty rather than colorful, integrated aspects of Ellington's tonal palate. Sensing that an audience that laughed at Tricky Sam's solos was not taking the attitude which his critical followers had hoped for, Ellington changed the program for the second half and included Lawrence Brown in *Trees*, Freddie Jenkins singing and dancing *Some Of These Days*, and such popular material as *Minnie The Moocher* and *Tiger Rag*. The serious devotees of Ellington's music were horrified; Duke had "debased himself"; he had commercialized his art! The most angry voice was that of Spike Hughes, and in the program notes for the second concert, held on July 16, 1933, members of the audience were advised by Hughes as to how to conduct themselves in a concert hall. "Don't laugh at Nanton," said Hughes, and "Don't applaud during numbers." He was promptly dubbed the "hot dictator," and his part in these events has been consistently maligned by almost every writer who has discussed the 1933 tour. However strongly one may disagree with the opinions Hughes later expressed about the decline in Ellington's music, there is no denying that in this instance he was right. Duke was able to create music wholly worthy of the time and attention of a concert audience, and the playing of Williams and Nanton was an integral part of it. Hughes's methods were drastic but well justified.

After the British tour, Ellington went on to France where he again found that his music was treated seriously and not simply as a passing show-business phenomenon. This sort of attention was very pleasing to Duke, but one wonders about Irving Mills's reaction. The last thing he wanted was for Ellington's music to be considered too "highbrow." Respect for his music, yes; however, Ellington's popularity could be seriously affected by too much of this sort of thing, and some of the criticisms of the Hughes approach came from within the Ellington camp. A delicate line needs to be drawn here. Success with concert music along the Paul Whiteman lines was desirable, as Mills had understood when in 1931 he had arranged for Ellington to record *Creole Rhapsody*. But too many comparisons with Delius or Stravinsky could be commercially dangerous, as these were "difficult" composers. There is no doubt, however, that Ellington himself was delighted with his reception:

> "The main thing I got in Europe was *spirit*; it lifted me out of a bad groove," he said. "That kind of thing gives you courage to go on. If they think I'm that important, then maybe I have kinda said something; maybe our music does mean something." (quoted in *Duke Ellington* by Barry Ulanov, p. 151)

On its return to the United States, the Ellington Orchestra embarked on a spell of tours and short-term residencies, the former including their first tour of the southern states. Accommodation problems in the segregated South did not exist for the Ellington musicians, due to Mills's provision of a set of Pullman cars; these were simply shunted on to a siding and the local electricity and water supplies linked up. Sleeping and cooking accommodations were included, so that the Ellington entourage traveled as a self-contained unit. This was to remain the pattern for Ellington tours during the whole of the band's time under the management of Mills. In 1934 they were featured in a group of films—*Murder At The Vanities*, *Belle Of The Nineties* (with Mae West) and *Symphony In Black*. This was the year in which Constant Lambert's study of twentieth-century music, *Music Ho!*, was published. While Lambert was lauding Ellington as an important composer and making his celebrated comparisons with Ravel and Stravinsky, Duke was engaged in playing dances for segregated audiences in the South and leading his band in brief snatches of undistinguished films.

* * *

While the large white dance orchestras were still playing straight dance music, the tradition of large black bands following a more jazz-inclined policy was by this time firmly established. Apart from the Ellington Orchestra, the most important were the Fletcher Henderson Band and the newly popular Jimmie Lunceford Orchestra, but Benny Carter, Cab Calloway, Earl Hines, Andy Kirk, Don Redman, and Chick Webb all led good bands, and Irving Mills had a fine group on the road known as The Mills Blue Rhythm Band. All these bands made good records at this time, but none of them was able to achieve a standard comparable with Ellington's. No matter how fine the arrangements—and Benny Carter and Lunceford's Sy Oliver were two of the very finest arrangers ever to grace the big band scene—the other bands sounded conventional beside Duke's, and their range of material restricted compared with his.

Sy Oliver was introducing a new concept of big band scoring in his work with the Lunceford Orchestra, a concept so widely imitated that people now have great difficulty in recognizing Oliver's originality, so familiar have his ideas become through their adoption by virtually every dance band, large jazz group or studio orchestra from the late thirties onwards. But the Lunceford records show how narrow a field Oliver was working in comparison with Ellington, his beautifully stylized miniatures being largely variations on a limited number of basic ideas. By comparison with such bands as Carter's, Redman's and Lunceford's, the Ellingtonians could sound very undisciplined, but in solo strength, in originality of material, and in range and adaptability they were incomparable.

An amusing story of Duke's ways of handling his musicians in this period is told by Barney Bigard. The first time Ellington met the Lunceford band in a battle of music, Lunceford led off with a string of Ellington compositions, plus their score of *Rose Room*, a feature for Willie Smith on clarinet which was clearly based on the recorded Ellington arrangement. When the Ellington band's turn to play came the leader persisted in calling slow, quiet numbers which made little impact on the audience. The band became increasingly angry at this policy and its effect until Cootie Williams shouted "For crying out loud, play something!" whereupon Duke turned his musicians loose—their blood well up—on *St. Louis Blues* and *Tiger Rag*. That was the end of the Lunceford challenge for that night (quoted in *The World of Duke Ellington*, by Stanley Dance, p. 89).

* * *

Although Ellington recorded for Brunswick, Victor, English Columbia (in the U.S.A.), and Decca (in England), his policy was different from that of earlier years when the recordings were often of a clandestine nature with pseudonyms on the labels. Now, with the band's recordings all issued under Duke's name, there are fewer different versions of the same compositions compared with the time when they were recording regularly for rival companies. The list of compositions extant in more than one version from this period—alternative takes excepted—is small: *Creole Love Call*, *Lot's O' Fingers* (alias *Fast And Furious*), *Slippery Horn*, *Harlem Speaks*, *Solitude*, and *Merry-Go-Round*. Of these, perhaps the different versions of *Harlem Speaks* and *Solitude* are the most interesting, the former finding the band giving two quite different readings of the same score, the latter showing differences caused by the continual state of change in which Ellington kept certain of his arrangements.

An interesting aspect of the band's recordings at this time is the different sound they assume under the contrasting studio acoustics of the various companies. The most marked contrast is between Victor and Brunswick recordings, particularly when Victor used its echo-ridden Camden studio. There is always a good deal of resonance in the Victor recordings and the effect is to give the music a very "public" sound, as if it were being played in a large dance hall. By contrast, the Brunswicks have a drier, more intimate quality, sounding as if the band really were playing in one's living room. Braud's gentle off-beat slap is as characteristic of the Brunswicks as the vigorous, stomping aspect of his playing is of the Victors. We are fortunate in having these contrasting sounds, for they serve to remind us that the true sound of the Ellington band of the early 1930s must have been different from either of these extremes. It should be emphasized that, with all their differences, the Ellington recordings are of a high overall quality for this period. Posterity has a good deal for which to thank the anonymous engineers, as did Ellington himself, who was always fastidious in such matters.

The reader who is not a record collector may have been puzzled by the frequent references to the many second and third takes which exist of Ellington recordings. In the 78 era, it was customary to record two, three or more versions or "takes" of a number. After selecting the one for issue, the others were either rejected or held by the company in case the selected master was lost or damaged. Quite a few of these second and third takes were issued on 78, and many of the rejected ones found their way into collectors' hands in the form of test pressings. In the microgroove era, many of these takes which had survived, either in company archives or in private collections, were issued for the first time. The value of such additional takes is hotly debated by jazz collectors and is a subject which can engender bitter arguments. One view is that the collector simply wants the best take, which is usually, although not always, the one originally issued. The contrary argument asserts that every take, no matter how similar to the known version, is essential source material in the task of understanding the many aspects of the art of a musician like Duke Ellington. Every take, even incomplete versions of a tune, should be made available, according to this view. The weakness of the first argument is that it evades the question "who decides which take is best?" In other words, the version presented to the record buyer may not be the one he himself would have chosen. The second argument is logically sound but ignores the fact that only specialists want to buy LPs full of rejected and sometimes incomplete takes. The ideal answer would be two sets of issues, one for the general collector, and a complete one for the specialist and the person who likes to make up his own mind on the question of the best take. Unfortunately, the sales figures for jazz records make this an economic absurdity. The musical value of these second and third takes varies: in some instances, for example the Perfect *When You're Smiling* or the Oriole *Them There Eyes*, they do no more than add a further three or six minutes of tedium to our lives. But who would be without the three takes of the Victor *Ring Dem Bells*, with their quite different versions of Cootie Williams's great solo? Who could accept that the slight increase in tempo would affect the sound of *Drop Me Off At Harlem* to such an extent without hearing the rare second take? In fact alternative takes, dull and uninteresting though they sometimes are, can on occasion throw a lot of light on Ellington's music. They tell us, for example, which of his soloists are improvisers and which stick closely to set patterns; how the individual's contributions to the music can vary from performance to performance; and how Ellington himself sometimes had second thoughts on an arrangement and made quite radical adjustments in the studio.

Sidemen

Hayes Alvis and Billy Taylor

The first of Ellington's experiments in using two string bassists with the band occurred when Billy Taylor joined Wellman Braud in January 1935. When Braud left in the spring of 1935, he was replaced by Hayes Alvis. Both Taylor and Alvis were bass players of the generation which had learned from such New Orleans pioneers as Braud and Pops Foster. While perhaps not competing with their mentors in drive, they were on the whole more accurate musicians and provided the jazz orchestras with sound, solid bass lines in the years prior to Jimmy Blanton's revolutionary innovations. After Alvis left the Ellington band in early 1938, Taylor carried on as sole bass player. During the time they were together in the band the two basses were not used on all recordings; some have Alvis alone, some only Taylor. (Standard discographies give details of these changes.) The prime attribute of both these players is sound musicianship, Alvis being the slightly more extroverted, Taylor having a smaller tone and a quieter musical personality. Neither possessed the swing or drive of Braud or Blanton, and the Ellington rhythm section is not one of the band's strengths in the late thirties.

Representative Recordings: Hayes Alvis—*Truckin'* (Brunswick, 1935); Billy Taylor—*Showboat Shuffle* (Brunswick, 1935); Alvis and Taylor—*I Let A Song Go Out Of My Heart* (Brunswick, 1938)

Ivie Anderson

When Ivie Anderson joined the Ellington Orchestra as its first featured vocalist in 1932, she had already acquired wide experience in show business, working as a dancer as well as a singer. Just prior to joining Duke, she had been on tour with a show of her own. Anderson was a musicianly and tasteful singer who had a way of imparting wholly individual zest to fast-tempo interpretations. She seemed to care very little for the fads and fashions of the day, and in consequence her art sounds unaffected and largely undated. Her singing has a cool, almost aloof quality, and her highly melodic phrasing was based on a poised and relaxed rhythmic base. Another outstanding feature of her style is her clear articulation of the lyrics. Ivie Anderson is the best known and the finest of the many specialist singers who worked regularly with the Ellington band.

Representative Recordings: It Don't Mean A Thing (Brunswick, 1932), *Troubled Waters* (Victor, 1934), *Truckin'* (Brunswick, 1935), *Kissin' My Baby Good Night* (Brunswick, 1936), *St. Louis Blues* (Fargo dance date, 1940), *I Don't Mind* (Victor, 1942)

Lawrence Brown

It is often thought by those unfamiliar with the music that the jazzmen of the twenties and early thirties were all rough, crude musicians. The fact is that an environment in which musicians did not go through a lengthy period of academic training produced a wide variety of types and a wide range of accomplishment. Lawrence Brown, for example, loved the sound of the cello and strove to make his trombone sound like one. The result is a tone which is as distinctive as any in jazz and not in the least crude or primitive. This mellow sound of Brown's was the vehicle for a wide-ranging musical sensibility. His entry into the band—at the insistence of Irving Mills, incidentally—created a three-piece trombone section in which he normally took the lead role. But in this section, as elsewhere, Ellington would ring the changes, giving the lead to Tizol or Nanton when a different effect was required, thus having three totally different sounds for the section at his disposal. Brown was a fine soloist whether on blues, ballads, or stomps, and his vocal accompaniments were of unusual sensitivity. He was also a brilliant section leader. Yet there is an inconsistency about Brown's work in that his occasional poor choruses will lack absolutely the poise and polish normally associated with his playing. On occasion he could sound pompous or excessively sentimental, but his contributions to such robust music as *Stompy Jones* or *Across The Track Blues* are happily more typical. He was a player who could cover virtually every facet of jazz trombone, including (in later years) the plunger style. He was highly valued by Ellington both for the range of his talents and for the sensitivity of his interpretations.

Representative Recordings: Ducky Wucky (Brunswick, 1932), *Stompy Jones* (Victor, 1934), *Rose Of The Rio Grande* (Brunswick, 1938), *Across The Track Blues* (Victor, and Fargo dance date, 1940), *Golden Cress* (Columbia, 1947), *Used To Be Duke* (Johnny Hodges group, Verve, 1954)

Rex Stewart

In 1932, the Fletcher Henderson Orchestra recorded a popular song called *Underneath The Harlem Moon*. The first chorus's middle eight is played by Rex Stewart, who concludes a solo full of mock tension with a perfectly placed "raspberry." This sums up the eight bars perfectly and is typical of the man in its outlandish and unorthodox humor. As we noted in the previous chapter, Ellington was quick to feature Stewart as a soloist, and one can only assume that in addition to having been friends for many years the two men had unusual musical rapport. In the Ellington band, Stewart quickly blossomed into a major jazz soloist with a wide range of style and technique. He was a fine melodist, could improvise with a Beiderbecke-like grace (he was a great admirer of Bix's playing), provide sharply crackling muted choruses of immense drive, or play open solos in a uniquely jaunty manner. Rex also became adept at the plunger-muted growl style which was, by the time he joined, a tradition in the Ellington orchestra. Most importantly, he developed a surprisingly accurate and elaborate manner of playing with the valves of his cornet only half-depressed. This is of course a trick style, producing a choked sonority, and Rex Stewart is the only player to date who developed it into an exact science. He also created a unique style of "talking" trumpet which was used very sparingly and usually for humorous effect. Such versatility was ideal for an Ellington sideman, and Duke was to exploit all the many aspects of Stewart's style during his ten years with the orchestra. Stewart's melodic language is based fundamentally on Louis Armstrong, but he was also a Beiderbecke admirer who listened to and learned from contemporary developments in jazz trumpet styles. Rex was essentially a musical eccentric, whose quirky, highly individual talent found its true home in the Duke Ellington Orchestra.

Representative Recordings: Kissin' My Baby Good Night (Brunswick, 1936), *Boy Meets Horn* (Brunswick, 1939; Fargo dance date, 1940; Carnegie Hall, 1943), *A Portrait Of Bert Williams* (Victor, 1940; Carnegie Hall, 1943), *Across The Track Blues* (Victor and Fargo dance date, 1940), *Mobile Bay* (Rex Stewart Orch, Bluebird, 1940), *John Hardy's Wife* (Victor, 1941)

Chapter 10

The Records—December 1936 to February 1940

IN LATE 1936, ELLINGTON BEGAN to record for Irving Mills's Master label, and introduced a new aspect of his recording policy by also instituting a series of recordings by contingents from the band on Mills's cheaper Variety label. These were nominally led by sidemen and appeared under the names of Barney Bigard, Johnny Hodges, Rex Stewart, and Cootie Williams; they will be discussed in the second part of this chapter. Although this recording contract lasted until February 1940, the records came out on a number of labels, a fact explained by changes in the ownership of the company. In the spring of 1937, Mills was bought out by ARC (the American Record Company) and from the summer of that year, the Mills labels were phased out and the Ellington band started to appear on ARC's main Brunswick label, the contingent recordings coming out on Vocalion. In December 1938, the Columbia Broadcasting System bought ARC and thus acquired the rights to the Columbia record label, which they reactivated in 1939. The Brunswick/Vocalion series were transferred to the Columbia/OKeh labels, and these were in use at the end of Ellington's stay with the company.

During the period of this contract, none of Ellington's contemporary recordings was issued in Britain or Europe as the company for which he was recording had no overseas outlets. Keen collectors imported discs, but by and large these records remained unknown outside the United States until the late 1940s, when they began, at last, to come out in Britain and Europe. The fact that many jazz writers and critics heard the Ellington Victors of 1940 as a direct development of 1936 Ellington music, without any knowledge of the intervening years, is responsible for some of the bizarre contemporary criticism of the 1940 records. It is because of this situation that the 1937–1939 period is sometimes known as "the Ellington gap" in non-American collecting circles.

* * *

At the start of the Master contract in December 1936 the personnel of the Duke Ellington Orchestra was:

Trumpets: Cootie Williams, Wallace Jones, Rex Stewart (cornet).

Trombones: Lawrence Brown; Juan Tizol (valve trombone); Tricky Sam Nanton.

Reeds: Otto Hardwick (alto and bass saxes, clarinet); Johnny Hodges (also and soprano saxes); Barney Bigard (clarinet and tenor sax); Harry Carney (baritone and alto saxes, clarinet, bass clarinet).

Rhythm: Duke Ellington (piano); Fred Guy (guitar); Billy Taylor (bass); Sonny Greer (drums).

Vocal: Ivie Anderson.

The new name here is that of trumpeter Wallace Jones, who had taken over Arthur Whetsol's responsibilities as lead trumpet and melodic soloist. During 1937 and 1938, both Whetsol and Freddie Jenkins made brief returns to the band, while at different times Danny Baker and Harold Baker joined the trumpet section.

* * *

After a couple of contingent dates for Variety, the full Ellington band assembled in the Master studio for the first time on December 21, 1936. Two titles were recorded, *Scattin' At The Cotton Club*, which was released only in the microgroove era, and *Black Butterfly*. This last is a very beautiful Ellington melody, yet for some reason it has never attained the popularity of *Mood Indigo* or *Sophisticated Lady*. On this initial recording, the main soloist is Brown, and Carney is also heard briefly. At this session Ellington recorded a piano melody which was originally issued on two sides of a 78 disc and which includes meditative and harmonically rich considerations of *Mood Indigo* and *Solitude* on the first side and *Sophisticated Lady* and *In A Sentimental Mood* on the second.

Next in the Ellington chronology come a group of soundtracks, one of which, *A Day At The Races*, is a doubtful Ellington item. This Marx Brothers classic includes Ivie Anderson singing *All God's Chillun Got Rhythm* accompanied by a choir and a large studio orchestra which, according to contemporary reports, includes the Ellington musicians. Aurally this seems improbable and the orchestra sounds distinctly un-Ellingtonian. The band's presence is certain, however, in the other two films. The first is a *Paramount Pictorial Magazine*, in which Ivie sings *Oh Babe! Maybe Someday*, and the second *Hit Parade Of 1937*, which features her in *I've Got To Be A Rug Cutter* and *It Don't Mean A Thing*; the band is also heard in this last film behind singer Dick Allen and in a short instrumental version of *Sophisticated Lady*.

Still in Hollywood, but back in the recording studios, the band recorded the new number, *I've Got To Be A Rug Cutter*. As in the film, this is given a pretty elaborate arrangement for a jivey pop song, with foot stamping fore and aft and with Ivie Anderson joined by the "Ellington vocal trio"— Stewart, Carney and Hayes Alvis—in one of their rare appearances. The foot stomping by the band is described, wrongly, in most discographies as "tap dancing by Freddie Jenkins." In addition to its more unusual features, *I've Got To Be A Rug Cutter* also has brief solos by Bigard, Hodges, and Carney, as well as spots of freak cornet by Stewart which open and close proceedings. There is a remake of *Scattin' At The Cotton Club* from this session, but the band's locale must have changed by the time the record was released as it came out as *Scattin' At The Kit Kat*. The piece is a medium-fast swinger played in very relaxed fashion and featuring both Williams and Stewart in open solos as well as contributions from Ellington, Nanton, and Carney. The two remaining titles made on this March 1937 date were revivals of earlier compositions—*The New Birmingham Breakdown* and *The New East St. Louis Toodle-oo*. *Birmingham Breakdown* is successfully revised in stylistic terms with Duke doing a very good takeoff of his early piano style and solos by Hodges, Williams, Carney, and Bigard before the clarinet trio enhances the musical impression of earlier Ellington days. The *East St. Louis Toodle-oo* arrangement is an extension of that which the band was using as its signature tune, with Williams and Bigard the only soloists, the latter playing an ad-lib part against the band on the second theme.

In March 1937, Ellington began a new residency at the Cotton Club, now situated in midtown New York rather than Harlem. From March 18 comes the first known air shot of the Ellington band—a half-hour broadcast from the new Cotton Club. Within a few years, recordings of broadcasts become commonplace in the Ellington discography; so far as 1937 is concerned, however, only this broadcast is known to have survived, apart from a couple of piano solos. Ivie Anderson is featured in three popular songs—*One, Two, Button Your Shoe*; *Pennies From Heaven*; and *Mexicali Rose*—while the band contributes *Harlem Speaks*, *Caravan*, *Sophisticated Lady*, and *Rockin' In Rhythm*. There are some good solos on the Ivie features, notably by Stewart and Carney on *Pennies*

From Heaven and by Hodges, superbly backed by the band, on *Mexicali Rose*. The versions of *Harlem Speaks* and *Caravan* are longer than the commercially recorded ones, and the *Rockin' In Rhythm* presents for the first time the arrangement which became familiar to concertgoers of the fifties, sixties and seventies. The announcer is the first of a succession of such gentlemen who are heard on Ellington broadcasts and who invariably make at least a couple of totally idiotic statements in the course of a half-hour broadcast. In this instance, the high spot is when the announcer advises us, with no elaboration, that *Sophisticated Lady* is a number which Duke "helped to make famous." One of the most valuable aspects of such air shots is that they find the band playing in a much more casual and relaxed manner than in the recording studios. Here the playing is beautifully poised, not without humor and full of obvious pleasure in music making.

Back in the Master studios on April 9, 1937, the Orchestra recorded three more popular songs, the first two with vocals by Anderson. *There's A Lull In My Life* is given conventional treatment so far as style is concerned, but the arrangement is unconventionally rich in musical substance, not least in the perfect backing to the vocal. The outstanding features of *It's Swell Of You* are the opening, with Bigard on the theme in the low register of the clarinet accompanied by the two altos in their high register, and the remarkably fierce eight bars of growl trumpet with which Cootie follows the vocal. The wholly instrumental *You Can't Run Away From Love Tonight* has a ravishing theme statement by Wallace Jones, Carney, and Hodges (on soprano), followed by an excellent Brown ballad solo. On neither this session nor the previous one (*The New Birmingham Breakdown*, etc.) do the alternative takes, which exist for all titles, add a great deal to our knowledge of the music.

From the next date (April 22, 1937) comes the first recording of Ellington's beautiful song *Azure;* for some reason, the arrangement of this was entrusted to Joe Lippman, who does a competent but not particularly imaginative job. Indeed *Azure* is one of the few Ellington compositions of which there is not a wholly satisfying recording by the band, the Chick Webb recording of 1938 being preferable to the Ellington versions. The uptempo *The Lady Who Couldn't Be Kissed,* another non-Ellington pop, has good workmanlike solos from Carney, Bigard, Stewart, Brown, and Hodges. The next title, *Old Plantation*, was one of two issued on the cheap Variety label as by Ivie Anderson and her Boys From Dixie. This band name might suggest that these are contingent recordings, but they feature the full Ellington band with Anderson vocals. *Old Plantation* opens with the sentimental melody stated in ironic fashion by Nanton. Towards the end of the middle eight played by the band, Bigard enters to conclude the chorus with one of those highly effective descant passages which Ellington scored so tellingly for him. Cootie and the brass comment laconically on the lyrics about the "beautiful South" and the record ends with a casual, relaxed half chorus by the saxophone section. A couple of piano solos have been issued from a broadcast of May 8, 1937, *Swing Session* and a medley of *Solitude* and *In A Sentimental Mood*. These are pleasant examples of off-the-cuff Ellington music making.

The first full band recording of Juan Tizol's *Caravan* (from May 14, 1937) is a relaxed affair with the composer's valve trombone stating the theme and with excellent solos from Williams and Carney. This was, of course, one of the band's big hits of the period. There are two different versions of *All God's Chillun Got Rhythm* in addition to the one from the soundtrack of *A Day At The Races*. These were both recorded on the same day—June 8, 1937—the first being a purely instrumental version released as by Duke Ellington and his Famous Orchestra on Master, the second a vocal version released as by Ivie Anderson and her Boys From Dixie on Variety. The band version is virtually an open house for the soloists; Nanton, Carney, Stewart, Brown, Bigard, and Hodges are all heard in excellent improvisations. On the other version, Ivie's vocal is backed by a small choir which is sometimes said to be the Alvis-Carney-Stewart trio, but the group is too distantly recorded for any certain identification to be possible. Hodges is the only soloist on this version. The other title from this session is *Alabamy Home*, an Ellington song which, despite the lyrics, inspires another great jazz performance capped by a wonderful Williams solo.

The last Ellington recording session in 1937, on September 30, produced six sides. Stewart's *Chatterbox* and Tizol's *Jubilesta* are perhaps the least important, but both contain good music. The composers have the major solo roles in their respective pieces, as may be expected, but Brown and Hodges on *Chatterbox* and Hodges and Bigard on *Jubilesta* also make important contributions. Duke's major work from these years is *Diminuendo And Crescendo In Blue* and the double sided 78 version—side one *Diminuendo*, side two *Crescendo*—comes from this session. The band sounds as if the work is pretty new to them, and they give a less effective performance here than those found on several mid-forties broadcasts. Nonetheless, the performance is a good one, although not helped by the poor dynamic range of the recording. *Diminuendo And Crescendo In Blue* is a thoroughly composed work like *Creole Rhapsody* and *Reminiscing In Tempo*, but otherwise it bears little resemblance to these previous Ellington concert pieces. It consists of a series of twelve-bar blues choruses—22 in all on this recording—which use altered harmonies and a wide variety of instrumental textures in between the brass-dominated climaxes which open and close the work. Williams, Carney, Ellington himself, and Bigard are heard in brief, functional solos. The varied scoring, including the imaginative use of the clarinet trio at the start of *Crescendo In Blue*, and the wonderfully apposite selection of melodic material, mostly blues riffs scored in antiphonal fashion, are important facets of the piece. Its success as an extended jazz composition is in some ways greater than either *Creole Rhapsody* or *Reminiscing In Tempo*, although in terms of variety it is less ambitious than the former and in terms of the development of material less so than the latter. In essence *Diminuendo And Crescendo In Blue* is a montage of blues riffs and it is remarkable that Ellington was able to create an extended composition without any dilution of the blues flavor.

A more conventional use of the riff is found in the admirable *Harmony In Harlem*, an essay in the conventional big band style of the early swing era by the music's least conventional group of musicians. Taken at a swinging medium tempo, *Harmony In Harlem* proves just how much music can be gotten into a three-minute riff number. The soloists are Hodges on soprano sax and Williams on growl trumpet. (A number which Cootie recorded in 1941 with members of the Benny Goodman band, *G-Men*, has its origin in the growl solo here.) On the alternative take of *Harmony In Harlem*, Cootie plays the same solo on open trumpet, which makes for fascinating comparison. On the air-shot versions of March and May 1938, we find that Cootie has fashioned a new solo, played on open trumpet in both broadcasts.

The final title from the session is another masterpiece, *Dusk In The Desert*. The title might suggest a quasi-oriental number in the manner of *Caravan*, but it is nothing of the kind. Like earlier pieces such as *Black Beauty* and *The Dicty Glide*, it has one of those utterly distinctive Ellington melodies which are so fully flavored in themselves that Duke usually gave the theme statement to someone who would play it reasonably straight—in this case Wallace Jones. Jones had now settled into the band; he had much of Arthur Whetsol's quality as a lead trumpet but was perhaps lacking a little in personality as a soloist. This is probably the reason why Duke did not use him very often in this capacity. After an introduction in which Ellington relishes the sounds of the trombone and saxophone sections—and how often his writing seems directed at just such delights—Jones enters with the theme of *Dusk In The Desert*. In the second chorus, riffs are used in a call-and-response pattern between muted trombones and muted trumpets, Bigard giving a perfect example of his big band clarinet style in counterpoint against the ensemble. Ellington may not have studied counterpoint academically, but he certainly liked multivoiced music, and it is rare to hear even a solo in the Ellington band without at least one independent part in accompaniment. *Dusk In The Desert* is a superb example of Ellington's voice writing, and it has a beautiful rhythmic poise, moving in an unhurried and easy manner throughout.

By early 1938, the swing era was well under way, and Ellington indicates his intentions at his first recording session of that year in *Steppin' Into Swing Society*. This is another riff piece, in the idiom of the time in some respects and yet utterly removed from it if one thinks of the vulgar "flag wavers" then in vogue. The delicate voicings and subtle variations on the basic riff are a delightful study in the use of the big band as a chamber ensemble. Duke's piano punctuations are sparse but effective, and there are brief, functional solos from Hodges's soprano and Carney's baritone. The remainder of this session is taken up by a double-length version of *Black And Tan Fantasy*, issued on two separate discs as *Prologue To Black And Tan Fantasy* and *The New Black And Tan Fantasy*, an error which was not only carried forward on all issues in the 78 era but into the LP period as well. Thirty years after they were recorded, it was still impossible to obtain a record with the two parts of the 1938 *Black And Tan Fantasy* together, and it was not until the issue by French C.B.S. of Volume 10 of their Ellington collected edition in 1977 that the two pieces were at last brought together on a disc. *Prologue* takes us up to the end of the two-chorus trumpet solo and features Hardwick and Williams. The tempo is slower than on the earlier versions and the mood more somber, while Ellington has filled out his previously sparse scoring. *The New Black And Tan Fantasy*, after a four-bar passage by Duke, has solos by Bigard, Carney, and Nanton before the peroration by Cootie and the band. The Nanton solo is accompanied, most effectively, by a long-held high-register note from Bigard and some pungent piano from the leader.

The first of two sessions from February 1938 opens with *Ridin' On A Blue Note*, a medium-tempo swinger which features Williams, using the straight mute and playing in magnificent style. The piece, a simple one, provides a perfect springboard for Cootie's playing. Others in big band jazz created great music in these years, Count Basie especially and also Fletcher Henderson and Jimmie Lunceford, but only Ellington was able to produce this kind of perfection. The ease and relaxation of *Ridin' On A Blue Note* are amazing, while Williams gives one of his greatest performances. This is not a harmonically complex, colorfully orchestrated number, but simply one which is full of the undiluted spirit of jazz. And the tempo is *exactly* right. The rare second take is nearly as good as the standard one. There are two longer air-shot versions of *Ridin' On A Blue Note*, one from 1938 which features Hodges on soprano as well as Williams on growl and open trumpet, and one from 1945, which features Hodges on alto and Stewart on both growl and open horn. These are excellent, but lack the perfection of the studio recording. Another medium-tempo swinger, *The Gal From Joe's*, features Hodges on alto and the brass section using plunger mutes. Hodges is in excellent form; his playing is starting to take on the sinuous quality of his later work. The third title from this session is a very fine Tizol melody called *Lost In Meditation*. It features solos by Hodges and Williams after the composer's valve trombone has delivered the initial theme statement.

The second February 1938 date is the first of two devoted to numbers from Ellington's music for *The Cotton Club Parade Of 1938*. *If You Were In My Place* was expected to be the hit from the production, but it was completely overshadowed in popularity by the little fancied *I Let A Song Go Out Of My Heart*. The Ellington recording of *If You Were In My Place*, a pleasant ballad, has good solos by Hodges and Brown before Williams enters at his most majestic to garnish the final ensemble, an effect somewhat spoiled by poor recording balance. As was the invariable custom with shows of this kind, *The Cotton Club Parade Of 1938* introduced a new dance routine in the fond hope that it would become the basis of a new craze. *The Skrontch* did not achieve any degree of success, and Ellington's recording of the piece is totally unmemorable.

The following month Duke recorded a second session of numbers from the show, and this was more fruitful in terms of quality. *I Let A Song Go Out Of My Heart* is one of Ellington's most beautiful popular songs and the instrumental version recorded at this March 1938 session is simply perfect. Hodges, Carney, Brown, and Bigard are heard in a lucid and balanced arrangement. The voicings in the ensemble are of the utmost beauty, while Duke's piano fill-ins complement the scoring perfectly. The recording ends with the saxes playing the theme pianissimo over effective work by the two bassists. Both takes are worthy of attention, as indeed is the case with the next number, *Braggin' In Brass*, the band's showpiece in *The Cotton Club Parade Of 1938*. This is a typical piece of late thirties big band virtuosity. The trumpet section is heard playing Freddie Jenkins's famous *Tiger Rag* solo in unison, while the centerpiece is a magnificent Stewart solo, which is the real reason why the two takes are important, for there is considerable variation in Rex's part. *Carnival In Caroline* was a chorus number in the show; on the Ellington studio recording, Ivie Anderson handles the vocal and there are solos from Williams, Bigard and Stewart, but the performance by the band is rather stilted.

From an April 1938 session come two more numbers from this show, *Swingtime In Honolulu* and *I'm Slappin' 7th Avenue With The Sole Of My Shoe*. The former was described in contemporary publicity material as "Duke's Polynesian swingaree" and the recording features a delicious first chorus with highly colorful scoring. The first sixteen bars have two trumpets and Nanton playing plunger muted in dialogue with the saxes, while a most effective third voice is added by Hodges; Stewart is heard briefly, the saxes casually play the middle eight and then Rex rounds off the chorus with judicious and humorous use of half-valve notes. The rest of the record is not up to this standard, but Ivie's vocal, Duke's piano and the final ensemble, with Barney riding high over the band, maintain that relaxed, casual swing which is so attractive a feature of many of the Ellington band's pop tune recordings. *I'm Slappin' 7th Avenue With The Sole Of My Shoe* honors the one-legged dancer Peg Leg Bates, the star of the show; this receives a rather stiff performance. The final title is *Dinah's In A Jam*, a band number on the chords of the popular song which evokes the casual atmosphere of a jam session in both the solos and the band riffing. Freddie Jenkins, who was making a brief comeback, and Brown have important solos here, while Bigard is also heard to admirable effect.

* * *

There are several broadcasts extant from the period March to July 1938. They include performances which are sometimes superb, sometimes instructive, and often both. One which falls into this last category is a version of *Dinah* from March which is incomplete but which features the vocal trio (said to consist here of Carney, Alvis, and Williams) followed by solos from Jenkins and Brown which clearly foreshadow those on *Dinah's In A Jam*. Unfortunately, the recording starts during the vocal and ends during Brown's solo so that one has no idea of the overall arrangement, even though the fragment is a lengthy one. Among the Ellington pops, we hear versions of *If You Were In My Place*, in an arrangement very different from the recorded one, and *Oh Babe! Maybe Someday*, by this time a fixed routine featuring delightful Hodges and vivacious Ivie Anderson. There are several performances of Edgar Sampson's *If Dreams Come True*, a number which was never recorded commercially by the band, and a couple of versions of *Harmony In Harlem*, which was familiar from the commercial recording although these broadcast performances have their own identity. There are several unlikely titles, including *You Went To My Head*, *Three Blind Mice*, *At Your Beck And Call*, *It's The Dreamer In Me*, and *Prelude In C Sharp Minor*. These show the band's repertoire to have been more extensive than even their large and varied recorded output of the period indicates. *Carnival In Caroline* and *I'm Slappin' 7th Avenue With The Sole Of My Shoe* both receive much more relaxed performances on these broadcasts than they did in the recording studio—indeed, the former is an outstanding performance, full of swing, despite the mediocrity of the number. *Dinah's In A Jam* is heard in a version which is the ultimate in relaxed band playing with Rex Stewart having taken over the trumpet solo. The three-chorus *On The Sunny Side Of The Street*—one each by Hodges, Anderson (superbly backed by Cootie), and Brown—is another masterpiece of casual jazz making not recorded commercially at this time. *Birmingham Breakdown* is brought forward from 1926 and *Rose Room* from 1932 in effective performances, while *The Gal From Joe's* and *Echoes Of Harlem* sound even better than in the celebrated studio versions. The recording quality of these broadcasts from the downtown Cotton Club, though obviously not as good as that of the contemporary studio recordings, is more than adequate for the purposes of hearing and enjoying the music.

* * *

The New York residence at the Cotton Club seems to have suited the Ellington band, for not only are the air shots full of dynamic playing, but the studio recordings from 1938 also find the band in a very happy frame of mind. *You Gave Me The Gate* is an ordinary pop song with a slight Lunceford flavor in the arrangement and one of Ivie's most lively vocals, as well as a first-class Williams solo. Cootie is also outstanding in a low-register solo during *When My Sugar Walks Down The Street* from the same June 1938 session. This also produced the very famous version of *Rose Of The Rio Grande* with its poised and perfected trombone solos from Brown and pleasant Anderson vocal. Another of Tizol's exotic pieces was recorded at this session, the beautiful *Pyramid*, which has the composer playing the exquisite melody and Ellington making his sole appearance on record as player of tom-toms. Good use is made of Brown's contrasting trombone style here.

Later in the month the band cut another excellent session which began with *Watermelon Man*, a simple Ellington arrangement of a very ordinary pop tune which swings tremendously, due in no small measure to Sonny Greer's admirable brush work. Hodges opens proceedings on alto and then switches to soprano to lead the saxes after Anderson's vocal in a passage which leads to a climax in the form of an exciting Stewart cornet solo. Tizol is cocomposer of both *A Gypsy Without A Song* and *The Stevedore's Serenade,* both slow ballad numbers without any trace of the exotic. The former features Brown at his most languorous, Williams at his most majestic, and Hodges at his most sensuous. Cootie and Hodges are also heard on the slow medium *Stevedore's Serenade* in which the featured soloist is Bigard. The final title from the session is a nonsense song, *La Di Doody Do*, with a pleasing Ivie Anderson vocal.

* * *

From the first of Ellington's August 1938 dates comes a rather unexpected recording of an old number never previously associated with him, *A Blues Serenade*. This was composed by members of the Original Memphis Five and recorded by them in 1926. Why Ellington used it twelve years later is not known—perhaps he just liked the song—but his reasons must have been pretty strong as the Hodges unit also recorded the piece. The full band score is an exquisite miniature with a lot of Duke's piano and brief solos by Hardwick, Williams, and Bigard. A much less distinguished non-Ellington pop tune, *Love In Swingtime*, celebrates a long-forgotten newspaper strip cartoon of the same name. Rex is heard on the theme, while the dreary vocal by Scat Powell is redeemed by the trombone solo which follows, featuring Brown in his most direct and forceful manner. By contrast with these last two songs, Duke had a hand in the composition of *Please Forgive Me*, which has fascinating changes of voice-leading within its rich sonorities and solos by Brown and Williams, interlocked with the orchestral texture.

From the next session, recorded on August 9, 1938, comes one of the more improbable Ellington recordings of the period—*The Lambeth Walk*. This was a popular Cockney novelty in Britain which did not catch on in the United States. Ellington simply used the piece as the foundation for a straightforward swing score and allocated the solo space to Williams, Brown, and Bigard. On Duke's new popular song *Prelude To A Kiss*—another which endured to become a standard—Brown's trombone and Hodges's soprano share the theme statement with Wallace Jones, while the composer is also heard to excellent effect. Two vigorous stomps conclude the session. *Hip Chic*, one of Ellington's punning titles, is a muted pianissimo study in the creative uses of the commonplace devices of the swing era. The piece—note the unusual structure of two twelve-bar blues joined by a middle eight to give a 32-bar chorus—is driven along by Greer's excellent drumming and spiced by two eccentric Stewart solos. The second piece, *Buffet Flat*, is also a study in pianissimo swinging but somewhat less striking. Carney is the main soloist, with Stewart appearing for a tightly muted solo in which the tone is cut down to a thin pencil point of sound. The structure here is again unconventional, on this occasion the choruses being 24 bars in length.

Boy Meets Horn, Ellington's famous concerto for Rex Stewart, was recorded at the next session under the provisional title *Twits And Twerps*—this version was not issued until the microgroove era. Its session mate is an attractive theme by jazz writer Leonard Feather called *Mighty Like The Blues*. It is given a beautiful and many-colored arrangement in which the unique low-register sounds of Bigard and Williams are heard to great effect.

When Irving Mills gave one of Ellington's numbers the title *Jazz Pot-pourri*, its outraged composer demanded to know "What the hell is a *pot-pourri*?" However the Mills title prevailed and the name given by Duke, *Myrtle Avenue Stomp*, was dropped. This piece is another Ducal essay in the swing style, an attractive riff theme framing solos by Cootie, Barney, and Tricky Sam and swung impressively by Greer's brushes. *T.T. On Toast* finds Hodges fully into his new rhapsodic style with a full, sensuous tone; he is abetted here by Brown, Williams, Bigard, and a colorful orchestral score. In *The Battle Of Swing* (the original title of this one was *Le Jazz Hot*), Ellington deploys a small group consisting of Stewart, Tizol, Bigard, and Hardwick against the full band in concerto grosso fashion. The idea works out well, although the arrangement is not particularly ambitious. One of Tizol's rare uptempo jazz solos occurs here, as well as contributions by Rex, suddenly jerking us into a new key, and Bigard.

The final session of 1938 produced more masterpieces. The first to be recorded was the delicate twelve-bar *Blue Light*, which opens with Bigard's rich low-register clarinet, followed by a chorus using the *Mood Indigo* voicing and then by a Brown solo over a trio of low-register clarinets. Finally, Ellington contributes one of his reflective piano solos full of beautiful harmonies. *Old King Dooji* is an uptempo number, the high spot of which is a chase chorus between Hodges and Williams. The first issued version of *Boy Meets Horn* comes from this session. This is indeed the perfect concerto for Rex Stewart, who uses his half-valve effects and perky phrasing with great wit and humor; the work conveys much of the character of the great cornetist. Finally comes *Slap Happy*, one of Ellington's masterly swingers with rich and concentrated scoring, full of dialogues between sections and between soloist and band. Carney is the main soloist but Cootie is heard briefly and Tricky Sam has a chorus of devastating eloquence.

The first recordings under Ellington's name in 1939 were a couple of piano solos dating from March 8 which remained unissued for many years. They are lightweight pieces, a reflective *Informal Blues* and a casual *Just Good Fun*. On March 20, the band recorded a four-title session, starting with a neat little jump number called *Pussy Willow*, featuring Bigard, Brown, Williams, and Hodges. A recording defect which causes wow on the piano part and makes the trombones sound out of tune mars *Subtle Lament*. A great pity, for this somber, reflective twelve-bar blues is an Ellington masterpiece with magnificent piano, a dark-toned solo from Rex Stewart, and brooding low-register clarinet from Barney Bigard. On the voluptuous *Lady In Blue*, Ellington indulges in some rich writing and sensuous scoring as well as contributing another effective piano part. Ellington, Stewart, and Brick Fleagle are the composers of *Smorgasbord And Schnapps*, no doubt written with the band's forthcoming visit to Sweden in mind, and Fleagle is credited with the arrangement. Nanton, Bigard and, more briefly, Williams are featured while the clarinet trio and Duke's percussive piano are both used to telling effect.

The March 21, 1939, date commenced with four titles by the Hodges unit, and then Hodges, Ellington, and bassist Billy Taylor combined to make up the Duke Ellington Trio for a recording of *Finesse*, a highly melodic piece featuring a rich Ellington piano solo. (This version, however, takes second place to the classic recording of the tune done in Paris in 1939 by Stewart, Bigard, Django Reinhardt, and Taylor under the band name of Rex Stewart and his Feetwarmers. It is a curious fact that on the labels of the trio version the composer credits go to Ellington and Hodges, while on the French recording Billy Taylor's is the name cited. Thus each member of the trio is given composer credits on different recordings.)

Following the recording of the trio version of *Finesse*, this very long session continued with three titles by the full band. The first of these is one of Ellington's celebrated portraits, that of Willie "The Lion" Smith, Ellington's early mentor and lifelong friend. Subtly incorporating some of Smith's favorite devices, *A Portrait Of The Lion* is a happy medium-tempo stomp with Ellington, Stewart, and Hodges the soloists. There are two takes, on the second of which Stewart indulges in some effective embellishments against the ensemble. The band next recorded a song for which young Billy Strayhorn wrote the words and Ellington the music. This is *Something To Live For*, the first fruit of the Ellington-Strayhorn partnership to appear on records. The vocal is by Jean Eldridge, and the recording remained a favorite of Duke's for the rest of his life. *Something To Live For* is an attractive melody lovingly arranged, but hardly one of the outstanding Ellington records of the period. The final title from the session, *Solid Old Man*, is not to be confused with the twelve-bar blues recorded under this title at Rex Stewart's Paris session and later done by the Bigard unit as *Honey Hush*. The present recording is of a spicy 32-bar jump number, with lots of good ensemble piano from Duke and solos from those two contrasting trombonists, Brown and Nanton.

* * *

On April 29, 1939, Duke Ellington celebrated his fortieth birthday; on that day the band was in Stockholm during the course of its second European tour. An interview and three performances from a concert were recorded from a broadcast on this date and have survived in very good sound. The interview shows Ellington to be a master of conversational gambits, and he adroitly deals with questions about swing and the future of jazz in his characteristically urbane way. The concert recordings feature long versions of three numbers, the first of which is an Ellington tribute to his hosts, *Serenade To Sweden*. Wallace Jones, Harry Carney and Lawrence Brown are heard in variations of this delightful melody, and Duke himself has a full chorus. *Rockin' In Rhythm* has a swinging piano introduction and is given a driving performance with Rex playing some wild cornet and Barney and Tricky Sam in their traditional solo roles. Rather surprisingly, the success from this broadcast is a performance of a long-forgotten pop song, *In A Little Red Cottage By The Sea*. This receives one of the most relaxed and easy jazz performances ever captured on record. The first chorus is a straight reading of the theme by the saxophone section, with Hardwick in the lead, sounding for all the world like a ballroom orchestra of the period. The identity of the band is disclosed in no uncertain manner in the second chorus which is by Carney, playing over muted brass. The third chorus is a masterpiece in itself as Nanton deliberates over the melody, using a great variety of tone colors, all of which sound perfectly natural and indeed inevitable. So easy does this solo sound that its skill and imagination could be underestimated; one has only to think of any other trombonist, including other plunger-mute specialists, playing such a melody chorus to begin to appreciate the artistry and skill Nanton displays here. The relaxation of the rhythm section is very noticeable at this point. The next chorus is a delightfully casual vocal by Ivie Anderson with clarinet backing by Bigard. Barney then goes on to embellish the final two ensemble choruses, notable for their perfectly judged dynamics. The relaxation of a performance like this is of a degree never approached by any other band. *Cottage By The Sea* is an example of the Ellington precept that one should never look down on material but always approach the task in hand with the maximum concentration and dedication, whether the work is a concert suite or an insignificant popular song.

* * *

On its return from Europe in mid-1939, the Ellington band was soon back in the Brunswick studios. The first two numbers recorded were remakes of *Cotton Club Stomp* and *Doin' The Voom Voom*. These are given effective arrangements in the late thirties swing style but do not equal the originals in impact; Williams and Carney are featured on the first title, the same two plus Hodges on the second. The great authority and the vehement accents of Williams's playing are very evident here. The session mates to these two revivals were both new compositions, the first being *Way Low*, an extraordinary blues creation. The chords which open the piece are interesting for the way in which one can hear the timbre of the different individuals in the voicing. Bigard's clarinet is used in a most imaginative manner in *Way Low*, and one can only regret that more opportunity was not given to the New Orleans clarinet stylists in the big bands; perhaps it needed an Ellington to grasp the potential which was there and a player of Bigard's imagination to realize it fully. Carney states the main theme of *Way Low* in incomparable style, dramatically interrupted by the band and by Bigard, while later the clarinetist and Stewart, the latter tightly muted, explore the unusual mood Ellington has created. Brown is heard on a contrasting theme, and the diverse elements are built into a totally coherent structure. The recording of *Serenade To Sweden* which follows is shorter than the broadcast version, mainly due to the deletion of Ellington's piano chorus. Williams shares the opening statement with Wallace Jones in this interpretation, while Brown remains the principal soloist.

The session of June 12, 1939, produced four popular songs, but this did not mean a sharp drop in quality as it might have four or five years earlier. Two of the four, *In A Mizz* and *You Can Count On Me*, are by outside writers and two, *I'm Checkin' Out, Goombye* and *A Lonely Co-ed*, are from Ellington's pen. *In A Mizz* is given an excellent arrangement: there are two eight-bar spots for Stewart's open horn in the first chorus and his use of a full, shining cornet tone in contrast to the coloristic half-valve effects is a real delight. The saxophones have a beautifully scored passage and Bigard is also heard on the theme before an Ivie Anderson vocal backed by full scoring for the band and a pungent commentary by Williams' plunger-muted trumpet. *I'm Checkin' Out, Goombye* is an uptempo song by Duke, given an arrangement full of happy, stomping music and a sparkling vocal by Ivie Anderson. Nanton, Bigard, and Ellington have supporting roles of great effectiveness, although there are no solos as such. The other two titles are equally rewarding, *A Lonely Co-ed* especially so with its Benny Carter-like saxophone writing and brilliant Williams theme statement. The dance band idiom of *You Can Count On Me* should not blind the listener to the excellent musical qualities of both score and performance. Ivie Anderson has excellent vocals on both these recordings.

* * *

On July 26, 1939, the band broadcast a half-hour spot from the Ritz-Carlton Hotel in Boston, and this has been preserved in very good sound. It provides an interesting insight into the band's repertoire in its public appearances in 1939. The numbers played are *East St. Louis Toodle-oo* (short version, used as signature tune), *Jazz Pot-pourri*, *Something To Live For*, *Old King Dooji*, *In A Mizz*, *Rose Of The Rio Grande*, *Pussy Willow*, *You Can Count On Me*, and *Way Low* (this is faded out as the broadcast comes to an end). *Something To Live For* is a nonvocal version featuring Brown's trombone, while there are Anderson vocals on *In A Mizz*, *Rose Of The Rio Grande*, and *You Can Count On Me*. The highlights include some humorous variations in the theme statement of *In A Mizz* by Rex, a superb version of *Rose Of The Rio Grande*, and a relaxed and swinging *Pussy Willow*. As in the earlier studio recording, *Rose Of The Rio Grande* features solos by Brown before and after Ivie's vocal; these solos were a planned routine by Brown and remained a feature for him even after Ivie's departure from the band.

* * *

Back in the studios the following month, the band recorded three excellent new scores. The first of these is one of Duke Ellington's most underrated masterpieces, *Bouncing Buoyancy*. This happy study in the use of ostinato figures behind the soloists has been strangely neglected by jazz writers—perhaps because, like most critics, they are inclined to shy away from happy art and concentrate their attention on the tragic. Williams is at his most brilliant here, and his solo work, along with that of Brown, Hodges, and Carney is perfectly dovetailed into the orchestral score. The use of Brown's muted trombone at the recapitulation of the primary theme, when the listener is expecting to hear Williams's growl trumpet, is a typical Ellington touch and enhances the impact of Cootie's later, delayed entry. *The Sergeant Was Shy* is a *Bugle Call Rag* variant which opens with a clarinet ensemble and then develops sundry military motifs into a montage which approaches chaos before Fred Guy's guitar takes a break—a rare occurrence indeed—and leads into a statement of the theme. Bigard, Stewart, and, most effectively, Nanton are the soloists in a score which is partly taken without amendment from Ellington's 1932 arrangement of *Bugle Call Rag*. The standard take -A is much the best performance of this piece, surpassing both take -B (in which Greer adds some quasi-military work on the snare drum at the start) and the two issued air-shot performances. The version of *Grievin'* cut at this date was not released for many years. It features Hodges, a vehement Williams, and Brown in the standard arrangement of this blues-impregnated Ellington ballad.

The band must have spent the greater part of October 14, 1939, in the studios, for no less than ten titles were cut—five by the full band, four by the Hodges contingent, and one piano solo. Two of the band numbers reflect Ellington's continuing interest in the musical portrait. *Little Posey* carries the subtitle *A Portrait Of Freddie Jenkins* and *Weely* that of *A Portrait Of Billy Strayhorn* ("Weely" was the nickname first given to Billy when he joined the organization). *Little Posey* is a most ingenious arrangement, featuring Brown playing a kind of quietly muted dixieland trombone part against the ensemble as well as taking an excellent muted solo. Bigard, Ellington, Carney, and Nanton are also heard briefly in a score which captures perfectly the musical character of Jenkins without resort to his stylistic mannerisms. *Weely* is an amiable medium-tempo jump number with some quite outstanding Stewart cornet solo work which incorporates highly skilled and quietly tasteful use of the half-valve technique. On *I Never Felt This Way Before* (two takes issued) Ellington uses the *Mood Indigo* voicing as an element in a rich and varied score, which includes admirable solos by Bigard and Brown. It is fascinating to compare this 1939 recording with the Victor version of the following year in which not only the arrangement but also the structure of the song have been altered. The recording of *Grievin'* which comes from this date—it has the same routine of melodic solos as the one from the previous session—is the standard one. *Tootin' Through The Roof* is in Ellington's happiest vein, with Carney stating the joyous theme and the whole band enjoying a score which is clearly derived from the stride piano style. The soloists are Carney, Williams, Hodges, and Brown, and the piece concludes with a series of chase choruses merging into a duet by Stewart and Williams which provides an ideal climax. There are two further recordings of this piece made while Cootie and Rex were together in the band and in the second of these the variations in the chase choruses are both fascinating and amusing. The piano solo from this session, *Blues*, is a pleasant but inconsequential ramble though Duke's favorite twelve-bar sequence.

A couple of days later, the orchestra was back in the studios to record three numbers, the first a Strayhorn score, *Killin' Myself*. This is unique in that it features Strayhorn singing; the main vocalist is Anderson and there are brief solos by Williams, Bigard, and Nanton. *Your Love Has Faded*, another Strayhorn arrangement, contains rich band scoring and an Ivie vocal; but, as was the case in *Killin' Myself*, the scoring lacks the balance and economy of Duke's writing. The third title is an Ellington blues, *Country Gal*, for long one of Duke's own favorites among his recordings. It is made up of solo choruses by Williams, Carney, Brown, Hodges, and Williams again, played over simple but effective backgrounds. Brown's muted solo is straightforward and melodic, yet delivered with such perfection of phrasing and nuance as to constitute the ideal centerpiece of the performance.

* * *

Bassist Jimmy Blanton had only been with the band a few weeks when, on November 22, 1939, Ellington took him into the studios for the first of their duet recordings. *Blues* and *Plucked Again* are essentially bass solos with discreet piano backing. Blanton's work reveals his revolutionary conception of the pizzicato bass as a melodic instrument and his ability to create melodically meaningful choruses. His full tone is also in evidence, although it is not captured so well as on the later Victor recordings. Also from this period come the versions of *I'm Checkin' Out, Goombye* and *Tootin' Through The Roof* which were first issued on V-Disc. On the former, the opening band chorus is replaced by an incredible dialogue between Ivie Anderson and Rex Stewart, who uses his "talking trumpet" technique. Ivie affects to be speaking to her boyfriend on the phone and is answered by Rex's cornet, the "words" being quite intelligible. This particular talent of Rex's is not used on any other Ellington record. Almost any other bandleader would have exploited its novelty value, but Duke was so sparing in his use of Rex's "talking" style that one suspects that he was not impressed by its musical potential. *Tootin'* differs from the earlier version in solo details and the absence of the trumpet chase.

A poorly recorded version of *The Sergeant Was Shy* from a Southland Café, Boston, broadcast of January 8, 1940, has been issued, but a full half-hour broadcast from the same location on the following day exists in very good sound. The titles are *East St. Louis Toodle-oo* (short version, used as signature tune), *Me And You, Grievin', Little Posey, My Last Goodbye, The Gal From Joe's, Tootin' Through The Roof, Day In Day Out* and *Merry-Go-Round*, the last title cut short at the end of the broadcast. There are vocals by Herb Jeffries on *Me And You* and *My Last Goodbye*, but Ivie is not heard at all. When the announcer tells us that Jeffries is about to sing "the story of *Little Josey*" as a lead-in to a band performance of *Little Posey* we begin to comprehend the level on which these radio hacks understood the music. Jeffries was Ellington's first regular male vocalist; the first of many more or less unfortunate choices. A melodramatic manner seems to have been Duke's one criterion in selecting male singers, and one can only wonder at the contrast between his taste in this matter and that which he showed in pretty well every other musical area. Jeffries' sentimentality on *My Last Goodbye* is characteristic, while his singing on *Me And You* is mediocre compared with Ivie Anderson on the later Victor recording. *Little Posey* is rather more robust than the studio version, while *The Gal From Joe's* receives a notably swinging performance. This *Tootin' Through The Roof* is outstanding. It is introduced, surprisingly enough, by the fanfare later used to herald the *Medley Of Popular Hits*. This pompous opening is followed by a brilliant stride piano solo, leading into the usual arrangement of *Tootin'*. The trumpet chase is restored, and Cootie indulges in a little half-valve work which prompts the expected riposte from his partner. *Day In, Day Out* is the kind of number in which every new chorus seems to threaten a Jeffries vocal, but is in fact a feature for Lawrence Brown in his ballad vein, muted at the outset, then deploying his mellow open tone. It is fascinating to hear the 1940 band tackle *Merry-Go-Round* and most regrettable that the performance is not a complete one.

* * *

The last full band session prior to the Victor contract is from February 1940, with Ben Webster now a regular member of the saxophone team. Four ballads were recorded, all long-standing favorites from the repertoire. The only non-Ellington song is *Stormy Weather*, long a feature for Ivie Anderson at shows and dances, but previously recorded by Ellington only in an instrumental version. Ivie presents her famous interpretation, preceded by Williams and accompanied by Webster. Ben makes his solo debut as an Ellington regular in a four-bar passage on *Solitude*, in which Anderson is again the featured artist. On *Mood Indigo*, the theme is stated by the saxophones with superb embellishments from Cootie's open trumpet, Ivie sings a chorus, and then Webster concludes the proceedings with a brief solo. There is no vocal on *Sophisticated Lady*, and the solo alto saxophone role previously taken by Hardwick is switched to Hodges. The other soloists are Carney, Ellington, and Brown.

* * *

By the middle thirties the band-within-a-band pattern had been used for many years, including a famous instance at a concert in 1924 when Paul Whiteman introduced a quintet of his musicians doing a "historical" re-creation of the music of the Original Dixieland Jazz Band. By 1936 there was quite a fashion developing for this type of presentation. The Benny Goodman Trio and Quartet were popular and well established, Tommy Dorsey had his Clambake Seven, and other bands were starting to use the idea. Quietly, and usually without any change in band name, Ellington had long utilized small groups from within his orchestra on numbers such as *Saratoga Swing*, *Mood Indigo*, and *Lazy Duke*. As recently as March 1935 the Duke Ellington Sextet had recorded a couple of sides, yet it was with a sense of embarking on a new undertaking that a group of Ellington musicians entered the Variety studios in December 1936. They were the members of a group under the direction of Rex Stewart inaugurating a new series of Ellington band-within-a-band recordings. Four Ellington musicians were involved as leaders, and at first they were given rather exotic-sounding band names on the record labels. Johnny Hodges was the only one whose group was simply billed as "his Orchestra" right through the series. But Barney Bigard's contingent started life as his "Jazzopators," while Rex Stewart led his "52nd Street Stompers," and Cootie Williams his "Rug Cutters." These were groups of from seven to nine pieces, most often featuring the nominal leader more than the other soloists. Ellington was usually at the piano, and he contributed much as arranger and composer. The musical policy was affected by the dual aims of providing small-band jazz records to meet an increasing demand and of catering to popular taste by providing "cover" versions of hit or potential hit records by other artists, or sometimes of those recorded for Master or Brunswick by the full band. The first Hodges date was made up of popular songs of the day, while many of Ellington's own songs, notably those from *The Cotton Club Parade of 1938*, were recorded by the units.

Despite the use of sidemen's names as leaders, Ellington was often at the helm to create a series of chamber-scale Ellingtonia. Even the least of the popular song recordings contain good jazz solos, and the instrumentals include several classics. As usual, Ellington turns the situation to musical advantage in the way he creates finished products rather than using the contingent dates as "workshop" sessions or treating them as purely commercial ventures.

An analysis of the material recorded shows that the Stewart unit made the fewest popular songs and the Hodges unit the most, with Bigard and Williams in between. The Hodges group, however, recorded far more titles than the others and was thus still able to turn out a large number of straight jazz records. Excluding alternative takes and air shots, 116 titles were recorded by Ellington units between 1936 and February 1940: 9 by Stewart, 26 by Bigard, 35 by Williams, and 46 by Hodges. The Bigard titles include two accompaniments to a vocal group, The Quintones.

* * *

Rex Stewart and his 52nd Street Stompers inaugurated the series on December 16, 1936, with *Rexatious* and *Lazy Man's Shuffle*. The group was made up of Rex, Lawrence Brown, Johnny Hodges, Harry Carney (who plays one of his rare clarinet solos on *Rexatious*), Ellington, Billy Taylor and Sonny Greer, plus Ceele Burke on steel guitar. Burke arranged *Lazy Man's Shuffle* as well as contributing some incongruous guitar work; this twelve-bar blues contains particularly fine playing from Stewart.

The Stewart group made only two more sessions during this period. On the first of these, Freddie Jenkins, making a brief unsuccessful attempt to return to full-time playing, is on second trumpet. He does not take any solos and sounds as if his lip is not wholly "in." The rest of the group consists of Hodges, Carney, Ellington, and Hayes Alvis plus two of Rex's friends from outside the band, Brick Fleagle on guitar and Jack Maisel on drums. *Back Room Romp* (subtitled *A Contrapuntal Stomp*) is a witty Ellington-Stewart creation with buoyant piano from Ellington and good solo work from Rex and the two reed players. The jaunty juxtaposition of riff figures is done in a most unusual and effective manner and the resources of the eight-piece band used in a remarkable way. The other three titles are more conventional—though Rex's own playing is not—with the cornet work on the second take of *Tea And Trumpets* one of the outstanding features of the section. This piece is an uptempo showcase for cornet, the other two items being conventional scores with liberal portions of unconventional cornet—*Swing, Baby, Swing* (or *Love In My Heart*) at medium tempo, and *Sugar Hill Shim-Sham* at fast tempo. Two takes of all four titles have been issued.

The final Stewart date was made in 1939 with another ex-Ellington trumpeter, Louis Bacon, sitting in. He and Rex are joined by Nanton, Bigard, Ellington, Taylor, and Greer for a session which produced three titles—the lively *San Juan Hill*, arranged by Brick Fleagle and with outstanding work from Rex and Tricky Sam; the ballad *I'll Come Back For More* with good work from Stewart and Ellington and a vocal from Bacon; and *Fat Stuff Serenade*, another Stewart-Ellington collaboration with Rex again featured at length. This last is a jaunty, lively stomp which could almost be a portrait of the cornetist, and indeed the title uses Rex's nickname in the band. A notable aspect of all these Stewart titles is the admirable piano playing by Ellington. As the unit routines were often head arrangements concocted in the studio, they are usually rather sparse and leave plenty of space for the pianist to fill in with embellishments. Duke is also heard to great advantage behind the soloists, and this whole series of contingent recordings is, among other things, a primer in band piano playing. There are also several personal, sometimes quirky, piano choruses of excellent quality.

* * *

Three days after the initial Stewart session, Williams, Tizol, Bigard, Carney, Ellington, Taylor, and Greer were in the studio masquerading as Barney Bigard and his Jazzopators. They cut four titles; the first a Bigard song, *Clouds In My Heart*, had been recorded by the full band in 1932. Barney is excellent on the theme and Cootie contributes a fine open trumpet solo. *Frolic Sam* is a Williams original, a riff number in the jump style of a kind which became characteristic of the Ellington units' output. The recording of Tizol's famous *Caravan* predates the full band version by some six months. It is treated in a very relaxed fashion as a vehicle for the soloists—Tizol himself (on the theme), Cootie (playing growl trumpet), Carney, and Bigard. There are two takes, the second (easily recognizable because its final chorus is played by the band instead of Tizol) being slightly superior, with a magnificent Carney solo among its high spots. The final title is a remake of *Stompy Jones* and two takes have been issued, the second slightly better. The soloists are Bigard in his most virtuoso vein, an ebullient Carney, and Cootie at his most Armstrong-like.

After this initial session the Bigard unit—later the Jazzopators became "his Orchestra" without any noticeable change in the music—settled into a regular personnel, with Stewart, Tizol, and Carney joining Bigard and the three-piece rhythm section. This was the lineup for their second session, which produced four delightful numbers, all issued in alternative takes. *Solace*, a Bigard ballad, finds Ellington using the small ensemble in a colorful way. Rex is cocomposer of *Four And One Half Street*, a jaunty uptempo twelve-bar piece with a characteristic Stewart theme. *Demi-Tasse* (*Each Day* or *Ev'ry Day* have been used as alternative titles) is a gem among these small-band recordings, with the second-chorus chase between Tizol, Bigard, Rex and the band a highlight. Tizol and the band play arranged figures while the other two improvise, Rex's eccentric phrasing adding a real spice to the mixture. *Jazz A La Carte* is another fast twelve-bar number, Rex stating the theme in a way which makes it seem conventional when played later by the ensemble.

Bigard's next session is marred by the presence of Sue Mitchell, whose vocals fail to enhance the value of *Get It Southern Style* and *If You're Ever In My Arms Again*. *Moonlight Fiesta* has Charlie Barnet playing maracas in a performance featuring Tizol and Stewart and generally superior to the full band version of 1935. Ellington's weirdly titled *Sponge Cake And Spinach* is probably the date's best side—a jump number with an unusual tune and good solo work. (*Moonlight Fiesta* is notable as the only one of the 116 contingent titles on which the leader, in this instance Bigard, does not take a solo.)

In January 1938, the Bigard group recorded two titles, *If I Thought You Cared*, a ballad with an excellent Carney solo, and a delightful jump score, *Drummer's Delight*, in which the various solos are divided by drum breaks. For some reason, the Bigard unit did not record again until June 1939, although recordings by the other contingents continued unabated. Their first two numbers from the June 1939 session are as accompanists to a vocal group, The Quintones, who have nothing to do with jazz and whose singing is as banal as their songs—*Utt-da-zay* and *Chew Chew Chew (Chew Your Bubble Gum)*. The instrumentals from this session are the languorous *Just Another Dream* and the easily swinging *Barney Goin' Easy*, where the beautiful mellow tone of the leader's clarinet is heard to perfection. This is actually a Billy Strayhorn arrangement of the melody to *I'm Checkin' Out, Goombye* with a musical climate totally different from that of the full band version. The mood is ultrarelaxed, the slightly somber instrumental colors glow, and solos by Rex and Duke further enhance a masterpiece of small-group Ellingtonia.

Later in 1939, the Bigard unit cut four titles, the first having only a six-piece band—Tizol is absent—playing *Early Mornin'*, an unusual Bigard theme with lots of the composer's clarinet. Strayhorn's *Minuet In Blues* is an unusual piece which boasts fine Bigard clarinet and remarkable Rex Stewart cornet. *Lost In Two Flats* is a Bigard essay in the standard Ellington small-band jump format, while *Honey Hush* turns out to be the same twelve-bar blues as that recorded by Rex Stewart at his Paris session of the previous year as *Solid Old Man*. On this version, solo choruses are provided by Bigard, who has two, and Stewart and Carney, who have one each.

The final Bigard session prior to the Victor contract was in February 1940 and produced good, solid Ellington small-band fare but no really outstanding titles. *Pelican Drag* is a Carney ballad featuring Bigard, while Strayhorn's *Tapioca* is a jump number with Stewart outstanding among the soloists. The final two titles are *Mardi Gras Madness*, a swinger by Bigard and Ellington with Stewart effective as soloist and ensemble leader, and *Watch The Birdie*, a popular song with Bigard featured and shorter solos for Tizol and Carney.

* * *

Cootie Williams and his Rug Cutters started to record in early 1937 and carried on through to 1940 without any change of band name. As with the Stewart unit, the personnel was inclined to be flexible, in this case usually Cootie plus two or three of the saxes and perhaps one of the trombonists, plus a three- or four-piece rhythm section. Their first recording was of a popular standard, *I Can't Believe That You're In Love With Me*, a classic performance with Carney on the theme and superb solos by Ellington, Nanton, Hodges, and Cootie in his most majestic style. *Downtown Uproar* is typical of the new instrumentals created for the Williams unit. At the start Nanton's open trombone sounds like the work of a rough New Orleans tailgate stylist as he plays against the ensemble. There are excellent solos by Hodges on soprano, Nanton in his more familiar muted guise, and Carney on baritone before Duke's stride piano, Greer's shouts of delight, and Cootie's high notes lead to the conclusion of a jubilant performance. *Diga Diga Do* is brought forward from the first Cotton Club period. After a droll introduction, Cootie's growl horn introduces a fine solo sequence to which Hodges (on soprano) and Tricky Sam are the most notable contributors. Hayes Alvis's bass is most effective on this performance. *Blue Reverie* is a slow twelve-bar blues with Hodges (soprano), Ellington, Carney, and Williams (growl) providing the solos. The fifth and final title from this session was not issued for many years—perhaps it was thought that the public would hardly appreciate such a surrealist version of *Tiger Rag*. It opens with a stride-gone-crazy piano introduction, followed by a brass duet between Williams and Nanton, both muted, in which Cootie plays the theme, breaks and all. The tempo is just too fast for a serious performance, the playing just too droll. Hodges plays the usual clarinet chorus on alto, and the performance ends with riffing brass after contributions from Nanton and Alvis.

Cootie's second session introduces vocalist Jerry Kruger, a member of the fair sex but not even a fair singer. Here she inflicts a vocal on only one number, Harry Nemo's (and Irving Mills's) *Watchin'*, musically distinguished by some superb trumpet from Williams in his Armstrong manner. Bigard is very effective here behind both trumpet and vocal. In the first chorus of *I Can't Give You Anything But Love*, Cootie, using (as he did in *Watchin'*) a straight mute of the kind used by Louis himself, comes as close as anyone ever has to the pure Armstrong style. He plays the melody differently from Louis but as an obvious Armstrong tribute. After a fine Carney solo and an interesting Bigard break, Hardwick plays the melody straight in a manner at once reminiscent of both the Ellington band of the *Blackbirds Medley* days and of the way Louis liked his saxophones to sound. Behind the alto, Duke introduces a passage of increasing vehemence for Cootie and Barney which builds to an unusual climax which again achieves an Armstrong flavor due to Cootie's note-placement and drive. The two other titles from this session are a version of Tizol's *Jubilesta*, more effective than the full band reading, and a blues-like 32-bar number by Duke and Mercer Ellington, *Pigeons And Peppers*, which has very fine Cootie growl trumpet.

One of the most remarkable recordings by the Williams unit is *Have A Heart*, dating from January 1938. The theme is actually Tizol's *Lost In Meditation*, taken at bounce tempo and completely transformed in character by the growls of Cootie and Nanton. Bigard, Carney, and Ellington make contributions before Cootie's open horn takes over. This performance is a perfect illustration of the melodic mastery of the Ellingtonians, and of how they are able to transform a theme. From the same session comes a small-group version of *Echoes Of Harlem* with excellent Cootie, but which is less effective without the full orchestral backing.

The next Williams session, from April 1938, features four numbers with vocals by Jerry Kruger. The first three are songs from *The Cotton Club Parade of 1938*—*A Lesson In 'C'*, *Swingtime in Honolulu*, and *Carnival In Caroline*. There is effective work from Hodges and Williams on the first title and fine Williams and Nanton on the second and third. The strident vocals are much less appealing than the Ivie Anderson choruses on the full band versions of the last two songs (*A Lesson In 'C'* was never recorded under Duke's name). The final title is a bizarre version of *Ol' Man River* in which the tedium of Miss Kruger's singing is relieved by her weird variations on the original lyrics; Cootie and Tricky Sam contribute excellent wa-wa work, and there is a nice stretch of Hodges alto.

According to Mercer Ellington, the vocalists on these contingent sessions were the choice of Irving Mills. The standards established by Kruger on two of the Williams dates are maintained by Scat Powell on a third; this was the session of August 1938, to which Powell contributes forgettable vocals on *Blue Is The Evening* and *Sharpie*. These also offer excellent Cootie solos, with straight mute on the former and in growl style on the latter. On *Sharpie*, Billy Taylor's bass is also heard to good effect. Two jump numbers (without vocals) from this date are more substantial: *Chasin' Chippies*, with a superb two-chorus Cootie growl solo, and the twelve-bar *Swing Pan Alley*. More good Cootie here and an excellent performance all-round, notable for the inclusion of an alto solo by Hardwick, sandwiched between two by Hodges on soprano. Apart from his playing of the theme on *The Sheik Of Araby* in duet with Nanton on the 1932 recording, this was Otto's only recorded uptempo solo between his return to the band in 1932 and his final departure in 1946!

A December 1938 Williams session produced two contrasting slow instrumentals and two more jump numbers. *Delta Mood* is a brooding, almost sinister piece by Ellington, who backs Cootie's snarling growl trumpet with heavy, steamy saxophone chords. In contrast, the slow, twelve-bar *Mobile Blues* features Cootie in two choruses of growl trumpet and one of open horn, all in the most forthright blues vein, with a rather rhapsodic piano chorus in between. *The Boys From Harlem* is an uptempo showcase for Williams's open playing in the conventional swing trumpet style of which he was such a master; there is more of the same in *Gal Avantin'*. On his next session, he makes up for this surfeit of open playing with a number largely given over to his growl trumpet, *Beautiful Romance*. Plenty of Cootie growl, too, on *Boudoir Benny*, which has good Bigard and Hodges solos, and very notable band piano from Duke. The last two titles from this session have vocals by Cootie himself—a Louis Jordan-type number, *Ain't The Gravy Good*, and a straight twelve-bar blues, *She's Gone*. Both have superb piano by Duke, and on the second he comes on in the style of a down-home blues pianist of the period.

From the next Cootie session comes a peculiar but very effective little number by Tizol and Jimmy Mundy, *Night Song*, which has some excellent growl trumpet by the leader. Cootie himself is the composer of *Blues A-Poppin'*, not a blues despite the title and with Strayhorn on piano instead of Duke, and the witty *Top And Bottom*, on which Duke returns, with telling effect. Cootie then brings forward *Black Beauty* from 1928 and offers a very slow reading in the sonorous low register of his trumpet. This sensitive performance is rather overshadowed by Cootie's version of *Black Butterfly* from his February 1940 date, another revival in which he is featured throughout on open trumpet, and the best version of a very beautiful Ellington ballad, notably superior to the 1936 full band reading. The oddly titled *Dry Long So* has another Williams vocal and fine playing by Cootie and Duke, while *Toasted Pickle* is a conventional jump number with solos all round. Finally, *Give It Up*, the very last number the Ellingtonians recorded before the 1940 Victor contract, features some excellent open trumpet.

* * *

The best known Ellington small-group sound is that of the Johnny Hodges unit, yet this was the last of the four to be recorded, Ellington not seeming to appreciate at first how well Hodges would function as leader in this situation. It may well be the experience and increased confidence which Hodges gained from these small-band recording dates which precipitated the blossoming of his art in the early forties; it also seems almost certain that Ellington came to look upon Hodges in a new light as the result of these sessions. The first session gave Hodges little opportunity to spread his wings; it consisted of three pop tunes undoubtedly intended as "cover versions" for other recordings and one unsuccessful novelty number. The vocalist on the ballads is Buddy Clarke, not a jazz singer in any sense. *Foolin' Myself*, *A Sailboat In The Moonlight*, and *You'll Never Go To Heaven* have good solo work by Hodges, Williams, and Bigard in very relaxed fashion, but Greer is not at his best on these performances. The novelty number is *Peckin'*, based on a riff from *Rockin' In Rhythm*. It was originally published as by Harry James and Ben Pollack, although Ellington later did get his name included in the composer credits. The vocalist is unknown—it is not Clarke—and his diabolical contribution was no doubt the reason for the rejection of this recording. Three takes have survived, Harry Carney being in particularly good form on the second and third. (The alternative takes of the earlier numbers from this session show only slight changes in the solos.)

In January 1938 the Hodges unit recorded another two pops, *My Day* and *Silvery Moon And Golden Sands*, with quality alto from Hodges and vocals by Mary McHugh of a sentimental kind far removed from the jazz idiom. In March 1938 Hodges brought into the studio the group which was to become his regular unit—Williams, Brown, Carney, and three rhythm. They recorded four titles. The first was *Jeep's Blues*, a considerable success which at once established the distinctive sound of the Hodges small band. It features all the front line in solos, with the leader on soprano sax. It was issued back-to-back with an uptempo number, *Rendezvous With Rhythm*, which introduced the Hodges unit's jump style. The other items from *The Cotton Club Parade Of 1938*, featured sweet vocals by Mary McHugh in the two most popular songs from the show—*If You Were In My Place* and *I Let A Song Go Out Of My Heart*. Hodges is fine on both, while Brown has eight bars of exquisite melody playing on the latter.

Mary McHugh is again on the next Hodges session, singing *You Walked Out Of The Picture* (nice accompaniment by Brown) and *Lost In Meditation* in her very straight manner. There is most effective Hodges alto on the former title. The outstanding numbers from this session are the instrumentals, *Pyramid* and *Empty Ballroom Blues*. Although not transformed so radically as *Lost In Meditation* had been to become *Have A Heart*, Hodges's *Pyramid* is totally different from the full band version. It features voluptuous soprano sax playing along with a very mellow Lawrence Brown-led ensemble. *Empty Ballroom Blues* is an uptempo piece on the *Stompy Jones* pattern, with solos from Hodges (again on soprano), Brown, Williams, and Carney, and fine supporting piano from Ellington. On this title, Ellington invented the "echo chamber" for recording purposes, achieving the effect by having a microphone placed in the adjacent men's room!

From this point on, Hodges's unit routine started to change, possibly as a result of the success of *Jeep's Blues*. The popular tunes with mediocre vocalists were gradually dropped in favor of nonvocal ballads and an increase in jazz instrumentals. The latter continued to produce the best music, although it would be foolish to ignore the popular song recordings. There is much good solo work on them, particularly from Hodges, one of those musicians who can transform the most base melody into pure musical gold. Of the jump numbers, *Swingin' In The Dell*, *The Jeep Is Jumpin'* (an archetypal Hodges riff tune), *Hodge Podge*, *Swingin' On The Campus*, and *The Rabbit's Jump* are the best. There are many excellent blues: *Jitterbug's Lullaby* is an outstanding example with particularly effective piano from Ellington, while *Rent Party Blues* is without doubt the best recording of this 1929 soprano feature. *Wanderlust* is a sad, rather nostalgic blues with one of Carney's best solos in the idiom. *Dooji Wooji*, with its eight-to-the-bar bass by Ellington, inspires passionate playing from all the front line soloists. *Tired Socks* is a rather menacing minor-key theme written by Hodges and featuring him on soprano throughout, backed by the other horns and rhythm section in a march-like accompaniment. The sinister *Krum Elbow Blues*, the rather theatrical *Good Gal Blues*, *Home Town Blues* (arranged by Hodges himself), and *Skunk Hollow Blues* (with very fine bass playing by Jimmy Blanton) are further excellent examples of Hodges blues from this period.

* * *

There are four surviving air-shot recordings of the Ellington units and as three of these are from Cotton Club broadcasts it is obvious that Ellington used the band-within-a-band idea in his public appearances at this time. There are two versions of *Ev'ry Day*, and one each of *Downtown Uproar* and *Frolic Sam*. All four performances follow the routines on the studio recordings exactly and there are only slight differences in the solos.

Outstanding Recordings

1. By the Full Band: Studio Recordings

Scattin' At The Kit Kat, *Old Plantation*, *All God's Chillun Got Rhythm* (nonvocal version), *Diminuendo In Blue*, *Crescendo In Blue*, *Harmony In Harlem*, *Dusk In The Desert*, *Steppin' Into Swing Society*, *Prologue To Black and Tan Fantasy*, *The New Black And Tan Fantasy*, *Ridin' On A Blue Note*, *I Let A Song Go Out Of My Heart* (both takes), *Dinah's In A Jam*, *Rose Of The Rio Grande*, *Watermelon Man*, *Hip Chic*, *Jazz Pot-pourri*, *Blue Light*, *Boy Meets Horn*, *Slap Happy*, *Pussy Willow*, *Subtle Lament*, *Portrait Of The Lion* (both takes), *Way Low*, *In A Mizz*, *I'm Checkin' Out*, *Goombye* (both standard and V-Disc versions), *A Lonely Co-ed*, *Bouncing Buoyancy*, *The Sergeant Was Shy*, *Grievin'*, *Little Posey*, *Tootin' Through The Roof*, *Country Gal*

2. By the Full Band: Broadcasts

a. The complete broadcasts of March 18, 1937, July 26, 1939, and January 9, 1940

b. *Dinah*, *Harmony In Harlem* (both March 24, 1938), *Carnival In Caroline*, *Dinah's In A Jam*, *On The Sunny Side Of The Street* (all from April 24, 1938), *Harmony In Harlem*, *The Gal From Joe's*, *Ridin' On A Blue Note* (all from May 1, 1938), *Rose Room*, *Echoes Of Harlem* (both from May 15, 1938), *Rockin' In Rhythm* (May 29, 1938), *Rockin' In Rhythm*, and *Cottage By The Sea* (both from a Swedish broadcast of April 29, 1939)

3. Duets with Jimmy Blanton

Blues and *Plucked Again*

4. The Contingents

a. Barney Bigard: *Demi-Tasse*, *Jazz A La Carte* and *Barney Goin' Easy*

b. Johnny Hodges: *Jeep's Blues*, *Pyramid*, *Jitterbug's Lullaby*, *The Jeep Is Jumpin'*, *Wanderlust*, *Dooji Wooji*, *Rent Party Blues*, and *Tired Socks*

c. Rex Stewart: *Back Room Romp*, *San Juan Hill*, and *Fat Stuff Serenade*

d. Cootie Williams: *I Can't Believe That You're In Love With Me*, *Downtown Uproar*, *Blue Reverie*, *Tiger Rag*, *I Can't Give You Anything But Love*, *Have A Heart*, *The Boys From Harlem*, *Mobile Blues*, *Top And Bottom*, *Black Beauty*, and *Black Butterfly*

Chapter 11

Steppin' into Swing Society

DURING THE LATE THIRTIES the Ellington Orchestra enjoyed great stability of personnel. In the middle of the decade Arthur Whetsol, Freddie Jenkins, and Wellman Braud had been replaced, after some shuffling about, by Wallace Jones, Rex Stewart, and the bass duo of Billy Taylor and Hayes Alvis. From 1936 to the end of 1939 the only important changes were the departure of Alvis in 1938; the arrival of Billy Strayhorn as lyric writer, arranger, composer and deputy pianist in 1939; and the replacement of Taylor by Jimmy Blanton that same year. Harold Baker's short stay in the trumpet section in 1938 did not affect the music heard on the records. In January, vocalist Herb Jeffries was added, and the following month Ben Webster came in on a permanent basis to bring the saxophones up to five pieces, but these changes came right at the end of the period we have been discussing.

The reasons why musicians stayed with the Ellington band for such long periods are various: they were well paid; Ellington was greatly admired and respected by his sidemen; the discipline was easy if a musician could hold down his chair in a responsible fashion; Ellington called for an imaginative response from his sidemen which could make their work highly stimulating; the music was good to play and had that full sound which big band musicians like so much; being in this band was an education, not least in the way Ellington helped to develop a musician's talent; and there was the prestige of being an Ellingtonian—a musician demonstrably at the head of his profession. This stability of personnel was most marked from 1930 to 1941, but to a lesser degree it remained a feature of the band in the years which followed. The periods of total stability were shorter, but at the very least, Ellington was able to keep a nucleus of long-serving members.

In the middle thirties the big band scene started to change. Previously, big white bands had played predominantly sweet dance music, big black bands alone featuring jazz in any quantity. The success of the Benny Goodman Orchestra in the middle thirties changed this pattern, for suddenly, playing big band jazz to white audiences became a very lucrative activity. The new craze was called "swing" and was contrasted with the sweet music of the postdepression years and the old-fashioned "jazz" of the twenties. The word jazz was very rarely used to describe the big band music of the late thirties in contemporary writing, and then only in the more serious magazines. The word itself was becoming rather musty and old in terms of show-business fashion, and musicians who played "jazz" were considered out of date. And in the entertainment world of the late thirties nothing was quite so disastrous. Duke Ellington had been around a long time in popular music terms, and there was a real danger that the public would start to regard his music as a relic of the twenties and thus "old hat." That Ellington's music was as contemporary in spirit as any—and more so than most—is clear enough from the viewpoint of later years. But care had to be taken about his image, which has always counted for more than musical content in the world of popular entertainment. So the Ellington Orchestra found itself being described as a "swing band," and Duke was soon *Steppin' Into Swing Society*, as his 1938 composition described it. The band was never as popular as Goodman's or Artie Shaw's or Tommy Dorsey's—not even in the opinion of those Americans who took the trouble to vote in the magazine polls—but it more than got by. The situation in Europe was different, and the magazine polls there showed that among jazz enthusiasts in Britain and on the continent Ellington's remained the most popular band.

* * *

In late 1939 Ellington broke his connection with the Irving Mills organization. There had been much criticism in the black press concerning the money Mills had made from Ellington, and Duke must have wondered if one of the other agencies which were doing so much for Goodman and Shaw—and for black bands like the up-and-coming Count Basie—might not do better for him. He made a careful study of the books of Duke Ellington, Inc., a Mills Music subsidiary, and then signed with the William Morris agency, which was already handling Basie. There was an improvement in terms of residencies for the band, but the Pullman train was no more, and the fact that the band now toured in the same fashion as any other may have affected some of the long-serving musicians who decided to leave during the next four or five years. But through 1940 and 1941, at least, Ellington was able to retain his stable personnel.

Up to this time all Ellington compositions had been published by Mills Music. At the time of the break with Mills, this responsibility was given to one of his rivals, Jack Robbins of Robbins Music, but in 1941, Duke and his sister, Ruth Ellington, founded Tempo Music. Their first publications were Edmund Anderson's *Flamingo*, Juan Tizol's *Perdido* and Billy Strayhorn's *Take The "A" Train*. Duke could not publish his own works until the Robbins Music contract ran out in 1942, but from that year on, he became his own publisher, and for the rest of his life his new work was published by Tempo Music.

The swing era affected Ellington musically as well as commercially. We noted earlier that Duke did not come from a jazz environment and that he based his style on music he had come to know at a comparatively mature age. As a young man, he listened to and learned from such musicians as Sidney Bechet and James P. Johnson, and what he learned he incorporated into his own musical language. While the effect of the show music he absorbed during his first years in New York should not be overlooked, the main influences on the young Ellington were jazz musicians. The pattern of what we might call "creative listening," which had become established with him in these years, continued throughout Ellington's life. In the swing era he listened to the newly popular bands and in particular to the music of Fletcher Henderson, Jimmie Lunceford, and Basie. Though nearing the end of its long and distinguished career, the Henderson Orchestra was a key group in the formation of swing styles, notably through the strong influence it had on Goodman, who employed Henderson as a staff arranger. Ellington had long been an admirer of the Henderson band, and in the middle thirties he urged Fletcher to capitalize on the potential popularity of the new arrangements he was then featuring. Henderson failed to do so; the person who did cash in, with due acknowledgements, was Goodman. Jazz writers often contrast the call-and-response patterns which are a basic feature of the Henderson/Goodman style with the blending of voices from various sections in which Ellington indulged. But they overlook the fact that Ellington wrote for straight sections, including call-and-response patterns, as well as using his famous blends and mixtures. A perfect example of this is the 1932 *Bugle Call Rag*, and Duke again employed Henderson style riffs—fully transformed into his own language—in the 1937 *Harmony In Harlem*.

The influence of the Lunceford band is more subtle; Lunceford's music was so highly stylized that it was always easier to imitate than to assimilate. There are Ellington records which are clearly in the Lunceford style, but overall this influence was less direct than Henderson's. During the middle thirties, the Ellington Orchestra became more adept at swinging convincingly at all tempos. At the same time, the division in musical quality between arrangements given to popular songs and to jazz numbers, often quite marked in the early years of the decade, disappeared altogether. In both these developments it is perhaps possible to trace an influence from Lunceford.

It is doubtful whether the early Basie band had much of an effect on Ellington's music, although the fact that Duke's band became much more proficient at swinging riffs during these years may be seen as more than a coincidence. But if Basie's collection of free-blowing jazz soloists had little influence on Ellington, the Count's own piano playing clearly had. In his less formal performances, for example at dances, Ellington was in the habit of playing long piano introductions which signalled the next number to the musicians and would continue while they had got their band parts ready. At first, these introductions were played in stride fashion, as we hear in the introduction to *Rockin' In Rhythm* on the 1937 broadcast. Basie's piano style was an implied stride style with the left hand largely omitted and the rhythm section given a prominent role. Ellington quickly saw the advantage of this for his own purposes and also grasped the rhythmic implications of Basie's placement of notes. By the time of the November 1940 Fargo dance date, Ellington had adopted a modified Basie manner for his introductions, and the increasing rhythmic potency of Duke's piano in the band from the mid-thirties on is clearly due to a refinement in timing which owes something to Basie principles.

The Basie Orchestra originated in Kansas City, although Basie himself was from New Jersey and played the piano in a manner derived from such New York pianists as James P. Johnson and Fats Waller. He can be heard playing pure Harlem stride piano on many of the later recordings of the Bennie Moten Kansas City Orchestra. Indeed the last recordings of that group, from 1932, prefigure the Basie band style in many ways. The transformation of the Basie Orchestra from a loose, soloist-dominated group to a more conventional but still outstanding big band can be traced fully on records.

This was the period when big bands with a jazz-based policy bloomed—in addition to the established bands of Calloway, Carter, Ellington, Henderson, Hines, Kirk, Lunceford, and Redman, there were such excellent new black bands as those of Willie Bryant, Edgar Hayes, Erskine Hawkins, Horace Henderson, Teddy Hill, Claude Hopkins, and Lucky Millinder, as well as Basie's. Chick Webbs' fine band from the famous Savoy Ballroom in Harlem also became more widely known at this time. The white bands which followed Goodman's remarkable breakthrough included Charlie Barnet, Bob Crosby, Jimmy Dorsey, Tommy Dorsey, Woody Herman, and Artie Shaw. Barnet was a zealous Ellington admirer and featured many Ellington pieces in his repertoire, although he was too astute to attempt an imitation of Ellington's style and methods.

The swing era also produced a number of notable small bands, including the highly contrasting groups of John Kirby and Al Cooper. Where the Kirby Sextet featured highly elaborate and tricky arrangements, sometimes based on themes from the classical repertoire, Cooper's Savoy Sultans concentrated on simple functional scores and solid swinging tempos. They were featured at the Savoy Ballroom, where they were the scourge of visiting bands. The other famous band from the Savoy, Chick Webb's, also knew all about swinging tempos.

To compare the Ellington band with its contemporaries becomes more obviously futile as time goes by, for it was clearly developing on the basis of its own unique traditions. The band was less disciplined than Lunceford's, and its music less obviously aimed at excitement than Basie's. The Ellington policy was less single-minded than Webb's, for Webb had only the Savoy Ballroom dancers to please, although they were, of course, a demanding audience. By comparison, Ellington's net was cast far, far wider. The drilled precision of the white bands was never Ellington's forte. What separates his band from all others at this time is not simply the solo strength—although only Basie, then at his peak in this regard, could even begin to rival him there—but the warmth and subtlety of the ensemble playing and the great variety of utterly original material which it handled.

* * *

There is a tendency among jazz critics to regard the Ellington records of the late thirties as being simply from a formative period which led to the great surge of Ellington creativity in 1940. There are several reasons for this attitude, including the fact that European audiences were denied new Ellington records in the late thirties. When these did become available many years later, they filled a gap between two blocks of known recordings, and European critics were inclined to see them primarily as demonstrations of how the long-familiar music of the mid-thirties led to the now equally familiar Ellington music of the early forties. Ellington's art was constantly changing in a way which can wrongly lead to such an interpretation. One can isolate any chronological block of Ellington recordings and view it as preparation for the music of the years to follow, for this is indeed one aspect of a developing and constantly evolving body of art. The danger is that this historical approach can lead to greater stress being laid on the evolutionary aspects of the music than on its intrinsic artistic worth. For aesthetic reasons, Ellington's output of 1940 and 1941 has for many years been given a preeminent place in critical evaluation of his work and it might seem perverse to regard this music as preparatory ground for that of 1942 and 1943. Yet, because of the continuing evolution and creativity of Ellington's art, this is indeed an aspect, and an important one, of the 1940–41 masterpieces: without them the music of 1942–43 could not have been what it was. In this instance, the "historical" value of the music is obviously secondary. Ellington's music continuously evolved but Duke was above all a working musician, writing music which "sounds good now," as he put it. His works should always be taken basically at face value and never as if they were parts of a project coming to full fruition only at some later date. The records cited at the end of the last chapter as the best from the late thirties are first and foremost important works in their own right. The period they represent was formative—or transitional, as it has sometimes been called—only in the sense that this is true of any other Ellington era.

* * *

In the late thirties we find, for the first time, broadcasts by the Ellington band which have survived in recorded form. Henceforth such recordings (or air shots) will become an increasing part of the Ellington output and indeed will soon start to outnumber records made for public release. By the mid-forties well over three-quarters of the Ellington discography consists of broadcast and concert recordings, each of which yields three or four times as many performances as the average studio session. The sources of this material vary. Some recordings were made by radio stations at the time of transmission, either for rebroadcast or sale to other stations. Some were recorded at dances, concerts, or special studio sessions by companies who produced material for sale to radio stations, a category usually referred to as "transcriptions." Then there are recordings made by private individuals, off the radio or recorded live at a club date, concert, or dance.

A good deal of this material has been issued on record in recent decades and offers an opportunity (as did the recordings for various companies in the twenties and early thirties) of hearing different versions of many of Ellington's new compositions. One also hears many, many pieces and scores which were never recorded for public issue. The number of such recordings which have already been identified is immense, and undoubtedly many hitherto unknown performances will come to light in the future. The sound quality of this material is variable. In the majority of cases, it was well recorded initially, but frequent taping and retaping by collectors may result in poor quality sound when the music is issued on disc, although often such records have been superseded by later versions in superior fidelity.

* * *

The last recordings under the Master-Brunswick-Columbia-Variety-Vocalion-OKeh contract were made less than a month before the first 1940 Victors, yet these Victors seem to mark the beginning of a new era, as if the band had been out of the studios for a year or more. A good deal of the credit must go to the Victor company itself for the superb recording quality of the 1940 discs. The late thirties Ellington band was well recorded by the standards of the time, but the Victors are exceptional; in particular the bass part—crucially important in this music—is clearly recorded. The band itself also sounds different, due to the effect of the playing of Ben Webster and Jimmy Blanton *within the ensemble*. Much has been made of Webster's contribution as a soloist, but we should remember that with his arrival the saxophones were increased to five and could now challenge the brass in terms of harmonic and coloristic resources. Webster's big, full tone and swinging phrasing were extra qualities to add to a team which had always been rather weak in section tenor playing. Blanton filled out the bass part and added to the swing of the rhythm section. He and Sonny Greer seem an odd partnership, but in practice they worked very well together, though if one listens carefully to some of the small-group recordings from late 1939 and early 1940 one hears that at first their rhythmic concepts did not blend. But soon they did, and along with Ellington's supremely imaginative piano and Fred Guy's reliable guitar a flexible, fully flavored, and swinging rhythm section was born.

Sidemen

Jimmy Blanton

During Blanton's tragically brief career—he died at the age of 23 of tuberculosis while on sick leave from the Ellington band—he revolutionized jazz bass playing. Blanton's conception of the pizzicato bass as a melody instrument, allied to his remarkable harmonic sense and his great virtuosity, impressed his fellow musicians to the extent that all succeeding jazz bassists have based their approach on his playing. But Blanton was also outstanding in the traditional role of the jazz bass in his ability to play within a band and lay down a rhythmic foundation of the greatest swing. Nor was his virtuosity achieved at the expense of tone; the mellow, singing sound he obtained on pizzicato bass is rich and full. If one plays through the Ellington records of the late thirties chronologically, the more vital rhythmic pulse can be felt from the moment Blanton joins. With the big band, the small units, or in duet with Ellington, Blanton is equally outstanding. All the recordings made by the Ellingtonians with Blanton are of special interest due to the brilliant bass playing.

Representative Recordings: Jack The Bear (Victor, 1940), *Concerto For Cootie* (Victor, 1940), *Sepia Panorama* (Victor and Fargo dance date, 1940), *Mr. J.B. Blues* (duet, Victor, 1940), *Subtle Slough* (Rex Stewart Orchestra, Bluebird, 1941), *Squatty Roo* (Johnny Hodges Orchestra, Bluebird, 1941)

Wallace Jones

His occasional solos show Jones to be a resourceful player, but it is as a section leader that he made his major contribution. He was one of those steady, reliable musicians on whom the big bands depended. As a rule, he was allocated solos in the ballad manner after the example of Arthur Whetsol, as on *Serenade To Sweden* and the arrangement of *Mood Indigo* which the band used during his stay. Another of Wallace Jones's traditional roles was to take over Whetsol's part in *Creole Love Call*. An unexpected aspect of Jones's talent was revealed in 1943, when he took over the growl trumpet parts in *Black And Tan Fantasy*. It seems ironic that one of his most noted solo roles, in *Mood Indigo*, was a cause of his giving up music. Apparently, one of Whetsol's talents was the ability to sustain long notes without apparent effort. The need to sustain the high D in the *Mood Indigo* solo drove Jones into cold sweats and nightmares, according to Mercer Ellington, and ultimately drove him out of the band and professional music (*Duke Ellington in Person* by Mercer Ellington with Stanley Dance, pp. 22–23).

Representative Recordings: Serenade To Sweden (broadcast, 1939), *Mood Indigo* (Fargo dance date, 1940, Carnegie Hall, January 1943), *Black And Tan Fantasy* (Carnegie Hall, December 1943)

Billy Strayhorn

Strayhorn was initially taken into the Ellington organization because Duke liked his song lyrics. He soon started writing scores for the small-band recordings and by early 1940 was established as a staff composer-arranger and deputy pianist, roles he held until his death in 1967. His success in adapting the unique Ellington methods to his own individual requirements was remarkable, and his association with Ellington was one of the great partnerships in jazz. (Billy Strayhorn's contribution to the music of the Ellington Orchestra is considered at length in Chapter 29.)

Representative Recordings: (For Strayhorn compositions, see the list at the end of Chapter 29. The following feature Strayhorn at the piano.) *Linger Awhile* (Rex Stewart Orchestra, Bluebird, 1940), *After All* (Victor, 1941), *Cue's Blue Now, Watch Your Cue, Gone With The Wind* (all Billy Strayhorn Septet, Felsted, 1959), *Strange Feeling* (solo, United Artists, 1961).

Chapter 12

The Records—March to November 1940

THE IMPROVED VICTOR SOUND QUALITY and the important new additions to the personnel are not the only factors which make the Ellington recordings from 1940 so outstanding. Ellington was now at the peak of his achievement as a composer, and the unique way in which his band functioned was an established and flourishing tradition. This owed much to Ellington's consistent musical methods and policy and the presence in the band of so many long-serving members. In his 1940 Orchestra, Ellington had an ideal instrument for the interpretation of his compositions, yet, even considered in isolation from its leader's genius, this was an absolutely outstanding big band. In solo strength alone, it far outshone its rivals, with the sole exception of the Basie band, and even that notable aggregation of superb soloists could not surpass Ellington in this respect. As an ensemble, the Ellington band of 1940 simply had no rivals within the jazz field. In March of that year, when the Victor recordings commenced, the personnel was:

Trumpets: Cootie Williams, Wallace Jones, Rex Stewart (cornet).

Trombones: Lawrence Brown; Juan Tizol (valve trombone); Joe Nanton.

Reeds: Otto Hardwick (alto sax, clarinet); Johnny Hodges (alto and soprano saxes); Ben Webster (tenor sax); Barney Bigard (clarinet, tenor sax); Harry Carney (baritone and alto saxes, clarinet, bass clarinet).

Rhythm: Duke Ellington (piano); Fred Guy (guitar); Jimmy Blanton (bass); Sonny Greer (drums); Billy Strayhorn (deputy pianist).

Vocal: Ivie Anderson, Herb Jeffries.

The first recording session under the new Victor contract took place on March 6, 1940, and the first title recorded was anything but a masterpiece, a non-Ellington pop song called *You, You Darlin'*. This features a Herb Jeffries vocal, relieved by an intelligent arrangement and good solos from those master balladeers Webster and Brown. The second title—Ellington's *Jack The Bear*—is much more representative. The core of the composition is framed by bass solos by Blanton which act as introduction and extended coda. The theme is presented by Ellington on piano, and the piece is carried forward by the soloists—Bigard, Williams, Carney, and Nanton—all of whom receive perfectly designed backing from the band, which takes a subsidiary role throughout. Despite the fact that the work is dominated by the soloists, the unity and the cohesive nature of the composition are retained. *Jack The Bear* is also important because the full effect of Blanton's contribution to the ensemble can be heard for the first time.

Nanton and Blanton are again featured in *Ko-Ko*, rumored to be a fragment of a projected jazz opera by Ellington. Basically a twelve-bar blues structure, *Ko-Ko* has a West Indian flavor and builds to a truly magnificent ensemble climax, exultant and ringing. Tizol's valve trombone and the leader's piano have minor roles, Nanton and Blanton more crucial ones in one of Ellington's most notable achievements, in which the harmonic innovations sound perfectly natural and not in any way self-consciously modish. *Morning Glory*, a pretty melody composed by Ellington and Rex Stewart, is scored as a showcase for the tender, melodic aspect of the latter's cornet style. (In later years, Rex maintained that the piece was by him, the rights having been won by Ellington in an all-night poker session on board ship returning from the band's 1939 European tour.) The final title is another non-Ellington pop song, *So Far, So Good*, with a pleasant vocal by Ivie Anderson and a nice half-chorus of Carney's baritone.

Congo Brava opens the second Victor session. This is an Ellington-Tizol collaboration with the valve trombonist introducing a characteristic Latin American melody. Soon the band takes over, and the rhythm changes gear into a swinging four-four. Bigard and Stewart have obbligato roles and Rex can be heard leading the trumpet section to good effect. Webster's loose, lissome solo contributes to the variety and substance of the piece before it closes with the return of the original melody, again played by Tizol. Next comes *Concerto For Cootie*, Duke's second feature for the trumpeter, which could lay claim to be the best of all Ellington "concertos." The main melody of this piece was later remodeled into the popular song *Do Nothin' Till You Hear From Me*. In the original *Concerto For Cootie*, this theme is played by Williams with the plunger mute, while a second melody demonstrates Cootie's magnificent open tone and majestic phrasing. *Concerto For Cootie* is so perfect an entity that to single out any one particular—Cootie's varied playing, Duke's original conception, the perfect orchestral backdrop, the sensitive playing of the band, Blanton's crucial contribution—would do an injustice to a marvelously cohesive and balanced whole. The third and final title from this March 15, 1940, session is *Me And You*, an Ellington pop song previously encountered in a rather dreary version complete with Jeffries vocal from the Boston broadcast of January 9, 1940. The Victor recording is vastly superior and is one of the best of all Ellington pop song performances. Ivie Anderson takes over the vocal and invests it with marvelous rhythmic life, while Cootie's theme statement and the chase chorus between Brown and Hodges are contrasting examples of high-grade jazz solo work. Bigard and Greer also make telling contributions to a swinging performance, just as enjoyable in its unpretentious way as the more formal instrumental pieces of the period.

The next session, of May 4, 1940, produced two more recordings of similar quality. *Cotton Tail* is an uptempo stomp with a classic two-chorus solo from Webster as its centerpiece, framed by a typically imaginative Ellington score in which the Hodges-led saxophone section has an important role. This is probably Webster's best-known solo—a superbly balanced, logical construction which is an acknowledged classic. The orchestration is perfectly judged, and the rhythm section is heard in a relaxed yet driving vein. Other brief solo contributions are made by Williams, Carney, and Ellington. The session mate to *Cotton Tail* is an equally celebrated classic, *Never No Lament*, which later became better known in pop tune guise as *Don't Get Around Much Anymore*. Musically, this original version remains the most important, another imaginatively conceived arrangement of a fine melody into which the solo contributions, themselves of superlative quality, are fitted with unerring taste and rightness. Hodges is the main soloist, giving a definitive demonstration of a melodic statement in which jazz values are paramount. By this time, Hodges had cultivated a tone of previously inconceivable richness and grandeur. It will always remain unique. In addition to Hodges's ravishing playing there are excellent contributions by Williams and Brown. This recording also offers an example of how Ellington's seemingly simple piano style can richly color a performance.

On this date, the band also recorded versions of *Bojangles* and *Blue Goose*, which were rejected and remade at later sessions. In the late seventies, the Meritt Record Society released these rejected takes. They differ only in detail from the more familiar recordings, but in the case of *Bojangles*, these are sufficient to make the alternative version an exciting listening experience, and Webster's solo is a gem.

It might stretch credulity to say that the next four-title session produced four more masterpieces, but such is indeed the case. It will have been noted that the variety of musical style and content so characteristic of Ellington's output had been further expanded in the late thirties and in early 1940. There is no question of cultivating just one area of the garden; the whole vast Ellington musical estate is thriving and blossoming more abundantly than ever before. The four items recorded on May 28, 1940, are typical in their wide stylistic contrast. The first, *Dusk*, is an Ellington tone painting of which two takes have been issued (-1 perhaps fractionally the superior). Important use is made of a variation of the *Mood Indigo* trio voicing, the theme being presented by Jones and Bigard, with Brown's muted trombone adding a harmony part above the muted trumpet and low-register clarinet. This trombone part is so quiet that the passages have often been credited to the duo of Jones and Bigard only, yet it is the subtle harmonies provided by Brown that give the theme statements of *Dusk* their distinctive flavor. Brown is also heard briefly in solo on muted trombone, and Ellington again has a crucial part on piano, but the main soloist is Stewart, playing in the low register of the cornet and evoking a suitably nocturnal mood over heavy, brooding orchestral harmonies. His imaginative use of the half-valve technique is characteristically excellent. The next two titles are Ellington "portraits"—*Bojangles*, depicting the distinguished dancer Bill "Bojangles" Robinson, and *A Portrait Of Bert Williams*, dedicated to the famous comedian. As befits a musical portrait of a tap dancer, *Bojangles* is taken at a lively pace and includes a soft-shoe routine played by the ensemble just after Webster's beautiful solo. Ellington, Blanton, and Bigard also make important contributions to this masterpiece of orchestral jazz. (The rejected version of *Bojangles* from the May 4 session differs mainly in the omission of Ellington's opening piano chorus and the addition of some ad-lib tailgate trombone smears from Brown during the soft-shoe passage.)

A Portrait Of Bert Williams is taken at a slow tempo. The principal thematic responsibility is assumed by Stewart, himself a great admirer of Williams. Rex presents the ever so slightly sentimental theme in the low register of the cornet, bursting out in the middle of the piece with a four-bar solo of the most eccentric kind. Bigard is used to excellent effect, and the droll plunger-muted trombone of Nanton captures exactly the right mood. Again the orchestral background is superlative in both conception and execution: note, for example, the varied tone colors of the saxophone section in the very brief introduction. *Blue Goose* is an Ellington ballad for orchestra; the first chorus contrasts Hodges on soprano saxophone with Carney in the lowest register of the baritone. Williams, Webster, and, more crucially, Brown are heard before the appealing, slightly melancholy sound of Hodges's soprano returns to close a multicolored, highly attractive performance.

* * *

During 1940, the British Broadcasting Corporation featured a series of radio programs called *America Dances*. As one of America's leading bands, the Ellington Orchestra was invited to participate. The result was a half-hour broadcast recorded on June 12, 1940, which has been issued on a Queen Disc LP. The numbers performed were all Ellington compositions, the oldest of which was *Boy Meets Horn* (from 1938), and so the broadcast gives a very fair cross-section of the contemporary Ellington output. The version of *Ko-Ko* which follows the signature theme is considerably faster than the studio recording of three months earlier, and it is a good deal less effective as a result. It has become a habit in some critical circles to denigrate the 1956 recording of *Ko-Ko* on account of its faster and less effective tempo, and to infer from this that Ellington's art had declined. Those who expound this view should listen to some of the *Ko-Ko* performances from later in 1940. The tempo went up almost as soon as the Victor recording had been made, but no critics seem to have found evidence of an Ellington decline at this time!

Blue Goose and *So Far, So Good* (vocal by Anderson) are very close to the studio recordings. *Cotton Tail* is less satisfying than the Victor, the tenor solo not being so well played. However, this version has the benefit of a second, concluding tenor solo, omitted from the studio performance to fit the piece into the time limits of a 78 disc. Other differences are in detail only, such as Ellington playing a totally different piano solo, as indeed he always contrived to do on this number. Only minor variants can be found in the radio versions of *Concerto For Cootie* and *Jack The Bear*, but *Boy Meets Horn* is played with much more assurance than on the earlier recordings. *The Sergeant Was Shy*, by contrast, is less successful than the 1939 Columbia recording.

* * *

Back in the Victor studios on July 22, the first title recorded was *Harlem Air Shaft*. Much has been made of the so-called "program" of this composition, following the lead of a statement by Duke himself:

> So much goes on in a Harlem air shaft. You get the full essence of Harlem in an air shaft. You hear fights, you smell dinner, you hear people making love, you hear intimate gossip floating down. You hear the radio. An air shaft is one great big loudspeaker. You see your neighbors' laundry. You hear the janitor's dogs. The man upstairs' aerial falls down and breaks your window. You smell coffee. A wonderful thing, that smell. An air shaft has got every contrast. One guy is cooking dried fish and rice and another guy's got a great big turkey. Guy-with-fish's wife is a terrific cooker but the guy's wife with the turkey is doing a sad job. You hear people praying, fighting, smoking. Jitterbugs are jumping up and down, always all over you, never below you. That's a funny thing about jitterbugs. They're always above you. I tried to put

all that into *Harlem Air Shaft*. . . . (Quoted in *Hear Me Talkin' To Ya*, ed. Hentoff and Shapiro, Peter Davies, London, 1955, p. 203)

As a scenario of the kind which often inspired Ellington's music, much can be learned from this quotation, but its application to the number we know as *Harlem Air Shaft* must be questioned. At the time of recording, the piece was known as *Rumpus In Richmond*, suggesting that Duke's famous program was something of an afterthought. He subsequently gave the title *Rumpus In Richmond* to another composition originally called *Brassiere*. The original *Rumpus In Richmond* was then retitled *Harlem Air Shaft*, and it is as such that it has become known to thousands of jazz enthusiasts.

Whatever the relevance of the program or the title, musically *Harlem Air Shaft* is a triumph. In an introduction of a mere twelve bars, Ellington provides sufficient melodic material to satisfy most jazz arrangers for several pieces. From this treasure trove he selects a little riff figure which he gives to the muted trumpets and garnishes with a strong countermelody in the lower saxophones, with tenor lead. Nanton is heard briefly in the middle eight of this opening chorus. The second chorus takes the form of a commanding and passionate open trumpet solo by Williams, the main sections of which are introduced by thrilling breaks for the saxophone section, now led by the altos. Cootie's open horn has rarely been heard to better effect, while Greer is at his most explosive. In the third chorus, Bigard's clarinet is heard playing against the trombone section, while the final chorus again features Williams, now muted, and then Bigard against a thrilling full band climax in which the original riff is now heard in the saxes.

While *Harlem Air Shaft* has long been recognized as one of Ellington's masterpieces, the next title has been unduly neglected. This is a non-Ellington popular song called *At A Dixie Roadside Diner*, with a vocal by Anderson. The reason that this fine performance—and the Ellington band really does make something out of a trifle here—has been neglected is that it is a recording of a popular song. While jazz fashion allows that small groups or soloists can make great music out of popular songs, there has always been a prejudice against a big band, even one of the caliber of Ellington's, playing popular material. This is probably an echo of the reaction against the pop rubbish served up in vast quantities by some groups—but not Duke's—during the big band era. The virtues of *At A Dixie Roadside Diner* are the straightforward ones of a simple but effective arrangement and a performance of maximum swing. Despite the banal lyrics, Ivie's vocal is good, and Stewart and Carney have excellent solos. But the highlight is the playing of the band, especially the rhythm section. This is one of the most swinging of all Ellington records. The next title is an Ellington ballad, *All Too Soon*, which has no vocal but on which first Brown and then Webster embroider and elaborate the melody in highly lyrical fashion. Webster's solo is one of the definitive ballad statements on tenor sax. The final item, *Rumpus In Richmond*, is perhaps slightly below the standard of the other three but still an admirable and original piece of big band jazz. Bigard and Brown are heard from, but Williams, muted and vehement, makes the major solo contribution.

Two days later the band was back in the Victor studios for a session which produced two titles only. The first is a non-Ellington popular song, *My Greatest Mistake*, in an arrangement which sounds very simple on the surface but contains many subtleties; the orchestration sounds like the work of Strayhorn. The soloists are Carney, Webster, and Brown. The second title is *Sepia Panorama*, an Ellington masterpiece which fits a tight formal structure into the slightly more than three minutes of a 10-inch 78. Three themes are introduced at the outset: a twelve-bar blues with breaks by Blanton, an eight-bar passage repeated twice with solo insets for Tizol and Williams, and a second eight-bar theme which has Carney playing a strong countermelody against the brass. The middle section is made up of two twelve-bar blues choruses, a piano-bass duet by Ellington and Blanton in the first, and a solo by Webster in the second. The original orchestral montage is then recapitulated in reverse order to provide a perfect conclusion. Two takes of *Sepia Panorama* have been issued and show great differences both in the solos and in the piano part. Not only are the piano-bass duet and the tenor sax solo improvised, as one would have expected, but so too are the parts for Williams and Carney in the ensembles. The vital importance of improvisation in Ellington's music can be clearly heard in a comparison of these two takes. The light they throw on *Sepia Panorama* also makes it clear why a band of jazz masters was absolutely essential to Ellington's artistic purpose.

The next Ellington recording date was not until September 5, 1940. This session opens with a non-Ellington popular song, *There Shall Be No Night*, which has a long and rather dreary vocal by Herb Jeffries, offset by some characteristic scoring; Webster is the soloist. Next comes a straightforward Ellington swinger which has become a standard for improvising jazz groups, *In A Mellotone*. This is a recasting of *Rose Room* into a swing era riff format. The riffing takes the form of a dialog between the Carney-led saxophones and the trombones with Brown in the lead. The solos by Williams and Hodges are notable for the way in which Ellington has built them into the overall conception. The orchestral parts, as always in this kind of Ellington score, are vitally important. The conception and execution of the saxophone parts during Williams's solo are of great brilliance. The whole performance is taken at a rocking medium tempo. If a hint of the Lunceford kind of swing is heard here, it becomes wholly manifest on the next title, a non-Ellington pop song, *Five O'Clock Whistle*. This is given an arrangement very much in the Lunceford manner with a vocal by Anderson and lots of Stewart cornet. It is a humorous performance, inclined to irritate the more solemn members of the jazz-collecting fraternity, who fail to realize that it is a finely turned-out piece of writing and a performance of great swing and verve. Also from this session come the first two takes of the Hodges feature, *Warm Valley*. These were not issued for many years and are studies for the approved and issued masterpiece of October 17. The second of the two September takes has an extra eight bars in the form of a beautiful passage for the saxophone section which does not appear on the other Victor recordings. The inspiration for this piece came from Ellington observing the contours of some hills during a train journey. To him, they looked like a reclining woman "unashamedly exposing her warm valley." The mood is appropriately sensual and Hodges the ideal soloist. There is also a muted Wallace Jones solo, which on some versions extends into an obbligato to garnish the succeeding ensemble.

* * *

From September 6 to October 24, 1940, the band was resident in the Panther Room of Chicago's Hotel Sherman, a venue from which it made frequent broadcasts. Many of these were recorded, and some items have been issued on LP in sound quality ranging from moderate to poor. The versions of *Sepia Panorama* and *Concerto For Cootie* from September 6 have several fascinating differences of detail compared with the studio recordings. From the following day's broadcast, *Stompy Jones* and *In A Mellotone* are particularly fine, while the incomplete *St. Louis Blues* gives an appetizing preview of the November Fargo version. *April In Paris*, featuring the Hardwick-led saxophones and Brown, and *Whispering Grass*, featuring Hodges, are among the unexpected numbers to be heard, while the versions of *Ring Dem Bells* from these broadcasts offer a last opportunity to hear Williams's later thoughts on his famous solo.

There is a pair of LPs on the Jazz Supreme label which contains 39 items from these broadcasts, most of which are not available elsewhere. Many of the titles are incomplete (some mere fragments) and the sound is poor, but the opportunity to hear this great band in an extended portion of its repertoire is not to be missed. Early pieces like *Black Beauty* (a piano solo), *The Mystery Song,* and *Echoes Of Harlem* rub shoulders with music from the late thirties and 1940, such as *Tootin' Through The Roof, Slap Happy, Solid Old Man, Subtle Lament, The Sergeant Was Shy, Bojangles, Blue Goose, Harlem Air Shaft, Ko Ko,* and *Cotton Tail*, plus the versions of *Sepia Panorama* and *In A Mellotone* already mentioned. There is also a good selection of current popular tunes and standards—both Ellington and non-Ellington in each case. The only reason why none of these items is cited among *Outstanding Recordings* at the end of this chapter is the sound quality; musically all are superb.

* * *

Duke Ellington used his next Victor session, of October 1, to show off the talents of his remarkable bassist Jimmy Blanton in a series of piano-bass duets. Four titles were recorded—a whimsical stride piano piece called *Pitter Panther Patter*; two ballads, *Body And Soul* and *Sophisticated Lady*; and the medium-tempo *Mr. J.B. Blues*. In the French RCA *Integrale* edition of Ellington's Victor recordings, two takes of each title are included. In the course of these duets Blanton not only demonstrates his virtuosity on pizzicato bass but also shows considerable mastery with the bow. On each of the ballads, he plays a full-chorus arco followed by a half-chorus pizzicato, and on *Mr. J.B. Blues*, he plays two choruses with the bow. The second take of *Mr. J.B. Blues* is not only very different from the well-known first take, but is arguably the finest of all these duets, with a particularly brilliant display from Blanton. On the whole, Ellington takes a secondary role here, although his playing is always apt and full of color, not least on *Pitter Panther Patter*, where the two instruments take equal parts in a joyous, effervescent performance. After decades of hearing bassists play in the Blanton-inspired style of later jazz, including some who have excelled their mentor in speed of execution, it is difficult for a listener to realize just how revolutionary Blanton's innovations were in his day. But one need only compare his work with that of any contemporary bassist—easy enough to do on records—to begin to fully grasp the impact Blanton had on his fellow musicians. When Jimmy first joined the Ellington band he played alongside Billy Taylor in one of Duke's two-bassist combinations. After a few nights, Taylor turned to Duke, said, "I'm not going to stand up here next to that young boy playing all that bass and be embarrassed," and left both the stand and the band. Taylor was at that time one of the best and most respected bassists in jazz.

* * *

On the October 17 session for the full band, the standard take of *Warm Valley* was recorded. From the viewpoint of Hodges's playing, this is the best of the three studio recordings. Three takes were also made—all on this one date—of *The Flaming Sword*, a rather surprising Latin American variation on *Stompy Jones*. This is a lighthearted romp with solos by Williams, Bigard, Tizol, and Nanton; in this instance, the existence of three takes adds little to our knowledge or enjoyment of the piece. On October 28 the full band entered the recording studio for the last time with the classic 1940 personnel. Another masterpiece opened the session—*Across The Track Blues*. This must rate among Ellington's greatest achievements in the blues idiom. The form of the piece develops naturally and organically, and at the conclusion one can see that the superbly imaginative handling of orchestral color plays a vital part in achieving so balanced a whole. Bigard, Stewart, and Brown are the soloists, Blanton and Ellington have important roles, and the ensemble plays magnificently. In *Across The Track Blues*, the two takes are interesting for the variations in the solos, but there can be little doubt that the first, used on 78 issues, is the superior reading of the score.

The arrangement of *Chloe* which follows seems rather

stagey and contrived by comparison, but it is a colorful and well-balanced piece of Strayhorn writing. Having Nanton deliver the melody in his wa-wa style is perhaps a rather obvious idea—albeit one realized with mastery—but later there are subtle uses of orchestral color and good solo spots from Bigard, Williams, Brown and—more crucially—Blanton and Webster. The session concludes with an Ellington pop tune which had been recorded for Columbia the previous year—*I Never Felt This Way Before*. Although this version starts (with a variation on the *Mood Indigo* trumpet-trombone-clarinet voicing) in the same way as the earlier recording, Ellington has in fact totally remodeled the song. The arrangement is excellent, and there are solo contributions from Webster, Tizol, Williams, and Brown, but the vocal by Jeffries is maudlin, sentimental, and faintly grotesque.

* * *

During the first part of this new Victor contract, the pattern of recording small-group sessions for the subsidiary label (in this case Bluebird) was continued. On November 2, 1940, the Hodges and Stewart units were in the studio. Hodges led his usual group of Williams, Brown, Carney, Ellington, Blanton, and Greer in four numbers. Strayhorn's *Day Dream* is a tone poem specifically written for Hodges, and for the first time we hear him indulging in the long glissandi and ultralanguorous phrasing which became so characteristic of his ballad playing from this time on. Some listeners feel that this style exceeds the boundaries of good taste, but the control of Hodges's playing and the sure sense of musical purpose of the works written for him by Strayhorn and Ellington in this style rule out any suspicion of cheap sentimentalism. *Day Dream* is a perfectly realized miniature, almost classical in its statuesque poise, and Strayhorn's melody is of particular beauty.

The two jump numbers from the session, *Good Queen Bess* and *Junior Hop*, are among the finest recordings by the Ellington units, definitive examples of the small-band Hodges jump style. The leader's alto provides solos of perfect balance and exciting swing. At this period Hodges had attained that command of his instrument which caused his fellow saxophonists to regard him as one of the greatest masters. The execution is perfect, down to the smallest nuance, and the tone incomparably rich and opulent. Williams and Brown, the latter using a felt hat as mute, are also heard in *Good Queen Bess*, of which two takes have been issued. The fourth title, *That's The Blues, Old Man*, is another classic of small-group Ellingtonia. This is the last recording on which Hodges is heard on soprano sax, and he and Williams provide superlative blues solos in the framework of a straightforward arrangement, enhanced by Ellington's thoughtful piano.

The Stewart group—no longer his 52nd Street Stompers, but now simply his Orchestra—consists of Brown, Webster, Carney, and the same three-piece rhythm section used by Hodges. *Without A Song* is a beautifully subtle arrangement from a melodic point of view with Stewart, tightly muted, and Carney the soloists. Ellington provides another highly melodic ballad for Rex's cornet in *My Sunday Gal*, which receives a performance recalling the delights of *Morning Glory*. *Mobile Bay* is the blues, with Rex's commanding, dramatic horn dominating the proceedings. His imperious work is perfectly set off by an ultrarelaxed tenor solo in Webster's best blues vein. The final title is the old standard *Linger Awhile*, on which Strayhorn takes over on piano from Duke and contributes a solo chorus. There are further solos by Webster and Brown (the latter notably fine), and plenty of Rex's incisive, swinging cornet. Both *My Sunday Gal* and *Linger Awhile* have brief, functional solo passages by Carney on alto sax; it is unusual to find him playing this instrument as late as this, and these are the last alto solos he recorded. Alternative takes exist of *Without A Song*, *Mobile Bay*, and *Linger Awhile*; they are well worth hearing for the considerable differences in the solos. In particular, the two takes of *Mobile Bay* are very different, especially in Ellington's crucial piano part.

This is a classic session with eight titles of superb small-group Ellingtonia. It was recorded in Chicago and after it ended, the musicians went on to play a one-night stand with the full Orchestra. When the gig was over, the band parted company with Williams, who was leaving to join Benny Goodman. His solo on the Hodges *That's The Blues, Old Man* was his last with the Ellingtonians for over twenty years. Cootie's departure marked the end of an era for the Ellington band, just as Bubber Miley's had done eleven years earlier.

Outstanding Recordings

1. By the Full Band—Studio Recordings

Jack The Bear, Ko-Ko, Morning Glory, Congo Brava, Concerto For Cootie, Me And You, Cotton Tail, Never No Lament, Dusk, Bojangles (both standard and rejected takes), *A Portrait Of Bert Williams, Blue Goose, Harlem Air Shaft, At A Dixie Roadside Diner, All Too Soon, Sepia Panorama* (both takes), *In A Mellotone, Five O'Clock Whistle, Warm Valley,* and *Across The Track Blues* (both takes)

2. By the Full Band—Broadcast

The complete BBC broadcast of June 12, 1940

3. Duets with Jimmy Blanton

Pitter Panther Patter and both takes of *Mr J.B. Blues*

4. The Contingents

a. Johnny Hodges: *Day Dream, Good Queen Bess* (both takes), *That's The Blues, Old Man,* and *Junior Hop*

b. Rex Stewart: *Without A Song* (both takes), *My Sunday Gal, Mobile Bay* (both takes), and *Linger Awhile* (both takes)

Chapter 13

1940—An Artistic Peak

IN THE BLACK BIG BANDS OF THE EARLY FORTIES the absence of academic training among most of the musicians was still an important factor. Academic tuition is designed to produce a standardized approach so that trained players will sound sufficiently alike; the composer in European art music would be placed at a great disadvantage if he did not know within rather strict limits how the various instruments would be played. There were no such restrictions on instrumental approach to limit the young jazz musicians of the twenties and thirties. Indeed there was quite a strong pull in the opposite direction from the achievements, both musical and financial, of the previous generation of jazzmen—especially the New Orleans players, such as King Oliver, Sidney Bechet, Louis Armstrong, and Jimmy Noone.

The absence of standardized tuition among the early generations of jazz musicians resulted in a wide variety of highly personalized techniques. A trumpet player for instance, might adopt an "incorrect" embouchure which would yield an unusually rich tone in the lower and middle registers of the instrument but caused doubtful command in the higher. Such a player could exploit the possibilities of the lower registers of the instrument as a soloist, and, provided his musicianship was good enough to hold a second or third chair in a trumpet section, his technical limitations would be neither apparent nor a handicap. This situation produced several generations of highly individual stylists, and indeed the playing of most musicians from these generations is instantly recognizable to the informed listener. In the late thirties and early forties the standard of jazz musicianship as judged by the academic yardstick continued to rise, but at first there was no apparent reduction in the individuality of the new soloists coming into the bands. Earl Bostic, Jimmy Blanton, Charlie Christian, and Charlie Parker were examples of brilliant musicians who came into jazz toward the end of the big band era. Their outstanding craftsmanship was that of men who had forged their own musical identities. It was on this kind of diversity that the Duke Ellington Orchestra was based, and Ellington himself was always exceptionally wary of the academy. When Ben Webster was thinking of enrolling at the Juilliard School of Music to study theory, Ellington advised him against it, much to Ben's chagrin. Later Webster came to agree that Ellington had been right, and that such study might have acted against his natural way of music making.

In addition to the featured soloists, the big bands also contained the more journeyman-type of musician—good, solid section men, usually better readers than the soloists, and often more reliable and less temperamental. Some leaders preferred this type of personality and would keep the number of volatile jazz stars to a minimum. But among the black bands, even the most commercial group would need some jazz soloists, since they were considered an integral part of any such band. Typical of the less jazz-oriented black bands was that of Noble Sissle. Such a group could get by with only a few hot soloists, and it seems ironic that it was Sissle who employed that most volatile of all jazz personalities, Sidney Bechet.

* * *

Sissle's orchestra was more a stage band than a dance band, and much of its repertoire consisted of vaudeville numbers featuring his vocalists. These were relieved by occasional band numbers and features of a rather showy nature for an instrumentalist, often Bechet. In the big bands styled for dancing, the strong rhythmic qualities of the jazz musician and his ability to extend numbers by improvised solos were important assets. In 1940, two of the most popular bands of this kind among black dancers were those of Jimmie Lunceford and Chick Webb. Lunceford's soloists were generally used in short, functional passages and the arrangements often featured the band's outstanding saxophone section. The Sy Oliver arrangements used by Lunceford were often complex but had the virtue of extreme lucidity, so that the audience was never puzzled by and rarely aware of their complexity. This band featured many popular songs and made extensive use of vocalists; but the intrinsic jazz qualities of its playing and of Oliver's scores resulted in a music vastly different from that made by nonjazz bands using a similar repertoire. The Webb band was resident at the Savoy Ballroom in Harlem. Its playing was looser, the arrangements more simple, and the soloists were given more room than Lunceford's. It swung just as powerfully, however, and one of the prime reasons for this was Webb himself, one of the great drummers in jazz history. Though musicians of the caliber of trumpeter Taft Jordan and trombonist Sandy Williams were regular members of the band, Webb did not rival Henderson, Basie, or Ellington in solo strength.

The Basie orchestra was the newest of the important black bands. It was much more of a soloists' group and more rooted in the blues than either Lunceford's or Webb's. The records from the Basie band's first years often feature a succession of brilliant solos within a spare orchestral framework. The effect is much like that of classical drama; each major actor steps forth to say his piece, with only occasional dialogue or interpolations from the chorus. Basie's band is often considered the heir to Fletcher Henderson's, which had a reputation for a similar kind of music making—outside the recording studios. Unfortunately, Henderson's records only rarely hint at this aspect of his band's work. As the Basie band matured, it too became more dependent on its arrangers, though these never became as important as Henderson's or Lunceford's.

The band Basie led in the late thirties has been said to contain the most brilliant group of soloists ever to play together regularly in a big jazz band: Buck Clayton and Harry Edison on trumpets; Dickie Wells and Benny Morton on trombones; Lester Young and Herschel Evans on tenor saxes. And there was the leader's piano, often underrated by critics as a solo voice. Basie could also call upon players like alto saxophonist Earl Warren and Jack Washington on baritone sax for a chorus of character and substance. Yet even with this powerful solo phalanx, Basie could not surpass Ellington in solo strength. In 1940, the Ellington band had Cootie Williams on trumpet and Rex Stewart on cornet, Tricky Sam Nanton and Lawrence Brown on trombone, and four world-class reed soloists in Barney Bigard, Johnny Hodges, Ben Webster, and Harry Carney. Here, too, the leader's piano was a voice of unique power, and Ellington could also call on Wallace Jones, Juan Tizol, and Jimmy Blanton for solos of a distinction quite beyond the capacity, ambitions, or opportunities of their Basie counterparts. Even Basie's celebrated rhythm section was not superior on all counts to the Ellington quartet—more consistent as a team, certainly, but with a narrower range and not as rich in individual character.

By 1940, these two groups had established themselves as the finest of all big bands. They continued to lead the field for the next thirty years, and more. The contrast between Ellington's band of 1940 and Basie's at its slightly earlier peak of 1937 to 1939 is striking and instructive. The Basie soloists step forward onto an almost bare stage and deliver their choruses against a utility backdrop of standard chord patterns. Almost all the great instrumental Basie records of this period are of this kind—for example *Honeysuckle Rose, One O'-Clock Jump, Out The Window, Every Tub, Swinging The Blues, Doggin' Around,* and *Texas Shuffle.* The Ellington soloists often improvised on similar basic chord progressions, but these would be used as parts of a more complex overall structure—compare the context of Webster's solo in *Sepia Panorama* or Cootie's in *Harlem Air Shaft* with those of Basie's tenor and trumpet soloists on any recordings from the period. And of course the orchestral accompaniments to the Ellington solos would vary from a sparseness reminiscent of Basie's to an opulence which never became obtrusive because of Ellington's genius for providing backgrounds perfectly tailored to the soloists' requirements. That Ellington's soloists played with the same relaxation and freedom as Basie's while contributing to a music vastly more complex was largely due to the atmosphere of freedom and creative involvement which Duke encouraged in his band.

Ellington's soloists were musical characters who contrasted with each other in much the same way as Basie's. Both Williams and Stewart were strong individualists who played with great passion and commitment; both habitually played with a rhythmic intensity that gave the Ellington trumpet section much of its remarkable vitality. Yet there is a great contrast between the brooding passion of much of Cootie's work and the frisky, skipping wit found in many of Rex's solos. The best illustrations of this contrast in musical temperaments can be found in the chase choruses on the various versions of *Tootin' Through The Roof.* In addition to these two, Ellington also had Wallace Jones on hand for the occasional more straightforward solo contribution.

The trombones showed even greater variation. Nanton was the "primitive" voice in the band and an unchanging reminder of its traditions and past glories. His voice often speaks more intimately to the listener than those of the other actors in the drama. During the thirties and forties, almost all of Nanton's solos were played with the plunger mute, but this was no limitation in his case. He was an artist of many moods, driving in *Jack The Bear*, laconic in *Hip Chic*, droll in *A Portrait Of Bert Williams*, and rousing in *Sidewalks Of New York*. Tizol was employed as soloist in the theme statements of the exotic Latin American specialities (often his own creations) but the other remaining trombone solos were taken by Brown, a highly versatile musician. Equally at home with smooth ballad theme statements, driving uptempo improvisations or slow blues choruses, he brought to all these a highly personal flavor.

The reed section offers still greater contrast. On the one hand there is Bigard, with his adaptation of the traditional New Orleans clarinet style to big band music; on the other there is Webster, one of the master tenor saxophone players and a very "modern" musician in 1940. Hodges was at the peak of his form and his alto and soprano work was flexible enough to fit perfectly into all the varied musical situations provided by Ellington. Carney's baritone playing was particularly magnificent at this time. Clearly inspired by the arrival of Webster, his work seems to have acquired a new dimension of rhythmic potency. Most of the section lead work was by Hardwick on alto, seldom a soloist by this time, but a man who gave the reeds a unique lightness of texture.

To back up this all-star roster of soloists the rhythm team of Ellington, Guy, Blanton, and Greer was close to ideal. On the 1940 recordings, Duke is unsurpassed as a band pianist, adding to the flavor and the substance of the music. Guy was a reliable player, but by this time the rhythm guitar had to some extent become superfluous in the band. We have discussed Blanton's contribution at some length, but in addition to his remarkable innovations, Blanton was a superb section player who always provided the most solid rhythmic and harmonic foundation. Greer, too, made a positive contribution: his use of cymbals, tom-toms, and percussive accessories as coloristic devices should not obscure the rhythmic potency of his best playing. One need only note the vital contributions made by Greer's drumming to *Harlem Air Shaft* and *At A Dixie Roadside Diner* to appreciate what a swinger he could be. He was loud at times, but this could be a very loud, shouting band. Before criticizing Ellington drummers for loud playing, a listener should remember Jo Jones's observation. When pressed on why he had declined Ellington's invitation to join the band, Jones remarked that "the drummer sits right next to that brass section, and that brass section hits him right in the stomach night after night and kills him." Clearly the Ellington band needed something other than the subtle, light touch which Jones so wonderfully brought to Basie.

In addition to this array of talent, Ellington had the services of Billy Strayhorn, an arranger of the first rank and also a fine pianist, and singers Herb Jeffries and Ivie Anderson. In the vocal category, though, Duke had to concede to Basie. For all of Ivie's qualities, Duke could not excel the Basie combination of Jimmy Rushing and first Billie Holiday, then Helen Humes. In the blues numbers featuring Rushing the Basie band reached its greatest heights. Ellington played the blues too, not just in a straightforward way, but expanding the tradition by using the blues language in an original, creative manner. The Basie band approached the blues in a straight, unvarnished fashion, and at this kind of blues playing they were unequaled in the late thirties and remained so for many decades to come.

* * *

The solo resources and the quality of ensemble playing the individuals brought to the band are only two aspects of the musical magnificence of this particular edition of the Ellington Orchestra. Equally important is the quality of the music they were called upon to play. In 1940, Duke produced a series of scores which equaled or surpassed the very best in his previous output. One of the features of Ellington's writing in 1940 is its tremendous melodic richness, a point sometimes overlooked by those who admire other attributes of the music. The thirties had established Duke as one of the leading American popular song writers, and if there is one thing at which such writers excel it is melody. In this, Ellington was a fully representative member of the school. Ellington's melodies are not just superb in themselves but also allow a jazz musician to make his instrument sing in a ravishing way—as, for example, Hodges on *Never No Lament* or Williams on *Concerto For Cootie*, both of which became hit songs for Ellington, respectively as *Don't Get Around Much Anymore* and *Do Nothin' Till You Hear From Me*. With Ellington, such melodies always seem perfectly designed for the musicians to whom they are entrusted—note how the principal theme of *Bojangles* is ideal for a Carney-led saxophone section, the opening melody of *Across The Track Blues* for Bigard's solo clarinet.

Harmonically, Ellington was very much his own man. He created some remarkable harmonic effects, but these were so bound up with his voicings and his mixtures of instrumental sounds that they were rarely innovations which other musicians could readily use. The bitonality of *Ko-Ko* is very effective, although, like much jazz harmony, it is elementary when compared with the use of that device in modern European concert music. Nonetheless, the use Ellington makes of harmonic resources is highly skilled and highly personal. His deployment of such musicians as Carney and Tizol as important inner voices has been noted on some of the earlier records, and this technique was developed to new degrees of subtlety in the early forties. Throughout the 1940 records there are countless delights of this kind to be relished in the scoring, both in band passages and in those unerringly apt backings for the soloists. Scores like *Congo Brava*, *Dusk*, *A Portrait Of Bert Williams*, *Blue Goose*, and *Sepia Panorama* reveal the resources of the band in terms of tone color: the different voice leadings in the sections, the subtle use of muted brass, of the clarinets, and of Ellington's famous mixtures of instruments and of personalities.

Among the outstanding qualities of these Ellington scores is their formal perfection, all the more remarkable when one considers the degree of improvisation going on in the band, and that many of the arrangements were tailored to fit the three-minute duration of the 10-inch 78 record. The economy of this music is another related attribute—not one note seems superfluous and every part adds something vital to the whole. The remarkable insight of the band into Ellington's creative processes is one of the reasons for this; the musicians could quickly adjust to any changes in an arrangement for the purpose of recording just as they could to the changes wrought outside the studio by the continuous state of flux in which Ellington kept many of his compositions. *Jack The Bear*, *Ko-Ko*, *Concerto For Cootie*, *Dusk*, *Bojangles*, *A Portrait Of Bert Williams*, *Harlem Air Shaft*, *Sepia Panorama*, and *Across The Track Blues*, to make but a brief selection, are truly remarkable for the amount of music they pack into their three-minute or so duration as well as for their beautifully judged formal balance.

Most of the compositions recorded for Victor in 1940 also exist in versions from broadcasts, concerts, or dances to which the three-minute time limit did not apply. Often an arrangement is extended by doubling the duration of the solos (e.g. *Bojangles* and *Sepia Panorama*), yet the concentration and economy of the scores is just as obvious here as in the shorter studio versions.

As we consider the masterpieces of the 1940 band, it becomes more and more obvious why Duke hired artists of character for his band rather than the solid journeyman musicians who might at first glance seem more suitable for a composer's purpose. Ellington had found strong musical personalities essential, because he used solos as building blocks within his compositions. He needed imaginative musicians who could respond to his promptings without needing every note or phrase spelled out in notation. Such artists are usually temperamental, and the personal relationships within the Ellington band were not always the happiest. The musicians got on well with Duke, but there was a good deal of internal dissension. Sometimes musicians did not speak to each other for months—in some cases for years—and the "nice guys" in the band, like Tizol and Carney, were often used as go-betweens in such matters as invitations to partake in the small-group sessions. Collectively, the band could be very hard on a newcomer, treating him, as Mercer Ellington has put it, like "a total slob" if he did not at once pick up on the eccentric musical procedures developed by the Ellingtonians. By tact, by refusing to get involved in or upset by the tempests created by his musicians, Duke held the band together. What he had wrought was something totally new—a collection of highly talented musicians led by a genius, playing, for the most part, dance hall and hotel engagements. It is unlikely that the world will ever see its like again.

As a specific illustration of why Ellington needed musicians of such caliber we might consider again the two takes of *Sepia Panorama*. We have seen that such vital parts of the compositional whole as Williams's short solos and Carney's countermelody to the brass are in fact improvised. During the years when only the originally issued take was known, these parts were held to be scored. Now we know that Williams and Carney were able, at Ellington's prompting, to create parts which were perfectly apt for their context and indeed as good as those any arranger—even Ellington himself—could have written. That musicians would so quickly and readily lend their full creative and imaginative powers to building parts of Ellington's structures speaks eloquently for how well he had built his band. One reason why Ellington was so prolific a composer was that he could communicate, in a kind of shorthand, musical details so complex that any other organization would have required them in full score, before careful rehearsal.

The harmonic basis of the jazz of this period allowed for a degree of development of tonal and melodic devices not possible in the more chromatic and harmonically fast-moving later styles. The grammar of this instrumental/melodic idiom was based on the language of Afro-American folk music in general and the blues in particular. In the work of the great jazz soloists, this musical style allowed for a concentration of emotional and expressive power which at its best renders their work among the most concentrated pieces of musical expression in existence. Ellington always employed masters of this kind of playing and carried over into his writing for the band the same kind of concentration. This made his three-minute 78 recordings wonders of artistic eloquence.

Sidemen

Herb Jeffries

Jazz enthusiasts have not, on the whole, approved of Duke Ellington's vocalists, particularly the males. The first specialist male singer Ellington employed was Herb Jeffries and his work with the band contains many of the negative qualities of his successors. He is a sentimental and at times excessively melodramatic singer; his pitching is not always secure and his vocal ornamentation often bizarre. Jeffries' style is wholly that of a ballad singer. But *Flamingo* was one of Ellington's biggest hit records.

Representative Recordings: My Last Goodbye To You (broadcast, 1940), *You, You Darlin'* (Victor, 1940), *Flamingo* (Victor, 1940)

Ben Webster

One of the great masters of the tenor sax, Webster was at the peak of his powers during his stay with Ellington from February 1940 to August 1943. An admirer of Ellington's music for many years, he had long wanted to become a member of the band. Twice in the thirties, Ben had deputized for Bigard and both times had been retained after Barney's return long enough to participate in a record session. He fitted in perfectly from the day he joined the band and created a tenor sax tradition later carried on by Paul Gonsalves and Harold Ashby—both Webster disciples. Ben himself was inspired by Coleman Hawkins, and his melodic language also reflected great admiration for Benny Carter. In his mature years, Webster's tone was softer than Hawkins's and was combined with a highly lyrical and sensitive melodic style. He recorded extensively in the thirties with the big bands of Bennie Moten, Willie Bryant, Fletcher Henderson, Cab Calloway, and Teddy Wilson, as well as with many small pick-up groups including some organized by Wilson. On joining Ellington he at once became one of the band's major soloists, and his effect on the saxophone section was remarkable and wholly beneficial. After three and a half years, Webster left and from then on worked mostly with small groups. He returned to Ellington for ten months in 1948–1949, again making an important contribution. Up to his death in 1973, Ben remained one of the established masters of the tenor sax. His later LP recordings with small groups allowed him to stretch out, and as a result the concise character of his solos of the 1940–1943 period was sometimes lost. Although he worked with Ellington for less than five years in all, Ben Webster is always thought of as a major Ellingtonian, and this reflects the magnitude of his contribution.

Representative Recordings: Congo Brava (Victor, 1940), *Cotton Tail* (Victor, 1940), *All Too Soon* (Victor, 1940), *Sepia Panorama* (Victor, both takes, and Fargo, 1940), *I Hear A Rhapsody* (Standard Transcriptions, 1940), *Just A-Settin' And A-Rockin'* (Victor, 1941)

Chapter 14

The Records—November 1940 to December 1942

AFTER COOTIE WILLIAMS HAD PLAYED HIS LAST DATE with the band, it had to make do for four nights with just two trumpets. On November 7, Ellington played a dance at the Crystal Ballroom in Fargo, North Dakota, at which Cootie's replacement made his debut. This was Ray Nance, a little-known musician at the time, though he had been with Earl Hines and Horace Henderson and led his own groups in Chicago. Nance doubled trumpet and violin and also sang and danced, and his versatility soon earned him the nickname "Floorshow"; he brought a new dimension to the band's performances with his humorous singing and cavorting. Underneath the clowning, however, Nance was a deeply serious musician with a poten-

tial obviously perceived by Ellington. The Fargo date is also important because virtually all of it was recorded by two local Ellington enthusiasts, Dick Burris and Jack Towers. These recordings were later issued and now stand as one of the most vital documents in the history of the Ellington Orchestra.

The band had traveled to Fargo from Winnipeg, Canada, where they had played a concert in the Civic Auditorium the previous night, and the musicians were rather tired. This, allied to the unsettled state of the trumpet section, perhaps served to enhance the untidiness characteristic of the Ellington band outside the recording studio. Burris and Towers were using a single acetate disc cutter, so there are breaks in the recording, sometimes during the course of a performance. The initial LP issues of the Fargo material were in very poor sound and sequenced out of performance order. More recently, the music has been issued on recordings made directly from the original acetates, revealing that the sound-quality is exceptionally good, considering the circumstances under which the two engineers were working. In addition to containing the most relaxed music recorded by the great 1940 Ellington ensemble, the Fargo discs give an invaluable insight into the repertoire the band used on its dance dates.

The first set was played without Ellington—the normal procedure at dances—and consisted of three of the band's vintage scores—*It's A Glory*, *The Mooche*, and *The Sheik of Araby*. Of these, only *The Mooche* was recorded complete, and it is fascinating to hear this 1928 composition played by the 1940 Ellington band. The interpretation has great vitality, with Stewart handling the plunger-muted obbligato to the first theme and Bigard's clarinet in counterpoint against the second. The soloists are Hodges and Nanton, who "sing" the blues in their contrasting yet equally authoritative ways. Brown spices the second theme with a little tailgate trombone, and there is more of the same on the fragment of *It's A Glory*. Again comparison with the original version is fascinating, especially so as the 1931 recording is the only other extant. Similarly, the 1932 arrangement of *The Sheik of Araby* is known only from the studio version and this incomplete recording of eight years later. Brown, Hodges, and Webster are heard from, but the introduction is missing and the recording is badly damaged, with most of Hodges's solo lost and much of Webster's distorted.

This short set is followed by a much longer one in which fourteen numbers are performed. Ellington is at the piano from the start, which coincides with the beginning of a half-hour broadcast over the local radio station, KVOX. A short version of *Sepia Panorama* is used as signature tune, followed by *Ko-Ko*, taken at the faster tempo and with the principal solos by Nanton and Blanton. Then Jeffries, well away from the recording mike, sings *There Shall Be No Night*, which also has brief solo spots by Wallace Jones and Webster. This is followed by a version of *Pussy Willow*, which is one of the most swinging Ellington performances ever caught on record. It has all the advantages of a live performance—an easy relaxation permeates the music, and there is a tangible and electrifying rapport with the audience. The rhythm section is in outstanding form, Greer refuting magnificently the claims that he was not a swinging drummer. After Duke has set the tempo and the mood, Nance, Hodges, and Blanton solo and there is some superb Bigard clarinet, especially in the passage played against the saxophone section in the final chorus. Next come two showcases, *Chatterbox*, featuring Stewart, and *Mood Indigo*, featuring Jones. On this evening, Stewart took over all the Cootie Williams solos except those on *Sepia Panorama* and *Pussy Willow*, and it is a measure of his stature as a musician that he was able to do so with success in addition to playing his own assigned solo spots. On *Harlem Air Shaft*, Rex is heard in a characteristic vein in a vigorous performance set up by a stimulating piano introduction. Ivie Anderson sings *Ferryboat Serenade*, a current pop number, and Hodges is heard in a long, sumptuous version of *Warm Valley*, in the course of which the radio announcer can be heard in the background bidding his listening audience farewell. *Stompy Jones*, *Chloe*, and a dancing *Bojangles* (with two choruses from Webster instead of the single one of the studio recording) lead up to an Ellington piece not recorded on any other occasion. Duke calls it *On The Air*, and it combines the melody of *You Took Advantage Of Me* with a riff from the Henry Allen/Fletcher Henderson *Rug Cutter's Swing*. This is another swinging performance with fine ensemble work spiced by contributions from Blanton, Stewart, and Bigard. The second set ends with a performance of *Rumpus In Richmond*, with Stewart again taking over the Williams solo spots.

The third set opens with *Sidewalks Of New York*. A cut occasioned by a change of acetates scarcely dims the historical and aesthetic value of the performance. It is historically important because comparison with the Victor version of December 28 provides a fine example of how Ellington remolded material. After *Sidewalks* and a somewhat perfunctory reading of *The Flaming Sword*, a sequence of feature numbers is presented: *Never No Lament* (Hodges); *Caravan* (Tizol); *Clarinet Lament* (Bigard); *Slap Happy* (Carney); *Sepia Panorama* (Blanton), and *Boy Meets Horn* (Stewart). Although these are showcases for the featured musicians, other soloists are heard from: Ellington and Brown on *Never No Lament*; Bigard and Stewart on *Caravan*; Nanton on *Slap Happy*; and Ellington, Webster, Nance, and Tizol on *Sepia Panorama*.

This version of *Clarinet Lament* is the only one recorded apart from the classic 1936 studio performance, and Bigard is in magnificent form. The *Boy Meets Horn* is one of the finest on record. On *Never No Lament*, Hodges launches patterns of soaring melody, and there is a brilliant pianissimo ending which had been cut from the 78 version due to the time factor. *Sepia Panorama* is magnificent too, with the piano/bass duet and the tenor sax solo twice as long as the studio version, and with vocal encouragement from Ellington in response to Webster's great blues playing. Next, Ivie Anderson takes over for a trio of short numbers—*Way Down Yonder In New Orleans*, *Oh Babe, Maybe Someday*, and *Five O'Clock Whistle*. A second group of vocal numbers, this time featuring Jeffries, is the only part of the dance which was not recorded because Jeffries was too far away from the recording mike for a reasonable sound to be obtained. Since we know that *Call Of The Canyon* and *Heaven Can Wait* were included, it is safe to assume that little of importance was lost.

The fourth set, much shorter, opened with versions of two pieces from the thirties, *Rockin' In Rhythm* and *Sophisticated Lady*, the latter giving Hardwick his only solo of the night. Webster follows with the inevitable *Cotton Tail*, and Hodges makes a lyrical ballad solo out of the then popular song *Whis-

pering Grass. *Congo Brava*, which follows, uses the same routine as the earlier studio recording, as does the version of *I Never Felt This Way Before* (vocal by Jeffries) with which the set ends.

The next set is shorter still. It opens with a wonderful extended version of *Across The Track Blues* in which all the solos are double the length of those on the studio recording. Bigard, Stewart, and Brown are all magnificent, responding brilliantly to the challenge of the extra solo choruses. Next are two numbers featuring newcomer Ray Nance, *Honeysuckle Rose* (on which he is heard on violin) and *Wham* (which features him as vocalist). Both find the bass less than fully prepared. *Honeysuckle* is a kind of jam session with Ellington's two opening choruses accompanied by an assortment of comments from the horns. *Wham* is either a head arrangement or a first readthrough of a stock. Both performances are redeemed, however, by their great spirit and gusto, with Nance inventive on violin and vivacious as vocalist. The swing is immense, with Blanton and Greer at their most effective. The final title from this set is a long improvisation on *Stardust* by Webster—one of the very best ballad solos ever recorded by this master of the art.

The sixth and final set opens with *Rose Of The Rio Grande* featuring Brown and Anderson in a vigorous if untidy runthrough of their famous routine. Then comes the climax of the evening, in the form of a long, exciting, and sometimes hilarious version of *St. Louis Blues*. Ellington and Stewart are heard at the start, followed by a mellow Bigard solo. Ivie wanders away from W. C. Handy's lyrics as she offers some forthright blues shouting. Then Webster comes in with a disorganized but exciting solo, only to be capped by Tricky Sam, who takes over in tremendous style. Gradually the band builds behind Nanton until his becomes the lead voice in what is in effect a collective improvisation for big band, foreshadowing the work of Charles Mingus by some fifteen or sixteen years. The tiredness and the excitement are both telling on the musicians by now, and the playing of the witty coda is very ragged. After this, they go into a quiet *Warm Valley*, which serves as a backdrop to Duke's goodnight speech to the audience, and the music ends with a patriotic *God Bless America*.

Recordings of the Ellington band at dances are rare from any period. To have this virtually complete recording is invaluable. The atmosphere is totally different from that of the recording studio or concert hall, and the ease, relaxation, and swing of the music is immensely impressive. The evening moves naturally to the climax of the long *St. Louis Blues* and the excitement generated by the band as reflected by the dancers and listeners can be sensed. Several of the performances are as fine as anything the Ellington band ever recorded—*Pussy Willow, Harlem Air Shaft, Warm Valley, Bojangles, On The Air, Sidewalks Of New York, Never No Lament, Clarinet Lament, Slap Happy, Sepia Panorama, Boy Meets Horn, Rockin' In Rhythm, Whispering Grass, Across The Track Blues, Stardust*, and *St. Louis Blues* are all classic performances. For all the greatness of the Victor studio recordings of 1940, in many ways the finest Ellington performances of that year are from the Fargo dance date. Dick Burris and Jack Towers certainly did posterity a favor when they captured this music.

* * *

The Ellingtonians concluded their 1940 recording activities with studio sessions in November and December. The first was by the Bigard contingent, on November 11. The unit consisted of Nance, Tizol, Bigard, Webster, Ellington, Blanton, and Greer, and the best of the four titles made are the two Ellington compositions, *Charlie The Chulo* and *A Lull At Dawn*. Bigard is featured heavily on both, and his work is complemented by brief band passages and highly pertinent piano comments. *Charlie The Chulo* is a jump number, with parts of the earlier *Downtown Uproar* incorporated into the arrangement. *A Lull At Dawn* is a gentle tone painting of great melodic beauty. Strayhorn and Bigard wrote *Lament For Javanette*, an exotic confection with a touch of Tizol's valve trombone and one of Webster's greatest solos. Bigard's *Ready Eddy* is arranged by Strayhorn who also plays piano; here Bigard himself is the only soloist. A large number of takes from this session, including incomplete ones, have been issued, and thus one can hear how the numbers were developed. This is particularly rewarding in the case of *A Lull At Dawn*.

* * *

The final 1940 session was by the full band on December 28 and it opens with a masterpiece, Ellington's arrangement of *Sidewalks Of New York*, greatly altered from the version heard on the Fargo date. On that occasion, five choruses of solos and ensemble followed one by Ellington's piano, but here the entire arrangement consists of three choruses and introduction. The routines are as follows:

Introduction
Fargo: piano vamp as recording fades in; one piano chorus, twelve-bar piano vamp behind bass.
Victor: sixteen bars of clarinet breaks alternating with band, a passage not included in the Fargo version.

First Chorus
Fargo: Nanton over saxophones.
Victor: Band with clarinet breaks, same as Fargo third chorus except that the clarinet plays a fuller part.

Second Chorus
Fargo: Blanton bass solo over muted brass figures.
Victor: Nanton over saxophones, as Fargo first chorus.

Third Chorus
Fargo: preceded by a two-bar clarinet passage, then full band with clarinet obbligato.

Victor: Short solos (eight bars each) by Webster, Hodges, Carney, and Bigard over the brass figures heard behind Blanton in the Fargo second chorus. The Victor performance ends with an eight-bar coda for the band not heard on the Fargo version.

Fourth Chorus

Fargo: Tightly muted cornet solo by Stewart over very quiet saxophone accompaniment.

Fifth Chorus

Fargo: Nanton over saxophones. As Fargo first chorus and Victor second chorus, except that Nanton plays a variant solo.

From this breakdown we can see that the pyramid structure of the arrangement in use at the time of the Fargo date, with its two Nanton solos flanking the performance and with the full ensemble chorus used as a central peak, is replaced by an episodic layout in which the ensemble chorus serves as a theme statement and the next two as variations. Blanton's chorus is replaced by one for the four reed soloists, and Rex's solo is eliminated. Yet, for all the radical alterations, the only fresh writing is in the introduction and the coda, both completely new. This kind of remodeling, usually of a less drastic nature, can be found throughout Ellington's recording career. Some numbers change only slightly, but those like *Ring Dem Bells*, which retained exactly the same arrangement over twenty-odd years, are very rare. (And even *Ring Dem Bells* did have a variant reading on the 1930 OKeh recording.) So far as *Sidewalks Of New York* is concerned, the Victor, despite a comparatively weak ending, is an accepted masterpiece. But the Fargo is superior in structure as well as being a performance of tremendous vitality. Even the gap while the engineers change acetates—the last eight bars of the first chorus and the first eight of the second are missing—hardly mars this piece of supreme jazz making.

The second December Victor recording became a hit for the band. It is Strayhorn's arrangement of *Flamingo*, a pop song with lyrics by Edmund Anderson with a long vocal by Herb Jeffries. Strayhorn is on piano here, and his scoring is highly imaginative, though lacking that firmness of texture and structure which Ellington himself brought to popular song arrangements. Brown and a swooning Hodges have brief, insubstantial solos. The third and final item is another popular tune with a Jeffries vocal, here restricted to one chorus. Mercer Ellington's *The Girl In My Dreams Tries To Look Like You* also features a Webster theme statement and a brief Stewart solo.

* * *

In 1941, the number of transcriptions and off-the-air recordings by the Ellington band increased dramatically. Typically, the first session of the year was for Standard Transcriptions, recorded in the Victor studios on January 15. Only two of the titles made were ever done on commercial recording dates and the session is a mine of little-known Ellington music. It also contains some less-than-classic popular material. The opening item is Strayhorn's first instrumental composition for the full orchestra, *Take The "A" Train*. This Henderson-style swing number became another hit for Ellington when recorded for Victor a month later. The piece was designed to feature Williams, Strayhorn no doubt being inspired by Cootie's work in numbers such as *Ridin' On A Blue Note*. But Williams had left by the time the score was ready, and the trumpet part was taken by Ray Nance. He produced a classic solo. It is formed in all essentials on the Standard Transcription performance, although the outline is perhaps fractionally less firm than on the Victor. *Take The "A" Train* was quickly adopted by Ellington as the band's signature tune. Towards the end of 1940 he seems to have decided that *East St. Louis Toodle-oo* no longer projected quite the required contemporary image. For a few months, he alternated this old theme with *Sepia Panorama*, and then, in early 1941, he started to use *Take The "A" Train*. It remained the Ellington signature tune for the rest of the band's life. (The only exception was a series of MBS broadcasts, "The Pastel Period," made in the summer of 1943; for these, Ellington used *Moon Mist* as the opening and closing theme.)

The next number on the Standard Transcription session is *I Hear A Rhapsody*, the first chorus of which is taken up by a typical effusion from Herb Jeffries. It is followed by one of Webster's finest solos, a long and masterly ballad statement. The pattern of scaling down compositions to fit the three-minute 78 would have had to be reversed had the band ever recorded *Bounce* for public release, for this delightful miniature lasts for less than a minute and a half. The title is wholly programmatic and the performance finds room for brief solos by Stewart's tightly muted cornet and Hodges in a laconic vein. Ellington's *It's Sad But True* is an instrumental in ballad style with Brown as featured soloist. The next two numbers are both Latin American popular songs. Each starts off as a rhumba, with Tizol stating the theme, but both *Madame Will Drop Her Shawl* and *Frenesi* change to a straight four-four rhythm before the end, which must have been rather confusing for dancers. Webster solos on both titles, and Stewart is heard on *Frenesi*. The Webster solo on *Madame* is particularly fine. This session offers a profusion of Webster, for on the next item, a ballad called *Until Tonight*, he is featured throughout. *West Indian Stomp* is a medium-tempo number with excellent work from Carney and Ellington and a fine solo from Nanton; this is the sole surviving version of this composition. *Love and I* is a ballad with solos by Stewart, Carney, and Brown built into a skillful arrangement. Finally, there is a version of *John Hardy's Wife*, shorter and less satisfying than the later Victor recording.

* * *

The versions of *Take The "A" Train* and *John Hardy's Wife* which were issued commercially by Victor were recorded on

February 15, 1941. This recording of *Take The "A" Train* was never surpassed by any of the excellent and varied arrangements which the band used over the ensuing years. Nance's trumpet solo is so familiar and established a part of the performance that it is easy to overlook its intrinsic value as a jazz solo. (One who never overlooked its quality was Ellington, who frequently cited this Nance solo as one of the classics.) *Jumpin' Punkins*, with composer credit to Mercer Ellington, is a medium-tempo piece written around the drumming of Greer. It begins and ends quietly, but its centerpiece is a *fortissimo* climax in the form of a dialog between Greer and the full orchestra. Greer refused to take drum solos but obviously relished the opportunities offered by the breaks in *Jumpin' Punkins*. On each of the many recorded versions he plays differently but always with zest and humor. The work is a delightfully good humored one and also has much fine playing by Ellington and Blanton, a chorus of warm dialogue between Carney and the trombone section, and a characteristic touch of Bigard's clarinet. This Victor recording has two takes, both excellent.

John Hardy's Wife (also credited to Mercer Ellington) is at a livelier tempo and in a similarly happy vein. Duke's piano is at its most sprightly here, and there is another good-humored conversation between Carney's baritone and the trombones. Brown has a short solo before the abrupt, almost brutal ending, but the main soloist is Stewart. Just as Freddie Jenkins had taken over the growl solos on Bubber Miley's departure, so Stewart assumed this responsibility when Williams left, although in time Nance was to become the band's plunger trumpet specialist. The vehement, energy-packed chorus on *John Hardy's Wife* is Rex's first major growl solo with the Ellington band and must be reckoned one of his best. This title is followed by a third composition credited to Mercer Ellington, *Blue Serge*—a brooding tone poem. The solos, all perfectly tailored to the requirements of the piece, are by Stewart, Nanton, Ellington, and Webster. The scoring is sheer perfection in its deployment of tone colors; a masterpiece of great richness. The final recording from the session is Strayhorn's *After All*, with the composer at the piano. Like many of Strayhorn's compositions, this approaches the border of sentimentality without quite stepping over; a holding back which Strayhorn did not always exercise in his popular song arrangements. *After All* is a languid, delicate, and very beautiful little piece with perfectly poised solos by Brown and Hodges, the latter giving another perfect example of his newly enriched ballad style.

* * *

The only Ellington recording session during the next three months found Duke alone in the studio. On May 14, 1940, two piano solos were cut: musing, reflective, and harmonically rich readings of *Dear Old Southland* and *Solitude*. Two takes each of these interesting if minor recordings have been issued. During the period under discussion, Ellington made several guest appearances on other people's radio shows as soloist. On these occasions he usually took Blanton along, and the resultant performances, some of which have been issued on LP, are virtually piano and bass duets with occasional accompaniment by large studio orchestras, including strings. The only recording of a slight Ellington piece called *Jive Rhapsody* comes from one of these broadcasts; another includes the first Ellington recording of his variations on the traditional *Frankie And Johnny*. Also from these broadcasts come versions of *Jumpin' Punkins* and *Take The "A" Train*, plus a fragment of a performance of *Flamingo*.

* * *

The Ellington band was on the West Coast from June 1941 until the end of the year, rehearsing for and appearing in Ellington's musical *Jump For Joy*. On June 5, they were in the Victor Hollywood studios to record four numbers. The first of these is an essay in Tizol's exotic vein, *Bakiff*, which features Nance on violin and the composer on valve trombone. This piece is typical of the kind of exotic Ellington which some jazz enthusiasts find extremely irritating. The musical content is anything but profound, and the odor of greasepaint in the playing is clearly deliberate. But the humor is strictly poker-faced. According to Eric Townley's book *Tell Your Story*, the title, far from being an exotic placename, is simply made up from the initial letters of Big Ass Kock I Floy Floy (Big Arse Cock-eyed Double Talk).

This is followed by the second of Ellington's showcases for Bigard. It also has a title based on word play, in this case, the slang term "blackstick" for clarinet. *Are You Sticking?* is a pleasant enough piece and features fine Bigard, but it is not on the level of *Clarinet Lament*. The masterpiece of this session is the ultrarelaxed *Just A-Settin' And A-Rockin'*, taken at a slow-to-medium walking tempo. It is an unpretentious piece of jazz making with really impressive swing. Blanton is the rock on which the performance rests, and the main soloist is Webster, who has two of the three choruses in nonchalant dialogue with the band. Nance has a soulful trumpet solo in the middle eight of the first of these, while the third and final chorus is split between Nanton and Bigard. The last title is a rather flashy piece at a tearaway tempo, *The Giddybug Gallop*. Nanton, Hodges, and Bigard are the soloists and the last two certainly demonstrate the speed of their playing in a piece of rather empty-orchestral virtuosity really untypical of the band. *The Giddybug Gallop* did not become established in the Ellington repertoire.

Three weeks later, the band was again in the Victor studios, this time to record two numbers from *Jump For Joy*, both with vocals by Anderson. *Chocolate Shake* (like all the songs from the show) has lyrics by Paul Francis Webster which were very smart and fashionable in 1941 but have dated rather badly. The performance is fine, and Greer's press rolls are more swinging than on some earlier recordings. The main soloist is Carney, and there is a very soulful middle eight from Nance. The second song, *I Got It Bad And That Ain't Good*, has become a standard. In this initial recording we are treated to a tasteful Anderson vocal and a Hodges solo replete with swooning glissandi.

On the very first title from the next session (recorded on July 2, 1941) Hodges contributes a swinging alto solo to Strayhorn's *Clementine*. This is Strayhorn's writing at its best—a straightforward score offering the maximum opportunity for the band to swing. In addition to excellent playing by Hodges, there is a superb chorus from Stewart's cornet, introduced by four bars of Nance's trumpet—a most effective device. Paul Webster's lyrics and Jeffries' vocal combine to make *The Brownskin Gal In The Calico Gown* an interesting Ellington popular song. Carney has a couple of brief solos. The title tune from *Jump For Joy* was recorded in two takes. On the first, the vocal is by Jeffries, on the second by Anderson. This magnificent score contains, in terms of color and concentration of material, some of Ellington's finest writing. Solos by Nanton and Hodges are woven perfectly into the orchestral fabric. The second take is superior, and not just because Ivie makes Jeffries sound pedestrian by comparison. The final recording from the date is a Tizol-Ellington collaboration which does not stem from *Jump For Joy*. *Moon Over Cuba* presents a tourist, pre-Castro image and is played over a rhumba beat, except for the last middle eight, taken by Webster. Tizol, inevitably, and Hodges are the soloists, and the scoring includes some nice passages for the clarinet trio.

* * *

On the following day—July 3, 1941—the Stewart and Hodges contingents cut four titles each for Bluebird. Stewart led the same group as on his previous date—Brown, Webster, Carney, Ellington, Blanton, and Greer. The first title, *Some Saturday*, is Stewart's composition and arrangement. He displays his solo cornet over shifting low-register patterns for trombone, tenor, and baritone. Brown and Webster split a chorus, and there is much first-rate cornet to be heard. *Subtle Slough*—according to its composer, Duke Ellington, the title means a subtle brush-off—is a theme which became known as *Just Squeeze Me* after it acquired lyrics. Rex indulges in growl cornet in a performance of tremendous swing, powered by Blanton but with every member of the septet contributing to great effect. *Menelik The Lion Of Judah* is a Stewart composition dedicated to the Ethiopian Emperor Haile Selassie. The piece is taken at jump tempo, and Stewart produces some pedal notes which are probably the closest one can get to the roar of a lion on cornet. He also plays some sprightly stuff in the instrument's more normal register. The scoring is simple but effective. The fourth title is a blues dedicated to the memory of Bubber Miley, *Poor Bubber*, with passionate Stewart-led ensembles, more of Rex's distinctive plunger solo style, and poised, elegant blues choruses from Webster and Brown.

The Hodges titles were made by a group consisting of Nance, Brown, Hodges, Carney, Ellington, Blanton, and Greer—the previous Hodges unit with Nance replacing Williams. *Squatty Roo* is the epitome of the Johnny Hodges jump number. The bright, bouncing theme statements are a garnish to some of the finest solo alto ever recorded. Hodges, at his magnificent best, plays with an endless flow of invention, perfect melodic poise and abundant rhythmic energy. His mastery of his instrument is complete. Every musician in the group has the Hodges jump style down to perfection, but special mention must be made of Blanton, who gives one of his most impressive performances. Strayhorn's *Passion Flower* is a tone poem for alto saxophone, sensuous, almost overripe in mood. By contrast, *Things Ain't What They Used To Be* is a basic blues, and a classic one. The ensemble statement is perfect, and Hodges pours out a stream of blues melody in a performance as great as that on *Squatty Roo*. Ellington has an economical, pungent solo, while Nance's chorus is played with great feeling and with a very beautiful, cloudy tone. The concluding title, another Hodges jump tune, *Goin' Out The Back Way*, has short solos by Ellington and Carney, and more brilliant playing by Hodges and Blanton.

* * *

Apart from air shots in pretty poor sound of *Raincheck*, a new Strayhorn composition, and *Just A-Settin' And A-Rockin'*, the next issued recordings by the Ellington band come from a long session for Standard Transcriptions of September 17, 1941. It begins with two Strayhorn compositions, a second recording of *Clementine*, and the first of *Chelsea Bridge*. The *Clementine* is perhaps fractionally less relaxed than the Victor, but Stewart's solo is again a lively, perky affair with clever use of half-valve notes. *Chelsea Bridge* was inspired by a famous painting by Whistler (actually of Battersea Bridge) and is one of Strayhorn's most attractive tone poems, harmonically rich and beautifully scored. Webster, Blanton, and Tizol are heard in the course of a gentle, reflective performance. *Love Like This Can't Last* is a pop song with Anderson featured throughout; she sounds less at ease than usual, possibly because she is not familiar with the song. Next comes a group of numbers already recorded for Victor. *After All* is heard without the prominent Strayhorn piano part which was such a feature of the Victor recording, and this illustrates how crucially recording balance can affect a jazz performance. The piano part itself is less elaborate on this version, but here it is barely audible whereas on the Victor it achieves an almost unnatural prominence. Otherwise there is little to choose between the two versions, and this can also be said of *The Girl In My Dreams Tries To Look Like You*. The Standard Transcriptions *Jumpin' Punkins* is an excellent complement to the two Victor takes; the tempo is slightly faster and the interpretation of Greer's percussion part particularly exuberant. Blanton is very well recorded here. *Frankie And Johnny* foreshadows several longer versions by the Ellington band; this forerunner is in the form of a concerto for Ellington's piano and the band, with Nanton and Blanton heard in subsidiary roles. There are two tempos: a slow central part framed by two fast sections. It is easy to see how Ellington developed the later versions from this first sketch (although the parts which were still later lopped off to make up *Metronome All Out* had not yet made their appearance). This *Frankie And Johnny* offers what is probably the best example of Ellington's work as a piano soloist from this period. The final two titles from this session are new versions of *Flamingo* and *Bakiff*, the first identical to the Victor in its routine. *Bakiff* is longer than the Victor with rather more of Nance's mock-oriental violin. The band seems to enjoy balancing on the edge of the outrageous in the later stages of this performance.

* * *

Back in the Victor studios twelve days later, four sides were cut by the full band and four by the Bigard unit. The first band item is a performance of a simple Ellington jump tune, *Five O'Clock Drag*, taken at a swinging medium tempo. Blanton is outstanding in the rhythm section, the orchestration is simple but in glowing colors, and the solos by Stewart and Webster are superb. Webster's four-bar break leading into Stewart's solo is brilliant, while the way in which the tenor solo is developed as a dialogue between soloist and orchestra is typically Ellingtonian in both conception and realization. Next, two numbers from *Jump For Joy*—*Rocks In My Bed*, a rather melodramatic blues with vocal by Ivie Anderson and atmospheric clarinet by Bigard, and *Bli-Blip*, with the now rather dated lyrics sung by Nance. The final title by the full band is a version of *Chelsea Bridge*, rejected at the time but issued in the French RCA complete edition of Ellington's Victor recordings.

Ellington plays on only one of the Bigard group titles from this date, *C Blues*, Strayhorn taking over at the keyboard for the other three. *C Blues* is by a considerable margin the best recording from the session; it is an embryonic version of *C Jam Blues* with Bigard and the ensemble heard to excellent effect, and with really outstanding solos by Nance and Carney. The other items are Mercer Ellington's *Brown Suede*, Strayhorn's *Noir Bleu*, and Bigard's *June*. All have pastel Strayhorn arrangements, very modern in their day, but sounding more than a little insubstantial now. Apart from a chorus of Tizol's trombone on *June*, the only soloist is Bigard himself, although Strayhorn has a prominent piano part in *Noir Bleu*.

These four titles were the very last recorded by an Ellington unit in this form. Johnny Hodges (regularly) and other sidemen (occasionally) continued to record with small groups drawn from the Ellington band, but the pianist would either be Strayhorn or someone from outside the organization. And of course Ellington would sometimes record with small groups from within the band, either for an odd title or a full session, but without any hint of coleadership with one of his sidemen. This was, of course, a development of a pattern go-

ing back to the twenties and such recordings as *Sloppy Joe* and *Saratoga Swing* rather than a continuation of the late thirties unit sessions. The Bluebird recordings of 1940 and 1941 by the Hodges and Stewart units are the epitome of this kind of small-group Ellingtonia, and it is perhaps because of their perfection that Duke never felt the need to return to this particular format. (The Bigard titles are less exceptional, though *Charlie The Chulo*, *A Lull At Dawn*, and *C Blues* are equal to the best of Barney's earlier output.) The work of the rhythm section on the Hodges and Stewart recordings is outstanding, and the excellent sound quality enables us to savor it in full. The musicians clearly have this kind of small band playing gauged to perfection, while the arrangements are models of small-band writing. The solo standard is of the highest, and Hodges's solos are among the very best he ever recorded.

* * *

When the next Victor session took place on December 2, 1941, Jimmy Blanton's illness had forced him to leave the band. He had been replaced by Alvin Junior Raglin, not a virtuoso of the same order, but a musician who grasped the essence of his predecessor's style and always played with great swing. The standard version of Strayhorn's *Chelsea Bridge* was recorded at this session. It is interesting to note the differences in the three 1941 recordings of this piece: the Standard Transcriptions version of September 17; the rejected Victor recording of September 29 [referred to as Victor (1) below]; and this Victor remake [Victor (2)]. Note that Blanton had left the band by the time of the last recording.

Introduction
Standard: Ellington piano solo, four bars.
Victor (1): Strayhorn piano solo, four bars.
Victor (2): Strayhorn piano solo, four bars.

First Chorus
Standard: muted trumpets over saxophone harmonies, sixteen bars; Webster tenor sax solo, eight bars; trombones with saxophone punctuations, eight bars.
Victor (1): Tizol valve trombone solo, sixteen bars; Webster tenor sax solo, eight bars; trombones with saxophone punctuations, eight bars.
Victor (2): muted trumpets over saxophone harmonies, sixteen bars; Ben Webster tenor sax solo, eight bars; trombones with saxophone punctuations, eight bars.

Second Chorus
Standard: dialogue between Blanton's bass and saxophones sixteen bars; Tizol valve trombone solo, sixteen bars.
Victor (1): dialogue between Blanton's bass and saxophones with clarinet lead, sixteen bars; Tizol valve trombone solo, eight bars; Strayhorn piano solo over saxophone harmonies, eight bars.

Victor (2): dialogue between Strayhorn's piano and saxophones with clarinet lead, sixteen bars; Tizol valve trombone solo, eight bars; ensemble with trumpet lead, eight bars.

All three versions have their particular qualities, and a comparison gives another illustration of the kind of revision to which material was subjected in the Ellington band. The final Victor version is the best, but the string bass/saxophone section dialogue and Strayhorn's closing solo are outstanding features of the earlier ones. On all versions Tizol's valve trombone sounds ideal for this theme, and Webster's eight-bar solo is a classic in miniature, although he, like the band as a whole, sounds a fraction less assured on the first recording.

* * *

On the Victor session of December 2, 1941, another important Strayhorn composition, *Raincheck*, was recorded. We have previously encountered it only in the form of a poorly recorded air shot. It is a very imaginative uptempo score which uses Tizol in the theme statement and Webster as the lead voice in the saxophone section. There are effective solos by Webster, Nance, and Strayhorn himself, again on piano for this recording. The two Strayhorn compositions were followed by a Strayhorn arrangement of a rather undistinguished pop tune, *What Good Would It Do?* There are some nice tone colors in the orchestration, but the performance is dominated by a long Jeffries vocal. Ellington takes over at the piano for the last title, a song by him in the twelve-bar blues format which features another vocal by Jeffries, *I Don't Know What Kind Of Blues I Got*. The attractive theme is presented by Carney on clarinet with a beautiful second part by Brown; muted brass take over for the second chorus with Webster in an obbligato role; the Carney/Brown combination returns for another chorus which leads into the vocal. Ellington presumably used Carney here rather than Bigard to give variety and to follow his lifelong philosophy of making use of all available resources. (On an air-shot recording of this song from 1943, Carney plays bass clarinet, which prompts the speculation that this may have been the way it was planned in the first place. It would be wholly characteristic of the casual ways of the Ellington band for Carney not to have known that the number was to be recorded and for him to have turned up without his bass clarinet as a consequence.)

The following day, the band was back in the same studio to record a long session for Standard Transcriptions. As usual with such sessions, it produced several numbers never recorded for commercial release. The opening *Stomp Caprice* is an instance of this. Duke's piano is featured in a delightfully casual performance of an attractive score credited to Mercer Ellington. *Bugle Breaks* is yet another Ellington variation on *Bugle Call Rag*, a number which seems to have interested him almost as much as *Tiger Rag* during the first half of his career. After Stewart's mocking bugle call, four soloists—Bigard, Webster, Brown, and Nance—are heard in a vigorous stomp. *You And I* is wholly given over to the vocal endeavors of Jeffries, but another popular song, *Have You Changed?* (also known as *Blue Tears*), features a good arrangement incorporating solos by Carney in his most Webster-like vein and Webster himself. The next two titles are already familiar in their Victor recordings—*Raincheck* and *Blue Serge*—and differ only in detail from the earlier performances. The initial recording of *Moon Mist* finds Nance featured on trumpet (in the first chorus) as well as violin and is without the Brown solo found on later versions. Another popular tune of the day, *I Don't Want To Set The World On Fire*, features Jeffries plus a touch of Jones. It is followed by a ballad feature for Stewart's cornet, *Easy Street*, of which this is the only recording. The final item is a brief first recording of Tizol's *Perdido*. There are only two choruses and the soloists are Tizol himself in the first chorus middle eight (Nance's province in subsequent recordings) and Stewart, also restricted to eight bars.

* * *

The first issued version of *Perdido* comes from the Ellington band's first Victor session of 1942, which took place on January 21. This theme was to become a favorite for jazz groups of all sizes and at jam sessions, while the Ellington Orchestra itself produced many different versions over the years. Yet none has ever surpassed the 1942 original. After a perfect four-bar piano introduction, Carney has the first half of the opening chorus—eight bars of theme and eight of variation. Nance takes a perfectly poised middle eight, and the band rounds off the chorus. A bouncing, eager Stewart and an easy, almost indolent Webster share the second chorus—note how Webster comes out of the middle eight into the last part of the chorus with such supple swing. The final chorus is an all-out climax by the band with Nance providing a point of repose in the middle eight.

C Jam Blues, another Ellington piece which became a jam session favorite, also receives its initial recording at this session. It opens with the riff from Bigard's *C Blues*, played first by piano and then by the saxophones, followed by a long solo sequence. Each soloist has a four-bar break to launch his solo chorus, and behind the last of the solos (by Bigard) the brass play a theme which emerges *fortissimo* in the final ensemble chorus. (This ensemble climax is less well played here than on some later versions.) There are countless recordings of *C Jam Blues* by the Ellington band, and the solo routine varies from performance to performance; usually each soloist takes two choruses after his four-bar break rather than just one, as on this first recording. Here the soloists are Nance (on violin), Stewart, Webster, Nanton, and Bigard. Nanton's four-bar break is remarkable in that it is played on one note throughout, varied only by rhythm and by the tonal shadings he gives to that note via the plunger mute.

The other two trombonists of this unique section—a section so full of character and contrast—can be heard on the next number, *Moon Mist*. This is a much more assured and poised performance than the Standard Transcriptions recording, the band obviously having become familiar with the piece. Tizol is heard leading the ensemble responses to Nance's violin in the first chorus, while the supple phrasing of the trombone section in the dialogue with Hodges in the middle eight is a sure indication that the lead is now in the hands of Brown, who also has a short muted solo toward the end of the piece. *Moon Mist* is one of Ellington's most attractive nocturnes. The scoring is unusually subtle even by his standards; note the quiet part given to Wallace Jones's solo trumpet during the first chorus. (The version issued in the French R.C.A. Complete Edition is a previously unissued take.)

These three masterpieces were followed by three of almost equal stature on the next Victor session, on February 26, 1942. The first is an Ellington medium-tempo piece, *What Am I Here For?*, in which Nanton, Ellington, Stewart, and Webster indulge in dialogues and solos. Then comes a ballad, *I Don't Mind*, for which Duke wrote the music and Strayhorn the lyrics. It receives an outstanding performance. The rhythmic authority of Ellington's piano in the introduction is remarkable, and so is the fact that he retained the figure he uses in it for 24 years before making it the basis of a composition called *Looking Glass*. *I Don't Mind* has one of Ivie Anderson's best vocals, and it receives ideal accompaniment from the band, while there are solos by Carney and Brown in the later stages of this magnificent performance. Almost as fine is the nonvocal *Someone*, in which a central solo by Nance is framed by choruses split between Hodges and Brown. All three soloists play in a singing, warmly melodic style while Hodges's two entries are equally breathtaking in their totally different ways.

Four months elapsed before the band was again in the Victor studios. This was for a session on June 26, 1942, which produced three titles. The first was Strayhorn's *My Little Brown Book*, a sentimental song with a sentimental vocal by Jeffries and solos by Brown and Webster. Ellington's *Main Stem* is the blues at a rousing medium-fast tempo featuring a marvelous sequence of solos in a performance of great swing—Hodges, Stewart, Bigard, Nanton, Webster, and Brown are featured. The orchestral colors are suitably bold, and this must be reckoned one of the Ellington band's best performances of the conventional kind. Almost as good is Strayhorn's *Johnny Come Lately*, a jump number with the ensemble led by the rich voice of Carney's baritone and the main solo roles featuring the contrasting trombone styles of Brown and Nanton.

* * *

This June 1942 session was the last on which Barney Bigard participated before he left the band in July. He was replaced by Chauncey Haughton, a veteran of the Chick Webb, Ella Fitzgerald, and Cab Calloway bands. Haughton appears to have been regarded as a stand-in as Duke tried to obtain the services of a New Orleans style clarinetist to replace Bigard; he is known to have offered the post to Edmond Hall and to Omer Simeon. Bigard's ultimate replacement was the academic stylist Jimmy Hamilton. But for the moment, Haughton, a sound jazz musician of no particular individuality, took over. The following month Ivie Anderson and Herb Jeffries also departed; Ivie was a major loss. Their replacements were Betty Roche and Jimmy Britton.

* * *

Several broadcast performances from the middle of 1942 have found their way on to record. None is particularly distinguished, although there is a performance of *Things Ain't What They Used To Be* by the full band at the same slow tempo as the 1941 Hodges recording, and the only known recordings of Jimmy Blanton's one score for the band, *The Strollers*, and of Ellington's *Swing Shifters Swing*.

In late 1942, the American Federation of Musicians imposed a recording ban on all its members, but before this came into force the Ellington band was able to get in one more Victor date. It featured two wartime songs with lyrics which have dated badly. *Hayfoot, Strawfoot* has an amusing Stewart introduction, Ivie's last recorded vocal with the band, fine Webster, and a stomping performance from the ensemble. Nance sings *A Slip Of The Lip (Might Sink A Ship)* and shares the solo honors with Hodges. A new showcase for Hodges, *Sentimental Lady*, finds the altoist in his most lyrical vein; there is also a half chorus from Stewart. This number was later given lyrics and retitled *I Didn't Know About You*. The final recording is a light Ellington jump theme, *Sherman Shuffle*, with solos by Brown and Haughton and a chase chorus between Nance and Stewart.

The only recordings between the July Victor session and the end of 1942 are air shots of rather variable sound quality. A sequence called *On Display* includes a remarkable version of *Tangerine* featuring Nanton, but this was not issued on LP. There is also an untitled clarinet feature for Haughton and popular songs of the day in versions featuring Brown and Webster. Betty Roche and Jimmy Britton are heard for the first time on the issued portions of a broadcast from Rhode Island State College in December 1942. The choice of material for this broadcast seems to have been particularly poor and the high spots are brief solos by Hodges and Nance on *A Slip Of The Lip*.

Outstanding Recordings

1. By the Full Band—Victor Recordings

Sidewalks Of New York, *Take The "A" Train*, *Jumpin' Punkins* (both takes), *John Hardy's Wife*, *Blue Serge*, *After All*,

Just A-Settin' And A-Rockin', *Clementine*, *Jump For Joy* (second take), *Moon Over Cuba*, *Five O'Clock Drag*, *Chelsea Bridge*, *Raincheck*, *Perdido*, *C Jam Blues*, *Moon Mist*, *What Am I Here For?*, *I Don't Mind*, *Someone*, *Main Stem*, *Johnny Come Lately*, *Sentimental Lady*, and *Sherman Shuffle*

2. By the Full Band—Standard Transcriptions

Take The "A" Train, I Hear A Rhapsody, Bounce, West Indian Stomp, Jumpin' Punkins, Frankie And Johnny, Stomp Caprice, and *Bugle Breaks*

3. By the Full Band—Location Recordings

The complete Fargo dance date of November 7, 1940

4. The Contingents

a. Barney Bigard: Charlie The Chulo, A Lull At Dawn, and *C Blues*

b. Johnny Hodges: Squatty Roo, Passion Flower, Things Ain't What They Used To Be, and *Goin' Out The Back Way*

c. Rex Stewart: Some Saturday, Subtle Slough, Menelik—The Lion Of Judah, and *Poor Bubber*

Chapter 15

Departures and Arrivals

THE DEPARTURE OF COOTIE WILLIAMS from the Ellington ranks was regarded by the music world as something approaching disaster. Raymond Scott, a purveyor of light music with a dash of jazz flavoring, went so far as to compose a dirge called *When Cootie Left The Duke*. From contemporary comments we can see that Williams was regarded as Ellington's major soloist. If we remember that Hodges was just developing the refinements to his style which were to be the basis of his later fame, and that Webster was a newcomer to the band, Williams's preeminence becomes easier to understand. Cootie was a more extroverted and powerful personality than any other Ellington musician, and it was probably a combination of natural exuberance and musical authority that so clearly made him a key member of the band during the late thirties. The enormous power and vitality of his playing is brilliantly caught on the high-fidelity recordings made in the sixties and seventies after he had rejoined the band. On these, particularly some of the live recordings, the sheer energy and authority of his playing are most impressive. The recording standards prevailing during Cootie's first tenure with Ellington do not allow him to make such an impact, but careful listening reveals the vital role he played in the orchestra.

Williams greatly admired Benny Goodman's approach to music and he left Duke to take up a year's contract with Goodman, followed by financial assistance from Benny in setting up a band of his own. He expressed doubts about this latter course to Ellington, but Duke, who had encouraged him to take the job with Goodman, with all that it offered in prestige and financial reward, also advised him to develop his career further by taking the opportunity to become a bandleader. Their parting thus was an amicable one, and Duke assured Cootie that there would always be a place for him in the band should he wish to return.

In musical terms, Cootie's departure was the greatest blow to the Ellington band since Bubber Miley had left eleven years earlier. In choosing a replacement Ellington followed the course he had adopted previously and selected a little-known musician of great potential, one who had no reputation as a growl specialist, rather than an established trumpeter with a style close to that of the departing star.

Even after Ray Nance had settled into the Ellington band his personality was less dominant than Williams's had been.

There is a subtle difference between the music of the 1940 band and that of 1941–42, the latter having a more relaxed, casual air. In part this was a consequence of Cootie's departure; among other things, he was noted for his insistence on the highest standards of band playing. In the autumn of 1942 Ellington added a fourth trumpet, Harold "Shorty" Baker. This may have been due to the conventions of the time, or to the additional scoring opportunities an extra instrument could offer, but it is more than possible that the loss of Williams's sheer physical power lay at the root of this change.

Another significant loss during this period was that of Jimmy Blanton. When the bassist's terminal illness forced him to give up playing, he had been before the public a mere two years. Yet so pervasive was his influence that Blanton disciples already were common enough for Ellington to find an ideally suited replacement in the person of Alvin (Junior) Raglin. Although Raglin did not have the virtuosity of his mentor, he was a powerful player capable of carrying the band in a manner fully equal to Blanton. Thus the loss of the young genius of the string bass was not so catastrophic as it easily could have been.

The third departure, however, did rob the band of a style of musicianship which it was never to acquire again. When Barney Bigard left, Duke tried, as we have noted, to obtain the services of other New Orleans clarinet stylists, and for a few months in the middle of 1943 he did use a musician called Nat Jones in this capacity. It is unfortunate that he was not able to obtain a player of the caliber of Edmond Hall or Omer Simeon, for the Ellington band provided the only opportunity in jazz for a further development of this beautiful style of clarinet playing. Bigard's ultimate replacement was Jimmy Hamilton, a brilliant musician who stayed in the band for a quarter of a century and made many important contributions to Ellington's music, but in a totally different manner from Bigard. From the late forties on, Russell Procope takes clarinet solos in a style close to Bigard. This contribution was valuable, providing dramatic contrast with Hamilton. But Procope was an alto sax specialist who doubled clarinet, not a virtuoso on the order of Bigard, nor an original or particularly imaginative player. The departure of Bigard meant the end of a fascinating development of the New Orleans clarinet style in big band terms.

The loss of Ivie Anderson was also a considerable blow, for she had proved to be the ideal vocal stylist for the band. Ivie's emotionally detached yet zestful way of singing was the perfect foil for the colorful, emotionally explicit playing of the Ellington instrumentalists. Duke was to employ a variety of singers without ever again finding one who blended quite so well with his music in terms of both personality and style. In Betty Roché and Joya Sherrill he came closest to finding a suitable replacement, but neither had Ivie's distinctive style or her rapport with his music.

Ellington's male singers tended to be highly dramatic balladeers with exaggerated styles. The reasons for what seemed to his followers to be unfortunate choices may have been that he looked for qualities in a singer similar to those he sought in instrumentalists, with strong emotional projection a high priority. The results were seldom happy.

Despite personnel changes and the gradual increase in the size of the band, discipline within the Ellington organization remained loose. It would be impossible to imagine occurrences such as Ben Webster's ceremonious dispatch of a cockroach with a hefty stamp of the foot while en route to the microphone for a ballad solo being so cheerfully accepted by other bandleaders. On another occasion, Webster chased Ellington from the stage because he did not like the chords Duke was laying down for his solo. One has only to imagine a sideman trying to chase Benny Goodman or Artie Shaw from the stage to see how differently the Ellington organization was structured. That this loose discipline paid off musically is obvious. Many an Ellington musician entertained the illusion that the band really depended on him, that Ellington was just the piano player and arranger. Duke encouraged such ego-boosting illusions—so subtle was his leadership, so light yet certain his holding of the reins.

* * *

In 1941 and 1942, Billy Strayhorn made his first major impact on the music of the Ellington band. In 1939 and 1940 he had made some arrangements for the contingent dates and of popular tunes for the full band, as well as contributing lyrics to some of Ellington's songs. With *Take The "A" Train*—first recorded for Standard Transcriptions in January 1941—Strayhorn began to contribute a series of instrumental scores for the full band. In the early forties there was a dispute between ASCAP (the American Society of Composers, Authors and Publishers) and the broadcast industry, and ASCAP banned the use of its members' compositions on the air. Duke was an ASCAP member but Strayhorn was not, and it is claimed that one of the reasons for the increase in the latter's output was the need to quickly create a library of material available for the band's very frequent broadcasts. The dispute is also considered a contributory cause of the sudden outcrop of Mercer Ellington compositions at this time. It is impossible, however, to find a record of any broadcasts by the band which did not use any Ellington compositions. It should be stressed that the band had always used a certain amount of material written by musicians other than Ellington; when this usage increased rapidly for a time in the early forties, the person gaining most in artistic terms was Billy Strayhorn. He quickly picked up Ellington's unusual methods of writing for the band and Duke encouraged the younger man, whom he henceforth described as "my writing and arranging companion." With new players coming into the band more frequently as the stability of personnel declined it became desirable to have more of the repertoire set down on manuscript paper and less of it reliant on the memories of long-serving sidemen. Strayhorn must have been a great deal of help in this regard, and his presence took a considerable workload off Ellington's shoulders.

To some degree, the position of Strayhorn in Ellington music is an ambiguous one. He became so close to Ellington in his musical language that even band members could not always tell which of them had scored what. Yet his influence on Ellington was not always in the most healthy direction. He contributed vigorous stomps such as *Take The "A" Train* and *Johnny Come Lately*, but many of his popular song arrangements were soft, sentimental, and of little substance, aspects only partially disguised by his fastidious craftsmanship. This softer side of Strayhorn's musical personality is illustrated in the writing he did for the last Bigard Bluebird session—*Brown Suede*, *Noir Bleu*, and *June*. These rather empty exercises in faintly decadent modishness are quite different in essence from Ellington's own much more strongly sinewed tone poems. Not all Strayhorn's mood pieces are in this vein; in *After All*, for example, the resigned melancholy is kept firmly under control. But there is a tendency for Strayhorn's music to dissolve into a rather vapid kind of formlessness, a kind of soft-centered romanticism. In the eyes of some, this was a feature of his personality and an influence which tended to draw Ellington's music away from its more robust traditions. Certainly the presence of Strayhorn and Jeffries serves to make many of the Ellington popular song recordings of the early forties less rewarding than those from the second half of the thirties, when the roles of these two were taken by Ellington himself and Anderson.

* * *

The presentation of Ellington's revue *Jump For Joy* in California in August 1941 was a major event. The show was judged a great success, but it has not been properly explained why it received just this one production. It ran for over three months in Los Angeles but was never staged in New York. Many reasons have been given for this, including wartime difficulties, racial prejudice, and managerial incompetence. Whatever the reasons, this brief spell on the West Coast was the nearest Duke ever came to realizing his lifelong ambition to create a successful Broadway musical.

***

In the early forties, as throughout the big band era, the best jobs and the maximum publicity went to white groups. The most popular swing bands at this time were Benny Goodman's, Artie Shaw's, and Tommy Dorsey's. This popularity bore no relation to musical values, for the best black bands were clearly superior. Goodman, Shaw, and Dorsey led superbly drilled orchestras, but in terms of swing, solo strength, and creative arrangements they were below the standard of several of the black orchestras. (This should not prevent the listener from realizing that bands like Goodman's, Shaw's, and Dorsey's produced music that was more than a production-line commodity based on a clever assessment of public taste.)

Fletcher Henderson had broken up his last important band in the thirties and now spent most of his time as staff arranger and occasional pianist with the Goodman organization. His later big bands were of slight import. Tommy Dorsey had lured Sy Oliver away from Lunceford in 1939 and that notable band had begun its slow, tragic decline. The finest of all bands apart from Ellington's remained Count Basie's. No longer the Kansas City blowing band of its earliest years, it still retained an impressive roster of soloists and its strong emphasis on the blues. Of the other black leaders, Cab Calloway, Earl Hines, Andy Kirk, and Erskine Hawkins continued to field fine bands, while those led by Lionel Hampton, Jay McShann, and Lucky Millinder were among the most interesting newer groups.

When the American Federation of Musicians (AFM) imposed its recording ban in 1942 the swing era was still flourishing. Although the music of many of the bands was of moderate interest from a jazz viewpoint, the standards of popular music were then amazingly high. If on the whole the music of the black bands was superior in jazzcraft and creativity, the music turned out by such bands as Goodman's, Shaw's, and Tommy Dorsey's in these years was also often of high quality and certainly superior to the various forms of popular music which succeeded it in public favor. Goodman and Dorsey were musical craftsmen of the highest order and led orchestras containing excellent soloists and good arrangers. Shaw had similar qualities and was a very imaginative musician with high artistic ideals. Perhaps these ideals were never fully realized, his music being too concerned with experiment for its own sake, but his bands certainly produced much worthwhile music.

The AFM ban was one of the contributory causes of the ending of the big band era since the public for popular records became accustomed to buying new discs by solo vocalists and vocal groups (singers were not AFM members). When the bands returned to the studios after the ban was lifted in late 1944, the swing era was clearly moving toward its end. But in 1942 only a tendency toward sameness and repetition among the popular bands and the rise of Glenn Miller-style instant pop gave a hint of the coming decline.

The bands were still flourishing, and to the casual observer the Ellington Orchestra was simply one among many. Its outstanding qualities were perhaps understood only by musicians and a handful of followers. And even among the knowledgeable, the band was liable to be misunderstood in that it was a constantly creative and evolving entity, presenting music which was always to some degree new or strange. There was usually a time lag of from five to ten years between the release of an Ellington record and its acceptance among collectors as a genuine part of the canon. It now seems amazing, but the great recordings of 1940 were at first greeted by some collectors as evidence of the band's decline into being no more than just another swing band! But such reaction from the more studious followers of the band rarely worried Duke. He was drawing good audiences at dances, hotel residencies, theaters, and concerts. Royalties were coming in from his substantial and growing library of popular songs, and the band was continuing to turn out music of a quality that met his own high standards.

Although the recording ban prevented the band from recording for public releases, it continued to record for transcriptions, and these, plus the broadcasts and concerts which have survived, are sufficient to give us a clear idea of Ellington's music during the 1942–44 period. During this span, three further important musicians, Ben Webster, Wallace Jones, and Juan Tizol, left the band. But as the records discussed in the next chapter show, the Ellington Orchestra remained the best of the big bands, turning out a body of music wholly in keeping with its previous achievements.

Sidemen

Chauncey Haughton

An orthodox jazz clarinetist in a pre-Goodman style, Haughton was not really equipped to take over the role of his predecessor Bigard, and did not try to do so. He simply played modest solos with a rather thin tone for his eleven months or so with the band. A sound musician, but not a particularly distinctive or distinguished one.

Representative Recordings: Sherman Shuffle (Victor, 1942), *A Portrait Of Bert Williams* (Carnegie Hall, January 1943)

Ray Nance

Seen in the context of his quarter century in the band, Nance is clearly one of the most versatile of all Ellington musicians. On trumpet, his playing varied from a swinging open-horn style to a highly personal version of the traditional Ellington plunger-mute technique. He was a magnificent ballad player, capable of investing a theme statement with a distinctive and appealing flavor, and he quickly established his credentials as a blues musician with his classic solo on the

Hodges recording of *Things Ain't What They Used To Be*. It seemed that there was no role in the Ellington trumpet section, solo or ensemble, which Nance could not perform in his prime. (He even essayed a little high-note trumpet in his early days in the band.) In 1961 Nance switched to cornet as his first instrument. His playing was always highly emotional and communicated with an audience in a most natural way. On violin, he could swing in a fashion few other jazz violinists have equaled. When playing this instrument on a ballad or during one of Ellington's more exotic confections, Nance would suddenly insert a phrase played with the maximum swing and delivered in a slyly humorous manner. Humor was an outstanding feature of Nance's personality, and this is seen most clearly in his singing. Nance's vocals sound very casual and offhanded, but they swing impressively and are full of fun and spirit. In fact, Nance was a first-class jazz singer and without doubt the best male vocalist Ellington ever employed. But for all his qualities as a violinist and singer, it is as a trumpeter that Nance will be best remembered, for his playing always represented the very finest aspects of the instrumental jazz tradition.

Representative Recordings: On Trumpet: *Take The "A" Train* (Victor, 1941), *Things Ain't What They Used To Be* (Johnny Hodges, Bluebird, 1941), *Black And Tan Fantasy* (Capitol, 1953), *Midriff* (Bethlehem, 1956), *Such Sweet Thunder* (title movement, Columbia, 1957), *I Wish You Love* (Reprise, 1962) On Violin: *C Jam Blues* (Columbia, 1959), *Lay By* (from *Suite Thursday*, Columbia, 1960) As Vocalist: *My Honey's Lovin' Arms* (broadcast, 1944), *Just A-Settin' And A-Rockin'* (Carnegie Hall, 1948)

Alvin Junior Raglin

Just as Nance fulfilled the seemingly impossible task of following Williams in the Ellington band, so Raglin fulfilled the equally daunting one of succeeding Blanton. Raglin based his style on Blanton's but did not attempt to emulate the latter's virtuosity, though he was well capable of handling the complex bass parts he was called upon to perform. Raglin seems basically a musician who liked to swing. He had an unusually full tone and this was matched by a commanding rhythmic authority, which enabled him to carry the full band without effort. The Ellington bass lineage is distinguished, and Raglin's place in it is a wholly worthy one.

Representative Recordings: Perdido (Victor, 1942), *What Am I Here For?* (Victor, 1942), *I'm Beginning To See The Light* (Victor, 1944), *Emancipation Celebration* (from *Black, Brown And Beige,* Victor, 1944), *In The Shade Of The Old Apple Tree* (D.E.T.S., both versions, 1945), *Frankie And Johnny* (D.E.T.S., 1945)

Betty Roché

On the evidence of her recordings with Ellington, Roché was a good singer with unusually secure pitching, who sometimes spoiled her work with an exaggerated manner of phrasing. She had two spells with the band. The first came during the first AFM ban; at the time, some journalists insisted that the Ellington discography was much the poorer for the absence of examples of her art. This assertion is not wholly borne out by the subsequent issue of transcriptions and air shots on which she sings, but this may be due to the poor material she was given most of the time. Her interpretation of *The Blues* in the premiere performances of *Black, Brown And Beige* is of a quality not to be discerned on her other records. Her second spell with the band was for some fifteen months in the early fifties. The few recordings she made then are excellent, although their virtues are those of standard jazz vocals rather than interpretations of Ellington's music.

Representative Recordings: The Blues (from *Black, Brown And Beige,* Carnegie Hall and Boston, January 1943), *Go Away Blues* (World Transcriptions, 1943), *I Love My Lovin' Lover* (Columbia, 1952), *All Of Me* (broadcast, 1952), *Take The "A" Train* (Columbia, 1952)

Chapter 16

The Records—January 1943 to September 1946

ON JANUARY 22, 1943, THE ELLINGTON ORCHESTRA played a concert at Rye High School, Rye, New York. The occasion was used as a public dress rehearsal for *Black, Brown And Beige*, Ellington's new 45-minute tone poem. The following night, the official premiere of what *Metronome* magazine described as "Duke Ellington's first symphony" was given at the first of what was to become a series of annual concerts at New York's Carnegie Hall. Four days later, a further performance of *Black, Brown And Beige* was given at Boston's Symphony Hall. After this, the full work was never performed again by the Ellington Orchestra. Excerpts, often extended ones, did remain in the repertoire, however, and in later years parts of *Black, Brown And Beige* were used in the stage show *My People* (1963) and in Ellington's first *Concert Of Sacred Music* (1965).

For some years prior to 1943 Ellington had mentioned his idea of a concert work depicting "the history of the American Negro—Africa to the present day." Parts of *Black, Brown And Beige* are said to derive from an earlier unproduced opera, *Boola*, sometimes also cited as the source of the 1940 *Ko-Ko*. Vague references to this opera occur from time to time in books and articles concerning Ellington but nothing definite is known, and one can only assume that any written parts have long since disappeared.

Ellington obviously regarded the *Black, Brown And Beige* project as vitally important and at first glance his abandonment of the work after three performances seems quite perverse. Did he overreact to some of the adverse criticism which appeared in the press? The audiences at the concerts were enthusiastic enough, as the recordings show, and it is clear that it was not their response that caused Duke to dismember his most ambitious creation. Critical reaction was mixed. The first Ellington Carnegie Hall concert was considered important enough for many newspapers to send their leading music critics. The majority of these wrote from a position of profound unfamiliarity with the jazz idiom, its musical devices and language. They were convinced that jazz—which to most of them comprised *all* popular dance music from the twenties to the forties—was an idiom incapable of sustaining a lengthy, serious composition. There was also much talk about the unsuitability of the dance band as a performing medium for extended concert music. Academic critics considered *Black, Brown And Beige* a failure, pointing to the episodic nature of the music and its loose formal structure, and they concluded that Ellington had overreached himself.

By contrast, the jazz press blew up a brash, show-business rave, in its own way equally superficial. The jazz critics were also unprepared for judging such a work. The *Down Beat* reviewer, for example, discussed much of the work in terms of other music he claimed to hear quoted or echoed—*East St. Louis Toodle-oo*, *Afternoon Of A Faun*, *Lullaby Of Broadway*, *Way Low*, *The Flaming Sword*, *Chelsea Bridge*, *I Know That You Know*, and *Rhapsody In Blue*, plus *Swannee River* and *Dixie* which *are* directly quoted. The review was intended to be favorable but the use of so much other music to describe *Black, Brown And Beige* gives the impression that it is a highly derivative work. So far as the general show-business publications are concerned, the headline in *Variety* indicates their attitude: "ELLINGTON, AT B.O. AND MUSICALLY, NIFTILY IN GROOVE AT CARNEGIE HALL CONCERT." "(B.O. stands for Box Office.) *Metronome* said the same thing more succinctly: "DUKE KILLS CARNEGIE CATS."

Duke Ellington never made public his reasons for deciding, after only three performances, that the public was not ready for his "tone parallel to the history of the Negro in America," so we can only guess at his motives. One factor must have been the difficulty of fitting a work of this duration into the average Ellington concert. A 45-minute tone poem would have seriously disturbed what Ellington clearly regarded as his ideal concert program balance. Typical of Ellington's pronouncements after the premiere was his spoken introduction to the second Carnegie Hall concert on December 11, 1943:

> I'd like very much to have a little word about the program. The numbers which have been selected for this particular program have been chosen because [pause] have been chosen for many or two or three different reasons. The first is that we picked things which we thought would be a great advantage to the soloists who are being presented in their individual responsibility; we have also been influenced by requests and a lot along the modern [pause] . . . ah, popular trend. Our program tonight is not a very heavy one, as usual, of course [laughs], but we're sincere about it. We think we have many of our good friends who are sincere about the things they do even if they are short.

He then goes on to introduce *Take The "A" Train*. The uncertainties in the construction and delivery of this speech are very marked. It is an attempt to reassure his audience that it was not going to be asked to listen to any 45-minute tone poems without appearing to deprecate *Black, Brown And Beige*. He also seems to want to convey that his more familiar shorter works are not being treated as inferior music, that the absence of an extended concert piece did not mean a reduction in the quality of the program. All this seems even more bizarre when we realize that Ellington was introducing an event which saw the premiere of another new concert work, *New World A-Comin'*, though this was only thirteen minutes long.

Equally strange is the way he introduces the two excerpts from *Black, Brown And Beige* played at this concert:

> Next we play a very short sketch from *Brown*, which is the second section of *Black, Brown And Beige*. We thought we wouldn't play it in its entirety tonight because it represents an awfully long and very important story. And it [pause] I don't think too many people are familiar with the story; we thought we would be better to wait until the story was a little more familiar before we did the whole thing again. Well now, however, in this story, I mean of course it is taken from the *Black, Brown And Beige* which is a tone parallel to the history of the American Negro.

The emphasis on length here—"an awfully long . . . story"—does seem to indicate that Ellington had been stung by complaints about the length of the full work, while the overall tone of these announcements indicates that he was afraid of being considered too highbrow.

In December 1944, after the AFM recording ban had been lifted, a *Black, Brown And Beige Suite* was recorded for Victor and issued on four twelve-inch 78s—a mere eighteen minutes out of the full 45. This was the only part of the work available to the record-buying public until thirteen years later, when Columbia Records invited Ellington to record the whole work. An LP entitled *Black, Brown And Beige* duly appeared, but it contained only the first part, the *Black* movement, from the original score. *Black* takes up the first side of the LP. The reverse is made up of two further variations on the spiritual theme from *Black*, the first by guest singer Mahalia Jackson, the second by Ray Nance on violin, and by a version of the *23rd Psalm*, sung by Jackson. By this time, tape copies of the full 1943 Carnegie Hall and Boston performances were beginning to circulate privately. But not until 30 years after the premiere was a good quality recording of the Carnegie Hall *Black, Brown And Beige* issued, on the Prestige label. (A decade earlier, an LP taken from a very poor tape copy had been issued by an Italian company.) Ellington again began recording *Black, Brown And Beige* in 1965. The final march was omitted, and *The Blues* was not recorded until 1971.

In 1972, a group of British musicians recorded the full work in London under the direction of Alan Cohen, a musician who has specialized in the interpretation of Ellington's music. This venture had been preceded by intensive research into existing sheet music and the then available recordings. The performance has been issued (on Argo and Monmouth Evergreen) and gives the listener an opportunity to hear the complete *Black, Brown And Beige* in a recording made with modern stereophonic techniques.

* * *

Ellington seems always to have feared that an undue concern with the formal aspects of music would have had an inhibiting effect on the performances of his musicians and on the spontaneity of his own writing. His mastery of form in the short pieces was so natural that no burning of the midnight oil was needed to achieve their remarkable cohesion and balance. But such an outlook has its dangers for a man working on extended compositions. Despite the fact that he had been talking about the project for several years, Ellington accomplished the actual writing of *Black, Brown And Beige* within the month before the premiere, during spare time available after performing his normal duties as a touring bandleader. There can be little doubt that the lack of formal unity, which is the most obvious defect of *Black, Brown And Beige*, is due to this hasty method of composition. And the uneven quality of the final *Beige* movement seems to be the consequence of the rapidly approaching deadline. Duke always maintained that he needed a deadline to inspire his best writing, but the later stages of *Black, Brown And Beige* suggest that he may well have been mistaken, at least on this occasion.

* * *

The personnel of the Ellington Orchestra at the premiere of *Black, Brown And Beige* was:

Trumpets: Wallace Jones; Harold Baker; Rex Stewart (cornet); Ray Nance (also violin and vocal).

Trombones: Lawrence Brown, Tricky Sam Nanton; Juan Tizol (valve trombone).

Reeds: Otto Hardwick (alto sax, clarinet); Johnny Hodges (alto sax); Ben Webster (tenor sax); Chauncey Haughton (clarinet, tenor sax); Harry Carney (baritone and alto saxes, clarinet, bass clarinet).

Rhythm: Duke Ellington (piano); Fred Guy (guitar); Alvin Raglin (bass); Sonny Greer (drums); Billy Strayhorn (deputy pianist).

Vocal: Betty Roché, Jimmy Britton (the latter not heard at the concert).

Black, Brown And Beige is divided into three movements; the first of these, *Black*, is itself in three parts. In the opening *Work Song*, the deep voices of Carney's baritone saxophone and Nanton's trombone are heard. This is a very rich movement musically, melodically fertile and with superbly varied scoring, and as a portrayal of hard physical labor it is also a total success. Greer's drums hammer out the work rhythm with a menace suggesting that the labor is anything but voluntary, the brasses have a whip-like urgency, and the brief moments of repose are beautifully captured. Nanton is brilliant and inimitable, and the use of his trombone as near-human voice is exceptionally subtle. A beautiful spiritual-like theme dominates *Come Sunday*—the second part of *Black*—and the hushed beauty of the Hodges solo captures Ellington's devotional mood to perfection. No less brilliant is the long orchestral introduction, with Tizol's valve trombone and Nance's violin heard before piano and muted brass simulate the church bells calling the congregation to prayer. The third section of *Black* is less successful, and the Carnegie Hall performance, with its uncertainties about basic tempo, tends to exaggerate this. Ellington seems to have been unsure about the title of this section, sometimes calling it *Light*, sometimes *Montage*. It uses themes from the first two parts of *Black* as the basis for variation and juxtapositions. In the main these are orchestral, although the opening trumpet solo offers brilliant examples of Baker's playing, both in the 1943 original and in the 1957 remake. While undoubtedly over-fragmented, this section contains some very beautiful passages and includes a reminiscence of the 1938 *Ridin' On A Blue Note*.

With the opening of *Brown* we return to the historical perspective. First Ellington offers a portrait of the West Indian blacks who have joined the American mainland community and a tribute to "the several hundred Negroes who came from Haiti to save Savannah during the Revolutionary War." This segment is known as *West Indian Dance* or *The West Indian Influence*. He then moves on to the Civil War with *Emancipation Celebration* or *The Lighter Attitude*. Here Ellington portrays the celebrations and the optimism of the young blacks and the doubts and fears of the older people whose social fabric had been destroyed by the

Civil War. This is one of the most vivid parts of *Black, Brown And Beige* and one of the most swinging from a jazz viewpoint. Stewart plays the opening theme with jaunty brilliance and is heard later with plunger mute in duet with Nanton. Their performance of this movement in the Carnegie Hall concert is one of the most brilliant examples of vocalized instrumental playing in the annals of recorded African American music.

The second part of *Brown* is *The Blues* (a section which Ellington originally called *Mauve*), which features probably his most successful essay in lyric writing. This is an Ellington blues, as much of mood as of tradition, and only the central instrumental section is cast in the traditional twelve-bar form. The vocal part was sung most expressively in the 1943 performances by Betty Roché and most beautifully on the Victor *Suite* by Joya Sherrill. The pyramidal structure of the lyric—the lines lengthening in the first part, shortening in the second—is beautifully brought off. The portions of the lyric cast as recitative receive a particularly finely judged accompaniment. Between the two parts of the vocal there is an instrumental interlude. First, Ben Webster states a ravishing Ellington blues melody. (This solo was later played by Al Sears, Harold Ashby, and Paul Gonsalves on different recordings, each bringing his own personal flavor to the theme.) It is followed by a twelve-bar riff chorus for orchestra which Ellington later detached and used as the basis for a short piece called *Carnegie Blues*. (This was never part of *Black, Brown And Beige* though it is sometimes so described by radio announcers and liner note writers. The twelve-bar theme from *The Blues* is used as the basis for a quite different arrangement from that found in *Brown*. A variation on the brass fanfare from *Work Song* also makes an unexpected and rather incongruous appearance in *Carnegie Blues*.) An excerpt from *Black, Brown And Beige* issued on the Jazz Archive label is said to come from the January 1943 Carnegie Hall concert. This consists of *The Blues* only, but Betty Roché's vocal and Ben Webster's tenor solo are both different from those on the Prestige recordings. Presumably, this excerpt comes from the January 1943 Boston concert.

The Blues brings to an end, in a slightly inconclusive fashion, the second part of *Black, Brown And Beige*. The final movement, *Beige*, illustrates aspects of African American life in the twentieth century. Ellington's piano tells a semi-autobiographical story here, with a snippet of stride piano included. In somewhat kaleidoscopic fashion, the Charleston, the loneliness of the city at night, the black thrust for education, and the kept woman in the *Sugar Hill Penthouse* are all depicted. After a couple of references to the *Come Sunday* theme, we arrive at the climax, a brassy, rather commonplace affair with Stewart's cornet stabbing out high notes. This *Beige* movement is a somewhat rambling structure with passages of quite breathtaking beauty side by side with music which seems to have been put together hastily. The attempt to impose unity by quotations from *Work Song* and *Come Sunday* succeed only in making it seem more diffuse. A final patriotic vocal section, *The Black, Brown And Beige Is The Red White And Blue*, was cut after the *Rye* runthrough.

* * *

The complete 1943 Carnegie Hall recording is the definitive *Black, Brown And Beige*. On the recordings of excerpts dating from the middle forties the band is obviously far more familiar with the music than in 1943, which usually results in superior performances. Of these selections, *Come Sunday* seems to have become the most popular, although quite often the whole of *Black* would be played. Other favorite extracts include *Work Song* from *Black*; *West Indian Dance*, *Emancipation Celebration*, and *The Blues* from *Brown*, and *Sugar Hill Penthouse* from *Beige*. Such extracts appear in recordings not only from concerts but also from broadcasts of club appearances and even dances, as well as in the Victor *Black, Brown And Beige Suite*. Many of these interpretations are of great interest, though there are fewer variations between different versions than in the recordings of most of Ellington's shorter works. The 1959 Columbia recording of *Black, Brown And Beige* is in superior sound, but Ellington ran out of studio time before the project was completed. The performance of *Black* is excellent, but the second side of the LP, featuring Mahalia Jackson and Ray Nance, is not at all successful and quite irrelevant as far as *Black, Brown And Beige* is concerned. In 1971, the band recorded a part of *Beige* as *Symphonette*, which included the *Sugar Hill Penthouse* scene. It is interesting that the solo part played by Carney on clarinet in the 1943 recordings is played by him on baritone saxophone in 1971. As with many later recordings, this has superior sound quality, but one needs to hear the original first in order to understand the relevance of these later extracts.

The recording of *Black, Brown And Beige* by the Alan Cohen Band offers an opportunity to hear the full work in excellent sound and to hear the actual notes Ellington wrote without the interpretative gloss of his own musicians with their long and intimate knowledge of his music. Much of the solo work is in a later jazz idiom in terms of phrasing and inflection, and the playing certainly lacks the strong character of Ellington's own versions. But this interpretation is a valid one, performed with great skill and devotion. The British musicians prove beyond any doubt that *Black, Brown And Beige* is fine music and not just overblown artistic pretension hiding behind the interpretative skills of the Ellington musicians, as has sometimes been claimed. Without the Ellington musicians the work sounds very different—less colorful and less subtle, but fine music still. This recording of Ellington's longest instrumental composition reveals a good deal about the composer and his methods. Like the complete Ellington recordings, it shows that, despite structural weaknesses and episodic construction,

Black, Brown And Beige is a single entity and not, as may sometimes be suspected, a suite masquerading as a tone poem. It is indeed unfortunate that Ellington did not record a fully prepared complete version of this work in later years. It would certainly have been interesting to hear what changes he would have made with decades of concert music experience behind him.

* * *

The change from the optimism of the prepremiere publicity about Ellington's new tone poem to Duke's conclusion that people were perhaps not ready for the story it told—that his 1944 pop tune *I'm Beginning To See The Light* was the new *Work Song*—was a rapid and apparently rather depressing one. But any fear that Ellington's new attitude might inhibit his production of new concert works was wholly unfounded, his postpremiere statements representing, in part at least, no more than an adjustment of his public mask. The concerts in New York and Boston at which *Black, Brown And Beige* was premiered also included *Blue Belles Of Harlem*, a concert work written in 1938 and commissioned by Paul Whiteman as part of a 40-minute anthology called *Those Bells*, written by six different composers who each conducted the Whiteman Orchestra in his own section at the work's premiere at Carnegie Hall in December 1938. Duke does not seem to have played the piano part in *Blue Belles Of Harlem* on that occasion, but in the 1943 revival, the work is cast in the form of a concerto for piano and orchestra. The music is Gershwinesque, with only a slight jazz flavor, and the three themes are developed in a rhapsodic manner. A similar format is used rather more successfully in *New World A-Comin'*, which Duke premiered at his December 1943 Carnegie Hall concert.

At all these 1943 concerts a very generous selection of Ellington's shorter pieces, old and new, was presented. The program for the first Carnegie Hall concert was an unusually long one, even by Ellington standards. Comparison between this and the programs presented at Boston and at the December Carnegie Hall concert is interesting:

Carnegie Hall, January 23, 1943

Star Spangled Banner
Black And Tan Fantasy
Rockin' In Rhythm
Moon Mist
Jumpin' Punkins
A Portrait Of Bert Williams
A Portrait Of Bill Robinson (*Bojangles*)
A Portrait Of Florence Mills (*Black Beauty*)
Black, Brown And Beige
Ko-Ko
Dirge
Stomp (*Johnny Come Lately*)

Are You Sticking?
Bakiff
Jack The Bear
Blue Belles Of Harlem
Cotton Tail
Day Dream
Boy Meets Horn
Rose Of The Rio Grande
Don't Get Around Much Anymore
Goin' Up
Mood Indigo

Symphony Hall, Boston, January 27, 1943

Star Spangled Banner
What Am I Here For?
On Becoming A Square (*Main Stem*)
Day Dream
Black, Brown And Beige
Jumpin' Punkins
Dirge
A Little Light Psalf (*Johnny Come Lately*)
Black Beauty
Bakiff
Black And Tan Fantasy
Blue Belles Of Harlem
Boy Meets Horn
Rose Of The Rio Grande

Carnegie Hall, December 11, 1943

Star Spangled Banner
Take The "A" Train
Moon Mist
Tea For Two
Honeysuckle Rose
Stardust
C Jam Blues
Extracts from *Black, Brown And Beige*: *West Indian Dance* and *Emancipation Celebration*
New World A-Comin'
Floor Show (*Goin' Up*)
Don't Get Around Much Anymore
Ring Dem Bells
Medley of Popular Hits: *In a Sentimental Mood*, *Mood Indigo*, *Sophisticated Lady*, *Caravan*, *Solitude*, and *I Let A Song Go Out Of My Heart*
Jack The Bear
Do Nothin' Til You Hear From Me
Summertime
Cotton Tail
Black And Tan Fantasy
Rockin' In Rhythm
Sentimental Lady
Trumpet In Spades
Things Ain't What They Used To Be

The most obvious feature of the last program is that it does *not* reflect the radical changes suggested by Ellington's opening speech.

The complete Carnegie Hall January 1943 concert has been issued on Prestige with the odd bits which have not survived in acceptable sound replaced by relevant parts from the Boston concert. Apart from these substitutions and *The Blues*, from *Black, Brown And Beige*, no other music from this Boston concert has been issued on disc. (The complete Carnegie Hall December 1943 concert has been released on the British Ember label.)

The interpretations of the shorter pieces heard at these concerts are by and large what one would expect, close to the studio versions in most instances, with the removal of the three-minute limitation often leading to a fuller arrangement and/or a more easy, relaxed tempo. The versions of *Black And Tan Fantasy* heard at all three concerts feature Wallace Jones as growl trumpet soloist, revealing an aspect of his talent not otherwise heard on record. Nanton is outstanding here, of course, and he is also the star of the vigorous performances of *Rockin' In Rhythm*, as vital and exciting a score in the forties as it had been in the previous decade. *Moon Mist, Jumpin' Punkins, A Portrait Of Bert Williams, Bojangles, Ko-Ko, Johnny Come Lately, Jack The Bear, Cotton Tail*, and *Day Dream* from the January 1943 concert are similar in overall pattern to the Victors. Bigard is missed on *Bert Williams*, although this version finds Stewart in particularly lively form. *Black Beauty* features Baker in a sensitive reading of this most beautiful melody. Strayhorn's *Dirge* sounds like a workshop piece, tentative in mood and featuring delicate pastel voicing and harmonization. *Are You Sticking?* has Chauncey Haughton taking over this not particularly memorable concerto role. *Bakiff* is much longer than the Victor, most of the extra time being devoted to tongue-in-cheek Eastern exoticisms from Nance on violin. *Boy Meets Horn* is yet another great reading and vies with the 1940 Fargo version as the best ever of this Stewart showcase. *Rose Of The Rio Grande* is the standard version with the vocal chorus excised. *Don't Get Around Much Anymore* is the Victor arrangement (i.e., *Never No Lament*) plus the final Hodges solo which did not fit onto the 78. Nance plays an expressive solo here, and Hodges is utterly exquisite. The closing *Mood Indigo* has Jones in Whetsol's role and a nice piano solo from Duke.

On the Prestige issue, the sound quality on *Black And Tan Fantasy* and *Rockin' In Rhythm* is only moderate, while *Black Beauty* and most of the first part of *Black, Brown And Beige* use the Boston recordings. Otherwise, the sound quality is excellent for a concert recording of this period. The Boston concert is also in good sound and the unissued versions of *What Am I Here For? Main Stem*, and *Johnny Come Lately* are among the many musical delights.

* * *

By the time of the December Carnegie Hall concert there were several important changes in the band. Taft Jordan had arrived to boost the trumpet section to five—the book always remained for four trumpets, but the section often expanded because of the need to capture or retain a particular talent. Jimmy Hamilton had taken over clarinet responsibilities, while the tenor chair vacated by Ben Webster was occupied pro tem by Elbert "Skippy" Williams (not to be confused with fellow tenor saxophonist Elmer Williams). The band had also acquired a new ballad singer in the person of Al Hibbler. At the concert, *Ring Dem Bells* joins *Black And Tan Fantasy* and *Rockin' In Rhythm* in a vintage trio. Three popular standards are used as showcases for Jordan (*Tea For Two*), Hamilton (*Honeysuckle Rose*), and Baker (*Stardust*). (According to a 1944 Leonard Feather article, these arrangements of standards are by Mary Lou Williams, who had married Shorty Baker in 1942.) The version of *Trumpet In Spades* heard at this concert is much superior to the 1936 Brunswick and features fine playing by Stewart. (It is preceded by a little speech from Duke who explains that the number is really a bit of program music representing a noonday street scene at the intersection of 47th and Parkway in Chicago.)

Rex is again outstanding in the excerpts from *Black, Brown And Beige*. The centerpiece of the concert is clearly *New World A-Comin'*. The title of this work is derived from a book on the future of the black American by Roi Ottley, and the music projects a gentle, reflective optimism. It is a concerto for Ellington's piano with four themes cast in a very loose rondo form. As was the case in *Blue Belles Of Harlem*, the orchestration does not make any significant use of the individual musicians in the band. In later years, Ellington performed this attractive composition as a piano solo. The shorter version broadcast as a memorial to President Franklin Roosevelt on April 14, 1945, simply consists of variations on the work's principal theme. But the solo versions from the sixties present the full composition, the one recorded at Goutelas in 1966 being probably the best interpretation of this particular work.

The December 1943 Carnegie Hall concert also saw the first known appearance of the *Medley Of Popular Hits*. On this occasion it consisted of six songs, but it was soon expanded and became a regular feature of Ellington concerts, sometimes incorporating multichorus performances of songs within its scope. Although offering an opportunity to hear Ellington playing melody at the piano, always worth the attention of the musical ear, in the opinion of many people the *Medley* took up an undue amount of time at Ellington concerts. It became one of the band's least highly regarded offerings, so far as Ellington connoisseurs were concerned. Duke always included it on the stated grounds that many people came to his concerts to hear his popular songs. But while he never said so in public, the performance of so many of his songs once or twice nightly was also a good way of boosting his income from royalties. Several recordings of the *Medley* have been issued on LP, all from concerts, and despite the reservations expressed about them they all contain a great deal of excellent piano playing.

Most of the other music at this concert is as expected. Nance is featured on *Take The "A" Train*, Skippy Williams on *Cotton Tail*, and Hodges on *Day Dream, Don't Get Around Much Anymore*, and *Sentimental Lady*. The new ballad singer Al Hibbler is heard on *Do Nothin' Til You Hear From Me* and *Summertime*.

* * *

The only studio sessions by the Ellington Orchestra during 1943 inaugurated their series for World Transcriptions. Like the earlier Standard and later Capitol Transcriptions, these have excellent sound quality. A number of them were issued on LP. The first sessions for World were on November 8 and 9, 1943. On the first, the trumpets were temporarily down to three—Jones, Stewart and Jordan—while bassist Wilson Myers subbed for Raglin. On the second, Nance and Baker returned to make the trumpets five, and Raglin was back in place of Myers.

The established Ellington repertoire recorded on these dates included *C Jam Blues*; *Mood Indigo* (with Carney playing the clarinet part); *Rockin' In Rhythm* (an exciting reading of the score with Carney taking over Bigard's part here too, as he had done on the Carnegie Hall performance); another excellent version of *Boy Meets Horn* (the one issued on V-Disc); *Do Nothin' Til You Hear From Me* (the pop version of *Concerto For Cootie* featuring Hibbler and Brown); *Sentimental Lady*; *Main Stem* (the excellent version used on V-Disc); *A Slip Of The Lip*; *Things Ain't What They Used To Be* (another excellent performance also found on V-Disc) and *Caravan*.

New numbers included three vocal features for Roché on *I Wonder Why, Go Away Blues,* and *I Don't Want Anybody At All*, while Hibbler is heard in Gershwin's *Summertime*. Johnny Hodges is featured in *Hop, Skip and Jump* (another V-Disc issue), a score later slightly modified and retitled *Rockabye River*. *Baby Please Stop And Think About Me* is a new Ellington song in a nonvocal version featuring Nance and Hamilton, as well as a rather conventional tenor solo by Skippy Williams. *Three Cent Stomp* (a number on the *Stompy Jones* chords written to celebrate the controversial issue of a three-cent stamp) remained in the book for a number of years; this initial version featured Baker, Nanton, Nance, Raglin, Stewart, and Williams. During the brief absence of Stewart in mid-1943, Jordan, a former star of the Chick Webb band, had been brought into the Ellington Orchestra, and he was retained on Stewart's return. He is featured on *Tea For Two* from the series of "Variations On Themes," which presented leading Ellington soloists on standard material. Another one of these, *Ain't Misbehavin'* featuring Baker, was also recorded at this session. (Other "Variations On Themes," apparently arranged by Mary Lou Williams, were showcases for Hamilton on *Honeysuckle Rose*, Brown on *Somebody Loves Me*, and Baker again, on *Stardust*.) The World Transcription recording of *Tea For Two* is an admirable setting for Jordan's playing, displaying his sprightly phrasing and powerful swing, while Baker's more mellow trumpet style is poised and restrained on *Ain't Misbehavin'*. Also recorded at the November 8 session was another arrangement by Mary Lou Williams destined to become famous. The score is based on Irving Berlin's *Blue Skies* and features Jordan, Brown, Williams, Stewart, Hodges, and Hamilton. Later it became a feature for the trumpet section under the title of *Trumpet No End* and as such was a regular showstopper at Ellington concerts.

A further session for World Transcriptions took place on December 1, 1943, and again mixed previously recorded Ellingtonia and new material. Fresh versions were cut of *It Don't Mean A Thing* (with vocal duet by Nance and Jordan); *Johnny Come Lately*; *Creole Love Call* (the version issued on V-Disc, with, unusually, Baker taking the growl solo and Carney both the clarinet choruses); *Jack The Bear*; *Harlem Airshaft* (a particularly fine version); and *Ring Dem Bells* (still in the 1930 arrangement). In addition there was a superb new *Rose Room*, based on the 1933 arrangement and featuring Hamilton, Brown, and Hodges. Two more of the "Variations On Themes" were recorded at this date—Hamilton's *Honeysuckle Rose* and Brown's *Somebody Loves Me*. A second showcase for Jordan, *Chopsticks*, is another enjoyable score—simple, swinging music which also features Ellington's piano and reminds us that as well as producing concert works Duke could always turn his hand to creating elemental jazz performances of incomparable quality.

* * *

The V-Discs mentioned in connection with some of these World Transcription items were records put out by the United States Armed Forces for the exclusive use of service personnel during and after the Second World War. The music was donated by the artists, and leading record companies provided recording facilities. The music on these V-Discs—including those by Ellington—was drawn from a variety of sources. Sometimes commercial recordings from various labels were used, including some from the thirties—alternative takes appeared on V-Disc with surprising frequency. Broadcast transcriptions were another source, and live recordings made at concerts and other venues were also used. Finally, there were special studio sessions set up for V-Disc recordings, although not in the case of the Ellington material. The reason for this is stated in George T. Simon's preface to Richard S. Sear's massive study, *V-Discs—A History And Discography* (Greenwood Press, 1980). Simon, a V-Disc producer, asked Duke if he would let the band make V-Discs. Duke suggested he ask "some of the guys." "And so I went over to Harry Carney and Lawrence Brown, whom I'd known for years, and asked them. Their reply in essence: 'George, if you are asking us to do this for free as a personal favor for you, of course we'll do it. But if you are asking us to do it for the Army, forget it—not when you consider the way they have been treating our people.' That's why I never had the privilege of recording the Ellington band for V Disc."

* * *

Several Ellington location broadcasts recorded during 1943 and 1944 have been issued on disc. Among the less familiar Ellington items heard on these broadcasts are a nonvocal *Jump For Joy*; *Tonight I Shall Sleep* (the later Victor recording features guest Tommy Dorsey); *People Will Say We're In Love* (a conventional arrangement with an unconventional sequence of ballad solos by Hamilton, clarinet, Carney, bass clarinet, and Nanton, plunger trombone); *Wait For Me Mary* (featuring Nanton and Hodges); *It's Been So Long*; *Barzillai Lew*; *You'll Never Know*; *Cabin In The Sky*; *On The Sands Of Time*; and *Design For Jivin'*.

During the summer of 1943, Ellington broadcast a series of half-hour shows entitled *Pastel Period*. Three have been issued on LP; while popular ballads and slow tempos predominate, there is at least one uptempo performance per broadcast. At the time of these broadcasts there were a couple of temporary personnel changes, Lawrence Brown and Otto Hardwick being replaced by Sandy Williams and Nat Jones. The latter doubled alto sax and clarinet, and broadcasts from this period show that Ellington did for a short time consider him as Bigard's replacement. On the *Pastel Period* broadcast of July 11, 1943, Jones, introduced as a New Orleans style clarinet specialist, plays his own arrangement of *Out Of Nowhere*. On other broadcasts Jones rather than Hamilton is given Bigard's choice clarinet parts, but his work is that of an imitator; his Bigard stylings lack both character and Barney's level of virtuosity. Sandy Williams received little exposure. Even the trombone solo on the then highly popular *Don't Get Around Much Anymore* was given to Nanton's plunger-muted horn, though it had been a Lawrence Brown open solo. A notable performance from this period is the relaxed *Five O'Clock Drag* from June 17, 1943, with a forceful essay in the Stewart half-valve style by Jordan. By August 1943, Brown and Hardwick were back. The full potential of their temporary replacements cannot be gauged from the few recordings they made with Duke. Among the highlights of the *Pastel Period* shows are a couple of performances of *Blue Belles Of Harlem*, a version of *Tonight I Shall Sleep* with vocal by Roché, and a fine, restrained *Dinah's In A Jam*, which features Nat Jones's best work with the band and a Nance vocal.

The 1944 Ellington broadcasts include *Fickle Fling* (a very swinging performance), *Jumpin' Frog Jump*, *Poinciana*, *G.I. Jive*, *Irresistible You* (a ballad showcase for Carney on bass clarinet), and *Too Much In Love*, while more familiar Ellington themes are often heard in superior versions. The recording of *My Honey's Lovin' Arms* (vocal by Nance) from a broadcast of May 21, 1944, is one of the most swinging Ellington recordings from this period.

There were several comings and goings in the trumpet section at this time, but the important changes were in the reed and vocal departments. Tenor saxophonist Skippy Williams was replaced by Al Sears in May 1944. Unlike the other long-serving occupants of the tenor sax berth, Sears was not a great virtuoso or innovator. His forte was straightforward, uncluttered phrases played with maximum swing, and he made his presence felt by means of a strong musical personality. Betty Roché left in April 1944 and was replaced, after a few months, by a trio of female singers—Joya Sherrill, a very young vocalist with an attractive style; Kay Davis, a schooled singer who sang ballads in a contralto range but was more often employed in wordless soprano parts; and Marie Ellington, a rather ordinary ballad singer, not related to Duke, who later became the wife of Nat King Cole.

On the first day of December 1944, the Ellington band was in the studio for its first Victor session in two-and-a-half years, the company having settled with the AFM. We will deal with the Victor recordings up to the end of 1945 *en bloc* before going on to consider music from other sources. Four titles were recorded at the first session, all Ellington popular songs: *I Ain't Got Nothin' But The Blues*, featuring Hibbler and Kay Davis; *Don't You Know I Care?*, featuring Hibbler; and two numbers for Joya Sherrill, *I'm Beginning To See The Light* and *I Didn't Know About You*. The most successful of these, commercially, was *I'm Beginning To See The Light*, given an attractive performance with good bass work by Raglin. Sears is heard in *Nothin' But The Blues*, Hodges on *Don't You Know I Care?*, and Brown on *I Didn't Know About You*. Comparison of the two issued takes of *Don't You Know I Care?* shows that Ellington replaced the Brown solo with a passage for the full trombone section on take 2. Later in the month the band moved to the opposite extreme of the repertoire, recording the selections from *Black, Brown And Beige* known as the *Black, Brown And Beige Suite*. The first three of the 12-inch 78 sides consist of *Work Song*, *Come Sunday* (both from *Black*), and *The Blues* (from *Brown*). The fourth side, *Three Dances*, contains *West Indian Dance* and *Emancipation Celebration* (from *Brown*) and *Sugar Hill Penthouse* (from *Beige*). The important trumpet solo in *Emancipation Celebration* is taken over, brilliantly, by Jordan as Stewart was again temporarily out of the band. These Victor selections, while no substitute for the whole work, make a good introduction to Ellington's most ambitious composition to date and have the advantage of being well recorded and played by a band by now thoroughly familiar with the music.

At the first Victor session of 1945 Ellington produced *Carnegie Blues*, the piece based on the blues theme from *Black, Brown And Beige*; Brown and Sears are featured in duet. The rest of the session is made up of concertos for Brown (*Blue Cellophane*) and Hodges (*The Mood To Be Wooed*), plus a non-Ellington pop tune, *My Heart Sings*, which features a vocal by Sherrill and violin by Nance. This session took place in January. The band did not return to the Victor studios until April 26, but then a heavy schedule followed, with sessions on May 1, 10, 11, 14, 15, and 16. Some of these dates produced only one issued title, which indicates that unreleased masters might repose in the Victor vaults. This view is encouraged by the history of *Blue Cellophane*, which remained unissued until 1961. The April 26 session produced one title only, a pop song by Strayhorn, Sherrill, and Stewart called *The Kissing Bug*. It is well sung by Sherrill, while Sears and Hamilton are heard briefly in the context of an effective arrangement.

A new Ellington song, *Everything But You*, was recorded at the next session. This is one of Duke's most attractive songs, with lyrics by Don George which are of a higher standard than those provided by most of Ellington's lyricists. Duke presents the theme on piano in his mock-pop style, Sherrill handles the vocal perfectly (notice the backing by Jordan in the second half of her chorus), and the performance ends with a vibrant solo from Carney backed by bold orchestral colors. Equally excellent is the studio version of *Riff Staccato* with its sharply swinging Nance and Jordan duet.

The session of May 10 yielded just one title, a remake of *Prelude To A Kiss*, heralding a short series of Ellington retrospects; here Carney, Nance, and Ellington are featured in a sumptuous arrangement. On the following day, *Caravan*, *Black And Tan Fantasy*, and *Mood Indigo* were recorded—the latter only to be hidden in the Victor vaults for sixteen years. This version of *Caravan* is one of the happiest of the many recorded by the band, the orchestral playing full of pastel colors and tonal shadings, the performance one of great relaxation and poise. Brown takes over Tizol's role, and the solo variations are provided by Hamilton on clarinet and Nance on violin. The *Black And Tan Fantasy* is dark and somber, the arrangement cut down to accommodate a slower tempo. Carney gives a massive reading of the second theme. Miley's two choruses are replaced by one for Nanton, who then leads the band in the peroration. In contrast to these heavily scored re-creations, *Mood Indigo* is a rather perfunctory affair with lots of Ellington piano and shorter contributions from Kay Davis's wordless soprano and Sears's tenor sax.

On the session of May 14, a version of *In A Sentimental Mood* opens with one of Hardwick's rare latter-day solos and develops into a complex score with solos by Brown, Stewart, and a flamboyant Ellington. On *It Don't Mean A Thing*, Ellington opens with a brilliant and unique chorus for the three girl singers and follows with a chase chorus for Nance (violin) and Jordan (trumpet), which is given a perfect orchestral framework. Sears then enters, backed by the rhythm section only, and proceeds to build to a driving, exciting climax, playing against the band in the final chorus—a superb piece of extroverted jazz making. The *Sophisticated Lady* that follows is also notable for orchestral tone colors. Hamilton and newcomer Cat Anderson on trumpet are heard after Duke's opening piano statement. The final title of the day, a recording of Ellington's *Tonight I Shall Sleep*, features Tommy Dorsey as guest soloist in a characteristic ballad statement; Hodges is heard briefly.

Ellington's aptitude for fresh musical thoughts on his compositions is next illustrated in a version of *I Let A Song Go Out Of My Heart*, recorded on May 15, 1945. Both this arrangement and that on the original 1938 recording consist of melodic statements with only the slightest variations. Yet there is no sense of monotony, each arrangement being utterly distinct and each inspiring a magnificent performance. The 1945 version opens with Carney's bass clarinet; continues with a vocal by Sherrill, given a perfect trombone obbligato by Brown; and concludes with brief solos by Brown and Ellington. There are two interesting takes of this arrangement. The other title from this date is a very unusual version of *Solitude* which features four vocalists, the three girls plus Hibbler. During the vocal chorus each voice changes function, sometimes used as lead with words, sometimes in a wordless supporting role. The only instrumental soloist is Hodges, who plays an exquisite half chorus backed by the girl singers.

The next session opens with a couple of titles performed by Ellington, Raglin, and Greer only: the sole commercial Ellington recording of *Frankie And Johnnie* (although the band arrangement was used extensively around this time) and a pleasant Ellington trifle, *Jumpin' Room Only*. To this last of the May Victor sessions the band contributed a remake of *Black Beauty* and a new Ellington pop song, *Every Hour On The Hour*. Harold Baker, now out of the band, had been the featured soloist in the 1943 revival of *Black Beauty*, so Duke again recast the arrangement, giving Brown the major solo role, with shorter passages for his own piano, Nance's violin, Hamilton's clarinet, and Carney's bass clarinet. Ellington's solo is an amusing pastiche of the piano styles of the late twenties, appropriate for a composition dating from 1928. *Every Hour On The Hour* is a more ephemeral Ellington creation, but when Hibbler is not singing, Hodges plays in the manner that ensures any performance a degree of immortality.

* * *

On July 24 and 30, 1945, the band recorded Ellington's and Strayhorn's *The Perfume Suite* for Victor. In a much lighter vein than *Black, Brown And Beige*, the work is cast in the form of a four-movement suite. According to Ellington, *Perfume Suite* does not depict the various perfumes in themselves, but rather illustrates how they affect the mood and character of the women wearing them. The first movement, by Strayhorn, is called *Balcony Serenade*, though *Under The Balcony*, *Love*, and *Sonata* were also considered as titles. Nance performs the introduction with a brief solo on warm-toned trumpet—he is less satisfactory on some other versions (e.g., the V-Disc) where he plays the passage on violin. Nance is followed by a solo by Ellington in his richest rhapsodic manner, which leads to Strayhorn's attractive melody, played by the Hodges-led saxophones and repeated with the addition of slight decorations from brass and piano.

Ellington observed that the woman pictured here feels that she is "the better half of Romeo and Juliet." The second movement is an Ellington-Strayhorn collaboration with some highly colored orchestration, vehement growl trumpet from Cat Anderson, and a Hibbler vocal in melodramatic style, perfectly matched by the lyrics. This section is called *Strange Feeling*, a title which replaced the original *Violence*. *Dancers In Love* (or *Naivety* or *Stomp For Beginners*) is a delightful piano solo accompanied only by string bass; it was written by Ellington, who plays with wit and charm in a simplified stride style. The final movement, *Coloratura*, takes the form of a concerto for Anderson's open trumpet and is a perfect musical portrayal of the prima donna temperament, of the woman who feels that "she is always making an entrance," as Ellington put it. This was written by Duke, who originally called it *Sophistication*, and both composer and soloist capture exactly the right mood. (The issued version of *Coloratura* is from the July 30 session, but a rejected take of July 24 has also been issued on LP. It is a slightly less polished performance.) *Coloratura* concludes a suite which, though musically lightweight, has the advantage of a consistent and even level of inspiration.

* * *

On the session of July 30, the band also recorded a version of *Things Ain't What They Used To Be* under the title *Time's A-Wastin'*. The reason for the change is not known; after the new title had been used for a couple of months, it was dropped and the original restored. On this vigorous performance the soloists are Hodges, Jordan, and Brown.

The remaining Victor recordings from 1945 are mostly of pop songs. On October 8, the band had Sid Catlett on drums as a temporary replacement for Greer. Catlett is one of the very greatest jazz drummers, and it is unfortunate that the only occasion on which he was in the studio with the Ellington band was given over to two non-Ellington pop songs. He did however play on one of the longer D.E.T.S. broadcasts, from October 13, 1945, which has been preserved and issued. The first of the two songs on the Victor date, *Come To Baby Do*, is very dated despite the inherent musicianship of Sherrill's vocal and fine playing by Brown, both in solo and accompaniment. The slower *Tell You What I'm Gonna Do* is even less interesting, but after the vocal Catlett's drums crack through the turgid texture like summer lightning on a dull, sultry day. Sherrill is again the singer and Brown the only soloist; his contribution here is brief.

The next Victor recording finds Duke playing piano with the Tommy Dorsey Orchestra in Sy Oliver's *The Minor Goes Muggin'*, and he indulges in the conventional swing piano style of the day with enthusiasm and humor. (This performance was issued back-to-back with *Tonight I Shall Sleep* from the May 14, 1945, session which featured Dorsey on trombone with the Ellington band.) Duke's final session of 1945—with his own band—produced recordings of three of his recent popular songs: *I'm Just A Lucky So And So*, featuring Hibbler with Hodges and Brown; *Long, Strong And Consecutive*, with Sherrill and Stewart in the major roles; and *The Wonder Of You*, featuring Sherrill, with Hodges and Brown. The first is an attractive song which became one of the standard Ellington ballads and one of Hibbler's perennials, but this session is not otherwise memorable.

* * *

In December 1944 and January 1945, the Ellington band took part in two important concerts. The first was in the annual Carnegie Hall series and included the premiere of *The Perfume Suite*. The concert side of the Ellington repertoire was also represented by *Blutopia* and over 30 minutes of selections from *Black, Brown and Beige*. Among the shorter pieces was a revival of *Creole Love Call* with a Kay Davis vocal and a trumpet solo by Nance which did not use Miley's original chorus as a model. A new number, *Suddenly It Jumped*, featured Jordan, and *Things Ain't What They Used To Be* had Hodges, Jordan, and Brown as soloists. Hodges was also featured on the voluptuous *The Mood To Be Wooed* and Brown in the rather inconsequential *Blue Cellophane*. The concert's climax was built on two non-Ellington numbers, *Blue Skies* and *Frankie And Johnnie*.

The January 1945 concert, at the Los Angeles Philharmonic Auditorium, was the occasion for the presentation of the annual *Esquire* magazine jazz awards. Ellington himself and five of his sidemen were among the recipients. Other award winners present were Billie Holiday, Anita O'Day, Art Tatum, Willie Smith, Al Casey, and Sid Catlett. These artists were featured at the concert in addition to the Ellington band. Louis Armstrong (in New Orleans) and Benny Goodman (in New York) were linked by radio to the Auditorium and joined the Ellington band in a not very impressive rendering of *Things Ain't What They Used To Be*. The concert featured some pleasant jam performances, but the most memorable music, along with some piano solos by Art Tatum, was provided by the Ellington Orchestra. (An exception is a mediocre performance of Leonard Feather's riff piece *Esquire Jump* in a setting by Esquire's "New Star" arranger of the year, Johnny Thompson.) The bulk of the concert is standard Ellington concert fare of the period: Hamilton is heard in his new concerto, *Air Conditioned Jungle*, and Anderson in *Coloratura* from *Perfume Suite*; there are selections from *Black, Brown And Beige* and long versions of *It Don't Mean A Thing* and *Frankie And Johnnie*, which serve to remind us of the high quality of music produced by the Ellingtonians in the more conventional aspects of their repertoire. Duke also takes a minor role in small-group jam session performances of *Honeysuckle Rose* and *I Can't Believe That You're In Love With Me*.

* * *

By January 1945, a number of further personnel changes had occured. Wallace Jones and Harold Baker had left the trumpet section, their places filled by Shelton Hemphill and Cat Anderson. Hemphill was a lead player greatly admired by Louis Armstrong, in whose orchestra he had held the first trumpet chair for some years. He rarely took solos during his five and a half years in the Ellington band. Anderson, in contrast, was featured as soloist in a great variety of roles and styles. He became famous for his high-register work, which encompasses notes few other trumpet players could reach. He was also a good soloist in the conventional Armstrong-inspired trumpet style and in the plunger-muted growl manner traditional in the Ellington band. In Anderson, Duke had acquired another brilliant all-rounder. Tizol left the band in April 1944, and contemporary commentators, not perceiving his great value as an ensemble player, were puzzled when Ellington expressed a strong sense of loss. His replacement was Claude Jones, a noted jazz trombonist who failed to make an impact on the band as soloist during a stay of four and a half years, doubtless because Ellington restricted his solo opportunities to a few theme statements in the Tizol style.

The full Ellington personnel in the early months of 1945 was:

Trumpets: Shelton Hemphill; Cat Anderson; Taft Jordan; Rex Stewart (cornet); Ray Nance (also violin and vocal)

Trombones: Tricky Sam Nanton; Lawrence Brown; Claude Jones (valve trombone).

Reeds: Otto Hardwick (alto sax, clarinet); Johnny Hodges (alto sax); Al Sears (tenor sax); Jimmy Hamilton (clarinet, tenor sax); Harry Carney (baritone sax, clarinet, bass clarinet).

Rhythm: Duke Ellington (piano); Fred Guy (guitar); Junior Raglin (bass); Sonny Greer (drums); Billy Strayhorn (deputy pianist).

Vocal: Al Hibbler, Joya Sherrill, Kay Davis, Maria Ellington.

Ellington recorded a further group of sessions for World Transcriptions in 1945, and the first took place on January 3 and 4. Duplications of repertoire with the 1944 and 1945 Victor include *I Didn't Know About You, I'm Beginning To See The Light, The Mood To Be Wooed, Blue Cellophane, Don't You Know I Care,* and *I Ain't Got Nothin' But The Blues.* From earlier years, *Pitter Panther Patter,* and *Subtle Slough* were revived. The latter, recorded by the Rex Stewart unit in 1941, is here given a full band arrangement virtually identical to the one used the following year, when the piece was given lyrics and a vocal chorus and the title changed to *Just Squeeze Me.* The "concertos" recorded at these sessions include the rich and sensuous *The Mood To Be Wooed* for Hodges, the cool and academic *Air Conditioned Jungle* for Hamilton, the rather slight *Blue Cellophane* for Brown, and the humorous *Frantic Fantasy* for Stewart. Strayhorn contributed *Midriff*, a new score with Brown as the only soloist, which features some particularly attractive scoring for the saxophone section. This is taken at a medium-fast tempo similar to Ellington's new *Let The Zoomers Drool*, but where Strayhorn's score calls for a light, jumping approach, Ellington's new piece is in the manner of the Buddy Johnson band and features a heavy, digging style with honking tenor and high-note trumpet. A couple of rather ephemeral pieces of Ellingtonia were also recorded, *Hit Me With A Hot Note And Watch Me Bounce* (vocal by Sherrill) and a brief nonvocal ballad with prominent lead alto from Hardwick, *You Never Know The Things You Miss.*

In marked contrast to these last pieces is a four-minute Ellington concert work, *Blutopia*, which here receives its only studio recording. Like *Blue Belles Of Harlem*, this piece was commissioned by Paul Whiteman. It was used by Ellington for a considerable period as the opener to his concert programs. *Blutopia* is an orchestral conception with three distinct thematic groups. On the World Transcription recording, the soloists are Jordan (in the short trumpet passage near the start), Sears (in a tenor sax obbligato), Nance (in the longer trumpet solos), and Ellington himself (in the brief but important piano statement).

The final Ellington World Transcriptions were recorded in July and August 1945. On the session of July 31, Duke recorded the three movements of his *Magazine Suite*, a tribute to three magazines which covered jazz in depth during this period—*Down Beat, Esquire,* and *Metronome*. It was also a celebration of the continuing success of Ellington and his sidemen in the polls run by these magazines to determine the most popular jazz artists. The three movements of the *Suite* were performed quite frequently by the Ellington Orchestra, but usually as separate numbers. *Down Beat Shuffle* is a medium-tempo twelve-bar blues with a theme statement by Hamilton on clarinet and Carney on bass clarinet; later Nanton, Hamilton, Jordan, and Sears are heard in solo. Strayhorn arranged *Esquire Swank*, a composition by Ellington and Hodges featuring the latter on alto. It is a 32-bar-with-bridge number with a strong blues flavor, and there is an important growl trumpet solo, played by Nance on this and other early recordings of the piece. (Later the solo was taken over most effectively by Anderson.) The finale to the suite is *Metronome All Out*, actually the second part of the long arrangement of *Frankie And Johnny* which the band had evolved over the years. The pace is a breezy uptempo, and there are infectious solos by Nance (violin), Ellington, and Raglin, as well as some spirited riffing by the band.

The two other titles from this July 1945 session are Anderson's *Teardrops In The Rain*, a medium-tempo swinger with solos from Sears, Raglin, Ellington, and the composer, and *Otto, Make That Riff Staccato.* The latter is a non-

Ellington nonsense song with truly imbecilic lyrics. It was given to Nance as a vocal feature and was so successful that it earned a prominent place in the repertoire for the next few months. Jordan provides a trumpet obbligato to Nance's singing, and it is always a pleasure to hear different versions of *Riff Staccato* for the variations in the witty interplay between vocalist and trumpeter.

The final World session introduces three new numbers—*Ultra Blue*, an Ellington composition (otherwise not recorded) with fine lead trumpet from Hemphill and short solos by Carney and Sears; a conventional *Hollywood Hangover* by Buck Clayton, with an *open* trombone solo from Nanton (his first on record since the twenties!), as well as contributions by Hodges, Nance, Hamilton, and Anderson; and Ellington's slight *Blues On The Double*, an uptempo romp featuring Hodges, Anderson, and Sears. The only "concertos" are Strayhorn's *Passion Flower*, with Hodges's solo heard in a big band setting, and *Frustration*, one of Ellington's more successful vehicles for Carney's baritone saxophone. Three popular songs were recorded—*Kissing Bug*, *Every Hour On The Hour*, and *Everything But You*—but the real delights of the session are the revivals of *In A Jam* and *In The Shade Of The Old Apple Tree*. *In A Jam* finds Nanton in prime form in the opening chorus, and there is a skillful and humorous version of the alto trumpet duet by Hodges and Nance before Stewart re-creates his final ride-out in impressive fashion. *In The Shade Of The Old Apple Tree* is even better. This is a longer version than the 1933 original, running for over five minutes. The theme statement by the saxes is relaxed and droll, while Stewart's muted commentary (based on Freddie Jenkins's part in the original) is full of wit and has a real rhythmic sting in its tail. Hodges has a wonderful chorus of very basic jazz alto, followed by one of Tricky Sam's greatest solos. His use of subtle variations of tone and rhythmic placing is as telling as ever, and the solo includes a gem of a break. One of the great jazz performances from the Ellington band of the middle forties, it concludes with a comic final ensemble embellished by Hamilton's clarinet.

* * *

In April 1945, Duke Ellington began what was to be the largest single recording project of his career, though it is most unlikely that he or anyone else thought of it in such terms at the time. At the beginning of the month, he opened at the 400 Restaurant and Supper Club in New York and signed an agreement with the newly formed American Broadcasting Company to broadcast a series of hour-long Saturday afternoon network shows under the title "A Date With The Duke." These were to be transmitted live and relayed from the band's current location (actually some of the later New York broadcasts were done from a Radio City studio), starting with this residency. They were "sustaining" (i.e. not commercially sponsored) broadcasts, financed by the United States Treasury Department. With the very first transmission on April 7, the Armed Forces Radio Service (AFRS) began to record the shows for the purpose of editing them into a series of half-hour broadcast transcription discs, again using the title "A Date With The Duke." The recordings of these complete broadcasts, preserved by either ABC or AFRS and augmented by the 78 half-hour "Date With The Duke" AFRS transcriptions, make up the largest single block of material in the Ellington discography.

The Treasury Department transmissions continued from a variety of locations up to November 24, 1945, after which Ellington went on a tour which would have made the weekly Saturday afternoon location broadcasts impossible. He had already made 33 broadcasts of one hour or more, plus a half-hour memorial to President Franklin D. Roosevelt, which had replaced the scheduled transmission on April 14, 1945. None of the music from this special memorial broadcast was used by AFRS. The ABC "Date With The Duke" broadcasts resumed on April 13, 1946, and the arrangement between ABC and AFRS continued as before. This second series consisted of seventeen programs, the last of which dates from August 31, 1946. Not all the music from the Treasury Department shows appear on the AFRS transcriptions, and since these were edited into programs tailored to fill exactly 30 minutes of air time, some selections were used more than once when their length was just what the engineers required. These "Date With The Duke" transcriptions are miracles of editing considering that tape technology had not yet become available.

Several individual items from these broadcasts appeared on V-Disc. The locations of the "Date With The Duke" broadcasts include theaters, ballrooms, radio stations, and U.S. Army posts, most with an audience, some without.

One feature of the series is the excellent sound quality. When excerpts from the transcriptions began to be issued on LP in the sixties, the sound was often poor, since the recordings were derived from tapes which had passed through several generations of copying before appearing on disc. But gradually the sources improved, and for some years an eight-LP set of DWTD selections on the Fairmont label led the field. Then, in 1980, a special Duke Ellington Treasury Series (D.E.T.S.) label was set up to issue entire broadcasts, by Jerry Valburn, an American collector and record producer who had been responsible for the engineering on a number of highly regarded LP issues. The D.E.T.S. releases, issued on a subscription basis by Valburn's Meritt Record Society, contain almost an hour's program per LP; indeed, each of the first 25 contains a full Treasury Department broadcast, but some programs of about 75 minutes duration disrupt this pattern from Volume 26 onwards. The recordings are taken directly either from surviving archival acetates or from AFRS transcription discs, whichever proved the better source for a given item when more than one could be found. Taken directly from originals and transferred with great skill and care, the sound quality of these discs is excellent, and the series, which runs to 48 LPs, is one of the most exciting ever produced.

***

The kind of programs Ellington presented on these "Date With The Duke" broadcasts can be shown from the first one, which is typical. There are two concert works, *Blutopia* and *The Perfume Suite*; a revival from the twenties, *Creole Love Call*; a couple of pieces from the early forties, *Subtle Slough* and *Passion Flower*; two of Ellington's current popular songs, *I'm Beginning To See The Light* and *I Ain't Got Nothin' But The Blues*; and four recent Ellington and Strayhorn compositions, *Midriff, Suddenly It Jumped, Frustration,* and *Air Conditioned Jungle*.

The Franklin D. Roosevelt Memorial Broadcast which replaced the second scheduled D.E.T.S. transmission has been issued several times and makes for fascinating listening. On the death of President Roosevelt, the American air waves were filled with solemn martial or classical music. The only dance band allowed on the air, the only one considered capable of offering music of an appropriate kind, was Ellington's. For that time, this was a very rare kind of recognition for black artists. The memorial program consisted of *Moon Mist, New World A-Comin'* (in a shortened version for solo piano), *Nobody Knows The Trouble I've Seen* (sung by Al Hibbler), *Mood Indigo* (one chorus), *Chant For F.D. Roosevelt* (piano solo), *Come Sunday, A City Called Heaven* (sung by Kay Davis), *Creole Love Call* (sung by Kay Davis, one chorus only), and *Moon Mist* recapitulated to close a historic broadcast.

***

One of the most important aspects of the D.E.T.S. broadcasts is that virtually the whole vast Ellington repertoire is brought into play. This repertoire ranges from lengthy concert works on the one hand to the slightest popular songs on the other, so that the series offers a complete picture of the 1945–46 Ellington Orchestra as a working band. So far as the performances are concerned, the listener should remember that the greater relaxation of the band's playing away from the recording studios sometimes resulted in a falling off in precision, which might surprise those unversed in the ways of the Ellingtonians. But the warmth and the surging, powerful swing so characteristic of these performances are qualities rarely captured fully in the more restraining climate of the recording studio. The D.E.T.S. broadcasts often find the band playing with a spontaneity and ease usually heard only in small improvising jazz groups.

Since the music in the D.E.T.S. series is so diverse, it is best discussed within the various broad categories into which it can be sorted—concert works, recent compositions, revivals from the twenties, thirties, and early forties, Strayhorn material, popular standards, Ellington's popular songs, and current popular songs.

***

We have already noted that *Blutopia* and *The Perfume Suite* were performed on the first D.E.T.S. broadcast. Both were repeated later, *The Perfume Suite* clearly gaining from the band's greater experience with the music when it reappears on the broadcast of July 7, 1945. A further advantage of the D.E.T.S. versions of *The Perfume Suite* is that the second movement, *Strange Feeling*, is heard complete while a whole chorus had to be omitted to fit it onto one side of the Victor 78 discs. Both of the Ellington "piano concertos" are heard, *Blue Belles Of Harlem* twice and *New World A-Comin'* in the excellent version which was also issued on V-Disc.

The selections from *Black, Brown And Beige* which appeared on V-Discs are from the D.E.T.S. broadcast of April 21, 1945, and Ellington presented excerpts from this work at intervals throughout the series. Overall, these are the finest of all interpretations of *Black, Brown And Beige*, the music by now more thoroughly absorbed by the band than on the earlier recordings. The extracts heard are *Work Song, Come Sunday, Light* (or *Montage*—these three pieces comprising the whole of *Black*), *The Blues, West Indian Dance, Emancipation Celebration,* and *Sugar Hill Penthouse*. As might be expected, the selections are more generously proportioned than on the 1944 Victor recordings. The first part of *Come Sunday*, for example, is heard complete on the D.E.T.S. broadcasts. Outstanding among these *Black, Brown And Beige* excerpts are several swinging performances of *Emancipation Celebration*, all with superbly alert and jaunty interpretations of the cornet part by Rex Stewart.

The band recorded the second of Duke's concert pieces, *Reminiscing In Tempo*, on July 21, 1945; the work dates from 1935, the year of the only previous recording. (This performance was considered along with the others of *Reminiscing In Tempo* in Chapter 8.) It is perhaps rather surprising that the only new concert piece from the D.E.T.S. broadcasts is *The Magazine Suite*. The first D.E.T.S. version (from July 14, 1945) predates the previously mentioned World Transcription recording and is definitive. The *Suite* reappears on August 4, 1945, but here the movements are scattered throughout the program. Duke also chose to revive *Diminuendo And Crescendo In Blue* at this time, and he now appears to have become dissatisfied with the two-movement formula. He started to experiment with the use of one of his other compositions as a "slow movement" between the two parts. *Rocks In My Bed, I Got It Bad, Carnegie Blues,* and *Transblucency* were all pressed into service at different times during these broadcasts, but Ellington did not settle permanently on any one. By 1947, he was using an extended piano solo as the central section. The problem was finally solved in the fifties by the Paul Gonsalves tenor saxophone interlude which caused such a sensation at the 1956 Newport Jazz Festival. The several combinations of *Diminuendo And Crescendo In Blue* with other material on the D.E.T.S. broadcasts are introduced as a *Blues Cluster*, and the radio announcer usually brings Duke to the microphone to explain the contents of the *Cluster*. Leaving aside the suitability of the various pieces used to divide the two sections, there can be little doubt that the finest recorded performances of *Dimin-*

uendo And Crescendo In Blue come from these broadcasts. That of June 9, 1945, (combined with *Rocks In My Bed*, vocal by Marie Ellington) has a very sensitive and mellow reading of *Crescendo*. The slightly more robust version of July 7, 1945, has *Carnegie Blues* as its centerpiece, and all three segments are well played; when this recording was used on V-Disc, *Carnegie Blues* was edited out and only *Diminuendo And Crescendo* issued. By October 13, 1945, one chorus of *I Got It Bad* (sung by Hibbler in a highly sentimental manner) had replaced *Carnegie Blues*; here the outer sections are taken slightly more slowly than on the previous version, powered by the great swing of Sid Catlett, who was deputizing for Sonny Greer. Perhaps the most exciting of all the *Blues Cluster* recordings stems from the broadcast of May 4, 1946. The filling in this particular musical sandwich is an excellent version of *Transblucency*, while *Diminuendo And Crescendo* is taken rather faster than before. The playing of the blues riffs that make up the melodic content of the work is of maximum swing and warmth, and the climax, topped by Cat Anderson's high-note trumpet, is tremendously effective.

* * *

Quite a number of the newer Ellington pieces heard on the D.E.T.S. broadcasts are cast in concerto form—*Frantic Fantasy* for Stewart, *Blue Cellophane* for Brown, *Air Conditioned Jungle* for Hamilton, *The Mood To Be Wooed* and *Hop, Skip And Jump* for Hodges, *The Suburbanite* for Sears, and *Frustration* for Carney. The only one not previously mentioned is *The Suburbanite*, premiered at a Carnegie Hall concert in January 1946 and subsequently also recorded for Capitol Transcriptions. It is a minor work, a bustling, busy piece which uses the resources and devices of Sears's tenor style rather less well than the later *Hiawatha*.

The D.E.T.S. series includes excellent versions of three of Ellington's stomps of recent vintage—*Three Cent Stomp*, *Stomp, Look And Listen* and *Suddenly It Jumped*. All these are in the tradition of Ellington orchestral pieces inspired by Duke's liking for the Harlem stride piano style. *Suddenly It Jumped* is a particularly impressive example and features Jordan as the main soloist, although Hamilton, Raglin, and Ellington himself also have important parts. This piece lost much of its effectiveness when Jordan left the band; his solos were taken over by Harold Baker who played them cleanly but without Jordan's drive and punch. *Fickle Fling* at medium-fast and *Riff 'n' Drill* at fast tempo are more conventional exercises, while *Let The Zoomers Drool* approaches the newly emerging Rhythm and Blues music in style and is reminiscent in places of the music of the Buddy Johnson Orchestra. Less conventional are *Fancy Dan*, a piece which was not fully realized until Duke created the 1951 arrangement, and *Unbooted Character*, which emerged in 1945 with an unusual theme and a concluding trumpet chase passage, played on the initial D.E.T.S. version by Jordan and Baker.

The blues are not as well represented in the contemporary Ellington output, the only notable new item being *Carnegie Blues*, a variation of *The Blues* from *Black, Brown And Beige*, which was sometimes introduced, wrongly, as a selection from that work. There is a new piece which is given a variety of titles—*Ultra Blue*, *Ultra Violet* and *How Blue Can You Get?*—with composer credits given to Jimmy Hamilton. The most effective new tone poem is without doubt *Transblucency*, which features Kay Davis's wordless soprano, although Ellington's song *Tonight I Shall Sleep* is given performances which more closely resemble this genre than is usually the case with his popular song arrangements.

* * *

Considering the number of revivals which Ellington worked into the D.E.T.S. broadcasts, it is perhaps surprising that only *Creole Love Call*, *Black And Tan Fantasy*, and *Black Beauty* come from the twenties. *Creole Love Call* is the most frequent of these, with Kay Davis featured in Adelaide Hall's old role along with Ray Nance on trumpet and, in Bigard's absence, Harry Carney on clarinet. There are two versions of *Black And Tan Fantasy*, both having solos by Hardwick on alto and Nanton on trombone. On that of May 5, 1945, Nance takes the trumpet choruses, while on August 25, Rex Stewart gave his only known interpretation of this solo with the Ellington band. *Black Beauty* is heard only as part of a piano medley on the broadcast of July 28, 1945, but Duke's performance is a loving one.

From the earliest years of the thirties *Rockin' In Rhythm*, *Mood Indigo*, and *Ring Dem Bells* are heard, but as these had remained standard items in the Ellington repertoire the excellent interpretations here have a familiar air; the *Mood Indigo* of August 25, 1945, includes a fine clarinet solo by Carney. On the broadcast of May 19, 1945, Ellington combined three of his thirties numbers, which he had revived for Victor recordings five days earlier—*In A Sentimental Mood*, *It Don't Mean A Thing*, and *Solitude*. Al Sears's solo on *It Don't Mean A Thing* is one chorus longer than on the Victor and also a shade more vulgar, the tenor working up to a honking and squealing climax as if this were a Lionel Hampton big band date. Otherwise the routines are identical to the Victors with three vocalists employed on *It Don't Mean A Thing* and four on *Solitude*. *It Don't Mean A Thing* was performed frequently during these broadcasts, often with the vocal chorus in the form of a duet between Nance and Jordan and with a Nanton solo added to its other delights. Between September 1945 and April 1946, Nance was out of the band; during this time Jordan took over the vocal chores on *It Don't Mean A Thing*, this being the only occasion on which Ellington took advantage of Taft's considerable abilities as a jazz singer. Jordan also takes a trumpet chorus here at the point at which on other versions he duets with Nance's violin. The version of this piece from April 21, 1945, is used on the first of the two V-Disc issues. Other revivals from the first half of the thirties heard on the D.E.T.S. broadcasts include *Sophisticated Lady*, *Stompy Jones*, *In A Jam*, and the Rex Stewart concerto *Trumpet In Spades*.

Of the Ellington pieces from the second half of the thirties, the D.E.T.S. broadcasts contain versions of *Prelude To A Kiss* (used on V-Disc) and *Caravan* very similar to those recorded for Victor in May 1945. It is interesting to note that while Nance was out of the band, the violin solo which he usually took on *Caravan* was allocated to Carney's baritone! There are pretty straight revivals of *Way Low* (which allow us to compare Hamilton's interpretation of the clarinet part with Bigard's and to enjoy some excellent Stewart cornet), *Solid Old Man*, *The Jeep Is Jumpin'*, and *Old King Dooji*.

The version of *Tootin' Through The Roof* from June 23, 1945, opens with a sprightly stride piano chorus from Ellington, but its most arresting feature is the trumpet chase played by Stewart and Jordan. Taft had joined Ellington when Rex departed temporarily in 1943 and in taking over many of Rex's solo spots had become quite adept at the half-valve technique. When they came to the duet in *Tootin' Through The Roof*, they seemed to regard it as a half-valve challenge match and utilize the tricks of that trade to excellent, humorous (and occasionally outrageous) effect. For all Taft's skills, however, Rex remained *the* master of half-valve and would undoubtedly have been proclaimed the winner if this had been a contest. He further reveals his mastery on the D.E.T.S. versions of *Boy Meets Horn*.

Another unexpected revival from the late thirties is *Ridin' On A Blue Note*, from the broadcast of October 13, 1945. This broadcast deserves special attention because on it Sonny Greer is replaced by Sid Catlett. Catlett had been on the Victor recording session five days earlier and seems to have worked as deputy drummer for about a week—Greer is clearly on the next D.E.T.S. broadcast of October 20, 1945. The recording from October 13 enables one to hear Catlett making a vital contribution to the music and he clearly knows the Ellington routines on such numbers as *Hop, Skip And Jump* and the *Blues Cluster*. The *Ridin' On A Blue Note* follows the pattern of the long version heard on the broadcast of May 1, 1938, rather than the truncated arrangement used on the studio recording of that year. The solos on the former were by Williams on trumpet and Hodges on soprano; on this new version they are taken by Stewart on cornet and Hodges on alto. Stewart is heavily featured, both with plunger mute and on open horn, in dialogue with Hodges and in solo. It is a brilliant performance, reminding us that underneath all the tricky stuff, Stewart was basically a swinging jazz musician. The band is also outstanding for its swing, and the performance overall suffers only in comparison with the 1938 studio recording, which remains, despite its brevity, the finest of all versions of *Ridin' On A Blue Note*.

* * *

Several of the outstanding compositions which Ellington had presented to the world in 1940 appear in the course of the D.E.T.S. broadcasts. From May 12, 1945, comes the version of *Harlem Air Shaft* issued on V-Disc. Stewart takes over Williams's role here and, though he is a trifle less effective, the band's performance is outstanding, full of fire and drive and revealing, compared with the 1940 original, different aspects of the work. Several versions of *Cotton Tail* have been issued from the series; the best being from June 16, 1945. With Ben Webster out of the band, the solo responsibility is passed to Al Sears. Although not a virtuoso in the Webster class, Sears was a very effective swinger, especially at medium tempos. Ellington therefore slows down *Cotton Tail*, and the band digs in and really rocks. This is one of those Ellington performances in which spirit and vigor take precedence over precise and tidy ensemble playing. Sears swings mightily in the long tenor passages, and Carney and Ellington sparkle during their brief solos, but primarily this is a triumph of swinging band playing, to which the fiery lead trumpet work of Cat Anderson makes an important contribution. *Cotton Tail* from November 10, 1945, is, by contrast, taken at a very fast tempo and again the band playing is outstanding. Once more Anderson makes a vital contribution, but the swing is less and Sears's solos, by comparison with the June recording, are mediocre. Other important 1940 compositions which receive first-class performances in the Treasury Series include *Pitter Panther Patter*, *Subtle Slough* (in the full band arrangement which became *Just Squeeze Me*), *Jack The Bear*, *In A Mellotone*, *Day Dream*, and *Ko-Ko*, the last at the faster tempo which seems always to diminish the impact of the piece. On the broadcast of November 17, 1945, the great bassist Oscar Pettiford was new to the band; on *Jack The Bear*, he reproduces Jimmy Blanton's original part note for note with great accuracy and swing. *Never No Lament* appears in its popular song guise as *Don't Get Around Much Anymore* from July 21, 1945, with Hibbler sounding unsure of the lyrics. The original *Never No Lament* arrangement is still used, and, after the vocal, Johnny Hodges gives a supreme demonstration of the art of melody playing.

Among the pieces from the early forties are several Strayhorn compositions. On the broadcast of June 30, 1945, a "Strayhorn Medley" was made up of *Chelsea Bridge*, *Something To Live For*, *Clementine*, and *My Little Brown Book*. Billy himself is on piano for this grouping, and it is unfortunate that *Clementine* is interrupted by a War Bond announcement, preventing us from hearing Nance's variation on Stewart's usual solo. A complete performance of *Clementine*, with Rex providing an outstanding version of this solo, is heard on the broadcast of May 5, 1945, while the Strayhorn medley (without *My Little Brown Book*) reappears on September 8, 1945, a station break cutting off the very end of *Clementine*. On this broadcast the versions of *Chelsea Bridge* and *Clementine* are outstanding.

Other Strayhorn compositions heard on these broadcasts include *Johnny Come Lately*, with fine Nanton, from June 9, 1945, and versions of *After All* from August 25 and October 13, the latter a rather disappointing interpretation. The most frequently performed Strayhorn piece heard on these broadcasts is *Midriff,* the version from May 26, 1945, being typical and including an easy performance by Brown of a solo which he sometimes played rather stiffly.

* * *

At this time, both *Perdido* and *C Jam Blues* were in the first years of their success, and there are several performances of each on these broadcasts. In *Perdido,* Duke was experimenting with separate choruses for the trumpet, trombone, and saxophone sections, and although only that for the trombones survived for any length of time (the chorus for saxophones used in the fifties is different from the one found here), all three can be heard on these recordings. The versions of *C Jam Blues* allow each soloist two choruses instead of the one on the studio recording and there are some fine solos to be heard here. *Things Ain't What They Used To Be* appears (under its temporary title of *Time's A-Wastin'*) on September 22 and October 13, 1945, and receives outstanding performances with extended solos for Hodges and fine contributions from Jordan and Brown. *Jump For Joy* is given a very relaxed, swinging performance on June 23, 1945, on which Nance proves that he is the ideal vocalist for the number. On August 18, 1945, Duke introduces an extended performance of the 1941 *Bugle Breaks* by holding a conversation with Stewart's "talking" cornet. Other outstanding performances of material from the early forties include fine versions of *Moon Mist, Main Stem, Blue Serge, Jumpin' Punkins, Just A-Setting' And A-Rockin', What Am I Here For?, Someone,* and the Hodges showcases *Warm Valley, Sentimental Lady,* and *Passion Flower.*

On the broadcast of October 20, 1945, Russell Procope is featured as guest star. This was eight months before he joined the band on a regular basis, and his appearance is due to the fact that he had just been demobilized from the U.S. Army. Duke tells his audience this and promises that from now on each broadcast will feature a guest musician returning to civilian life after a spell in the armed forces, yet no other such broadcasts seem to have taken place. Procope is featured on *Honeysuckle Rose* and also joins the band for a version of *Perdido* in which he takes a couple of solo choruses. The arrangement of *Honeysuckle Rose* used here had become a Jimmy Hamilton clarinet showcase and appears as such on other D.E.T.S. broadcasts.

One of the features of these broadcasts was the interruption of the music, sometimes in midperformance, by War Bond promotion announcements. After the first few broadcasts these were done live by Duke himself, and a particularly annoying example occurs during the course of an excellent *Body And Soul* from the June 23, 1945, session. This is a long performance at medium-fast tempo which opens with an Ellington piano solo, continues with a chase chorus between the warm, emotional trumpet of Nance and the cool, detached clarinet of Hamilton (an excellent contrast), and is climaxed by a long tenor solo by Sears. Big bands at this time often featured a tenor saxophone soloist in heated, declamatory solos in the manner pioneered by Illinois Jacquet with Lionel Hampton. Al Sears did this job for Ellington with an admirable lack of complication, and this *Body And Soul* is one of the best examples of his work in this vein. Unfortunately, Duke makes his appeal for War Bonds just as Sears's solo starts to build to its climax. (This performance has also been issued with the bond appeal edited out; on at least one issue, it appears complete under the title *Bonds, Body And Soul.*)

A second version of *Body And Soul,* from September 1, 1945, was unknown to collectors prior to its D.E.T.S. issue. It follows the same routine up to and including an Ellington bond announcement during Sears's solo, the latter in a rather more mellow mood. But here Sears is followed by Lawrence Brown, starting quietly but building to a shouting trombone climax, unfortunately cut off by a station break.

* * *

One of the best of the many Ellington adaptations of standard material on the D.E.T.S. broadcasts is *Frankie And Johnnie.* The version from May 26, 1945, was used on V-Disc and is definitive. By now the multitempo structure of the 1941 Standard Transcription arrangement had been extended from a mere three minutes to over seven and incorporates solo parts for Nanton, Nance (violin), and Raglin (who has an important role throughout) in an arrangement which also features Duke's piano in a variety of moods. Jazz enthusiasts often complained that Ellington did not feature himself enough on piano, but in the forties he gave many superb demonstrations of his abilities using this arrangement as his setting. An equally brilliant adaptation of a popular standard is *In The Shade Of The Old Apple Tree,* in fact a revival of Ellington's 1933 score. There are two D.E.T.S. versions, from May 26 and July 14, 1945. Both feature Stewart, Nanton, and Hodges, plus outstanding bass from Raglin. These are very close to the version for World Transcriptions in August 1945, already noted.

During the early and middle forties Duke employed a series of arrangers to assist Strayhorn and himself in the preparation of popular songs, mainly for broadcast use. They included Dick Vance, Chappie Willet, Luther Henderson, Buck Clayton, and Bobby Williams. One of the best of these is *My Honey's Lovin' Arms,* by Williams, who was in the same U.S. Army band as Clayton and Mercer Ellington. It would appear that Mercer was responsible for several of the highly talented players in this unit being given arranging commissions by Duke. *My Honey's Lovin' Arms* is heard on the broadcast of May 26, 1945, with solos by Hodges and Anderson and a very swinging vocal by Ray Nance. This D.E.T.S. version is perhaps fractionally less good than the air shot of May 1944 or the Victor recording of September 1946, but all three are different in ways which show how the Ellington band continually adjusted even a conventional score by an outside arranger. And they show, too, how Nance's vocals are varied in just the same way that an instrumental solo would be.

Another outstanding recording of a popular standard is *On The Sunny Side Of The Street*, from June 16, 1945. This is an extension of the version heard on the Cotton Club broadcast of April 24, 1938, with the vocal omitted but with two choruses each from Hodges and Brown instead of one. Both soloists are in top form. The Treasury Series also includes an excellent *On The Alamo* with some delightful Hodges, playing against the trombone section, and versions of *Blue Skies* which show the arrangement moving nearer to *Trumpet No End* with the introduction of a final chorus of high-note trumpet by Anderson. A selective listing of titles will suffice to indicate the range of standards covered by the band in this series: *Sentimental Journey*, *Yesterdays*, *Laura*, *Summertime*, *Indiana*, *Tea For Two* (featuring Jordan), *Dancing In The Dark*, *I Can't Believe That You're In Love With Me*, *How Deep Is The Ocean* (featuring Hamilton and Jordan in a very swinging performance), *Between The Devil And The Deep Blue Sea* (featuring Stewart), *Time On My Hands* (featuring Hamilton), *I Can't Get Started*, and *Just You, Just Me*.

The best known outside arranger Ellington employed at this time was Buck Clayton, who contributed a number of instrumental scores. The most famous is his arrangement of *One O'Clock Jump*, which remained in the band's performing repertoire over several decades. This extensive use of Count Basie's famous signature tune is eloquent expression of the regard in which Basie was held by Duke, and it allowed the band, including its leader (who always took a prominent part on piano), to exploit yet another way of playing the blues. The title *One O'Clock Jump* makes its first appearance in the Treasury Series on June 30, 1945, with solos by Ellington, Sears, Brown, Hodges, and Jordan, and it is interesting to note how the character of the Ellington band is immediately established in music so closely associated with the Basie style. On later recordings, there is a coda consisting of two-bar breaks for drums, trumpet, and trombone plus a two-bar ensemble tag; the first version simply has six bars of drums and two of ensemble, and one assumes that this is the way it was originally scored. Later D.E.T.S. versions have similar solo routines and the final version of the coda. There are excellent *One O'Clock Jumps* from July 28 and September 1, 1945, and April 20, 1946, but the most remarkable version from the forties is from an air shot dated July 9, 1947, done after the D.E.T.S. broadcasts had finished. This must be the slowest version of the number on record. (Collectors should note that late in the 78 era some of these Ellington broadcast recordings of *One O'Clock Jump* were issued on disc as *Half Past Midnight Tempo* and *Two O'Clock Jump*, titles which were also used on some early LP releases.)

In addition to arranging *One O'Clock Jump* and Earle Warren's *9:20 Special*, Clayton also contributed two originals to the Ellington book—*Hollywood Hangover* and *Blues On The Double*. Both are uptempo numbers in the twelve-bar format and feature soloists plus riff ensembles; both appear several times in the D.E.T.S. broadcasts. *Hollywood Hangover* was taken from the broadcast of May 26, 1945, for use on a V-Disc; the recordings of this number are unique in being the only Ellington items since the very early thirties to feature open trombone solos by Nanton.

There seems to have been very little new material written by the musicians in the band at this time, the few exceptions including Hamilton's previously mentioned *Ultra Blue* and a slight piece by Carney, called *Jennie*. One number heavily featured by Ellington on the D.E.T.S. broadcasts but never recorded for public release was Cat Anderson's *Teardrops In The Rain*. Despite the title, this is a sprightly piece and the various versions all have good solos by the composer. It is interesting to note that in introducing solos by Anderson at this period both the station announcers and Duke himself refer to him as "Bill." The feline nickname had apparently not yet been fully established.

* * *

Some jazz enthusiasts have objected to the number of popular songs on the D.E.T.S. broadcasts, but it is essential to realize that these were the staple diet of the big bands of the day, and Ellington's was no exception. Actually he featured fewer of them than most leaders, and many of these were his own or Strayhorn's usually superior examples of the genre. As is usual when jazz groups use even the most ephemeral pop tunes, many such Ellington performances feature good solos or bits of fine scoring or band playing. Of the Ellington songs, those most heavily featured are *I'm Beginning To See The Light*, *Kissing Bug*, *I Ain't Got Nothing But The Blues*, *Every Hour On The Hour*, *Everything But You*, and Strayhorn's sentimental *My Little Brown Book*. Less frequently heard are *I Don't Mind*, *Don't You Know I Care*, and *Go Away Blues*. The version of *I Don't Mind* from August 25, 1945, has a particularly fine trombone solo by Brown. Ray Nance is best of the singers on the pop tunes, but he appears less frequently than the specialist singers. Of these, Joya Sherrill shows a degree of taste and artistry no matter how dire the song. Some of her vocals are superbly judged interpretations, and she is certainly a singer well suited to the needs of Ellington's music.

Among the best of the non-Ellington pop songs on D.E.T.S. are those which have Nance vocals, outstandingly several versions of the nonsense song *Riff Staccato*, with its swinging dialogue between Nance's singing and Jordan's trumpet. On the first from April 21, 1945, no vocal appears, and Sears plays the chorus usually taken by Nance and Jordan. On a couple of the D.E.T.S. versions of *Riff Staccato* from October 1945, Sherrill takes the vocal in Nance's absence, but the song is not suited to her style. It was then dropped until Nance's return in April 1946, when it enjoyed a brief revival. Another song which features Nance's vocal abilities (and his trumpet too) is *Candy*; there are three recordings of it from the first few months of the Treasury broadcasts.

It would be tedious and unnecessary to list all the popular songs in the Treasury series, but the following selection gives some idea of the variety in terms of both the quality and types of songs heard: *Accentuate The Positive, A Friend Of Yours, All At Once, Autumn Serenade, Blue Is The Night, Can't You Read Between The Lines, 11:60 PM, Homesick That's All, I'd Do It All Over Again, If I Love You, If You Are But A Dream, I'll Buy That Dream, I Miss Your Kiss, I Should Care, Out Of This World, Tell It To A Star, The More I See You, There's No You, The Wish I Wish Tonight*, and *Waitin' For The Train*.

Some of these popular songs are dull, some of the performances of Ellington compositions are not as good as the better-known studio versions, and some of the solo work is uninspired. But the majority of the pop tunes have at least some positive musical features; most of the instrumentals are played with a greater swing and flow than in the more staid studio versions; and not only are the solos often more inspired but they also benefit from the ease and relaxation of the environment. These solos are often longer than on contemporary studio recordings, for here the length of the performances is dictated by musical considerations rather than by the duration of the 78. Typical of the unexpected delights these broadcasts offer is *Get On Board Little Children*, an otherwise forgettable feature for a guest vocal group, the Mellotones, backed by a beautifully pointed trombone obbligato by Brown.

The D.E.T.S. broadcasts show the band to have absorbed the lessons provided by Jimmy Blanton when he brought new ideas and a dynamic personality into the Ellington rhythm section five years earlier. The band swings powerfully, with the little appreciated Junior Raglin playing a vital part as Blanton's successor. Oscar Pettiford is superb when he takes over on bass, while the long session with Sid Catlett finds the band responding to the playing of one of the master jazz drummers in an odd way. Catlett said afterwards that he did not find Ellington's band easy to play with, and clearly his few days with them did not give him time to really settle in. His fills and decorations do not always sound appropriate, and one is aware that the band swings fully in its own fashion irrespective of the drummer. To listen to this session and the one that followed with Sonny Greer back on drums throws into relief the eccentricity of Sonny's style and its rightness for the band. The trumpets play with bite and power as well as great sensitivity of phrasing and dynamics through a wide range of music. The trombones, as always with Ellington, are at the heart of affairs and the saxes contribute greatly, not least in rhythmic terms. As usual, the band was packed with top soloists and even those of lesser stature, such as Al Sears, were sure swingers. Even when important musicians like Rex Stewart and Ray Nance were out of the band, there were always deputies fully capable of taking over their roles. The great range of material on the Treasury series is a challenge with which the orchestra deals in a delightfully casual manner, enhancing its reputation as a truly great musical ensemble without diluting in any way the jazz qualities of its playing.

* * *

The Treasury series dominates the Ellington broadcasts of 1945 and 1946, but the band also frequently appeared on other shows and made regular contributions to such AFRS series as *One Night Stand* and *Spotlight Bands*. The repertoire heard on such broadcasts is not as wide as that on D.E.T.S., since Duke did not have completely free choice. One of the most interesting recordings surviving from this period is a curiosity from August 1945—a club jam session with Duke on piano. This has been issued on Jazz Archive in an anthology of recordings featuring Ben Webster. The musicians involved are Stuff Smith (violin), Webster, Don Byas, Dexter Gordon (tenors), Herbie Fields (clarinet and tenor), Buster Bailey (clarinet), Al Lucas (bass), and Eddie Nicholson (drums). On *The Romp*, Duke is heard in a functional opening chorus, in a couple of bridge passages, and faintly behind the other soloists, but he is virtually inaudible on the second title, *Honeysuckle Rose*. The whole affair is rather disappointing with only Byas among the soloists playing up to his best form. As an Ellington item, the recording is only of slight interest.

* * *

At the beginning of 1946 the Ellington personnel was:

Trumpets: Shelton Hemphill, Taft Jordan, Cat Anderson, Francis Williams, Bernard Flood.

Trombones: Lawrence Brown, Wilbur De Paris, Claude Jones (valve trombone).

Reeds: Otto Hardwick (alto sax, clarinet); Johnny Hodges (alto sax); Al Sears (tenor sax); Jimmy Hamilton (clarinet, tenor sax); Harry Carney (baritone sax, clarinet, bass clarinet).

Rhythm: Duke Ellington (piano); Fred Guy (guitar); Oscar Pettiford (bass); Sonny Greer (drums); Billy Strayhorn (deputy pianist).

Vocal: Kay Davis, Al Hibbler.

The absence of Ray Nance was temporary. He returned in April 1946, and apart from a spell of enforced absence in 1961/1962 he was to remain a pillar of strength in the band for the next seventeen and a half years. But Rex Stewart had left permanently in December 1945. In the trombone section, Wilbur De Paris was sitting in Nanton's chair due to the latter's illness. When Nanton came back in April, De Paris remained, making the trombones four. Ellington's decision to keep a deputy on hand in the section proved all too right when the great Tricky Sam Nanton died suddenly in July 1946. Harold Baker made one of his frequent returns to the Ellington band in May, a month which also saw the introduction of a second girl singer, Marion Cox. Hardwick, another of the Ellington veterans, left in June, and his place was filled for the remaining twenty-eight years of the orchestra's existence by Russell Procope. Junior Raglin had left in October 1945, and for a month or so the bass chair was held by Lloyd Trottman until Oscar Pettiford joined in mid-November. Pettiford was the greatest of Blanton's disciples and one of the outstanding bass players in jazz history. His two and a half years as an Ellington regular yielded many musical riches.

* * *

Ellington's 1946 Carnegie Hall concert took place on January 4. Most of it has been issued on a Prestige two-LP album. The selections from *Black, Brown And Beige* on this occasion were *Come Sunday*, *Montage*, and *The Blues* (*Montage* is wrongly titled *Work Song* on the Prestige issue). With no plunger trombone specialist, Ellington presumably felt that he could not perform *Work Song* satisfactorily. This concert saw one of the few complete performances of *Suite Ditty* or *A Tonal Group*, a new three-movement work consisting of *Mello-ditty* (or *Rhapso-ditty*), *Fugue-a-ditty*, and *Jam-a-ditty*. The first movement presents the development of two melodic motifs with the contrasting alto saxophone voices of Hardwick and Hodges in solo. *Fugue-a-ditty* has a solo quartet of trumpet (Jordan), trombone (Brown), clarinet (Hamilton), and baritone sax (Carney) in a staid piece of counterpoint, and the finale uses this quartet in a concerto-grosso setting against the full band. Only this fast movement entered the regular repertoire; the first two were dropped after a few January 1946 concert performances. This seems less a reflection on their quality than an instance of the usual policy of quickly dropping complete concert works to make way for new ones, thus ensuring that this sort of music did not monopolize the programs.

This concert also featured revivals of *In A Mellotone* with Anderson in the growl trumpet role, and *Solid Old Man* in an especially sprightly version. The most important showcases were *Rugged Romeo* (Jordan), *Sono* (Carney), *The Suburbanite* (Sears), and the magnificent *Magenta Haze* for Hodges. In the absence of Nance, the main solo on *Take The "A" Train* is by Ellington, in a really exceptional performance. Al Lucas was added as second bassist for this concert, but the performance of *Pitter Panther Patter* with Pettiford proclaims that a master Ellington bassist is in residence—a fact which is indeed in evidence on all Ellington recordings of this period. Another highlight is a stirring performance of *Diminuendo And Crescendo In Blue* in its *Blues Cluster* format, with the coolly beautiful *Transblucency* as the not wholly apposite centerpiece.

A fortnight later the Ellington band was in Los Angeles, participating in another *Esquire* Award Concert. Two V-Discs come from this event: a fine version of the Hodges feature *Esquire Swank*, with Cat Anderson taking the growl trumpet solo, and a recording of *C Jam Blues* by the combined Ellington and Woody Herman orchestras, a performance more notable for novelty than musical value. The Ellington repertoire at this concert was basically selected from the Carnegie Hall program, and this was also the case at the Chicago Civic Opera House on January 20, 1946. (The AFRS used some of the broadcast portions of this concert in their "A Date With The Duke" series. That music appeared in Volume 33 of Jerry Valburn's D.E.T.S. LPs, which contains all surviving recordings from the concert.)

* * *

Ellington's first 1946 appearances in the Victor studios were as a participant in sessions to celebrate successes in the *Esquire* and *Metronome* polls. On January 10, he appears on two sides by Leonard Feather's *Esquire* All Americans, a pick-up band which also included Jimmy Hamilton, Johnny Hodges, and Sonny Greer. One of them was a Feather blues, *Long, Long Journey*, which featured Louis Armstrong on vocal and trumpet. On the original 78 release, Ellington did a short spoken introduction, but this was edited out of some LP reissues. Duke's main contribution is a pleasant piano chorus in a performance naturally dominated by Armstrong. Louis is not present on the other title, *The One That Got Away*, another Feather number. Duke is confined to the introduction and some judicious comping behind the soloists. At this session Ellington and Strayhorn also recorded a couple of pleasant but slight piano duets, *Tonk* and *Drawing Room Blues*. *Tonk* is a sharp, spry composition with something of the air of twentieth-century academic piano music, while the second title, a Strayhorn composition, is a piece of rather vapid impressionism, owing nothing other than its basic structure to the blues idiom.

Five days after the *Esquire* session, a ninteen-piece band was assembled in the Victor studios to celebrate the winners of the *Metronome* poll as The Metronome All Star Band. Hodges and Carney were present, and Duke was invited to arrange and direct one of the two numbers, his own *Metronome All Out*. The arrangement is a variant of that used by the Ellington band. The principal difference is the addition of an introduction and coda played out-of-tempo by trombonist J. C. Higginbotham. Duke does not play the piano, which is in the capable hands of Teddy Wilson.

The first Victor sessions that year by the full band did not take place until July 9 and 10, when it cut a total of eight titles. First was *Rockabye River*, a development of *Hop, Skip*

And Jump, which features Hodges in peak form and some ferocious growl trumpet from Anderson. Next was *Suddenly It Jumped*, with Jordan to the fore, followed by a feature for Kay Davis, *Transblucency* (*A Blue Fog You Can Almost See Through*). Based on the 1938 *Blue Light*, it features Davis's wordless singing in a trio voicing with clarinet (Hamilton) and trombone (Brown). This brilliant Ellington composition receives a fine performance, but the Capitol Transcription of March 1946 is better, having the advantage—important in this piece—of the best recording quality, while not being tied, as the Victor is, to the three-minute 78 time limit. Ray Nance sings on *Just Squeeze Me—Subtle Slough* with lyrics added. A fine vehicle for Nance's humorous singing, the performance also features Jordan and Hodges, the latter contributing a delicious half chorus.

The July 10 session opens with a feature for Anderson, *A Gathering In A Clearing*. At this period, Ellington used the range of Anderson's artistry more fully than at any other, and this is a gospel-flavored number featuring Cat's plunger-muted trumpet. Sears is heard in some basic, down-home responses, and the band, with Carney's huge tone anchoring it, is unmistakably a great jazz ensemble. Anderson's ferocious growl playing in this little-known masterpiece displays a different aspect of his skills from those found on Coloratura from *The Perfume Suite* or *Trumpet No End*.

Despite some fine instrumental work, neither *You Don't Love Me No More* nor *Pretty Woman* can be enjoyed with unalloyed delight from a jazz point of view due to the Hibbler vocals, but the second title has a muted solo of great delicacy by Harold Baker. *Hey! Baby* is another ballad, a rather more jivey affair than the last two, and boasts a vocal by Ray Nance. It's not one of Ray's best, but does demonstrate his superiority to the kind of singing we hear down the years from Duke's featured male ballad singers.

The final sessions from this Victor contract, which had begun so explosively with the brilliant 1940 Ellington band, were cut on August 26 and September 3, when a total of thirteen titles was recorded. *Indiana* is one of a group of arrangements which Dick Vance contributed to the Ellington book, mainly for use at dances—a straightforward, rather ordinary score with solos from Anderson and Hamilton. Both this and *Blue Is The Night*, a popular song of the day which receives similar treatment, are given vigorous performances. The solos on this number are by Brown, Carney, Nance, and Hodges and the trumpet section is in particularly good form; this score is probably also by Vance. A third performance in similar vein is Luther Henderson's arrangement of *Just You, Just Me*, with solos from Hamilton (on tenor sax), Carney, Jordan and Anderson on trumpets. Harold Mooney's once highly regarded *Swamp Fire* is heard in a somewhat over-fussy arrangement (probably by Strayhorn) in which Hamilton, Sears, Ellington, and Pettiford are the principal contributors. The popular ballads recorded at these sessions are *Lover Man* and *Ghost Of A Chance*, the former featuring Marion Cox, the latter Kay Davis.

At this time, Ellington was presenting a tribute to W. C. Handy in the form of a suite of three of his most famous numbers—*Beale Street Blues, Memphis Blues*, and *St. Louis Blues*. This was presented at concerts as *Mr. Handy's Medley* or *Mr. Handy's Big Three*. All were recorded in suitably tailored three-minute versions on these Victor dates. *Beale Street Blues* receives a charming, characteristic Ellington treatment with Hamilton and Baker as main soloists. Baker is heard both muted and open, and his glorious tone is as impressive as his impeccable phrasing; the growl trumpet in the coda is by Nance. *Memphis Blues* is also seen in a new light when viewed from a Ducal perspective. It opens with a ravishing introduction by Hodges; there are also solos by Anderson on growl trumpet and Hamilton on clarinet. The most conventional of the three arrangements is *St. Louis Blues*, an uptempo affair with a vocal by Marion Cox and very pungent piano by Duke behind Sears's biting tenor solo.

In the book for a couple of years by now, the Bobby Williams arrangement of *My Honey's Lovin' Arms* was finally recorded for public release at the second of these Victor sessions. A new half-chorus for Jordan's trumpet is placed ahead of the main arrangement; Carney and Sears also solo, and Nance's casually swinging vocal is superbly backed by Duke. The Ellington version of *Royal Garden Blues* breathes new life into what had become an overworked Dixieland warhorse. An arrangement full of wit and humor is laid out in a way that encourages the band to swing; solos are by Jordan, Brown, and Anderson.

The last two titles were recorded in the Victor studios for the French Swing label, co-owned by the French writer and critic Charles Delaunay, who was in the United States on a visit. The numbers chosen were the Hodges/Ellington composition *Esquire Swank*, with Hodges and Anderson featured in Strayhorn's arrangement, and Strayhorn's own *Midriff*. Both are fine performances without having quite the ease of the best "live" versions.

* * *

In 1946 and 1947, the Ellington band recorded seven sessions for Capitol Transcriptions. These were studio recordings and involve some duplication of numbers made for commercial release at this time. It is always interesting to hear different performances of the same number from a band as creative as Ellington's, where variations of interpretation in ensemble passages are almost as common as in solos. As with the earlier Standard and World Transcriptions, neither the striving for perfection nor the time limitations of the commercial recordings is to be found in these Capitol Transcriptions. As a consequence, the duration of the numbers varies greatly, but there are no second and third takes. The sessions also contain a number of compositions and arrangements never recorded commercially.

The first of these dates from March 28, 1946. It opens with a Hodges composition, *Crosstown*. The arrangement is good, if conventional, with notable accompaniment to Johnny's own excellent solo; Anderson, Nanton, and Sears are also heard, and the value of Anderson as a lead trumpeter can be appreciated from his work here. Hodges is then featured on Strayhorn's 1941 *Passion Flower* and Ellington's new *Magenta Haze*. Compared with the earlier Bluebird version, *Passion Flower* benefits from the full orchestration here, while this version of *Magenta Haze* presents the complete arrangement, in contrast to the better-known recording done later for Musicraft, which was cut to fit a 78. *Everything Goes* was written and arranged by Cat Anderson when he was with Doc Wheeler's Sunset Royals. Taken at a swinging Luncefordian tempo, it has fine solos by Hodges and Sears. But the star is without doubt Cat himself who, both in solo and in dialogue with the band, lays down one of the most exciting performances of his career.

Next is one of the less distinguished of Ellington's features for Anderson, *The Eighth Veil*, which was not recorded commercially for another five years. This version is unusual in that Anderson plays muted throughout. *Riff 'n' Drill*, never recorded commercially at any time, is a sprightly uptempo Ellington piece featuring the talents of Brown and, especially, Hodges. Anderson rides out the final ensemble with some of his biting ultra-high-note trumpet, while at the opposite extreme of the orchestra's range, Pettiford gives a particularly noteworthy display. As if being rewarded, the bassist is given a good deal of solo space in the next number, *Blue Abandon*, a light, airy Ellington blues at fast tempo. The Capitol version of *Transblucency* is followed by *Embraceable You*, featuring Kay Davis in the role of conventional ballad singer. *Rugged Romeo*, a modest jump number, is the only piece written by Ellington designed to feature Taft Jordan in the half-valve style. *Jenny* is an uptempo composition by Carney with some conventional swing trumpet by Anderson. Hodges is featured in his most lively vein in a revival of *The Jeep Is Jumpin'*, which also has more fine Pettiford. This is followed by the standard arrangement of *Take The "A" Train* but with Jordan in the featured trumpet role: this makes an interesting contrast with the familiar versions featuring Nance. At this period, the arrangement of *Perdido* seemed to change almost day by day; this Capitol Transcription finds Nance absent, so Anderson plays the lyrical middle eights as well as the high notes. The first session ends with a trio performance, *Tip Toe Topic*, in which Pettiford's virtuosity is shown off to fine effect.

The remaining 1946 Capitol Transcription sessions are a group of three, recorded in July. Quite a lot of numbers duplicate the current Victor output: *Rockabye River*, *A Gathering In A Clearing*, *You Don't Love Me No More*, *Pretty Woman*, *Just Squeeze Me*, *Suddenly It Jumped* (a very fine interpretation), *Hey, Baby!*, *Indiana*, *Ghost Of A Chance*, *Lover Man*, and *Just You, Just Me*. Among the new material is a rather ordinary ballad performance by Kay Davis, *Come Rain Or Come Shine*. There is a version of *Fickle Fling* featuring Ellington and Hodges; this number had appeared on some earlier broadcast recordings. These sessions also include two of the scores written by Buck Clayton of numbers associated with the Basie band. *9:20 Special* features Jordan, Sears, and Pettiford and shows how well the Ellington band could swing in the conventional manner of the time. The second Clayton score is the only studio recording by the Ellington band of *One O'Clock Jump* dating from the forties. The variables in the band's performances of this piece at the time are tempo, length of Ellington's opening piano solo, and choice of trumpet soloist; the other solos are always by Sears, Brown, and Hodges. In this instance, Ellington contents himself with a couple of choruses at the start, obviously delighting in the performance of this prime piece of Basie music. A swinging fast-medium tempo is established, and Jordan is the trumpet soloist in this outstanding performance. Another number which Ellington never recorded commercially during the 78 era was his own *Unbooted Character*, a somewhat eccentric medium-tempo swinger. This version has solos by Brown and Hamilton and an excellent chase chorus by Jordan and Baker. An Ellington composition never recorded commercially at any time is *The Suburbanite*, a feature for Sears's tenor, and part of the contemporary concert repertoire. The Capitol version is the only studio recording of the piece.

The final Capitol Transcriptions session of 1946 opens with *Moon Mist* in a particularly sensitive reading; it is interesting how different the ensemble textures sound now that Tizol is no longer in the band. Another remake follows, a fine version of *In A Jam* with a rather tired-sounding Nanton. Jordan takes over from Nance in the duet with Hodges, with a contribution from Sears and a humorous solo from Anderson to conclude. Next come two standards—*On The Alamo*, with solos from Hodges, Anderson, and Hamilton and *I Can't Believe That You're In Love With Me*, which features two choruses of swinging baritone from Carney, a superb solo from Jordan, and sprightly clarinet from Hamilton. There are excellent remakes of *Someone* and *Tea For Two*, the former featuring Hodges, Brown, and Nance, the latter Jordan's tightly muted trumpet. *Double Ruff* is an unusual new number by Strayhorn, which utilizes the new solo voice of alto saxophonist Russell Procope; Nance is also heard to fine effect, both in solo and in a chase sequence with Jordan. Hodges is featured in *A Flower Is A Lonesome Thing*, a Strayhorn composition which does not seem to have been performed very often by the band at this time.

The final title is the very last Ellington recording on which Tricky Sam Nanton participated; he died suddenly in his hotel room three days after this session. His trombone is heard for a chorus in *The Mooche*, his playing clearly affected by ill health. Hodges embellishes the trombone solo and then goes on to play an outstanding blues chorus. On this version of *The Mooche*, Ellington tries out for the first time the idea of a duet between two contrasting clarinet stylists. This routine was to become well established in the hands of Russell Procope and Jimmy Hamilton, but here the lead is taken by veteran Ellingtonian Carney rather than by newcomer Procope. One of the outstanding features of this version is Nance's growl trumpet against the clarinet trio in the opening and closing ensembles. This is one of the finest early examples of Nance playing in the growl style, and it is so effective that one can well understand why Ellington later used Nance to the almost total exclusion of other trumpeters who could play in this manner.

Outstanding Recordings

1. Victor Recordings

I Ain't Got Nothin' But The Blues, *I'm Beginning To See The Light*, the *Black, Brown And Beige Suite*, *Carnegie Blues*, *The Mood To Be Wooed*, *Everything But You*, *Riff Staccato*, *Black And Tan Fantasy*, *In A Sentimental Mood*, *It Don't Mean A Thing*, *I Let A Song Go Out Of My Heart* (both takes), *Solitude*, *Frankie And Johnnie* (trio version), *Black Beauty*, *The Perfume Suite*, *Time's A-Wastin'* (*Things Ain't What They Used To Be*), *Rockabye River*, *Suddenly It Jumped*, *Transblucency*, *Just Squeeze Me*, *A Gathering In A Clearing*, *Blue Is The Night*, *Beale Street Blues*, *My Honey's Lovin' Arms*, *Memphis Blues*, *Royal Garden Blues*, *Esquire Swank*, and *Midriff*.

2. Concert Recordings

a. Complete Concerts: the Carnegie Hall concert on January 23, 1943, including the complete *Black, Brown And Beige*.

b. Selected Items from Concerts: *Black Beauty* (Boston, January 27, 1943), *Moon Mist*, *Tea For Two*, excerpts from *Black, Brown And Beige*, *New World A-Comin'*, *Trumpet In Spades* (Carnegie Hall, December 11, 1943), *Blutopia*, *Creole Love Call*, excerpts from *Black, Brown And Beige*, *Frankie And Johnnie* (Carnegie Hall, December 19, 1944), and *Suite Ditty* (Carnegie Hall, January 4, 1946)

3. World Transcriptions

Tea For Two, *Hop, Skip and Jump* (the V-Disc version), *Rockin' In Rhythm*, *Boy Meets Horn* (V-Disc), *Main Stem* (V-Disc), *Three Cent Stomp*, *Ain't Misbehavin'*, *It Don't Mean A Thing*, *Johnny Come Lately*, *Creole Love Call* (V-Disc), *Somebody Loves Me*, *Jack The Bear*, *Harlem Air Shaft*, *Rose Room*, *Chopsticks*, *Let The Zoomers Drool*, *Down Beat Shuffle*, *Esquire Swank*, *Metronome All Out*, *Riff Staccato*, *In A Jam*, *In The Shade Of The Old Apple Tree*, and *Frustration*.

4. Duke Ellington Treasury Series (D.E.T.S.) Recordings

All these broadcasts are of great interest and most contain several outstanding performances. To detail each one, including the many versions of individual titles, would be of little value. The following alphabetical list of titles indicates the cream of the D.E.T.S. output; unless otherwise stated, the reference is to *all* D.E.T.S. versions: *Black And Tan Fantasy*, *Black Beauty*, excerpts from *Black, Brown And Beige*, *Blue Belles Of Harlem*, *Blutopia*, *Body And Soul*, *Bugle Breaks*, *Candy*, *Chelsea Bridge*, *C Jam Blues*, *Clementine*, *Cotton Tail* (June 16, 1945), *Creole Love Call*, *Diminuendo And Crescendo In Blue* (*Blues Cluster*), *Don't Get Around Much Anymore*, *Everything But You*, *Fancy Dan*, *Fickle Fling*, *Frankie And Johnnie*, *Frantic Fantasy*, *Harlem Air Shaft*, *How Deep Is The Ocean?*, *I Can't Believe That You're In Love With Me*, *In A Jam*, *In The Shade Of The Old Apple Tree*, *It Don't Mean A Thing*, *Jack The Bear*, *The Jeep Is Jumpin'*, *Jump For Joy*, *Jumpin' Punkins*, *Let The Zoomers Drool*, *Magazine Suite* (*Down Beat Shuffle*, *Esquire Swank*, *Metronome All Out*), *Main Stem*, *Midriff*, *Mood Indigo*, *My Honey's Lovin Arms*, *New World A-Comin'*, *One O'Clock Jump*, *On The Alamo*, *On The Sunny Side Of The Street*, *The Perfume Suite*, *Pitter Panther Patter*, *Reminiscing In Tempo*, *Ridin' On A Blue Note*, *Riff Staccato*, *Rockin' In Rhythm*, *Stomp, Look and Listen*, *Suddenly It Jumped*, *Things Ain't What They Used To Be* (*Time's A-Wastin'*), *Tootin' Through The Roof*, *Transblucency*, *Trumpet In Spades*, *Unbooted Character*, *Warm Valley*, *Way Low*, and *What Am I Here For?*

5: Broadcasts Other than D.E.T.S.

a. Complete Broadcasts: the "Pastel Hour" broadcasts of June 6, 1943, June 27, 1943, and July 11, 1943, and the Franklin D. Roosevelt Memorial Broadcast of April 14, 1945

b: Selected Items from Broadcasts: *Five O'Clock Drag*, *Wait For Me Mary* (June 17, 1943), *My Honey's Lovin' Arms* (May 21, 1944), and *Fickle Fling* (May 21, 1944)

6. Capitol Transcriptions

Everything Goes, *Rugged Romeo*, *Sono*, *Tip Toe Topic* (trio), *Magenta Haze*, *Transblucency*, *Rockabye River*, *A Gathering In A Clearing*, *Just Squeeze Me*, *Suddenly It Jumped*, *One O'Clock Jump*, *Unbooted Character*, *Moon Mist*, *In A Jam*, *On The Alamo*, *I Can't Believe That You're In Love With Me*, and *The Mooche*.

Chapter 17

New Territories and New Musicians

THE ELLINGTON ORCHESTRA PERFORMED two contrasting and apparently incompatible functions—that of an all-star jazz band exhibiting the creative and instrumental skills of its musicians, and that of a specialist ensemble designed for the interpretation of its leader's compositions. The music that Ellington and Strayhorn wrote ensured that these were two sides of the same coin. We have already seen that the Ellington band had much greater solo strength than any other big band—with the possible exception of the early Basie band—or even than those ad hoc groups of jazz virtuosos brought together for concert performances and tours from the middle forties onward. Ellington's was an expensive organization which needed a degree of commercial success to survive. To please its audience at any of its varied venues and functions, the band required a wide range of material. Duke was always aware of fashion in popular music, partly because of his innate musical curiosity, but also because he needed to please his audiences, some of whom had no interest in Ellington music as an artistic entity.

One consequence of this situation is that a part of the Ellington recorded repertoire—not the most important nor yet a wholly negligible one—finds the orchestra playing in conventional big band style. In the forties, such performances were sometimes of popular songs and sometimes of swing instrumentals.

An instance of how changes in big band fashion could affect Ellington can be found in the developments in the trumpet section during the swing era. In the later part of this period, it became fashionable for big bands to have large and loud trumpet sections, usually featuring a high-note specialist. This was a development which covered the whole stylistic range from Lionel Hampton to Stan Kenton. By the mid-forties, Ellington had five or even six trumpets in the section, including Cat Anderson, one of the finest and most individual high-note specialists. The Ellington book was for four trumpets, and the extra men were either on hand because someone had lip trouble or because Ellington liked their playing and was reluctant to let them go when the player they had been deputizing for returned. Even with four men, the Ellington trumpets of the mid-forties could blow up a rousing climax, but unlike some other leaders, Duke also demanded soft and subtle music from his trumpets. The Ellington brass retained the ability to produce the quiet, delicately colored playing for which it had become renowned. But if the audience and/or the leader wanted a rousing, shouting brassy climax, the section was equipped to compete with and usually to beat the best of the competition. This development in the Ellington trumpet section was obvious even before Anderson joined; for example, Rex Stewart can be heard doing high-note endings on several mid-forties versions of *Diminuendo And Crescendo In Blue*. And it was Rex who originally played the high-note climax to *Blue Skies*, which later became one of Anderson's most popular specialities. In later years, if Anderson was out of the band, Ellington usually saw to it that another high-note man, such as Al Killian or Fats Ford, was brought into the section. It is typical of Ellington that in choosing Anderson as his high-note trumpeter, he picked a man who was skilled not only in this department, but who was also a versatile all-round musician and an artist of skill and humor.

Anyone playing a selection of Ellington recordings from 1946 alongside a similar selection from ten years earlier is bound to notice great changes in the ensemble. These changes are evolutionary, and therefore much less obvious if we play a chronological group of recordings covering the intervening years. It is not simply that the band now has a louder brass section and that the ensemble reflects in its phrasing and general musical style the fashions of the later period. The balance between orchestra and leader has also changed in subtle and interesting ways. In an interview in the forties, Ellington confessed that many of his early published compositions had been transcribed from recorded performances which had been accomplished without ever being written out in score. The ensemble of ten horns and four rhythm of the early and middle thirties was made up of men well versed in the Ellington style—indeed, by men who had contributed to the creation of that style. In this band, much was accomplished by discussion of a piece and by the throwing of phrases from musician to musician in the course of a rehearsal or a recording session. Barney Bigard recalled that *Rockin' In Rhythm* came about when he, Carney, and Hodges were just warming up and doodling. By 1946, the brass section alone consisted of ten pieces on occasion, and the band was now too large for this kind of thing to succeed regularly.

And, even more crucially, many of the players were new to Ellington's methods. They were joining a musical organization with established traditions which they had to master before they could make a significant contribution. This inevitably led to a situation where Ellington relied more and more on the long-serving members of the band for the realization of his more subtle musical concepts. Hayes Alvis, in an interview with Johnny Simmen, drew a distinction between the "real Ellingtonians" and those musicians who "just happen to play with Duke," a distinction clearly already apparent during his years with the band. Rex Stewart, in conversation, reaffirmed this and said that even though he was with the orchestra for ten years and had been a friend of Ellington's long before joining it, he never felt himself to be one of the band's inner circle.

As more and more of the original Ellingtonians left, the band inevitably moved towards a less collective kind of music making. Duke continued to select highly skilled musicians for the band, men of distinctive styles, and men who were capable of making an imaginative contribution as well as being competent professionals. Discussions of musical material and suggestions from sidemen remained a vital part of the Ellington way of making music, but by 1946, the emphasis had changed. The band was now less like a chamber ensemble and more like a full orchestra.

The increased frequency of personnel changes can easily be seen if we compare the six years from 1935 to 1940 with the following six. In the former period, Ellington employed seven trumpeters: Arthur Whetsol, Cootie Williams, Rex Stewart, and Wallace Jones were the regulars; Charlie Allen and Harold Baker came in for short spells, and Ray Nance joined right at the end of the period. In the second six years, Ellington employed eleven trumpeters of whom Stewart, Jones, Nance, Baker, Taft Jordan, Shelton Hemphill, Cat Anderson, and Francis Williams were all regular members, and Bernard Flood and Dizzy Gillespie short-stay musicians. Of the trombones, three men were used in the first six-year period—Joe Nanton, Lawrence Brown, and Juan Tizol—while in the second period this was doubled, with these same three plus Sandy Williams, Claude Jones, and Wilbur De Paris. From 1935 to 1940, Ellington used five reed men: Otto Hardwick, Johnny Hodges, Barney Bigard, and Harry Carney, plus Ben Webster, who joined in February 1940. More than double this number of musicians played in the Ellington reed section from 1941 to 1946: Hardwick, Hodges, Bigard, Carney, Webster, Chauncey Haughton, Nat Jones, Jimmy Hamilton, Elbert Williams, Al Sears, and Russell Procope—eleven in all. The rhythm section, although it too changed considerabiy in style, was comparatively stable with changes only among the bass players plus the addition of Billy Strayhorn as deputy pianist. Both of these periods saw Ellington use four bassists—Wellman Braud, Hayes Alvis, Billy Taylor, and Jimmy Blanton in the first; Blanton, Junior Raglin, Lloyd Trottman, and Oscar Pettiford in the second. The changes in vocalists were even more noticeable although this was a much less significant factor. In the first period, Ivie Anderson, Herb Jeffries, and Jean Eldridge sang with the band; in the second Anderson, Jeffries, Betty Roché, Jimmy Britton, Al Hibbler, Joya Sherrill, Kay Davis, Marie Ellington, and Marion Cox were featured.

In the course of these many personnel changes, a number of musicians who were to become major Ellingtonians were introduced. They include Ray Nance, Harold Baker, Taft Jordan, and Cat Anderson on trumpets; Jimmy Hamilton, Al Sears, and Russell Procope in the reed section; and Junior Raglin and Oscar Pettiford on bass. Duke continued to pick up the essentials of a new man's musical personality, to provide him quickly with perfect settings for his solos and to utilize his sound in the ensemble. But the comparatively unsettled state of the band meant that this was often done in bolder colors and with less subtlety than before. Although Nance, Jordan, and Baker were given the major roles in such pieces as *Take The "A" Train*, *Suddenly It Jumped*, or the revival of *Black Beauty*, none of the concertos written for the trumpet soloists in this period was of the caliber of *Echoes Of Harlem*, *Boy Meets Horn*, or *Concerto For Cootie*. Perhaps the nearest approach would be *Coloratura* from *The Perfume Suite* for Cat Anderson. Often the musicians would be given standard non-Ellington songs for their features—usually in the "Variations On Themes" sequence. The majority of the new compositions in the concerto format were for the two long-serving members of the reed section, Johnny Hodges and Harry Carney. Billy Strayhorn's predilection for soaring romantic melody lines designed for Hodges's alto was one reason for this, but these were also the two men whose styles Ellington knew best. It is surprising that Duke did not make more use of Lawrence Brown's versatility in this kind of context during these years, but the only two concertos for the trombonist are *Blue Cellophane* and *Circe*, both slight pieces.

In some ways the constant changes of personnel—typical of big band practice and unusual only by Ellington standards—had a depersonalizing effect on some of the music. Whereas in the thirties every performance would be recognizably Ellingtonian from the sound of the individual musicians, this was not always the case by the mid-forties. The performances with the least Ellington flavor are those of the scores by outside arrangers like Bobby Williams, Chappie Willet, Luther Henderson, Dick Vance, and Buck Clayton. On such numbers, the Ellington orchestra sounds more like a typical big band of its period than the band of the thirties or the first few years of the forties had ever done. Only when Hodges, Carney or one of the other long-serving members of the band takes a solo does the casual listener identify the music with Ellington. And the larger sections inevitably led to a slightly less personalized sound in the ensemble. Although Bigard, Webster, and Hardwick left the band during this period, the reeds seem to have been less affected, although Bigard's soaring ensemble clarinet was never replaced. It was only when Hardwick departed that the sound of the reed section changed to any marked degree, his replacement, Russell

Procope, seeming to give the saxes a heavier, more dense sound. Of all the Ellingtonians, Hardwick is the one whose contribution usually is least appreciated. In the section he was a good deal more than a competent lead alto. He was a master saxophonist with a very individual tone and a light, airy sound which contrasted perfectly with the thicker sonorities of Hodges, Webster, and Carney. Often, when Hodges, Webster, or Carney has the lead, Hardwick's distinctive sound will stress the harmony part which gives the passage its flavor. By contrast, Procope's sound and style were much more conventional, if deployed with exceptional skill. Both Hardwick and Procope were outstanding and stylish melody players.

* * *

It seems to have been in the middle forties that Ellington developed his never-quite-to-the-point style of public (and often private) communication. His reaction to the hostile reception to *Black, Brown And Beige* in 1943 was in some ways a lasting one. And his continued development of concert music isolated him from popular trends in jazz development. He spoke in an oblique manner, from a position which was itself oblique to the direction in which most jazz musicians were moving. He continued to be a major innovator in jazz, but the influence of his concert music on his fellow musicians was slight. And despite the token respect shown by journalists and critics, this concert music seems to have made only a slight impression on the jazz public. Yet Ellington clearly felt that the future of jazz lay in the concert hall.

This belief was given further practical expression in the spring of 1945, when Duke Ellington invested $16,000 in the Boyd Raeburn band, a "progressive" big band which was briefly a rival to Stan Kenton. Ellington's interest probably lay in Raeburn's concert music and in his racially integrated personnel, which featured several black jazzmen in what was basically a white big band. Raeburn's music was not a popular success and whatever artistic merit it may have possessed was not strong enough to prevent its disappearance into limbo, remembered only by connoisseurs. Ellington, with a broad financial base resting securely on his royalties from his many popular songs, was able to weather public indifference to his concert works.

With a steady output of shorter works from the pens of Ellington and Strayhorn, it seems odd that Duke should have employed Bobby Williams, Dick Vance, Buck Clayton, and other outside arrangers. The reason seems to have been the need to have a large number of current popular songs on hand for broadcasts. Ellington was intensely patriotic, and it is no coincidence that many of these arrangers were servicemen or exservicemen. Another motive may have been to ensure that he would have a repertoire of conventional big band arrangements on hand at a time when conformity was starting to take a strong grip on popular entertainment. And he may have been curious to see how his musicians would tackle such material.

According to the established conventions of jazz history, the Ellington band was supposed to have been in decline around this time due to the loss of such stars as Cootie Williams, Barney Bigard, Jimmy Blanton, and Ben Webster. Yet the records show that the band continued to produce a flow of great jazz performances, and it now becomes obvious to even the most doubting observer that Ellington himself was the real strength of the band—rather than the soloists, great as they were. Just as he had adapted to changing social and environmental patterns in the past, so he adjusted to the loss of these long-serving musicians, kept the band filled with creative and imaginative players, and continued to write superb music.

* * *

The end of the swing era was heralded by a change in public taste. The new popular music of white America was provided by the solo vocalist, that of black America by the emerging small rhythm and blues groups. The big bands were to a degree the victims of this change, which was however itself related to a public dissatisfaction with the fare most big bands were serving up. The technical standards of some of the bands had deteriorated when the draft took away key musicians, and the frequent changes of personnel ultimately led to the recruitment of inexperienced or substandard players. White public taste had already moved away from the jazz-oriented bands of Goodman and Shaw toward the bland musical commonplaces of Glenn Miller. Change was in the air. Small jazz groups were thriving in the clubs— another drain on the supply of accomplished sidemen for the big bands. The Henderson-Goodman swing style had been around for the better part of a decade and was becoming dated by the standards of popular music. Jazz was now recognized as an art form by its own small audience, and new trends in the music reflected this in ways which were often commercially disastrous.

Jazz would soon cease to be a popular music in any real sense, yet its long trek to full public acceptance as an art music had only just begun. The tendency to treat jazz seriously can be seen not only in the evolution of bebop, the first "modern jazz" style, and one built deliberately on esoteric antipopular aesthetics, but also in the intense activity in jazz history and research, resulting in the revival of interest in early jazz and its musicians. For years, jazz had been scorned by academic musicians for its harmonic crudity and for the poor (by academic standards) tones produced by its practitioners. The cultural proximity of the harmonically sophisticated music of the post-Wagnerian European academic tradition was a constant reminder to the more alert jazz musicians of their music's apparent naivety in this respect. For the new generation of jazz musicians, jazz evolution was seen primarily in terms of increased harmonic complexity. Such big bands as Dizzy Gillespie's and Stan Kenton's, on different sides of the still very real racial barrier, exemplified this antipopular trend. Throughout the jazz world, the new soloists were concentrating on speed of execution and complexity of harmonic reference, and on a smoothness and evenness of tone which was in marked contrast to the blues-based sonorities and sensual tone colors of previous generations. The rough tones of the blues tradition were out, especially in the music which later arose in modern jazz as a complementary form to bebop, so-called cool jazz. Not even the smooth, bland tones of the Miller band were further from the rough and expressive music of earlier jazz than those used by the cool jazz ensembles. The middle forties were, for jazz, a time of cultural transformation. Antipopular forms of the music were evolving, and the public ceased to support the big bands—both phenomena being aspects of the same overall pattern of change.

Duke Ellington's place in all this change reflects the position he often seemed to hold in relation to the development of jazz and to its immediate social surroundings. He stands off at some distance, not unduly affected by what is happening around him, even through a time of violent upheaval. The Ellingtonians simply seemed to go on, creating their own music for their own audience and staying aloof from the maelstrom. Ellington's superior business sense was clearly a factor in his ability to dictate, to a large degree, his own musical policy. As Leonard Feather has pointed out, Ellington's concert music presented an answer to the cultural dilemma of the time, an answer which was just as viable as the small band music which became the symbol of the "new jazz." But like many of Ellington's previous innovations, those of the forties proved to be unique and inimitable. There was no lack of big band concert jazz in the late forties; but none of it approached Ellington's in terms of mastery and imagination. Nor did it have the creative vitality of the music of Charlie Parker and his associates—the music which was to become the touchstone of jazz development over the next two decades.

At first Ellington's band, despite the personnel changes, was not much affected by the new developments in jazz. Duke did have a characteristically oblique influence himself on the music's development at this point, for he was the prime inspiration of the most important pianist in the early days of modern jazz, Thelonious Monk. But neither Monk's importance nor Ellington's influence on him was realized by the jazz public at this time. Indeed, Ellington was still considered a mediocre pianist, the weakest soloist in his band, and an outdated player in an era when stride piano was considered distinctly old-fashioned.

Among the Ellington sidemen we can discern more than a trace of modern jazz phrasing, for example, in some of Harold Baker's playing and in Jimmy Hamilton's clarinet solos. Duke's new bassist, Oscar Pettiford, had been the bassist with the first regular bebop band, but Ellington's band was a more important arena for innovations on the bass than bop. Pettiford was persistent in trying to persuade Ellington to employ some of the new-style players in his band. It is reported that approaches were made to some of the most notable bop musicians with offers to join the band, including Charlie Parker and Fats Navarro, but negotiations supposedly foundered on the financial question. To have heard such musicians in the context of the mid-forties Ellington band would have been fascinating indeed; their reaction to Greer's drumming, for example, could have been of great interest. But even personalities as strong as Parker and Navarro could not have fundamentally altered the nature of Ellington's music. In later years, several players in the modern idiom worked with the band, but the music still remained basically and essentially Ellingtonian.

While all these changes were going on, the band continued to function in the traditional Ellington way, playing dances, theaters, clubs, and concerts. Other big bands did not fare so well. Between the pretensions of Stan Kenton and the somewhat frenetic music of the first and second Woody Herman "Herds" on the one hand, and the primitivism of the Lionel Hampton and Buddy Johnson bands on the other, there was little middle ground. (Johnson's blues-based group was the last big band to become popular with the black public and retained its popularity well into the sixties, very much against the pattern of the times.)

The swing era was falling apart as it fell into oblivion. There were still good bands on the scene in 1946, although fewer than four or five years earlier. Count Basie's was one of the few which reflected the old musical values, and even Basie's band was heading for decline and disbandment. In his case, both were temporary, but for most of Basie's contemporaries they would prove permanent.

Sidemen

Cat Anderson

Cat Anderson was a featured musician in the Ellington band—with occasional leaves of absence—for over a quarter of a century. He is known above all for his ultra-high-register playing, achieving a range on the trumpet which has been equalled by very few and mastered by even fewer. But Anderson was a real jazz musician and his playing retained its personal qualities even when he was playing in the trumpet's highest register. And with Cat, these personal qualities were often of a humorous kind. His high-register work was often the subject of ignorant criticism; on British tours he used to collect reviews in which local journalists described how he had "ruined" Ellington concerts with the vulgarity of his playing. Anderson was in fact a trumpet player of remarkable all-round talents. He was an excellent growl player with the plunger mute, and often played with great drive and vigor in the middle register. He was also used occasionally as a ballad player and as a Latin American style trumpeter. Cat was also a very fine arranger, with a talent for writing scores which allow the band to swing in the most natural fashion.

Representative Recordings: Coloratura (from *The Perfume Suite,* Victor, 1945), *A Gathering In A Clearing* (Victor, 1946), *Jam With Sam* (Columbia, 1951), *Don't Call Me, I'll Call You* (with Johnny Hodges, Verve, 1957), *Madness In Great Ones* (from *Such Sweet Thunder,* Columbia, 1957), *Jungle Kitty* (from *Virgin Island Suite,* Reprise, 1965)

Harold Baker

Harold "Shorty" Baker was a first-class musical craftsman held in the highest esteem by his fellow musicians. As a lead player he was without peer, his superb tone and finely judged phrasing making him an ideal first trumpet. On ballads Baker's rich, golden sound allied to his lyrical phrasing and impeccable musicianship made him an instantly recognizable soloist. So radiant was Baker's tone that it seemed like a form of sacrilege whenever he played with a mute. Yet even muted Baker's sound had a certain indefinable "class." He was also quite adept in the growl manner, although Ellington did not use him in this style. His recorded solos reveal immaculate craftsmanship in their construction which typifies the excellence of all aspects of this admirable musician's work. He had several spells with Ellington, and in each his contribution was of great value. His solos have a special distinction and their own kind of rather gentle swing.

Representative Recordings: As Time Goes By (Carolltown dance recording, 1957), *All Heart* (from *A Portrait Of Ella Fitzgerald*, Verve, 1957), *Willow Weep For Me* (Columbia, 1957), *Red Shoes* (from *Toot Suite*, Columbia, 1958), *Cue's Blue Now, You Brought A New Kind Of Love To Me* (both by the Billy Strayhorn Septet, Felsted, 1959)

Kay Davis

When heard as a contralto singing popular ballads, Kay Davis seems an ordinary, rather anonymous vocalist, albeit a musically competent one. But her wordless soprano work brought a new sound to the Ellington band; in this role her background as a trained singer became obvious. Wordless singing in itself was not new to the Ellington tonal palette, but Davis's type of voice certainly was. Ellington utilized her talent both in adaptations of established Ellington classics and in new compositions inspired by her soprano voice.

Representative Recordings: Transblucency (Victor, 1946), *Minnehaha* (from *The Beautiful Indians,* Musicraft, 1946), *On A Turquoise Cloud* (Columbia, 1947), *Creole Love Call* (Columbia, 1949)

Wilbur De Paris

Wilbur De Paris replaced Tricky Sam Nanton with the Ellington band—an almost impossible assignment which he performed with competence if not brilliance. He inherited Nanton's solos on the standard arrangements but was otherwise not much used in a solo capacity. Prior to his eighteen months with Ellington, he had worked with many leading big bands; from 1951 he achieved great success with a small band, Wilbur De Paris and his *New* New Orleans Jazz.

Representative Recordings: The Mooche, Ring Dem Bells (both from Cornell Concert, April 1947)

Jimmy Hamilton

Jimmy Hamilton took over as principal clarinetist in the band in June 1943, rather less than a year after Barney Bigard's departure. It would be difficult to imagine two more contrasting stylists. Hamilton had an academic approach to his instrument. The virtues of his playing are perfect musicianship and a cool, unruffled virtuosity. Although he was not able to create clarinet parts in the manner of Bigard's magnificent ensemble style, Hamilton was a tasteful and constructive player within the band. As a soloist, he was a clean, perfectly organized musician whose style reflects the influence of Benny Goodman. Yet for all its virtues, his playing was often lacking in warmth and in that strong personality which is the hallmark of the great jazz soloist. While his clarinet work was characterized by an even, pure tone, Hamilton played tenor sax with a coarse, rough sound. For him, at least, the tenor was a "barrelhouse" instrument and his attitude to it was casual, in great contrast to his approach to the clarinet. Yet he was sufficiently skilled on tenor to sound impressive when playing chase choruses with tenor specialists. During his 25 years as an Ellington bandsman, Hamilton contributed many arrangements to the book, often of a very basic, swinging nature.

Representative Recordings: On clarinet: *Flippant Flurry* (Musicraft, 1946), *The Tattooed Bride* (Columbia, 1950), *Smada* (Columbia, 1951), *Take the "A" Train* (Johnny Hodges, Verve, 1956), *Ad Lib On Nippon* (Victor, 1966). On tenor sax: *Taffy Twist* (M.F. Productions, 1962)

Shelton Hemphill

Although he played with the Ellington band for over five years, Hemphill was hardly ever heard as a soloist. His forte was lead trumpet, and he was considered the outstanding black practitioner in this field by no less an authority than Louis Armstrong. Ellington was fortunate to have such outstanding trumpet section leaders in his band at the same time—Hemphill, Harold Baker, and either Cat Anderson or Al Killian.

Representative Recordings: Memphis Blues (Capitol Transcription, 1947), *Azalea* (Capitol Transcription, 1947), *Trumpet No End* (Carnegie Hall, 1948; Shelton Hemphill plays the trumpet solos in the first chorus)

Al Hibbler

Hibbler was often introduced by Ellington as "our romantic baritone," and this description was all too accurate so far as the jazz enthusiast is concerned. Although not a particularly distinguished vocalist, Hibbler's sensitivity to lyrics on some Ellington songs make his versions preferable to those by more famous singers. On the few opportunities he was given on Ellington records, Hibbler proved himself a better blues singer than might have been anticipated from his ballad work. Perhaps his greatest attribute, so far as Ellington was concerned, was his strong musical personality, and while his work has been much criticized by jazz writers, none has ever accused Hibbler of anonymity.

Representative Recordings: I Ain't Got Nothin' But The Blues (Victor, 1944), *Strange Feeling* (from *The Perfume Suite*, Victor, 1945), *Don't Get Around Much Anymore* (Columbia, 1947), *I Like The Sunrise* (from *The Liberian Suite*, Columbia, 1947), *Ballin' The Blues* (Capitol, 1953)

Claude Jones

Like Shelton Hemphill, trombonist Jones was used by Ellington primarily as a section man, although he had considerable experience as a soloist. He was a veteran of such first-class bands as McKinney's Cotton Pickers, Fletcher Henderson, Chick Webb, Don Redman, and Cab Calloway. On joining Ellington he inherited Juan Tizol's chair, and as a consequence took up the valve trombone, but he received very few solo opportunities. He was with the band some four and a half years.

Representative Recording: Come Sunday (from *Black, Brown And Beige*, Carnegie Hall, 1944)

Taft Jordan

After establishing his reputation with the Chick Webb band, where his playing was dominated by the influence of Louis Armstrong, Jordan joined Ellington at a time when he had developed into an individual and mature trumpet stylist. With Webb, he had been the featured soloist for a period of some six years, and even in the star-studded Ellington trumpet section of the mid-forties, he had no difficulty in holding his own. A forthright player with a full, broad tone and a stinging attack, Jordan is heard to best advantage on medium to fast numbers, where he is revealed as one of the outstanding swingers among jazz soloists. Jordan was also an accompanist of unusual sensitivity; his playing behind Ray Nance's vocals offers prime examples of this skill. The Webb records show Jordan to have been a jazz singer of character and humor, but Ellington made little use of this aspect of his talents. After leaving Duke, he fell into quite undeserved obscurity, working for the most part in theater orchestras, though his infrequent post-Ellington recordings show that he remained a fine jazz player.

Representative Recordings: Tea For Two (World Transcriptions, 1943), *Emancipation Celebration* (from *Black, Brown And Beige*, Victor, 1944), *Riff Staccato* (accompaniment to Ray Nance's vocal, Victor, 1945), *Rugged Romeo* (Capitol Transcription, 1946), *Suddenly It Jumped* (Victor, 1946), *Jam-A-Ditty* (Musicraft, 1946)

Oscar Pettiford

Foremost among the bass players inspired by Jimmy Blanton, Pettiford naturally graduated to the Ellington Orchestra, which in a very real sense was the home of the virtuoso bass player. Pettiford did not have as big a tone as either Blanton or Junior Raglin, but he had a beautifully clean articulation which seemed to cut through the heavy textures of the band. His harmonic sense was remarkable and his bass part often adds a distinctive flavoring to a performance. The all-round mastery, the swing, and the imagination displayed by Pettiford mark him as one of the great bass players in jazz history. After he had left the band, Ellington would often include him as guest soloist at concerts, on which occasions he would sometimes be featured on pizzicato cello.

Representative Recordings: Pitter Panther Patter (Carnegie Hall, 1946), *Tip Toe Topic* (Capitol Transcription, 1946), *Suddenly It Jumped* (Victor, 1946), *Royal Garden Blues* (Victor, 1946), *Sultry Serenade* (Columbia, 1947), *Air Conditioned Jungle* (Columbia, 1947)

Russell Procope

From the departure of Otto Hardwick in 1946 until Duke Ellington's death in 1974, the first alto chair in the Ellington band was held by Russell Procope. He had previously worked with a variety of leaders including Jelly Roll Morton in the twenties and Benny Carter, Chick Webb, Fletcher Henderson, and John Kirby in the thirties. With Ellington he was at first heard mainly in the section and in a very occasional alto sax solo, but from 1950 onwards, he began to be featured as a clarinet soloist. Although a New York musician, Procope had been inspired by the New Orleans clarinet school, and his playing provided a contrast with the more formal style of Jimmy Hamilton, which Ellington utilized to good effect. Procope was not a virtuoso clarinet player, and was indeed a soloist with real limitations. But his warm low-register clarinet playing contributed vitally to many of Ellington's finest late-period scores. Procope was an outstanding section man and an important member of the famous Ellington saxophone section of the fifties and sixties.

Representative Recordings: on clarinet: *Mood Indigo* (Columbia, 1950), *Blues To Be There* (from the *Newport Jazz*

Festival Suite, Columbia, 1956), *Black And Tan Fantasy* (with Cat Anderson, French Columbia, 1958), *More* (Reprise, 1964). On alto sax: *Things Ain't What They Used To Be* (Capitol, 1954), *Indian Summer* (Bethlehem, 1956)

Al Sears

Sears was an unusual figure in the Ellington saxophone section in that he was a primitive stylist. Unlike such Ellington tenor saxophone virtuosi as Ben Webster and Paul Gonsalves, he concentrated on playing in a straightforward manner with maximum swing. At medium tempo he is at his most successful, using incisive phrasing to good effect, but Ellington also used his brooding slow tempo tellingly on occasion. Sears was with the band for five years, from 1944 to 1949.

Representative Recordings: I Ain't Got Nothin' But The Blues (Victor, 1944), *The Blues* (from *Black, Brown And Beige*, Victor, 1944), *It Don't Mean A Thing* (Victor, 1945), *Cotton Tail* (D.E.T.S., version of June 16, 1945), *Hiawatha* (from *The Beautiful Indians*, Musicraft, 1946); *Dance No. 1* (from *The Liberian Suite*, Columbia, 1947)

Joya Sherrill

Although very young during her stay with the Ellington band in 1944 to 1946, Joya Sherrill was one of the more satisfactory singers Duke employed. Despite the fact that she was often given trite pop songs to perform, she never made less than a musicianly impression on the listener. She gave several notable performances of Ellington's own songs and must be rated among the few successes Ellington achieved in the recruiting of vocalists. Joya was a gracious, lively stylist.

Representative Recordings: I'm Beginning To See The Light (Victor, 1944), *The Blues* (from *Black, Brown And Beige*, Victor, 1944), *Everything But You* (Victor, 1945), *I Let A Song Go Out Of My Heart* (Victor, 1945)

Elbert Williams

Elbert "Skippy" Williams played in the Ellington Orchestra between the departure of Ben Webster in August 1943 and the arrival of Al Sears the following May. His solos reveal him as a rather conventional tenor stylist of the time, playing in a competent but not particularly individual manner. This musician's name has often been given as Elmer Williams, which has led to his being confused with the tenor saxophonist of that name who had been featured with the Chick Webb Orchestra. Skippy Williams had worked with Count Basie, Edgar Hayes, Earl Bostic, and Lucky Millinder prior to joining Duke.

Representative Recordings: It Don't Mean A Thing (World Transcriptions, 1943), *Cotton Tail* (Carnegie Hall, December 1943)

Francis Williams

Williams was in the Ellington trumpet section for some three and a half years, from 1946 to 1949, unfortunately for him at a time when it was packed with better-known soloists. On records, his solo appearances were for the most part confined to one of the trumpet solos in *Trumpet No End*. Here, as on records made away from Ellington, he appears to be a soloist of a swinging if not outstandingly individual kind.

Representative Recording: Trumpet No End (Musicraft, 1946—Francis Williams plays the trumpet solo in the third chorus)

Chapter 18

The Records—October 1946 to December 1950

ON OCTOBER 23, 1946, THE DUKE ELLINGTON orchestra recorded the first session under a new contract with the Musicraft label. At this time the personnel was:

Trumpets: Shelton Hemphill, Francis Williams, Taft Jordan, Harold Baker, Cat Anderson, Ray Nance (also violin and vocal).

Trombones: Lawrence Brown, Wilbur De Paris, Claude Jones (valve trombone).

Reeds: Russell Procope (alto sax, clarinet); Johnny Hodges (alto sax); Al Sears (tenor sax); Jimmy Hamilton (clarinet, tenor sax); Harry Carney (baritone sax, clarinet, bass clarinet).

Rhythm: Duke Ellington (piano); Fred Guy (guitar); Oscar Pettiford (bass); Sonny Greer (drums); Billy Strayhorn (deputy pianist).

Vocal: Kay Davis, Al Hibbler.

Thirteen titles were recorded in October, November and December 1946, making up fifteen sides in all, since two of the titles were double-sided 78s. The repertoire was dominated by new instrumental material, including selections from three of the most recent suites. The series started with its one revival, a recording of *Diminuendo In Blue* without its *Crescendo* companion. This is a good performance, but semiredundant as it is really only one-half of a composite whole. Its session mate is the first of two new Ellington concertos for Hodges, *Magenta Haze*; the second, *Sultry Sunset*, was recorded at the session of November 25, 1946. Both scores were cut down owing to the time limits of the 78 format, but Hodges is in superlative form. He plays with a pure, crystal-like tone and phrases with a classical beauty which keeps the music clear of the sentimentality towards which these melodic lines might tempt a lesser artist. (Of the recordings which contain these compositions in full, the Capitol Transcription and Carnegie Hall versions of *Magenta Haze* are both excellent, but for *Sultry Sunset*, the Capitol Transcription recording is to be preferred.)

The second Musicraft session also includes music from two Ellington suites. The first is the two-sided *Happy-Go-Lucky Local*, the only part of Ellington and Strayhorn's *Deep South Suite* ever recorded commercially. Two of the three movements of Ellington's *The Beautiful Indians* suite were recorded for Musicraft—*Minnehaha*, a feature for Kay Davis's wordless soprano, and *Hiawatha*, an uptempo concerto for Sears. *Hiawatha* is based on the harmonies of *It Don't Mean A Thing* and is remarkable for its insight into Sears's style and for the perfection of the way the orchestral part projects the soloist.

At the time of issue, the most famous of the Musicraft recordings was Mary Lou Williams's arrangement of *Blue Skies*, which had become a feature for the trumpet section under the title *Trumpet No End*. Jordan, Baker, Nance, Williams, and Anderson are featured in what had obviously developed into something of a showstopper. The greatest possible contrast is a new Strayhorn concerto for Jimmy Hamilton, *Flippant Flurry*, a cool, unemotional composition highly suitable for Hamilton's academic clarinet style. In this piece Strayhorn and Hamilton examine several clarinet clichés of the swing era in a clinical, detached, and rather droll fashion. Ellington also contributes a new concerto, *Golden Feather*, for Carney's baritone sax. This was recorded on the December 5, 1946, session and contains some beautiful music.

The fourth Musicraft date was on December 11, 1946, and produced the only two vocal numbers recorded for the label. *It Shouldn't Happen To A Dream* has a vocal by Hibbler and some timeless alto from Johnny Hodges. *Tulip Or Turnip*, with a vocal by Ray Nance, is much better; in addition to witty, satirical lyrics and lively singing, this medium-tempo score allows the band the maximum opportunity to swing. The final Musicraft session, on December 18, 1946, produced Billy Strayhorn's *Overture To A Jam Session*, which covered two sides, and *Jam A-Ditty* from *A Tonal Group* (or *Suite Ditty*). The Strayhorn piece is rather lightweight, with some nice scoring for the saxophone section and rather a lot of indeterminate violin music performed by Nance. The other soloists are Pettiford and Baker. *Jam A-Ditty*, subtitled *Concerto For Four Jazz Horns*, is a development of the concerto grosso principle first used by Ellington in the 1938 *Battle Of Swing*. On this recording there is some good playing from soloists Jordan, Brown, Hamilton, and Carney; Jordan, in outstanding form, contributes a gem of a break.

* * *

An LP of broadcasts from October 11 and 25, 1946, just before the first Musicraft session, has been issued on the Fanfare label. The striking feature of these broadcasts is the repertoire, with popular ballads dominating, mostly of an ephemeral nature. There are some Ellington numbers—*Just Squeeze Me*, *In A Mellotone*, and *C Jam Blues*—but these are in a minority. The scores for the pop songs do not sound particularly Ellingtonian and are probably the work of one or more of the outside arrangers. They are treated as showcases for different soloists: Hodges on *A Garden In The Rain*, Carney on *The Whole World Is Singing My Song* and *I'll Buy That Dream*, Brown on *The Things We Did Last Summer* and *Love Letters*, and Baker on *This Is Always*. The LP is of particular interest in that it features a part of the Ellington repertoire rarely heard on records—the scores by the outside arrangers reserved for radio and dance hall use.

* * *

In late 1946, Ellington invited the great gypsy guitarist Django Reinhardt to the United States to tour with his band. Owing to Reinhardt's unreliability, no rehearsals took place, and indeed the guitarist only played a handful of concerts with Ellington. At these he was featured as a soloist with no attempt to integrate his playing with that of the band. No commercial recordings were made, but the music from a concert at the Chicago Civic Opera House on November 10, 1946, has been issued. Reinhardt's contribution consists of four solos, one unaccompanied, the others supported by the rhythm section and occasional riffing from the band. In no way is Reinhardt used *with* the band, which is a great pity. The addition of his guitar, with its highly distinctive flavor, to the Ellington tonal palette could have been rewarding in many ways. The only indication of what such a combination might have been like are the recordings made under Rex Stewart's name during the Ellington band's stay in Paris in 1939 by a quartet of Stewart on cornet, Barney Bigard on clarinet, Billy Taylor on bass, and Django on guitar. It is music with a strong Ellington flavor, and Django's contributions, especially on *Finesse* and *Solid Old Man*, show how congenial he found these surroundings. The 1946 Chicago concert finds Django on amplified guitar—he was actually playing on a borrowed instrument which he disliked—and he produces a rather perfunctory set. Though these solos are not Reinhardt's best, they are nonetheless indicative of the inventive genius of one of the greatest jazz soloists, here supported by a superb rhythm section.

The music recorded by the Ellington band at this Chicago concert is of greater interest. The opener is Strayhorn's *Overture To A Jam Session* in a somewhat more relaxed reading than on the studio recording. Then, as was customary at Ellington concerts, a number from the band's early days is revived: *Ring Dem Bells*, still in its original arrangement. Greer is heard on chimes here, and is featured on drums in an ebullient *Jumpin' Punkins*. Then the band plays the three-part Handy tribute of *Memphis Blues, Beale Street Blues,* and *St. Louis Blues*. These make interesting comparisons with the 1946 Victor and Capitol Transcriptions. Surprisingly, it is the best of the three arrangements, *St. Louis Blues*, which proves most rewarding here, although purely because of the placement of the recording microphone. The arrangement is that on the Victor recording, for the most part, backing to singer Marion Cox. The vocalist is, however, so far from the recording mike as to be almost inaudible, and it would be quite possible for someone to hear this recording without being aware of the vocal. So rich in tone colors and so lively in articulation is the accompaniment that (the last chorus apart) it makes a totally coherent musical fabric in itself; the quality of the sound clearly derives less from the scoring than from the rich sonorities which were a hallmark of musicians chosen to play in the Ellington band. The program continues with a group of concertos, sandwiched among which is a fine version of *Unbooted Character*. The concertos are two rather moderate examples of the genre—*The Eighth Veil,* for Cat Anderson, and *Air Conditioned Jungle*, for Jimmy Hamilton—and two rich and sensuous pieces—*Sultry Sunset*, for Johnny Hodges, and the new *Golden Cress*, for Lawrence Brown.

Two new Ellington suites received their premieres at this concert, *The Beautiful Indians* and *The Deep South Suite*. We have already mentioned the Musicraft recordings of two movements of the former, *Minnehaha* for Kay Davis's wordless voice, and the Al Sears showcase *Hiawatha*. The additional movement is the opening *Chaugogagog Maushaugagog Chaubunagungamaug*, a feature for Taft Jordan's trumpet, with a little exotic valve trombone from Claude Jones in the manner of Juan Tizol.

The Deep South Suite is a more substantial piece of work. The first of four movements presents what Ellington calls "the Dixie Chamber of Commerce view of the South": *Magnolias Dripping With Molasses*. This is a comfortable medium-tempo piece, probably written by Strayhorn. Its relevance to its title is tenuous, apart from the rather obvious device of a few quotations from Stephen Foster. *Hearsay* is a grim slow movement in which the soloist—Harold Baker at his most majestic—sings a sad lyrical trumpet song against a somber background, with a violent introduction and interruptions from the orchestra. The harsh aspect of black life in the South, the lynchings and the persecution, are evoked in this unusual but very effective movement. The combination of menace, violence, and just slightly overheated lyricism strikes precisely the right note.

Ellington said that *The Deep South Suite* was in two parts, presenting what he and Strayhorn had heard about the South in its first two movements, and what they had actually seen there in its last two. The third section is a piano solo portraying the harmony between people of different races and backgrounds, when *Nobody Was Lookin'*. This is a kind of rondo, with some beautiful themes, played with quiet mastery by Duke. The final *Happy-Go-Lucky Local* provides a perfect climax, and it is noticeable how relaxed and easy the band sounds at the premiere performance. This last piece survived in the band's performing repertoire long after the rest of *The Deep South Suite* had been consigned to that very crowded limbo of neglected Ellington compositions. Duke himself said that *Happy-Go-Lucky Local*

> told a story of a train in the South, not one of those luxurious, streamlined trains that take tourists to Miami, but a little train with an upright engine that was never fast, never on schedule, and never made stops at any place you ever heard about. After grunting, groaning and jerking, it finally settled down to a steady medium tempo. The train had a Negro fireman who loved to pull the string that blew the whistle, and since he seemed to know every house, and to recognize someone watching him go by in every window—in every house and in every window on *his* side of the tracks, that is—he was forever pulling that string. He played tunes on the whistle, too—blues, a little *Shortenin' Bread*—calling somebody as the train rattled along with more than a suggestion of boogie-woogie rhythm. (*Music Is My Mistress*, pp. 184–85)

Happy-Go-Lucky Local is an exhilarating ride on the twelve-bar blues. The main soloists are Ellington, Pettiford, Nance, Hamilton, and Anderson, the last supplying the sound of escaping steam as the locomotive pulls into the station. The warm, rugged, swinging blues performance by the band on this first night is a tribute to the efficacy of Ellington's informal methods of bandleading—and to his unerring judgment in selecting musicians. No other group could have approached a new concert work of this character and brought it off with such ease and panache. This piece manages to be at one and the same time the most brilliant train portrayal in all music and a very basic, rugged, boogie blues. (A main strain from *Happy-Go-Lucky Local* was used by Jimmy Forrest for his popular *Night Train* of a few years later.)

Ellington obviously attached a good deal of importance to *The Deep South Suite*. Like many of his longer works, it is bound together by a programmatic idea rather than by strictly musical means. Yet the four movements are nicely contrasted and complement each other well. It is unfortunate that he never found time to revive this suite in later years.

Of the many versions of *Happy-Go-Lucky Local* issued on record, a balanced selection of the best would include the Musicraft and Capitol Transcription versions of 1946, the Capitol of 1954, and the Atlantic *Paris Concert* recording of

1963. So far as complete recordings of *The Deep South Suite* are concerned, they are restricted to that from the Chicago Civic Opera House concert of November 10, 1946, and that from Carnegie Hall thirteen days later, the latter used on the V-Disc issue. There is little to choose between them, either as performances or as recordings.

The Civic Opera House concert was of typically generous Ellington proportions. Still to come after the suites were *Things Ain't What They Used To Be*, the *Medley of Popular Hits*, the Reinhardt segment, four numbers by Hibbler and one vocal by Nance, and finally, *Trumpets No End*. The event was also typical in that it presented a wide variety of music and demonstrated the unbroken Ellington tradition of relaxed, individualistic music making—in contrast to the highly drilled precision playing now becoming almost the only kind of big band jazz heard outside the Ellington camp. It is interesting to note that the two concert suites introduced at these concerts met the fate of *Black, Brown And Beige*—one or two complete performances, followed by the entrance of selected excerpts into the regular concert repertoire. From *The Beautiful Indians*, the second and third movements were used in concerts for about a year, but of the four movements of *The Deep South Suite*, only *Happy-Go-Lucky Local* survived after the initial performances.

* * *

The Carnegie Hall concert of November 23, 1946, largely duplicated the music played at the Civic Opera House. Among numbers issued on record, the only ones not also done at the earlier event are two features, for Carney on *Golden Feather* and for Hamilton on *Flippant Flurry*. (The V-Disc recordings of *Golden Cress*, *Sultry Sunset*, and *The Deep South Suite* were taken from this concert.)

On April 30, 1947, the band did a concert at Cornell University. The program makes interesting reading, both in comparison with the two concerts discussed above and as a typical example of a 1947 Ellington concert program:

Blutopia
Overture To A Jam Session
The Mooche
Diminuendo And Crescendo In Blue
Frustration
Rugged Romeo
Flippant Flurry
Golden Cress
Jam A-Ditty
Passion Flower
The Blues (from *Black, Brown And Beige*)
Dancers In Love (from *The Perfume Suite*)
Frankie And Johnnie
Things Ain't What They Used To Be
Take The "A" Train
Beale Street Blues

Minnehaha (from *The Beautiful Indians*)
Transblucency
Hiawatha (from *The Beautiful Indians*)
My Little Brown Book
Don't Take Your Love From Me
Summertime
I'm Just A Lucky So And So
Flamingo
Ring Dem Bells

The trombone solos on *The Mooche* and *Ring Dem Bells* are by Wilbur De Paris and offer a rare opportunity to hear his plunger style. *Diminuendo In Blue* and *Crescendo In Blue* are separated by a long, reflective piano solo by Ellington. *The Blues* from *Black, Brown And Beige* includes the tenor sax and trombone duet otherwise heard only in *Carnegie Blues*; the vocalist is Kay Davis. Parts of this concert have been issued on the Stardust label, but the sound quality is not good.

The change from Victor to Musicraft in 1946 had resulted in a lowering of recording quality, and the best records of the band between the Victors of late 1946 and the Columbias of 1947 are those from the final sessions for Capitol Transcriptions. One of these was held in January 1947, two in June of that year. The January session duplicates many of the Musicraft recordings—*Golden Feather*, *Flippant Flurry*, *Jam A-Ditty*, *Happy-Go-Lucky Local*, *Overture To A Jam Session*, and *Sultry Sunset*. These versions are to be preferred to the Musicrafts due to the superior recording quality; on purely musical grounds, there is little to choose between them. The elusive *Fugue A-Ditty* and the Lawrence Brown concerto *Golden Cress* were also done at this January session.

The June recordings look a little further back for material and there is considerable duplication with the late Victors—*Beale Street Blues*, *Memphis Blues*, *St. Louis Blues*, *Royal Garden Blues*, and *Blue Is The Night*, all in effective performances with sufficient variations to give them an identity of their own. Ray Nance is the vocalist on *St. Louis Blues* and on a new recording of *Jump For Joy*. The trombone solo previously played by Nanton on this last number is taken by Brown, despite the fact that both De Paris and Tyree Glenn were in the band. For some reason, Ellington preferred Brown's orthodox trombone to that of his new plunger specialists, possibly because Brown was more familiar with the piece.

Jumpin' Punkins has Pettiford taking over Blanton's role to great effect, plus admirable work from Carney and the irrepressible Greer. *The* fashionable theme in instrumental jazz at this time was *How High The Moon*, and in the 1947 Ellington version, Baker and Hamilton are the main soloists. *Blue Lou*, an Edgar Sampson piece famous from classic 1930s recordings by Benny Carter, Fletcher Henderson, and Chick Webb, makes a slightly surprising Ellington debut here, with solos by Nance, Ellington, and Pettiford. *Who Struck John?*, *Far Away Blues*, and *Frisky* are given the Hodges small-group treatment, with solos by alto and piano. *Violet Blue* is the first recording of a piece written by Strayhorn for Hodges, which became better known a decade later (in somewhat extended form) as *Multi-Coloured Blue*. There is an excellent version of the Carney feature *Frustration* and a couple of new pop tunes, *Azalea* and *Orchids For Madame*, which feature vocalist Chester Crumpler (who was with the band for a few months only) in a style typical of Ellington's male ballad singers. The last of these Capitol titles is a midtempo twelve-bar blues, *Park At 106th*, a casual riff piece with an obbligato role for Nance's plunger trumpet, a duet by Ellington and Pettiford, and a solo by the ever reliable Carney.

During the course of a broadcast on May 10, 1947, four titles were recorded by V-Disc. Three were typical Ellington showcases—*Sophisticated Lady* for Carney, *On The Sunny Side Of The Street* for Hodges and Brown, and *I Can't Give You Anything But Love* for Jordan. On *It Don't Mean A Thing*, Duke tried to persuade Greer to revert to his old Cotton Club role of vocalist, but he graciously declined and much of the record is taken up by Ellington and Greer talking. These verbal exchanges are followed by the usual concluding tenor solo by Sears. On some LP issues, the first part of the Ellington-Greer discussion is cut out. Issues from broadcasts for this period are few and tend to add little to our knowledge of the band and its music. An exception is a *One O'Clock Jump*, from July 9, 1947. This version, originally issued on 78 as *Two O'Clock Jump*, is taken at a solid medium tempo, surely the slowest ever for this famous blues. The performance lasts over seven minutes and features a long piano solo by Duke as well as two chorus contributions from Sears, Brown, Hodges, and trumpeter Francis Williams. The band riffing at the end reaches such a degree of nonchalance that if the musicians relaxed any more, one feels that they would fall off the bandstand.

* * *

Ellington's stay with Musicraft was brief. On August 14, 1947, he was in the Columbia studios, initiating a series of recordings for that label which was to run for just over five years. Those years saw the introduction of the long-playing record, though at first it was used only as an adjunct to the standard 78 single. One feature of this long Columbia series, especially when compared with the Musicrafts, is the superb recording quality. These are certainly the technically best recordings to date of the Ellington Orchestra, just as outstanding for their era as were the 1940 Victors for theirs.

Among a few personnel changes by the time the Columbia contract got under way, the most important were the departure of Jordan and Anderson from the trumpet section and the replacement of De Paris by Tyree Glenn, a trombonist who also doubled on vibraphone. The replacements in the trumpet section did not bring any important musicians to the band, but Glenn's appearance in Nanton's old chair was significant. Glenn has said that he joined the band specifically to play Nanton's role, and while his musical personality was very different, he brought to the plunger trombone parts a skill and artistry second only to Nanton's. Glenn's plunger style was smoother and less gutty than Nanton's, and he was also a skilled soloist on open trombone. The middle to late forties were bad times for big bands, and Ellington's was almost the only one to survive the problems of the period intact, the single other exception among jazz-oriented bands being Buddy Johnson's. The desperate situation demanded desperate measures, and the Ellington discography of this period contains several examples of records made with the sole intention of creating a juke box hit or an impact on the popular record charts. There had always been a proportion of popular songs in the Ellington output, but the difference now was that pieces were created with the aim of quick popularity; pieces which were never played outside the recording studio and which often had little in common with Ellington's musical traditions. For example, when in the early days of the Columbia contract, Duke used Woody Herman—another contract bandleader struggling against adversity—on a session as vocalist, one of the songs was a piece of ephemera entitled *Cowboy Rhumba*. There is, inevitably, some interesting music on the popular-song recordings of the period 1947–1950, but before considering these we will look at the instrumental items which, as always, produced the most substantial music.

* * *

The first recording made at the first Columbia session was a blues, *H'ya Sue*. It features Glenn's plunger trombone, backed by Hamilton's rough-toned tenor sax, and a superbly eloquent blues solo from Hodges. Glenn establishes himself at once as an authoritative Ellington voice, and the performance is only slightly marred by the rather stodgy delivery of the final ensemble chorus. Two previously unreleased takes have appeared on Jerry Valburn's Up-To-Date label. The first is a longer performance with the composition in a state of flux; it has solos by Ellington on piano and Baker on plunger trumpet, in addition to the contributions by Glenn and Hodges. The second has an arrangement identical to the issued version's, but the performance breaks down in the final ensemble. The stiffness at this point in the performance is obviously due to the band phrasing the riffs in a careful, almost cautious, manner. These rejected takes are of interest; the first, with its series of new solos, especially so.

Lady Of The Lavender Mist is a warm and melodious Ellington tone poem, and the performance benefits greatly from the superior recording quality. The scoring is especially rich, and in the massive central ensemble the lead is played by Baker, and there is characteristic deployment of Carney's baritone. At the start, Hodges has the lead role and Hamilton and Carney decorative parts, while after the ensemble, with its curiously somber overtone, Brown takes a perfectly poised eight-bar solo. The next number, a concerto for Brown called *Golden Cress* (a dedication to the wife of Ellington's then personal manager), is without doubt the most successful of Ellington's several showcases for the trombonist. There are slightly longer versions of *Golden Cress* from transcriptions or concerts, but the Columbia is to be preferred, due to a recording quality which reveals every detail of a sumptuous and colorful score. The interpretation of the orchestral part here is among the miracles of Ellington music, the saxophones in particular displaying an almost unbelievable richness and variety of tone color as well as the characteristic Ellington warmth and thrust.

In *Boogie Bop Blues*, one of the more conservative stylists in the band, Russell Procope, plays a "bop" alto part in ensembles which frame a solo sequence by Nance, Hamilton, Glenn, and Pettiford. The rhythm section plays in a manner which owes nothing to bop and there is not a trace of boogie to be heard, this being simply a fine medium-tempo blues performance. Glenn plays plunger trombone, but on *Sultry Serenade* we have an opportunity to hear his open horn at length. Ellington provides a perfect setting for Glenn. The theme is one which the trombonist later recorded himself as *How Can You Do A Thing Like That To Me?*, and indeed he shares composer credits with Duke for *Sultry Serenade*. Hodges and Pettiford also make vital contributions to a swinging medium-tempo performance of a score which fits the personalities of its executants to perfection. (Two additional takes of *Sultry Serenade* have been issued on the Up-To-Date label; the main differences are in the trombone solo, which is clearly less developed on these earlier attempts. One of the takes breaks down for that rarest of reasons, a fluff by Hodges.)

Duke's essay in the powerhouse big band style of the day, *Stomp, Look And Listen*, is a number whose stride piano origins can be discerned behind its late swing period stylistic facade. This is the first studio recording of the piece, and the Ellington band gives a performance which shows that it is second to none in this kind of music. There are several fine individual contributions, notably a chase chorus between Nance and Baker. A concerto for Hamilton follows, *Air Conditioned Jungle* (from 1945), a vehicle for clarinet virtuosity which also has an important role for the string bass. Hamilton and Pettiford perform their parts with unruffled brilliance.

Perhaps the most successful of the uptempo pieces from these sessions is *Three Cent Stomp*, an essay on the *Stompy Jones* chords which, like *Stomp, Look And Listen* and *Air Conditioned Jungle*, had been in the performing repertoire for the past few years. This Columbia is a superb version, with solos from Baker, Glenn, Nance, and Pettiford in a nicely diversified setting. The band performs beautifully, not least in the marvelous passage for the saxophone section. Strayhorn's *Progressive Gavotte* is neither progressive nor a gavotte, but it is a very pleasantly melodic piece of writing. There is a glorious Baker theme statement and a Hodges solo in which we hear for the first time that note of slightly bland detachment which later became characteristic of much of his work. As is the case with several of these performances, some different takes of *Progressive Gavotte* have appeared on LPs in recent years. There are two interesting rare takes, which, so typically, tell us more about the band's attitude to performance than about the work itself.

At another November 1947 session, Ellington recorded versions of three popular standards—*I Can't Believe That You're In Love With Me*, *How High The Moon*, and *Singin' In The Rain*. The first two had previously been recorded for Capitol Transcriptions, but the Columbia versions are perhaps to be slightly preferred, again owing to the superb recording quality. *I Can't Believe* is given a very uninhibited performance, while the highlight of the rather commonplace Dick Vance arrangement of *How High The Moon* is an excellent Baker solo. *Singin' In The Rain* receives a suitably droll performance, with solos from Hodges, Nance, Brown, and Carney.

The third and final of the Ellington tone poems featuring the trained soprano voice of Kay Davis was recorded with a small group from the band at this time. This is the exquisite *On A Turquoise Cloud*, the most successful of these pieces. It contains some masterly and highly original scoring. Davis's wordless voice is blended with Brown's trombone and Hamilton's clarinet in the manner already familiar from *Transblucency*, while additional coloring comes from Nance on violin and Carney on bass clarinet. These various instruments are used in a contrapuntal passage behind the voice, and the result is a beautiful mosaic of sound. Brown provides a perfect reading of the second theme.

* * *

On December 24, 1947, the band recorded *The Liberian Suite*, an Ellington work commissioned by the government of Liberia to celebrate that country's first 100 years of existence. The work was premiered at Carnegie Hall on December 26 and 27, and the performance from the 27th has been issued on one of the Prestige Ellington Carnegie Hall albums. Although done after the Columbia recording, the performance is rather untidy. In this instance, the studio version is to be preferred in every way.

The suite consists of an introductory vocal movement, *I Like The Sunrise*, and five instrumental dances. On both the Columbia and Carnegie recordings, *I Like The Sunrise* is sung by Hibbler, and although his contribution is neither a brilliant vocal demonstration nor the kind of singing jazz enthusiasts much care for, it is notably more successful as an interpretation of Ellington's song than later recordings by such eminent singers as Frank Sinatra and Ella Fitzgerald. Carney's interpretation of the baritone saxophone parts is beyond compare. For some reason, Hibbler's vocal was not recorded at this time but was added to the orchestral part at a later date. A strange error was made when *I Like The Sunrise* was issued on V-Disc, for Columbia provided V-Discs with the original recording *without the vocal added*. No one seems to have realized this error, and some critics have treated this

V-Disc issue (reissued on microgroove in recent years) as if it were a second instrumental version. This and a number of genuine alternative takes from *The Liberian Suite* have been issued on an Up-To-Date LP; the most interesting is an embryonic version of *Dance No. 1*.

This first of the dances is a remarkable creation; a brooding minor-key blues which features Sears's tenor in a solo which develops into a honking, squealing climax in the rhythm-and-blues style. In this *Dance No. 1*, Ellington creates a mood of latent menace with occasional and perfectly judged flashes of violence. It is as if he were demonstrating that he could use the growls and tonal distortions of rhythm-and-blues tenor just as successfully as he had employed the snarls and growls of plunger-muted brass for the past two decades. In this sense, *Dance No. 1* is part of that Ellington tradition inaugurated by *Black And Tan Fantasy* and *The Mooche*. The orchestral preamble to Sears's solo is also of the utmost mastery. (The rejected take is clearly of an earlier performance; Sears shows a less certain grasp of his role, and the integration between band and soloist is less well developed.)

Dance No. 2 is an uptempo, stomping piece opening with a train motif and some interesting orchestral ideas, but petering out in a swinging but rather commonplace vibraphone improvisation by Tyree Glenn. The third dance has a very rich melody, played first by Nance on violin and then developed into a huge orchestral climax led by Al Killian's high-note trumpet. Killian had just joined the band and was given the high-note role previously assigned to Cat Anderson. The fast *Dance No 4*, a sparse and rather perfunctory-sounding piece, features Greer on timpani (not one of Ellington's most successful uses of his musicians' resources) and Hodges on alto. The final *Dance No. 5* features Glenn once more, this time on plunger trombone. This piece, a blues, is the ancestor of such Ellington creations of the sixties as *La Plus Belle Africaine* and *Ad Lib On Nippon*. The dialogue in one-bar phrases between the muted instruments of Nance and Glenn and the interjections of Baker on open trumpet are among the striking ingredients of this highly original composition, which however lacks the feeling of climax expected from the finale of a six-movement suite.

The Liberian Suite is a loosely constructed and uneven work in terms of both content and balance, yet despite this (and the arbitrary air of some of the writing) the suite deserves better than the few words of denigration which have usually been its lot among jazz critics. The best parts of *The Liberian Suite* are wholly worthy of their creator.

* * *

The remaining instrumental recordings from the 1947 Columbia sessions consist of a trio of contrasting pieces done by a small group from the band. The first two feature Ellington on piano. *The Clothéd Woman* paints a musical portrait of a sophisticated, experienced and dignified woman and contains a little "depth psychology" in the form of a ragtime middle section. The inspiration of this piece is clearly close to that of *The Perfume Suite*, and there are also similarities in the musical idiom. *The Clothéd Woman* is one of Ellington's most successful compositions, with a harmonic usage which is very modern in conception, but so apposite to the musical content that it never sounds in any way bizarre or modish. The conception and execution of the piano part are of great mastery. In contrast to the outer sections, which approach atonality, the central ragtime section is harmonically very static. *The Clothéd Woman* is an extremely imaginative piece in which hints of melodic shapes and harmonic directions are conveyed in a most subtle manner. It was performed at the November 1947 Carnegie Hall concerts and that version, issued on Prestige, is performed with the full band and is longer than the Columbia. The Columbia alternative take (heard complete and in good sound on Up-To-Date, incomplete and in poor sound on some other issues) is also longer and contains a fascinating development of the ragtime middle section. Both these versions of this masterpiece are of great interest, but the standard Columbia issue remains the definitive one, a supremely concentrated piece of musical thinking.

The companion piece to *The Clothéd Woman* is similarly available in three versions, of which the Carnegie Hall recording is expanded and for full orchestra. This is *New York City Blues*, not a blues in the traditional sense but an evocation of the emptiness and loneliness of the big city, its mood sad and nocturnal. Again Ellington features himself at the piano and again he displays that rarest form of virtuosity which makes every note and every chord count. All three versions are worth hearing, the differences between the two Columbia takes being less marked than in the case of *The Clothéd Woman*.

The musicians who had recorded *The Clothéd Woman* and *New York City Blues* for Columbia were encouraged by Duke to indulge in an end-of-session uptempo blues which everyone, including the piano player, obviously enjoyed. Never intended for public release since it was not allocated either a title or a master number, it nonetheless survived and was included in the Columbia album, *The World Of Duke Ellington*, under the title *Let's Go Blues*. As informal a piece of jazz making as can be imagined, it has solos by Ellington, Baker, Hodges, Killian, Sears, Glenn, and Hamilton.

* * *

Some of the popular songs Ellington recorded for Columbia in 1947 were from *Beggar's Holiday*. This was Ellington's adaptation of John Gay's *The Beggar's Opera*, which transformed the work into the idiom of the American musical. The lyrics were by John Latouche. Duke is said to have written 78 pieces for this show, only half of which were used. Strayhorn did the scoring for the pit orchestra, and it is perhaps because neither Duke nor the band was involved in the actual production that *Beggar's Holiday* has attracted so little attention among Ellington devotees. Although $35,000 was invested in it and the reviews were good, the show was a flop. The multiracial nature of both the cast and the production team was radical in 1947, but it would seem that the three-and-one-half-hour running time was the most likely cause for the failure.

From the mid-forties on, Ellington's output of popular songs declined in quantity and to a degree in quality. There are good songs to be found among his later output, but there are fewer of them, and they are joined by some fairly commonplace specimens. At times it seems as if, consciously or not, Duke was reworking his earlier hits. In 1947, the band recorded a mixture of Ellington and non-Ellington songs for Columbia. On many of these the band and its soloists play superbly, but the overall effect is often of mediocrity. Sometimes this is due to the material, sometimes to the vocalists, sometimes to both. On *Women, Women, Women* (from *Beggar's Holiday*), *Antidisestablishmentarianismist*, *You Gotta Crawl Before You Walk* (which has singer Mel Tormé as one of the cocomposers), and *Kitty*, Ray Nance is the vocalist, and at times even his vitality is dimmed by the material. *Women, Women, Women* is the best of these, with superb work by the saxophone section and solos by Hodges and two of the trumpeters—Nance and Dud Bascomb. The most amusing thing about *Antidisestablishmentarianismist* is its title and there is nothing much in the way of instrumental delight here, but *You Gotta Crawl* boasts a solo roster of Glenn, Hodges, Bascomb, Baker, and Carney, while the same two trumpet soloists and Hodges are heard on *Kitty*.

The two numbers with Woody Herman are substandard, even though the second title, *I Fell And Broke My Heart*, includes a nice Hodges passage. A rather less distinguished song is *Put Yourself In My Place, Baby*, but this performance includes a full chorus of Baker's open trumpet in which his wonderful tone and perfect phrasing are heard to excellent effect. The girl singer with Ellington at this time was Dolores Parker, and, although the numbers she recorded during her six months or so with the band were not particularly inspired, she is revealed as a lady who could sing, by no means a certain attribute of an Ellington vocalist. On *Once Upon A Dream*, she is supported by pleasant solos from Hodges and Brown; she makes rather more of this song than of *A Woman And A Man*. The Parker vocal on *I Could Get A Man* is supported by richly scored saxophones and a passionate solo from Hodges. *It's Mad Mad Mad* is typical of the material recorded in an attempt to achieve popular success; despite Parker's vocal and a Brown trombone solo, it fails to add up to very much.

In addition to *Women, Women, Women* there are three other numbers from *Beggar's Holiday* in this group of records. Of these, *Change My Ways* is the most interesting. This is a very attractive Ellington theme for which arranger Strayhorn seemed unable to find the right combination of soloists. Four takes have been issued from various Columbia sessions. The final version, which remained in the book for a number of years, features Nance on violin and Brown on trombone. The earlier recordings, including one with a vocal and one with Nance playing trumpet, had been rejected. The other *Beggar's Holiday* pieces are *Brown Penny*, with a pleasant vocal by Kay Davis but little musical substance (Strayhorn is the pianist) and *Take Love Easy*, which has a nice Dolores Parker vocal and solos by Hodges and Nance. *He Makes Me Believe He's Mine* is also by Ellington and Latouche but does not seem to be from *Beggar's Holiday*; the Columbia recording has nice Brown in his ballad vein but nothing else to commend it, despite the professionalism of Parker's vocal.

Of the recordings featuring Hibbler, *It's Monday Every Day* and *It's Love I'm In* (neither of them Ellington songs) are both pretty drab. Much livelier are the remakes of two of Duke's most famous numbers from 1940—*Do Nothin' Til You Hear From Me* and *Don't Get Around Much Anymore*. These had been adapted from *Concerto For Cootie* and *Never No Lament* some years before and given lyrics by Bob Russell. Although the titles on the labels of some Victor 78 reissues had duly been changed, Ellington himself had not recorded vocal versions of these songs for commercial release until now, despite the popularity of such recordings by other artists. On this recording of *Do Nothin' Til You Hear From Me*, Nance is heard on growl trumpet and Brown in a superb, floating trombone solo; *Don't Get Around Much Anymore* is a good example of how the strong personalities of the Ellington musicians can be used to set an atmosphere as Nance (again on growl trumpet) and Hodges introduce the piece with supreme authority.

***

The bulk of a concert played by the Ellington Orchestra at the Hollywood Bowl on August 31, 1947, has been issued on Unique Jazz. The program was similar in many ways to that at Cornell University on April 30, listed previously. Differences include the reappearance of the complete *W.C. Handy Medley* and the use of three excerpts from *Black, Brown And Beige*—*Come Sunday*, *The Blues*, and *Emancipation Celebration*. This last is of particular interest as the roles previously assigned to Rex Stewart (or Taft Jordan) and Tricky Sam Nanton are given to Ray Nance and Tyree Glenn; their interpretations are characteristically skilled. The *Blues Cluster* form of *Diminuendo And Crescendo In Blue* is used, with *Transblucency* returning as the centerpiece. Other revivals include *Jumpin' Punkins*, *Golden Feather*, *Air Conditioned Jungle*, and *Moon Mist*. The concert is well recorded and the performances full of interest. For example, the *Frankie And Johnnie* heard here (like that at the Cornell concert) is a somewhat recast arrangement. A rather tedious handclapping routine which had crept into some of the 1945 performances had disappeared, while Nance's violin solo has been replaced by Hamilton on clarinet. Duke's piano work and the bass playing of Pettiford are outstanding features of both this and the Cornell performances.

At both these events, Ellington had used his standard concert format of the period, but when he appeared at Carnegie Hall on December 26 and 27, 1947, some changes were inevitable, as almost all of this routine had been heard at previous Carnegie concerts. For this reason, the December concerts were notable for the amount of new material presented, though some of this was ephemeral in the extreme. Some numbers seem never to have been played outside these concerts, among them Strayhorn's diffuse *Triple Play*, Ellington's concertos *Mella Brave* (for Carney) and *Kickapoo Joy Juice* (for Hamilton), and his feature for two bassists, *Basso Profundo* (Junior Raglin had joined Oscar Pettiford for these concerts).

Several of the revivals were grouped into medleys—a *Johnny Hodges Medley* consisting of *Wanderlust, Junior Hop, Jeep's Blues, Squatty Roo,* and *The Mood To Be Wooed*; and what is described as a *Theme Medley*, consisting of *East St. Louis Toodle-oo, Echoes Of Harlem, Black And Tan Fantasy,* and *Things Ain't What They Used To Be*. Although the medley format is an unsatisfactory way of presenting these numbers, there is much fine music here. The *Hodges Medley* contains the expected feast of top quality alto playing and includes a version of *The Mood To Be Wooed* with more variation in the solo part than usual. The first part of the oddly titled *Theme Medley* features Nance playing growl trumpet. He is heard in the first part of *East St. Louis Toodle-oo* before the trumpet section plays the second theme, in a way which anticipates the 1956 Bethlehem recording. Ellington then introduces the bass figure from *Echoes Of Harlem* over which the band delivers the first theme of *Black And Tan Fantasy*, before Nance returns with a chorus of *Echoes Of Harlem* itself. Lawrence Brown then enters with two blues choruses which lead into the final ensemble from the standard *Things Ain't What They Used To Be* arrangement. Neither of these medleys was repeated at later concerts.

In addition to these concoctions there were plenty of other revivals, including *Blue Serge, Midriff, Rockin' In Rhythm, On The Sunny Side Of The Street, It Don't Mean A Thing, Harlem Air Shaft, Bakiff,* and *Cotton Tail*. The standard Ellington *Medley Of Popular Hits* was performed and there were several vocal features for Parker and Hibbler, as well as *Tulip Or Turnip* for Nance.

Strayhorn's *Snibor* made an appearance here under its original title, *The New Look*, while the uptempo band piece recorded for Columbia as *Stomp, Look And Listen* was presented as *Stomp, Look And Glisten*. The version of *On A Turquoise Cloud* is slightly longer than the Columbia recording, as are the previously discussed performances of *The Clothéd Woman* and *New York City Blues*. The version of *The Liberian Suite* discussed above, and a concluding *Trumpet No End* with Killian performing the high-note parts, made up the rest of a typically generous Ellington concert program.

* * *

A second recording ban by the American Federation of Musicians kept the band out of the studio for all of 1948 and most of 1949. Duke was hospitalized for a spell in early 1948. In June and July of that year he, Ray Nance, and Kay Davis toured Britain while the others in the band split up to take a variety of jobs. Duke did not take the band to Britain because the dispute between the British and American musicians unions, which had caused a ban on touring since the mid-thirties, was still in force. Ellington, as a solo piano act, and Nance and Davis as cabaret artists were able to evade the ban. An initial two-week residency in variety at the London Palladium was followed by a tour of Britain and Europe with an Anglo-Canadian trio. This was led by Jack Fallon (bass), with Malcolm Mitchell on guitar and Tony Crombie, drums.

On the return of the three Americans to the United States, the band re-formed but for some reason no 1948 broadcasts or concert recordings dating from earlier than November, have been issued. Indeed, there do not seem to be *any* recordings of the Ellington band in any form from between January and November 1948. The last two months of the year found Ellington again presenting concerts at Carnegie Hall and at Cornell University, and recordings from both these events have been issued. The full personnel at the time of the concerts was:

Trumpets: Shelton Hemphill, Francis Williams, Harold Baker, Al Killian, Ray Nance (also violin and vocal).

Trombones: Lawrence Brown; Tyree Glenn (also vibes); Quentin Jackson (valve trombone).

Reeds: Russell Procope (alto sax, clarinet); Johnny Hodges (alto sax); Al Sears, Ben Webster (tenor saxes); Jimmy Hamilton (clarinet, tenor sax); Harry Carney (baritone sax, clarinet, bass clarinet).

Rhythm: Duke Ellington (piano); Fred Guy (guitar); Wendell Marshall (bass); Sonny Greer (drums); Billy Strayhorn (deputy pianist).

Vocal: Kay Davis, Al Hibbler.

The presence of six saxophones is unusual, the addition being a second tenor saxophone specialist in the distinguished person of Ben Webster. Hal Singer had held this chair for a short while prior to Ben's reengagement. In a 1966 interview, Singer explained that he was brought in to play Jimmy Hamilton's saxophone parts. Hamilton's dislike of the saxophone was a recurrent theme during his long stay with Duke, but that this was a reason for the six-man reed team is brought into question by the many tenor solos by Hamilton on Ellington's 1948–49 recordings. If this was Ellington's way of showing Hamilton that tenor solos were expected of him if he was to remain with the band, there seems little point in the hiring of an extra saxophonist, but whatever the reason, Duke now had a six-piece reed section.

The other major change is less ambiguous—Jimmy Blanton's cousin Wendell Marshall replaced Oscar Pettiford on bass. As when Junior Raglin replaced Blanton, the new man maintained the standards established by his predecessor.

The repertoire of the two late 1948 concerts shows a number of changes from those of the previous year. The musical low spot is Hibbler's singing of *Trees* during the course of an extended medley of undistinguished songs. From the opposite end of the spectrum comes a new Ellington concert work, *The Tattooed Bride*.

* * *

The Tattooed Bride was premiered at the Carnegie Hall concert of November 13, 1948, in a performance issued on V-Disc. It was performed again at Cornell University on December 10, and both performances have been issued on LP. A one-movement work, *The Tattooed Bride* runs for about twelve minutes. It is an exceptionally balanced and coherent piece of musical thinking. In his extended compositions Ellington liked to present contrasting thematic material, often inspired by the contrasts inherent in the idea behind the works. Examples include the varied aspects of African American life portrayed in *Black, Brown And Beige* or the contrasting impressions of *The Deep South Suite*. Although it has a literary "program," there is no such diversity in *The Tattooed Bride*. The work is virtually monothematic, the structure being built from the four-note motif introduced by the piano at the outset. The twelve minutes of highly varied melodic development, encompassing several changes in tempo and instrumental texture, are beautifully paced and structured. Perhaps the simplicity of the story the work purports to tell, and its lack of "political" importance when compared with *Black, Brown And Beige*, *New World A-Comin'*, or *The Deep South Suite* allowed Ellington to concentrate more on the purely musical aspects of the composition. *The Tattooed Bride* also lacks the thrown-together-to-meet-a-deadline feeling of either *The Liberian Suite* or the closing pages of *Black, Brown And Beige*.

When considering the "program" of *The Tattooed Bride*, it is best to recall the skepticism which a study of the circumstances of the recording of *Harlem Air Shaft* casts on the "program" of that work. When presenting *The Tattooed Bride* to his concert audiences, Ellington used two totally different introductions. The more elaborate one claimed that the piece described the early married history of an exceptionally athletic gentleman so devoted to hiking, swimming, and other outdoor activities that on the first two nights of his honeymoon he fell asleep the instant his head hit the pillow. The increasing tempo of the first part portrays his athletic endeavor, while the slow section which follows describes the third night of his marriage, when he discovers that his bride is tattooed from head to foot, the moment of discovery signified by the long-held high note on the clarinet. This leads into the most warmly sensual part of the score, followed by a return to the extroverted music of the earlier parts, perhaps indicating that the hero's lifestyle was ultimately unaffected by his somewhat unusual discovery. The orchestra tell this story, which Duke described as "a musical striptease," with wit and elegance, and the final chord is clearly the bow of a storyteller who has held his audience's attention with a well-told if somewhat outlandish tale.

In his alternative explanation, Ellington informed his audience that the lady of the title is tattooed in an unusual way. "Rather than having an assortment or variety of pictures and diagrams and so forth, she had the continuous repetition of the same sort of zig-zaggy figure," reminiscent of an *M* or a *W*. From this formation Ellington claims to have derived the four notes which make up the thematic motif of the piece. At this point various solo instruments, culminating in Glenn's plunger-muted trombone, play the four notes, and Ellington tells the audience that they will "now hear the development, but *that* is the theme"—and the performance commences.

Among Ellington's extended compositions *The Tattooed Bride* is unique in that it is conceived as a concerto for one of his sidemen, clarinetist Jimmy Hamilton. Two earlier works, *Blue Belles Of Harlem* and *New World A-Comin'*, were written as concertos for piano and orchestra, but the orchestral parts were mere backdrops, contributing little of importance to the musical argument; this became abundantly clear when Ellington began to play *New World A-Comin'* as an unaccompanied piano solo. By contrast, *The Tattooed Bride* is a thoroughly integrated concerto for soloist and orchestra with the clarinet having the main voice in a basically orchestral argument. Both Ellington on piano and Lawrence Brown on trombone have roles of importance in *The Tattooed Bride*. There are also brief solo contributions from Baker, Procope, Sears, and Carney. The role of the bass is quite crucial throughout. The use of Hamilton as featured soloist in this piece is a pattern which Ellington did not repeat in subsequent concert works. It may be that the strong personality which is the hallmark of most of the Ellington soloists would have created problems had he tried to use them in this way. Hamilton's virtuosity and imaginative musicianship are clear for all to hear; but he is not a strongly individual stylist, and his academic virtues make him a soloist better suited than most other Ellington musicians to the interpretation of a work in which the composer's personality is dominant.

Of the several recorded versions of *The Tattooed Bride*, the Columbia studio version of 1950 (included on the *Masterpieces By Ellington* LP) is the best overall. Anderson leads the trumpet section in a fiery manner and Wendell Marshall's bass work is superlative, but it is the excellent recording quality which wins out over the rival versions. A very useful second recording is from the 1948 Cornell University concert. It finds the band in a very relaxed frame of mind and delightfully illustrates that Ellington's concert works are wholly of jazz, in that they lend themselves to a relaxed swinging interpretation, just as do his less formal pieces.

* * *

The rest of the programs from the late 1948 concerts contain a characteristic mix of old and new. The vintage piece chosen for performance is *Creole Love Call*; here Davis's vocal part is extended to include the statement of the second theme, usually given to the clarinet. After playing the Miley plunger chorus, Nance goes on to add a chorus of open trumpet at double tempo, backed by handclapping from the band; although pleasant enough in itself, this passage makes an incongruous middle section for *Creole Love Call*. Other revivals include *Cotton Tail*, with solo responsibilities back with Ben Webster, *Tootin' Through The Roof*, *Suddenly It Jumped*, and *Trumpet No End*. The *Medley Of Popular Hits* was also used. A surprising revival at the Cornell concert is *Reminiscing In Tempo*, which had been recorded only twice previously. A new arrangement of *How High The Moon* features Webster's tenor at slow, medium, and fast tempos.

Of the numbers recorded commercially around this time, these concerts featured *Lady Of The Lavender Mist* and *Three Cent Stomp*, plus a version of *H'ya Sue* with a long Hamilton tenor solo appended. Strayhorn's famous *Lush Life*, a brilliant if oversophisticated ballad never recorded commercially by Ellington, is sung by Davis with the composer at the piano. Ellington subjects Strayhorn's *Take The "A" Train* to some surprising variations in *Manhattan Murals*, while a new Strayhorn composition, *Paradise*, is given ravishing treatment by Carney in the role of featured soloist. Another Strayhorn piece premiered at the Carnegie concert is *Brown Betty*, perhaps best known in the 1951 Columbia recording, but here used as a showcase for Hodges at his most eloquent. Another showcase for a member of the saxophone section is *My Friend*, in which Sears's tenor is heard in a fervent gospel-style performance. Dvorak's *Humoresque* is taken for a rumbustious ride in which the wit of Nance's violin playing is outstanding. Probably the best of all vocal versions of *Just A-Settin' And A-Rockin'* comes from the Carnegie Hall concert; the singer is Nance, whose performance provides a definitive lesson in what swing is about, while his phrasing is full of wit and humor. Webster and Glenn are Nance's assistants here.

The remarkable continuing creativity of Ellington and his associates is brought home forcibly by the sheer quantity of new material heard at these concerts. This includes many items which were never recorded commercially and others which are so different from commercial versions as to constitute a new listening experience. To most people *the* Ellington version of *Limehouse Blues* is the famous 1931 Victor, but he revived this number in 1948 as a feature for Glenn on vibraphone in a little-known arrangement. And then there is *Fantazzm*, which was introduced by Ellington as the "resulting sound of . . . two people living a lush life"; it is a piece of richly scored exotica featuring Carney on bass clarinet, Nance on violin and Brown on trombone. Two more instrumentals are of a straightforward swinging kind—*You Oughta*, featuring Hodges, Brown, and Killian, and the remarkable *She Wouldn't Be Moved*, which has Hodges accompanying the string bass in one episode and features brilliant writing for the band throughout. Glenn's plunger-muted playing here approaches the drive and authority of Tricky Sam himself. The version of *You Oughta* from a broadcast of November 6, 1948, is notable for having a long and excellent solo by Webster following the standard routine. (On the World Record Club issue of parts of the Cornell concert, this number is mistitled *Dancers In Love*.) So far as *She Wouldn't Be Moved* is concerned, the remarkably swinging and vital version from the Cornell Concert is the best.

At these events Duke also introduced a minor concert work, *Symphomaniac*. In two movements, the first finds Ellington's piano set against some mock-symphonic writing for the band. Ellington called this part *Symphonic Or Bust* and claimed it reflected the urge of some musicians, under the influence of Paul Whiteman, to give their music a rather desperate symphonic build-up. (It incorporates the theme Ellington was to use in 1958 for the basis of *Princess Blue*). The second movement is designed to illustrate "music as it is today" or "the modern trend," and is entitled *How You Sound*. It is a typical Ellington/Strayhorn jump piece of the period; the soloists are Nance, Hamilton and Ellington himself. The remaining items from the 1948 concerts are popular songs featuring Al Hibbler or Kay Davis, the latter in her contralto ballad style.

* * *

A large amount of broadcast material from late 1948 and 1949 has been released on LP, most notably in a batch of four albums on the Raretone label. Along with the concerts discussed above, these help fill out our picture of the band during a period when the second AFM ban was keeping it out of the recording studios. Much of the broadcast repertoire duplicates that from the concerts, but inevitably there are surprises and new highlights. From a series of November 1948 broadcasts from The Click in Philadelphia comes a *S'posin'* featuring Hibbler. The combination of Hamilton's clarinet and Glenn's vibraphone here reflects, surprising in an Ellington context, the sound of the Goodman small groups. There is also an excellent *Rockabye River*, slower than earlier versions, and with Nance taking over the growl trumpet from the absent Anderson. Hodges is in great form here as he is in his two choruses during a fine *H'ya Sue*.

From Hollywood broadcasts of early 1949 we find exceptionally lively versions of *Just Squeeze Me*, on which the humor of Nance's singing is caught perfectly, and *Rockin' In Rhythm* (these have been issued on the Ozone label). On a version of *Take The "A" Train*, Hamilton is heard both in clarinet and tenor sax solos, and there is a rare extended solo for

Killian. *Clementine* (with Baker in Stewart's old role) and *Main Stem* receive rather unexpected revivals, while many of the popular ballads have brief but brilliant Webster solos. In August 1949 the band was back at The Click in Philadelphia and the broadcasts include the only known solos with the band by tenor saxophonist Jimmy Forrest: a brief spot on *St. Louis Blues* (on which Nance has taken over vocal responsibilities) and a longer, rousing contribution to *It Don't Mean A Thing*. Hopes of a new composition are raised by the title *Tribal*, but this turns out to be *Dance No. 2* from *The Liberian Suite*. Among the standard pleasures is a version of the original arrangement of *Take The "A" Train*, with a beautiful performance of the trumpet solo by Nance. This is from September 3, 1949, but is unfortunately not complete.

* * *

Following the lifting of the second AFM recording ban, the band returned to the Columbia studios for sessions in September and December 1949. The familiar voices of Hibbler and Davis are heard on the first two titles. *You Of All People* is a commonplace Ellington ballad featuring Hibbler, but the Davis feature is the first studio recording of *Creole Love Call* in sixteen and a half years. In this version, the tiresome double-tempo trumpet solo featured at contemporary concerts is dropped, although on a rejected take (issued on Up-To-Date) one hears some of the musicians preparing for it. Apart from Davis's high soprano voice the only soloist is Nance, who offers an impassioned version of Miley's old solo. A new girl singer, Lu Elliott, is heard on *He's The Greatest Thing There Is*, a rather inconsequential Ellington blues. Although both Charlie Rouse and Jimmy Forrest were in the band as replacements for Sears and Webster, the tenor solos are by Hamilton. The highspots come from Nance, with plunger behind the vocal, and Baker, open, in solo. The most important contemporary Strayhorn composition is *Snibor*, recorded at the September 1949 Columbia session. This piece had been heard at the 1947 Carnegie Hall concert as *The New Look*; the new title is a dedication to Ellington's music publisher, whose last name, Robbins, it reverses and misspells. The scoring is in Strayhorn's richest vein, and the outstanding players are Hodges, in a brief obbligato role; Nance, in a long, lyrical trumpet solo; and Baker, whose trumpet provides the lead in the thickly harmonized ensemble.

The five titles from December 22, 1949, are by a small group of Nance, Glenn, Hodges, Hamilton, and Carney, plus rhythm section and vocalists. Hibbler sings *The World Is Waiting For The Sunrise* and an Ellington blues, *Good Woman Blues*. The instrumental contributions by Hodges (obbligato) and Nance (solo) are the choice parts of the latter, although Hibbler's blues singing is effective. Lu Elliott, a rather average singer, is heard on an Ellington song so banal it must be satirical. This is *Joog, Joog* and the use of a vocal group enhances this feeling; there is also a good deal of Hamilton's solo tenor sax. (However, it is possible that the satirical effect of *Joog, Joog* was unintented, and that both song and treatment were serious attempts to join the hit parade.) *On The Sunny Side Of The Street* had been in the repertoire since the late thirties, a consequence of the famous 1937 recording by Hodges with Lionel Hampton. This 1949 recording is, surprisingly, the first Ellington had done in the studio. Hodges gets two half-choruses, between which Elliott sings a full one, backed by Glenn's vibes. Additional takes from this session (released on Up-To-Date) show that Ellington had intended to use the vocal group on this number; fortunately, that idea was dropped. The session concludes with another blues, an instrumental out of the *C Jam Blues* stable, *B Sharp Boston*. The word "Boston" is musicians' slang for a solo, and it is the soloists who have the major say here. They are Glenn (on plunger trombone) and Carney, both of whom simply swing one riff for their twelve bars, and Nance and Hamilton (the latter still on tenor), who essay rather more.

One of those curiosities which crop up from time to time in the Ellington discography dates from January 1950—a recording of Duke in a hotel room in Detroit, singing and playing two of his current pop tunes—*I'm Afraid Of Loving You Too Much* and *Joog, Joog*. Duke does not seem to have recorded the former commercially. These two items are on the Up-To-Date label, in a collection including a complete broadcast from the same month, made up of mostly familiar material. An exception is *B Sharp Boston*, in its only other known recording.

* * *

Ellington's contract with Columbia was not exclusive, and in late 1950 he started to record with various groups for a new label, Mercer, founded by his son Mercer Ellington and Leonard Feather. The first Mercer date was with a group led by Oscar Pettiford, featured on cello. Ellington is on piano, Lloyd Trottman on bass, and Jo Jones on drums, while Strayhorn is heard playing celeste on two of the five issued items. These performances are showcases for Pettiford on pizzicato cello, with the other musicians in supporting roles. Ellington, Pettiford, and Strayhorn indulge in a lighthearted chase chorus on *Take The "A" Train*, and Duke has a solo on *Oscalypso*. But Ellington's best work is heard on a couple of slow blues. The first is *Blues For Blanton* where the piano introduction, solo, and backing have a much more committed air than his work on the other titles. In the course of this session, an untitled blues was recorded. Its existence would probably never have been known if one copy of *Oscalypso* had not been found on which this item was pressed in error. The indefatigable Jerry Valburn issued this recording on Up-To-Date; it contains some of Pettiford's best solo work and a fine Ellington chorus.

A few days later, Duke was back recording for Mercer with Pettiford on cello, as well as a group of musicians from his current band and two Charlie Parker alumni, Red Rodney and Max Roach. Of the eight recorded titles, seven have vocals by Chubby Kemp, Al Hibbler, or Sarah Ford—and these were issued under four different band names. The eighth title has a fifth such name and is the only piece of musical substance from the session. There is no vocalist, and Duke is featured throughout on a "mandoline" piano. This was an instrument with the hammers so treated as to give the sound of an old, tinny, honky-tonk piano; such instruments had a brief vogue at the time and continue to be used whenever an old-time, good-time atmosphere is required in popular music. The overall effect is of a second-rate player piano. Duke calls his improvisation *The New Piano Roll Blues* and characteristically uses the old-time piano as vehicle for one of his most modern performances of the period. This is a percussive, probing solo with jagged lines and unsettled harmonies, which shows how much Thelonious Monk owes to Duke. Rodney has a brief spot here, but little use is made of the soloists on this session.

Much the same can be said of an October date for Mercer in which a group including Benny Carter on alto is heard backing Hibbler with virtually no attempt to utilize the instrumental talent on hand.

The most interesting Mercer recordings are those by the Billy Strayhorn Trio, actually piano duets by Ellington and Strayhorn with discreet accompaniment from bass (on one session) and bass and drums (on the other). Eight numbers were recorded: four standards from the band repertoire (*Cotton Tail, C Jam Blues, Flamingo, Johnny Come Lately*); an Ellington-Strayhorn duet often played in public and recorded previously for Victor (*Tonk*) *Bang Up Blues*; *Great Times*, a contrasting trio of blues which was in the band repertoire at this time; and *In A Blue Summer Garden*. This last features the blues riff which was to become the basis of *Blues To Be There*, the second movement of the 1956 *Newport Jazz Festival Suite*. The treatment of the piece in this duet version is quite different from that found on the 1956 band recording; here the primary motif emerges from a thick mist of impressionist harmony in the opening chorus. The effect is beautiful, but the piece sounds insubstantial, though the casual air, typical of these duet performances, is pleasant. On most of the other numbers, Ellington and Strayhorn coast along and ideas are tossed from one to the other without being seriously developed. These recordings should perhaps be looked upon as light-hearted entertainments—albeit highly civilized ones—rather than the basic statements of the Ellington-Strayhorn musical creed which some writers have claimed to see in them. The duet on *Johnny Come Lately* is typical in its urbane humor and gentle inventiveness, a pleasant item, but of lesser stature than the orchestral versions. It is also typical that *Tonk*, an exercise in modernized stride piano, is given a more casual performance here than on the 1946 Victor recording. The recording quality of these duets is poor, although not bad enough to seriously mar our enjoyment of the music.

* * *

In November 1950 the band was back in the Columbia studios to record four titles, one of which—a version of *Solitude*—remains unissued. The first item reflects the new popular interest in folk songs. With his eye ever on the chance for a popular success, Ellington writes a railroad worksong—*Build That Railroad (Sing That Song)*. Hibbler delivers the vocal in melodramatic fashion, not all that far from the histrionics of some popularizers of folk music. This is one of Ellington's lesser-known railroad pieces, and the orchestral score is good, with particularly effective use of the trombones. A few bars of tenor sax on *Build That Railroad* mark the entry of Paul Gonsalves onto the Ellington recording stage—an important moment, as Gonsalves was destined to become one of the major Ellingtonians. The title *Love You Madly* became a catch phrase in the last twenty years of Ellington's career, much better known than the song itself. On this version Yvonne Lanauze is the vocalist; she is a pleasant stylist out of the early Sarah Vaughan school, but her singing has an unfortunate nasal quality. Gonsalves is heard briefly here too and is the outstanding soloist, along with Nance (on violin), in the end-of-session blues from this occasion, *Great Times*. Another new soloist is heard here: Quentin Jackson makes his debut on plunger-muted trombone.

* * *

The final recordings of 1950 were important in two ways. They are the first done by Ellington with release on LP in mind, and three of them are extended arrangements of Ellington standards. Columbia had already issued the *Liberian Suite* on a ten-inch LP, and now they had chosen Ellington to inaugurate the jazz section of their twelve-inch long-playing catalog, an imaginative yet risky choice. Duke's last-minute solutions to commissions had not always produced happy results in the past, and there was a danger that such an attitude might mar this project. Or he might treat the occasion as he had the duets with Strayhorn and produce pleasant but lightweight music. The *Medley Of Popular Hits* was already a regular part of the concert repertoire and could easily have been pressed into service, had Ellington been in the mood to pass off the occasion in a trouble-free way. Fortunately, he took a very different attitude and produced a twelve-inch LP made up of four concert-length performances. One of these is the definitive recording of *The Tattooed Bride*; the other three are arrangements of *Mood Indigo* (over fifteen minutes), *Sophisticated Lady* (over eleven), and *Solitude* (just over eight minutes the shortest track on the record). The LP was called, simply and accurately, *Masterpieces By Ellington*.

When the band entered the recording studio on December 18, 1950, to record this music the personnel was:

Trumpets: Harold Baker, Nelson Williams, Fats Ford, Cat Anderson, Ray Nance (also violin and vocal).

Trombones: Lawrence Brown, Quentin Jackson, Tyree Glenn.

Reeds: Russell Procope (alto sax, clarinet); Johnny Hodges (alto sax); Paul Gonsalves (tenor sax); Jimmy Hamilton (clarinet, tenor sax); Harry Carney (baritone sax, clarinet, bass clarinet).

Rhythm: Duke Ellington (piano); Wendell Marshall (bass); Sonny Greer (drums); Billy Strayhorn (deputy pianist).

Vocal: Albert Hibbler, Yvonne Lanauze.

It should be noted that Glenn was no longer a regular member of the band but was brought back specially for this recording project, and that when guitarist Fred Guy left in May 1949, he was not replaced. Neither Strayhorn nor Hibbler is heard on the *Masterpieces* LP, and Nance's contribution is confined to trumpet.

* * *

Masterpieces By Ellington opens with *Mood Indigo*. This has as its centerpiece three vocal choruses by Yvonne Lanauze which are not particularly outstanding. They are the weakest part of the performance, but so perfectly set by Ellington that they provide an ideal nucleus to the structure. Prior to the vocal, we have a theme statement by one of those variants of the traditional *Mood Indigo* trio voicing which Ellington liked to use; on this occasion, two muted trombones and bass clarinet make up the trio. From this time onwards, Russell Procope started to emerge as an Ellington clarinet soloist, and here he plays what used to be Barney Bigard's chorus, using a thick, broad tone and a blues-impregnated melodic style. He is beautifully backed by Ellington who is at his most brilliant as a keyboard accompanist throughout these performances. Procope goes on to play a low-register obbligato against the brass in the next section. This passage is scored for muted trumpets, and with Ellington's shifting harmonies some wonderful sounds are heard. The next two choruses are given over to Johnny Hodges, again with brilliant piano backing; this solo is a minor masterpiece in itself. The full band is used for the first time in the sixth chorus, which has superb lead trumpet from Baker and constantly moving and changing counterpoint among saxes, trumpets, and trombones, scored with breathtaking beauty and originality. In the reeds, the lead is changed about from clarinet to alto to tenor to baritone, with Carney's deep sound creating a magnificent basis for the multistructured writing. The greatest possible contrast is heard in the next chorus, given over to piano variations, calm in spirit with beautiful chording and balanced, inventive melodic structures. The band's newest soloist, Gonsalves, takes the bulk of the following chorus in a rich-toned, highly rhapsodic solo played against a brooding orchestral backdrop, but Ellington himself has the last four bars to set up the vocal entry. The first vocal chorus is backed by piano and rhythm only, the second by powerful plungered brass, and the third by sultry, stilled saxophone harmonies. The contrast as Glenn's plunger-muted trombone takes over at the conclusion of Lanauze's vocal is dramatic. One chord from Ellington immediately changes the mood, and Glenn's two choruses, again with trenchant support from the pianist, are among his best on record. This trombone solo is followed by a long ensemble section in 3/4 time during which Nance's trumpet is briefly heard. Duke's piano then leads back to the recapitulation of the theme by two trombones and bass clarinet, but this time, improvised countermelodies by Procope and Ellington create a rich three-part counterpoint with the trio as lead voice. This is followed by a brief, incisive piano coda. This *Mood Indigo* must be reckoned among the very finest of all Ellington arrangements.

Sophisticated Lady also has a vocal by Lanauze, this time in the third chorus. It is preceded by a theme statement in which Carney (on bass clarinet) and Ellington have important roles, and by a beautiful solo by Baker. The trumpeter's magnificent tone is perfectly caught by the recording, and his melodic lines are full of beautifully sculptured phrases which lie perfectly over the rich sound of Ellington's orchestration. This is a ballad solo of outstanding quality. It is followed by the vocal, and then Ellington has a reflective piano chorus, broken into rudely by the brass section to herald a passage of vintage Ellington scoring in which Hamilton's clarinet has a prominent role. The final statement is given to Brown, who plays with magnificent poise in a beautiful solo, behind which the orchestral ideas worked out in the preceding chorus continue to develop. These lead to a climax capped by a few final bars of solo piano.

The trombone section and the robust voice of Carney's baritone make the major contributions to the theme statement of *Solitude*. Ellington has the second chorus, Gonsalves the third, and in the fourth, Nance plays a solo which is a perfect complement to that by Baker on *Sophisticated Lady*. (Rare indeed is a band which can boast two such brilliant ballad soloists on the same instrument.) A feature of this Nance solo is the warm lyricism which he projects in a most direct manner; his phrasing is so perfect that each phrase is turned to the maximum melodic effect. The final chorus of *Solitude* is split between Hamilton and Brown, the latter losing his poise and ending the performance on a rather crude note. In *The Tattooed Bride*, the fine recording quality enables one to hear details of the scoring not apparent on the "live" versions, and, as previously noted, this is the best of the several recordings of this piece. The sheer power and punch of the band, led by Anderson's stinging trumpet, is caught beautifully.

Masterpieces By Ellington is one of the peaks of Duke's achievement. The three ballads represent just about the fullest extent to which jazz techniques can be applied to ballad performances without starting to sound like pseudosymphonic light music. Within their scope they incorporate great jazz solos—Hodges in *Mood Indigo*, Baker in *Sophisticated Lady*, and Nance in *Solitude* being outstanding. The structure of the arrangements of *Mood Indigo* and *Sophisticated Lady* is masterly and quite the equal of any of Ellington's more obvious compositional triumphs. From this time onward, Ellington seems less interested in remakes of his earlier songs. These remain part of the recording repertoire, but only rarely are they treated with the care and attention found in the series which started with the 1945 Victor revivals and culminated with this collection. It is as if with *Masterpieces By Ellington* Duke felt he had achieved a level of excellence he could never surpass.

Despite these musical triumphs this was not a good time for the Ellington band. There was a lot of internal dissension. Duke was heading a more than usually undisciplined team, and frequent personnel changes worked against the sort of music making which Ellington's art demanded. Some years later, however, Ellington remarked that these musicians always came through for him and really played on the occasions that mattered. They certainly do so on the *Masterpieces* LP, playing with a sensitivity which is the equal of any band in Duke's long history. The bass playing, so vital a part of all Ellington music, is of the very highest class, and if one musician other than Ellington could be said to be the star of the collection it would be Wendell Marshall. With Greer unusually subdued, Marshall often carries the rhythm section single-handed while also responding in a most imaginative way to the playing of the band and of the piano player. Anderson was newly returned to the band, and it is he, Baker, and Nance who contribute the individual voices within the trumpet section. Baker is heard playing lead on all tracks except *The Tattooed Bride*, where the task is performed by Anderson. The trombones are beautifully led by Brown, who plays all the solos except Glenn's plunger choruses on *Mood Indigo*. The saxophones had just been stabilized by the introduction of Paul Gonsalves. It is interesting to note that his deep understanding of Ellington's music was already in evidence after only a few months in the band. We also find Ellington starting to use Procope's blues-impregnated clarinet as a solo voice, a development which gave him an excellent foil to Hamilton's more academic approach. Already we find that pattern familiar in the last decades of Ellington's career of a brass section consisting of two kinds of musician—the Ellington "characters" and the rest—the latter only rarely used in solo.

The arrangements for *Masterpieces By Ellington* are rich in harmony and color, in melody and counterpoint. There is hardly a moment when only one line is used. The solos are accompanied by rich orchestral scoring or by Ellington's endlessly resourceful piano; ensembles will sometimes have an obbligato from one of the soloists, while Duke's piano passages, with or without the rhythm section, provide contrasting highlights. For all the richness of texture the music never sounds cluttered, and the solos are performed with the jazz musician's natural ease of expression. The Duke Ellington Orchestra of 1950 was clearly a great jazz ensemble, different from that of ten years earlier, but with a range which was, if anything, even broader than that of its predecessors. And the peaks within that range were, if less frequent, just as commanding. *Masterpieces By Ellington* is one of these, a supreme and unique achievement in a long recording career.

Outstanding Recordings

1. Musicraft Recordings

Magenta Haze, *Sultry Sunset*, *Happy-Go-Lucky Local*, *The Beautiful Indians* (*Minnehaha* and *Hiawatha*), *Flippant Flurry*, *Tulip Or Turnip*, and *Jam A-Ditty*.

2. Columbia Recordings

H'ya Sue (all three takes), *The Lady Of The Lavender Mist*, *Women, Women, Women*, *Golden Cress*, *Change My Ways*, *Boogie Bop Blues*, *Sultry Serenade* (all three takes), *Stomp, Look And Listen*, *Three Cent Stomp*, *Progressive Gavotte*, *I Can't Believe That You're In Love With Me*, *Singin' In The Rain*, *On a Turquoise Cloud*, *The Liberian Suite*, *The Clothéd Woman* (both takes), *New York City Blues*, *Creole Love Call*, *Snibor*, *B Sharp Boston*, and the four performances on the *Masterpieces By Ellington* LP— *Mood Indigo*, *Sophisticated Lady*, *The Tattooed Bride*, and *Solitude*.

3. Mercer Recordings

Take The "A" Train, *Blues For Blanton*, untitled blues (with Oscar Pettiford), *The New Piano Roll Blues*, and the eight duets with Billy Strayhorn

4. Capitol Transcriptions

Golden Cress, *Fugue A-Ditty*, *Jam A-Ditty*, *Happy-Go-Lucky Local*, *Beale Street Blues*, *Memphis Blues*, *Who Struck John?*, *Jumpin' Punkins*, *Royal Garden Blues*, *Blue Is The Night*, *Jump For Joy*, *Far Away Blues*, *Frisky*, and *Park at 106th*

5. Concert Recordings

Overture To A Jam Session, *Jumpin' Punkins*, *Beale Street Blues*, *Memphis Blues*, *Unbooted Character*, *The Deep South Suite*, *The Beautiful Indians*, (Chicago Civic Opera

House, November 10, 1946), *The Deep South Suite, Unbooted Character* (Carnegie Hall, November 23), *The Mooche, Diminuendo And Crescendo In Blue, Frankie And Johnnie* (Cornell University, April 30, 1947), *New York City Blues, The Clothéd Woman* (Carnegie Hall, December 27, 1947), *My Friend, Manhattan Murals, Fantazzm, Humouresque, Just A-Settin' And A-Rockin', Symphomaniac Suite* (Carnegie Hall, November 13, 1948), *Reminiscing In Tempo, The Tattooed Bride, The Lady Of The Lavender Mist, She Wouldn't Be Moved, Paradise, You Oughta* and *Brown Betty* (Cornell University, December 10, 1948)

6. Broadcasts

It Don't Mean A Thing (V-Disc) (May 10, 1947), *One O' Clock Jump* (July 9, 1947), *H'ya Sue* (November 22, 1948), *Rockabye River* (November 26, 1948), *Rockin' In Rhythm, Just Squeeze Me* (February 6, 1949), and *It Don't Mean A Thing* (August 31, 1949)

Chapter 19

Consolidation

BY 1946 THE BIG BAND ERA was drawing to a close. If Duke Ellington was to keep his orchestra in existence, he would soon have to adapt to functioning in a new environment. For the working jazz musician, the changes which occurred in the mid-forties were much more drastic than a mere shift in public taste, a simple decline in the popularity of "swing music." The demand for live music in prodigious quantities had been a constant factor in American entertainment since the time of the First World War. Not only small improvising groups and large dance bands employed jazzmen; theater bands like Erskine Tate's and show bands like Will Marion Cook's had also been eager to employ the competent jazz musician. The arrival of efficient amplification for musical instruments, especially after the end of the Second World War, coupled with the simultaneous improvements in the use of recorded sound, coincided with a drastic decline in ballroom dancing as a popular pastime. These factors were major causes in the breakup of an employment pattern for the working musician which had existed long before the years of the swing music boom. In the mid-forties, the capacity of the American entertainment industry to employ jazz musicians shrank suddenly and drastically. The changes in public entertainment patterns, which included the rapid spread of television, also swept away large numbers of cinemas and theaters which had featured big bands. Records were still popular, but solo vocalists dominated the best-selling charts. With so many outlets closing, popularity declining, and amplification now making a handful of musicians or even a phonograph capable of doing a job which once would have called for a big band, the bands suddenly found themselves obsolescent. They became a subject of instant nostalgia, and, in all but a handful of cases, an economic impossibility. If Ellington's music was to have a future, he had to ensure by hook or by crook, that his band was one of that handful.

In 1949 Duke Ellington celebrated his fiftieth birthday in characteristic fashion—by working. On his birthday, he and the band played six shows at the Paramount Theater in New York City. Duke's success in keeping the band in existence in these hard times was signaled in an unusual fashion in 1950. He found himself the only big band leader among those who had collected awards in the previous year's *Down Beat* poll whose band was still in existence and was given a special scroll to commemorate the fact. Ellington's motives for carrying on were musical rather than commercial, and he often had to use royalties from his songs to subsidize his payroll. Yet, with or without subsidy from other sources, he needed a degree of commercial success simply to meet that payroll for the top-quality musicians in the band.

It is this casting about for a commercially successful formula in a changing entertainment world that gives so strange a look to certain pages in the Ellington discography of the late forties. The instrumental pieces carry on the Ellington tradition in a musically logical manner, but the popular song recordings seem more concerned with current trends than with either quality or the Ellington tradition. The degree of banality of some of the items recorded is a measure of the concern with which Ellington surveyed the scene. Unfortunately for Ellington's financial peace of mind, these recordings were misses rather than hits, despite the considerable efforts which went into trying to solve the band's economic problems in this way. Among the Ellington popular-style recordings of the late forties there are items of real quality, such as some of the songs from *Beggar's Holiday*—pleasant trifles from the hand of a master. And it should be stressed that for all the variable quality of the would-be popular recordings, there is no falling off in overall musical standards. Any reasonable selection of the best recordings from these years makes nonsense of the view that this was a musically poor period for Ellington.

Although Duke was successful in holding his band together, these were not happy years within the Ellington organization. The only musical evidence of this is found on some location recordings, where the playing shows a nonchalance and disregard for precision unusual even for this band. In the studios, it continued to produce first-class performances, right through from the Musicraft sessions of 1946 to the Columbia *Masterpieces* recordings of December 1950. Yet contemporary interviews and later recollections by bandsmen suggest that there was a lot of discontent and disillusionment among the personnel. In some ways, this was a reflection on the new instability of the band business. In others, it reflects the fact that the easy-going discipline of the Ellington band was becoming an excuse for laziness on the part of some of its members. With the benefit of hindsight, the survival of the band seems quite natural when Ellington's motivation, his business acumen, and his large royalties are taken into account. To the Ellington musicians, the stability of their jobs at a time when all other bands with a jazz policy were folding must have seemed doubtful, a factor which certainly could weaken loyalty and involvement. And some of the newer members clearly felt trapped since virtually no other employment was readily available.

Another source of discontent was the allocation of existing roles within the band to specific musicians. For example, Anderson, during his first spell with the band, had established a need for a high-note trumpet specialist. For a good deal of the period under review, this role was taken, with less than total enthusiasm, by Al Killian, who resented the emphasis on this aspect of his playing. He felt that Ellington should give him an opportunity to do more than, to use his own words, "blow my top." The high-note trumpet chair was just the most recently established of the traditional positions within the Ellington band. The changing personnels meant that Duke had to continually find musicians capable of filling these traditional posts, an additional problem in these changing times. Sometimes it was almost impossible to find a suitable musician, while at other times several players in the band might fight for the same solo role. In later years, as certain styles went out of favor with practicing jazz musicians, role replacements became almost impossible. But in the late forties, and indeed for a further decade, Ellington's answers to such problems were in the main triumphantly successful.

During the late forties, discontent and indiscipline seem to have been particularly rife in the trumpet section. Francis Williams was a member of this section from 1945 to 1948 and also for a period in 1951. He tells (in an interview with Eric Townley in *Storyville* 80, April–May 1977) of a booking at the Regal Theater in Chicago during 1947, when the band had six trumpet players on the payroll. Shows were frequently played with only two trumpeters present, and it was not until the penultimate day of a full week's engagement that all six bothered to attend. Williams also states that a couple of years earlier, Ray Nance had done so much jamming on 52nd Street that he was hardly ever seen during a six-month residence at the Zanzibar Club in New York. The band did three shows a night, and Williams estimates that Nance appeared in fewer than twenty in six months. At the end of this engagement, Nance was dropped by Ellington and formed his own quartet. Due to some unbelievable bungling by club owners, Nance was forced to disband and returned to the Ellington fold. Thus Duke almost lost, after a mere five years, a man who was to become one of his key long-serving musicians. Despite such goings on, the playing of the trumpet section of this period sounds quite outstanding—not really surprising with three such skilled section men as Al Killian, Shelton Hemphill, and Harold Baker often working together.

In April, May, and June 1950, the band made its first European tour since 1939. Ellington took along a second drummer, Butch Ballard, as insurance against Sonny Greer's increasingly erratic behavior. Only two trombonists traveled, and when they arrived in Europe a third was hired; tenor saxophonist Don Byas was also brought into the band. He became the sixth saxophone, sharing the solos with the incumbent tenor, Alva McCain. The continuing dispute between the British Musician's Union and the American Federation of Musicians again prevented the band from visiting the British Isles.

* * *

One of the most noticeable aspects of the second half of the forties is the minimal influence then current developments in jazz had on Ellington's music. One would hardly know bop was in the air, apart from a satirical reference in *Boogie Bop Blues* and a few new-sounding figures in the writing for the trumpet section. It was not that Ellington shared the antibop sentiments of many musicians of earlier generations—"I always liked the bop" he says in his autobiography—but simply that the latest jazz developments were some distance removed from Ellington's own musical idiom. Bop used harmonic innovations in an aggressive manner—Duke's were subtle; bop melodic lines were spiky and usually played in unison—Ellington's were voluptuous and used warm harmonies; bop rhythms were jerky and tight—Duke's rhythmic penchant was for easy and relaxed playing; bop musicians favored thin, cutting tones—Duke liked his horns to have rich, fat sounds; bop piano favored many notes and fast, fleet playing—Ellington favored a concentrated style, with much musical meaning condensed into one epigrammatic phrase; bop rhythm sections were light and fleet—Duke liked a big, gutty sound from his bassist and a drummer with a big sound, giving him a two-man section weighty enough to carry the band in full cry when the pianist was indulging in a little conducting or even some extramusical activity during a performance. The importance attached to melody playing in Ellington's music was in direct contrast to the boppers' neglect of this art; this may be one reason why no horn player from the first generation of "modern jazz" musicians ever found a home in the Ellington Orchestra. So, while finding bop—and especially Dizzy Gillespie's brand, for Dizzy had humor, and this was a quality greatly valued by Duke—interesting and entertaining, he did not at once use its innovations in the way he had quickly adapted the techniques of some earlier developments in jazz. In later years, Ellington was to employ many of the devices of modern jazz, but at first his music was almost totally unaffected by the biggest changes in the jazz vocabulary since Louis Armstrong had rewritten and expanded it over twenty years before.

The fact that Duke was not conforming to the current fashion as to what constituted modernism in jazz did not mean that his art was stagnating or moribund, indeed, in such works as *The Clothéd Woman* and *The Tattooed Bride* he was creating music as fresh and as vital as at any time in his career. But Ellington's modernism was only rarely of a fashionable kind, while his effect on jazz fashion was always slight for so prodigious an innovator. Duke's stylistic development was always inspired by his own evolution as a composer and by that of his orchestra rather than by any outside factors, and consequently his devices did not export well. When used by other composers or arrangers outside the Ellington organization, they frequently lost their power and indeed their musical coherence. In the late forties, Lester Young and Charlie Parker had so many imitators among jazz saxophonists as almost to defy belief. Clearly, many jazz critics did not agree and heaped praise on some remarkably derivative musicians as if they were true innovators. But no such school of Ellington disciples could ever have been possible. Duke's art and methods were always too personal, too individual, and too original for that.

Despite the changing fortunes of the band business and the startling changes in jazz music, Ellington sailed on, seemingly impervious to contemporary trends. Yet circumstances were conspiring in ways which were to cause, in the very first year of the new decade, the biggest upheaval in the long history of the Duke Ellington Orchestra.

Sidemen

Dud Bascomb

Although his stay in the band was short, Dud Bascomb showed every sign of being an artist who would have fitted well with the Ellington way of music making. He could play swinging open trumpet in a style similar to that of Taft Jordan and growl trumpet of a rather more individual kind. Ellington is said to have regretted that he did not record *East St. Louis Toodle-oo* while Bascomb was in the band, so impressive was the latter's interpretation of this piece. At the time of writing, no recording of any broadcast or concert featuring such a Bascomb performance has come to light, although the quantity of previously unknown recordings of the Ellington band discovered each year makes it possible that one may yet be found.

Representative Recording: Women, Women, Women (Columbia, 1947—Bascomb plays the trumpet solo after the vocal)

Tyree Glenn

With the arrival of Tyree Glenn as a member of the trombone section in 1947 Ellington once again acquired a first-class plunger trombonist. Tyree had known Tricky Sam Nanton back in the Cotton Club days and had occasionally substituted for him when Tricky's social engagements had been pressing. In return for these favors, Nanton had given him instruction in the subtleties of the plunger mute. This stood Glenn in good stead during his years with Ellington. He did not use the style in a simple imitation of his predecessor and mentor, but imparted to it his own musical character. His playing is less primitive in spirit than Nanton's and is quite without Tricky's rough-hewn sound. The plaintive, rather smooth sound of Glenn's plunger was highly distinctive and his mastery of this difficult art comprehensive. Like Tricky, he was a masterly blues player, an essential quality for a plunger-mute specialist in Ellington's band. On open trombone Glenn was also a highly personal stylist and made several important solo contributions in a rather graceful, swinging style. He was also occasionally heard on vibraphone, on which he was an accomplished if less individual player.

Representative Recordings: On trombone—*H'ya Sue* (Columbia, 1947), *Sultry Serenade* (Columbia, 1947), *Three Cent Stomp* (Columbia, 1947), *Mood Indigo* (Columbia, 1950); on vibraphone—*Dance No. 2* (from *The Liberian Suite*, Columbia, 1947), *Limehouse Blues* (Carnegie Hall, 1948)

Al Killian

A trumpet player of tremendous accuracy and drive, Al Killian was probably a more potent influence in a band as a section man than as a soloist. Prior to joining Ellington he had played in the trumpet sections of Don Redman, Count Basie, Charlie Barnet, and Lionel Hampton. As a soloist in the Ellington band, Killian was usually assigned the high-note role previously taken by Cat Anderson. In these parts Killian proved to be a more accurate player than Anderson, but he lacked the latter's personality and humor.

Representative Recordings: Dance No. 3 (from *The Liberian Suite*, Columbia, 1947), *Trumpet No End* (Carnegie Hall, 1947; Killian plays the final trumpet solo), *Let's Go Blues* (Columbia, 1947), *You Oughta* (Cornell University concert, 1948)

Wendell Marshall

Wendell Marshall was a notable member of the distinguished line of Ellington bass players. He possessed a full, ample tone and an unerring harmonic sense. His playing had great swing and an inherent rhythmic vitality. During his time with the band the drummers changed far more than was usual with Ellington, and Marshall remained the backbone of the rhythm section as Sonny Greer, Louis Bellson, Butch Ballard, and Dave Black each made his individual contribution from the drum chair. It is often said that the baritone saxophone of Harry Carney was the rock upon which the Ellington band rested, but in fact it is in the string bass lines that the music is rooted. This vital role was performed with great distinction by Wendell Marshall, a musical virtuoso in the fullest sense.

Representative Recordings: She Wouldn't Be Moved (Cornell University concert, 1948), *Mood Indigo* (Columbia,

1950), *The Tattooed Bride* (Columbia, 1950), *Take The "A" Train* (Columbia, 1952), *Kinda Dukish* (Capitol, 1953)

Nelson Williams

A trumpeter of pleasant style but no particular individuality, Nelson Williams gained greater fame as an ex-Ellingtonian than as a Ducal sideman. He was in the band from 1949 to 1951, after which he worked mainly in Europe, residing in France for many years.

Representative Recordings: Great Times (Columbia, 1950—Nelson Williams plays the second trumpet solo), *Fancy Dan* (Columbia, 1951), *Brown Betty* (Columbia, 1951)

Chapter 20

The Records—January 1951 to Spring 1956

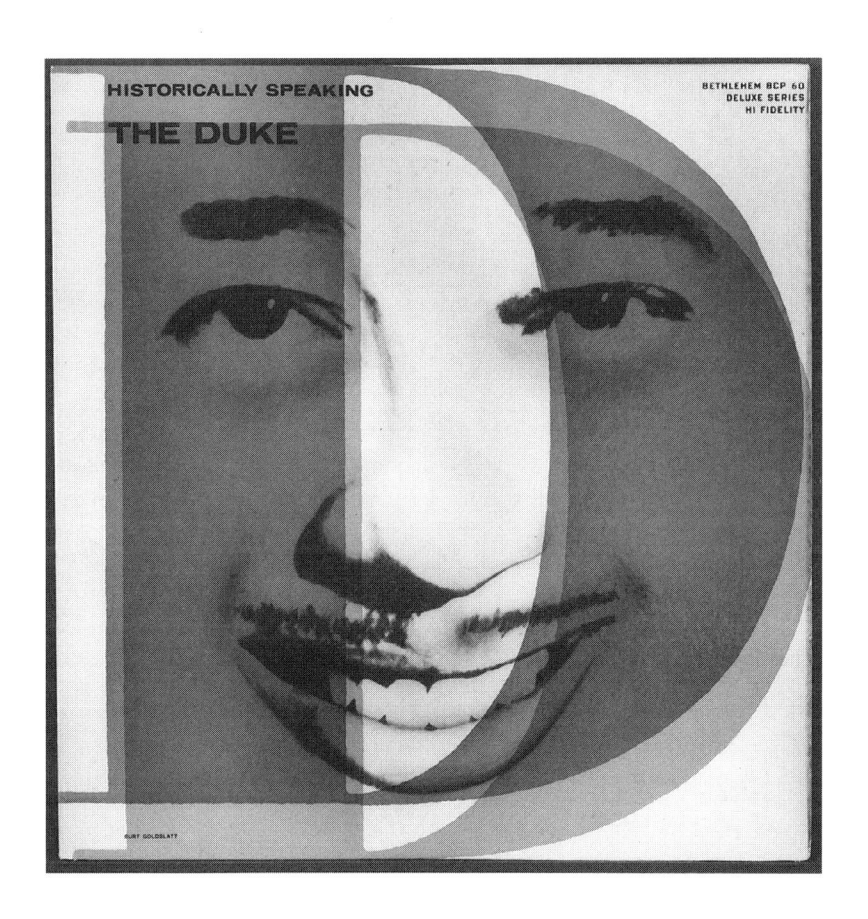

FEW RECORDINGS BY THE ELLINGTON BAND from early 1951 have survived, and of those few the most important are from a concert given for the National Association for the Advancement of Colored People at the Metropolitan Opera House in New York City on January 21. The concert was recorded by the Voice Of America and has been issued on LP. The personnel on this date was basically that of the *Masterpieces By Ellington* session of the previous month, the only changes being the absence of Tyree Glenn (there are only two trombones) and the addition of Joe Benjamin (bass) and Bill Clark (drums) for the concert only. Benjamin was a long-standing Ellington "back-room boy," having been employed in copying parts as far back as the 1943 *Black, Brown And Beige* premiere. It is not clear why Duke wanted a second drummer, but it should be remembered that he had seen fit to take Butch Ballard on the European tour of the previous years as cover for Sonny Greer, who had become rather unreliable.

The centerpiece of the Metropolitan Opera House concert was the premiere of *Harlem*, a fifteen-minute long tone poem. This is one of the major Ellington concert works and was to be performed frequently down the years. Ellington varied the title, sometimes calling the work *A Tone Parallel To Harlem*, sometimes *The Harlem Suite*, but most often simply *Harlem*. The January 1951 version is, like so many Ellington first performances, rather untidy and more of historical than strictly musical importance. The *Controversial*

Suite, a minor Ellington concert work, also made its debut at the same concert. This is in two movements, *Before My Time*, which features a Dixieland trumpet-trombone-clarinet front line, and *Later*, a somewhat satirical view of contemporary jazz concert music. (Both works will be discussed in detail when we consider the studio recordings made later in the year.)

The remainder of this concert consisted of the usual Ellington mixture of shorter pieces, old and new. His earliest period was represented by *The Mooche* and by the last performance recorded by Ellington of *Ring Dem Bells*. This number was used by Ellington to feature Greer as "the man who introduced hot chimes in 1930" (a rather dubious assertion, by the way). Greer's refusal to take drum solos, which he considered to be unmusical, was the main reason why Ellington kept this number, with its emphasis on the tubular bells, in the performing repertoire so long. As none of Ellington's later drummers shared Greer's reluctance to take solos, *Ring Dem Bells* vanished when Sonny left the band. Perhaps the most unusual thing about this piece is its unchanging format. The arrangement heard at this 1951 concert is exactly the same as the one recorded for Victor in August 1930.

The usual quota of showcases was presented, including a brilliant performance of *Coloratura* from *The Perfume Suite* by Cat Anderson and a rather perfunctory *Rose Of The Rio Grande* from Lawrence Brown, while Paul Gonsalves is heard in a new variation on *Take The "A" Train*. Ellington seems to have been fascinated, almost obsessed, by *Take The "A" Train* at this time. He had presented the variations known as *Manhattan Murals* a couple of years earlier, and then used an arrangement featuring Strayhorn on piano which does not seem to have been performed very frequently. This was followed by the *"A" Train* featuring Gonsalves, and by yet another version featuring Betty Roché, which was recorded for Columbia in 1952 with the Gonsalves showcase version welded on to it. And then there was the long version heard on a 1949 broadcast, with solos by Jimmy Hamilton on both clarinet and tenor sax. All these in addition to the standard arrangement featuring Ray Nance, which was used as the signature tune.

After the Gonsalves *"A" Train*, Yvonne Lanauze is heard on *Love You Madly* and then Duke recites his new *Monologue*, the story of *Pretty And The Wolf*, against a background of three clarinets. This was used at the concert as the first part of a trilogy—*Monologue*, *Duet*, and *Threesome*. *Duet* features Jimmy Hamilton and Wendell Marshall playing in the manner made familiar by the clarinet-bass duet in *Air Conditioned Jungle*, while *Threesome* is in two parts, which were soon to be divided and given the titles *V.I.P.'s Boogie* and *Jam With Sam*. Al Hibbler contributes a selection of popular songs, Duke does his now statutory *Medley Of Popular Hits*, and Nance sings *St. Louis Blues* before the concert ends with *Trumpet No End*, capped once more by Anderson's ultra-high-register playing.

The Voice Of America recording shows this to have been a fine concert. Yet the thrust and surge of the best Ellington performances are heard only intermittently. The playing often lacks that electrifying immediacy which usually overpowered any reservations a listener might have about the untidy moments. By Ellington's own standards, the concert is rather below par. Even though it was bolstered by extra bass and drums and strengthened by the arrival of Gonsalves and the return of Anderson, the Ellington Orchestra was clearly not enjoying one of its best periods. A broadcast transcribed on January 2, 1951, for the U.S. Treasury Department has Oscar Pettiford added on cello for *Great Times* and also contains an interesting version of *Take The "A" Train* featuring Strayhorn on piano and Gonsalves on tenor sax. The date of this recording is sometimes wrongly given as February 11, 1951, the date of the broadcast *transmission*.

* * *

Matters came to a head a few weeks after the NAACP concert when three of the band's longest-serving members gave their notice. These were Sonny Greer, who had been with Ellington from the beginning of his bandleading career and was the last survivor of the original Washingtonians apart from Duke himself; Johnny Hodges, who had been in the band since 1928; and Lawrence Brown, an Ellingtonian since 1932. All three were musicians with a deep and sympathetic knowledge of the leader's music—distinctive musical personalities whom the public identified with the Ellington band. Their departure to work for Norman Granz in a group led by Hodges constituted the biggest single crisis in the band's history. Musicians, critics, and collectors all over the world wondered how Ellington would react. His band without these three, it was suspected, would hardly sound like an Ellington band at all. In the event, Duke's reaction was simple—he just carried on, signing the best replacements available, and within a few months the Ellington Orchestra had been reconstituted and revitalized. It is interesting to note that *Down Beat* reported Strayhorn's presence in the Hodges group in March 1951 and quoted him the following month as saying that he was going to stay with the Hodges band.

After using some temporary replacements Ellington acquired three musicians from the Harry James Orchestra to take the places of his departed stars—Juan Tizol (valve trombone), Willie Smith (alto sax), and Louis Bellson (drums). An equally important new addition was that of Britt Woodman on trombone, thus bringing the section back to its full complement of three. What actually happened in the trombone section was that Quentin Jackson had moved to the plunger chair on Tyree Glenn's departure, Woodman took over Brown's duties, and Tizol took up his original role, now vacated by Jackson, of valve trombonist.

Willie Smith's name is important in the annals of jazz saxophone. He is considered one of the greatest lead altos, a reputation he had gained as leader of Jimmie Lunceford's magnificent saxophone team. While a thorough all-round musician, Smith was an uneven soloist and certainly not in the Hodges class.

Of all these changes, it was the addition of Bellson on drums which provided the greatest contrast with what had gone before. His cleanly articulated, driving, rather conventional drumming was the antithesis of Greer's almost archaic individualism. The most important gain was the spirit these new men brought to the band, and Bellson was a vital factor in this respect. The Ellington Orchestra had become a group of temperamental virtuosi, liable to show up late and then to play in a sloppy fashion. In 1951, all that changed. According to Ellington's own testimony, the musicians started to arrive on the stand promptly, and the playing of the ensemble suddenly became clean, fresh, and bright. Most important of all was the new enthusiasm and zest which permeates the performances from this period; these indeed indicated a true Ellington renaissance.

The fact that Smith stayed only one year with the band—he reported that after six months or so they started to slip back into their former ways—and Bellson only two years is no indication at all of their importance in the Ellington story. Their contribution cannot be evaluated in terms of length of service. They helped to give the band new spirit and a new sense of purpose; with their aid Duke survived the departure of three of his major sidemen. How he would have fared if a fourth key musician, Harry Carney, had left—as he almost did—is a question which there was never a need to answer. Yet for all the contributions made by the new bandsmen it is clear that Ellington's genius lay at the root of this renaissance; it was he who selected the new men and provided the scores which so clearly inspired them to such spirited music making. And of course the band they joined was already packed with jazz talent.

* * *

The full personnel on the first recordings of the reorganized band, from a Birdland broadcast of May 2, 1951, was:

Trumpets:	Harold Baker, Nelson Williams, Fats Ford, Cat Anderson, Ray Nance (also violin and vocal).
Trombones:	Britt Woodman, Quentin Jackson, Juan Tizol (valve trombone).
Reeds:	Russell Procope; Willie Smith (alto saxes, clarinets); Paul Gonsalves (tenor sax); Jimmy Hamilton (clarinet, tenor sax); Harry Carney (baritone sax, clarinet, bass clarinet).
Rhythm:	Duke Ellington (piano); Wendell Marshall (bass); Louis Bellson (drums); Billy Strayhorn (deputy pianist).
Vocal:	Al Hibbler.

The press reaction to the "new" Ellington band was universally favorable and its appearances brought superlatives from writers and musicians alike. In a changing world of jazz fashion, Ellington was again considered a "modern" attraction. One of the musicians who was most impressed was Count Basie. He recalled in 1956:

> My biggest thrill as a listener came one night back in, I think it was 1951. The so-called progressive jazz was going big then, and here comes Duke Ellington on opening night at Birdland. He had just revamped his band and no one knew just what he'd have. We all dropped in to catch him—and what we heard! What a thrill that was! The Duke was swinging. All this "progressive" talk, and the Duke played the old swing. He scared a lot of people that night. It was just wonderful. Of course, the Duke has always had the greatest band at all times. There's never been any other band for me, year in and year out. (*Down Beat*, May 16, 1956)

* * *

The studio recordings made during 1951, particularly the singles, are rather disappointing when compared with the rave reports of the new Ellington spirit. We will consider these in two groups: first the three-minute pieces recorded for release as singles, then the extended performances made for LP. The first studio session by the Bellson-powered band took place on May 10 for Columbia, and the opening title was a new arrangement of a piece which had been heard on several broadcasts in 1945—*Fancy Dan*. This is a superb score, and the way in which the material has been reorganized from the arrangement used in 1945 is brilliant, transforming a commonplace composition into a masterpiece of jazz arranging. Two solos by Gonsalves frame a solo sequence featuring the contrasting styles of trumpeter Nelson Williams and trombonists Woodman and Jackson in a perfect orchestral setting, the whole being rounded off by a few bars of pungent, understated piano by Duke. The tempo is on the fast side of medium and the band swings superbly; *Fancy Dan* is certainly the pick of the 1951 Columbia singles. *V.I.P.'s Boogie* is a lesser Ellington work with Carney and Hamilton featured and a fine passage for the Smith-led saxophone section. It is the misfortune of this pleasant piece to have been accompanied throughout its long life in the Ellington book by its companion from *Threesome*, *Jam With Sam*, a rough and unsubtle essay by Ellington in the rather frenetic big band style of the early fifties. The soloists are Baker, Gonsalves, Woodman, Procope, Jackson, and Anderson, the last finishing off in his ultra-high register. For reasons known only to its creator, this item remained one of the most performed of his compositions, appearing regularly for decades in his concert programs. Recordings of *Jam With Sam* are legion and very much alike, although the original 1951 recording at least lacks the staleness which characterizes many of the later versions. Yet Anderson's playing was always so full of spirit and fire that, thanks to him, even the worst versions end on an exciting note.

Even less typical of Ellington was Bellson's *The Hawk Talks*, a conventional score which the band performs with fire and precision. Anderson and Nance are the soloists. (The piece was written by Bellson for the Harry James band and the title refers to the nickname by which James was known to his bandsmen.) *The Hawk Talks* was the most popular of this batch of recordings and caused many observers who relied on records rather than live appearances to conclude that Ellington's music had lost its identity, that Duke's band now sounded more like Woody Herman's than his own! Both drummer and band are more relaxed on *Fancy Dan* (which was coupled with *The Hawk Talks*), but this was the less fashionable piece at the time. Duke also recorded *Monologue* at this session; this is a formalized piece of Ellington humor recited over a background scored by Hamilton for two clarinets and bass clarinet. A delightful trifle.

The very first studio recordings with Smith and Bellson had been made a month earlier on a contingent date for the Mercer label. On the labels, the band was called "The Coronets"; the session was the first of four under this name. On this occasion, the personnel consisted of Anderson, Tizol, Smith, Gonsalves, Ellington, Marshall, and Bellson. Two Latin American–styled numbers were recorded, Tizol's *Moonlight Fiesta* (from 1935) and Bellson's *She*. The Tizol piece has been issued in two takes; the longer has some beautiful playing by Gonsalves, while the shorter contains one of Anderson's best solos. Cat often recorded in the style of a Latin American trumpeter, but never so effectively as here, where he concludes his chorus in a poised manner which owes everything to Louis Armstrong and provides a perfect climax. On both takes, Smith has good solos, Tizol is perfect in the theme statements, and Ellington most effective in his supporting role. The shorter of these versions is perhaps the best of all recordings of *Moonlight Fiesta*. Bellson's exotic *She* is more suitable material for the Ellingtonians than anything else he wrote for them and again has beautiful playing by Tizol on the theme. Both these Latin American performances are notable for Bellson's magnificent drumming, poised and incisive, colorful and imaginative.

Night Walk (or *Cat Walk*) is a somber blues with Anderson's impassioned growl trumpet featured throughout in a performance of great vehemence and power. The fourth title is *The Happening*, five choruses of tenor saxophone by Gonsalves on the chords of *Get Happy* at a driving fast tempo. Although Gonsalves had been heard in solo on previous records by Basie and Ellington, *The Happening* served notice on the jazz community that a major new voice had arrived. The writers and the public seemed little impressed, but musicians were soon talking about the inventive and swinging solos of Duke's new tenor player. In the perspective afforded by hindsight, it seems that the most important event in the Ellington band during 1951 was not the arrival of any of the musicians recruited in that year but the maturing of Paul Gonsalves into a major Ellingtonian.

A further Coronets session from May 1951 was rather less notable, although the recording quality of two of the titles—*Swamp Drum* and *Britt And Butter Blues*—is such as to impair the listener's pleasure. The former is a piece of Strayhorn exotica with Tizol and Smith in the solo roles, while the latter, despite its title, has Smith as the main soloist in a jump-tempo blues—the two musicians referred to in the title, Britt Woodman and Quentin "Butter" Jackson having just one chorus each. The personnel on this date consists of the three-piece trombone section, Smith on alto, and the rhythm section with Duke again on piano. The other two titles are showcases, for Woodman in Tyree Glenn's *Sultry Serenade*, a nice performance if less fine than the original, and for Smith in a pleasant ballad version of *Indian Summer*.

The second Columbia session for the full band is disappointing. *Brown Betty* had been heard in concert as a Hodges feature a few years before; its revival as a showcase for Nelson Williams on trumpet is not wholly successful, but this is the best recording from this date. Bellson's *Ting-A-Ling* is a rather monochrome piece of big band writing with none of the color of the Ellington ensemble utilized, although this arrangement is superior to *The Hawk Talks* in terms of swing, and there are solos by Gonsalves, Anderson (playing muted), and Wendell Marshall. The Ellington-Strayhorn *The Eighth Veil* is an exotic feature for Anderson's open horn, which remained in the book for some twenty years. It is not of any great musical substance.

The last four titles by The Coronets stem from June 1951. *Caravan* was the sole issued title from the first of that month, the remaining three sides being the product of a session on the nineteenth. *Caravan* features theme statements fore and aft by composer Tizol and variations in the middle by Smith. Strayhorn makes his only recorded appearance on organ in the accompaniment here, with Ellington, Marshall, and Bellson making up the rhythm section. On the other session, Strayhorn alternates with Ellington at the piano and Hamilton, doubling clarinet and tenor, is added. *Alternate* is a blues featuring choruses in alternating keys by Smith on alto and Hamilton on tenor; taken at a fast medium tempo, it also contains a couple of nice piano choruses by Duke. The second title, *Hoppin' John*, is a brisk jump performance with Hamilton's clarinet and Smith's alto as solo voices. Lester Young's *Jumpin' With Symphony Sid* was one of the fashionable jazz riffs of the fifties, and the Ellington version is heard on this Coronets session. Strayhorn plays the ensemble piano, and Smith and Hamilton are again the soloists, the latter back on tenor.

The recording quality (at least on European 78 and all microgroove issues) of The Coronets items is very variable, inconsistent indeed within each session. This would appear to be because of the disappearance of the original masters and the rarity of master pressings in anything like mint condition. The Coronets offer a most interesting insight into Ellington's music of the early fifties, and are the first series of Ellington contingent records since the Bluebird sessions of ten years earlier. Since that time, only units led by Hodges had made any substantial number of recordings; these were all without Ellington, having either Strayhorn or an outside pianist at the keyboard. Though they contain good playing, these Hodges records add little to the totality of Ellington music, being in the main variations on patterns established in the thirties and early forties. But The Coronets represented something new, reflecting 1951 Ellington music in small-band terms. It is fortunate that the best titles—*Cat Walk, Moonlight Fiesta, She*—enjoy the best sound quality.

By contrast, the Columbia issues from this period are all superbly recorded, but for much of the time they continue the pop-oriented policy which was a feature of the late forties output. From early August 1951 come two non-Ellington pop tunes and a couple of new Strayhorn jump numbers. *Deep Night* features Tizol leading the ensemble, followed by solos from the other members of the trombone section, Jackson (with plunger) and Britt Woodman (open horn). *Please Be Kind* is a similarly relaxed and highly melodic affair featuring contrasting voices, this time from the saxophone section in Smith, the main soloist, and Gonsalves with a most effective obbligato to the muted brass in the middle section. The two Strayhorn pieces are pretty conventional. *Smada* (the dedicatee's name spelled backwards) is from the *"A" Train* mold with Hamilton featured; the band plays with great verve over Bellson's highly propulsive beat. *Rock Skippin' At The Blue Note* is a shade less convincing: Nance's plunger trumpet does not fit well into the solo role, and the performance by the band is also a trifle awkward.

By December 1951, when the next singles were recorded, several important changes had taken place in the trumpet section. Nelson Williams had left, Francis Williams was back for another brief stay, but most important was the addition of two players who were to make vital contributions during the next decade—Clark Terry and Willie Cook. Both were influenced by current trends in jazz trumpet playing but had deeper stylistic roots than most of their contemporaries, which was essential for Ellington's music with its wide stylistic references. Sound was equally important, and fortunately both came equipped with superb and individual trumpet tones. Both were also excellent and distinctive players of melody, another Ellington essential not much cultivated by the fashionable musicians of that day.

The first single recorded with Terry and Cook in the band was *Bensonality*. This is a driving blues of a kind not often heard and even less often brought off with success, at least outside the music of Sidney Bechet, which it recalls in its rolling passion. The soloists are Hamilton, doing his robust blues routine on tenor; Terry with plunger mute; and another trumpet soloist who is probably Francis Williams. Paul Gonsalves plays a characteristic role here, entering with a magnificent break, then playing a free-wheeling obbligato against the ensemble before closing the performance with a magnificently executed coda. The band plays with great vigor and spirit, especially the trombone section and Bellson at the drums. *Blues At Sundown* was revived in 1963 for Duke's *My People* stage show; the centerpiece of the 1951 recording is a vocal by Lloyd Oldham, and its musical highlights are Baker's obbligato to that vocal, some nice alto from Smith, and a striking introduction by Terry. (From the same session come two further numbers with poor vocals by Oldham. Never issued by Columbia, they have appeared on Up-To-Date. The titles are *Azalea* and *Something To Live For*, the latter with a beautiful theme statement with Juan Tizol's valve trombone leading the ensemble. Up-To-Date has also released an otherwise unissued uptempo piece by Tizol recorded on this date, *Vagabonds*. The main soloists are Clark Terry, Willie Smith and Jimmy Hamilton.) This session also saw the recording of *Duet*, the Hamilton clarinet showcase which started life as a part of *Threesome*.

By this time we are well into the microgroove era and singles—either 78 or 45 rpm—by big bands like Ellington's were beginning to be phased out. As a consequence many of the items the band recorded for singles were either never issued at all or only put out years later as part of LP compilations. An instance of this is *I Love My Lovin' Lover*, a highly satirical and amusing blues sung by Betty Roché, the humor superbly pointed up by the band accompaniment. The high-note trumpet by Anderson in the last chorus sustains the mood perfectly. Unfortunately this item lay unissued in the vaults for many years and its release on a 1976 Columbia LP is taken from a rather rough test-pressing. The take issued on Up-To-Date is in much better sound. The session mate to this is a Jimmy Grissom ballad, *Come On Home*, with Nance providing a sensitive introduction and Hamilton's tenor heard in the unusual role of ballad accompanist. Up-To-Date (and later French CBS) have issued a couple of vocal numbers from this period which had never previously been published—a version of *Body And Soul* for Roché and a *Blues* at fast-medium tempo featuring Grissom's blues shouting and containing one of Woodman's best solos. The final session from this Columbia contract, and coincidentally of what we now call "The Bellson Period," took place on December 22, 1952, a date on which the band seemed to be burdened with a large number of substitutes. *Primpin' For The Prom* is an Ellington jump number with a Strayhorn-like predilection for pastel shades of tone color. Hamilton's rough-toned tenor combines with Ellington's piano in an effective introduction, but the musical meat is again provided by the specialist tenor player, Gonsalves. The final Columbia singles were a couple of Grissom ballads the second of which—*Follow Me*—is redeemed by a superb score and a Gonsalves tenor solo.

* * *

The most important Ellington LP from the Bellson period is known either as *Ellington Uptown* or *Ellington Uptown In Hi Fi*. One of the main features of *Ellington Uptown* is a performance of *A Tone Parallel To Harlem*, but *Ellington Uptown In Hi Fi* has this item replaced by the *Controversial Suite*. Thus, even with Ellington material from the microgroove era, the serious collector has to maneuver this way and that in an attempt to build a complete collection while avoiding duplication. If the collector has the version of *Ellington Uptown* which includes *A Tone Parallel To Harlem*, then he can find the *Controversial Suite* on *The Complete Duke Ellington 1947–1952*, a six-LP boxed set on French CBS. This contains all Ellington's Columbia recordings (alternative takes are omitted) apart from those on *Masterpieces By Ellington* (1950) and *Ellington Uptown* (1951–1952). The *Liberian Suite* of 1947 is also included in this set.

On all issues of *Ellington Uptown* the remainder consists of four items recorded in August 1952 (the suites were done in December 1951)—*Skin Deep, The Mooche, Take The "A" Train,* and *Perdido*. *Skin Deep* is a Bellson number showcasing his drumming in a stunning display of virtuosity. (It is odd that after having a drummer who refused to take solos Ellington should replace him with one of the most brilliant drum soloists.) *Skin Deep* was also issued as a two-part 78 single and was a considerable hit. As a consequence of its popularity, every Ellington concert from this time forward included a drum solo, but few of them even began to approach the brilliance of Bellson's virtuosity. The other three titles are more characteristic of Ellington's music in both content and quality.

The version of *The Mooche* is a brilliant one. Nance indulges in an eloquent dialogue with the band, and Ellington has the clarinet duet played by Procope close on mike and Jimmy Hamilton distant and heard through an echo chamber. Jackson has an excellent plunger solo with support from Gonsalves, and there are choruses from Carney and Hilton Jefferson, who had replaced Willie Smith on alto. The pungent alto solo here shows how suited Jefferson's music was to the Ellington band, but unfortunately his stay lasted less than a year. A brilliant section leader and an accomplished soloist with an acute melodic sense, Jefferson is perhaps foremost among the players who flitted briefly through the Ellington ranks but would seem to have been capable of more substantial contributions.

Take the "A" Train presents two versions welded together. The first features an Ellington piano solo and then Betty Roché in three choruses, singing and scatting with vocal support from the trumpet section. (This vocal was performed in later years by Nance, whose use of Roché's mannerisms was often hilarious.) Bellson's drumming is very effective on this 1952 recording. The second section features Paul Gonsalves in both slow- and fast-tempo variations on Strayhorn's theme. Although this hardly seems an ideal vehicle for his talents, Gonsalves plays brilliantly.

The *Ellington Uptown* version of *Perdido* is one of the most exciting of all Ellington recordings. It lasts for eight and a half minutes and finds the band using the additional time available on LP to good effect, building a roaring big band performance to a magnificent climax. All the virtues of classic big band jazz playing are present and the rhythm section of Ellington, Marshall, and Bellson is superb throughout. Ellington opens with a chorus of solo piano. Then the usual *Perdido* first chorus is played, with Nance on the middle eight. A brilliant, witty solo by Terry precedes choruses by the saxophone and trombone sections, played with easygoing, nonchalant swing. Terry then returns for two more choruses and Wendell Marshall, with wonderful support from Duke, takes one. This is followed by a five-way brass chase by Nance, Anderson, Cook, Terry, and Woodman (in that order). This in turn leads to the final band chorus, in which the all-out playing of the ensemble is garnished with high-note extravaganzas from Woodman and Anderson. This arrangement was used in truncated form as a feature for Terry for many years and became rather stale in the process, but the 1952 recording is a vital, swinging performance which gives a more vivid idea of the kind of excitement generated by this "new" Ellington band than any other studio recording.

* * *

Harlem or *A Tone Parallel To Harlem* is in one continuous movement and lasts just under fifteen minutes. It is built on two themes, a two-note motif, which Ellington always introduced as spelling out the word "Harlem," and a beautiful spiritual theme. The first part of the piece is a representation of various aspects of Harlem life and presents a brilliant kaleidoscope of orchestral color and pattern, initially derived from the basic two-note motif but later including other material. A nocturnal passage introduces the spiritual theme, a really beautiful melody, heard first on solo trombone. The development of this theme is an example of Ellington's writing at its most resourceful, notably in its use of the individual clarinet styles of Procope and Hamilton, which are brilliantly exploited. Carney's bass clarinet is also used, and a very beautiful trumpet solo, interpreted here by Harold Baker, is woven into the texture. The orchestration in this section is of the utmost brilliance, individuality, and beauty. The final part of *Harlem* is a gigantic climax in which the two themes are heard together over a driving march rhythm which Duke claimed represented the citizens of Harlem "making our civil rights demands."

This tone poem must be counted among the finest of all Ellington's achievements. It is a fully integrated whole, and, if not so finely structured as *The Tattooed Bride*, it has no weaknesses and is a work of considerably greater variety and substance. Like *Black, Brown And Beige* it remained in the repertoire until near the end of Ellington's career, although it was not subjected to the chopping and abridgment which was the fate of that work. In *Harlem* only details were altered, and Ellington's assessment of the work implied by these repeated revivals seems wholly justified. Along with *The Tattooed Bride* it is one of his finest pieces of extended writing.

Harlem was written as a result of a commission from the NBC Symphony Orchestra, and the recordings of the work include a version by a symphony orchestra and one by the Ellington band combined with a symphony orchestra.

The versions issued at the time of writing are:

January 21, 1951	Ellington Orchestra	Recorded by Voice of America at a concert at the Metropolitan Opera House, New York
December 7, 1951	Ellington Orchestra	Columbia studio recording
December 7, 1951	Ellington Orchestra	Columbia alternative take, issued on Up-To-Date
March 25, 1952	Ellington Orchestra	Recorded by RCA at a concert in Seattle
April 30, 1955	Ellington Orchestra	Recorded at a concert at the Armory, Washington, D.C., and issued on the Jazz Guild and Phontastic labels
January 31, 1963	Ellington Orchestra plus the Paris Symphony Orchestra	Reprise studio recording
February 23, 1963	Ellington Orchestra	Recorded by Reprise at a concert at the Olympia Theatre, Paris, and issued on Atlantic
May 28, 1970	Cincinnati Symphony Orchestra, conducted by Erich Kunzel with Duke Ellington (piano)	Decca studio recording

In addition to these, there are several unissued recordings by the Ellington band, with and without symphony orchestras, some of which will no doubt be released in the future. Of the versions listed above, the last is in some ways the least satisfactory, but it is fascinating to hear a symphony orchestra playing a work which has become familiar through these performances of the Ellington Orchestra. Although not realized so vividly, *Harlem* stands up very well to orchestral treatment, the final section retaining much of its convincing swagger.

(The reason for Ellington's presence as piano soloist seems to be compliance with the description of the performers on the LP: Duke Ellington, piano; Cincinnati Symphony Orchestra, Erich Kunzel, conductor. Unlike the other two Ellington works performed on the disc, *Harlem* has no piano part; during stage performances, Ellington was busily engaged in conducting. In this version, he makes a brief appearance as pianist and then retires to allow the Cincinnati Symphony Orchestra to get on with what is essentially an orchestral work.

The Reprise version, with the Ellington Orchestra and the Paris Symphony Orchestra, has the advantage of Ellington musicians in the solo roles and the propulsive drumming of Sam Woodyard, but for all the extra tone colors provided by the symphony orchestra, the overall effect is one of dilution when compared with the versions by the Ellington Orchestra alone. It must be said, however, that Ellington himself seems to have been very fond of this way of presenting the work, and the performance is in no sense a failure.

Of the recordings of *Harlem* by the Ellington band, the debut performance of January 1951 is mainly of historical interest; neither the quality of the recording nor of the playing can be compared with later versions. Of these, the Columbia studio recording has the best balance and gives the clearest impression of the details of the score. The second take (on Up-To-Date) is also in good sound and contains interesting differences in the details of the interpretation. All three concert versions are more fiery and spirited but less cleanly articulated. The Seattle recording is of special interest because of its proximity to the Columbia studio version. A comparison gives a clear impression of the difference of approach by the band—even to one of Ellington's more formal concert works—when away from the recording studio. The playing of the trumpet section at the end is untidy but full of fire. The 1955 version by a slightly later edition of the Ellington band is a good one. The 1963 Paris recording is very vivid and immediate and, like the two versions with symphony orchestra, is in stereophonic sound. It also has Lawrence Brown's reading of the spiritual theme and Sam Woodyard at the drums—the latter a musician who always injected great spirit into this particular work. All these recordings present different aspects of *Harlem* and all are worthy of study. If one version only is required, the standard take of the 1951 Columbia studio recording is recommended. Of the concert performances, the 1963 Paris issue is to be preferred, especially as a contrasting version to the Columbia.

* * *

The *Controversial Suite* is one of Ellington's minor works, a miniature affair in two short movements, *Before My Time* and *Later*. This suite did not remain in the Ellington book for long, and the only alternative recording to the two Columbia takes is the one from the Metropolitan Opera House concert of January 1951. This tells us nothing more about the piece and is not nearly so well recorded as the Columbias. *Before My Time* is a humorous look at Dixieland jazz in which Dixieland favorites are parodied in slightly disguised and rather affectionate take-offs. A trumpet-trombone-clarinet front line is called for here, and these parts are handled by Baker, Jackson, and Procope. Terry and Nance are heard in solo, and portions of the 1945 *Rugged Romeo* are incorporated in the score. Then Procope takes up the soprano sax to lead the band into a weird and wonderful variation on *Tiger Rag*, with a brass break recalling Ellington's 1929 Brunswick recording, before the band is precipitated into a hilarious coda. By contrast, *Later* is one of the enigmas of the Ellington output, a satire on the "progressive" big bands of the period. It has a mock-pretentious aura and is as monotonous and unswinging as any record by an accredited practitioner of the idiom. But its monotony is self-defeating, and any humor it may once have had has faded away over the years. Yet the *Controversial Suite* will always have a special place in Ellington's music for the lively satire and wit of the *Before My Time* movement. The alternative take of the Columbia recording (issued on Up-To-Date) shows minor differences of detail and has the movements in the order recorded, a reversal of the usual sequence. With *Before My Time* as the second movement, the reversal of chronological sequence is at least partly compensated for by the avoidance of anticlimax.

* * *

So far as the major record companies are concerned, the only other LP from this period—excluding, of course, later collections of singles or from broadcasts—is an RCA record of part of a concert given in Seattle in March 1952. *Harlem* (already discussed) and a performance of the *Medley Of Popular Hits* take up a good deal of the LP. For the rest, a rather commonplace selection from the current band repertoire is heard—*Skin Deep* and *The Hawk Talks* are not pieces of which alternative versions provide the listener with many new pleasures, although Ellington's oral and pianistic introduction to the latter is diverting. There is a pleasant version of *Sultry Serenade* featuring Woodman, Smith is heard in *Sophisticated Lady*, and Terry goes through his *Perdido* routine. Tizol, Hamilton, and Nance (on violin) are soloists in the standard arrangement of *Caravan*, which has some effective Anderson trumpet in the ensembles. Anderson also closes *Jam With Sam* with an exciting foray into his highest register. The music is played with great spirit, and the LP gives considerably more pleasure than its repertoire might suggest. Even so, it is unfortunate that the selection was not a little more imaginative.

This "new" Ellington band soon became a favorite in clubs such as Birdland which were considered modern jazz houses, with a clientele previously thought to be skeptical of a veteran like Ellington. The new spirit of the band can be heard on some of the records we have just discussed, but is manifested continuously on the air shots from such locations which have appeared in recent years on a variety of labels. These have done much to bring Ellington's music of this period into clearer perspective. Such issues inevitably present more versions of *Skin Deep*, *The Hawk Talks*, and *Jam With Sam*, but they also include many performances of Ellington compositions not otherwise associated with this particular Ellington band. For example, there are several fine versions of *Just A-Settin' And A-Rockin'* with impressive solos from Gonsalves as well as Jackson's plunger trombone and Nance's swinging vocals; that from May 5, 1951, is especially noteworthy. Anderson is heard in a version of his menacing growl trumpet blues, *Night Walk*, even better than the studio recording by The Coronets. The several recordings of *Fancy Dan* reveal that the crucial Gonsalves solos are pure improvisation, with fresh melodic delights in every version. An exciting recording of *Things Ain't What They Used To Be* has wonderful blues solos by Smith, Baker, and Woodman before Gonsalves indulges in the first of his many recorded tenor saxophone marathons, a matter of nine choruses. Baker is featured in *Harlem Air Shaft* and *Boy Meets Horn*, the latter a particularly interesting interpretation of the old Rex Stewart concerto in which Baker finds some unexpected pockets of lyricism. Gonsalves is heard in his best ballad vein in *Warm Valley*, while the 1952 version of *Cotton Tail* is notable not only for Paul's playing but also for the drive and attack of the entire orchestra, especially the trumpet section. (This is a more considered version than that of the 1956 Bethlehem recording.)

The first recording of *Diminuendo And Crescendo In Blue* with the Gonsalves interlude is heard on a June 1951 broadcast, thus predating the famous Newport Jazz Festival explosion by five years. The orchestral playing is superb here, as indeed it is in several exciting versions of *Rockin' In Rhythm* from 1951 and 1952. On a Carnegie Hall recording of January 5, 1952, we get another chance to hear the Ellington Dixieland front line, this time in a version of *Basin Street Blues* featuring Ray Nance. Terry is the ensemble trumpet, and he offers a humorous view of old-style jazz trumpet, while Nance plays some very lyrical trumpet as well as indulging in a Louis Armstrong–style vocal. Ellington introduces this item as "Ray Nance's Perdido Street version of the *Basin Street Blues*." Willie Cook is not heard in solo very much on commercial records from this period, but a feature number written by Jimmy Hamilton, known at this stage simply as *W.C.*, appears on these broadcasts and exhibits the trumpeter's clean-cut ballad style; this composition was later titled *Moonstone*. Even better is a version of *Tenderly* by Cook, playing muted and accompanied by piano, bass, and drums only; on this performance the Ellington-Marshall-Bellson team sounds like an ideal rhythm section. *Moonlight Fiesta*, *Chelsea Bridge*, and *Lady Of The Lavender Mist* are among the numbers from earlier years which can be heard in excellent versions on broadcasts from 1951 and 1952. Also among the delights from these broadcasts are a casual Ellington piano solo of *Black Beauty*, an exciting revival of the Buck Clayton arrangement of *One O'Clock Jump*, and a fine version of *C Jam Blues*, this last from April 29, 1952. Among the new pieces by Ellington is a number called *Felanges*, which was recorded by Columbia but never released by them; a pity, for the broadcast reveals it to be a piece in Duke's best contemporary vein with Clark Terry and Louis Bellson featured.

In February 1952, Ellington made a group of Snader Telefocal Transcriptions—these were films for use by television stations. They feature good Ellington performances, but unfortunately the LP issues from this source suffer from atrocious recording quality. Nor are the performances from the two Carnegie Hall concerts of November 14, 1952, particularly outstanding, although Strayhorn's arrangements of two of the fashionable jazz standards of the day, *How High The Moon* and *Lullaby Of Birdland*, are played and there is a very good version of *The Tattooed Bride*. The issue of an LP on the Aircheck label of the complete broadcasts of July 30 and August 13, 1952, from Chicago's Blue Note is of greater interest, for these give a very vivid impression of the band's club appearances at this time. The sound is excellent on these broadcasts, which cover the Ellington repertoire from *Mood Indigo* and *Rockin' In Rhythm* to *Bensonality* and *Ting-A-Ling*.

* * *

After the Columbia sessions of December 1952, the Ellington band did not make any records for commercial release for over three months. When it next entered a recording studio it was to inaugurate the new contract with Capitol records on April 6, 1953. There had been several personnel changes, and the departure of Louis Bellson marked the end of an era for the Ellington band. The full personnel now was:

Trumpets: Cat Anderson, Clark Terry, Willie Cook, Ray Nance (also violin and vocal).

Trombones: Britt Woodman, Quentin Jackson, Juan Tizol (valve trombone).

Reeds: Russell Procope (alto sax, clarinet); Rick Henderson (alto sax); Paul Gonsalves (tenor sax); Jimmy Hamilton (clarinet, tenor sax); Harry Carney (baritone sax, clarinet, bass clarinet).

Rhythm: Duke Ellington (piano); Wendell Marshall (bass); Butch Ballard (drums); Billy Strayhorn (deputy pianist).

Vocal: Jimmy Grissom.

For all the excellent playing of the band in 1951 and 1952, it is clear that the constant changes in personnel must have been unsettling. If we compare the personnel of May 2, 1951, with the band of April 1953 we find several interesting changes. Only Anderson and Nance of the 1951 trumpets remain, while such players as Dick Vance and Francis Williams have been in and out since that date. The trombones remain unchanged. In the reeds, the unsettled chair was the one filled by Willie Smith and then Hilton Jefferson for one year each. It is now occupied by a little-known player, Rick Henderson. Smith had done an important job for Ellington, but his loss was not so great as that of the other catalyst of the 1951 revival, Louis Bellson, who departed in March 1953. The new drummer was Butch Ballard, a sound technician who had already played with Ellington during the band's 1950 European tour. Ballard was Ellington's regular drummer from March to July 1953 only, a period which included an unusually large amount of recording activity under Ellington's new contract.

Coincidentally, the period during which the band recorded for Capitol covers exactly the time when the second alto chair was held by Henderson and the drummer was either Ballard or his successor, Dave Black. Apart from this change of drummers the only important personnel movements during these years were the departure of Tizol, who was replaced briefly by Alfred Cobbs, then more permanently by John Sanders, and the arrival of a new bassist, Jimmy Woode, who replaced Marshall on the final Capitol date.

After the contract had been signed, Capitol issued a fairly heavy publicity barrage concerning Ellington's new artistic freedom under the new arrangement. Many jazz enthusiasts expected a stream of uncompromising jazz releases and were puzzled and angry when Capitol issued such commercial items as *Bunny Hop Mambo*, *Isle Of Capri*, and *The Echo Tango*. *The Echo Tango* is a performance which challenges strongly for the honor of being the least distinguished of all Duke Ellington's records. The jazz enthusiasts and critics blamed Capitol for this commercial policy, but these recordings were Ellington's own idea—further attempts to break into the hit parade and juke box markets. The idea that they were foisted on a reluctant artist by a rapacious record company is totally false.

Artistically, such records amount to very little and, alas, financially they were failures too, unable to attract a popular audience. They brought forth loud condemnation from jazz critics, who announced the long-expected decline of Duke Ellington. One result of this critical reaction has been that Ellington's Capitol period is often considered to be characterized by blatant commercialism. However, the orchestra recorded much fine music for this label, and though this was not one of the greatest of Ellington bands, it was far ahead of anything his competitors could field. Its qualities are clearly heard on these well-engineered Capitol recordings. The brass was truly outstanding, with a trumpet section of extraordinary power and versatility. The trombones were a fine team, with Jackson now settled into Nanton's chair and Woodman covering the wide range previously handled by Brown. When Tizol left, Ellington was fortunate in obtaining the services of John Sanders, a young musician who took over the chair with musical taste and a strong sense of tradition. Although not an original stylist or a brilliant improviser, Sanders was a fine bandsman and the possessor of a rich and distinctive tone.

Among the reeds, Gonsalves was the outstanding soloist, and the section could also call upon the solo talents of Procope, Hamilton and Carney. Any rhythm section containing Ellington and Marshall was bound to be outstanding, and in Butch Ballard and Dave Black, it had two excellent drummers. On the vocal front, Jimmy Grissom, a singer whose mannerisms often bordered on the grotesque, was featured. The band did not have a female vocalist at this time, and from now on Ellington normally carried only one specialist singer. Much more to the taste of the discerning jazz listener were the vocals by Ran Nance, but these were unfortunately much rarer than Grissom's.

* * *

Like the Columbias of the preceding couple of years, the Capitols can be divided into two categories, those intended for use as singles, and those intended for issue as part of LPs. Generally speaking, these latter items are longer than the singles, but this was not always the case. For example, all the tracks on Ellington's first Capitol LP were of approximately three minutes duration. These were collected on a 10-inch LP, and the disc contains eight remakes of non-Ellington numbers recorded by the band in previous decades and entitled *Premiered By Ellington*. Duke did not go back to his old arrangements here, he and Billy Strayhorn preferring to approach each number afresh. This pattern was followed even on a song like *Stormy Weather*, where the original 1933 arrangement had been so distinctive and imaginative.

Ellington's very first Capitol session produced one of the tracks for the *Premiered By Ellington* set, *Cocktails For Two*, in which contrasting theme statements by Tizol and Nance, a dash of Hamilton's clarinet, and a longer improvisation by Gonsalves are heard in the context of a nicely balanced arrangement. *Flamingo* was one of Ellington's best-selling recordings of the early forties, and on this totally different (and superior) remake he features himself on piano along with Nance on violin and an inventive Gonsalves. Short solos by Terry, Gonsalves, Carney, Ellington, and Henderson and a long one by Woodman are among the gems fitted into the arrangement of Gershwin's *Liza*. Gonsalves has a ravishing theme statement in *My Old Flame*, a track on which Jimmy Hamilton also has a prominent part. On *I Can't Give You Anything But Love* Ellington provides another gem of an arrangement, wholly of the fifties without doing the slightest violence to what is usually thought of as a typically twenties song. Nance's open trumpet is heard at its most soulful, and the main solo voice is that of Procope's clarinet. The score also clearly shows Ellington's love of the clarinet in ensemble textures; notice the way in which he briefly uses the contrasting sound of Hamilton, just before Quentin Jackson starts his solo.

Stormy Weather is another example, among hundreds in Ellington's output, of how to make brilliant jazz without departing from the melody. Carney, Cook, and Nance combine to present the song in contrasting styles, while the main soloist is Anderson, opening in his ballad manner but ascending to the high register at the climax of this imaginative score. *Stardust* is a showcase for Terry which makes one wish that Ellington had featured him more often in ballads. The influence of Charlie Shavers on Terry's style is more evident here than is usually the case. The final recording for this set was *Three Little Words*, a concise, swinging arrangement with Cook and Gonsalves in the solo roles. *Premiered By Ellington* finds Ellington, Strayhorn, the ensemble, and the soloists applying themselves collectively to a traditional task for jazz musicians, that of playing popular songs. The result of this application is a colorful, varied, and highly imaginative collection.

The recordings for *Premiered By Ellington* were made at three sessions in April 1953. Most of the other items from these dates were issued on 78, and the very first of them became Ellington's last really popular single. It was *Satin Doll*, the last of his songs which came to be regarded as a standard and the last which, after it had acquired a few years seniority, was admitted to a place in the *Medley Of Popular Hits*—a dubious distinction, some might say, but an undoubted sign of worldly success. It is arguable that this original version of *Satin Doll* is the best of the many Duke recorded. In later years the piece had a long stint as a showcase for the bass player, and when it returned to an ensemble context the tempo went up and the performances seem a little rough. But this Capitol *Satin Doll* is perfectly proportioned. Gonsalves leads the saxes, and Nance has a gorgeous eight bars of theme, but basically it is a triumph for the band.

The version of *Without A Song* recorded immediately afterwards bears no relation to the brilliant Rex Stewart contingent version of 1940 and is no more than a vehicle for Grissom's vocal eccentricities with no instrumental solos. Anderson's *Bluejean Beguine* recalls the band's earlier Latin American explorations, with its Tizol theme statement and the reversion to a straight four-four beat on the entry of Gonsalves's tenor sax. A pleasant minor piece this, with some fiery trumpet from its composer, who finishes off the performance with a Latin American cliché delivered from the highest register of the trumpet. There exists a recording from around this time, in very poor sound, of Ellington himself singing and talking his way through *Nothin', Nothin', Baby Without You*, accompanied only by his own piano. It is tempting to say that there is no improvement in the vocal on the Capitol version, but in fact this kind of number is much more in Grissom's line than *Without A Song*, and his bluesy bawling is appropriate here and on the 78 backing, *Ballin' The Blues*. Grissom is a moderate blues singer, but the instrumental work on these titles is of interest, with Anderson heard on *Nothin', Nothin', Baby*, while *Ballin' The Blues* features Ellington's boogie-woogie piano, Terry's trumpet, Woodman's trombone, and Hamilton's rough-toned tenor sax before Anderson enters with an appropriately climactic effect. This performance has the inestimable value of sounding as if the players are enjoying themselves, although by Ellington standards it is a pretty trite piece of work.

Strayhorn's *Boo-Dah* is another theme out of the *"A" Train* stable, with a pleasant solo by Nance and assorted flavoring by Hamilton and Anderson. *Warm Valley* is heard in a version totally different from the 1940 original. The main reason is the difference in the musical personalities of the soloists—Hodges on the older versions, Gonsalves here. This is one of the finest Gonsalves ballad solos on record, and Nance handles the solo trumpet part with sensitivity and warmth. The remaining few titles from these April 1953 sessions were used by Capitol for later LP compilations. *Orson* became part of *Dance Date With The Duke* and *Blossom* part of *Ellington Showcase*, collections otherwise made up of tracks from 1954 and 1955 respectively. Both pieces are specimens of Ellington's "mood music," Tizol having the theme statement on *Orson*, with Nance and Gonsalves also heard briefly. *Blossom* has an unobtrusive Latin beat and Duke as the only soloist, though Woodman has a prominent role as lead voice in the soft, shifting tone colors of the orchestration.

* * *

The next group of Capitol recordings represents something of a new departure for Ellington in that they are piano solos, accompanied by bass and drums. Twelve titles in all were cut at two late-night sessions during April 1953 and issued on an LP called *The Duke Plays Ellington*. Individual piano solos were not new to the Ellington discography, but a dozen in a row certainly was an innovation: there are more piano solos from these two sessions than can be found in the previous thirty years of Ellington recordings. Duke had rarely featured himself with the band and his two extended concert works with prominent piano—*Blue Belles Of Harlem* and *New World A-Comin'*—had not been commercially recorded. The issue of this Capitol LP was therefore a considerable event. Ellington had long been recognized by a handful of discerning listeners (and more generally by his fellow musicians) as one of the best jazz pianists. But even this limited reputation was based on his work in the band with just the odd chorus or half-chorus solo, supplemented by an occasional feature such as *Frankie And Johnnie* or *New York City Blues*.

Ellington was not the most dexterous jazz pianist on record, but his inherent musicality makes him one of the most fascinating. In terms of musical rather than digital virtuosity, he is unexcelled. His timing is astonishing in its absolute rightness, and his touch can vary from the most delicate caress to a positively brutal attack. Perhaps the most remarkable feature of Ellington's pianism is the way in which he plays with a very precise dynamic placing of each note within a chord to give a great variety of voicings. The parallel with his writing for saxophones is very marked.

The 1953 piano solos for Capitol are of modest dimensions and demeanor, their considerable subtlety and depth apparent only to those who listen beneath the surface. Three of the pieces are of a quiet, reflective nature—as if Ellington were musing in private at the piano—and unusual in mood and texture. These are *Retrospection*, *Reflections in D*, and *Melancholia*, and along with the version of Strayhorn's *Passion Flower* they display Ellington's harmonic mastery and pianistic control to a marked degree. Three standard Ellington ballads are included in the program—*Prelude To A Kiss*, *In A Sentimental Mood*, and *All Too Soon*—and here Ellington repeats at the piano what he had so frequently done with the band, basing whole performances on varied theme statements. Superficially the three solos sound rather bland, yet beneath the surface lie many delights of creative melodic, harmonic, and rhythmic variation. Any one of them could stand as a definitive performance of the song in question; *In A Sentimental Mood* is particularly notable, outstanding even among the many fine versions of this beautiful ballad. The sprightly *Dancers In Love* from *The Perfume Suite* is heard in a swinging version which incorporates a finger-snapping routine, which Ellington had just started to use in his public performances of the piece.

There are two blues, a slow *Things Ain't What They Used To Be* and an uptempo *B-sharp Blues*. These reveal a good deal about Ellington's musical thinking. In neither performance are there any choruses of improvisation in the usual sense. Instead, each chorus is given a melodic germ cell which is its province alone and which is repeated with variations until the next chorus takes up another idea, sometimes complementary, sometimes contrasting. On *B-sharp Blues* especially, it is as if Duke were musing over potential riff themes for the band, some of which, as the title hints, had already featured in piano solos introducing performances of *C Jam Blues*. *Things Ain't What They Used To Be*—a particularly fine piece of piano playing in its quiet way—also incorporates the *Blues For Blanton* riff which was often used in band performances of this number. Blanton's successor plays an important supporting role during these performances, nowhere to better effect than on this track. The thoughtful nature of much of this music and the structural emphasis in the blues performances have caused many writers to regard these recordings as examples of "composer's piano," as examples of Ellington using the keyboard as a kind of public workshop. There is an element of truth in this, but in another and more subtle sense they are "pianist's piano" also.

The compositional aspect is to the fore on the remaining two numbers, *Who Knows* and *Janet*. According to the original (anonymous) sleeve note both these were "spontaneous, ad libbed compositions . . . created in the privacy of the dimly lit studio"—a description also extended to *Reflections In D* and, dubiously, to *B-sharp Blues*. Indeed this description is also questionable when applied to *Janet*, as its main theme is played by Ellington as part of a long introduction to a March 1952 recording of *Cotton Tail* made at a dance date. The delightful *Who Knows* is possibly the most conventional of these Capitol solos. It is an uptempo piece with some stunning variations, structured in the manner of *B-sharp Blues*, but looser and with some quite startling ideas. The brusque, discordant manner which Ellington uses here is clearly that aspect of his piano style which had earlier affected Thelonious Monk's development. *Janet* is one of Ellington's "portraits"; apart from her name, we can deduce from the music that she was a sprightly, vivacious lady, although the lyrical central section points to other, more specifically feminine attributes. This is one of Ellington's most successful two-tempo compositions, the outer sections in a neo-ragtime style with implied stride in perfect contrast with the slow, rhapsodic central portion. The variations in the main part are brilliant, and they epitomize that air of gentle understatement which makes these Capitol solos so attractive a part of the Ellington output of the early fifties.

* * *

Duke Ellington's next visit to the Capitol studios was toward the end of June 1953, when the band recorded two non-Ellington ballads featuring Grissom: *Give Me The Right* and *Is It A Sin? (My Loving You)*. These are not important, and the main points of interest are some mock-pop piano playing by Duke on the first title and a Nance trumpet solo on the second, surprisingly good considering the context. These were recorded in Chicago, as was the sole product of a session on July 1, Ellington's *The Big Drag*, a title in some ways more descriptive of the recordings from the previous session. The piece is an uptempo swinger with an unusual use of the twelve-bar blues sequence as its base. The orchestra sounds rather stiff in the riff ensembles and the rhythm section swings less than usual. The soloists are Hamilton, Gonsalves and Cook, with Hamilton and Anderson also heard in characteristic obbligato passages.

By the time of the Capitol recordings of December 1953, Ballard had been replaced by Dave Black. The effect of this change was to loosen up the rhythm section; this is most noticeable on live recordings. The first studio date with Black on drums produced a trio version of an Ellington piano trifle called *Kinda Dukish*. This later became the regular piano prelude to the orchestra's onslaught on *Rockin' In Rhythm*. The next session featured units from the band. Versions of *Just A-Settin' And A-Rockin'*, *Blue Moon*, and *Lady Be Good* were recorded by an ensemble varying from a quartet to a septet. The first title features Nance singing with the rhythm section, and if the vocal here is perhaps fractionally less swinging than those recorded live it is far and away the best singing on the date. *Blue Moon*, a pleasant enough tune, is butchered by a Grissom vocal so grotesque it must have been intended as an assault on the hit parade. In between the extravagant and eccentric singing, Nance contributes a tasteful violin solo; there is a refreshing feeling about this chorus which may not be due entirely to its context. The group here consists of Grissom, Nance and rhythm. For the five-minute *Lady Be Good*, Nance switches to trumpet and Procope (alto sax) and Jackson (trombone) are added. Grissom has four choruses, and even on an uptempo performance, when choruses pass quickly, this does seem four too many. Procope and Jackson have one chorus each and Nance two, all good without being outstanding. The drumming by Black is excellent throughout.

The full Ellington band was in the studio for the next session, and the first number recorded was a new Ellington tone poem of standard three-minute length, *Ultra De Luxe*. This is full of haunting harmonies and brooding tone colors; Carney, Hamilton, Nance, and Gonsalves are heard in solos which are subservient to Ellington's overall design. For some reason, Ellington again brought in arrangements from outside sources at this time and, as in the middle forties, Dick Vance was given a number of assignments. His score of *Flying Home* is in the spirit of Lionel Hampton's big band, which had had such a success with the number, and the driving performance by the Ellington band is in greatest possible contrast to the gentle *Ultra De Luxe*. On *Flying Home*, the soloists are Hamilton, Terry, and Anderson and although they all play well, the most impressive feature is the quality of the fiery ensemble playing in an orthodox big band style. The full impact of the outstanding trumpet section is certainly felt here.

Three recordings featuring Grissom follow. None is particularly noteworthy, and only one is of an Ellington song. *September Song* has a spot of Hamilton behind the vocal, *What More Can I Say?* (by Ellington) has some impassioned plunger-muted Nance trumpet behind Grissom's opening chorus, and *Coquette* features Terry with plunger in a similar role, as well as a touch of Procope's clarinet. It sometimes seems that the band, in addition to recording the myriad compositions of their leader, has recorded virtually every well-known jazz standard. Their recording of *Moten Swing* can be found behind the second of Grissom's vocal choruses on *Coquette*. This is one of Grissom's better recordings, and while the singing is not too secure, his view of the song has a sharp satirical edge, and he is backed by a swinging band performance. The *Honeysuckle Rose* which concludes the session is the standard Ellington score featuring Hamilton on clarinet—he displays his customary skill and again the brass play with truly remarkable fire.

Capitol sessions on December 28 and 29 conclude the band's studio activities for 1953. These produced one piano solo and three band items. The solo is the rather slight *Night Time*, a pleasant trifle with a Latin American rhythm. The band follows this with another Vance arrangement, this time of *Stompin' At The Savoy*, given a driving performance much in the manner of *Flying Home*. The soloists are Hamilton, Terry, Carney, Gonsalves and, briefly, Rick Henderson. Ellington's own *Don't Ever Say Goodbye* could hardly be in greater contrast. This is a characteristic Ellington ballad, played by the band in an arrangement which recalls the conventional big band styles of ten or fifteen years earlier. Willie Cook, muted, plays the theme in that clean-cut way of his, and then the pianist and the band take over. The alto-led sax section shows its class even in this Hodges-less period. The final title from 1953 is a remake of the 1927 *Black And Tan Fantasy*. This must be considered one of the finest of all versions of this Ellington classic. Ray Nance's playing of the solo trumpet parts is an outstanding example of the kind of creative remodeling which was the hallmark of the leading Ellington musicians. His playing is second only to that of Bubber Miley on this work, his most sensitive interpretation of the two-chorus solo being notable for tonal shading, beauty of phrasing, and strong emotional flavor. The other soloists are Procope, on alto on the second theme and on clarinet during the blues solo sequence, Ellington himself in a rather playful mood, and Jackson, who here proves a worthy successor to Tricky Sam Nanton.

During January and February 1954, the Ellington band recorded six more titles in the Capitol Chicago studios. *Frivolous Banta*, Ellington's only composition written to feature Rick Henderson, is a conventional swinger with some skilled alto playing in the then modern manner. Joe Garland's famous *In The Mood* is given a very casual arrangement and performance, with solos by Terry, Procope, Hamilton and Nance. The Procope alto solo, with its unusual vibrato, is a real oddity; it apparently came about when Ellington heard Procope fooling around in this fashion while warming up. A rather more familiar item came next, the Buck Clayton arrangement of *One O'Clock Jump* which the band had been using for the past decade. Rather surprisingly, this Capitol recording is the first made for public release. The solos are by Ellington, Hamilton (on tenor sax), Woodman, Gonsalves, and Nance. Only a below-form Nance fails to reach the general level of excellence, and the band work is both relaxed and spirited: the brass section roars to fine effect here.

The session mate to *One O'Clock Jump* is an equally famous blues, *Things Ain't What They Used To Be*. This is the long version already heard in a 1951 broadcast with an extension in the form of an eight-chorus tenor solo by Gonsalves. Such marathons became popular as a result of the success of the tenor extravaganzas by such musicians as Illinois Jacquet and Flip Phillips with Norman Granz's "Jazz At The Philharmonic." As we have seen, Ellington started to use them in the early fifties; their frequency in the Ellington output increased sharply after the great success of the Gonsalves sequence in *Diminuendo And Crescendo In Blue* at the 1956 Newport Jazz Festival. Musically, these marathons can be very monotonous, and they certainly do not show Gonsalves at his best. The tenor solo at the end of the Capitol *Things Ain't What They Used To Be* is a superior example of the genre, but in no way compares in terms of musical richness or emotional content with the Gonsalves blues solos in a more restrained mood. The first part of the performance, which uses the 1945 arrangement, offers a fine example of big band blues playing. Solos are by Procope, with his pleasantly rooty alto style; Cook, whose balanced conception is matched by superb execution; and Woodman, in one of his most fiery statements.

Two more remakes followed: *Happy-Go-Lucky Local* and *Rockin' In Rhythm*. The former had been reintroduced into the performing repertoire owing to the huge public success of *Night Train*. This piece was a rhythm-and-blues hit for Buddy Morrow's band, with composer credit to one-time Ellington tenor saxophonist Jimmy Forrest, who also recorded it with his own group. It is actually one of the themes from *Happy-Go-Lucky Local*, with an added interlude. When the 1954 Ellington band set the old engine in motion again, it had become even more rickety, and it protests vigorously at the slightly faster ride it is given here. The brakes are more rusty, and Anderson's trumpet shrieks a loud protest as the train draws to a halt. This is fine, rugged blues music, and the band plays with uninhibited verve and obvious enjoyment. These qualities are also marked in the playing of *Rockin' In Rhythm*, one of the few Ellington numbers never out of the regular performing repertoire—it is something of a surprise to realize that this 1954 Capitol recording is the first made for public release since 1931. Certainly Ellington collectors were surprised to find that the gentle medium-tempo stomp of the early thirties had been transformed into a romping, roaring essay for modern big band, played with overwhelming power and drive. (The noncommercial recordings of *Rockin' In Rhythm* show that the transformation was gradual, but these were not known to the collectors of the mid-fifties, so the contrast between old and new was stark. We can sense the impact by playing one of the original versions and following it with the 1954 Capitol.) Amid the roaring excitement, we should note that Carney has taken over Bigard's old clarinet solo and Jackson that of Nanton. Yet again, this is a triumph of band playing, a sure indication to those with ears that Ellington's was still a great jazz ensemble, still the best of the big bands by a considerable margin. The version of *Rockin' In Rhythm* selected for issue by Capitol was a rehearsal run-through, considered more exciting than the final, more carefully played take. An alternative has been issued on an Up-To-Date album, which also includes valuable second takes of *Ultra De Luxe* and *Flying Home*; this *Rockin' In Rhythm*, more staid than the standard one, may well be the version originally intended for release. The last title from this session is *Fallin' Like A Raindrop*, a pleasant Ellington song with the composer's piano and Carney's baritone in the melodic solo roles and an orchestration full of Ellington pastel effects.

Anderson's playing on *Happy-Go-Lucky Local* and *Rockin' In Rhythm* is worth some consideration. Cat is often praised for performances like *Coloratura* and the later *Madness In Great Ones* because in them he is performing Ellington's unorthodox concert music and the artistic aims are clear, while his high-note contributions to more orthodox scores are frequently decried as tasteless. But Anderson adds unique excitement to the music—unique, because in place of the usual violence of high-note trumpet endings he provides wit and humor. The train effects on *Happy-Go-Lucky Local* are both programmatic and amusing, and Anderson's sudden eruption from the driving ensemble on *Rockin' In Rhythm* adds tremendously to the excitement of the climax.

Two months after these largely retrospective triumphs,

the first in the Capitol series of Ellington attempts at juke box hits, *Bunny Hop Mambo* and *Isle Of Capri,* were made. Their banality indicates the degree of Ellington's desperation at this time, as the early fifties revival of interest in his music gave way to rounds of one-night stands before poor audiences. All things are relative, however, and if the Ellington version of *Bunny Hop Mambo* sounds dull, one should hear the actual hit record of this tune by its composer, Ray Anthony. (His version was also made for Capitol, and when the British World Record Club put out an Ellington LP called *Band Call* from this period, the Anthony recording was used in error.) The Ellington version has solos by Duke and Hamilton (clarinet) before Anderson's high-note trumpet supplies a satirical conclusion. *Isle Of Capri* is turned into a mambo but does not have the sardonic edge of *Bunny Hop Mambo;* even the use of Carney and Jackson fails to enliven a very dull recording. Two new compositions were recorded at this April 1954 session: Strayhorn's *All Day Long* and Ellington's *Band Call.* Both are fastish jump numbers featuring Terry as the only horn soloist. On the Strayhorn piece Terry plays the theme at the outset on open trumpet, displaying great sensitivity and an excellent, distinctive tone. (Theme statements were not often given to Terry, and *All Day Long* is of particular interest because of this; otherwise, it is a fairly ordinary performance.) *Band Call* is based on a piano lick used by Duke to call the band back to the stand after an intermission. The piano playing is much in the vein of the solos recorded the previous year, with the brief ensembles and the trumpet solo sounding almost like afterthoughts. The final title from the session is the best, a superb *C Jam Blues,* one of the very finest on record. Ellington, Nance (violin), Cook, Gonsalves, Jackson, and Hamilton are the soloists—all at their best in a performance also notable for the vigor of the band playing.

Although the *It Don't Mean A Thing* from June 1954, first released on Pickwick International, lasts over five minutes, it is an edited version; the complete take issued on Up-To-Date runs for over ten minutes. Outstanding features are the long chase sequences, first by Nance and Cook on trumpets, then by Hamilton and Gonsalves on tenors. Capitol only issued one title from this session, the first of what became an obligatory series by Ellington drummers attempting to recapture the success of Bellson's *Skin Deep.* This item, *Gonna Tan Your Hide,* features Dave Black, and the musical interest is low. This was yet another Ellington disc which failed to become a hit record. But Ellington, in the face of continuing financial losses, was still trying, and the next Capitol date, done in Chicago on September 1, produced several more attempts at the charts—desperately uncharacteristic music by Ellington standards. The session opens with Ellington adopting his best cocktail-lounge piano style for *Smile,* the Charlie Chaplin song which had given Nat Cole a big hit; Nance's violin and Carney's baritone make brief appearances before a huge brass climax, Cat Anderson and all, which simply leads back to more cocktail piano. The next title is probably the most uncharacteristic Ellington record since *Ragamuffin Romeo* of 1930: *Echo Tango* might be recognized as an Ellington recording from Carney's tone on baritone sax, but this is the only clue. The alternative title of the piece, *Tyrolean Tango,* indicates the genre. One could imagine the band dressed in Tyrolean costumes for this number—a sight which would doubtless have been more interesting than the music.

More of the Ellington cocktail piano is heard on another non-Ellington pop tune, *If I Gave My Heart To You,* at this time a hit for Doris Day. Once more, a very unambitious arrangement is used, and as on *Smile,* the sheer volume of the trumpet section's playing would seem to rule out popular approval; maybe Duke had Stan Kenton's pop-tune successes on Capitol in mind at such moments. Ellington's own *Chile Bowl* is a somewhat half-hearted attempt at blending choruses in Latin American rhythms with medium-tempo swinging sections. Ellington plays nice piano here and Nance has a twelve-bar chorus on open trumpet. Finally, in another remake, Duke conjures up *Bakiff* from 1941. This is an extended version with rich and varied scoring and much humorous Nance violin, accompanied by spiky piano and an augmented percussion section. John Sanders plays beautifully in the theme statement originally handled by the composer, Juan Tizol. The following month a final, desperate bid was made for a commercial hit with *Twelfth Street Rag Mambo,* which boasts an arrangement as bizarre as its title. Sanity is restored by a new version of *Caravan,* with Sanders again on valve trombone; the other soloists are Hamilton (clarinet) and Nance (violin). Duke is still using the arrangement which had become standard in the mid-forties, and the performance includes some pungent piano playing.

The band's final Capitol sessions took place in Chicago in May 1955, a year in which the Ellington band hit its lowest level in terms of popularity and income. The two titles issued from the first of these dates are both trumpet features. Anderson's *La Virgen De La Macarena* is an arrangement of traditional Spanish bullfight music—one of a series of numbers on which Anderson's considerable talents were frittered away in displays of virtuosity on musically weak material. Clark Terry is heard in an arrangement of *Harlem Air Shaft* which had been used a few years earlier as a feature for Harold Baker. Well though Terry plays here, one feels, with Cootie Williams's fiery work on the 1940 original inevitably brought to mind, that such cool, emotionally detached trumpet playing is not right for this composition. It is also unfortunate that Ellington is here using one of his best orchestral scores as a backdrop for a trumpet showcase. Yet such is the strength of *Harlem Air Shaft* that had we never heard another version, this would no doubt have been hailed as a great piece of big band jazz.

The final Capitol date was on May 18, 1955. Three more showcases were recorded—Ellington's *Serious Serenade,* for

Carney, plus two scores by Hamilton, *Clarinet Melodrama* for himself, and *Theme For Trambeam* for Woodman. The best of these is the Ellington composition, one of the most attractive of Carney features, with strong melodic lines superbly realized by the master baritone saxophonist. *Clarinet Melodrama* is as stagey as its title suggests and features highly expert clarinet playing in a composition of some variety. *Theme For Trambeam* is less ambitious and a rather more successful composition for the most part, though the long coda offers no more than demonstrations of Woodman's phenomenal range and his agility in jumping big intervals.

According to Dave Dexter, a jazz journalist turned record company executive who was responsible for Ellington's Capitol recordings, at this final date Duke slyly produced a number called *Discontented Blues* to indicate his imminent break with the label. Location recordings show that this number—also known as *Trombone Trio*, *Daddy's Blues*, and *Bass-ment*—was already in the book, but no Capitol recording has ever been issued or listed in the discographies.

* * *

The beautiful *Satin Doll* of 1953 and the admirable *Serious Serenade* of May 1955 stand at the extremes of the series of recordings Ellington made for Capitol. As often happened with Ellington, a contract with a particular record company marked off a distinct period in the history of his band. Louis Bellson and Willie Smith left before he joined Capitol; Johnny Hodges and Sam Woodyard are in the band on the first post-Capitol recordings. These personnel changes are important milestones in the story of the Duke Ellington Orchestra.

As we have seen, the Capitol recordings have not been well received by jazz critics. An exception is the collection of piano solos, which has always been highly regarded. Yet the Capitol period produced many gems of orchestral Ellingtonia. Shortsighted critics were frightened off by *Isle Of Capri Mambo* and the like, but another reason for the neglect of the Capitol output is that at the time the jazz world had its mind and ears on other things. The renaissance of Count Basie was under way, and this band seemed to many jazz lovers more significant and more "modern" than what Ellington was doing. The fact that the Basie phenomenon was in many ways a false dawn could not possibly have been seen then. Apart from Basie, contemporary jazz, now very much a minority interest, was dominated by a rather bland music which was very much favored by the writers for the modish magazines. Against such a background, the Ellington Capitol output stands out for its vitality and for the continuing creativity of its soloists. The work of these individual musicians is framed at the very least by good arrangements and at best by scores permeated by Ellington's genius.

It is a pity that Capitol did not record Ellington's new concert work of 1955, *Night Creature*, written for the band and symphony orchestra. It took him eight years to find a company that would record and issue this work. The comparative shortage of new Ellington compositions in the Capitol period is offset by the brilliance of the remakes and the outstanding recordings of such non-Ellington scores as *One O'Clock Jump* and *Flying Home*. These last show aspects of the orchestra's versatility which had not previously been heard on commercial recordings.

A final word about the Capitol issues. Ellington was with Columbia when microgroove recordings were introduced, and that company's policy had been for most of his issues to be in the form of singles. Only a limited number of specially recorded items, such as those for the *Masterpieces* and *Ellington Uptown* collections, were made for LP. After the Capitol period this pattern was reversed, with the bulk of Ellington's recordings made for LP, with just the odd single supplementing the LPs up to 1959. The Capitols represent the halfway stage in this process. Roughly half of them came out originally on singles, the other half on LPs. As with the Columbias, many of the singles were later collated as LP sets. Sometimes these have been mixed up with items from the original Capitol LPs, while at the same time many of the LPs continued to be reissued in their original format, usually also retaining their original titles. For the purposes of identification, therefore, the details of the Capitol LPs as originally released are listed below; the list should also be useful to the collector who wishes to avoid duplication. (All issues are 12-inch LPs unless otherwise stated.)

PREMIÈRED BY ELLINGTON

This LP has been issued in 10-inch form only and contains the following tracks: *My Old Flame*, *Three Little Words*, *I Can't Give You Anything But Love*, *Liza*, *Flamingo*, *Stardust*, *Stormy Weather*, *Cocktails For Two*.

THE DUKE PLAYS ELLINGTON

This was originally a 10-inch LP containing the following eight tracks: *Who Knows?*, *B Sharp Blues*, *Passion Flower*, *Reflections In D*, *Prelude To A Kiss*, *In A Sentimental Mood*, *Things Ain't What They Used To Be*, *Janet*. The later 12-inch version has become standard and has four additional items: *Retrospection*, *Dancers In Love*, *Melancholia*, *All Too Soon*. All these solos date from April 1953. Some late editions of this LP also include the two trio items from December 1953: *Kinda Dukish* and *Night Time*.

ELLINGTON '55

Rockin' In Rhythm, *Black And Tan Fantasy*, *Stompin' At The Savoy*, *In The Mood*, *One O'Clock Jump*, *Honeysuckle Rose*, *Happy-Go-Lucky Local*, *Flying Home*.

DANCE TO THE DUKE

C Jam Blues, *Orson*, *Caravan*, *Kinda Dukish* (trio), *Bakiff*, *Frivolous Banta*, *Things Ain't What They Used To Be*, *Night Time* (trio).

ELLINGTON SHOWCASE
Harlem Air Shaft, Serious Serenade, Clarinet Melodrama, Blossom, Theme For Trambeam, Gonna Tan Your Hide, Falling Like A Rain Drop, La Virgen De La Macarena, Don't Ever Say Goodbye, The Big Drag.

* * *

A number of live recordings by the band from this period have been issued on disc, with a rather more generous sample of music from dance dates than is usually the case. Such music has a very relaxed air, as typified by two excellent recordings of *Liza* which use the same arrangement as the Capitol version. Each has a long and fascinating piano introduction by Duke—three choruses on one and two on the other. There are also fine recordings of *Creole Love Call* and *H'ya Sue*, the latter with the Hamilton tenor sax marathon attached, as well as a rather unexpected *Change My Ways* which shows that this pleasant melody survived in the Ellington book, if not in the public's affections, for a few years. *Please Be Kind* had been a Willie Smith feature, but the 1953 recording finds Russell Procope in the solo role. From the same year there is a particularly relaxed performance of *Boo-dah* and one of *Stomp, Look And Listen* with a piano introduction which highlights the piece's affinity with stride piano techniques. There is also a second superb Gonsalves *Warm Valley* from a 1953 dance date and, from a similar source two years later, the first recording of Paul's two-tempo version of *Body And Soul*.

On April 30, 1955, the band gave a concert at The Armory, an ex-Army building converted into an auditorium in Washington, D.C. Mention has already been made of the version of *Harlem* from this source. Other numbers issued from the concert include *Happy-Go-Lucky Local*; a six-minute *Perdido* (with many of the features of the 1952 Columbia, including the chase between the four trumpets and Woodman); *All The Things You Are*, featuring Rick Henderson; *Just Squeeze Me* with a Nance vocal; the Anderson showcase *La Virgen De La Macarena*, and a seven-minute *"A" Train*, similar to the 1952 Columbia, with Nance taking the vocal instead of Betty Roché and including the long tenor solo by Gonsalves. But perhaps the most interesting item from this concert is a blues piano improvisation which Ellington played to close the proceedings. Accompanied by the rhythm section only and taken at a loping slow to medium tempo, it demonstrates Ellington's very personal mastery of the blues idiom and his remarkable inventive capacity. His harmonic and rhythmic resources seem endless. The piece is called *John Sanders Blues*, but we do not know whether or not this was because Sanders suggested the musical idea to Duke. This was a kind of performance which had never been heard from Ellington before; happily it was followed by several blues piano solos in a similar vein over the next few years.

* * *

After the final Capitol dates of May 1955, the band was not in the recording studios again until the following January. In the meantime, an important change had occurred in the saxophone section when Johnny Hodges returned to replace Rick Henderson. The performances by the orchestra since 1951 had shown that Hodges was not *essential* to Duke's music; even so, his qualities as a band musician and his long experience of Ellington's methods made his return a major event. The new bassist, Jimmy Woode, was a player with the knack of finding exactly the right note, phrase, or sequence for any Ellington context.

The band also had a new drummer, Sam Woodyard. After a trio of rather conventional drummers in Bellson, Ballard, and Black, Ellington had acquired a percussionist of pronounced character and eccentricity in Woodyard. As Duke himself observed on more than one occasion, Woodyard was a swinger, but while his initial contributions to Ellington's recorded output were universally welcomed, in later years he became a controversial figure. He was not a musician of the "reliable craftsman" variety, but rather an emotional artist who could on one night make the *Harlem* suite swing as much as *One O'Clock Jump*, and on the next sound pedestrian, dull, and heavy even when the rest of the band was swinging. The main reason why Woodyard was criticized so severely was that he was not a fashionable kind of musician, his basic, "primitive" approach being in direct contrast to the increasingly intricate and complex methods of the modern drummers of the day. In retrospect, we can see that Woodyard was the last major Ellingtonian recruited by Duke. Cootie Williams and Lawrence Brown were later to rejoin the band, and Duke kept up his supply of marvellous bass players. But Woodyard was the last musician to come into the band who could make it sound different by his very presence; others who had this quality include Johnny Hodges, Harry Carney, Cat Anderson, Lawrence Brown, and of course, Sonny Greer. Louis Bellson's tremendous dynamism and drive had their very positive effects on the music, but the overall effect of Bellson's drumming was to make the Ellington Orchestra sound less distinctive and more like other big bands. With Hodges and Woodyard added to its ranks, the Ellington band which recorded for Columbia and Bethlehem in early 1956 sounded very different from that of the last Capitol sessions. (Actually, the band with Hodges and Woodyard recorded a session for the United States Treasury Department in October 1955, but only a handful of titles have been issued.) The full personnel at this time was:

Trumpets: Cat Anderson, Willie Cook, Clark Terry, Ray Nance (also violin and vocal).

Trombones: Britt Woodman, Quentin Jackson, John Sanders (valve trombone).

Reeds: Russell Procope (alto sax, clarinet); Johnny Hodges (alto sax); Paul Gonsalves (tenor sax); Jimmy Hamilton (clarinet, tenor sax); Harry Carney (baritone sax, clarinet, bass clarinet).

Rhythm: Duke Ellington (piano); Jimmy Woods (bass); Sam Woodyard (drums); Billy Strayhorn (deputy pianist).

Vocal: Jimmy Grissom.

* * *

The first three Ellington LPs recorded in 1956 were done on a freelance basis, one for Columbia and two for Bethlehem. The Columbia set, *Blue Rose*, is a collaboration with the popular singer Rosemary Clooney, the first of many such meetings with artists from outside the Ellington orbit which we find in the LP era. In the next dozen years, Ellington was to record sessions with artists as diverse as John Coltrane and Frank Sinatra, Charles Mingus and Ella Fitzgerald. The Clooney LP has generally been disregarded by jazz buffs, who have been inclined to classify it among Ellington's purely commercial ventures. No doubt the record was made to sell, but musically Miss Clooney does no harm to the Ellington songs selected. She sings in a relaxed and straightforward fashion which gives the melodies room to breathe, and the unpretentious manner of her approach is preferable by far to the convoluted distortions of many latter-day "jazz" singers. The band accompanies her in magnificent fashion, every one of the standard Ellington ballads provoking new ideas from Ellington and Strayhorn.

The impact of the return of Hodges is most marked in the saxophone section playing in the theme statement of *I'm Checkin' Out, Goombye*, where the tone, energy and zest of the section work are outstanding. The way Woodyard kicks the band along here indicates that new things are afoot in the rhythm section. Hodges is the soloist on the LP's only non-vocal track, a remake of Strayhorn's *Passion Flower*. *Mood Indigo* has a long solo improvisation by Willie Cook on muted trumpet and the now established trio voicing for this number is used—two muted trombones and bass clarinet. The title tune, *Blue Rose*, is the only new composition in the set and proves to be a pleasantly melodic medium-tempo piece to which Clooney contributes a wordless vocal. Perhaps the pick of the items in the Clooney-Ellington collection is *Grievin'*, a revival which features a totally different arrangement from that on the 1939 original. Carney, Gonsalves, and briefly Hodges are heard in addition to the singer, but Anderson's contribution is astounding. Making an urgent entry after the vocal chorus, the trumpeter contrives to fit a passage in the highest register of the instrument into this ballad performance without any sense of incongruity. The selection of numbers on the *Blue Rose* LP maintains a nice balance between Ellington standards and his lesser-known songs. In addition to the titles mentioned the set includes *Sophisticated Lady* (with Ellington as the only soloist); *Me And You* (Nance); *Hey, Baby* (Carney); *I Let A Song Go Out Of My Heart* (no solos); *It Don't Mean A Thing* (Hodges, Hamilton on tenor, Terry, and Carney); and *I Got It Bad* (no solos).

The band recorded these numbers on January 23 and 27, 1956, and the vocals were added at a later date. In addition to the material included in the *Blue Rose* LP, three further items from these sessions have been released. Columbia has issued *If You Were In My Place* and Up-To-Date two alternative takes—*Passion Flower* and *Hey, Baby*—both nonvocal, the second title clearly in the form in which Ellington left the music, with room for Clooney's vocal. Although the vocals are pleasant, the prime impression of the music from these sessions is the superb form of the band, each section sounding full and rich and never seeming to miss a trick in the interpretation of the music.

* * *

If *Blue Rose* was aimed at the popular music audience, the two LPs for Bethlehem which followed were clearly directed at the jazz market. The first, *Historically Speaking: The Duke*, presents a continuation of the Ellington retrospectives which had been a feature of the Capitol recordings. Among the Capitol output, the following Ellington compositions from the mid-twenties to the mid-forties had been rerecorded: *Warm Valley*, *Just A-Settin' And A-Rockin'*, *It Don't Mean A Thing*, *Black And Tan Fantasy*, *Things Ain't What They Used To Be*, *Happy-Go-Lucky Local*, *Rockin' In Rhythm*, *C Jam Blues*, *Bakiff*, *Caravan*, and *Harlem Air Shaft*.

Historically Speaking: The Duke is made up of a further selection of material from the same period plus two new numbers. From the twenties come *East St. Louis Toodle-oo* and *Creole Love Call*, from the thirties *Stompy Jones* and *The Jeep Is Jumpin'*, and from the forties no less than six numbers: *Jack The Bear*, *In A Mellotone*, *Ko-Ko*, *Midriff*, *Stomp, Look And Listen*, and *Unbooted Character*. (It should be noted that the last title had never before appeared on a commercial record, although it had been featured on transcriptions and V-Discs plus recordings of broadcasts, concerts, and dances. The two new numbers are *Lonesome Lullaby* and *Upper Manhattan Medical Group*.

The performances on this LP continue in the spirit evident in the orchestra's contribution to the *Blue Rose* set. *East St. Louis Toodle-oo* sets the tone with a magnificent muted trumpet solo by Ray Nance on the first theme. The second theme is here taken over by the other three members of the trumpet section—playing open—and they produce an affectionate lampoon of twenties jazz, accomplished with humor, wit, and no little skill. Nance's reading of the Miley part here is matched by his version of Bubber's solo in *Creole Love*

Call, another beautiful band performance which also features Procope's clarinet in solo and Cook and Hodges in obbligato roles. The multicolored coda is superbly executed.

This version of *Stompy Jones* is the first recorded commercially by the band since the 1934 original, although again air-shot and transcription versions show the gradual evolution of the arrangement. In place of the rough, vigorous exuberance of the original, this interpretation opens in superbly poised fashion with Woodman's trombone in dialogue with muted trumpets as an aperitif and a theme statement from Hamilton's emotionally detached clarinet as the first course. The warm voices of Nance's trumpet and Carney's baritone precede a juxtaposition of the contrasting trombone styles of Woodman and Jackson, their choruses divided by a witty ensemble interlude. Finally, Anderson enters in his most magisterial manner to drive the performance to an exciting conclusion over the traditional band riffs, which are decorated by Hamilton's swirling clarinet. This version of *The Jeep Is Jumpin'* is based on the 1938 recording by the Hodges unit, and the saxophonist is heavily featured.

Jack The Bear and *Ko-Ko* are not up to the standard of the original 1940 recordings, although the former has some nice moments. *Ko-Ko* is the disappointment of the set, a careless performance taken at the faster tempo which the band had adopted for this number soon after the 1940 Victor recording. *In A Mellotone*, with magnificent solos by Nance and Hodges and wonderful and expressive playing by the trombone and saxophone sections, follows the outline of the original pretty closely, but the spirit is vigorous and new. Strayhorn's *Midriff* is superior to the 1946 Victor and indeed the finest version on record; Nance is once more the outstanding soloist and the work of the saxophones, led by Hodges, is again superlative.

Stomp, Look And Listen almost became one of those numbers which combined below-average Ellington musical content with a longer-than-average stay in the repertoire. The original 1947 recording is a pleasant enough swing-style performance, but by 1956 the tempo had speeded up sufficiently to introduce an element of farce. The resulting piece of big band virtuosity sounds like a satire on bebop at times, although Woodyard's drumming, hardly ever at its best at such a tempo, fails to substantiate this impression. Cook and Nance have a chase chorus here, and Hamilton and Woodman also solo before Anderson delivers a telling climax. By contrast, *Unbooted Character* proceeds in leisurely, relaxed fashion; Ellington and Hamilton have good solos and the concluding trumpet chase between Nance and Cook is full of poised and swinging music. The new compositions form a contrasting pair: *Lonesome Lullaby* is one of Duke's rather melancholy tone poems, with Nance's violin and Hamilton's clarinet heard against the band, while *Upper Manhattan Medical Group* is a rather unconventional swinger by Strayhorn with Cook as principal soloist and Hamilton and Carney in minor roles. It provides a fine ending to a celebrated Ellington collection. Nance is the star of the set, but all the soloists are in excellent form, and the ensemble playing is of the finest Ellington quality. It is some measure of the solo strength of the band at this time that such outstanding players as Terry and Gonsalves do not take a single bar of solo between them in the course of these ten performances.

The companion Bethlehem LP, *Duke Ellington Presents*, is less consistent in quality. It contains an assortment of Ellington revivals and popular standards rounded off by a rousing end-of-session medium-tempo blues. The Ellington retrospective continues with *Everything But You*, *Frustration*, *Cotton Tail*, and *Day Dream*. On *Everything But You*, Jimmy Grissom produces one of his better vocals over a score which is conventional for Ellington but on which the band swings in impressive fashion. *Frustration* is the Carney feature from 1944 in a superbly played new interpretation. *Cotton Tail* is taken at a ridiculously fast tempo, which once again brings out the worst in Woodyard's drumming. The trumpet and reed sections show a hair-raising kind of virtuosity here, Gonsalves gives a frantic rendition of the featured tenor solo, and Duke, as usual in this number, improvises a new eight-bar solo. *Day Dream* is an excellent new version of one of Strayhorn's best Hodges showcases.

Of the standards, a rather vulgar *Summertime* featuring Anderson over a Latin beat is the least interesting. *Laura* is given a deep, brooding arrangement quite different from that used on the 1945 D.E.T.S. broadcast. Paul Gonsalves is featured here in a masterly ballad interpretation.

The choice tracks on *Ellington Presents* are *I Can't Get Started* and *My Funny Valentine*. It would be difficult to imagine two more contrasting approaches to popular standards. The first is a casual, off-the-cuff improvised performance of the kind usually offered by small jazz groups, the second a meticulously scored orchestral tone poem. Ellington opens *I Can't Get Started* with an ingenious piano chorus in which the theme is stated and variations sketched in an easygoing manner. Nance sings a vocal chorus with his usual skill backed by the rich tones of Procope's low-register clarinet, then he takes a half-chorus of humorous violin before rounding off the piece with a vocal climax in the Louis Armstrong manner. Woodyard on brushes is a tower of strength in this performance. In Strayhorn's arrangement of *My Funny Valentine*, Hamilton is featured in the first of the two choruses, Jackson, with a beautifully poised eight bars of trumpet by Nance, in the second. The soloists are supported by a highly colored orchestral score of breathtaking beauty and imagination, played quite perfectly.

The remaining standards are of less interest. Hamilton plays *Deep Purple* in his cool, detached manner, and Procope is given a rare opportunity to demonstrate his skills as an alto soloist in the arrangement of *Indian Summer*, which Willie Smith had recorded with the Coronets in 1951. The final

Blues opens with functional piano from Duke, setting the scene for a long solo sequence of Hamilton (tenor), Woodman, Terry, Hodges, Nance, and Gonsalves; Terry returns to trade fours with Woodyard, and Anderson provides a high-note conclusion.

These Bethlehem LPs gave a clear indication that the Ellington band was at one of its peaks. The next time it appeared on record would be to inaugurate a new exclusive Columbia contract with an album which would spread the news of this Ellington renaissance far beyond the small community of jazz record collectors.

Outstanding Recordings

1. Mercer Recordings

Cat Walk, *Moonlight Fiesta* (both takes), *She* (all with The Coronets)

2. Columbia Recordings

Fancy Dan, V.I.P.'s Boogie, Monologue, Smada, Bensonality, Harlem, Controversial Suite, I Love My Lovin' Lover (both takes), *Take The "A" Train, The Mooche, Perdido, Me And You, I'm Checkin' Out, Goombye, Grievin', Mood Indigo* (the last four titles with Rosemary Clooney)

3. Capitol Recordings

Satin Doll, Cocktails For Two, Liza, My Old Flame, I Can't Give You Anything But Love, Stormy Weather, Stardust, Three Little Words, Boo-Dah, Warm Valley, all twelve recordings on *The Duke Plays Ellington* LP, *Kinda Dukish* (trio), *Ultra De Luxe, Flying Home, Coquette, Night Time* (trio), *Stompin' At The Savoy, Don't Ever Say Goodbye, Black And Tan Fantasy, One O'Clock Jump, Things Ain't What They Used To Be, Happy-Go-Lucky Local, Rockin' In Rhythm, C Jam Blues, Band Call, Bakiff, Serious Serenade*

4. Bethlehem Recordings

East St. Louis Toodle-oo, Creole Love Call, Stompy Jones, In A Mellotone, Midriff, Unbooted Character, Lonesome Lullaby, Upper Manhattan Medical Group, I Can't Get Started, Frustration, My Funny Valentine, Day Dream, Blues

5. Concert Recordings

Basin Street Blues (Carnegie Hall, January 5, 1952), *Harlem* (Seattle, March 25, 1952), *Perdido, Happy-Go-Lucky Local, Harlem, John Sanders Blues* (solo) (Washington Armory, April 30, 1955)

6. Broadcasts and Recordings from Dances

Take The "A" Train, Great Times (January 2, 1951), *Sultry Serenade, Just A-Settin' And A-Rockin'* (May 5, 1951), *Night Walk, Things Ain't What They Used To Be* (June 11, 1951), *Fancy Dan, Harlem Air Shaft* (June 23, 1951), *Warm Valley, Boy Meets Horn, Diminuendo And Crescendo In Blue* (June 30, 1951), *Fancy Dan* (August 19, 1951), *W.C., Chelsea Bridge, Bensonality, Cotton Tail, Moonlight Fiesta, Lady Of The Lavender Mist, One O'Clock Jump* (March 10, 1952), *Black Beauty* (solo), *Fancy Dan, Tenderly* (March 22, 1952), *Felanges, C Jam Blues, Passion Flower* (April 29, 1952), the complete broadcasts of July 30 and August 13, 1952, *Liza, Creole Love Call, Booh-Dah, H'ya Sue, Change My Ways, Stomp, Look And Listen, Warm Valley, Sultry Serenade* (April 1953), *Liza* (April 29, 1954), *Body And Soul* (June 11, 1955)

Note

This selection covers the period when record companies gradually switched their jazz releases from singles to LPs. In the above list, individual titles have been cited as in previous chapters, even if these are from LPs. *In subsequent chapters, complete LPs rather than individual titles will be cited in the Outstanding Recordings sections.* Complete LP titles are listed in italic capital letters. For the period under review the following LPs (which include some of the titles cited above) would be included. (*N.B.*—In this instance, collections of previously issued singles and of concert and broadcast material are *not* included: see Appendix 2 for details of these):

1. Columbia Recordings

ELLINGTON UPTOWN
ELLINGTON UPTOWN IN HI FI (The only difference between these is the substitution of the *Controversial Suite* for *Harlem* on the latter.)
BLUE ROSE (with Rosemary Clooney)

2. Capitol Recordings

PREMIÈRED BY ELLINGTON (10-inch)
THE DUKE PLAYS ELLINGTON
ELLINGTON '55
DANCE DATE WITH THE DUKE

3. Bethlehem Recordings

HISTORICALLY SPEAKING THE DUKE
DUKE ELLINGTON PRESENTS

4. RCA Recordings

SEATTLE CONCERT

Chapter 21

Revolution and Evolution

THE DEPARTURE IN FEBRUARY 1951 of Lawrence Brown, Johnny Hodges, and Sonny Greer seemed to many people at that time to sound the death knell of the Duke Ellington Orchestra. The paucity of post-1947 Ellington on record in Britain and in Europe, plus the commercial nature of some of the records which were issued there, caused Ellington watchers far from the scene of action to rely unduly on reports in the jazz press. These were often written by people involved in the cult of modernity to whom Ellington was a rather curious survivor from the age of the Charleston. It was usual at this time for the Ellington situation to be described as a lot worse than it really was. So when Brown, Hodges, and Greer left, it seemed to many jazz followers a fatal blow to an already ailing orchestra. The Ellington technique of using the individual sounds and styles of his musicians as compositional components, and the understanding he had built up with the long-serving members of his band, made the idea of replacements for these men seem impossible. Johnny Hodges, for example, had a unique sound, and no other musician could bring such a tone to the saxophone section. Nor could any outsider replace Hodges's experience and expertise in the eccentric Ellington methods of music making. It would be equally impossible for Ellington to engage new musicians, no matter how skilled, who could come in to the band and assume the roles of Brown or Greer. Superficially, Greer seemed the least likely to be missed. His playing had become rather erratic and for the 1950 tour of Europe Duke had engaged a second drummer as cover against Greer's unreliability. Yet Greer was the only percussionist whom Duke had ever employed (other than short-term deputies) and, as was the case with Brown and Hodges, his sound had become totally identified with the Ellington style.

It was not without good reason that jazz musicians regarded Ellington as the greatest of all bandleaders. The most important factor in the 1951 situation was how Duke himself would react. What he did was to follow his previous practice—he made no attempt to replace the departed players with inferior imitators but hired good, experienced big band musicians as replacements. And then he simply carried on making Ellington music.

Ellington's orchestra was always the home of the eccentric and the unexpected. What other big band of the fifties and sixties would have featured a clarinet player like Russell Procope, who played in the New Orleans style? Equally anachronistic by normal standards was the playing of Greer in the Ellington band of the forties. Greer had become an oldfashioned stylist, yet he still sounded at home in a band which featured what were then considered "modern" musicians and which was a hotbed of creative innovation. His rightness stemmed in part from the fact that many of his techniques had been developed in response to the particular demands of Ellington music, and he seemed to have an instinctive understanding of Ellington's musical requirements. Greer was often criticized for heavy drumming, but Ellington's band was always based on a heavy rhythm section. Even when partnered by Oscar Pettiford, a pioneer "modern jazz" musician who had been featured in the first bop group to play outside Harlem, Greer sounded like the right drummer for Ellington's rhythm section.

Not least of Sonny's virtues was the way in which he would lie back and allow the band to relax and swing in a casual, nonchalant way; this is most noticeable on the recordings made at Ellington dance dates. To replace his long-serving percussionist, Ellington hired Louis Bellson, and this seemed a sensational signing at the time. That Bellson was a white musician playing in a black band was something of a talking point in 1951, but, more importantly, he was the stylistic antithesis of Greer, a master virtuoso of the new school of superefficient big band drummers. No casual-sounding collection of mysteriously appropriate tone colors emerged from Bellson's kit: all was precision and light. And he brought to the Ellington band a kind of drive which it had never had before. With that master disciplinarian Willie Smith leading the saxophones, a reconstituted trombone team of very high class, and a trumpet section which was to stabilize into one of the finest in jazz history, Bellson and Wendell Marshall found themselves in the engine room of a "new," bright-sounding Duke Ellington Orchestra. Now that Hodges and Brown had gone, some of the richness of ensemble texture had inevitably been lost, but the leaner sound fitted well with the fifties concept of jazz. Some subtlety had been lost, but the new men were inspired by the challenges and rewards of playing Ellington scores. This inspiration showed in the music. Not the least important factor was that Duke was delighted with his new band.

During 1951 the Ellington band played an engagement at Birdland in New York City which set the music world by the ear. The band suddenly became a favorite of the jazz press, and musicians spoke in awe of the spirit and precision with which the new band tackled Ellington music old and new. On the record front, the singles of *The Hawk Talks* and *Skin Deep* sold well and thus helped to publicize the band. There was no sign of a big band revival, but a much reduced roster of bands was touring the country. All seemed set for a new decade of Ellington popularity and prosperity. But fortunes changed with uncomfortable rapidity, and by the middle fifties the band was at an all-time low so far as finances were concerned, with Duke regularly making up the payroll from his composing royalties. Ellington always had the most expensive band in the business. The majority of his men were stars in their own right and needed pretty large financial inducements to stay on the road as sidemen. There were, of course, musical rewards too, although the soloist called upon to play the same feature once or twice nightly for months on end might begin to have reservations on that score. (Some time after Clark Terry had left the Ellington band, a jazz writer suggested to him that he must miss playing Ellington's marvellous music. Clark replied, with some seriousness behind the humor, that he sure did miss playing *Perdido* twice every night of his life.) The Ellington band's decline in popularity after the successes of the early fifties is only partly explained by the fickle nature of the jazz audience. The specialist jazz audience in itself was nowhere near big enough to keep a band as expensive as Ellington's in business 52 weeks a year, although its more vocal members frequently forgot this fact when criticizing Duke's musical policy.

The departure of Louis Bellson in early 1953 could have affected the band's popularity. Bellson was a considerable draw with his superb musicianship and showmanship, and of course the two Ellington hit records of the early fifties were of Bellson compositions, one of them a drum feature. But the loss of a sideman, even one so popular as Bellson, cannot itself account for this sharp decline. The main cause seems to have been that there simply were not enough outlets prepared to pay the kind of money Ellington needed; the band was not yet well enough established as a concert attraction on the one hand, while on the other the number of dance halls and theaters requiring a band of this size and style had dwindled to almost nil. This problem remained until July 1956, when Ellington's huge success at the Newport Jazz Festival established him as a major concert attraction. Another point is that by the middle fifties, the band had gone back into its now traditional casualness of manner after the sudden bout of self-imposed discipline in 1951, but this never seems to have alienated audiences apart from a rather prim segment of the jazz fraternity. The full story of this period will be known only if and when details of the financial aspects of the Ellington organization become public knowledge.

In late 1955 the band played an engagement which was probably the least distinguished and least musically interesting of its entire career, one which showed the desperate remedies Ellington needed in order to keep his band working. For the summer season, the Ellington Orchestra appeared in an Aquacades show at Flushing Meadows, Long Island, with substitutes for Willie Cook, Britt Woodman, Rick Henderson, Paul Gonsalves, and Dave Black. A string section, a second pianist, and two female harpists, who also did imitation swimming effects, augmented the band. After Ellington had delivered his famous *Medley Of Popular Hits*, the Aquacades conductor took over the musical direction and Duke went home. Earlier in the year, a series of Ellington concerts with the Symphony of the Air and the Philadelphia Symphony Orchestra had included the premiere of *Night Creature*, as well as revivals of *New World A-Comin'* and *Harlem*. These must have been the musical highlights of 1955 for Duke. In retrospect the situation is hardly credible. With typical resourcefulness Ellington took advantage of the regular hours the Aquacade show afforded him, enjoyed his free time and got on with writing music and, surprisingly even for this man of surprises, a play. Called *The Man With Four Sides*, it has never been produced. (A partial description and some quotations can be found in Mercer Ellington's *Duke Ellington In Person* [p. 113ff.].)

This is perhaps a good moment to pause, while considering a time when the struggle to keep the band together was so difficult, to review Duke Ellington's achievements simply as a bandleader. For little short of 50 years he had a band on the road. Occasionally, as when he was working on a film or during the British tour of 1948, it would be laid off for a period. But Ellington was a believer in working 52 weeks in the year and the band maintained a schedule close to this exhausting norm most of the time. Although it did have some prestigious residences—the Cotton Club in the band's early days and the Rainbow Grill in the later years are among the most obvious examples—it also did its share of grinding one-nighters. The musicians in Ellington's band were a highly temperamental bunch who were frequently warring with each other, often under the conditions of touring by coach, with long distances between gigs and not much sleep. Yet Ellington kept them working together. Respect was, of course, a crucial factor, which stands out in all interviews with Ellington musicians. Whatever they may have felt about each other, they all respected the leader. But it cannot have been easy for Ellington. Through good times and bad, through the easy gigs and the apparently endless one-night stands, he kept his aggregation of star jazz musicians together, more like a huge if not altogether harmonious family than a commercial enterprise. Yet this had to be a business operation, one which needed a very high standard of commercial expertise to keep it in existence at all. In this sphere, as in the musical one, Duke remained the man in charge, though obviously delegating more responsibility.

Other leaders employed a "straw boss" within the band, who could take rehearsals and deal with day-to-day musical chores. The leader could then sit back and enjoy the trappings of fame and a little of the leisure which affluence can bring. Not Ellington. His personality demanded that he remain fully in charge of all aspects of the music. Fortunately he had the energy to take on this work in addition to composing, arranging, administrative duties, and endless public appearances. Compared with other bands, the musical discipline was loose. Rehearsals might be few, premieres might be untidy, but Ellington got the music into performance in prodigious quantities. There were years like 1955 when things looked bleak, but such were surprisingly rare, and for the most part Duke Ellington and his Orchestra were national and international box office draws. To have kept such an organization together with such success over such a long period is more than any other musician in the jazz field has been capable of. That Ellington accomplished this while also being one of the great creative artists of the century is a measure of his vast ability.

Following the Aquacade season the band returned to the road, with Johnny Hodges back after his own venture into bandleading and Sam Woodyard settling into the drum chair. They participated in the third Newport Jazz Festival in July 1956, and both their appearances at the festival and the subsequent *Ellington At Newport* LP were great public successes, finally stimulating the kind of demand Ellington had been needing so badly. This, plus a great increase in the overseas touring schedule from the late fifties onwards, provided sufficient momentum to keep Ellington and his musicians occupied for the remainder of the band's career—a matter of eighteen years.

* * *

Ellington's major rivals on the big band jazz scene were now narrowed down to three: Count Basie, Woody Herman, and Stan Kenton. Kenton's favored approach was indicated perfectly by his styling of his presentations as "Music For Moderns" concerts by his "Innovations Orchestra." He featured a large and superbly drilled brass section and arrangements which, by an emphasis on the bizarre, were able to persuade the jazz audience—always inclined to be naive in such matters—that his was indeed an important form of "modern" music. Kenton also featured popular songs and a girl singer—attempts to hit the financial jackpot in order to keep his band going, just as Ellington tried to do with his popular recordings. With occasional exceptions, the soloists featured by Kenton were more notable for their virtuosity than for their jazz qualities. The lack of swing in Kenton's bands has always been marked, although there is no lack of drive or enthusiasm in their playing. Kenton's Orchestra did not set out to swing in the manner of the great black bands.

As one of the few big bands still around in the fifties and sixties playing under the "jazz" banner, Kenton unquestionably affected the taste and expectations of the audiences. An audience used to Kenton's programs would hardly feel intimidated by Ellington's concert works, as the jitterbugs of the swing era had felt. On the other hand, listeners would be unlikely to appreciate the earthy and rhythmically resilient kind of swing purveyed by the Ellington band if their concept of rhythmic vitality was based on Kenton's example. And such an audience would also be unlikely to appreciate the subtleties of phrasing nurtured by the jazz tradition or the musical language of such musicians as Ray Nance and Johnny Hodges.

Kenton saw himself as Ellington's successor in some respects. He returned from his first European tour in the fifties claiming that his band meant more to European audiences than Ellington's and that his music was more advanced in melodic and harmonic content. André Previn, for one, did not agree: "Stan Kenton can stand in front of a thousand fiddles and a thousand brass and make a dramatic gesture, and every studio arranger can nod his head and say 'Oh, yes, that's done like this.' But Duke merely lifts his finger, three horns make a sound, and I don't know what it is." It is doubtful if Kenton ever had an effect on Ellington's music other than perhaps suggesting that a loud trumpet section might be a means to commercial success. There are satirical references to Kenton in at least two of Ellington's recordings: *Later*, from the *Controversial Suite* of 1952, and the 1958 arrangement of *The Peanut Vendor*.

In the reduced big band jazz scene of the fifties and sixties, Woody Herman occupied a position roughly halfway between Kenton and Basie. Like Kenton, Herman favored loud brass sections and high-precision musicianship, but his music had none of the pretentious edge of Kenton's "modernity." Although he sometimes featured music of a frantic nature, Herman also presented a good deal of straightforward jazz. His concert music was often by Ralph Burns, a man with a different musical outlook than Kenton's writers. Taken overall, Herman's music had a humor lacking in Kenton's, and his scores were often designed for swinging. Until the production line anonymity of the American musical colleges became the sole source of supply, Herman also featured soloists of considerable individuality. Although always willing to deal with demands for ballad singing himself, Woody made no serious attempts at popularity through this medium after the forties. He was an Ellington admirer, and while the two men always seem to have been on good personal terms, it is doubtful if Woody's music ever had any effect on Ellington's work.

Both Kenton and Herman were forced to disband temporarily during this period, but Basie adopted a different solution to the problems of the time. While Kenton started to run a big band for only part of each year and Herman led a big band only when sufficient engagements were on hand, Basie rode out the storm by fronting an octet from 1950 to 1952. Prior to this there had been changes in the style of his band, particularly after the great rhythm section of Freddie Green, Walter Page, and Jo Jones had broken up. When Basie reorganized a big band on a regular basis in 1952, the break with the music of the 1937–1947 era was complete. A heavier (though still swinging) rhythm section was the basis of a band which, in great contrast to its predecessor, often lacked major soloists. The emphasis was on the arrangers and indeed the arranger remained the key man in Basie's music from here on. Despite many changes of personnel, the band remained much the same kind of unit through the years—always swinging whenever the arranger gave it half a chance and outstanding on the blues. The limitations of Basie's music since the fifties are reflected by his band's rather modest output of recordings of the highest class and in the narrow range of its stylistic mastery. Even so, his band remained capable, on the right night and with the right material, of playing with the swing, spirit, and zest which always were the hallmarks of Count Basie music.

* * *

Big bands outside the jazz idiom also survived to a limited degree, and along with Kenton, Herman, Basie, and Buddy Rich, these were the contemporaries of Ellington in the last two decades of his career. With these bands he shared the few outlets in dances, night clubs, and theaters, as well as those in concert halls. In the early fifties, Ellington adopted a standard format for concerts which varied little in later years. All the soloists in the band would be given at least one feature number—his most popular soloist, Johnny Hodges, always had two or three features per concert. A three-part medley of *Black And Tan Fantasy*, *Creole Love Call*, and *The Mooche* would be provided for lovers of old Ellingtonia, occasionally varied by a complete performance of one or the other of these pieces. Those who enjoyed Ellington's long list of popular songs, from *Mood Indigo* to *Satin Doll*, would be catered to in the *Medley Of Popular Hits*. This was subject to much variation and would often include full-length performances of songs like *Sophisticated Lady* and *Just Squeeze Me*. Most of the time at Ellington concerts was taken up by the medleys, the showcases, the obligatory drum solo, and such warhorses as *Rockin' In Rhythm* and *Jam With Sam*. The rest consisted of selections from the latest Ellington LPs, revivals of one of the concert works, and responses to requests for such Ellington classics as *Harlem Air Shaft* or *In A Mellotone*. This concert routine was reflected on records only by the live albums; for his studio recordings, Duke and Billy Strayhorn continued to create a seemingly endless stream of new material. The wide-ranging nature of Ellington music was in part a reflection of its creator's versatility. But it was also a reflection of the need for the band to succeed in vastly differing circumstances and before widely varying audiences. At need, Duke could play the pop-tune medleys with all the show-business presentation of the sweet bands; he could swing the blues in a way which was just as potent as Basie's, or he could produce concert works in programs just as "serious" as Kenton's. Among other things, the Ellington Orchestra continued to be the one which could turn its attention to any kind of music and play it superbly.

* * *

The increased rate of personnel changes in the band which had been a feature of the forties continued in the early fifties, though from 1953 onwards the situation began to stabilize. Ellington's music was so strongly based on the individuality of his musicians that a personnel change was always more of an event in his band than in others. One of the reasons why the "Ellington renaissance" of the early fifties faded so soon, while that of the later part of the decade thrived, is the much more stable personnel of the later period. While the idea that Ellington was dependent on certain specific musicians was refuted by the events of the early fifties, there is no doubt that stability of personnel was highly beneficial to his music. The replacements he chose in the early fifties confirmed his continuing ability to find suitable musicians. Apart from Juan Tizol, who was of course an old hand, the only musician of the early 1951 intake to stay for more than a couple of years was Britt Woodman. He, along with Quentin Jackson and first Juan Tizol and then John Sanders, helped to create what became the best Ellington trombone section since the Brown-Tizol-Nanton team. Although without a soloist of the stature of Nanton or Brown, this unit could muster a fine plunger specialist in Jackson, a man who could handle the open-horn jazz solos in Woodman, and a valve trombone specialist in Sanders. But the glory of this particular trombone trio was its work as a team, both in the skill of its section playing and in its mastery of Duke's scores—so profound that they sounded just as natural in Ellington's music as did his own left hand at the piano. And of course (as Duke himself liked to point out) there were really three trombone sections, since the group took on a totally different character as the lead switched from one musician to another.

Ellington's basic need was for skilled jazz musicians with strong musical personality, plenty of imagination, and big sounds on their instruments. By the fifties, jazz was no longer producing a Cootie Williams or Johnny Hodges, but there were still a lot of highly individual characters around. In 1951 alone, Duke picked up Britt Woodman, Clark Terry, and Willie Cook, as well as Willie Smith and Louis Bellson. With these musicians and their fellow bandsmen he created a series of Ellington recordings of a quality wholly comparable with those of his glorious past. In doing so he proved, if proof were still needed, that great though many of his sidemen were, the true genius came from the leader. For the full realization of his music the only person whose presence was *absolutely* essential was Ellington himself.

Sidemen

Butch Ballard

Butch Ballard spent two spells in the band, from March to July 1950, when he acted as second drummer to Sonny Greer during a European tour, and from March to July 1953 in the more usual role of solo percussionist. This second period coincided with a busy recording schedule, and thus Ballard looms larger in the Ellington discography than his rather short stays with the band would imply. He was a pleasantly swinging and rather unobtrusive stylist, effective without having any markedly personal or imaginative traits.

Representative Recordings: Satin Doll (Capitol, 1953), *Liza* (McElroy's Ballroom recording, 1953)

Louis Bellson

In the history of the Ellington band the conventional stylists and brilliant craftsmen have usually taken second place to the characters and the eccentrics. The main exception is Louis Bellson. A member of the highly professional school of drumming established by Gene Krupa and refined by Buddy Rich, Bellson was the greatest possible contrast to his predecessor, Sonny Greer. Greer did not read music and was an eccentric individualist whose technique reflected a twenties vaudeville background. For him to be replaced by a virtuoso master craftsman was a revolution indeed, and it changed the sound of the Ellington band to a marked degree. But Bellson was more than a brilliant virtuoso; he was also an artist who played a sensitive and imaginative part in Ellington music. He and Willie Smith were the two catalysts who whipped the band into new shape in 1951. In his all-too-brief spells with the band in later years, Bellson showed himself still capable of playing a major role in Ellington music. While there are many superb studio recordings in which Bellson plays an important part, one needs to hear the location recordings of the 1951–1952 period to realize the full extent of his contribution. His spirit is a constant inspiration to the band and his playing is beautifully blended with the ensemble. Curiously enough his writing for the band, although of a highly professional standard, was quite lacking in any distinctive quality and seems oddly barren when compared with the richness of his contribution as a drummer.

Representative Recordings: Moonlight Fiesta (Coronets; Mercer, 1951), *She* (Coronets; Mercer, 1951), *Fancy Dan* (Columbia, 1951), *Take The "A" Train* (Columbia, 1952), *Skin Deep* (Columbia 1952), *Used To Be Duke* (Johnny Hodges; Verve, 1954)

Dave Black

One of the few white musicians to have held a key role in Ellington's band, Black followed Butch Ballard in the drum chair and stayed until Sam Woodyard's arrival in the summer of 1955. A drummer clearly influenced by Dave Tough, Black brought drive and vitality to the Ellington band at a time when declining popularity could easily have had an adverse effect on morale.

Representative Recordings: Flying Home (Capitol, 1953), *Stompin' At The Savoy* (Capitol, 1953), *Liza* (McElroy's Ballroom recording, 1954)

Willie Cook

The jazz community has largely overlooked the merits of Willie Cook's playing despite its considerable exposure in the Ellington band. That Cook was in a section of better-known players for much of his stay may be the cause, and his joining at the same time as Clark Terry no doubt minimized the impact of his arrival. Although his virtuosity is less flamboyant than Terry's and his lyricism a shade less warm than Harold Baker's, there can be no doubt at all that Cook is a fine jazz artist. His pure tone, clear articulation, and unstrained facility mark him as an outstanding craftsman. Like Baker, he is one of the "straight" men among Ellington trumpet stylists, not in the academic sense but rather because his playing lacks the eccentricities of the Rex Stewart-Clark Terry-Cat Anderson variety on the one hand and those of the plunger specialists on the other. No matter what the context, Cook's solos with Ellington are always delightful and his work is beautifully poised rhythmically. In style he is an interesting amalgam, having the harmonic command and instrumental facility of the postbop trumpeters while retaining the superior tonal values of the big band era.

Representative Recordings: Tenderly (Salem, Mass. dance recording, 1952), *Things Ain't What They Used To Be* (Capitol, 1954), *Mood Indigo* (with Rosemary Clooney, Columbia, 1956), *Unbooted Character* (chase with Ray Nance; Bethlehem, 1956)

Paul Gonsalves

When Paul Gonsalves joined the Ellington band, he surprised the leader with his ability to play all of Ben Webster's solos note for note. Like Webster himself, Gonsalves was a discipline of Coleman Hawkins and must be rated as one of the most creative members of that school of tenor playing. His prior experience included a spell with Basie. Although lacking the big sound of Hawkins or Webster, his tone was of such inherent quality that he could lead the entire Ellington band with just as much success and distinctiveness as a powerful player like Hodges. To the general public, Gonsalves was best known for his extended marathon performances, but he recorded tenor solos at every tempo and in every mood while a member of the Ellington band. They always fitted perfectly into the musical context. It seems amazing in retrospect that during his Ellington years vastly inferior artists were paraded before the jazz public as "stars" while Gonsalves was looked upon as something of a vulgarian because of the notoriety of his marathon solos, most notably that on *Diminuendo And Crescendo In Blue* from the 1956 Newport Festival. Gonsalves was a soloist of wonderful and endless invention, tremendous melodic taste, and great rhythmic potency. His harmonic approach had considerable influence on Ellington's musical thinking. Like Clark Terry and Jimmy Hamilton, he was regarded as being among the modern segment of the Ellington band. But neither Hamilton nor Terry had anything like so profound an effect on the Ellington style. He was also a superb ensemble musician: even when given just a few melodic phrases or a brief lead part he would bring to the ensemble a unique personal flavor. His ballad style must be accounted one of the most beautiful in jazz history. No sideman contributed more to the Ellington Orchestra than Gonsalves, and his combination of a strong musical personality with the ability to be thoroughly involved in every ensemble situation made him, in many ways, a model Ellingtonian.

Gonsalves used heroin and was also a heavy drinker, yet until the closing years of his life he rarely allowed these factors to affect his playing, although he often seemed to teeter on the edge of disaster. On one Ellington tour, the band played a piece which opened with a long piano solo followed by a very fast, intricate passage for the saxophones. After a few concerts, it became obvious that Duke varied the length of his solo and alerted his saxophonists by inserting a prearranged phrase toward the end of it. As this phrase sounded, the five musicians would slowly mobilize from their varied contemplation of the world—Carney benign, Procope composed, Hodges seemingly indifferent, Hamilton stoical, and Gonsalves dreamy—and at the appropriate moment make their entry. At one concert, as Duke's solo moved toward its end, it became obvious that Paul was in fact asleep. The piano sounded the warning phrase, the other four saxophonists adjusted their straps and prepared to play while on the end of the section Gonsalves slumbered on. At the last millisecond Hamilton gave Paul a nudge, and five saxophones made a perfect entry.

Representative Recordings: Fancy Dan (Columbia, 1951), *Jones* (Columbia, 1958), *Happy Re-Union* (Columbia, 1958), *I've Just Seen Her* (Columbia, 1962), *West Indian Pancake* (Verve, 1966), *Mount Harissa* (from *The Far East Suite*, Victor, 1966)

Jimmy Grissom

One of the Ellington succession of "romantic baritones," Jimmy Grissom was true to the tradition he inherited—his ballad singing displayed no jazz characteristics. He was an eccentric and highly individual singer, whose work with Duke ran the gamut from the conventional to the bizarre. Unfortunately the latter quality predominated in his ballad work, and his singing at medium tempo is to be preferred overall.

Representative Recordings: Without A Song (Capitol, 1953), *Ballin' The Blues* (Capitol, 1953), *Blue Moon* (Capitol, 1953), *Coquette* (Capitol, 1955), *Everything But You* (Bethlehem, 1956), *Rock City Rock* (Columbia, 1957)

Rick Henderson

Rick Henderson followed Hilton Jefferson into Hodges's chair. A disciple of Charlie Parker in his solo style, Henderson exhibited more traditional values as a band player. His solos lack strong individuality, but their musical soundness and craftsmanship point to his virtues as a section player. Henderson left the band in the summer of 1955 on the return of Hodges.

Representative Recordings: Frivolous Banta (Capitol, 1954), *All The Things You Are* (Washington Armory concert, 1955)

Quentin Jackson

After a long and distinguished career in such top bands as McKinney's Cotton Pickers, Don Redman, and Cab Calloway, Quentin Jackson joined the Ellington Orchestra to take over Claude Jones's duties in Tizol's old chair. After Jackson had been with the band about eighteen months, Tyree Glenn departed and bequeathed the plunger duties to him. So successful was Jackson in this role that, after a lifetime of section work, he suddenly found himself a famous soloist. His plunger solos with Ellington are in marked contrast to those of Glenn. In place of his predecessor's rather smooth, sophisticated approach, Jackson restored some of Nanton's earthiness. The longer he stayed with Ellington, the more Jackson mastered this rare and esoteric art. His section playing was, naturally enough for a man with his credentials, a tremendous asset, for he was a thorough professional with (according to Paul Gonsalves) perfect pitch. Both in the traditional plunger roles and in parts written specially for him in this idiom, Jackson produced solos worthy of this distinguished Ellington succession.

Representative Recordings: Fancy Dan (Columbia, 1951), *The Mooche* (Columbia, 1952), *My Funny Valentine* (Bethlehem, 1956), *Donkey Serenade* (Columbia, 1958), *Red Carpet* (from the *Toot Suite*, Columbia, 1959)

Hilton Jefferson

As a replacement for Willie Smith, Ellington obtained the services of another man with a superb record as a first alto—Hilton Jefferson. As a soloist, Jefferson featured a basic, rather dry version of the Benny Carter style, incorporating many of Carter's virtues. As a melodist he was rated among the very best by Ben Webster, who was certainly an authority on that subject. There is unfortunately only one solo contribution from Jefferson on the issued recordings by the 1952 Ellington band, on the long version of *The Mooche*. It is a solo well in keeping with the best Ellington traditions.

Representative Recording: The Mooche (Columbia, 1952)

John Sanders

John Sanders took over from Juan Tizol a few months after that worthy's second departure from the band, and shortly after joining he switched to valve trombone. His rare excursions into the realm of the improvised solo are not particularly distinguished—at least not by Ellington standards—but Sanders was well up to the highest Ellington demands as an ensemble player. His theme statements, often on numbers associated with Tizol such as *Caravan* and *Bakiff*, show a trombonist with a fine melodic taste and a full, rich tone. Sanders was one of a group of younger musicians who fully appreciated Ellington's contribution to music and the honor of being a member of the band. During his time in the Ellington organization Sanders also acted as librarian.

Representative Recordings: Bakiff (Capitol, 1954), *Total Jazz* (from *A Portrait Of Ella Fitzgerald*, Verve, 1957), *Come Sunday* (from *Black, Brown And Beige*, 1958), *Caravan* (Travis Air Force Base dance recordings, 1958)

Willie Smith

Although a famous saxophone soloist, Willie Smith is perhaps even better remembered as one of the very finest lead altos in big band history, arguably the best of all. His contribution to the Ellington band during his rather short stay was felt more in the ensemble than through his solo efforts, good though these were. On joining the band, Smith rehearsed the saxophone section and disciplined it into a beautifully cohesive team. Previously it had been noted for expressive playing, individuality of timbre, and richness of overall sound, but Smith welded it into a tightly knit unit. His influence at this vital time in the band's history, when morale could have hit rock bottom, was wholly salutary, and despite the absence of solos of the first magnitude, Smith's contribution to the Ellington band was a very important one.

Representative Recordings: Indian Summer (Meadowbrook broadcast, 1951), *Things Ain't What They Used To Be* (Meadowbrook broadcast, 1951), *Alternate* (Coronets, Mercer, 1951), *Please Be Kind* (Columbia, 1951), *Tea For Two* (Salem, Mass. dance, 1952), *Sophisticated Lady* (Victor, 1952)

Clark Terry

When he joined Ellington, Terry had experience with the big bands of Charlie Barnet and Count Basie as well as with the latter's Octet. During his stay with Ellington, he became a remarkable all-rounder. There was virtually no role in the extensive Ellington trumpet repertoire which he did not take over at one time or another. He could deliver beautiful melodic theme statements; create superb variations on ballads; play bop trumpet, high-note trumpet, or plunger-mute trumpet; or simply improvise swinging no-nonsense jazz solos in his own personal style. This versatility was greatly appreciated by Ellington, as was Terry's ability to double effectively on flugelhorn. During his years with Duke he was usually a member of a trumpet team of four outstanding virtuoso soloists. Although he was such a versatile musician, he received only about a quarter of the trumpet solos in the book, where in any other band, he would certainly have been given the lion's share. His abilities were such that he *could* have handled all solos in the Ellington book, but this was clearly impossible with players of the caliber of Ray Nance, Cat Anderson, and either Harold Baker or Willie Cook also in the section. Ellington's insight into Terry's musical character is perhaps best seen in his casting of the trumpeter's two solos in the 1957 Shakespeare Suite, *Such Sweet Thunder*, but the student of the Ellington discography from 1951 to 1959 knows that Terry can be heard in a great variety of roles, always contributing to the delights of the music.

Representative Recordings: On trumpet—*Perdido* (Columbia, 1952), *Stompin' At The Savoy* (Capitol, 1953), *Up And Down, Up And Down* (from *Such Sweet Thunder*, Columbia, 1957), *Lady Mac* (from *Such Sweet Thunder*, Columbia, 1957), *Total Jazz* (from *A Portrait Of Ella Fitzgerald*, Verve, 1957). On flugelhorn—*Juniflip* (Columbia, 1958).

Dick Vance

A member of the Ellington trumpet team for a few months during 1951, Dick Vance's most important contribution to the music of the Ellington band is as an arranger. He worked for Duke in that capacity on and off from the middle forties onwards, his scores being distinguished by fine musicianship and confident jazz craftsmanship.

Britt Woodman

Although Ellington claimed that he never went out of his way to hire a musician in his life, simply engaging the best men available wherever he was playing, his associates insist that he cabled to the West Coast to ask Woodman to take over Lawrence Brown's chair. In Woodman he obtained a young musician who was already a highly skilled and accomplished jazz stylist. Owing to the presence of Quentin Jackson, Woodman did not solo with the plunger mute, although he subsequently showed (on records made away from the Ellington band) that he had mastered this technique. Although he produced some good solos and displayed an individual style, Woodman never became a major Ellington voice. It could be that he was too conscious of the need to carry forward the Lawrence Brown tradition. In fact, he was a different kind of musician from Brown, a more forthright, rougher kind of player with a less lyrical approach. His contributions to the band were valuable and varied indeed, yet his potential as an Ellingtonian never seemed fully realized.

Representative Recordings: Sultry Serenade (Victor, 1952), *Things Ain't What They Used To Be* (Capitol, 1954), *Theme For Trambeam* (Capitol, 1955), *Sonnet For Hank Cinq* (from *Such Sweet Thunder*, Columbia, 1957), *Red Garter* (from the *Toot Suite*, Columbia, 1959)

Chapter 22

The Records—Summer 1956 to February 1959

THE PERSONNEL WHICH RECORDED FOR Columbia and Bethlehem in early 1956 was still unchanged when the Duke Ellington Orchestra played the Newport Jazz Festival in the summer of 1956. For the next four years, this group of musicians settled down to the sort of permanence associated with earlier Ellington bands. The only major change was the replacement of Willie Cook by Harold Baker in 1957. Minor changes involved the vocalists, rarely an important factor in Ellington's music after the forties, and short periods away from the band by Hodges (in 1958) and Woodyard (in 1959). This stability of personnel was an obvious advantage compared with the situation over the previous ten years and coincided happily with a steady recording contract with Columbia. Although subject to less ballyhoo at the time than the earlier Capitol association or the later one with Reprise, Ellington's arrangements with Columbia enabled him to record a great variety of music. He seems to have had freedom to record whatever he wanted.

The one thing Columbia would not do was to record some of his major works using a symphony orchestra. The company typically saw Ellington as a jazz artist and could not envisage him succeeding "out of category." So we had to wait until the sixties and seventies to hear recordings of *Harlem* as scored for symphony orchestra, or any version at all of *Night Creature*. Ellington appears to have particularly enjoyed recording with the various artists who appeared as guests with the band. These included Rosemary Clooney,

Mahalia Jackson, Dizzy Gillespie, Jimmy Rushing, pianist Jimmy Jones, a selection of percussionists from leading New York Symphony Orchestras, and Count Basie and his entire band! Much of the success of the Ellington recordings of this period must have been due to the presence at Columbia of Irving Townsend, a man who appreciated the importance of Ellington's music and also understood the personality of its creator and his unorthodox methods.

Some idea of the scope of the Columbia output can be seen in the following list of the LPs Ellington made for Columbia from 1956 to 1961:

Blue Rose (1956)—featuring Rosemary Clooney. (Discussed in Chapter 20.)

Newport (1956)—the *Newport Jazz Festival Suite* plus revivals, the latter including the famous performance of *Diminuendo And Crescendo In Blue*.

A Drum Is A Woman (1956)—Ellington's TV spectacular on the history of jazz, the band augmented by extra vocalists and a choir.

Such Sweet Thunder (1956–57)—the new Shakespearean Suite by Ellington and Strayhorn.

Ellington Indigos (also known as *Solitude*) (1957)—a set of ballad performances combining Ellington songs with other standards.

Black, Brown And Beige (1958)—a remake of part of the 1943 work, with Mahalia Jackson added.

At The Bal Masque (1958)—a humorous collection of Ellington versions of the most unlikely songs.

The Cosmic Scene (1958)—a contingent called Duke Ellington and his Spacemen is featured; it consists of Clark Terry, Jimmy Hamilton, and Paul Gonsalves with the trombone and rhythm sections.

Ellington At Newport 1958—a collection of new compositions.

Jazz At The Plaza, Volume Two (1958)—the second LP from a party thrown by Columbia for some of its leading jazz artists. Volume One contains non-Ellington performances.

Jazz Party (1959)—Ellington and guests in a program of old and new music.

Anatomy Of A Murder (1959)—Ellington's score for the film.

Festival Session (1959)—a mixture of old and new.

Blues In Orbit (1958–59)—a scaled-down version of the band in a mainly impromptu collection.

The Nutcracker Suite (1960)—Ellington's and Strayhorn's rescoring of Tchaikovsky's ballet music.

Piano In The Background (1960)—a retrospective collection with Ellington's piano featured more than usual.

Peer Gynt Suite/Suite Thursday (1960)—Grieg's incidental music to Ibsen's play, rearranged and coupled with a new Ellington/Strayhorn suite.

The Unknown Session (1960)—Ellington leads a septet in a program of brilliantly conceived and executed miniatures. (Not released until 1979.)

Piano In The Foreground (1961)—a collection of piano solos with bass and drums, combining new compositions and standards.

Battle Royal (1961)—the combined Basie and Ellington Orchestras in alternating selections from their respective repertoires.

The Girl's Suite And The Perfume Suite (1961 & 1957)—a new suite of swinging music and a revival of a concert suite from 1944. (Not released until 1982.)

"All American" In Jazz (1962)—Ellington's contribution to the then popular fashion of having jazz artists record albums of songs from Broadway musicals.

Midnight In Paris (1962)—a mixture of new Ellingtonia and old standards, all with Parisian connections.

During the years spanned by these LPs, Ellington also recorded for Verve, Roulette, and United Artists. In addition to all these releases, more recent years have seen issues from film soundtracks, live recordings from dances and concerts, and selections from studio sessions recorded by Ellington at his own expense—all from this period. But the backbone of the Ellington output from the second half of the fifties and the start of the sixties was this outstanding series for Columbia.

* * *

So far as the record-buying public were concerned, *the* success of the series was the 1956 *Ellington At Newport* LP. The circumstances surrounding this recording read like a Hollywood script of a great artist pulling out of the shadow of public neglect. The Ellington Orchestra was making its first appearance at the Newport Jazz Festival, this 1956 event being the third in an already world-famous series. The festival producers had their doubts about Ellington's drawing power with the new jazz audience. In typical fashion, the band turned up minus several members and played a perfunctory first set before giving way to an array of small groups. These ran over time, and the situation was anything but promising when the Ellington band returned to play the final set of the long evening. The band was complete now and playing at the top of its form. Ellington sensed the mood of the audience; with the experience of his long years in show business, he selected the number which he knew was right for the occasion—*Diminuendo And Crescendo In Blue*. This was presented with an "interlude" of uptempo blues improvisation by Paul Gonsalves between the two parts. This was a deeply swinging and immensely exciting performance, and during the long tenor saxophone solo the audience erupted, dancing, clapping and cheering in response to the exuberance of the music. A riot was feared, but Ellington calmed everybody down by playing a slow blues followed by a set of encores. This spontaneous demonstration became a major news item, and once more Ellington's name was on everyone's lips. Following this Newport success Duke appeared on the cover of *Time* magazine—then one of the supreme accolades of American society.

It has often been stated that the tenor saxophone interlude was an inspiration of the moment, but as we have noted in a previous chapter, earlier recordings have the Gonsalves interlude between the two parts of *Diminuendo And Crescendo In Blue*, one of them dating as early as June 1951. That this routine was used at other Ellington concerts is confirmed in a report by the English writer Charles Wilford, who attended an Ellington concert at Pasadena Civic Auditorium in March 1953. In the course of his report, he wrote: "In the in-between of *Diminuendo In Blue* and *Crescendo In Blue*, [Gonsalves] played a seemingly unending succession of choruses that must have lasted quite five minutes, and duly aroused the fans as intended" (*Melody Maker*, April 18, 1953, p. 3). So the routine was clearly established well before the 1956 Newport event. Another precursor of these events occurred at a Randall's Island concert in May 1938, when *Diminuendo And Crescendo In Blue* roused the crowd to a similar pitch of excitement. No doubt Ellington had such occasions in mind when he called for the piece at Newport. By 1956 jazz had become a more cerebral, less emotional music, and the Ellington band's uninhibited playing, with its sensuous phrasing and earthy vitality, contrasted with the milder musical mixtures served up by the fashionable jazz artists of the day. The Newport performance bowled over an audience caught totally unprepared for such an experience.

On record, the Newport *Diminuendo And Crescendo In Blue* comes over with all the excitement of the event, but the loud and continuous audience roar which starts up during Gonsalves's solo makes listening difficult from that point onwards. This is a pity, as the performance of *Crescendo In Blue* is a vital one with the magnificent musical spirit of the ensemble fully in evidence. The famous—or infamous—Gonsalves interlude follows the pattern he always used on extended solos. He introduces and repeats blues phrases, examining various ways of phrasing them and investigating countless variants. His rhythmic attack is very swinging, but over a solo of such length the lack of sustained development becomes rather trying. Of course the Newport audience did not feel this, but on record the long tenor solo fails to induce the ecstacy which they obviously felt. Gonsalves is backed superbly by the rhythm section, Ellington giving a magnificent display of band piano playing throughout. His terse, spare yet eloquent and swinging introduction and linking passages are the foundation on which the entire performance is built. Indeed the *Ellington At Newport* LP presents Duke at the very pinnacle of his keyboard mastery, a mastery deployed entirely in the service of the band and its soloists.

On the LP, *Diminuendo And Crescendo* shares a side with a revival of the 1938 Johnny Hodges number *Jeep's Blues*. Hodges, featured throughout, combines his rich tonal resources and peerless command of the instrument with a beautiful singing blues style and a perfect sense of solo architecture. The band plays superbly here too, while Ellington's piano backing is of such rightness as to almost unwittingly steal the show.

The second side of the record is devoted to a new Ellington work, *The Newport Jazz Festival Suite*. The version of the LP was recorded in New York a few days after the Festival, with crowd noises added to make it sound like a live recording. One presumes that this was because of an untidy performance by the band at the premiere, or engineering problems. The *Suite* is in three movements. The first is a medium-tempo twelve-bar theme, *Festival Junction*. It is introduced by Hamilton's clarinet first in solo and then with the band. The development is mainly in the form of solos by Willie Cook, Gonsalves, Woodman, Carney, Jackson, Procope, and Anderson. The flighty *Newport Up* which closes the suite became the segment most often performed by Ellington. This features his trio of "modern" soloists—Hamilton, Terry, and Gonsalves—in a lively uptempo setting.

The musical core of the suite, however, is its central movement, called *Blues To Be There*. Here, Ellington on piano, Procope on clarinet, and Nance on plunger-muted trumpet are the soloists, and the orchestral writing and playing is that intriguing Ellington blend of the traditional and the new. No blues performance quite like this had ever been heard before, yet both soloists and orchestra "sing" the music with the unrestrained eloquence of a country blues singer. Procope and Nance are excellent, the latter playing one of his most glowing solos, but Ellington's opening two choruses are the outstanding contribution. This is piano playing rooted in the purest blues tradition, yet at the same time striking in its originality.

Owing to the notoriety achieved by the near-riot at the festival, *Ellington At Newport* became a best-selling LP, and the attendant publicity served to reinstate Ellington as a major jazz figure in the public eye, not just briefly, as in 1951, but on a permanent basis. The image of Ellington as a figure towering above the whims of jazz fashion dates from this time.

In addition to *Ellington At Newport*, four further Ducal titles were put out in the series of Columbia LPs which covered the 1956 Festival. These made up one side of an LP shared with trumpeter Buck Clayton and an all-star group. *Skin Deep* is less successful in the hands of Sam Woodyard than in those of its composer, Louis Bellson. This is a mediocre drum feature, though Woodyard's band drumming on all these Newport recordings is superb. *Take The "A" Train* features Ray Nance in the standard arrangement, but its highlight is the long Ellington piano solo which serves as introduction, a solo of great swing and vivacity. The other two items are ballad features, for Hodges on *I Got It Bad*, and for Carney on *Sophisticated Lady*. Both saxophonists play beautifully and receive perfect backing from the band. Ellington's piano work on *I Got It Bad* must be singled out for its ideal conception of the role of the accompanist as well as for its great intrinsic beauty. A version of *Black And Tan Fantasy* from this concert was issued in an anthology of Newport recordings in the early eighties; it features Cat Anderson in the solo trumpet role. Among the 1956 Newport Ellington recordings which have not yet been issued are *Tea For Two*, *Day In, Day Out*, and *Tulip Or Turnip*.

* * *

Eight days after the Newport Festival the Ellington Orchestra played a concert at the Berkshire Music Barn in Lenox, Massachusetts, as part of a summer jazz festival which extended from July 1 to September 2, 1956. The first two-thirds of Ellington's concert have been issued on a couple of Queen Disc LPs. The first contains a *Black And Tan Fantasy* with Nance back in the solo trumpet role; *Take The "A" Train* following the pattern of the 1955 Washington Armory version, featuring Nance's singing plus the Gonsalves tenor solo at two tempos; *Monologue*; and a sequence of showcases—*Harlem Air Shaft* (Terry), *Clarinet Melodrama* (Hamilton), *Theme For Trambeam* (Woodman), and *Sophisticated Lady* (Carney). The second disc has a full performance of *The Newport Jazz Festival Suite*, which finds the brilliant Ellington two-chorus solo on *Blues To Be There* reduced to one chorus of perfunctory introduction, although Nance is outstanding in this performance. The *Suite* is followed by a scrappy *The Hawk Talks*, three Hodges features (*Prelude To A Kiss*, *Things Ain't What They Used To Be*, *I Got It Bad*) and Anderson's *La Virgen De La Macarena*. (The unissued portion includes the *Medley Of Popular Hits*.) The surprising thing about this concert—which, unlike the Newport performances, was recorded in stereo—is the absence of the hit of the Newport festival, *Diminuendo And Crescendo In Blue*.

On July 28, 1956, the Ellington Orchestra played at the Connecticut Jazz Festival. Among the handful of issued recordings from this source is a driving version of *Diminuendo And Crescendo In Blue*. The recorded sound has occasional flaws, but the overall quality is good and the Gonsalves solo is in much better sound than the famous Newport version; here it extends to 37(!) choruses. The final part of *Crescendo In Blue* is acoustically dominated by Anderson, who masks the band by standing in front of the recording mike when he comes down front to add his high-note trumpet to the final ensemble.

* * *

As was so often the case, Ellington's next Columbia release was in total contrast to its predecessor. With his band augmented by Rick Henderson on alto, a harpist, two extra percussionists, three solo singers, and a full choir, Ellington as narrator presented his fantasy on the origins and history of jazz, *A Drum Is A Woman*. This was broadcast as a television spectacular in 1957 on the CBS network in what seems to have been its only complete performance. The recorded version was made at a series of sessions in September, October, and December 1956, some of the later dates presumably taken up by Ellington dubbing his narration over music recorded earlier. *A Drum Is A Woman* is of particular interest as it is the only one of Ellington's dramatic works which exists in a complete recording under his direction. The Columbia version is complete with the exception of one number, *Pomegranate*, although this was recorded and can be found on some 45 rpm EP selections from the work. When asked in later life to name what he considered to be his major artistic achievements, Ellington almost always included *A Drum Is A Woman* among his choices.

The structure of *A Drum Is A Woman* is based loosely on the history of jazz, and this provides a succession of pegs on which Ellington is able to hang his fantasy and sense of irony. The central character is Madame Zajj, who has the habit of transforming herself into a drum. She is passionately in love with Carabee Joe, who lives in and loves the jungle: "He talks to the animals in their jungle slang." Together, Zajj and Joe experience New Orleans and Congo Square, the *Ballet of the Flying Saucers* (part of a satire on progress), and a music devised by Joe after visiting 52nd Street, *Rhumbop*. Ellington's comments are couched in typically flowery, ornate language, spiced with sharp asides and ironic references. When it was first released, *A Drum Is A Woman* was severely treated by critics expecting a new and serious instrumental work, not a whimsical show with chunks of choral singing and spoken narrative. Their negative view of *A Drum Is A Woman* has persisted despite Ellington's references to the work as among his best. Listeners who are aware of the issues with which Ellington deals in *A Drum Is A Woman* almost invariably find it a rewarding work, not least in terms of humor.

The choice part is that running from the start of *New Orleans* to the end of *Congo Square*. This is in fact one long section, as the recapitulation of Procope's clarinet blues and Ellington's opening words clearly indicate. The satire on the white man's association of black people and jazz with primitivism and the pasteboard Africa of popular entertainment is concentrated into a stunning send-up of the New Orleans myths so beloved of jazz historians. Only the red-light district is omitted, this being reserved for a later section entitled *Madam Zajj*. The New Orleans portion opens with a long blues solo, unaccompanied, by Procope on clarinet. Mardi Gras day is described, and it is found that the carnival King of the Zulus for that year is Buddy Bolden, celebrated in song with *Hey, Buddy Bolden*. In this song a few stinging asides are fired in the direction of the clichés of the American musical. The representation of Bolden's trumpet playing is handled by Clark Terry in one of his very best with the Ellington band. The half-valve playing at the end is executed with great brilliance, and the note-placing engenders great swing. There is a brief muted passage by Ray Nance, but otherwise Duke entrusts the role of the most traditional of jazz trumpeters to a man usually considered a modernist in his band. This illustrates Ellington's contention that such categorizations are at best convenient half-truths and at worst completely misleading. The *Congo Square* sequence is highly colorful both orchestrally and verbally, and concludes with an unaccompanied tenor solo by Gonsalves—another of the "modernists" by conventional standards—which is perhaps the most basic piece of jazz making in the whole extravaganza. Finally Ellington, whose comments throughout are full of wit and humor, draws us back to his original picture of New Orleans at dawn, and Procope's New Orleans-style clarinet concludes the section as it had begun.

Among the many delights of *A Drum Is A Woman* are the beautiful middle section, *Ballet Of The Flying Saucers*, and the cunning deployment of the drum solo in this section. Ellington makes use of chimes here, reminding us of Sonny Greer and the Cotton Club all those many years ago—years which were, of course, well within the lifespan of Madam Zajj. Two of Ellington's best songs since the forties—*What Else Can You Do With A Drum?* and *You Better Know It*—come from this score. On the LP, they are sung by Ozzie Bailey, a young man of West Indian descent whom Ellington had brought in to replace Jimmy Grissom. Bailey's work is free from the contorted style which most of Duke's male vocalists adopted; while he was not a jazz singer in any sense, Bailey's unaffected singing was an asset to the band, although he is not heard a great deal on record. The other singers on *A Drum Is A Woman* are Margaret Tynes, a trained contralto, and Joya Sherrill. Both sing well, the latter with that stylistic affinity with Duke's music which had marked her work with the band in the middle forties. (It is a great pity that Joya did not stay with the band, for her vocal qualities and her understanding of the music suggest that she could have been to later decades what Ivie Anderson had been to the thirties and early forties.) It seems unlikely that posterity will rate *A Drum Is A Woman* quite so highly in its creator's output as he did himself. But it is a very humorous work, full of joy and vitality and a real storehouse of Ellington verbal and musical wit. In the fifties, jazz enthusiasts and especially jazz critics had a tendency to take the music very solemnly indeed, and in this climate it was unlikely that critical reaction to such a work would be favorable. The tragedy is that many people have noted the exotic aspects of *A Drum Is A Woman*, and its use of harps and choirs, and have accepted the critics' negative judgment without actually listening to the work. Yet for anyone in sympathy with Ellington's outlook, this witty and urbane creation yields great pleasure—as well as fresh perspectives on its subject matter.

The potential buyer should be warned that Columbia/CBS have issued two versions of *A Drum Is A Woman* nearly always with identical packaging. The differences are all on side one. In the incomplete version, both *Hey, Buddy Bolden* and *Carribee Joe* are missing; the section called *Zajj: A Drum Is A Woman, Part Two* is used twice on these pressings, on side one to replace the missing segments and on side two in its proper place. This incomplete version is apparently a rejected pressing which was used on reissues in error. It also contains scraps of Ellington piano and bits of narrative not on the full version, as well as some variations in those parts of the spoken narrative which are common to both. There is also about ten seconds of New Orleans marching music which is heard only in the background of the fuller recording. The Ellington specialist will want both versions of the LP, but the general listener will prefer the full version with *Hey, Buddy Bolden* and *Carribee Joe*. Identification is not easy. All issues contain identical annotation and label information, which refer to the content of the full version. Apparently, the original U.S. issue on Columbia CL-951 at first used the incorrect version, but this was quickly withdrawn and most copies of this LP in circulation contain the full version. The correct version was also issued on Philips (European) B-07253-L, Philips (English) BBL-7179, and CBS/Sony (Japanese) SOPU-90. The incomplete version reappeared on some reissues in the late 1970s and is used on CBS (European) 65185 and CBS (French) 84404. The U.S. Columbia Special Products issue, JCL 951, also from the seventies, has appeared with both versions. (Those wishing to check on this should examine the numbers printed on the surface near the label: 39156-1AJ indicates the incomplete version; XLP 39156-1K the complete one.)

* * *

In some ways, *A Drum Is A Woman* was overshadowed by the paean of praise which greeted the next Columbia release, the new Ellington/Strayhorn work on Shakespearian themes which had been commissioned by the Shakespeare Festival of Stratford, Ontario, Canada. Entitled *Such Sweet Thunder*, the suite is in twelve short movements. Each one is a portrait of a dramatic situation, or of one or more characters, in a light and mildly satirical vein.

The opening *Such Sweet Thunder* is a magnificent curtain raiser, an Ellington blues at medium tempo with rich writing for the saxophones, a mysterious passage with John Sanders's valve trombone in the lead, and an eloquent trumpet chorus from Nance as the centerpiece. Although the title of the suite and of this opening movement are taken from *A Midsummer Night's Dream*, the movement itself was, Ellington tells us, inspired by *Othello*, by "the sweet and swinging, very convincing story Othello told Desdemona." Ellington's choice of Nance's trumpet to tell this story was a stroke worthy of his genius. The next two movements are entitled "sonnets"—the four movements in the suite so designated are its less weighty components. The first two are greatly contrasted: a somber, statuesque *Sonnet For Caesar* with Jimmy Hamilton stating a distinguished melodic line with taste and austerity, and the light mercurial *Sonnet For Hank Cinq*, with Hamilton in a scurrying subsidiary role and a bluff and forceful statement from Woodman's trombone, which has just the tone and style of phrasing this subject demands.

"We suspect there was a little ragtime in her soul" was Ellington's comment on *Lady Mac*, the next of these Shakespearian portraits. This is one of the most successful parts of the suite, although the association with its subject is rather tenuous. *Lady Mac* is cast in the form of a jazz waltz and Ellington certainly proves his point that a waltz could be swung with the same vigor as a piece in 4/4. The introductory piano solo is a brilliant conception in itself, a perfect example of jazz in triple time and an ideal opening to the movement. The main soloist in *Lady Mac* is Terry, poised and articulate, Procope's alto providing him with a perfect lead-in. The coda's hint of the more sinister aspects of the subject's personality is suitably theatrical. *Sonnet In Search Of A Moor* is a string bass feature, one of the most imaginative of the many Ellington wrote. Here Jimmy Woode is featured against an accompaniment by a clarinet trio of Hamilton, Procope, and Carney, the latter on bass clarinet. Ellington described his solo here as a "hi-fi piano introduction," which again sets up the movement to perfection.

There is no piano in *The Telecasters* in which Ellington claims to combine the character of Iago with those of the three witches from *Macbeth*. Why this combination and this title? "They all had something to say," observed the composer. Again the relationship to Shakespeare is tenuous, but the music is magnificent, with Carney (as Iago) and the three trombones (the witches) featured along with quizzical interludes of silence. The next movement is one of the great triumphs of the suite. *Up And Down, Up And Down,* is a sound parallel to the situation in *A Midsummer Night's Dream,* Act 3, Scene 2, in which Puck plays havoc with the couples. The musical couples are Hamilton and Nance (on violin), Procope and Gonsalves, and Hodges and Sanders, while Puck is played brilliantly by Clark Terry. Even Ellington rarely made so judicious a choice of soloists, and the entire movement is brought off with deliciously light wit. At the end, Clark's "talking trumpet" renders Puck's famous observation, "What fools these mortals be."

Sonnet For Sister Kate, a rather plaintive lament for Quentin Jackson's plunger trombone, is one of the less successful movements. Jackson himself wanted another attempt at the piece, but Ellington was satisfied, and that was that. If we encountered this performance in other surroundings we too might be satisfied, but between *Up And Down, Up And Down* and *The Star-Crossed Lovers* it does seem rather slight. The latter piece is the inevitable Hodges feature from the suite. As often with Ellington, he dipped back in the repertoire for one of the movements of a new work. On a recording date for Norman Granz's Verve label, Hodges had recorded a brief instrumental ballad by Strayhorn entitled *Pretty Little Girl*. Given an orchestral backdrop, this now became the musical portrait of Romeo and Juliet, *The Star-Crossed Lovers*, in the Shakespearian suite. Alternative takes and rehearsal sequences of a slightly earlier Columbia recording of this number (still under the title *Pretty Little Girl*) have been issued on the Up-To-Date label. These make a fascinating and very beautiful supplement to the standard recording of *The Star-Crossed Lovers*. The melody is exquisite, and the scoring is of the highest Ellington-Strayhorn standard. The publicity always cited Hodges's alto as portraying Juliet and Gonsalves's tenor portraying Romeo, which puzzled many people since Hodges is the only soloist. But Gonsalves has the lead in the beautiful orchestral passage in the middle of the movement.

"In those days, crazy didn't mean the same thing as it means now," noted Ellington apropos of Hamlet and the movement which portrays him, *Madness In Great Ones*. Over an orchestral tapestry of great thematic richness, Cat Anderson ties the piece together with a statement of the strong melody, only to move into a coda where his high notes are set against a repetitive figure from the other trumpets, with the rest of the orchestra silent. It would be difficult to find a more brilliant conception or a more inspired performance in all of Ellington's music. The opening orchestral section of *Madness In Great Ones*, before Anderson's entry, contains some of Ellington's most skillful and imaginative writing. *Half The Fun* is a painting of Cleopatra on the Nile, exotic barge and all, of typical Ellingtonian sensuality. The Woode-Woodyard team is very important here, as is the brief but heady solo by Hodges, but most important of all is the rich, many-colored and beautifully shaded orchestration. (There is an alternative take of this movement on Up-To-Date.) The final *Circle Of Fourths* makes a deliberately perfunctory close to this fabulous suite. It is a lithe, dancing number with Gonsalves in the solo role, following a blues progression through a series of restless key changes.

Such Sweet Thunder must be accounted among the most successful of all Ellington-Strayhorn concert pieces, indeed among the most successful of all their works. It was recorded at a time when the orchestra was in peerless form, and the performance is one of the justifications for the view that this particular orchestra was Ellington's finest since the early forties.

* * *

A series of recordings from a dance in Carrolltown has been issued on the Doctor Jazz, Jazzy, and Koala labels. These date from June 1957, just after the recording of *Such Sweet Thunder* had been completed. The contrast between the casual playing at the dance date and the much more precise playing on the studio recordings is most marked. Of particular interest among the Carrolltown recordings are versions of the popular standard *As Time Goes By*, which features the newly returned Harold Baker on trumpet, and a version of the Cat Anderson number, *The Happy One*, which was recorded commercially only under Johnny Hodges's name. A second showcase for Baker's open trumpet, *Stardust*, uses the same arrangement as that which featured Terry in 1953 (and Nance in 1960).

* * *

Ellington's next recording project took him away from Columbia to act as accompanist to Ella Fitzgerald for Norman Granz's Verve label. Granz had been recording Fitzgerald in a series of *Songbooks* issued in multi-LP sets. These celebrated such important American songwriters as George Gershwin, Harold Arlen, and Richard Rodgers. Both singer and impresario agreed that Ellington belonged in this group and should be represented in their *Songbook* series. The

During a Swedish visit. (*Courtesy of Reportage Foto.*)

Bigard, Hodges, Webster, Hardwick, Carney.

Concert, Royal Tennis Hall, Stockholm, 1958. (*Courtesy of Pressens Bild.*)

Jimmy Blanton on bass and Herb Jeffries on mike, Fargo, North Dakota, 1940. (*Courtesy of Jack Towers.*)

Duke's drummer Sonny Greer, Fargo, North Dakota, 1940. (*Courtesy of Jack Towers.*)

Sam Woodyard and the trumpet section, 1961. (*Courtesy of Ray Avery.*)

Ray Nance with Ellington.

At a recording session.

Johnny Hodges, senior and junior.

The Hodges smile, rarely seen in public.

"My favorite tune? The next one."

In Stockholm, June 1963. (*Courtesy of Folkparkema Central Organisation.*)

Anatomy of a Murder Swedish premiere. (*Courtesy of Sven Tollin*)

During the 1963 tour of the Middle and Far East.

Rehearsal, Malmo, 1966. (*Courtesy of Reportage Foto.*)

With Arthur Fiedler, Hotel Kramer, Malmo, 1965. (*Courtesy of Reportage Foto.*)

The famous orchestra.

Adelaide Hall with Alice Babs, at the international Ellington conference, Birch Hall, Oldham, UK, 1985. (*Courtesy of Patricia Willard.*)

With son Mercer, Malmo airport, 1968. (*Courtesy of Reportage Foto.*)

Duke in an exultant mood.

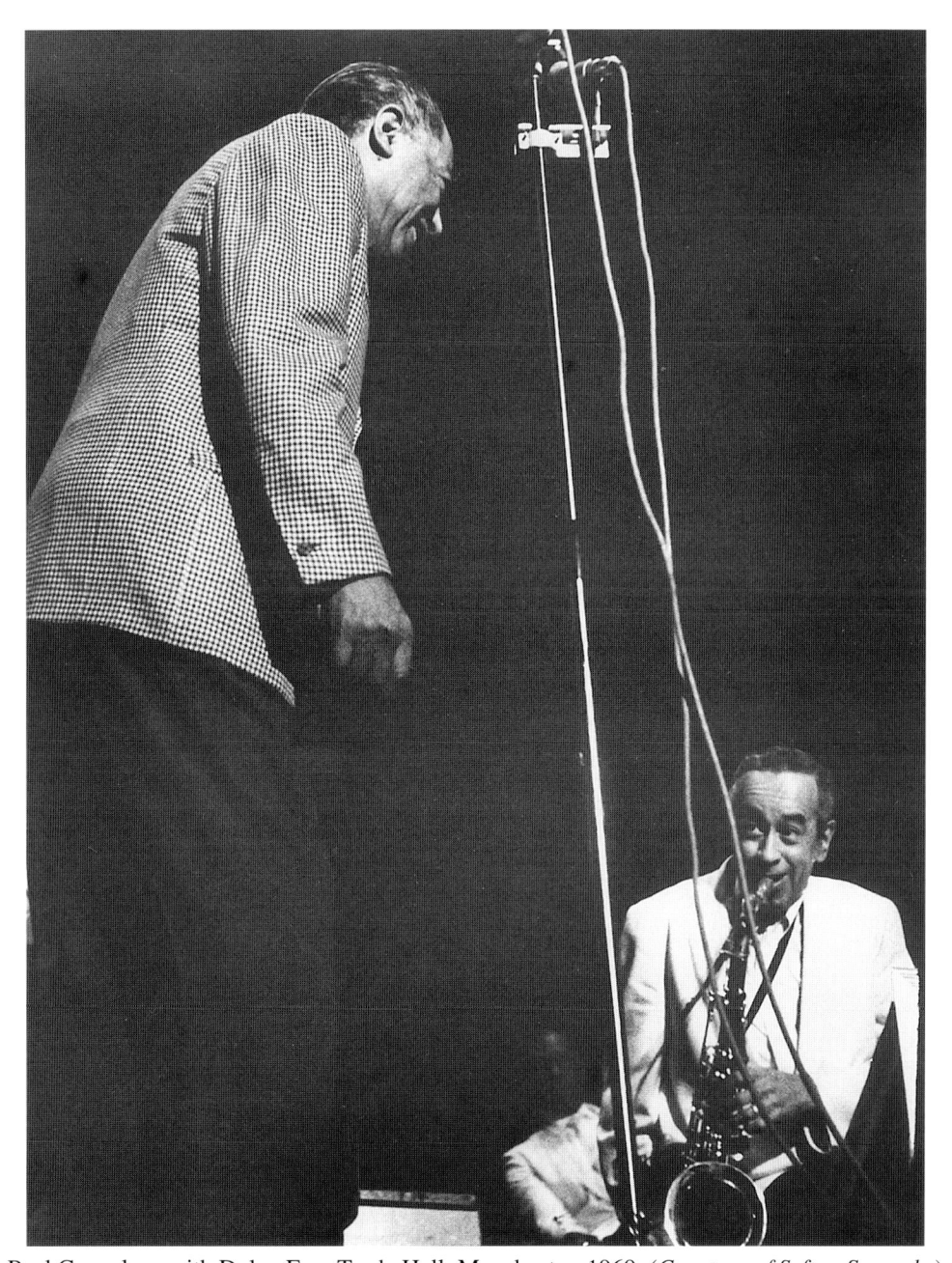

Paul Gonsalves with Duke, Free Trade Hall, Manchester, 1969. (*Courtesy of Sefton Samuels.*)

"In Triplicate," Free Trade Hall, Manchester, 1969. (*Courtesy of Sefton Samuels.*)

At the Free Trade Hall, Manchester, 1969. (*Courtesy of Sefton Samuels.*)

Ellington project produced two sets of two LPs, each containing one disc with Fitzgerald accompanied by a small studio group and one on which she was featured with the Ellington Orchestra. Almost a full side in the second set is taken up by an Ellington-Strayhorn suite commissioned by Granz and dedicated to Fitzgerald.

When the singer joined the band in the studio in the summer of 1957, she had already recorded enough Ellington material for three LP sides in the company of Ben Webster, violinist Stuff Smith, and a rhythm section headed by pianist Paul Smith. The sessions with the band took up four days in June; the suite *A Portrait Of Ella Fitzgerald* was done a couple of months later, and a final session, with Ella accompanied by Webster, the Oscar Peterson Trio, and drummer Alvin Stoller, completed the program in October 1957. It is obvious that Granz and Fitzgerald took a lot of time and trouble over *Ella Fitzgerald Sings The Duke Ellington Song Book*. Ellington seems to have taken the matter rather more lightly, and most of the weaknesses of the set can be laid at his door.

With the small groups, Fitzgerald is in fine voice, obviously relaxed and feeling in tune with the world. The uptempo pieces such as *Cotton Tail*, *It Don't Mean A Thing*, and *Squatty Roo*, on which Ella offers long stretches of scat singing, are the least successful, but they are outnumbered by the many fine medium and slow interpretations. Among these, *Just A-Settin' And A-Rockin'*, *I Let A Song Go Out Of My Heart*, *Don't Get Around Much Anymore*, and *Do Nothin' Til You Hear From Me* are outstanding. On the ballads and medium swingers, Webster is in ravishing form, and the humorous violin of Stuff Smith—an unusual but imaginative choice for these sessions—is a constant source of delight. The rhythm section is up to the high standard expected on a Granz date, and so is the recording quality. The titles with Peterson and Webster are also excellent and well recorded, although the sharp flavoring of Smith's violin is missed.

The dates with the Ellington band, by contrast, began to go wrong from the start. First, Granz could not obtain either the studio or the recording engineer he preferred for any dates on which both Ella and the band were free. So he had to put up with second-best. And then Duke turned up unprepared. He asked which songs and which keys suited Ella, and then he was off, starting his copyists transposing, and stimulating the memory of his musicians regarding numbers they had not played in years. This was the typical Ellington way of working, of course: taking chances, ensuring spontaneity, and leaving maximum room for the inspiration of the moment. Ella must have found it appalling. Throughout her professional life, she had been used to the most careful and painstaking presentation; even in her early days with Chick Webb, special arrangers were engaged for her feature numbers. Most of the hundreds of recordings under her own name had been accompanied by well-rehearsed bands playing tailor-made arrangements. What she must have thought of the chaos of the Ellington band involved in a collective memory exercise can only be imagined. Granz has said that at one point she burst into tears, only to be placated by Ellington.

As if all this were not sufficient, the choice of some numbers was less than ideal—for example, *Rockin' In Rhythm*. Here Ellington did a slight re-jigging of his standard arrangement and Ella was obliged to sing into the microphone over the combined fortissimo playing of the Ellington brass section, Cat Anderson's high notes and all. *Clementine* was another unfortunate choice, an instrumental piece not enhanced by Ella's scat singing. *Take The "A" Train* and *Perdido* have little to recommend them vocally, while the wordless singing on *Chelsea Bridge* seems perfunctory. Of Ellington's actual songs, as opposed to instrumental numbers with and without words added, *Everything But You* comes off badly due to an overfussy arrangement that sounds new to the band. *I Didn't Know About You* and *All Too Soon* find Ella approaching her best form, and on *I Ain't Got Nothing But The Blues* and *I'm Beginning To See The Light* she sings very well indeed. But *Caravan* and *Drop Me Off At Harlem* are further instrumental numbers less than ideal for a vocal collection, and do nothing for the singer.

Ella Fitzgerald Sings The Duke Ellington Song Book is a unique and valuable document for the student of the Ellington band. It finds the men doing some rather hasty memory acts, recording some unrehearsed new Ellington scoring, and reacting to a whole series of new musical situations. With more rehearsal and preparation, this obviously could have been a near-perfect collection, but as a document of the Ellington band it would have been less interesting and less revealing. As it is, we hear them setting the perfect mood time and time again by the skill and strength of personality of the soloists involved. This is particularly true of *Lost In Meditation* (Sanders, Baker, Carney); *I Ain't Got Nothing But The Blues* (Carney, Hodges), and *I'm Just A Lucky So And So* (Ellington, Hodges, Terry)—a contrasting trio of numbers each requiring totally different treatment. The band is here revealed as an ensemble which can, with just a brief outline from its leader, set up any mood or emotional climate. The soloists are given a good deal of room, and there are contributions from Baker on *Perdido* and Gonsalves on *All Too Soon* which must be reckoned among their best work. Willie Cook had returned to increase the trumpet section to five, and on *Take The "A" Train* guest Dizzy Gillespie makes it six in an extended trumpet chase. Although full of fascinating things, this chase is a victim of less than expert recording technique. On *I'm Beginning To See The Light*, which, like *"A" Train*, is given a totally new arrangement, the band swings superbly with outstanding bass work from Woode. There are brief high-class contributions from Hodges on *Day Dream* and *I Got It Bad*. The one new piece is *The E And D Blues*, a casual Ellington medium-tempo romp with Ella scat singing and sharing the solos with Hodges, Nance and Hamilton, the last on tenor.

Norman Granz tells us that the night before *Portrait Of Ella Fitzgerald* was to be recorded, Ellington had not written a note. He turned up for the session with a few things scribbled on the backs of envelopes, and with the aid of his copyists and his special kind of musical shorthand, the band managed to turn out a four-movement suite. This may not be the best of Ellington's suites, but it is a minor work of quality. The first movement, *Royal Ancestry*, is an unusual 32-bar piece with distinctive ensemble writing and a fine solo by Paul Gonsalves. The second movement, *All Heart*, is one of Ellington's finest settings for the glorious open trumpet of Baker. *Beyond Category* is an amusing essay in the bop idiom: Terry is obviously Duke's inspiration here, and he and Hamilton are the main soloists, with Gonsalves and Carney also heard. The main indication of Ellington's unpreparedness for the *Portrait* is found in the last movement, another improvised blues similar in mood and tempo to *The E And D Blues*. Called *Total Jazz*, it features an outstanding plunger-muted solo by Terry and an unexpected excursion by John Sanders into the world of solo improvisation. Gonsalves and Hamilton complete the solo roster. On the original issue of the *Portrait Of Ella Fitzgerald*, there are spoken introductions to each movement by Ellington or Strayhorn. Embarrassing in their maïveté, they describe Ella as if she were a heroine in a tale for very young children. Duke's coy delivery serves only to increase the listener's discomfort.

* * *

After this fascinating digression for the Verve label, Ellington returned to Columbia with a new collection of ballad interpretations, recorded in September and October 1957, except for one track (*The Sky Fell Down*) which dates from March. In America this set was issued on an LP called *Ellington Indigos*, but for some reason the British Philips company, which then had the rights to U.S. Columbia material, changed the title to *Solitude*. This set found little favor among reviewers in the jazz press. There is a definite prejudice among jazz lovers against ballads by big bands; they seem incapable of distinguishing between genuine musical contributions and the more insipid pop song recordings prevalent in the swing era. For soloists to record ballad collections, including current pop songs, is acceptable, but if a big band, even one so distinguished as Ellington's, does it, the automatic response of many listeners and most reviewers is to regard the product as tainted with commercialism. In fact, *Ellington Indigos* is an LP of exceptional music making, albeit a different proposition from either *Such Sweet Thunder* or *A Drum Is A Woman*.

Ellington's Columbia releases from *Such Sweet Thunder* onwards had been made available, in the United States at least, in both stereo and mono versions, and in the case of *Ellington Indigos* two of the titles, *Mood Indigo* and *Willow Weep For Me*, are heard in different takes on the stereo and mono releases. *Mood Indigo* is one of four Ellington titles among the nine items presented (eight on the original pressings of the stereo version which omit *The Sky Fell Down*, ap-

parently recorded in mono only). This *Mood Indigo* takes the form of an extended muted solo by Baker of quite outstanding quality—a beautifully melodic construction. *Prelude To A Kiss* becomes a Hodges feature and receives a melodic interpretation of the highest distinction. Ellington himself takes the solo role in *Solitude*, playing lightheartedly with both melody and harmony, creating combinations of apparently incongruous elements and blending them perfectly. The fourth Ellington song is *Someone* from 1942, now with the title *The Sky Fell Down*. The writing here is superficially conventional—saxes with strong alto lead, lyrical trumpet soloist—but the playing of his musicians makes for a performance beyond the grasp of any other band. The poise of the phrasing, the richness of tonal quality, and the warmth of the emotional projection are outstanding, and Nance proves an ideal choice as soloist.

The rather heavily textured score of *Where Or When* is a showcase for Gonsalves in a vein similar to that of *Laura* from the previous year, while in *Tenderly* the cool clarinet virtuosity of Hamilton is provided with a perfect orchestral context. *Willow Weep For Me* is one of the highlights of the LP, featuring Duke's casual-sounding piano in most subtle thematic touches, Baker at his best, and a touch of passionate Hodges alto. The two takes are very different, the mono the more cohesive, the stereo with superior solo playing. Baker is heard on muted and open trumpet on mono but remains open on the stereo take, much to its advantage. (On a recording from a U.S. Air Force dance the following March, this same arrangement is heard without the Ellington and Hodges solos—Hodges was out of the band temporarily—and features Baker on open trumpet throughout. As a band performance it is much less impressive than the Columbia versions, but as a piece of ballad trumpet playing it is simply glorious.)

Vocalist Ozzie Bailey is heard on *Autumn Leaves*, in which the rather sparse orchestral textures are handled with skill. Nance on violin gives forth in his most romantic vein. On the final track, *Dancing In The Dark*, Carney's baritone and Nance's trumpet are heard in another imaginative arrangement. Throughout this LP the Ellington soloists, including Duke himself, show how wonderfully they can present a program of ballads—beautiful theme statements combined with rich and imaginative improvisations. The orchestral writing by Ellington and Strayhorn is equally creative and tasteful. A beautiful set!

* * *

The next Ellington project on the Columbia schedule should have been a triumph—a remake of *Black, Brown And Beige*, with gospel singer Mahalia Jackson brought in to participate in the *Come Sunday* section. The resultant LP is a considerable disappointment, though full of interesting things. Not for the first time it would appear that Ellington's dilatory behavior resulted in an untidy and imperfect final product. Of the three sections of *Black, Brown And Beige*, only the first, *Black*, is on this LP. Possibly the parts for *Brown* and *Beige* were lost and there was insufficient time for them to be transcribed. Whatever the reason, the time allocated by Columbia for the project ran out with only one of the three movements recorded. This occupies the first side of the LP; the reverse contains *Come Sunday* (already heard in its original place on side one) sung by Mahalia Jackson, a third version of *Come Sunday* played by Ray Nance on violin, and *The 23rd Psalm* sung by Jackson. All three sound like spur-of-the-moment creations.

The performance of *Black* follows the pattern of the earlier recordings in all essentials, except that the extended solo normally taken by Hodges in *Come Sunday* is played by Carney and Baker. Hodges was on temporary leave from the band, working in a trio with Billy Strayhorn. (His replacement, Bill Graham, an experienced big band musician, does not take solos on any of his recordings with Ellington.) Carney's reading of the spiritual theme from *Come Sunday* is as impressive as Hodges's, but the switch to Baker's muted trumpet for the middle part seems unnecessary, and Woodyard's percussion effects at this point sound decidedly out of place. The solos on *Work Song* are by Carney, Baker, and Quentin Jackson; those at the start of *Come Sunday* by John Sanders and Nance (violin); and those in the *Montage* (or *Light*) section by Baker (open trumpet), Anderson (with plunger mute), Woode, and Woodman. Baker's playing is outstanding throughout *Black*, and the band plays with expected ensemble expertise. The Mahalia Jackson vocals and the Nance violin solo on the second side are pleasant enough but make a poor substitute for *Brown* and *Beige*.

It is difficult to conjecture why Ellington let this project tail off in so abject a fashion. It is true that he was not usually happy looking backwards and often said that he played his old numbers only to satisfy a section of his audience. But this "tone parallel to the history of the Negro in America" was a work he always considered an important statement of his creed, and he had no hesitation in presenting further revivals in the sixties. Yet he allowed the best opportunity he ever had to get the complete work down on record to peter out. It may be that he had doubts about the form of the work, or about the structure of *Beige* in particular (this part was never revived in full after the premiere performances) and felt disinclined to undertake a major revision. Or maybe he was just too busy with other work, including the time-consuming business of keeping the band on the road 52 weeks of the year. Whatever the reason, the result of this promising project is an unsatisfactory LP—despite the excellent performance of *Black*.

* * *

During the second half of the fifties, the band also recorded other material for Columbia than that issued on the series of LPs listed at the beginning of this chapter. Some things were put out on singles and others remained unissued; in later years some of these items have been released as part of LP anthologies, yet there is a good deal of unissued Ellingtonia from the fifties still languishing in the Columbia vaults.

Typical of the excellent music which was kept on ice for over a decade is *A-flat Minor*, a delightful uptempo piece in which the brass section's boppish theme is contrasted with a very basic Hodges solo. This is from a 1956 session which also produced *Suburban Beauty*, an attractive, swinging, medium-tempo piece which just might have become a hit had it been issued as a single at the right time: certainly the simple melodic content and lack of development, either solo or ensemble, seems the correct recipe for popular success. The trombone section is heard to excellent effect on this. Another attractive item unissued for years is *Cafe Au Lait*, with tuneful thematic material and fine writing for the saxophone section. These three pieces appear in the U.S. Columbia/European CBS two-LP album *The World Of Duke Ellington, Volume Two*. All three also appear on Up-To-Date in alternate takes, with fascinating snatches of rehearsal surrounding the first and third titles.

Also appearing for the first time in *The World Of Duke Ellington, Volume Two*, is *Improvisation In Three Parts*, a piano suite recorded in March 1957. Ellington is accompanied by bass and drums, and his playing accurately reflects the use of the word *Improvisation*—less formal than, for example, the Capitol solos of 1953. The work is diffuse even by Ellington's standards, the movements lacking any unifying element. The "three parts" are a fast blues, a slow blues, and a piece of stride virtuosity. The rhythmic strength of these performances is marked, as are Ellington's highly individual harmonic usage and melodic invention. His playing on the two blues is perfect jazz piano, with every aspect in proportion and balance. Humor is to the fore in the final movement, a really remarkable piece of stride piano with hints of James P. Johnson's *Carolina Shout* and Ellington's own *Dancers In Love*; the closing is sheer rhythmic magic. This *Improvisation In Three Parts* rates very highly among Ellington's recordings from this golden period. Actually, five segments were recorded, and the original title was *Improvisation: Blues-Ragtime-Rhumba*. The two played over a rhumba beat were not used by Columbia but have been issued on Up-To-Date.

Also from this March 1957 session come three band recordings. *Cop Out* is an uptempo showcase for Gonsalves in the manner of his marathons, but here the performance is kept down to less than three minutes, since it was recorded for issue as a single. In that form, its backing was one of the first of Ellington's commercially unsuccessful attempts at rock and roll, *Rock City Rock*, in a performance driven along powerfully by Woodyard. The band plays with great punch, and the vigorous work by vocalist Grissom and Hamilton on tenor sax makes for an exciting performance, if one of slight musical depth. The third title, *The Sky Fell Down*, was used for the *Ellington Indigos* LP.

Ellington made two further attempts at hit parade success later in 1957 with *My Heart, My Mind, My Everything* and

Together. Grissom is heard at length, and only a short Gonsalves solo on the second title sheds much musical light. The following year saw the issue on a single of *Duke's Place*, the vocal version of *C Jam Blues*, with Ozzie Bailey featured; but again popular success proved elusive. Later in 1958, Bailey and Lil Greenwood shared vocal duties on a single which contained two of Duke's latest songs—*Hand Me Down Love* and *Walkin' And Singin' The Blues*. Despite some ingenious writing for the brass section on the former and a touch of class by Hodges on the latter, these cannot be regarded as important Ellington recordings.

* * *

A considerable amount of nonstudio material has become available on disc from these years. Three titles from a broadcast from the Chicago Blue Note in mid-1957 are pleasant enough but add very little to Ellingtonia, being very close to the studio versions. These are *Rock City Rock* (vocal Grissom), *You Better Know It* (vocal Bailey), and *I Got It Bad* (the usual showcase for Hodges).

November of the same year saw a TV show by Ellington, the music from which has been issued on a Joyce LP with only the *Medley Of Popular Hits* and a brief closing version of *"A" Train* missing. A short opening version of this theme is followed by *Jam With Sam*, suggesting that we are about to be treated to the usual selection of Ellington favorites. But after a conversation with the announcer Duke plays half a chorus of *Soda Fountain Rag* and follows with excerpts from *Such Sweet Thunder* and a surprising revival of *The Perfume Suite*. The selections from the Shakespearian suite are the title piece, somewhat faster than on the LP and with Nance's solo played muted; *The Telecasters*, very close to the original; and *Lady Mac*, in a performance which brings out the power of the climax and has solos by Duke and Terry that differ from those on Columbia. *The Perfume Suite* had been out of the repertoire for many years; the announcer tells us that Ellington had to consult his old recordings prior to the performance as the original sheet music was lost. The band performs its collective memory act, and only the first two movements seem adversely affected. The long opening passage by Nance and Ellington from *Balcony Serenade* (or *Under The Balcony*, as it is called here) is replaced by a four-bar piano introduction. *Strange Feeling* is cut down to a single chorus sung by Grissom, with Anderson adding distant muted comments in a faint echo of the important part his plunger trumpet played in the original. *Dancers In Love* had been regularly used by Ellington as a piano feature, and on this occasion he is joined by the studio audience in the finger-snapping routine which had become a part of the piece. Ellington delivers a sparkling interpretation of the piano part. The last movement, *Coloratura*, had also stayed in the repertoire longer than the first two, and the performance here by Anderson and the band is that of men playing a fairly familiar piece. These excerpts from the Chicago TV program end with a couple of vocals by a local singer accompanied by the band, and a short version of *Satin Doll*.

* * *

The reason for the inclusion of *The Perfume Suite* on the TV program seems to have been that the band was preparing the work for a Columbia recording, which took place on December 2 and 9. For some reason, the version of *Strange Feeling* was considered unsatisfactory and a remake was done three and a half years later, in June 1961. The Columbia version of the suite was not issued until 1982, on an LP with the also previously unissued *The Girl's Suite*. It adds little to the recordings of *The Perfume Suite* from the mid-forties, and *Strange Feeling* is distinctly inferior. On *Dancers In Love*, Ellington verbally encourages the band's finger-snapping, and there is even an ensemble coda. Neither this nor slight changes in orchestration in the other movements is an improvement, but this version does have the benefit of superior sound.

* * *

Recordings of the Ellington band playing for dancing are of particular value, as the Fargo recordings of November 1940 demonstrate so well. At concerts the band may often play in a relaxed fashion, but the tendency of the audience to demand virtuosity, plus Ellington's habit of springing unrehearsed works on the band, are negative factors. And sometimes the band sounds bored. On dance dates, the very relaxed attitude of the band often leads to outstanding performances, though they can also be rather untidy. In the dance hall situation, rhythmic vitality is a primary consideration, and this tends to bring out the best qualities in a jazz ensemble.

The Doctor Jazz label has issued a two-LP set from a dance in Carrolltown, Pennsylvania, in June 1957; some music from this date has also appeared on Jazzy and Koala. Anderson and Woode are absent, but Joe Benjamin subs for the latter, most noticeably on *Bass-ment*. Cook has a fine solo on *Mood Indigo* and Baker, newly returned to the band, is featured on both *Stardust* and *As Time Goes By*. There is a version of Anderson's rarely heard *The Happy One* (without the composer) and another exciting version of *Diminuendo And Crescendo In Blue* with 26 choruses of Gonsalves between the two parts. The sound quality is superb for a location recording.

On March 4 and 5 1958, the band played dances at the Travis Air Force Base and we are very fortunate that these have also been preserved in excellent stereo sound. Although no complete edition of these recordings has yet been published, several have come out in rather haphazard fashion, on LPs on the Jazz Connoisseur, Unique Jazz, and Koala labels. Unfortunately the music issued on Jazz Connoisseur is taken from a poor copy of the tapes, but the issues on the other two labels are in excellent sound. The Koalas are particularly good in this respect, but the music is mixed up with material from other sources, there is no discographical information, and the titles are sometimes wrong.

At the time of these dances, the band was without two of its key members, Hodges and Anderson, both on temporary leave. Bill Graham came in for Hodges on alto but took no solos; Anderson was not replaced, and as Willie Cook had left, the trumpet section was down to three—Baker, Terry, and Nance. It speaks volumes for the quality of the Ellington band at this time that two such strong personalities as Hodges and Anderson were not missed at all.

Some numbers in the Ellington repertoire were used both at concerts and dances, and the Travis recordings include a good selection of Ellington standards from this category. Among these are *Satin Doll* (the original arrangement, followed by a bass feature for Woode); two versions of *Caravan*, both much slower than usual and both with amusing spoken introductions by Duke (Nance is heard on violin on one, trumpet on the other, and there is some fine John Sanders valve trombone on the melody); *Mood Indigo* (featuring Procope on clarinet in one of his best solos and a magnificent contribution from Baker on open trumpet); *Perdido* (featuring Terry); *C Jam Blues*; a combined *I Let A Song Out Of My Heart/Don't Get Around Much Anymore* (Nance vocal on the second); *Sophisticated Lady* (featuring Carney); *Just Squeeze Me* (another fine Nance vocal); and *"A" Train* (the standard arrangement, featuring Nance on trumpet and a long and excellent introductory piano solo by Ellington).

A portion of the Ellington repertoire was used almost exclusively for dances, as represented here by *Smada*, *Honeysuckle Rose* (both featuring Hamilton's clarinet), *Frivolous Banta* (which had become a feature for Hamilton's tenor after the departure of Rick Henderson), *Boo-Dah*, *Suburban Beauty*, and *Main Stem*. It is particularly interesting to hear a revival of *Main Stem* with Hodges out of the band as it gives Procope an opportunity to play a couple of choruses of basic swing alto. Nance handles the trumpet parts, and the solos originally taken by Webster, Nanton, and Brown are given to Gonsalves, Jackson, and Woodman.

Any extended selection of Ellington performances can be expected to yield a number of new compositions and such is the case here. One of the numbers from the March 5, 1958, dance is so obscure that its title has not survived, and it seems destined to be known to posterity as *Unknown Title*. Neither this nor the number known as *Wailing Interlude* are more than conventional bread and butter big band scores, though pleasant enough within their modest scope. *Vivi* is another little-known piece, cast in the unusual form of a showcase for John Sanders on valve trombone. This is of less interest than two other new numbers, both to be featured in the Ellington program at the 1958 Newport Jazz Festival four months later—*Juniflip* and *Just Scratchin' The Surface*. The former is a showcase for Terry on flugelhorn, the latter another rather conventional band number. Both sound good here, but the Columbia recordings on the *Newport 1958* LP are superior.

A dance hall is not where one would normally expect to hear excerpts from concert works, but in this regard (as in so many others) Ellington was a law unto himself. Here we are treated to a beautiful performance of *All Heart* from *A Portrait Of Ella Fitzgerald*, with lyrical trumpet playing from Baker in the featured role, and *The Star-Crossed Lovers* from *Such Sweet Thunder*. The latter is a most unusual choice as it was written to feature Hodges, who of course was absent on this date. Instead, the main statement is allocated to vocalist Ozzie Bailey. The vocal is wordless, and Bailey sounds a trifle uneasy; the use of the voice cannot be accounted a success, but the recording does serve to bring out the fine orchestral backing, so easily missed when a listener's attention is focussed on Hodges's superb playing.

The Ellington band featured many popular standards on dance engagements, and Bailey is heard again in conventional vocals on three of these—*Autumn Leaves*, *Together*, and *Blue Moon*. The versions of *Where Or When* and *Dancing In The Dark* are, like that of *Autumn Leaves*, very close to those on the slightly earlier *Ellington Indigos* LP, but *Willow Weep For Me* is changed, owing to Hodges's absence. On the Columbia versions, the altoist had taken a prominent role, but here what is basically the same arrangement is used as a frame for a beautiful trumpet feature for Baker. Both here and on *All Heart* Baker plays open trumpet, and his fine tone is heard to great advantage.

The most unusual item from the Travis Air Force Base recordings is *The Beer Barrel Polka*, performed in true polka fashion. Stanley Dance has told of an occasion when Duke, preparing for a dance for an audience of East European descent, sent him out to obtain some authentic polka records so he could study them and compete with the polka band with which he was to alternate. Despite the authentic style, the band sounds uninterested in polkas, but Terry sees the humor inherent in the situation, and with sound backing from Hamilton and Woodyard the day is saved and *The Beer Barrel Polka* receives what must be its most hilarious performance on record.

The other three items which have been issued from these dates are all blues, and as might be expected they are among the best of the recordings. There are two excellent performances of *Blues To Be There* from *The Newport Jazz Festival Suite*, featuring Procope and Nance; *Bass-ment*, featuring Jimmy Woode and heard here in the version for full band which includes the two-chorus passage for the saxophone section later used in the *Red Carpet* movement of *Toot Suite*; and *Blue Star* (alias *Star Blues* alias *Blues In Orbit*), which features Duke on piano.

* * *

In 1977, a five-LP box of previously unissued Ellington performances was released on the MF Productions label. This includes both studio and concert performances and although the discographical information supplied with the box is minimal, it has become obvious that some of the recordings come from Swedish concerts given during the band's 1958 and 1959 tours. The sound quality is first class, and while these recordings are of familiar material there are some notable performances. *Things Ain't What They Used To Be* is by a considerable margin the best of the versions of this number using the Hodges showcase format. Johnny is in a witty and inventive mood here and the band plays with a wonderful control of dynamics and an infectious swing. This is a great performance. *Diminuendo And Crescendo In Blue* is perhaps a little too fast for the orchestral performance to be considered definitive, but the Gonsalves solo is superbly recorded, far better than that on the Newport version, and is one of his best solos in this vein. The other recordings from 1958 in the MF set are mainly versions of familiar solo showcases: *Perdido* (Terry), *Sophisticated Lady* (Carney), *Sonnet For Hank Cinq* (Woodman), and *Satin Doll* (Woode). There is also an edited version of the *Medley Of Popular Hits* which includes a *Just Squeeze Me* with a lively Nance vocal. A number of these recordings come from a concert in Göteborg on November 6, 1958, a part of which was issued on an LP on the Italian Musica Jazz label. Some of the tracks duplicate those on MF, but the disc also includes the *Black And Tan Fantasy/Creole Love Call/The Mooche* medley, *Boo-Dah*, *On The Sunny Side Of The Street* (a Hodges feature), and *El Gato*, none of which appears in these versions on MF.

The 1959 recordings from the MF box include good but not outstanding versions of *Such Sweet Thunder*, *Rockin' In Rhythm*, and two more Hodges showcases—*Jeep's Blues* and *Passion Flower*. (Other material from this set will be dealt with according to date of recording.)

* * *

If the response of jazz critics to *A Drum Is A Woman* was cool, their reaction to Ellington's next essay of a humorous nature, the *At The Bal Masque* LP, was distinctly frigid. In contrast to many of his followers, Ellington set great store by humor and regarded it as an indispensable quality for a jazz musician. In *At The Bal Masque* wit and humor are the dominant qualities, and the disc has never been popular with the more solemn members of the jazz fraternity. The format is indeed one which would lure most jazz groups into the depths of disaster, for Ellington selects a group of improbable songs which would normally be fare for a light novelty orchestra. He presents them in a supper-club manner and himself assumes a mock-cocktail piano style. Leading from the front, Duke plunges the band into such selections as *Who's Afraid Of The Big Bad Wolf*, *Satan Takes A Holiday*, and *The Donkey Serenade*. The idea for this LP and its title is said to have been inspired by an Ellington residence in the supper room of the American Hotel in Miami Beach, which was decorated with a sequence of masks. The musical masks which Ellington uses are fortunately very transparent, and just below the surface of the music lie all the familiar Ellington musical features. It is obvious that Ellington and the band relish the ironies of the situation. The element of parody is, however, handled gently, but, even when Duke is giving the most simple theme statement at the piano, he manages to include quirky harmonic and rhythmic twists. The orchestral writing is of the best Ellington class and even the most banal tune is given a sumptuous score. According to Irving Townsend's liner notes, the repertoire is based on the actual decor of the American room, Ellington conceiving a "musical masquerade of Alice and the wolf, an angel, a butterfly and a peanut vendor, a satin doll and a donkey, the lady in red with her Indian, and a gypsy and a clown." This cast of characters is portrayed by the following numbers (in addition to the soloists shown, Ellington is featured on every track on piano): *Alice Blue Gown* (Hodges), *Who's Afraid Of The Big Bad Wolf* (Terry, Gonsalves), *Got A Date With An Angel*, *Poor Butterfly* (Hamilton, Nance on violin, Gonsalves), *Satan Takes A Holiday* (Carney), *The Peanut Vendor* (Nance), *Satin Doll* (Woode), *The Lady In Red* (Hamilton, Terry), *Indian Love Call* (Baker, Hamilton), *The Donkey Serenade* (Jackson), *Gypsy Love Song* (Nance on violin, Hodges), *Laugh, Clown, Laugh* (Carney).

At The Bal Masque is a total success primarily because the band responds so well to the humor of the situation which Ellington has set up. Another advantage is that the drums are recorded in their proper perspective so that Woodyard can be heard to excellent effect. The scoring by Ellington and Strayhorn is a compound of deliberate hamming, light wit, and subtle stylistic satire. The takeoff on the Hal Kemp style on *Got A Date With An Angel* is a masterpiece of musical irony; *Poor Butterfly* has dazzling flights by Hamilton and incorporates one of Gonsalves's most exquisite solos; the wit of *Satan Takes A Holiday* and the easy swing of *Peanut Vendor*, with its evocation of the Louis Armstrong version by Nance's trumpet and its brief allusion to the ponderous Kenton recording, are very special; *Satin Doll*, the only Ellington composition, is heard in the format then used at concerts—as a showcase for Woode's bass. The conception of *The Donkey Serenade* as a feature for plunger-muted trombone is amusing enough in itself, but with the skills and wit of this orchestration we have a masterpiece of musical humor: Hodges's ballad style has never been heard to better effect than on *Gypsy Love Song*; and *Laugh, Clown, Laugh* is transformed into a swinger with which to end the masquerade. Not the least remarkable facet of this unique set of performances is the way the band swings throughout, and for so unusual a venture, the poise of the music is remarkable. Ellington will always be remembered as a man of real humor, and this aspect of his personality is given full rein in *At The Bal Masque*. It is a collection which saw the only billing on record of "Duke Ellington, His Piano and His Orchestra" and the fact that the jazz world has failed to see the joke for 30 years is not the least revealing aspect of this LP.

* * *

After this extravaganza, Ellington's next project was much more conventional in jazz terms: a set by a medium-sized group from the orchestra. It seems that Ellington was determined to show a different aspect of his genius with each succeeding issue. So far for Columbia, he had done a collection with a pop singer, a jazz festival LP, a fantasy on the history of jazz, a Shakespearian suite, a selection of ballads, a revival of a major concert work, and a set of satirical pop performances. Now he appeared with his "Spacemen," an unusually constituted group, on an LP called *The Cosmic Scene*—both band name and LP title celebrating the successful launching of the first American space satellite. The group is built around a front line of Terry (trumpet), Hamilton (clarinet), and Gonsalves (tenor) with the trombone and rhythm sections in accompaniment. This novel combination produced an LP of dazzling jazz with brilliant solos from the trio of principals, varied and punching backing from the trombones, and ideal support from Ellington, Woode, and Woodyard.

Three of the titles—*Avalon, Early Autumn,* and *Midnight Sun*—are arranged by Hamilton, and *Perdido* also has the sound of a Hamilton score. There are three new Ellington themes, the first of which is *Bass-ment*, featuring Woode against trombone figures and including some inventive Ellington piano blues; this is the number reputedly recorded at the last Capitol session and is also known as *Discontented* and *Daddy's Blues*. Terry plays an important part in the other two new numbers, as cocomposer of *Jones* and as soloist in the uptempo *Spacemen*. *Jones* is the blues at fast medium tempo with a brilliant solo by Gonsalves; an alternative take, issued on EP, has great differences in this solo. *Body And Soul* is a Gonsalves showcase; he plays a hushed and beautifully melodic slow chorus followed by three in his uptempo manner. (This routine became established for a while in the band repertoire.) The longest track on *The Cosmic Scene* is a version of *St. Louis Blues* with Ellington contributing a characteristic theme statement and Terry and Gonsalves taking excellent blues choruses; Gonsalves is outstanding. Hamilton's arrangement of Ralph Burns's lovely ballad *Early Autumn* is given a superb performance.

The Cosmic Scene is wholly successful, and the danger that a medium-sized group might sound like either an undernourished big band or an overgrown small group is avoided. The music has all the spontaneity of a small-band date, with the contribution of the trombone section a delightful bonus. This is another collection on which the Columbia engineers resisted the temptation to overrecord Woodyard's playing; as a result, his vital contribution is tellingly heard in its true perspective.

* * *

The standardized format of Ellington concerts from the fifties onwards caused a good deal of adverse criticism; it was sometimes said that audiences at dances heard a more varied selection of current Ellingtonia than at his concerts. One concert audience which heard a very different program, however, was the one present at the 1958 Newport Jazz Festival. Here Duke returned to the scene of one of his greatest triumphs, and for the occasion he produced a whole batch of new music. Columbia again recorded the Festival but once more it was considered that the live Ellington recordings were technically below the standard required for release. Only two of the Newport performances were used on the LP, issued as *Newport 1958*; the remainder came from a New York studio date held eighteen days later, with crowd noises dubbed in.

It would be wrong to question Columbia's judgment in remaking the recordings without having heard the originals, but the two tracks from the Festival, *Just Scratchin' The Surface* and *Prima Bara Dubla*, suggest that the standard of band playing was quite acceptable. *Just Scratchin' The Surface* was the opening number, and finds Duke indulging in conventional big band scoring with the sections used as self-contained blocks; the performance is full of vitality, with a deep relaxed swing and tremendous punch from the ensemble. Paul Gonsalves has a fine solo and Woode and Woodyard in their contrasting ways lay the soundest of foundations. *Prima Bara* features Carney and guest star Gerry Mulligan in a piece for two baritones written by Ellington. There is no element of competition, and the piece emerges as a friendly collaboration between two masters of the baritone sax.

Of the studio remakes, the most impressive are *Multicolored Blue*, *Mr. Gentle and Mr. Cool*, and *Happy Re-Union*. *Multicolored Blue* is a development of *Violet Blue*, a Strayhorn ballad in twelve-bar form used as a Hodges feature in the mid-forties. Hodges recorded the piece under this name in 1947 on one of his small-band dates. In the new arrangement, the original ballad mode is used at the beginning and end, with glowing orchestral colors behind the solo alto. Framed by these passages are two vocal episodes by Ozzie Bailey and a central alto solo which treats the melodic material in a forthright blues manner, backed by stinging trumpets and a propulsive walking bass. *Mr. Gentle And Mr. Cool* is a very simple, swinging number taken at a loping, slow to medium tempo designed by Ellington to display the talents of Baker on trumpet and Nance on violin—Nance stated that neither ever learned from Duke who was who! This is the kind of performance inexplicable to anyone lacking a feeling for jazz, for the entire purpose of this operation is to swing. Baker, who had a distinct talent for ornate phrasing, simply concentrates on swinging riffs in his solo, while Nance swings with particular power in a solo full of light, humorous touches. Ellington fills in wonderfully on piano, while Woode and Woodyard provide a sound yet flexible base.

The title *Happy Re-Union* refers to Gonsalves's return to Newport after his 1956 triumph. Yet this piece is totally different in mood and substance from his *Diminuendo And Crescendo In Blue* solo. An Ellington ballad for tenor sax accompanied by piano, bass and drums only, it is one of the most beautiful tenor solos ever recorded and one of the high spots of Gonsalves's recording career. The beauty of the melodic statement, the sensitivity of the phrasing, and the aptness of the variations all enhance a performance of rare warmth and grace. Ellington's important contributions—as composer and in his perfect piano accompaniment—are apt to be overlooked in the flow of Gonsalves's lyricism.

Princess Blue is the longest track on the LP, a little-known Ellington concert piece dedicated to Princess Margaret, whom he had met at the Stratford (Ontario) Shakespeare Festival. The main melodic material, a theme containing some subtle twists, is derived from an episode in the first movement of *Symphomaniac* (1948). It is stated by Duke's piano at the outset and developed by the band in a subtle, pastel-colored score. Hamilton's clarinet has an important role, and there are solos by Procope (alto), Woodman (trombone), and Terry (trumpet). These are not jazz solos in the usual sense, but passages in which the distinctive solo style of each musician is used by Ellington as part of the development. Finally, Ellington and Hamilton re-create the stilled mood of the opening. There are many moments of superb music in *Princess Blue*, an underrated minor masterpiece of great charm.

The remaining pieces are of a slighter cast: *Juniflip* is an Ellington showcase for Terry's flugelhorn with a highly individual melodic line; *Hi Fi Fo Fum*, for Woodyard, has some nice writing for the band before the percussion onslaught, and *Jazz Festival Jazz* is Ellington's impression of the music heard at a jazz festival. This has Terry, Hamilton, and Gonsalves in a "cool" first part; a front line of Nance, Jackson, and Procope in the second "Dixieland" segment; and Anderson's high-note climax in the brief third part. Anderson is the composer of *El Gato*, in which he alternates a Latin American theme with jazz solos for the four members of Duke's superb trumpet section. On record, this piece loses something of its impact and excitement as compared to the spectacular concert presentations with the four contrasting virtuoso trumpeters lined up at the front of the stage.

Newport 1958 is an outstanding collection of fresh and creative jazz, but this, too, was largely overlooked by a critical fraternity busily extolling the latest ephemeral jazz fashion. Without doubt, such critics did their readers little service in passing over an Ellington collection containing such valuable and contrasting works as *Princess Blue, Happy Reunion,* and *Mr. Gentle And Mr. Cool.*

* * *

Shortly after the 1958 Newport Jazz Festival, Columbia threw a party for its jazz roster at the Hotel Plaza in New York City. The artists who performed at this chic function were Miles Davis and his sextet, the Ellington Orchestra, Jimmy Rushing, and Billie Holiday. In 1973, two LPs were released of recordings from this event. The first featured the Miles Davis portion, but *Jazz At The Plaza, Volume Two,* contains the Ellington performances as well as those by Rushing and Holiday. The main item on the Ellington agenda is what later became known as *Toot Suite,* here called *Jazz Festival Suite.* The first movement, *Red Garter,* has a smoky, sultry melody played by Woodman over a distinctive bass figure; Carney and Hamilton handle the variations; and there are flashes of contrasting color from Baker's muted trumpet before Woodman returns for the recapitulation. The second movement, *Red Shoes,* is a typical latter-day Ellington stomp played with great verve and drive. The melody is tricky, but that seems to put the musicians on their toes and the surge and spirit of the performance are impressive. Hamilton and Baker are the soloists, and Ellington's use of Hamilton's clarinet as an ensemble voice is very effective. The third movement is a slow blues, *Red Carpet,* itself in three sections, each of the first two ending with a cadenza. This is in the great Ellington blues tradition. Its first part features Procope's clarinet against trombones and baritone sax. This is followed by a passage for the reed section in which one of Ellington's richest mixings of saxophones and clarinets is heard; this is taken from the full band version of *Bass-ment.* Jackson is the second soloist, and his mastery of plunger technique has never been heard to better effect. The final section of *Red Carpet* has Nance preaching the blues on plunger-muted trumpet against the main riff, now played by the clarinet trio. The whole movement is full of wonderful jazz making, but its continuity would have been enhanced by omission of the cadenzas. *Toot Suite* ends with *Ready Go,* a Gonsalves marathon of the type which jazz concert audiences now expected from him. This one lasts for over six minutes, and the orchestra cooks up a couple of storms while Paul goes relentlessly on his way. Whether the finale of a four-movement suite is the best place for this kind of display is questionable; indeed, *Ready Go* represents a considerable drop in musical quality in what is otherwise a very fine suite. The performance of *Toot Suite* on *Jazz At The Plaza* is excellent, although it is less well recorded than the slightly later one for the *Ellington Jazz Party* LP. On the Plaza recording, Woodyard is too forward, and some of the solos are somewhat off-mike.

The *Suite* is followed by *Jones,* the Terry-Ellington piece heard on *The Cosmic Scene,* presented in a new guise as accompaniment to an Ellington seminar on finger-snapping and earlobe tilting. Duke used it as a very effective closer for his concerts, but here his voice is so faint that most of the words are inaudible. But the band is certainly swinging!

On the second side of the LP, Jimmy Rushing sings *Go Away Blues,* the Ellington song written for Betty Roché in the mid-forties; *Hello, Little Girl;* and an impromptu encore, *Love To Hear My Baby Call My Name.* On all three, the band plays in a disorganized fashion which at times approaches chaos. Three further numbers without Rushing follow: *El Gato,* Anderson's extravaganza for the trumpet section; *All Of Me,* a Hodges feature; and *"A" Train* in its standard guise.

There is some admirable trumpet playing on the Anderson piece, Hodges is as always impeccable, and on *"A" Train*, Nance injects warm lyricism into a much-played routine.

* * *

One of the discographical curiosities of the Ellington fifties output comes from December 1958, in the form of an LP which first appeared on the Roulette label as *Billy Strayhorn Live!*, but even the most perfunctory listening reveals that it is by the Ellington band, with Duke at the piano. The music was recorded at the Blue Note in Chicago, and the person who compiled the LP was obviously a Hodges enthusiast, for he has included no less than five Hodges showcases among the eight selections. All five are numbers Hodges was using regularly at this time: *Things Ain't What They Used To Be*, *Jeep's Blues*, *All Of Me*, *Passion Flower*, and *On The Sunny Side Of The Street*. These are all excellent versions with that extra dimension of liveliness characteristic of nonstudio recordings. There is a sixth showcase number, *Sophisticated Lady*, featuring Carney; the other tracks are a fast *In A Mellotone*, featuring Nance and (once again) Hodges; and *Mr. Gentle And Mr. Cool*. The latter is marginally to be preferred to the performance on the *Newport 1958* set, if only for the way the trombones, which have an important supporting role in this piece, rip out their phrases in the last chorus, to the accompaniment of grunts of approval from the piano bench.

* * *

Columbia's *Duke Ellington Jazz Party* LP is made up of material from a couple of sessions. These were done in the studio with a guest list consisting of nine symphonic percussionists, two jazz instrumentalists, and a jazz singer. The percussionists are used in two numbers, Dizzy Gillespie appears in a remake of *Upper Manhattan Medical Group* (here designated by its initials, *U.M.M.G.*), and pianist Jimmy Jones and singer Jimmy Rushing join Gillespie and the band in an extended blues routine. From the Ellington Orchestra alone, we have a Hodges standard and the four-movement *Toot Suite*. The suite is heard in a version to be preferred, on the whole, to the one in *Jazz At The Plaza*, if only because of the superior recording quality. There is a typically Ellington moment during the clarinet cadenza which concludes the first section of *Red Carpet*. On the day this was recorded, Procope's clarinet had a broken key. Duke insisted that the trill on which the cadenza ends should die away to silence with nothing sounding but the rattle of the broken key. Duke described this as an instance of making use of all available resources.

Of the other items on the *Ellington Jazz Party* LP, the most rewarding are those featuring the nine percussionists. The charmingly titled *Tymperturbably Blue* is a minor masterpiece, with the full resources of a symphonic percussion section hurled into vigorous dialogue with the Ellington band.

Marimbas, xylophones, vibraphones, and glockenspiel vie with the Ellington brass in the exciting central section, while in the outer parts thematic fragments are presented via the lugubrious tones of the tympani, with hollow chords on muted brass as the somber accompaniment. The clarinet soloist is Jimmy Hamilton. The uptempo *Malatoba Spank* is even more of a virtuoso display, if without quite the musical substance of its sister piece.

Hodges takes *All Of Me* as a showcase and offers his usual heady concoction of thick sensuous tone, beautifully decorated melodic phrasing, and almost arrogant rhythmic poise. This piece of casual jazz mastery is taken at a strolling medium tempo and is admirably supported by the trombone section. Gillespie is excellent in the main part of *U.M.M.G.*, although his contribution has no greater effect than Willie Cook's had on the original. Dizzy also contributes some muted musings before and after his solo. It is unfortunate that he did not remove his mute for *Hello Little Girl*, where his quiet entry after Rushing's first vocal is a distinct letdown. But otherwise this long blues is a successful climax to the LP, with fine solos from Gillespie and Jimmy Jones and roaring blues shouting from both Rushing and the Ellington ensemble.

The applause Columbia chose to dub onto these recordings to give the impression of a studio party is particularly annoying on the percussion titles—the opening and closing of *Tymperturbably Blue* are almost ruined. One hopes the original tapes for this LP (and those for *At The Bal Masque* and the studio recordings for *Newport 1958*) have been preserved and can some day be issued without these distracting and wholly unnecessary noises.

Outstanding Recordings

1. Columbia Recordings

NEWPORT 1956 RECORDINGS:
    Take The "A" Train, Sophisticated Lady, Diminuendo And Crescendo In Blue, I Got It Bad, Jeep's Blues, Newport Jazz Festival Suite (especially Blues To Be There), Black And Tan Fantasy.
A DRUM IS A WOMAN (especially the New Orleans sequence from *New Orleans* to *Congo Square*: see text regarding the different versions of this LP).
SUCH SWEET THUNDER
DUKE ELLINGTON: THE STUDIO RECORDINGS, VOLUME FIVE (Up-To-Date) (includes many rare takes of Columbia recordings from this period).
ELLINGTON INDIGOS (see text regarding the differences between the stereo and mono versions of this LP).
BLACK, BROWN AND BEIGE (especially the first side, which contains the complete *Black* movement).
AT THE BAL MASQUE
THE COSMIC SCENE
NEWPORT 1958

JAZZ AT THE PLAZA, VOLUME TWO
ELLINGTON JAZZ PARTY

Columbia Singles And Miscellaneous Items:
Suburban Beauty, A-Flat Minor, Cafe Au Lait, Improvisation In Three Parts.

2. Verve Recordings

From ELLA FITZGERALD SINGS THE DUKE ELLINGTON SONG BOOK, VOLUMES ONE AND TWO: Caravan, Take The "A" Train, I Ain't Got Nothin' But The Blues, I'm Beginning To See The Light, Lost In Meditation, Perdido, I'm Just A Lucky So And So, Portrait Of Ella Fitzgerald.

3. Roulette Recordings

BILLY STRAYHORN LIVE!

4. Concert Recordings

Black And Tan Fantasy, Blues To Be There (Tanglewood Concert, July 15, 1956), *Diminuendo And Crescendo In Blue* (July 28, 1956), *Things Ain't What They Used To Be, Diminuendo And Crescendo In Blue, Jeep's Blues* (1958–1959 recordings, MF Records).

5. Recordings from Dances

As Time Goes By, The Happy One, Stardust, Mood Indigo, Diminuendo And Crescendo In Blue (June 1957), *Willow Weep For Me, Blue Star, Beer Barrel Polka, Caravan* (two versions), *Bass-ment, Suburban Beauty, Blues To Be There* (two versions), *Satin Doll, Mood Indigo, Main Stem, All Heart* (March 4 and 5, 1958).

Chapter 23

The Ellington Units since 1941

THE PRACTICE OF RECORDING SMALL CONTINGENTS from the band under the names of certain sidemen had been dropped after the Bluebird dates for the Stewart, Hodges, and Bigard units in 1941. Ellington continued to employ small groups from time to time—for example, on the 1946 Victor recording of *Transblucency* and on a considerable number of titles for Columbia between 1947 and 1949. In 1951 came the recordings by The Coronets, followed by a series stretching into the sixties and including such notable LPs as *The Cosmic Scene*, *Blues In Orbit*, and *The Unknown Session*. But with the exception of The Coronets sessions, these were a continuation of the policy of using small bands under Ellington's own name, which goes back to the twenties and early thirties with such titles as *Saratoga Swing*, *Mood Indigo*, and *Rocky Mountain Blues*. (Even The Coronets bore little relation to the old contingent recordings, Ellington's role being less crucial and Strayhorn seeming to act as musical director.)

Much closer in style to the original contingent dates were a group of sessions by Johnny Hodges in 1947 and 1950 using musicians from the Ellington band. As well as being a sideman in Duke's band, Hodges was looked upon, rightly, as a major jazz artist in his own right. He continued to record under his own name, and the discs he made with units from the orchestra often throw an interesting light on that organization. This is not true of the 1947 and 1950 recordings, however, which do little more than echo the style of earlier Hodges units. The 1947 sessions, done for the Mercer and Sunrise labels, feature Hodges with either Taft Jordan or Harold Baker on trumpet, Lawrence Brown on trombone, and Al Sears on tenor, plus a rhythm section of Strayhorn (piano), Oscar Pettiford (bass), and Sonny Greer or Wilbur De Paris on drums. (The presence of trombonist De Paris as Greer's substitute suggests a hasty reorganization following Greer's nonappearance.) The music is very much that of men going through well-established routines, and the creative spark which Ellington had brought to the earlier Hodges contingent recordings is absent. This said, much excellent music is to be heard here, mostly from Hodges but with good shorter contributions from the other soloists and fine bass playing from Pettiford. Among the most interesting titles are the initial recording of a Strayhorn ballad which was to receive more famous recordings later by the full band, *Violet Blue*, and a comparatively intimate small-scale version of the full band's rousing *Let The Zoomers Drool*.

The 1950 recordings were all made in Europe during an Ellington tour. Harold Baker (trumpet), Quentin Jackson (trombone), Don Byas (tenor sax), and Wendell Marshall (bass) are heard on most sessions, with the French pianist Raymond Fol as Strayhorn's usual replacement; Jimmy Hamilton is present on one date, and the drumming is split between the two men Duke had with him, Greer and Butch Ballard. These records were made for the French Swing and Vogue labels, and for Danish Tono. Again the music is predictable overall, but with much good solo work from both Hodges and the sidemen. Baker is as always magnificent, and among the best tracks are a revival of *In The Shade Of The Old Apple Tree* and *Last Legs Blues*, which was issued on two sides of a 78 disc. This is the first of many extended Hodges blues performances which were to become a prominent part of his output in later years. (Microgroove reissues of *Last Legs Blues* have usually presented it in ludicrously truncated form lasting just over two minutes; the first reissue of the complete version was not published until 1978, on French Vogue's Jazz Legacy series JLA 59).

When Hodges left the Ellington Orchestra in March 1951, he formed a small band which worked under the management of Norman Granz, and a couple of months before this he had started a series of recordings for Granz's labels under an exclusive contract. From 1951 to 1955 these recordings were by Hodges's regular band, sometimes augmented by additional Ellingtonians, and the entire Hodges output from this period has been reissued in a six-LP chronological series on Verve (with a useful supplement in the form of a couple of LPs on Enigma containing live recordings).

Though occasionally marred by heavy drumming, these recordings offer high-quality middle-of-the-road small-band jazz with a slight Ellington flavor. This flavoring is the result of an Ellington-inclined repertoire and of the natural association of such soloists as Hodges and Brown with Ellington music. It is the soloists who provide the musical meat here: Hodges is just as exceptional as he was with Ellington, while the playing of that fine trumpeter Emmett Berry has hardly ever been caught so well on record. One of the best sessions is from August 1954 (with Louis Bellson on drums), which includes an exciting performance called *Used To Be Duke* with some of Brown's most extroverted playing in a group performance of wonderful swing and vivacity.

Hodges rejoined Ellington in August 1955 and the following month his Verve series continued with an LP by a contingent of Clark Terry (trumpet), Brown (trombone), Hodges (alto), Hamilton (clarinet, tenor sax), Carney (baritone sax), Strayhorn (piano), Woode (bass), and Greer (drums). All but Brown and Greer were from the current Ellington band. Apart from an unissued Hodges session, this is the last occasion on which Sonny Greer recorded in an Ellington context, and the music is therefore of particular interest. The drumming imparts a surging swing to the proceedings and sounds a little odd stylistically behind Terry's then-modern trumpet playing. The best track is the slow blues *No Use Kickin'*, and this plus the two jump numbers are long performances. The LP is rounded off by a couple of brief Strayhorn originals and a ballad medley; issued under the title *Creamy*, it was the herald of a whole series of superb Hodges contingent recordings.

The next Hodges LP issued by Granz was *Ellingtonia '56*. One side features a small group similar to that on *Creamy*, except that Ray Nance and Sam Woodyard replace Terry and Greer, while the reverse finds Hodges directing the full Ellington band (with Strayhorn on piano). Three tracks by the smaller group are usually included on the album—two Hodges originals, the jump tune *H'ya* and the slow *Texas Blues*, and a remake of Strayhorn's *Snibor*. A fourth item, *I'm Gonna Sit Right Down And Write Myself A Letter*, was originally released as a single but has been added to some later editions of the LP. The music of this group has a real Ellington small-band sound, although one can be sure that had Duke been around something more original would have been devised. The outstanding performance is the long *Texas Blues*, which has a magnificent solo sequence, although the repetitions of the riff theme between the solos become a shade tedious.

The vigorous spirit of this music is carried over to the big band performances, recorded the following day. The brass section in particular is in extroverted mood, and this rough, exciting music is perhaps the closest the Ellington band ever came to the spirit of Lionel Hampton's big bands. Cat Anderson's *The Happy One* has some choice writing for the trumpet section which plays with great power and drive; the soloists are Nance, Carney, and Hodges. *Duke's Jam* has an outstanding trumpet chase, five choruses long, by Terry, Cook, and Anderson. During its course, Terry delivers some of the most forthright trumpet of his career while Cook combines melodic grace with fierce blowing. Anderson is the spark plug of the entire sequence and plays with tremendous fire and attack, setting up his high-note forays perfectly. This is great jazz playing, the musicians blowing hard and sounding very excited while remaining in complete control. The trumpet chase is preceded by a long solo sequence by Hodges, Cook, Gonsalves (outstanding), Woodman, Jackson, and Carney, followed by each of the three trumpeters taking twelve-bar solos as limbering-up exercises before the fray. The closing riff ensemble is, unfortunately, something of an anticlimax. Anderson's *Night Walk* is given new treatment as a showcase for Hodges, while Hodges himself contributes *You Got It Coming*, in which Cat's growl trumpet is the main solo voice. *Ellingtonia '56* is an exceptional LP. The full band tracks find the Ellington Orchestra playing in an unusually forthright manner, with a very different musical flavor from any heard when Duke is in charge.

* * *

The Hodges date that followed *Ellingtonia '56* comes closest of all to the music of the old contingents. The LP is usually known as *Duke's In Bed*; its initial British release was titled *Johnny Hodges And The Ellington All Stars*. The "All Stars" are Terry, Nance, Jackson, Hodges, Hamilton, Carney, Strayhorn, Woode, and Woodyard. Despite the similarity in personnel, this group exhibits none of the rough-and-tumble spirit which characterized the small-band music on the previous LP, and the ensemble achieves a beautifully cohesive and finished sound. This issue features some of Terry's best work with the Ellingtonians and much tasteful, understated drumming from Woodyard, giving the lie to those who consider him vulgar and overloud. Perhaps the outstanding track is the long *"A" Train*, which utilizes a riff first heard in *The Flaming Sword*. There is a long, impressive solo sequence commencing with a superbly inventive contribution from Hodges; the later soloists can be heard using phrases from this solo as the basis of their own improvisations. Other notable tracks include an extended blues, *Meet Mr. Rabbit* (note how the sound of Woodyard's drums sets the tone for this performance), and a beautiful chamber music version of *Black And Tan Fantasy* with a most delicate statement of the second theme by Carney. (The trumpet solos on these last two performances are by Nance, not Terry as stated in the notes.) There is also a nicely arranged version of the tune used by the full band as a Gonsalves feature known as *Cop Out*, here called *Duke's In Bed* and featuring solos by Hodges and Nance. Taken overall, this is a small-band collection of consistently high quality.

The next Hodges Verve release contains contributions by three different groups—the full Ellington band and two medium-sized units from it. This LP has been given three different titles—*Johnny Come Lately*, *The Big Sound*, and *The Big Band Sound Of Johnny Hodges*. On the full band sides, which again have Strayhorn on piano, the orchestra plays with more discipline but scarcely less fire than on *Ellingtonia '56*. Of these four tracks, three feature Anderson compositions and arrangements, which underline Cat's great talent for creating well-balanced scores and encouraging maximum swing from the band. *Don't Call Me, I'll Call You* is from the same stable as *The Happy One* with a beautiful statement by the trumpets and solos by Hodges (with pungent brass punctuations), Carney, and the composer. *An Ordinary Thing* is cast in a gospel mode with a theme statement by the two altos in unison, a telling contribution from Hodges, and some preaching trombone by Jackson in one of his most eloquent solos. *Waiting For Duke* is less original—it is actually an Anderson arrangement of the old Chu Berry flag-waver *Christopher Columbus*, made famous by Fletcher Henderson and Benny Goodman in the thirties; here Hamilton, Baker, and Carney join Hodges in a typically fine solo sequence. Hodges's own *Dust Bowl* is given a rich and brooding arrangement, presumably by Strayhorn, with solos by the composer and Nance, the latter making a particularly soulful contribution on trumpet.

The tracks by the smaller bands contain much fine music but from the point of view of the student of the Ellington Orchestra, the big band recordings are of the greatest interest. But one thing the other tracks illustrate perfectly is the remarkable poise of Hodges's music. Poise is present in the work of all major jazz musicians, but Hodges's playing embodies it in a very strong and very individual fashion. The rather offhand, take-it-or-leave-it quality of his later work tends to mask this facet of his playing. This rhythmic strength is one of the qualities he brought to the Ellington ensemble, and the difference in the band's sound with or without Hodges is at least as much concerned with rhythmic values as it is with tonal richness.

* * *

For his next Verve LP, issued as *Blues-A-Plenty*, Hodges reverts to the small-band format. The disc is the product of a single session which featured Roy Eldridge (trumpet), Vic Dickenson (trombone), Hodges, Ben Webster, Strayhorn, Woode, and Woodyard. Hodges was a prolific creator of melodic cells of a highly distinctive flavor and on his record dates these were worked into melodic patterns, usually of a riff construction, which made up the bulk of the repertoire. The association of such riffs with the Hodges/Ellington partnership, and the fact that most of the soloists are Ellington sidemen, are factors which give this music its Ellingtonian sound. When the personnel is made up wholly of Ellingtonians and Strayhorn is on hand to do the arranging—as in *Duke's In Bed*—the music is wholly in the Ellington tradition. On the other LPs, the music is more on the lines Hodges developed when leading his own band in 1951–1955. The later recordings are on the whole superior to those with Hodges leading his regular band and have the additional advantage of allowing us to hear Hodges and other leading Ellingtonians working in an informal context. The *Blues-A-Plenty* LP is typical in the high quality of the solo work, not least on the four slow blues tracks *Cool Your Motor* (Hodges was as much the master of the witty verbal epigram as of the musical), *Honey Hill*, *Blues-A-Plenty*, and *Reeling And Rocking* (an extended performance).

Two more Hodges dates follow a similar pattern to *Blues-A-Plenty*, if without the same emphasis on the blues. The first features Eldridge, Brown, Hodges, Webster, Strayhorn, Wendell Marshall, and Jo Jones and was issued as part of the *Side By Side* LP. The outstanding tracks are two long ballad performances, *Just A Memory* and *Let's Fall In Love*, and there is also a fine small-band version of Mercer Ellington's *Ruint*.

On the second date, issued on the *Not So Dukish* LP, Nance and Hamilton are added and Marshall and Jones are replaced by Woode and Woodyard. Here the outstanding track is a long blues with a slight gospel flavor, *Preacher Blues*. It includes Brown's best recorded interpretation of a solo he recorded on several other occasions (e.g. on *Texas Blues*), and a really magnificent, stinging contribution from Roy Eldridge. After these two dates, Granz recorded Hodges with the Stuttgart Light Orchestra in a selection of standards at a session done during the Ellington band's 1958 European tour. Then, in February 1959, he organized two Hodges sessions which are the most important of the series from an Ellington viewpoint, for the simple reason that Duke is on piano.

* * *

Duke Ellington's presence on the two Verve sessions which make up the whole of *Back To Back* and part of the *Side By Side* LP was the result of an exchange deal. Columbia allowed Ellington to appear as a *quid pro quo* for the presence of Dizzy Gillespie (a contracted Granz artist) on the *Duke Ellington Jazz Party* LP. Thus Dizzy's seemingly unnecessary participation in a session by an Ellington band already boasting four top trumpet soloists had a very important consequence.

Although the two sessions for the *Back To Back* and *Side By Side* LPs were set up as Hodges dates, the saxophonist encouraged Ellington to exercise his skills in musical organization. There must have been a temptation to use the format of the old Hodges unit dates, but instead the music is cast in the mold of a loose jam session. For all the casual nature of the music, the hand of the master is discernible in the skillfully varied routines and in the ideal choice of tempos. The personnel consists of Harry Edison (trumpet), Hodges (alto sax), Ellington (piano), Les Spann (guitar and flute), and Jo Jones (drums), with Sam Jones and Al Hall alternating on bass. On the *Back To Back* LP, the repertoire is heavily weighted with blues standards such as *Beale Street Blues*, *Basin Street Blues*, and *St. Louis Blues*. There are only two nonblues on the disc, *Wabash Blues* and the old Artie Mathews rag, so popular with New Orleans style bands, *Weary Blues*, the latter given an astonishing transformation at slow tempo.

The outstanding soloist on these two LPs is unquestionably Ellington. Here he plays as a jazz soloist without any hint of "composer's piano" or of just being around as accompanist to the other musicians, a pose he often liked to affect. Duke's performance here is one of the most inventive displays by a jazz soloist in the entire history of jazz. Ellington does not have the virtuosity of Art Tatum, Oscar Peterson, or Earl Hines, but he has a balance in his musical vocabulary which none of these possesses, as well as invention which surpasses that of any other jazz soloist except Louis Armstrong. In these piano solos, everything is in proportion—melody, harmony, and rhythm combine in a remarkably articulate language. And Ellington improvises with all three elements, creating new melodic patterns, new rhythmic shapes, and unusual harmonic blends. On *Weary Blues* and *St. Louis Blues,* his response to the melodies is amazing and he creates totally new ways of looking at these familiar themes. His beautiful touch is also in evidence, as is his subtle way of playing chords with each note given a different weight. Ellington's solo mood on these performances varies from the musing intimacy of *Beale Street Blues* to the wild, driving conclusion to *Stompy Jones*. Not the least impressive aspect of Duke's playing on these sessions is his absolute mastery of the blues idiom. It is fascinating too to hear his accompaniments in such an impromptu setting, exactly the right chord, figuration, or riff pattern always effortlessly to hand.

Hodges also plays magnificently, and his unique tone is particularly well recorded. Like Duke, he finds the perfect phrase for any musical situation, if without quite the same inventive genius, and the sheer vigor and strength of his playing here are particularly impressive. The ability to state a familiar melody with all the freshness of a newly created song was one of Hodges's greatest gifts and it is heard to wonderful effect on these recordings. He makes *Wabash Blues*—not the world's greatest melody—sound like the epitome of feline grace.

Harry Edison is a trumpet player who has often been criticized for a lack of melodic invention, and his contribution to *Back To Back* and *Side By Side* has sometimes been cited as an instance of this. Yet if Edison is rather sparing in bestowing melodic creations on his audiences, at least there can be no doubt that these creations are his own, not always the case among musicians who are reputedly more inventive. Edison's tone, swing, and authority carry the day here, and in the daunting company of Ellington and Hodges in prime form, he makes an impressive contribution to the music. Not many jazz trumpeters would have made more of this situation.

Jo Jones swings superbly on drums and seems more concerned with percussive coloring than usual, no doubt a reflection of Ellington's presence. The two bassists are excellent, and only the young Les Spann seems a little outclassed. But despite their other virtues, especially the ravishing playing by Hodges, these are basically Ellington's sessions, the music throwing new and unique light on his artistry. It is known that several alternative takes were made, and it is to be hoped that these have survived. Stanley Dance's firsthand account of the sessions indicates that Ellington's solos were fresh and quite different on every remake.

* * *

The next small-band recording by the Ellingtonians after *Back To Back* and *Side By Side* was under Strayhorn's name for the Felsted label. The LP title, *Cue For Saxophone*, indicates its flavor. "Cue Porter" was Johnny Hodges's pseudonym when recording away from Norman Granz, to whom he was still under contract, and the music is very much a development of the Hodges small-group style. (This session by the Billy Strayhorn Septet is discussed fully in Chapter 30.)

* * *

Hodges recorded a further two sessions for the Verve label in 1959, but these were not released until 1979 in a double album, *The Smooth One*. Both use the format established on such LPs as *Not So Dukish* and the bulk of the numbers played are Hodges originals. The sequence *First Klass, Second Klass, Straight Back, Steerage,* and *Third Klass* from the first of these sessions is a virtual primer in the Hodges method of composition in his later years. Johnny himself is heard in top form throughout, especially on the first date, which produced fractionally the better music. The personnel is Baker and Vance (trumpets), Sanders and Jackson (trombones), Ben Webster (tenor sax), Hamilton (clarinet and tenor sax), Jimmy Jones (piano), Les Spann (guitar and flute), Ray Brown (bass), and Jo Jones (drums). Baker and Webster play particularly well, and in the rhythm section Brown and Jones are outstanding. The second session has Baker, Lawrence Brown, trombonist Booty Wood, Hamilton, tenor saxophonist Harold Ashby, Jimmy Jones, Woode, and Woodyard. The drumming of Woodyard is rather uneven, confirming an impression from the Ellington Orchestra records of the period that this was not one of his vintage years.

In 1961, while Duke was working on the film *Paris Blues*, Hodges led a band of Ellingtonians on a brief European tour. A very good selection of their music, recorded at a concert, can be heard on *Johnny Hodges At The Sportpalast, Berlin*, a two-LP Pablo package. The personnel is Nance, Brown, Carney, pianist Al Williams, bassist Aaron Bell, and Woodyard. The program offered on this tour contained a wide selection of numbers associated with Hodges and Ellington. The Pablo set includes a Hodges blues, *In The Kitchen*, and the popular standard *Blue Moon*, not otherwise recorded by Johnny, but the rest of the tracks are Ellington themes or standards associated with particular musicians—*On The Sunny Side Of The Street* and *All of Me* for Hodges and *Rose Of The Rio Grande* for Brown are examples. Despite the hackneyed program, and the format of long sequences of solo showcases, the musicians play with remarkable freshness, and the performances are highly enjoyable.

* * *

During 1961, Hodges made his first recordings with the organist Wild Bill Davis. They were successful both musically and commercially, and from this year on the majority of recordings made under Hodges's name were away from the Ellington environment, the bulk of them with Davis. They feature much fine music but their relevance to Ellington's art is nil. Three major exceptions are provided by other Hodges collaborations, the first at this time an LP made in late 1961, issued as *Johnny Hodges With Billy Strayhorn And THE Orchestra*. Here Hodges is featured with the full Ellington band, with Jimmy Jones on piano and Strayhorn as musical director. The band does little more than provide backings for the alto solos, and the set is very disappointing from an orchestral point of view. In 1964, Hodges again used the full Ellington band in a session for the Impulse label at which he also recorded some small-group titles. The small band consists of Nance, Anderson, Brown, Gonsalves, Jimmy Jones, Ernie Shepard (bass), and Grady Tate (drums). This rhythm section is also heard on the big band recordings. The LP is called *Everybody Knows Johnny Hodges*, and by 1964 everybody did indeed know what to expect from a Hodges LP—a selection of Ellington standards leavened with Hodges originals on the familiar riff pattern. There is much excellent jazz on this LP with notably fine solos by Hodges and Gonslaves. The full band contributes a deeply swinging version of *Main Stem* and also provides the only new piece, apart from the Hodges themes. This is a Latin American number by Anderson, *Open Mike*, which has some blistering high-note lead trumpet but is otherwise rather undistinguished. Anderson also contributes as trumpeter, composer, and arranger to the third of this group of late-period Hodges recordings with an Ellington flavor. This is the series recorded with Earl Hines from 1957 onward. Again, some fine music is made within well-established frameworks. It is particularly fascinating to hear Hines's band piano, so different from Duke's yet highly effective, in this Ellingtonian context.

* * *

The sessions recorded by Ellington musicians under the leadership of Brown, Carney, Gonsalves, and Nance are not particularly interesting from an Ellington point of view, although, like the Hodges sessions, they contain good solo work. This is particularly true of those done under Gonsalves's name, and one in particular has the sound of the traditional Ellington small-band session. It was recorded in New York in February 1960 and features Nance, Booty Wood, Hodges, and Gonsalves with a rhythm section of Jimmy Jones (piano), Al Hall (bass), and Oliver Jackson (drums). An outstanding version of Billy Strayhorn's *Day Dream* features Gonsalves throughout. Recorded in 1960 the LP remained unissued for over ten years, finally appearing on French RCA (who managed to get the composer credit of *Day Dream* wrong, confusing it with a song called *Day Dreams*). This LP was issued as *Ellingtonia: Moods And Blues*.

* * *

A very unusual session took place during the Ellington Orchestra's visit to Paris as part of their 1950 European tour. On April 15 of that year a young enthusiast, Daniel Filipacchi, recorded the Ellington trumpet section with just the rhythm section as accompaniment for a label which he created solely to issue these performances, called Mood. The discs were issued under the name of Nelson Williams, who was with Ellington for less than eighteen months. The five trumpeters involved are Williams, Nance, Baker, Al Killian, and Ernie Royal, with the American expatriate Art Simmons on piano and two members of the Ellington band—Wendell Marshall and Butch Ballard—rounding out the rhythm section. Three titles were recorded, *Five Horn Groove*, *Big Al*, and *Chumba Leezy*, and in 1979 they were reissued in French Vogue's Jazz Legacy series, with solos from alternative takes added. The routines are basically sequences of trumpet solos, with Baker providing most of the choice moments. Although the session is rather ordinary as far as musical quality goes, it is certainly unique in the annals of Ellingtonia.

* * *

A more rewarding session was recorded on the Ellington band's next visit to Paris, in 1958, under the direction of a trumpet player who missed the 1950 trip—Cat Anderson. This initiated a series of recordings by Anderson with fellow members of the band which is second in interest only to the Hodges series from an Ellington point of view. Like the Hodges recordings, these Anderson sessions are inclined to fall into a set pattern, but the LPs recorded in 1958, 1964, and 1965 provide excellent examples of small-group Ellington music, usually of a rather more rugged kind than that found on the Hodges discs. The 1958 session features Anderson, Jackson, Procope on clarinet, the French pianist Georges Arvanitas, Woode, and Woodyard. The rhythm team of Woode and Woodyard is well recorded and is heard to maximum advantage. The two brassmen have fine solos, both open and in the plunger style, while Procope's clarinet has rarely been heard to such advantage on record. Anderson performs with great fire and drive on an unusual recording of *Black And Tan Fantasy*. The whole session displays a surprising freshness, not least when we consider the hour at which the music was recorded, as indicated in the LP title—*Cat Anderson Plays At 4 A.M.*

After a very disappointing LP recorded in New York in late 1959, issued on the Wynne and Fidelio labels, Cat did not record again under his own name until the Ellington band's visit to Paris in March 1964. On that occasion, he made a second LP for French Columbia, *A Chat With Cat*. Anderson, Procope (doubling clarinet and alto), and Woodyard remain from the 1958 session, with Buster Cooper on trombone, Gonsalves on tenor, and Roland Lobligeois on bass, plus Joe Turner and Claude Bolling alternating at the piano. A Bolling arrangement of *Muskrat Ramble* and a couple of Anderson originals are used along with a trumpet feature on *Confessin'* and three Ellington numbers. The most interesting of these is *A Gatherin' In A Clearing*, the Ellington showcase for Cat's plunger-muted trumpet recorded in 1946. This revival is pleasant enough, but lacks both the immense vitality and the assurance of the Ellington version. Overall, *A Chat With Cat* is a fine collection of small-band jazz performances with an Ellington flavor. Of the many fine solos, those by Paul Gonsalves are outstanding.

In January 1965, Anderson made an LP for French Philips titled *Cat Anderson, Claude Bolling And Co.* Bolling is the French pianist, composer, arranger, and Ellington enthusiast who here creates a more organized basis for the music than had been the case on Cat's two previous French sessions. There is no attempt to create a mock-Ellington flavor, but the structuring of the music beyond the casual ensemble-plus-solos pattern ensures a firm context for the solos, while on an emotional level the inspiration of Woodyard's drumming ensures the music's warmth and vitality. The personnel varies from track to track through the ten titles, but its basis is the Claude Bolling Sextet plus Anderson, Gonsalves, Buster Cooper, Chuck Connors (bass trombone—he does not solo), and Woodyard from the Ellington band. Cat is in prime form, offering a wide variety of trumpet styles including much fine work in the Rex Stewart half-valve manner. His solo on Strayhorn's *Clementine*, a straightforward re-creation of the original 1941 arrangement, is a quite masterly essay in this style. There is a recording of *Hello, Dolly* with a vocal by Woodyard of a distinctly unsober variety and a theme statement by Cat which moves into the trumpet's highest register—and when the trumpeter is Cat, that's pretty high! The LP contains several originals by Cat and by Bolling, including a very pretty ballad for Gonsalves by Bolling, called simply *Paul's*. Cat's contributions include *De De Da Da*, closely modeled on Sy Oliver's *Organ Grinder's Swing*, and an uproarious showcase for Cooper called *Trombone Buster*, a piece also used by the Ellington band at concerts. The solo standard is very high, with Gonsalves again outstanding. This excellent LP is in reality more in the Ellington tradition than many which essay a more deliberately Ellingtonian style.

* * *

During 1958 and 1959 the Ellington musicians formed the core of a big band which recorded two LPs for the Coral label under the direction of Mercer Ellington. Styled "Mercer Ellington and his Orchestra," the band includes the full Ellington brass section (except for Nance) and the full reed section (except for Gonsalves). There is no replacement for Nance, but Ben Webster and Harold Ashby alternate as substitutes for Gonsalves. The rhythm sections vary but are non-Ellington, apart from the inclusion of Strayhorn on piano or celeste on a few tracks. Jimmy Jones is the pianist on the majority, with Skeeter Best, Carl Lynch, or Les Spann on guitar; Wendell Marshall or George Duvivier on bass; and Joe Marshall or Gus Johnson on drums. The 1959 recordings produced an LP called *Steppin' Into Swing Society* and those from 1959 one entitled *Colors In Rhythm*.

The arrangements are by Mercer Ellington, Luther Henderson, Dick Vance, Jimmy Hamilton, Jimmy Jones, Andy Gibson, and Strayhorn. There are no attempts to create an Ellington atmosphere, even in the Strayhorn arrangement of *Blue Serge*. It is fascinating to hear what is virtually the Ellington band with another rhythm section performing this non-Ducal music. The richness of the saxophone section is, if anything, even more striking than usual. The trombones are equally impressive, while the three trumpets—Baker, Terry, and Anderson—prove totally adequate in situations which would normally call for a four- or five-piece section.

The repertoire consists of Ellington standards and Mercer Ellington originals, leavened by an occasional outside song. Vance's arrangement of *Yearning For Love*, which features Carney at his most delicate, is alone among the versions of Ellington themes in equaling the original. Other excellent scores include Mercer Ellington's *Afternoon Moon*; Gibson's version of Mercer's *Ruint*; Luther Henderson's light, frothy *Aqua-tonic*, and the same writer's nicely balanced arrangement of *Little White Lies*. Henderson also contributes an amusing arrangement of Mercer's *Got My Foot In The Door*, which has vaudeville overtones and a dancing Terry flugelhorn solo. The solo work on both LPs is of the expected standard, with Baker heard on many tracks, most notably *Afternoon Moon*, *Blue Serge*, *Golden Cress* (all on open trumpet), and the Vance arrangement of *Black And Tan Fantasy* (with plunger mute). Webster, Carney, and Hodges are all heard to advantage, and Webster has a particularly outstanding ballad solo on *Be Patient*, where Henderson at one point brings in the saxophone section behind the soloist to excellent effect. Woodman is featured on the beautiful *Black Butterfly*, while Procope is heard on bamboo flute in *Dawn Of A Greenhorn*. When one considers that these scores were new to the musicians, the quality of the band playing and the cohesive nature of many of the interpretations are astonishing. They clearly reveal the reserves of sheer musicianship which lay behind the casual facade of the Duke Ellington Orchestra. Some of these tracks, especially those on the *Colors In Rhythm* LP, contain commonplace arrangements played in a competent but commonplace manner, but there are also many good things. Perhaps the best performance is that of Mercer Ellington's *Ruint* on the *Steppin' Into Swing Society* collection. Here Hodges is the soloist in one of the most vigorous, rugged, and swinging big band records from this period.

* * *

It has often been noted that Duke Ellington, alone among the great musicians of jazz, has fathered no school of imitators nor been responsible for any major stylistic developments in the music. The records discussed in this chapter help to illuminate why this is so. They are all by Ellington musicians, on some of them the full band is present, and many performances are in a deliberately Ellington style. Yet even the records with Strayhorn on piano—and Billy often substituted for Duke with the band—could never be mistaken for the work of the Duke Ellington Orchestra. They demonstrate just how inimitable Ellington's music was, even though they come closer to that music than any other non-Ellington recordings. The arrangements, the performances, and indeed the basic approach to music making are all different. Under Ellington, the musicians relax to an extent and in a manner quite different from the way they tackle music—even simple (*Duke's Jam*) or familiar (*Main Stem*) music—away from his direction. His arranging, his personality as a leader, and the vital way in which his piano playing nudges and inspires the ensemble are among the reasons for this. Yet even if one takes these factors into account, the difference Duke's absence makes to a group of current Ellingtonians, even with Strayhorn at the piano, is truly amazing.

The best examples are the big band recordings under the direction of Hodges or Mercer Ellington, for these clearly show how vital Ellington's presence was for the full projection and realization of the "Ellington effect." Just as a famous symphony orchestra can sound totally different under the batons of conductors of contrasting temperament, so Ellington impressed his personality on a jazz group in the most authoritative manner. In his case there can be no comparison with other masters. In the Count Basie Orchestra there is invariably a decrease in rhythmic vitality and swing on the rare occasions when the Count is replaced, no matter how skilled a pianist that replacement may be. But with Ellington it is not just a matter of rhythm. The textures, the quality of the section phrasing, and the overall sonority are different; the music is much warmer and more relaxed when Duke is present—even though the Ellington musicians certainly could play in a very relaxed style without him.

The small-band sides tell a similar story, although when Strayhorn has an important role in the arranging and also plays the piano, the results can be very close to the sound of the earlier small groups with Duke at the piano. The 1956 *Duke's In Bed* LP by Hodges is the most Ellington-like of all the recordings discussed in this chapter. But if one compares this (or any of the other Hodges groups from the late fifties) with the *Unknown Session* LP recorded by Ellington with a small group from the band (Nance, Brown, Hodges, Carney, Bell, and Woodyard) the differences are striking.

Another obvious conclusion from a study of the records discussed in this chapter is that the Ellington *soloists* play in the same way on these impromptu sessions as with the Ellington band. The musicians' natural way of making music was not in any way constricted or distorted by Ellington's arrangements; quite the reverse, for his scores actively encouraged a soloist to develop and display his musical individuality. Yet for all the light they throw on important aspects of Ellingtonia, the ultimate criterion for these records is the quality of the music they contain. And by this criterion they—and especially those recorded under Hodges's leadership—are outstanding jazz records.

Outstanding Recordings

1. Johnny Hodges, 1947–1950

The Hodges 1947 Mercer recordings have been reissued from time to time, notably on French and English Vogue and Fantasy. The 1950 French Vogue recordings have been collected on a French Vogue Jazz Legacy LP called *The Rabbit In Paris*.

2. Johnny Hodges Verve Recordings

Used To Be Duke can be found on the LP of that name and also on *RABBIT'S WORK ON VERVE IN CHRONOLOGICAL ORDER, VOLUME 4*. The remaining items cited are all LPs.

CREAMY
ELLINGTONIA '56
DUKE'S IN BED or JOHNNY HODGES AND THE ELLINGTON ALL STARS
JOHNNY COME LATELY or THE BIG SOUND or THE BIG BAND SOUND OF JOHNNY HODGES
BLUES-A-PLENTY
NOT SO DUKISH
BACK TO BACK (with Ellington)
SIDE BY SIDE (with Ellington—these two LPs have sometimes been issued as a double album)
THE SMOOTH ONE (double album)

3. Johnny Hodges on other Labels

JOHNNY HODGES AT THE SPORTPALAST, BERLIN (Pablo double album)
EVERYBODY KNOWS JOHNNY HODGES (Impulse)

4. Billy Strayhorn

CUE FOR SAXOPHONE (Felsted, Master Jazz)

5. Cat Anderson

CAT ANDERSON PLAYS AT 4 A.M. (French Columbia/Emidisc)
A CHAT WITH CAT (French Columbia)
CAT ANDERSON, CLAUDE BOLLING AND CO. (French Philips)

6. Mercer Ellington

STEPPIN' INTO SWING SOCIETY (Coral)
COLOURS IN RHYTHM (Coral)

Chapter 24

The Records—March 1959 to October 1962

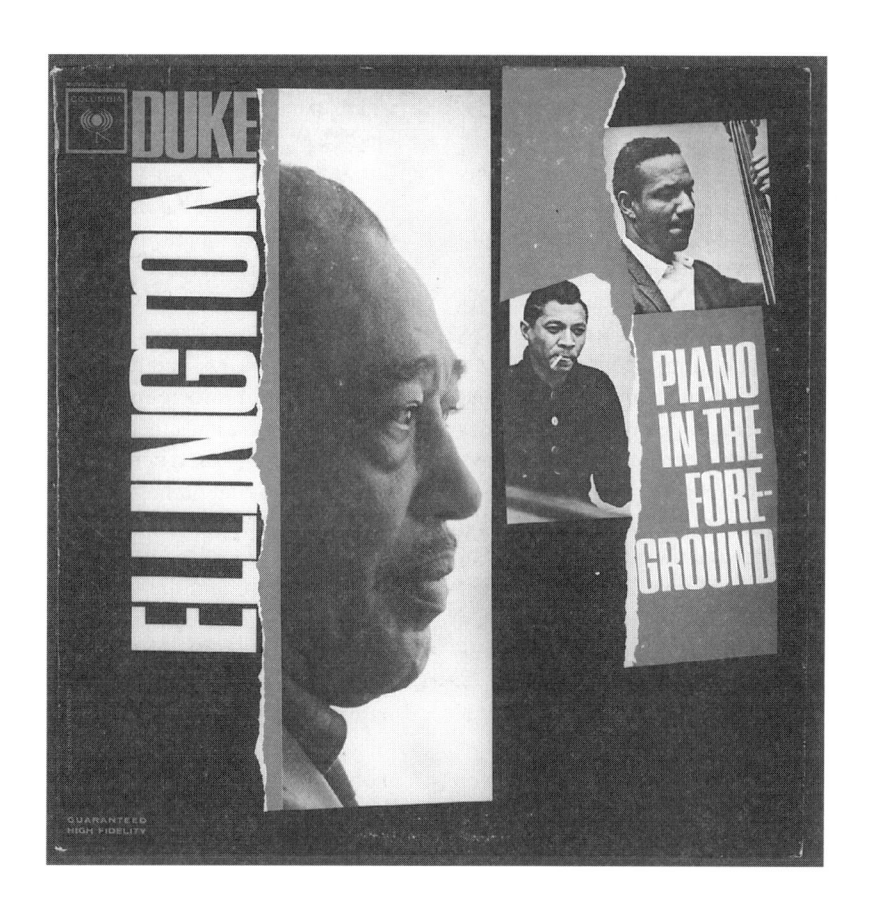

IN MARCH 1959, THE ELLINGTON ORCHESTRA recorded an unusual session for SESAC, a transcription company. What made the session unusual was that under the terms of this performance rights organization's policy, a band could record only material licensed by SESAC, or traditional themes in the public domain. The full name of the organization—Society of European Stage Authors and Composers—indicates its original aim: to employ writers from outside the U.S. copyright system. When the company became international in scope, the full name was dropped and only the initials used. One consequence of this policy was that Ellington could not use any of his standard material. The tunes had to be new so that they could be copyrighted by SESAC, and consisted of four by Jimmy Hamilton, three by Dick Vance, one by Duke himself, and four by writers not associated with Ellington, probably SESAC staff men. The Ellington piece, *She Was A Tinkling Thing*, was originally attributed to "Ellis," using the name of his common-law wife, Evie Ellis, due to Duke's AS-CAP membership. The music on these SESAC recordings, which have been reissued on a variety of labels, is rather conventional by Ellington standards. Prior to the SESAC recordings Sam Woodyard had been replaced by Jimmy Johnson, a heavy drummer of the kind Duke liked, but unsubtle and lacking Woodyard's imagination and swing.

Hamilton provides his four compositions with effective arrangements. Jimmy had a marked talent for writing very basic jazz scores; *Little John's Tune* is a good example and stimulates incisive phrasing and easy swing from the band. The solos are by Hodges, Terry, and Gonsalves. Equally pleasant is the Hamilton ballad *Moonstone*, an attractive theme that features Shorty Baker as trumpet soloist. This number had been heard previously on an air shot from 1952, when it featured Willie Cook; at the time it was known simply by the code name *W.C.* Ellington's *Tinkling Thing* has a light theme, a spacious arrangement, and a long and excellent solo by Gonsalves. Of the three compositions by Dick Vance, *Lullaby For Dreamers* (arranged by Strayhorn) and *Still Water* (superbly scored by Ellington) are highly melodic balladlike themes presented as Hodges features. The creation of Hodges showcases was usually the province of Ellington or Strayhorn, but the quality of Vance's melodies fully justifies the commissions and reveals a little-known side of his talent. By contrast, his *Fat Mouth* (arranged by Ellington) is a conventional swinger with solos by Baker, Gonsalves, and Hamilton. Bassist Jimmy Woode is particularly effective on Ellington's arrangement of *Jet Strip* (a composition attributed to White); the solos are by Terry, Gonsalves, and Hamilton. Hamilton's *Dankworth Castle* receives a rather conventional arrangement, but his *Jamaica Tomboy* has Anderson in his Latin American style and Hamilton himself indulging in some rough rhythm-and-blues tenor. *Frou Frou* is a brooding tone poem arranged by Strayhorn who also contributes a rather unusual piano solo. Strayhorn's scoring is outstanding on *Lost In The Night*, a ballad with lots of Baker's open trumpet and the attractive sound of Gonsalves leading the saxophone section. Ellington himself arranged the uptempo *Night Stick* (credited to "Swanston"), a rather conventional score with solos by Terry and Gonsalves.

* * *

In 1958 the Duke Ellington Orchestra visited Britain for the first time since 1933. During the tour the band played at the Leeds Music Festival, where Ellington was presented to Queen Elizabeth the Second. Earlier that year Ellington had premiered *Princess Blue*, dedicated to the Queen's sister, Princess Margaret. His meeting with the Queen was even more productive; he and Strayhorn wrote a suite of six movements for her and recorded it at Duke's own expense in the early part of 1959. At Ellington's insistence, only two copies of the record were pressed, one of which was presented to the Queen. *The Queen's Suite* was, in Ellington's eyes, a purely personal gift, a wholly personal mark of his appreciation of the grace with which he had been greeted by the monarch and her subjects. He steadfastly refused suggestions for subsequent public release of the piece, despite much urging from his friends. It was only after Ellington's death that *The Queen's Suite* was issued on Norman Granz's Pablo label and revealed as an outstanding achievement of the Ellington-Strayhorn partnership. An outline of the suite and of the sources of inspiration for each movement—remember that Ellington said that his music was always about something—were revealed by Duke in his autobiography published in 1973, the year before his death.

The first movement, *Sunset And The Mocking Bird*, was inspired by the call of a bird heard by Ellington and Harry Carney one evening during a beautiful sunset in Florida. It was included in *The Queen's Suite* as "one of the beauty experiences of my life." The main theme, with its poignant mockingbird motif, is played by Ellington over hushed, low saxophone harmonies. Although Hamilton has a key role here and the ultimate presentation of the full melody is entrusted to Hodges, the main voice is that of Ellington's piano, masterly in every note and chord. The beautiful tone and phrasing of the saxophone section and the warm harmonies and unusual voicings given to them each represents a special kind of perfection. The superlative playing of the orchestra throughout *The Queen's Suite* is an instance of what happened when this collection of sometimes wayward masters decided to devote their full abilities to the work at hand. The result is incomparable.

The second movement recalls a time when, traveling to a gig, Ellington and Carney got lost and "ran into an area where the sultry moon was half hidden by the trees it silhouetted. We stopped short, for there in this huge arena, with the trees as a backdrop, were, it seemed, millions of lightning bugs, dancing in the air. It was a perfect ballet setting, and down below in a gully, like an orchestra pit, could be heard the croaking of frogs. The number this inspired was called *Lightning Bugs And Frogs* (*Music Is My Mistress*, page 112). Hamilton sets the atmosphere and the frogs are impersonated, very musically, by Carney's bass clarinet. A chord is built up in steps of low trombone, bass clarinet, trumpet, and tenor sax, and the resultant melodic outline is the main thematic substance of the movement. Quentin Jackson, Jimmy Hamilton and Jimmy Woode have important ensemble parts. With glowing harmonies and graceful melodic twists, Ellington paints a nocturnal scene with unusual shades and colors. It is interesting how the "straight" academic voice of Hamilton's clarinet is used so frequently by Ellington in concert works. One is reminded of his remark to Juan Tizol many years before that it was essential for him to have at least one musician in the band who played his melodies as written, in a "legit" fashion.

The third movement, *Le Sucrier Velours*, is another superb canvas in this series of Ellington tone paintings of the images of beauty. The title, Ellington says, "is the name the French have for a bird whose song is sweet as sugar and who feels as soft as velours." For this section Ellington turns to his incomparable saxophone section whose sound is rich and heady, the opulent tone of Hodges's alto used as lead voice over warm, glowing harmonies. The melodic contours of this luscious movement are long and sensuous. Ellington's piano complements his rich reed writing and then returns in solo to provide a perfect coda.

Northern Lights, the fourth movement, was originally given the more specific title *Northern Lights As Seen From Quebec, Canada*. It recalls an unusually brilliant display of the aurora borealis seen by Ellington and Carney on a Canadian journey. Ellington related the experience to Strayhorn, who wrote the music. Duke has said that this movement and this experience represented majesty, and the tremendous climaxes of the introduction, with brass figures over Carney's baritone saxophone, strike exactly the right note. As so often in the scoring of Ellington and Strayhorn, the saxophone section is divided into groups: alto and tenor (Hodges and Gonsalves), two clarinets (Hamilton and Procope), and baritone (Carney, who as always sounds like a section himself with his massive tone). The actual melody, a spiky, pithy affair, is stated with maximum rhythmic awareness by Gonsalves. The piece is full of rich, sustained orchestral harmonies contrasted with tangy voicings for the divided reeds. Strayhorn enhances the richness of the sound by allocating the lead voice in the trumpet section to Baker. After a reprise of the massive climaxes of the opening, Gonsalves's tenor slides into the chords of the closing section.

For the fifth movement, Ellington performs a piano solo which he calls *The Single Petal Of A Rose*, which he said represented wonder. There is indeed a hushed sense of wonder as the pianist picks out a moving, simple theme with open harmonies. Again we are aware of Ellington's beautiful touch, which can give to the keyboard so varied a palette. And, as always, Duke is supreme at putting the listener in touch with the music at a far deeper level than any other jazz pianist. The final movement, *Apes And Peacocks*, brings back the orchestra in a piece of highly flavored exotica based, Ellington tells us, on the biblical account of the presents brought by the Queen of Sheba to King Solomon (Kings I, 10). Along with quantities of gold, silver, and ivory were apes and peacocks—"to us," said Ellington, "apes and peacocks seemed like the splendor of all time." In *Apes And Peacocks*, it seems as if the "splendor of all time" passes before our ears in an incredible pageant of wild and outlandish riches, a cavalcade of colorful materials and people. Three clarinets are used here, and the crucial solo part for low saxophone is entrusted to Gonsalves, who plays brilliantly. As the procession passes, the Ellington band develops the material in a fascinating canvas of dazzling, heady colors.

No royal personage can ever have received a more splendid gift than this suite. In Ellington's public appearances at this time the emphasis was, as previously noted, on the great solo personalities of the band. In *The Queen's Suite*, the Ellington band demonstrates why it was still an ensemble of the very highest quality. *The Queen's Suite* is one of the greatest examples of scoring for jazz orchestra that Ellington and Strayhorn ever gave to the world.

* * *

In 1959 Ellington wrote the music for the Otto Preminger film *Anatomy Of A Murder*. The Columbia recording by the Ellington Orchestra—with Gerald Wilson as fifth trumpet and both Ellington and Strayhorn at the keyboards—is a suite of brilliantly colored but often inconclusive vignettes. The hammering off-beat of the title music, preceded by what could be taken as a satire on film score openings, gradually softens into a characteristic piece of Ellington writing; Carney maintains the initial riff figure against clarinets and plunger-muted brass as a background to a hushed, delicately phrased Gonsalves solo. Following this the music is allowed to trail off inconclusively. An important theme which recurs several times (it is reminiscent of Gershwin's *They Can't Take That Away From Me*) is first heard under the title *Flirtibird* with Hodges as the featured soloist and Terry's trumpet working as part of the saxophone section. This theme also opens *Way Early Subtone* which develops into a Procope clarinet solo with highly colored accompaniment in which Hamilton's clarinet leads the sax section. The music is first class, but its organization, clearly built around the action it accompanies on the screen, seems haphazard and rambling when heard in isolation. *Hero To Zero* has some of Gonsalves's most ravishing ballad playing, with effective backing by muted brass and clarinets. *Midnight Indigo* also has interesting voicings, this time of the solo instruments; Nance's muted trumpet is in the lead, and Carney's bass clarinet functions as the main harmonic voice. Both piano and celeste are heard on this track. A further version of *Flirtibird* features Shorty Baker's poignant, full-toned trumpet. A reprise of the title music is led first by Baker and then by Anderson, who moves it into the extreme high register and leads to a conclusion with isolated ultra-high-note trumpet notes over heavy, low organ harmonies. This is effective scoring, but once again disconcertingly organized from a formal point of view.

The other movements are on the whole less impressive: *Low Key Lightly* features a languorous violin solo by Nance; *Happy Anatomy*, in its first appearance, has conventional jazz solos by Terry and Gonsalves and some very loud brass playing. *Sunswept Saturday* is a "landscape piece," effective but unmemorable, with Hamilton featured, while *Grace Valse* is also little more than well-concocted background music. The second *Happy Anatomy* has a small group (Nance, Hamilton, and rhythm) and heavy drumming (Jimmy Johnson). A further Hodges feature, *Haupé*, is pleasant and has a distinctive melodic line.

The initial impression of the *Anatomy Of A Murder* LP is of an inventive and brilliantly colored Ellington creation. Closer investigation confirms these qualities but reveals that this is music with less commitment and of a much lower emotional voltage than is usual with Ellington. The fragmented, inconclusive nature of the movements is perhaps inevitable with the inner demands of the music taking second place to the happenings on the screen. Yet if the overall impression is of rather uninvolved music, Ellington's melodic inventiveness, his colorful scoring, and his absolute mastery of big band instrumentation are heard clearly and vividly. Less satisfactory overall than most of Ellington's LPs, *Anatomy Of A Murder* is nonetheless a treasure trove for the listener who delights in the tone colors of the Ellington Orchestra.

* * *

A two-LP set has been issued on the Foxy label of Ellington performances from the 1959 Newport Jazz Festival. The sound is rather poor, and much of the repertoire can be heard in superior fidelity on other issues. Among the more interesting items are a set of accompaniments to Jimmy Rushing and a version of *Launching Pad* in which the central trumpet solo is by Baker rather than Nance, who takes it on the familiar Columbia recording of two months later.

* * *

Continuing the pattern of offering great contrast in succeeding Ellington issues, Columbia next recorded the band in a collection designed to reflect the material they had played at various jazz festivals during the summer of 1959; this was issued as *Festival Session*. For this date, Willie Cook and Fats Ford bring the trumpet section up to six pieces, and both Woodyard and Johnson are present on drums. The recording took place early one September morning in 1959. The band was ready to record but without a bass player. While urgent telephone calls were made, a long showcase for the two drummers, *Duel Fuel*, was recorded with Quentin Jackson on bass and Clark Terry taking his place in the trombone section on flugelhorn. Jackson returned to trombone for the first part of a new suite, *Idiom '59*, which has substitute bassist Joe Benjamin sitting in. By the time the second and third sections of *Idiom '59* were recorded, the regular bassist, Jimmy Woode, had arrived.

Idiom '59 is not one of Ellington's great compositions, but a minor work with enough fine music to deserve more than the neglect and obscurity which have been its lot. The first movement, *Vapor*, is the most satisfying—a brief melodic fragment for Procope's low-register clarinet. In the main section Procope is accompanied by the tightly muted and hushed trumpets of Nance and Baker, while in the middle part trombones and baritone sax contrast their more solid, somber tones with the ethereal sounds heard before and after. Neither of the following movements was titled: the second, based on a riff theme, is in the main an uptempo display of standard swing style clarinet by Hamilton—brilliantly executed but thin stuff for an Ellington suite. The third movement combines the virtues and defects of what has gone before. Its opening slow section over a tango rhythm features brilliant orchestration as Ellington builds up pyramid chords with contrasting voices and colors, but there is no development, and it simply leads to a Terry improvisation on flugelhorn with a stirring orchestral conclusion. This is good jazz but compositionally below the standard one would expect for the conclusion of an Ellington concert work.

The highlight of *Festival Session* is a piece sometimes ascribed to Clark Terry and sometimes to Duke himself—probably a collaboration—called *Launching Pad*. A quartet of Terry, Woodman, Gonsalves, and Hamilton is set against the band in a concerto grosso role. This was a pattern to which Ellington returned from time to time and one of its most successful applications is found in *Launching Pad*, a less stilted performance than the 1938 *Battle Of Swing* and a less academic conception than the 1946 *Jam-A-Ditty*. For *Launching Pad*, Ellington establishes an easy medium tempo, and the dialogue between the solo group and the full band is conducted in swinging terms, Terry's melodic concept evident in the light, airy lines for the quartet. In a typical Ellington juxtaposition, the middle section is a long solo by the totally contrasting voice of Nance's trumpet.

The rest of the LP is more conventional fare. The three-part drum suite, *Duel Fuel*, is unusual only in that there are two drummers; they are given suitable stereo separation. The central section has a swinging medium-tempo passage for the band. *Perdido* is given over to Terry, who parades all his festival tricks in skilled fashion, while Gonsalves does his festival chore in the eight-minute *Copout Extension*. The mood here is less frenetic than on some other Gonsalves marathons, and those whose tastes run to these exhibitions might consider this to be a choice specimen. Finally, Hodges plays *Things Ain't What They Used To Be*; both he and the band work the old magic without saying anything new.

* * *

Two groups of recordings have been issued which feature music from the 1959 Ellington European tour. On Affinity, there is a two-LP set from the Paris concerts of September 20, while the Swing House label offers two single LPs from the Berlin concert of October 4. Apart from Lil Greenwood singing *Bill Bailey Won't You Please Come Home?*, a distinctly slight affair heard on both sets of records, nothing new is added to the Ellington repertoire. There is, however, plenty of good music including several items common to both collections. These include the now-established medley of *Black And Tan Fantasy, Creole Love Call*, and *The Mooche* (with Nance stealing honors); the *Medley Of Popular Hits; Such Sweet Thunder; Rockin' In Rhythm; El Gato; Walkin' And Singin' The Blues; VIP's Boogie; Jam With Sam;* and *Skin Deep*. The Paris recordings also feature *Newport Up* and *All Of Me*, while those from Berlin include *Things Ain't What They Used To Be, Hank Cinq, Flirtibird, St. Louis Blues, Satin Doll*, and an amusing encore featuring Nance singing *Basin Street Blues*. Jimmy Johnson was the drummer on this tour, and he is featured on this dull version of *Skin Deep*. The drumming during this tour was substandard and threw into relief the contribution Sam Woodyard had made over the preceding years.

* * *

The stability of personnel which the band had enjoyed for the past four years was now at an end, and the autumn of

1959 marks the close of a distinct period of Ellingtonia, just as the 1956 *Blue Rose* LP had marked its beginning. During this time, Duke had led the best band he had had since the early forties. The magnificent brass section was built up during the Capitol period, the reed team was clearly invigorated by the return of Johnny Hodges, and the rhythm section fired by the formidable swing of Sam Woodyard. Once the changes began in 1959, they accelerated sharply. By September 1960, Nance was the only surviving member of the great brass team, although Willie Cook had returned to the band for a spell at this time. Harold Baker and John Sanders had left in September 1959, Clark Terry and Quentin Jackson the following month, and Cat Anderson in November. Woodyard was in and out of the band during this period, leaving for a second time in September 1959, only to rejoin the following April. Jimmy Woode left in January 1960 and Britt Woodman in September.

Fortunately the reed section held together. The five musicians of this section had first played together when Gonsalves joined Ellington in September 1950, and the only changes since then had been in the alto chair during Hodges's absence from 1951 to 1955. In fact this team was destined to stay together until the summer of 1968 when Jimmy Hamilton left the band. In replacing the departing musicians, Ellington had at first much greater fortune with trombonists than with trumpeters, and for a while the Ellington trumpets were weak as a section, a weakness cured by the return of Anderson in 1961 and of Cootie Williams in 1962. But at first Fats Ford (alias Andres Marenguito), Eddie Mullins, and Cook joined Nance in the trumpets. At this time Nance was still a great soloist, but his section activities were restricted by an aging lip and only Cook was an all-round trumpeter of the expected Ellington class. Trombonists Booty Wood and Matthew Gee joined Woodman, giving Duke a fine section and three good soloists.

At the end of 1959 the Ellington personnel was:

Trumpets: Willie Cook, Fats Ford, Eddie Mullins, Ray Nance (also violin and vocal).

Trombones: Britt Woodman, Booty Wood, Matthew Gee.

Reeds: Russell Procope (alto sax, clarinet); Johnny Hodges (alto sax); Paul Gonsalves (tenor sax); Jimmy Hamilton (clarinet, tenor sax); Harry Carney (baritone sax, clarinet, bass clarinet).

Rhythm: Duke Ellington (piano); Jimmy Woode (bass); Jimmy Johnson (drums); Billy Strayhorn (deputy pianist).

Vocal: Ozzie Bailey, Lil Greenwood.

Lil Greenwood was a singer who stayed with Ellington for a couple of years without making much of an impact. She was employed on ballads and in more lively songs such as the previously noted *Bill Bailey*.

* * *

Ellington's next visit to the recording studios was for a couple of sessions in December 1959 which provided the bulk of the material for an LP called *Blues In Orbit*. On these occasions Duke brought his full trombone, reed, and rhythm sections into the studio but on trumpet used only Ray Nance. He gave this group the title "Award Winners"; Gonsalves did not make the second date, having gone home for the weekend. Even with Paul in the group, however, Duke thought enough of Hamilton's tenor playing to feature it on the opening uptempo romp, *Three J's Blues*. The driving, rough-toned tenor must have pleased the leader because it shares the limelight on the second title with Nance's plunger-muted trumpet. This number is also known as *Pie Eye's Blues* and is the *Flirtibird* theme transformed into a twelve-bar blues and taken at a fast tempo. This version concludes with a final ensemble of Mingus-like chaos. After two uptempo blues, why not a third? The remake of *C Jam Blues* which follows is one of the very best versions of this much-recorded Ellington standard. The clarity of texture in the closing ensemble with just the one trumpet is an unexpected bonus and the tempo is exactly right. The soloists are Ellington, Nance (violin), Matthew Gee (open trombone), Gonsalves, Booty Wood (plunger trombone), and Hamilton (clarinet). Nance, Gee, and Gonsalves contribute outstanding solos, while Nance and Hamilton also make useful contributions behind the other soloists. The final title from this date is a Strayhorn piece for the saxophone section and Wood's plunger trombone, a combination Strayhorn describes as *Sweet And Pungent*. The trombonist is heard to good effect and here he seems the ideal replacement for Quentin Jackson. (Hodges—who had sat in front of Tricky Sam for so many years—always rated Wood's playing very highly.)

The second session opens with *Smada*, completely recast from its 1951 format as a straightforward big band swing piece featuring Hamilton's clarinet. Here Hodges is given a Latin American rhythm as he states the theme, and he and Nance take care of the solo parts in an attractive new version. The next title, *Blues In Blueprint*, is an outstanding Ellington creation. In the first chorus, bass and bass clarinet spell out a harmonic/rhythmic sequence of typical Ellington quirkiness, accompanied by the composer marking time by finger snapping. Then these two instruments provide a background to a melancholy chorale-like theme on two clarinets, a melody of an unusual and highly appealing nature, with a solitary tom-tom also joining the group. The middle section is another beautiful Ellington melody, this time of a wistful character, played by Nance on muted trumpet over a rich backing of trombone, clarinets, and rhythm. The first two choruses are then repeated in reverse order, and Ellington's final snap of the fingers is followed by a solitary piano chord played by Strayhorn. This is a brilliant and captivating fragment of genius, in total contrast with its informal session mates.

The performance of *In A Mellotone* which follows emphasizes, as did *Smada*, the tremendous punch of a new trombone section. Carney introduces the theme with decorations, and Nance plays the traditional trumpet solo, on this occasion without the usual accompanying saxophone figures. Matthew Gee not only brought a new solo trombone conception into the Ellington band but he also introduced a new instrument, the baritone horn. (At one point, the Ellington trombone section was equipped with these instruments and for some years it was no surprise to see one or the other of the Ducal trombones doubling on baritone horn. As late as the European tour of 1967, Buster Cooper was taking solos on this instrument. Although Duke seems to have looked on these doings favorably, he did not choose to make much use of this instrument in the recording studio. There is a Hamilton LP made in 1960 which has a section of Booty Wood, Britt Woodman, and Dave Wells on baritone horns in a group which also includes Gonsalves, bassist Aaron Bell, and Sam Woodyard.) The only important contribution by Gee on baritone horn to the Ellington discography is on a number he and Duke put together for this *Blues In Orbit* LP, called *The Swingers Get The Blues Too*. Apart from theme statements by baritone horn, this item, a slow blues, has passionate solos by Nance with plunger and by Hodges. The final title of those which have been issued from these "Award Winners" dates is a fast blues called *The Swinger's Jump*, with solos by Hodges, Nance, Hamilton on tenor, and Wood, with Hamilton's clarinet decorating the final ensembles.

After the varied experiences of *At The Bal Masque*, *The Queen's Suite*, and *Anatomy Of A Murder*, the music on *Blues In Orbit* finds Ellington and his musicians indulging in the most basic of jazz experiences, impromptu music with an emphasis on the blues. And of course there is always the unexpected item, in this case the highly original *Blues In Blueprint*. The seven items which were to be issued from these sessions—there are versions of *Brown Penny* and *Sentimental Lady* which are not yet published—were not sufficient to make up an LP, so a couple of earlier unissued tracks were used. These are *Blues In Orbit*, which comes from the *Black, Brown and Beige* sessions of 1958, and *Villes Ville Is The Place, Man* from the following year, actually done at the session with the percussionists for the *Jazz Party* collection. *Blues In Orbit* (also known as *Star Blues*) is said to have been inspired by the high-pitched bleeps emanating from early spacecraft, and features Ellington playing the blues in the piano's highest register over a background in which Terry's flugelhorn leads the saxophone section. The amusingly titled *Villes Ville* does not feature the *Jazz Party* percussionists or even the full band but simply Nance, Hodges, and Carney with trombones and rhythm section. This makes an interesting comparison with the slightly earlier *Spacemen* LP which had a front line of Terry, Hamilton, and Gonsalves with the same backing. The mood of the Nance-Hodges-Carney group is, not surprisingly, more basic, and they produce an outstanding performance of great drive and swing with solos of the expected quality.

There is a lot of fine jazz in the *Blues In Orbit* collection despite its casual atmosphere. It is a set which emphasizes the continuing importance of Nance as a major force in the Ellington band at a time when it had just lost a trio of great trumpet stylists.

* * *

The choice of material for Ellington's next Columbia LP was enough to surprise even the most experienced Ellington watcher: nothing less than an arrangement of Tchaikovsky's *Nutcracker Suite*, or to be more exact, nine of its movements. Much of the critical reaction was hostile: some objected on the grounds of "jazzing the classics," while others held that Tchaikovsky's music was Tchaikovsky's and could not be improved upon. Some claimed that such an enterprise was a waste of Ellington's time when he could be writing fresh music of his own. All these attitudes reflect a lack of understanding of what kind of artist Duke Ellington was. The question of "jazzing the classics" was a dead one in an age when Beethoven was used to advertise breadcrumbs, but a comparison between the Ellington ensemble and the dance bands of the twenties and thirties who were castigated for "jazzing the classics" also shows that such criticisms were irrelevant. Cheap commercial gimmickry was far from the minds of Ellington and Strayhorn when they embarked on this venture; nor were they trying to "improve" Tchaikovsky. Their purpose was to translate the music into the idiom of the Ellington band without destroying its character or cheapening it. The idea that in recording other men's music Ellington was preventing us from hearing his own works is absurd. He had ample opportunity at this time to record any of his own compositions except those which required a symphony orchestra. If the preference is to his earlier compositions, one can only observe that at the time of *The Nutcracker Suite* sessions a selection of Ellington standards was also being recorded for the *Piano In The Background* LP which proved to be a good deal less rewarding than the Tchaikovsky arrangements.

Both Ellington and Strayhorn always stressed that one should approach any material with respect, including a popular ballad. They certainly approached Tchaikovsky's music with care and dedication, and their scoring of it is among the most detailed and precise they ever wrote for the band. The trumpets on these sessions were the now-regular quartet of Nance, Cook, Ford, and Mullins with Gerald Wilson added as an extra; Nance handles all the trumpet solos, while as a section the trumpets have a more mellow sound than that of the departed team of high-powered virtuosi. The trombones were temporarily up to four: Matthew Gee had departed but in his place we find two long-serving Ellingtonians, Lawrence Brown and Juan Tizol. This section was completed by Britt Woodman and Booty Wood. The reeds and piano were in the usual hands, with Aaron Bell coming in on bass and Sam Woodyard back on drums.

A notable feature of the band's performance on this LP (and some others from this period) is the seemingly heavy and loud drumming by Woodyard. It is hard to believe this is the same man who drummed with such sensitivity on *At The Bal Masque* or on *Such Sweet Thunder* or indeed on the small-band Johnny Hodges *Duke's In Bed* date. No one who knows Duke Ellington's approach to a rhythm section would expect to find light, airy drumming; a big sound and a deep-digging swing were what Ellington required from a drummer. One reason for this preference was that on many occasions the bass and drums would have to carry the full band (as indeed they do most of the way through *The Nutcracker Suite*) because Ellington would often be absent from the keyboard, perhaps conducting or maybe in the engineer's booth at a recording session. Another aspect of Ellington's preference for heavy drummers is that such a player liberates the bassist from simply playing time, and frees him to use figures and melodic patterns. These are some of the reasons why Woodyard could be the ideal Ellington drummer. But there was a disturbing tendency, clearly heard on *The Nutcracker Suite*, for the engineers to overrecord him. In addition, Woodyard was a highly strung, moody musician whose attitude and performance could be extremely variable. Persons close to the band were aware of the way Woodyard was overrecorded; bassist Aaron Bell, who was in a pretty good position to judge, was one of several musicians who pointed this out. Yet one cannot help but feel that Ellington was fundamentally responsible. He always supervised his recordings closely and was very well aware of the problems of balance posed by his band, and these Columbia recordings were approved by him. So far as *The Nutcracker* is concerned the drumming is overly loud on almost all the uptempo performances, but in the slower movements Woodyard's playing is seen in a kinder light.

The suite opens with the *Overture* and side one of the LP ends with an *Entr'acte*. The other seven movements were all retitled by Ellington: *Dance Of The Reed-pipes* as *Toot Toot Tootie Toot*, the *March* as *Peanut Brittle Brigade*, *Dance Of The Sugar-Plum Fairy* as *Sugar Rum Cherry*, the *Russian Dance* as *The Volga Vouty*, the *Chinese Dance* as *Chinoiserie*, the *Waltz Of The Flowers* as *Dance Of The Floreadores*, and the *Arabian Dance* as *Arabesque Cookie*. By characteristic usage of clarinets, muted brass, and divided reed and brass sections, Ellington and Strayhorn manage to create the impression that the tonal palette of the seventeen-piece band is equal to that of a full symphony orchestra—with the added advantage of jazz soloists available to contribute improvised variations. How these soloists are integrated into Tchaikovsky's music is perhaps best seen in the brief and delightful *Entr'acte* where the main theme of the overture is passed around between Hodges, Carney, Gonsalves, Brown, and Hamilton before the band brings the movement to a gentle conclusion. (Brown's solo here is his first on record with the band since the *Masterpieces By Ellington* LP of 1950.) Ellington's aim in *The Nutcracker Suite* seems to have been to give full value to the three principal features of Tchaikovsky's score—its rich melodic content, its colorful textures, and its humor. This music is delightfully lighthearted without being insubstantial. *Chinoiserie* is a piece of poised, sharply etched contours in which Hamilton's clarinet and Gonsalves's tenor duet over discreetly scored trombones and bass clarinet. A sound foundation is provided by Bell and Woodyard with pungent comments from Ellington at the piano. Similarly, the use of the plunger-muted "pep" section—Nance, Cook, and Wood on this occasion—on *Sugar Rum Cherry* is brilliantly set off against the saxophone duo of Gonsalves and Carney. More brilliant writing for these two players can be heard on *Toot Toot Tootie Toot*, but perhaps the richest, most lush scoring is reserved for *Arabesque Cookie* with solo trombones, plunger-muted trumpets, clarinet duets, and bass clarinet all contributing to a colorful and varied display.

Tchaikovsky's *March* is directly transformed into an uptempo stomp, while the *Overture*, the richly scored *Russian Dance*, the frothy *Entr'acte*, and the powerful *Dance Of The Floreadores* are also fast-tempo swingers. This last piece, the transformation of *Waltz Of The Flowers*, is played in 4/4 time, there being no Ellington waltzes in this suite. Of the soloists, Nance and Gonsalves are outstanding in their different ways, while Carney is exceptional in the ensemble, and Hodges has solos of characteristic excellence on *Entr'acte*, *The Volga Vouty* and *Arabesque Cookie*, the last played over one of the richest backings ever given to a jazz soloist.

The humor and wit of the Ellington-Strayhorn version of *The Nutcracker Suite* are qualities which have evaded many jazz lovers. The band contains players who are natural humorists and some whose styles could be used in a grotesque fashion in Tchaikovsky's music, but Ellington ensures that the humor is wholly musical, giving an elegant glow to a set of performances of characteristic Ellington quality.

* * *

At the same sessions which produced *The Nutcracker Suite*, a retrospective LP, *Piano In The Background*, was also recorded. It is difficult to know why this collection proves to be so disappointing. The format is familiar—a selection of well-known Ellington band numbers, mostly in familiar arrangements but with a few new touches. The performances are designed to throw the spotlight on the leader's piano, the piano which is usually in the background, rather more than usual. The disappointing performance by the orchestra is all the more puzzling when compared with its excellent work on the Tchaikovsky LP and the selections from Grieg's *Peer Gynt* music, which was also recorded at some of these sessions. Most probably the fact that most of Ellington's and the band's time was taken up by the new scores led to the standard material for *Piano In The Background* being thrown off in a hasty, overly casual manner. The selections are not particularly inspired—for the most part, Duke seems to have fallen back on older pieces which were still in the repertoire—the *Kinda Dukish-Rockin' In Rhythm* pairing, *Take The "A" Train*, *Happy-Go-Lucky Local*, *Midriff*, and *Main Stem*. All these are heard in their standard arrangements, as is the rather less well tried *What Am I Here For?* Two outside arrangers are employed. Gerald Wilson contributes a version of *Perdido* which became part of the concert repertoire, and Bill Matthieu provides arrangements of *I'm Beginning To See The Light* and *It Don't Mean A Thing* which disappeared after the sessions were completed. The band does not sound particularly thrilled by this repertoire. Nor does Duke. He provides piano introductions to all the performances, including some of considerable length. His playing is casual to a degree but lacks the vitality of the sketchy but often intriguing introductions we hear on live recordings, especially from dances. Duke's playing here has its usual harmonic twists and sly melodic variants as well as lots of punch and invention, but he does not sound inspired. Apart from the piano introduction, the first part of *Happy-Go-Lucky Local* is missing, and this cannot be considered an important version of the piece. *Rockin' In Rhythm* derives no benefit from the fast tempo, and the climax fails to make its full impact in the absence of Cat Anderson; Woodyard's drumming is relentless and monotonous. *Midriff* is inferior in every respect to the 1956 recording despite the return of Lawrence Brown to play the trombone solo. *Main Stem* is played over loud and relentless drumming and is lackluster compared with the 1940 original. *Take The "A" Train* starts with Ellington adding new thoughts to his piano introduction and continues with a very assured version of Ray Nance's familiar trumpet solo.

The Gerald Wilson arrangement of *Perdido* is preceded not only by Duke's piano but also by the Hamilton thematic variant familiar from recordings of the fifties, played on this occasion by the two tenors. Wilson provides a rousing big band arrangement without any Ellingtonian characteristics. The two Matthieu scores are not particularly distinguished. On this LP the trumpet section sounds new and unsettled, the trombones distant, and the saxes bored—compare the saxophone section on the celebrated Hodges-led passage on *Midriff* with its work on *Volga Vouty* from *The Nutcracker Suite* for an example of the different attitude of the Ellington musicians toward the two projects. Apart from Ellington, the pick of the soloists on *Piano In The Background* are again Gonsalves, Hodges, and Nance, with Booty Wood seeming skilled in the use of the plunger without sounding quite at home with the music.

* * *

At this stage, some doubts might have been entertained about Ellington's recording policy, because hot on the heels of *The Nutcracker Suite* came an arrangement of Grieg's incidental music to *Peer Gynt*. Ellington and Strayhorn arranged five segments from the two *Peer Gynt Suites*, taking up one side of an LP. In the event this proved to be Ellington's final adaptation of music from the European concert repertoire, and the danger of his becoming preoccupied with this kind of enterprise to the neglect of his own creations proved to be illusory.

As was the case in the Tchaikovsky recordings, Grieg's music is wholly transformed into the Ellington idiom and Hamilton's legitimate clarinet is again used to admirable effect. The opening movement is from the first *Peer Gynt Suite—Morning*, retitled *Morning Mood*. Certainly the initial presentation of the main melody here, with the warm voice of Paul Gonsalves's tenor replacing the flute of the original, suggests some change of perspective. According to Irving Townsend's notes, dawn is represented by the climax of this section with Harry Carney on baritone in the lead. The scoring, especially for the solo voices—Hamilton's clarinet in addition to the tenor and baritone—and for low brass, is very sensitive. *In The Hall Of The Mountain King* is transformed into a rousing swinger, the "pep" section of two trumpets and trombone with plungers being separated from the rest of the brass section, while Ellington himself is the main soloist. It is no coincidence that when Ellington decided to orchestrate and transform parts of the classical repertoire for the band, his choice landed on composers who, like himself, were brilliant melodists. *Solveig's Song* is one of Grieg's most beautiful miniatures, and here it is scored for plunger-muted trombones in both solo (Wood) and ensemble, with Hamilton's clarinet in a virtuoso role which includes some brilliant cadenzas. Nowhere in the recordings of Ellington is Hamilton's worth to the band displayed so clearly as on the *Nutcracker* and *Peer Gynt* suites.

Solveig's Song is the only piece from Grieg's second suite in Ellington's selection. The somber *Ase's Death* is music of an unusually tragic nature for this band, but Ellington's handling of it cannot be faulted. There are no solos, but Nance's trumpet provides an expressive lead voice in several sections, while Hodges is heard to wonderful effect in a similar role towards the end, and Carney provides the foundation for a rich and sonorous ensemble. The final *Anitra's Dance* is taken at a lively fast-medium tempo with solos by Hodges, Hamilton, and Gonsalves; again the music is beautifully adapted to the jazz idiom and there are moments of pure Ellington magic in the voicings of the instruments. Appropriately, the penultimate note, the last solo note, is by Hamilton who is heard in his happiest vein throughout this suite.

The Nutcracker Suite and *Peer Gynt* confirm that whatever the quality of the other changes in the band, Ellington had once more obtained the services of a magnificent bass player. It is true that after the Second World War good jazz bass players were common, but the requirements of Ellington's music demanded a kind of bass playing which differed in emphasis from the fashionable style. It also required an artist of unusual imagination and creativity, able to respond in a positive manner to Ellington's unusual musical demands. Aaron Bell had a fuller sound than Jimmy Woode and at once teamed up with Woodyard to maintain the traditions of the Ellington rhythm section while putting the stamp on his own individuality and musical authority on the bass work. The high standard Bell set on these first two recordings with the band was maintained throughout his stay.

* * *

In 1979 Columbia put out a previously unissued collection on an LP with the rather odd title *Duke Ellington: The Unknown Session*. This had been recorded in Hollywood in July 1960—between *Peer Gynt* and the following project, *Suite Thursday*—by a contingent from the band consisting of Nance, Brown, Hodges, Carney, Ellington, Bell, and Woodyard. In many ways, this is the ultimate in small-group Ellingtonia. It seems incredible that twelve such perfectly balanced and polished performances of totally new arrangements could be turned out at one recording session, but of course Duke was working with brilliant virtuosi who knew his music and his methods intimately. The opening *Everything But You* sets the perfect note with its mellow and relaxed mood. Then Duke delves even further back into his past, to 1928 for *Black Beauty*. This is given a perfect reading with Ellington and later a muted Lawrence Brown on the main melody, separated by an authoritative statement of the subsidiary theme by Nance and the ensemble. *All Too Soon* features Brown in both theme statement (as on the 1940 original) and variations, and the ensemble playing is of uncommon vigor. Carney and Nance share solo responsibilities on *Something To Live For*; both are in superb form, Carney using his huge tone with rare gentleness and Nance displaying his great musical eloquence. The recent return of Brown to the band is no doubt the reason for his heavy exposure here; *Mood Indigo* becomes a feature for his open trombone until a variation on the famous trio voicing leads to a familiar conclusion. A trio of Brown, Ellington, and Bell is heard on *Neo Creole*, an unexpected revival of the second theme from the 1931 *Creole Rhapsody* in a totally new arrangement.

Don't You Know I Care has Hodges in the main solo role, with contributions from Carney, Nance and a well-bottomed ensemble. Carney is featured in an effective arrangement of *A Flower Is A Lovesome Thing*, before Leonard Feather's *Mighty Like The Blues* is revived in a magnificent performance with some wonderful blues piano from Ellington in both solo and ensemble. *Tonight I Shall Sleep* becomes an exquisite Hodges ballad feature. *Dual Highway* is a miraculous Hodges blues feature, an Ellington masterpiece thrown off with astonishingly casual ease. A final uptempo *Blues* provides a perfect climax with solos for all except the drummer. The *Unknown Session* presents an astonishing display of easy, relaxed musical creativity, with a front line of infinitely resourceful Ellingtonians backed by a perfect rhythm section. On piano Ellington gives a performance wholly characteristic of his genius, inventive and unfailingly stimulating to the other musicians. Bell provides a foundation full of contrasting patterns and fresh conceptions which add both variety and rhythmic impetus. Sam Woodyard echoes the music's moods in a most sensitive way, the sound of his drums when he is playing quietly having the same gutty, basic jazz sound which is found in the pianissimo ensembles of the front line. His swing and rhythmic punch, his relaxation and judgment of dynamics are those of a great jazz drummer.

* * *

A group of recordings made at a dance at the Mather Air Force Base on July 22, 1960, has been released in good stereophonic sound on the Koala label. They include two movements from *The Nutcracker Suite* given very easy, casual-sounding readings. The arrangement of *Stardust* which had been used as a Terry feature on Capitol is here utilized as the framework for a Nance trumpet solo. (The finest recording of this arrangement of *Stardust* is that from the Carrolltown dance of July 1957 released on the Doctor Jazz label. It features Harold Baker as soloist.) The July 1960 Mather recordings include an excellent version of *Paris Blues*, as well as much easy jazz making on such contrasting Ellington fare as *Such Sweet Thunder*, *Tulip Or Turnip*, and *All Of Me*. One of the best recorded examples of Booty Wood's playing with the Ellington band is to be found on the *Black And Tan Fantasy-Creole Love Call-The Mooche* medley; this is in fact a fine all-round performance with excellent work also from Ray Nance.

* * *

Not many broadcasts have been issued on disc from this particular period. There is a Rarities LP of a broadcast from the Philadelphia Quaker City Jazz Festival of August 1960, which includes such Ellington perennials as *Perdido*, *VIP's Boogie*, *Jam With Sam*, and the *Medley Of Popular Hits*. The item which makes this broadcast interesting is a performance of the concert version of *Congo Square* from *A Drum Is A Woman*, otherwise unavailable on disc. Despite the poor recording, *Congo Square* is most impressive in its stark, evocative scoring.

* * *

The most important new concert work from this period is an Ellington-Strayhorn collaboration called *Suite Thursday*. This had been commissioned by the Monterey Jazz Festival and was premiered there in September 1980. The work is based on John Steinbeck's novel *Sweet Thursday*, which is set in Monterey, although the music reflects its literary associations only in the loosest manner. The suite consists of four movements unified by a motif stated at the outset by Brown's trombone. The introductory orchestral texture hints of fog horns and thick mists, a suggestion of locale which recurs from time to time during the four movements. These are in medium tempo (*Misfit Blues*), fast tempo (*Schwiphti*), slow tempo (*Zweet Zursday*), and fast medium tempo (*Lay-by*). After the introduction and a lead-in of two choruses by Ellington, the first movement is given over to the saxophone section, the full band entering only for the final chord. Accompanied only by the rhythm section and a touch of trombone color, the saxes have a long development with some intriguing voicings, including the discreet use of Willie Cook's trumpet within the section. Hodges was out of the band due to illness at the time of the *Suite Thursday* studio recording but Ellington works his magic through the reed scoring as surely as ever. This music swings and has real substance and balance. The fast *Schwiphti* contains some clangorous, percussive piano from Duke and some brilliant scoring for the band. Nance's solo seems a trifle hurried and that by Gonsalves rather off-the-cuff, but the meat here is in the orchestral writing and playing.

The slow movement is Ellington at his greatest, with an awed stillness which could be a reaction to the scenery in the Monterey area. Bell and Woodyard provide a perfect foundation, the pianist garnishes the music as only he knew how, and the orchestral filigree is finely wrought. Brown has a solo here which hints that the heavy wear on his lip over the years is beginning to take effect. Gonsalves by contrast provides a perfect eight bars, while Hamilton has the final statement, poised and sensitive to Ellington's every requirement, as Carney's baritone gently hints at the Monterey fog.

The final movement is a swinger, with Duke's piano and the band setting up a perfect scenario for an extended violin solo by Ray Nance. This is a great solo in itself as well as being a perfect development of the material of the suite. The pizzicato section, which develops into a brief duet with Bell's bass, is brilliantly done, as is the climax, ending with the fog horn sounds and then just Nance, pizzicato, picking out the skeleton of the suite's basic motif.

There is a second version of *Suite Thursday*, recorded live at a Paris concert some two and a half years after the Columbia studio version and issued on Atlantic. The performances differ in the expected ways, the studio recording giving a clearer and more precise account of the score, the concert version more spirited but less balanced and with some untidy patches. The band is obviously much more familiar with the piece and of course the long saxophone passage in the first movement sounds all the better for Hodges being back in the section. (Here this is almost too much of a good thing as Hodges is overrecorded to a degree that endangers the sound of the section.) Both Brown and Nance are less than convincing in their solos in the second and third movements, but Gonsalves is so perfect that a pause for breath is filled by a cry of approval from the composer. The last movement is played with great swing in this version, for although the bass part as conceived by Ernie Shepard is less elaborate than Aaron Bell's version, it is no less swinging.

These two recordings offer an interesting comparison of the band playing one of Ellington's concert works in formal and informal fashion. The constant high level of musical interest, the skilled use of jazz solos of the conventional kind as developmental agents, and the overall structural unity combine to give *Suite Thursday* an important place among Ellington's concert works.

* * *

Duke Ellington's next recordings for Columbia were a set of piano solos not released for a couple of years. They came out on an LP called *Piano In The Foreground*, and, like all Ellington's solo collections, this is of the greatest musical interest. Here Ellington is accompanied by Aaron Bell (bass) and Sam Woodyard (drums). This collection marks the first public appearance of the interest in Africa which Ellington showed in his later years. There are two titles with specific African references—*Cong-go* and *Springtime In Africa*—although it would be foolish to attach too much importance to the titles themselves. They were the result of deliberations by Ruth and Mercer Ellington and Stanley Dance, since Duke was abroad when Columbia decided to issue the set.

There are three non-Ellington songs in the *Piano In The Foreground* collection. The first is *I Can't Get Started*, on an Ellington band recording from 1956, which had included an excellent piano solo. The 1961 version is notable for the wide range of the pianism—for example, the alternation of violent and delicate chords in the second chorus. More substantial is *Body And Soul*, which also runs through a wide variety of moods. There are references to the styles of other jazz pianists along with some harmonic developments which are wholly Ellingtonian. Here and throughout the LP, the bass playing of Bell is ideal, while Woodyard responds to the changing levels of emotional intensity with great sensitivity. Ellington's wide summation of the potentials lying dormant in a ballad such as *Body And Soul* is concluded by a coda of delicate impressionism.

These two performances are typical of Ellington's approach to ballads, but there is nothing at all typical about *Summertime*; Woodyard's drums rat-tat like a continuous tattoo of machine-gun fire, Bell's bass figures are stuttering and deliberately disruptive, and the melody is heavily discordant and fragmented. Ellington's final chord is the very epitome of desolation and despair. (Sinclair Traill claimed that Ellington had once told him that this performance was his reaction to the war in the Congo.) By contrast, *Springtime In Africa* is a warm tone painting, full of steamy, dreamy harmonies without any distinct melodic core. It is played with a wonderfully delicate touch over percussion patterns evocative of the dark continent. A comparison of Bell's bass figures here with some of those used by Charles Mingus on the 1962 *Money Jungle* LP is very interesting and suggests that Ellington himself, the common factor in the two collections, may have had more to do with the bass parts than is usually realized. The other impressionistic piece from *Piano In The Foreground* is *Fontainebleau Forest*, a slight, innocent little composition. *Cong-go* combines exotic rhythm with wide-ranging piano styles, from the sparse opening statement to the dark harmonies which precede the climax; from the vigor of thought and playing at this climax to the "Africanized Basie" ending. *It's Bad To Be Forgotten* (taken at a swinging medium tempo), *A Hundred Dreams Ago*, and *Pleading For Love* (an uptempo number), incorrectly labeled *Yearning For Love* are short, pithy pieces whose musical content is much greater than their playing time or the easy, laconic manner of their performances would suggest.

The other two titles are blues—a walking, slow medium performance, *Blues For Jerry*, and a masterpiece at slow tempo, *So. Blues For Jerry*, in which Bell plays superbly, contains much rich Ellington improvisation, using obsessive riffs, violent chording and brusque, crushed left-hand notes in contrast to passages of gently played, singing melodic lines. At this stage of his career Ellington's mastery of blues piano was second to none, and *So* is probably his greatest recorded blues solo. It combines a comprehensive and individual command of the traditional language of the blues with original invention, beautifully detailed playing, and a simple but effective formal unity. Duke's sensitive touch, in which every note of a chord has just the right weight, is caught perfectly here, while his use of the trill is remarkable in its rhythmic mastery.

* * *

Ellington's next project was a collaboration with Louis Armstrong for the Roulette label. These sessions with the Louis Armstrong All Stars mark the start of a spell in which Ellington concentrated his recording activities on collaborations with other notable jazz artists; after Armstrong came Count Basie, Coleman Hawkins, Max Roach and Charles Mingus, and John Coltrane. On some of these sessions the full Ellington Orchestra participates, on others just a contingent is heard, and on others still Duke appears without any of his own sidemen.

For many years, Duke Ellington and Louis Armstrong had shared the distinction of being the two leading figures in jazz music. In many ways they were very different kinds of artists: compare Louis's perfection at an early age with Duke's late development; the trumpeter's indifference to his accompanists with the pianist's great concern with selecting high-class musicians; Armstrong's roaring gales of laughter with Ellington's subtle, often oblique, wit. Yet they had a lot in common: their firmness of artistic purpose, their ability to combine great art with popular success, and their pride in the achievements of blacks in America. It is surprising that they had not recorded together previously, apart from one cursory meeting at an Esquire Award Winners session in 1946. On the 1961 sessions, Armstrong plays with astonishing facility for a sixty year old, but he is clearly past his peak as a trumpet player; his last truly great solos were some four or five years behind him. Yet it is simply impossible to imagine any other artist contributing what Louis brings to this music. The authority of the master is there, the imprint of a man using an idiom he had forged himself. In their later years, the Louis Armstrong All Stars often failed to live up to their name, but with Trummy Young on trombone and Barney Bigard on clarinet this is not the case here. The group is rounded off by Mort Herbert on bass and Danny Barcelona on drums.

Ellington liked to chuckle about these sessions and claim that he had stolen the gigs from Billy Kyle, Armstrong's regular pianist of the time and another bona fide All Star. Yet it is obvious that Ellington's contribution to this music is a good deal more than simply that of pianist. The arrangements, although they are casual "heads," show a freshness of approach which contrasts with the usual staid routines of the All Stars. The balance of the arrangements is impressive too, not least on *The Beautiful American*, Ellington's one new composition in the set, where the performance is built around the peaks of Armstrong's majestic leads. The trumpet solos on this number and on *Black And Tan Fantasy* and *The Mooche* are the best from these sessions, although there are other passages of commanding and incomparable trumpet playing. The two early Ellington pieces receive interesting performances, with Young playing plunger solos as if this had been his lifelong specialty. Throughout the two sessions Young shows an awareness of the total needs of the music, as opposed to just simply playing good solos, and this makes his contribution a vital one. Bigard plays beautiful clarinet but seems much less involved than he had been in his Ellington years, yet responsive as always to positive direction. Bass and drums supply a sound foundation. With the exception of the titles mentioned, the repertoire is mainly taken from Ellington's output as a songwriter, with *C Jam Blues* masquerading as *Duke's Place* and *Azalea*, a little-known ballad from the forties, the only surprise. This last item has just about the poorest lyrics—written by Ellington himself—of any Ducal song. They are the epitome of that overblown, overcolored manner which characterized Ellington's verbal expression at its worst. Fortunately they are quite overshadowed by Armstrong's majestic statement of the theme.

Throughout the two LPs which these sessions yielded, Duke is in superb form on piano, heard mostly as band pianist and accompanist, but also occasionally and tellingly as soloist. *Duke's Place* has a concluding solo in which the music gets progressively more sparse and economical, while on *The Mooche* Duke plays the first theme in a way which throws new light on this venerable subject. Of Ellington's accompaniments, that on *I'm Just A Lucky So And So* must take pride of place. Young and Bigard do not play on this track, which is devoted to Armstrong's singing accompanied by piano, bass, and drums. Ellington provides a backing which is full of interest in itself as well as complementing the voice to perfection; this represents another peak in Duke's recorded output. The other titles all provide interesting piano, and the unique qualities of Ellington's harmonic and rhythmic usage are very apparent in this conventional jazz setting. The other titles on these two LPs are *Cotton Tail, Mood Indigo, Do Nothin' Til You Hear From Me, Drop Me Off In Harlem, In a Mellotone, It Don't Mean A Thing, Solitude, Don't Get Around Much Anymore, I'm Beginning To See The Light, Just Squeeze Me*, and *I Got It Bad*.

An interesting appendix to these LPs is the appearance on a Louis Armstrong LP on the Pumpkin label of a couple of titles by Duke Ellington and the Armstrong All Stars deriving from a December 1961 TV show. *Duke's Place* and *In A Mellotone* find both principals in a mellow mood and the music is more relaxed than on the studio recordings. Duke's solos are excellent, although they do not break any new ground.

* * *

Around the time of the Roulette sessions, Armstrong and Ellington were involved in another joint venture, the film *Paris Blues*. As with *Anatomy Of A Murder*, Ellington wrote the music for the soundtrack, but for this production it was recorded by three different groups: a studio band in California, a mixture of French musicians and American expatriates in Paris, and some final material by a studio band including current Ellingtonians and alumni in New York. For contractual reasons the New York recordings for this soundtrack were nominally conducted by Lawrence Brown.

The film concerns the fortunes of two American musicians and their girlfriends in Paris. Armstrong appears as a famous trumpet player, Wild Man Moore, who sits in at a jam session with the two musicians, Paul Newman, cast as a trombonist, and Sidney Poitier, who plays the part of a tenor saxophonist. Their music was dubbed by Murray McEachern and Guy Lafitte. The soundtrack LP is a very mixed affair containing two tracks, *Take The "A" Train* and *Mood Indigo*, featuring McEachern with a rhythm section and tenor sax (probably Lafitte); an uncredited guitar solo of *Guitar Amour*; two items by Armstrong with the big French band, *Battle Royal* and *Wild Man Moore*; and six items from the New York sessions. The music is naturally rather episodic, but there are brilliant moments. Armstrong is in good form on the two tracks on which he is featured, although there is no particular integration with the Ellington scores.

The music recorded in America has a more distinctly Ellington flavor, with some interesting scoring for oboe (Harry Smiles), flute (Les Spann), and clarinet (Hamilton), as well as typical solos by Nance, Woodman, Brown, Hodges, and Gonsalves. The latter's reading of his part is clearly that of a great interpreter of Ellington's music.

In the film itself there are many sections of impressive Ellington music which did not find their way onto the LP. At one point Ellington plays a fascinating version of *The Clothéd Woman*, which would be a particularly welcome addition to the Ellington discography.

The two tracks on the *Paris Blues* soundtrack LP marked the end of the recorded collaborations between Duke Ellington and Louis Armstrong. The music they made together is of a high standard, if perhaps below that expected from the two greatest musicians in their field. Yet one wonders if an earlier collaboration, made when Armstrong's playing was unaffected by age, would have produced anything better. The art of each musician was complete in itself. An Ellington score behind one of Armstrong's great solos might have been an unnecessary enrichment, while a soloist of Armstrong's blazing genius in an Ellington score might well have distracted the listener from the writing. In any event, their meeting late in life produced some music which was much more than a genial geriatric get-together. In particular *The Beautiful American* and *I'm Just A Lucky So And So* hold important places in the output of both artists on grounds which have everything to do with music and nothing to do with nostalgia.

While in France working on *Paris Blues*, Duke was commissioned to write the music for a play, *Turcaret* by Alain Le Sage, which was being revived by the Theatre National Populaire for the first time since 1709. In his autobiography Duke recalls the pleasure of this task and notes that he recorded the music with a group of French musicians. It has never been issued on record.

* * *

When the Ellington Orchestra entered the Columbia studios on July 6, 1961, it was for their first session in nine months. The lineup in the reed and rhythm sections was as before, while the brass consisted of the newly returned Cat Anderson plus Cook, Mullens, Ford, and Nance on trumpets, and Brown, Tizol, and Louis Blackburn, the latter a new plunger specialist, on trombones. On this particular date the Count Basie Orchestra was also in the studio. The session was a collaboration between the two bands, the second in the series of musical meetings between Ellington and other leading jazz figures. Basie was under contract to Roulette, and his Columbia appearance was in exchange for Ellington's appearance on Roulette with the Armstrong All Stars. The Basie-Ellington LP offers four titles from the repertoire of each leader. Basie contributed *Corner Pocket* (retitled *Until I Met You*), *Segue In C*, and *Jumpin' At The Woodside*, plus Thad Jones's new *To You*; Ellington produced *Take The "A" Train*, two pieces from *Paris Blues* (*Wild Man* and *Battle Royal*), and a new piece, *B.D.B.* (Basie, Duke, and Billy), for which composer credit is shared by Ellington and Strayhorn. The LP was originally titled *Battle Royal*, but some reissues are labeled *First Time*.

The most fascinating aspects of this collaboration are the piano duets by Basie and Ellington. The two numbers from *Paris Blues* sound much more impressive than on the soundtrack LP. *Battle Royal* is an uptempo swinger with rather relentless Woodyard drumming, duets by the pianists and drummers, and a Cat Anderson high-note ending. *Wild Man* is a gem, with a rich theme statement by first Frank Wess on flute and Hamilton on clarinet, second by Lawrence Brown, and then by the ensemble with a Hodges obbligato. This sequence is used at the end in a modified reverse order; the middle part is taken up by trumpet solos and duets by Thad Jones and Anderson and tenor sax solos and duets by Frank Foster and Gonsalves. For *"A" Train*, Basie declined to play piano as this was Ellington's feature piece. This resulted in a bit of horseplay with Ellington pursuing the reluctant Basie around the studio. Strayhorn, who was in the control booth, was hastily dispatched to the scene of the action, and it is he who joins Ellington as piano duetist. The arrangement, a new one, makes some use at the start of the two bands as separate units; Strayhorn, the composer, is the principal pianist with Ellington taking a subsidiary role. Chase choruses between musicians from the two bands are used: Nance and Sonny Cohn on trumpets, then Hamilton on clarinet and Budd Johnson on tenor. The new piece, *B.D.B.*, is taken at a swinging medium tempo which suits both bands perfectly; Brown and Quentin Jackson are the soloists and there is some admirable writing for the ten saxophones, both *en masse* and as separate sections. The piano duetists close the performance with characteristic reticence.

Of the Basie pieces, *Jumpin' At The Woodside* is the least important as it is used as a flag-waving closing number with the tenors of Foster and Gonsalves to the fore over the roar of the combined Basie and Ellington brass. *Until I Met You* is a Basie score with Ellington soloists—Willie Cook in a cleanly articulated solo and the admirable Gonsalves. The number contributed by Thad Jones, *To You*, is a brooding ballad with somber tone colors and some excellent lead trumpet, presumably by Snooky Young. The outstanding track on the LP, however, is Frank Wess's *Segue In C*, a strolling medium-tempo blues. This piece was recorded by the Basie band "live" at Birdland later in the month with solos by Budd Johnson and Quentin Jackson, in a performance which more than any other on record demonstrates the virtues of the Basie orchestra of this period. Basie was greatly strengthened by the presence of Johnson on tenor, and he is the main soloist on the Basie-Ellington *Segue In C*, with four choruses of classic quality. Louis Blackburn's plunger-muted solo is one of the very few he recorded with Ellington, and he is followed by Quentin Jackson in fascinating contrast. Jackson was now a Basie sideman, and he uses a different approach from that he had featured with Ellington, employing the plunger alone, without the straight mute all Ellington plunger trombonists from Nanton on have utilized. The effect is heavier, more somber and in the hands of Jackson a droll, humorous dimension is introduced. Among such superb band playing, the way in which Nance leads the Basie trumpet section on violin is notable. Perhaps the most important feature of *Segue In C* is the opportunity it affords for extended piano duets by the two leaders between the various solos and ensemble passages.

Two additional tracks were recorded at this session. Ellington's *One More Once* was unissued until Stanley Dance included it in his *World Of Swing* anthology LP in 1974. It is a showcase for the five tenor saxophonists—Foster, Wess, Johnson, Gonsalves, and Hamilton. They and the very large band shout the blues over Woodyard's driving shuffle rhythm—exciting but hardly classic stuff. The other piece, Basie's *Blues In Hoss' Flat*, features Snooky Young, Foster, Gonsalves, and Louis Blackburn as soloists. Issued only on a U.S. Columbia double album, *Black Giants* (an anthology by various artists), it is wholly in the Basie style. The only important contribution by an Ellingtonian is the solo by Paul Gonsalves.

* * *

The two items from *Paris Blues* on the Basie-Ellington LP were also issued as a single. By this time, the practice of making up Ellington singles from tracks from his LPs was normal. Occasionally recordings were still made specifically for release as singles, but these were now rare. One instance was a coupling recorded during the sessions for *The Nutcracker Suite* and *Piano In The Background*—*Lost In Loveliness* and *Just One More Chance*. Both feature the vocal talents of Milt Grayson, with only a brief Gonsalves solo on the second title of real interest to the jazz enthusiast. The only other item recorded and issued as a single during this period was the *Asphalt Jungle Theme*. (*The Asphalt Jungle* was a TV series for which Ellington had written the theme music.) It was issued as a two-part single; the second part has also appeared on some LPs as *Asphalt Jungle Twist*. This cannot be counted among Ellington's masterpieces, but he obviously carried out his commission in a thoroughly professional manner and the recording is full of beefy scoring for the band. Clark Terry sits in with his former colleagues and joins the sax section to excellent effect. At the end of 1961, Ellington recorded a version of *Paris Blues* which was put out as a single. This is different from the one used on the *Midnight In Paris* LP and is probably the last Ellington recording made and issued as a single.

* * *

At a Monterey Jazz Festival appearance on September 7, 1961, Ellington introduced a new suite, *The Girls*. This was in five movements: *Introduction*, *Sarah*, *Lena*, *Mahalia*, and *Dinah*. No recording from this festival concert has been issued. The new suite was recorded in expanded form for Columbia on September 19 and 20 (the dates on the LP liner are incorrect) but was not released for over twenty years. The work was shrouded in mystery prior to the LP issue and was not even mentioned in the list of Ellington compositions in *Music Is My Mistress*.

Columbia finally brought out the work in 1982, along with a previously unissued version of *The Perfume Suite*. On the LP, what was styled *Introduction* at Monterey is called *Girls*, and the piece dedicated to Sarah Vaughan (a piano solo) had disappeared. The dedications to Mahalia Jackson, Lena Horne, and Dinah Washington are mixed in with new movements, all arrangements of non-Ellington songs: *Peg O' My Heart*, *Sweet Adeline*, *Juanita*, *Sylvia*, *Clementine*, and *Diane*. This suggests that Columbia asked Ellington to expand the work to fill an LP and that he and Strayhorn responded by quickly arranging the six non-Ellington songs. The result is rather jumbled as a suite, but the music is superb.

Lawrence Brown makes his recording debut as plunger-trombone soloist on *Sweet Adeline* in a duet with Johnny Hodges. The trombonist is heard to better effect on *Diane*, a loping medium-tempo showcase for his mellow and melodic open horn. All the soloists are in fine form, and the suite includes top-drawer muted solos from Ray Nance on *Mahalia* and *Peg O' My Heart*. Procope (on clarinet) and Hodges are effective duetists on Ellington's brilliant arrangement of *Clementine*, but, so far as the soloists are concerned, *The Girls Suite* is most notable for the superlative playing of Gonsalves. His work on *Juanita* and *Dinah* is of the very highest quality. The band is in fine form, the brass responding with skill and artistry to Ellington's demands for a wide variety of tone colors. The ensemble swings marvellously, and the Bell-Woodyard team is an inspiring powerhouse.

By the early sixties, the demand for *swinging* jazz had declined—the jazzmen of that era had no Savoy Ballroom dancers or Apollo Theater chorus lines to satisfy. But a few leaders, notably Basie and Ellington, continued to supply swinging music in varied packages designed to appeal to the sixties concert jazz audience. Some of Duke's most swinging (and most melodic) music of this period is to be heard in such concert suites as *Suite Thursday* and *The Girls*. That the latter lay neglected on the Columbia shelves for so many years has no bearing on its quality. It is full of distinctive and highly imaginative music.

* * *

The switch of the jazz record-buying public from singles to LPs was now virtually complete. Some jazz LPs, among them the 1956 *Ellington At Newport*, had been big sellers. One of the most popular was a collection of songs from the musical *My Fair Lady* performed by Shelly Manne, André Previn, and Leroy Vinnegar. By jazz standards, this LP was a huge success and it stimulated a whole spate of albums of music from Broadway shows by jazz artists. Soon Duke Ellington was recording a set of selections from a Broadway musical. Unfortunately for Ellington's overseas admirers, the vehicle Duke and Columbia decided to use for this venture was a short-lived show called *All American*. It ran for only 60 performances and was never performed outside the United States. Nor was Ellington's LP, *All American In Jazz*, released in Britain or continental Europe until 1979. Thus, in many parts of the world, this is among the least-known of Ellington's recordings, which is unfortunate since Duke reacted in a positive manner to the stimulus of ten songs by Charles Strouse and Lee Adams. When the band assembled in the Columbia studio in January 1962 to record the pieces from *All American* the full personnel was:

Trumpets:	Harold Baker, Bill Berry, Cat Anderson, Ray Nance (cornet, violin, vocal).
Trombones:	Lawrence Brown, Leon Cox, Chuck Connors (bass trombone).
Reeds:	Russell Procope (alto sax, clarinet); Johnny Hodges (alto sax); Paul Gonsalves (tenor sax); Jimmy Hamilton (clarinet, tenor sax); Harry Carney (baritone sax, clarinet, bass clarinet).
Rhythm:	Duke Ellington (piano); Aaron Bell (bass); Sam Woodyard (drums); Billy Strayhorn (deputy pianist).
Vocal:	Milt Grayson.

It will be noted that Nance switches to cornet from this time onward. The newcomer in the trumpet section is Bill Berry, who was rarely used as a soloist during his ten months in the band. There are two new faces in the trombone section: Leon Cox, who played plunger-style solos and stayed for six months, and Chuck Connors, who played bass trombone and stayed for the rest of the band's lifespan. The bass trombone gave Ellington's brass section new depth, and he was quick to utilize this. Connors was a valuable addition to the band although he was no soloist. The reed and rhythm sections are unchanged.

The ten selections from *All American* begin with one of Ellington's best jazz waltzes, his arrangement of *Back To School*. This has a genuine 3/4 feel—it does not sound like 4/4 music pushed into the wrong meter, as jazz waltzes so often do—and it swings. Carney has an important role, there is a good deal of Ellington piano, the scoring is top Ellington quality, and humor abounds. If anyone should think that Ellington would look down on this material and produce a substandard LP, the second track seems designed to allay any doubts. It is a ballad, *I've Just Seen Her*, which Ellington sets up as a showcase for Gonsalves. The full, rich and active backing is most unusual and inspires the tenor saxophonist to deliver one of his very best ballad solos. After this number was completed, the musicians in the band burst into spontaneous applause, so impressed was even this group of hardened professionals with the brilliance of Paul's playing. The brief trumpet solos are by Baker, who also plays the beautiful open solo on the uptempo *Which Way?* Ellington's quirky introduction at half-tempo and the busy scoring—note the trombone section here, with the bass trombone adding depth to the sound—are designed to cover the melodic paucity of the song.

If I Were You, on the other hand, is a very pleasant melody. Brown states the theme with a very familiar Ellington sound in accompaniment, that of Hodges leading the saxes. Hodges has a couple of solo spots, but the main variations are entrusted to Jimmy Hamilton, who is given some boppish accompaniment from the brass; there is nothing boppish, however, in the deep swing provided by Messrs. Bell and Woodyard. For the simple, folklike melody of *Once Upon A Time*, Ellington uses the primary colors from his tonal palette. The interplay of muted trumpet (Baker), clarinets (Hamilton and Procope) and trombone is succeeded by a short solo of the utmost beauty by Gonsalves. These soloists, along with the trombone section and Carney's bass clarinet, combine in an intricate development which never loses the innocent quality of the melody. Bass trombone is heard behind muted brass and saxes in the introduction to *Nightlife*, which after a little hesitation settles down to a swinging medium tempo and builds to an impressive climax. The next ballad, *Our Children*, has solos by Hamilton, Gonsalves, and Baker plus some unusual scoring. Here, as on all these tracks, Bell plays magnificently. *I Couldn't Have Done It Alone* is one of a distinguished line stretching from *Goin' To Town* via *Bojangles* in which Ellington writes vaudeville music in a mildly satirical vein. Here the theme statement is by Gonsalves, whose versatility and expertise in very varied Ellingtonian roles is fully demonstrated on *All American In Jazz*. Sam Woodyard does the soft-shoe shuffle; he is another musician who enters fully into the spirit of the delightful performance.

The melody of *We Speak The Same Language* is entrusted to Harry Carney, and this is yet another example of his magnificent artistry. Baker is heard both open and muted on this track, and it is interesting to note the intriguing way in which Ellington works Carney's solo baritone into the orchestral texture during the trumpet solos. The finale is an uptempo romp, *What A Country!*, featuring Nance, who solos on open cornet, and Hodges, who leads the saxes and solos in his inimitable fashion. Nance is used surprisingly little on this LP, probably because it was recorded just after he had a brief spell out of music. As a result, Ellington calls on Baker as soloist rather more than normally. But for all the fine solos—and those by Gonsalves are truly outstanding—*All American In Jazz* is a product of the Ellington *team*, with the arrangements by Ellington and Strayhorn its most impressive feature, closely followed by the skill and sensitivity of the ensemble playing.

* * *

In January 1962 the Ellington band made a promotional film for Goodyear Tires. The soundtrack has been issued on LP, taking up one side of a disc shared with Bobby Hackett. Duke plays it ultrasafe with the repertoire. The only new number is *One More Time*, temporarily masquerading under the title *Goodyears Of Jazz*; it is given a brief and perfunctory performance. The two opening tracks are probably the best—a version of the standard arrangement of *"A" Train*, minus the now familiar opening piano solo but with Nance offering a good interpretation of his standard trumpet solo,

and a *Satin Doll* in the bass showcase version heard on *At The Bal Masque*, now with Bell in the solo role. For the rest, *Blow By Blow* is a version of the Gonsalves marathon in which Paul's tone is particularly well recorded; Hodges plays *Things Ain't What They Used To Be* at a medium tempo with shuffle rhythm by Woodyard; the overworked twosome of *VIP's Boogie* and *Jam With Sam* appear; the piano solo of *Kinda Dukish* is followed not by *Rockin' In Rhythm*, its usual sequel, but by an unadorned Woodyard drum solo. The *Jam With Sam* is unusual in that it contains choruses by Bill Berry and Eddie Mullens, not often heard on solo, plus one by Ray Nance, who disliked this number intensely. Berry takes the first trumpet solo, Nance the second, and Mullens the third. The fourth and final trumpet contribution is by Anderson, who delivers his high-note climax with a humor which eradicates much of the tedium of this Ellington warhorse.

* * *

While continuing to present his concert, TV and radio audiences with repetitions of his standard repertoire, Ellington went on recording fresh material. As in the case of *All American In Jazz*, it had none of the pretentiousness then found in the presentation of much contemporary jazz, and its importance and worth failed to register with many jazz lovers. Yet much fine Ellington music is to be found both in *All American* and the somewhat similar Columbia LP called *Midnight In Paris*. This is a collection of songs with Parisian connections. Only three are by Ellington or Strayhorn and only one—Strayhorn's *Midnight In Paris*—is a new composition. As in *All American*, the scoring is typical Ellington, with rich tone colors and unexpected voicings allied to untiring invention, warmth and humor. Again the opening piece is a waltz, this time *Under Paris Skies*, another lesson in how to play jazz naturally in triple meter. Baker and Carney solo and the scoring for reeds is particularly delightful.

I Wish You Love is one of the most beautiful Ellington records, easy-sounding music of a kind unique to this ensemble. The format is simple—solos by Harry Carney, Jimmy Hamilton, and Ray Nance, with the band in a supporting role. Carney introduces the melody; Hamilton plays filigree decorations of the verse, backed by the trombones; and Nance contributes a solo of mellow warmth and beautifully poised phrasing which ranks with his very best work. Note the use of the bass trombone behind Ray's cornet. The bright flash of clarinet in the coda is just the right color after Nance's burnished brass. Nance's tone here shows one reason why he switched from trumpet to the more mellow cornet. The next track introduces us to the swinging *Mademoiselle De Paris* with several trumpet soloists and the ardent Gonsalves among her admirers—more lovely scoring for the incomparable saxophone section here. On *Comme Ci, Comme Ca* Duke shares the theme statement with the band, and there are typical solos by Hodges and Brown. Again the orchestration makes good use of Connor's bass trombone. *Speak To Me Of Love* is another melody ravishingly presented by the band—Woodyard on hand drums, the theme in tightly muted trumpets backed by rhythmic figures from the trombones, and a breathy, sensuous countermelody by Gonsalves. Short cadenzas fore and aft frame Hamilton's clarinet solo, presented with contrasting orchestra colors.

The title tune, *Midnight In Paris*, makes full and rich use of the ensemble, notably the saxophone section, in an impressionistic Strayhorn piece with the composer at the piano. *My Heart Sings* is a brief vignette featuring Nance on cornet with touches of Baker's trumpet among the thickly scored trombones and reeds. Only one of these numbers gained a regular place in the Ellington concert repertoire, *Guitar Amour*, an arrangement of a piece from *Paris Blues*. It features Nance on violin over an orchestral background to which exotic percussion makes a colorful contribution.

The arrangement of *Petit Waltz* is one of Ellington's charming miniatures, laconic, droll, and harmonically audacious with the theme treated with a marked lack of respect. A long thematic solo by Brown closes a performance in which Ellington's harmonic virtuosity is used to satirical ends. More unusual voicings are heard on *Paris Blues* along with the bass trombone, exquisite saxophone section playing, and solos by Brown, Gonsalves (outstanding), and Hodges. More fun and more bass trombone parts are present in *Javapacha*, Ellington's version of the famous Apache dance. Hodges states the theme in nonchalant fashion, and Nance is also heard in solo in this extremely witty score. *No Regrets* features Brown playing the melody with all the class and elegance a top-flight Ellingtonian brings to such a task. Finally, we have the uptempo *River Seine*, a kind of sing-along tune which is given over to wa-wa brass and Hodges. A gentle, warm humor permeates *Midnight In Paris*. Beneath its benign exterior we find the Ellingtonians at work with imagination and vigorous creativity.

* * *

It appeared for many years that *All American In Jazz* and *Midnight In Paris* had completed the issue of studio recordings by the Ellington band from 1956 to 1962. But in 1977 MF Records released a boxed set of LPs which included several studio recordings from 1962 done at sessions privately recorded by Ellington himself. Two such from May of that year feature Ray Nance in a variety of settings. *Flirtibird* from *Anatomy Of A Murder* features his open horn against an arrangement similar to that used in the film, with one of the other trumpets again playing an integral part in the saxophone section. The version of *Smada* is reminiscent of the one on *Blues In Orbit*, except that the full band is deployed and Nance is the only soloist. There is some confusion in that Nance plays his final solo over an orchestral part which is complete in itself, clashing at times with the riffs of the trumpet section. But the band really swings on this performance, and these sessions are indeed notable for an exhilarating swing not often found in studio recordings. Bell and Woodyard make a vital contribution. (Throughout these sessions, Woodyard's drumming is of the highest class and is also well placed in the recording balances.)

A Nance improvisation over bass and drums introduces *What Am I Here For?* in a lovely arrangement given a wonderful band performance. Nance, playing with great expressiveness, is again the only soloist. For *"A" Train*, Nance even takes over the introduction from Ellington's piano as well as playing, with great taste, the traditional trumpet solo he himself had created 22 years earlier. *I'm Gonna Go Fishin'* is the name given to the main theme from *Anatomy Of A Murder* after lyrics had been added. On this MF version, Nance is heard playing impassioned growl trumpet over a background arrangement of superb quality, the whole driven along by Woodyard's tremendous vitality. *Boo-Dah* is a sister-piece to *Smada* and receives a similarly swinging performance, the final trumpet solo again clashing with the already self-sufficient band parts. *Black And Tan Fantasy* finds Carney playing the second theme and Nance contributing some fresh ideas to the growl trumpet choruses.

A slightly later session produced a fine recording of *The Feeling Of Jazz* at a relaxed and swinging tempo with Hodges, Brown, Nance, and Hamilton as soloists. Duke seems to have been unsure as to the best way to present this composition: several unissued vocal versions were recorded around this time, as well as those found on the *Violin Session* and on the LP with John Coltrane. This band arrangement is probably the most satisfactory. An amalgam of *I Let A Song Go Out Of My Heart* and *Don't Get Around Much Anymore* was featured at concerts around this time, and a studio recording is heard on the MF set. *Don't Get Around Much Anymore* had originated in the late thirties (when it was known as *Never No Lament*) in an accompaniment devised for *I Let A Song Go Out Of My Heart*; more recently, a combination of the two themes had become the standard ending of the *Medley Of Popular Hits*. Here *I Let A Song* is played by Carney on baritone, with brief assistance from Gonsalves and Ellington in the middle eight, then Nance sings a chorus of *Don't Get Around Much*, followed by his muted cornet solo and a reprise of the vocal.

Mr. Gentle And Mr. Cool is revived on the MF set with the part originally taken by Baker's trumpet handled by Gonsalves on tenor sax. There is some superb tenor playing here, but this version of the piece is less satisfying than the original, partly because the band playing is less effective. *Taffy Twist* is one of Duke's more successful ventures into rock-and-roll, a tremendously dynamic performance powered by the Woodyard shuffle rhythm. Nance's open horn is heard, but Hamilton on tenor is the main soloist. Another revival concludes the issued portion of these sessions, a version of *Jump For Joy* featuring Nance on cornet and vocal. The arrangement is revised but still highly effective and a fine alto solo by Procope is another highlight of a powerfully swinging performance.

* * *

The session which produced the *Duke Ellington Meets Coleman Hawkins* LP was supervised by Bob Thiele for the Impulse label and recorded on August 18, 1962. Duke and his guest are backed by a group of experienced Ellingtonians: Nance (doubling cornet and violin), Brown, Hodges, Carney, Bell, and Woodyard. The session came about through a remark Hawkins had made in a magazine interview with Stanley Dance, expressing his hope of recording with Ellington some day. There was, of course, much in common between the two men. Both had long been among the most eminent and respected of jazz musicians; both had always insisted on the highest musical standards; both understood the process of change and had encouraged the new in art without being carried away by the wind of fashion. While Hawkins was new to the Ellingtonians they were well prepared for him, as the band had nurtured two of his finest disciples in the persons of Ben Webster and Paul Gonsalves. This session was an event in which the greatest tenor saxophonist in jazz played alongside the greatest alto and baritone exponents. The Ellington musicians were a proud group, and there is plenty of evidence in the music that Hodges, especially, and Carney were determined not to be outshone by their distinguished guest. For the session Duke produced five new numbers, making up the balance with standard Ellington pieces.

The opener is an apparently new piece called *Limbo Jazz*—actually based on Stompy Jones—and, apart from a shuffle rhythm during the Coleman Hawkins solo, it is powered by an infectious Caribbean beat. So exuberant was the run-through for this number that Sam Woodyard can be heard singing to himself throughout the performance. Stanley Dance advises us in his liner note that the first part of this track was recorded while Hawkins was changing a reed, but the huge sound of the Hodges-Carney duo really makes a third saxophone unnecessary. Hodges and Brown are heard before Hawkins enters, but the star soloist of the track is Nance, playing Latin American cornet with a pure jazz sound and compelling warmth of expression. On *Mood Indigo* the traditional trio for the theme statement consists of Hodges, Brown, and Carney, the latter on bass clarinet. Once they have performed their opening task, however, the piece is taken over by Hawkins in a saxophone improvisation that reconstructs the harmonic and melodic fabric of *Mood Indigo* with great skill and beauty. This performance would have to be included in any list of major Hawkins solos and in any list of outstanding performances of *Mood Indigo*. *Ray Charles' Place* is a rocker with insistent drumming by Woodyard and fine solos by Nance, Hodges, Brown, and Hawkins. Brown's trombone is heard in the presentation of the rather unusual theme.

The blues *Wanderlust* (from a 1938 Hodges unit date) is another spirited performance with solos by all the horns. Brown sounds as if he has lip trouble here, but the others are in peak form, Carney making an entry which could have daunted a lesser musician than Hawkins. Duke's blues piano is perfect in support, and the big sound of the ensemble has to be heard to be believed. Nance adds greatly to the flavor and expressiveness of this blues performance. *You Dirty Dog* is another new number, this time of a very casual nature. Here Hodges follows Hawkins in the solo routine and plays an alto solo of tremendous verve with a tone bigger than that of most tenor players. "Bean" was the nickname of Coleman Hawkins, yet *Self-Portrait Of the Bean* is a joint production by Ellington and Billy Strayhorn. Hawkins has no difficulty in making the piece his own, however, doing full justice to the beautiful melodic curves of the theme. In *The Jeep Is Jumpin'* Ellington calls for what sounds like a cruelly fast tempo for a band of aging horn players, but the three saxes revel in the situation, Hodges opening the solo round with a challenging contribution. Carney leaps in with one of the best solos of his career, and Hawkins calmly delivers a solo of immense authority. The brass players sound less at ease. *The Ricitic* is performed by a quintet of Hawkins, Nance (on violin), and the rhythm section; it features more Latin rhythms and some lovely Ducal piano. Hawkins seems indifferent to the Latin touches but plays a beautiful solo of detached dignity. The final title from the session was not issued on the *Duke Ellington Meets Coleman Hawkins* LP but came out on an Impulse anthology. It is a performance of *Solitude* by the quintet of *The Ricitic*, and it contains a solo by Hawkins of quite ravishing beauty.

Duke Ellington Meets Coleman Hawkins provides an excellent opportunity to study the methods and style of the Ellington rhythm section of the early sixties. For all his occasional crudities, Woodyard lays down a big, swinging beat and contributes color and excitement. Bell plays with intelligence and musical vigor throughout the set: one could cite *Mood Indigo*, where his choice of notes is superb; or *Ray Charles' Place*, where he seems to have quickly devised a bass part of the utmost perfection; or *Wanderlust*, where his Spanish rhythms create a beautiful bass pattern beneath the swell of a great blues performance. And then there is Duke, his ensemble piano directing the course of events with a subtle authority.

This music has a very impromptu feeling, the air of a casual meeting of a group of highly talented musicians, yet it bears the stamp of authentic Ellington style and quality.

* * *

The Ellington-Charles Mingus-Max Roach session for United Artists is not particularly well recorded for an early sixties date. For this occasion Ellington wore his "modern jazz pianist" mask, and, as on the infrequent occasions in the past when this had been donned in public, the extent of his influence on the music of Thelonious Monk is very apparent. Three of the seven titles are new Ellington compositions at uptempo—*Money Jungle* (the title of the LP), *Very Special*, and *Wig Wise*—all quirky little themes of the kind associated with Monk. Ellington's theme statements are frequently brusque, even brutal, and his variations are inclined to be fragmented into power-packed, angular phrases. The harmonies are lean and harsh; the total effect is of spare, attenuated, driving music. Roach plays busily and with considerable drive, and it is interesting to note Ellington's reaction to this drumming, so different from that in his own bands. The bass playing is greatly skilled but Mingus's elaborations are at odds with the essentially concise Ellington language. Over the busy playing of his partners, Ellington delivers percussive, dry, laconic statements using the bass and drums as a background without getting involved in any kind of dialogue with either. It is interesting to hear *Caravan* subjected to this kind of treatment, stride piano elements and all; Duke as usual reveals new aspects of the theme, and his work is full of drive and spirit. The collection is completed by three ballads, *Les Fleurs Africaines* (also known as *Fleurette Africaine*), a new composition by Ellington in which an attractive little motif is used to build a gentle pastoral mood, and two standards, *Warm Valley* and *Solitude*. The former receives a brief reading, with thick harmonies and sensuous lines; the latter is a long performance with a rigorous examination of the harmonic substructure. This is a very attractive *Solitude* — one of the best of the many Ellington recordings.

It is not simply because Ellington solo recordings were so infrequent that *Money Jungle* was an important addition to the Ellington discography. Its particular quality lies in the fact that it features Duke in the role of conventional jazz pianist, away from his usual musical environment. There is not a great deal of rapport between Ellington, Mingus, and Roach, but this turns out to be an advantage, at least in that we hear Duke playing with rhythm section accompaniment rather than functioning *within* the section as was his wont. Mingus was a great admirer of Ellington, and this is the only occasion on which they are heard together on record. But Ellington plays no particular attention to the bass work and much of the interplay which might have been expected between these two is lost in the welter of Roach's noisy drumming. Mingus is on record as saying that the choice of drummer for this session was unfortunate, but much of his own playing is less than ideal, making overmuch of vocalized effects in the higher register of his instrument. One suspects that, for all Mingus's worship of Duke's art, the music of the two men was basically incompatible. Yet this lack of rapport with his partners does not affect the quality of Ellington's solo work.

* **

In the early sixties Charles Mingus represented the most advanced style of ensemble jazz; the most "far out" soloist was considered to be saxophonist John Coltrane. Many musicians and listeners consider Coltrane to be the first man to alter significantly the language of the jazz solo since Charlie Parker. Coltrane was Ellington's partner on his next record date for the Impulse label in September 1962. Although a part of Coltrane's apprenticeship had been spent in Hodges's band during the early fifties, his connections with Ellington's music were virtually nonexistent. As if to insure against a feared incompatibility, producer Bob Thiele asked both Ellington and Coltrane to bring their own bassist and drummer to the session. The contrast in drummers is particularly fascinating: Elvin Jones was *the* name in modern drumming at the time, a figure as respected for his innovations as were Mingus and Coltrane, while Sam Woodyard was one of the last drummers whose values reflected the days when a swinging beat meant one which would inspire the dancers.

The Ellington-Coltrane meeting of apparent extremes is conducted on the basis of five themes by Ellington, one by Strayhorn and one by Coltrane. In the opening *In A Sentimental Mood*, Bell and Jones are on bass and drums, but on the rest more familiar partnerships are heard, either Bell and Woodyard or Jimmy Garrison and Jones. Coltrane plays the melody of *In A Sentimental Mood* in rather austere fashion, creating an emotional climate different from the one usually associated with this voluptuous melody. Coltrane's variations are firmly controlled, but Ellington's solo is not improved by the drummer's restless double beat, as if he were impatient to get on to the next uptempo number. The melody of Strayhorn's *My Little Brown Book* is also treated with great respect, but here Coltrane changes the mood even more radically into one of dark, almost despairing, subjectivity. On two new Ellington pieces, *Take The Coltrane* and *Angelica*, there are Coltrane solos of a harmonically free variety during which Ellington drops out to give the soloist his head. *Big Nick* is a Coltrane original on which the composer plays soprano sax. Perhaps the most integrated performances are *Stevie* and *The Feeling Of Jazz*, although the restraint of both principals indicates that they were conscious of their lack of familiarity with each other's methods. Ellington is strangely tentative throughout this partnership; the musical languages of the two musicians were probably too far apart for any singleness of purpose to emerge during the course of an isolated recording session.

* **

An LP on the Varese label, released in 1976, contains a 35-minute interview with Ellington by Jack Cullen of radio station CKNW in Vancouver, recorded in October 1962. The interview was obviously done to work in with the playing of Ellington records during a broadcast and is cast in the form of a conversation about various Ellington compositions, so that it could be edited to fit in with records of these works. The LP sounds totally unedited and catches Ellington in a loquacious mood, chatting about his compositions from *East St. Louis Toodle-oo* to *Such Sweet Thunder*. Duke talks away and often gets started on some interesting dissertation only for Cullen to cut him off with a mention of the next number to be covered. Despite this, the LP is a fascinating document in which Ellington talks about his music in greater depth than in the other, shorter interviews released on record. It will be interesting to see what further Ellington interviews and conversations will be issued in the future, for his comments on his music, though couched in the smooth language of the popular music world, are always of great interest.

Outstanding Records

1. Columbia Recordings

ANATOMY OF A MURDER
FESTIVAL SESSION (especially *Idiom '59—Part One*-[*Vapor*] and *Launching Pad*)
BLUES IN ORBIT
THE NUTCRACKER SUITE
PEER GYNT SUITE
THE UNKNOWN SESSION
SUITE THURSDAY
PIANO IN THE FOREGROUND
BATTLE ROYAL—WITH COUNT BASIE AND HIS ORCHESTRA (especially *Wild Man* and *Segue In C*)
ALL AMERICAN IN JAZZ
MIDNIGHT IN PARIS

2. Pablo Issues

THE QUEEN'S SUITE

3. SESAC Transcriptions

Little John's Tune, She Was A Tinkling Thing, Lullaby For Dreamers, and *Still Water*

4. Roulette Recordings

LOUIS ARMSTRONG AND DUKE ELLINGTON (especially *Duke's Place* [alias *C Jam Blues*], *I'm Just A Lucky So And So, Mood Indigo, The Beautiful American, Black And Tan Fantasy, The Mooche,* and *Just Squeeze Me*

5. Impulse Recordings

DUKE ELLINGTON MEETS COLEMAN HAWKINS
DUKE ELLINGTON AND JOHN COLTRANE

6. United Artists Recordings

MONEY JUNGLE (with Charles Mingus and Max Roach)

7. Goodyear Recordings

Take the "A" Train and Satin Doll

8. Studio Recordings Issued on MF Records

Flirtibird, Smada, What Am I Here For?, Take The "A" Train, Boo-Dah, Black And Tan Fantasy (May 24–25, 1962), *The Feeling Of Jazz* (July 3, 1962), *Taffy Twist,* and *Jump For Joy* (ca. July 1962)

9. Concert Recordings

Launching Pad (Newport, 1959; Foxy), *Black And Tan Fantasy-Creole Love Call-The Mooche* (Berlin, 1959; Swing House)

10. Broadcasts and Recordings from Dances

Stardust, Paris Blues, Overture, Dance Of The Floreadores (Mather Air Force Base Dance, July 22, 1960), *Congo Square* (Quaker City Jazz Festival, August 27, 1960)

11. Interview

October 1962 interview with Jack Cullen (Varese)

Chapter 25

Triumphs and Travels

FROM HIS MID-FIFTIES ON ELLINGTON liked to share a joke with his audiences about his age. He referred to numbers like *Black And Tan Fantasy* and *Creole Love Call* as being "before my time," denying knowledge of the early days and claiming that "Sonny Greer was the leader then." When asked his age directly, he would reply that he had been born at the Newport Jazz Festival of 1956. Because Ellington never felt himself to be an old man, he strongly resented being presented as some kind of aged wonder. The Newport reference was wholly characteristic in that it revealed a truth about his life while appearing to be no more than an evasion. In a very real sense, the 1956 Newport Jazz Festival represented a rebirth of Ellingtonia. An enduring art like Ellington's experiences many rebirths but this Newport Festival triumph reestablished Duke as a public figure, and from this time on, Duke Ellington and his Famous Orchestra (as they were usually billed) were once again a top drawer international attraction. It seems strange that we should be discussing a rebirth of the Ellington band in 1956 when such a phenomenon had been noted just five years earlier, when Louis Bellson and Willie Smith had joined. But in commercial terms, that rebirth had been short-lived, and the band took a steep dive from the triumphs of 1951 to the slough of 1955. Fortunately, the successes of 1956 had a permanent effect so far as economic viability was concerned.

The combination of the band's new popularity with the musical stimulus of the return of Johnny Hodges and the arrival of Sam Woodyard unleashed in Ellington a new surge of creative endeavor, and the second half of the fifties was one of his most prolific periods as a composer. The appearance of *A Drum Is A Woman* in 1956 and of *Such Sweet Thunder* the following year brought fresh publicity and prestige as well as being purely musical events of major importance. The idea of a jazz musician writing and presenting his own TV fantasia was unusual enough to attract wide attention, while the commission from the Shakespeare festival at Stratford, Ontario, was even more newsworthy and prestigious. So the important first condition for the continued existence of the Duke Ellington Orchestra—plenty of well-paid employment—was met, and in a warm climate of critical and public approval, Ellington was inspired to work, along with Billy Strayhorn, on a great variety of new musical projects.

The European tour by the Ellington band in 1958 was the first since 1950. It was built around the Leeds Triennial Music Festival of that year, at which Duke was presented to Queen Elizabeth II. It was the prospect of this presentation which tempted Ellington into making the tour; without this inducement it is doubtful whether Ellington would have brought his band to Europe at all in 1958. Some writers have interpreted Ellington's attitude to royalty and other titled persons as a kind of snobbery. In fact his view, like that of many of his generation, was that it was important for the black jazz artist to be seen to have respect. In hindsight, this may seem naive, but Ellington was a man of his time and anything but naive about racial problems. He always saw himself as an African American in the public eye, with responsibilities which he would never shirk. He had faced racial prejudice all his life. From an early age he had been a wealthy man and this meant that he could avoid many of the most unpleasant consequences of racial prejudice which were the everyday lot of less affluent blacks. These last included his bandsmen, whose problems in getting food and accommodation in the segregated South and the often prejudiced North have been documented elsewhere.

Despite the pressures, Duke Ellington never compromised either in artistic or in behavioral terms. His partnership with Irving Mills was castigated in the black press, as was his employment of white lyric writers for his songs. We can hear on the *Night At The Cotton Club* recording of 1929 Irving Mills referring to Ellington in just the condescending terms one would expect to be used of a black performer at that time. But one cannot find in 1929, or in any other year, an instance where Duke's own behavior was anything but dignified. When attacked for his apparent lack of involvement with civil rights militancy, he replied that he had done his freedom marching in the South 30 years before—without benefit of a police escort. It is wholly consistent with his attitude that he should regard an invitation to be presented to the Queen of England, or a commission for a suite for a Shakespeare Festival, as effective means to combat the ignorance which lies behind racial prejudice. Ellington's own personal delight in meeting the Queen was compounded by the honor which this did him, coming from the head of a country which had given him so much encouragement a quarter of a century earlier, and the fact that he found the Queen to be a wholly charming person. The nature of his reaction to the meeting can be clearly perceived in the writing and dedication of *The Queen's Suite*. That Ellington clearly enjoyed associating with royalty and titled persons is of little significance. He was a gregarious man who relished the company of people from all parts of the social scale.

The public release of *The Queen's Suite* after Ellington's death revealed the work to be one of his and Strayhorn's masterpieces. Similarly, the Shakespearian suite *Such Sweet Thunder* was of the highest standard, and was indeed recognized and acclaimed as such at the time. In *A Drum Is A Woman* Ellington had clearly broken new ground. With the film scores for *Anatomy Of A Murder* and *Paris Blues* further challenges were accepted and transformed into successes. The band enjoyed a brief layoff while Duke was in Paris working on the latter film. During this break from bandleading, Ellington wrote some incidental music for a classical French drama, but none of this seems ever to have been played by the Ellington band. The commission from the Monterey Jazz Festival for a suite based on John Steinbeck's writings resulted in another musical triumph, *Suite Thursday*. All these activities came from the years in which Ellington also created *The Newport Jazz Festival Suite*, *A Portrait Of Ella Fitzgerald*, *Princess Blue*, *The Toot Suite*, and *Idiom '59*, as well as arranging music as diverse as *The Nutcracker Suite* and *Who's Afraid Of The Big Bad Wolf?* and writing shorter jazz pieces of the standard of *Blues In Blueprint* and *The Beautiful American*. Other Ellington achievements in these years include the piano improvisations on *Back To Back* and *Side By Side*, as well as on the solo piano LP *Piano In The Foreground*. Then there are such marvelous and diverse LPs as *All American In Jazz*, *Midnight In Paris*, *Battle Royal*, and the *Peer Gynt* suite. Even for a man with a collaborator of the caliber of Billy Strayhorn, this was a prodigious output. One can well understand why Duke did not like to be thought of as an old man.

* * *

The Ellington Orchestra of 1956 to 1959 was the best band Duke had led since the early forties. It was so full of strong soloists that its concerts were inclined to become a series of showcases—a kind of superior Jazz At The Philharmonic presentation with the solos backed by Ellington scoring. Much of the best playing of this band was heard in the recording studios, where it proved itself an ideal ensemble for the performances of Duke's new work, able to produce a solo voice or an ensemble voicing to meet perfectly any of the composer's wide-ranging demands. The virtuosity of the trumpet section occasionally led to a flamboyance which could unbalance the ensemble, but Ellington saw to it that such occasions were not the important ones. The quality of this ensemble can be heard not only on Ellington's own recordings but also on the more conventional music they recorded under the direction of Johnny Hodges and Mercer Ellington.

In solo terms the band could boast four top-class trumpet soloists, three outstanding trombone stylists of the highest quality, and a reed team which included three of the greatest players ever heard on their instruments—Johnny Hodges, Paul Gonsalves and Harry Carney. This same reed section also included the clarinet virtuoso Jimmy Hamilton (who was a fine tenor sax soloist too) and the thoroughly professional Russell Procope, a craftsman with long experience in jazz ensembles of many kinds. With the skilled and inventive Jimmy Woode and the volatile Sam Woodyard firing the rhythm section, this clearly comes close to being an ideal jazz ensemble, one which could also boast the finest of all band pianists.

It is interesting to compare this band with the Ellington Orchestra of 1940, usually considered to be the best of all Ellington bands. Such a comparison is difficult because Ellington's music had changed so much in the intervening years. It is a fact that the band of the late fifties would not have played the 1940 book as well as the old band, as Ellington always wrote for particular soloists and for a particular ensemble. And before we chalk up a victory for the established favorites, we should note that the 1940 band would not have coped any better had this hypothetical situation been reversed. The surprising thing about the two bands is that the fifties group sounds so much more a *big* band, despite the fact that it contains the same number of instrumentalists (the rhythm guitar of Fred Guy being replaced by a fourth trumpet). To some extent this is because of the slight but perceptible decline in the importance of the individual musician within the Ellington band over the years. But it must be stressed that this was a minor change of emphasis, for the individual creative jazz musician remained a figure of vital importance in the Ellington ensemble. The recorded history of the band clearly shows how the importance of the individual musician was gradually diminished in relation to that of the composer-leader. The most dominant sideman in the history of the Ellington band was Bubber Miley, and after his departure in 1929 no other single soloist was ever of comparable importance. The man who replaced Miley, Cootie Williams, was a spark plug of the band and a musical personality on whom Ellington relied heavily, but he was a less commanding figure in the band overall than Miley had been. The departure of Williams and of Barney Bigard in the early forties tended to accelerate this process, and when in the middle of that decade Ray Nance, the man who replaced Williams, took time off, the effect on the music was minimal. As Ellington's mastery of composition grew the creative contributions of the sidemen, while still of great importance, assumed a less obvious place in the scheme of things. Partly because of these changes of emphasis and partly due to the accelerated rate of personnel change, the playing came to have less of the chamber-music quality of the earlier Ellington bands. One can see how important a part the individual still played in the band by noting, for example, Clark Terry's impact, but no one would have thought of writing a dirge when Clark departed.

To a certain extent the changes in the Ellington Orchestra reflected the situation in jazz as a whole. Soloists with an individual and original style and big, commanding personalities clearly did exist, but there were now far fewer of them. In the future this would pose problems for Ellington as the shortage of jazz personalities became more and more acute. An allied problem was that few musicians from the postwar schools of jazz concerned themselves much with melodic presentation and that few of them achieved the degree of excellence in this regard that had been commonplace among the musicians of the twenties and the thirties. Many of the musicians of the new aesthetic persuasion regarded the playing of a melody at best as a perfunctory prelude to an examination of the music's harmonic structure. This was not Ellington's way. Another disadvantage that the new musicians had compared with their predecessors was a lack of big band experience. The generation of Clark Terry, Willie Cook, and Paul Gonsalves was the last on which Ellington could draw for experienced big band players. After this generation, Ellington would have to rely on veterans or on younger players who might lack big band seasoning, the requisite type of tone and melodic ability, and the individuality which had characterized the traditional Ellington sideman.

Despite these portents, the breakup of the great late-fifties band was not a disaster. Sam Woodyard soon returned, Aaron Bell joined on bass, and the vastly talented and experienced saxophone section held together, becoming the real core of the band as it moved into the new decade. The changes in the trombones were such that high standards were constantly maintained as far as section playing was concerned, while the wide-ranging styles of the newly returned Lawrence Brown covered any shortcomings in solo ability among his section mates. Section playing was vitally important here, for in the Ellington band the trombone section was always treated as an entity in its own right and not, as in many big bands, as a sort of adjunct to the trumpets. Much of the quality of Ellington's trombone section of the sixties was due to Brown's abilities as a leader. The greatest instability was in the trumpets, but the frequent changes between 1959 and 1962 were inclined to revolve around Cook, Nance, Anderson, and Baker, all experienced Ellington hands. Fats Ford, Eddie Mullins, and Bill Berry also made contributions to the trumpet section at this time, although none made a great impact as a musical personality.

Berry, in an article published in 1980, stressed how he found Ellington's to be a "pure jazz" band:

> the music certainly was created as it went along. I had a huge book of music—I don't think we played any of it at all.... [This] book must have been ten inches thick, and nothing was numbered or titled.... When I first went on the band, I said to Cat Anderson "What note do I play on the end of this tune?" He said, "Grab a note that sounds wrong and hold on." (*Crescendo*, January 1980, p. 22)

This insight into the workings of the band shows why academy-trained musicians were of so little use to Duke. Later in the article, Berry tells how, at a recording session, each musician was given a stave of whole notes to read, "then Duke sang the rhythms to us, and by the time he got through, it was a gem."

Another factor which was starting to affect Ellington's music was the aging of the established soloists within the band. The most vulnerable area was the brass section. The consequences for a trumpeter's or trombonist's lip of playing in a band like Ellington's for a long period are far from beneficial. Some, at least, of the slight inconsistency in Nance's playing from the Capitol period can be ascribed to this cause, as can the fluffs which were increasingly heard in Brown's work as the years went by. By the time they left Ellington, both were well past their peak as brass players. In the last couple of years that Brown was in the band, he could hardly be relied on as a soloist, although right to the end he remained a wonderful section leader. In the period from 1956 to 1962, most of these problems were still in the future. But the signs were there.

An enormous variety of music, some of it created by Ellington and Strayhorn, some of it translated by them into the Ducal language, was produced in these years—at a rate which was never again equaled. When one considers that in addition to the issued recordings there still is much from this time yet to be released, one begins to grasp the magnitude of the creative achievement of Ellington and his team. Unfortunately, the jazz audience's conception of creativity is limited and conditioned by the practices of the majority of jazz artists, who happen to be solo performers. To such an audience, records like *At The Bal Masque*, *All American In Jazz*, and *Midnight In Paris* appeared to be mere "commercial" ventures and were disregarded. Even those who took the trouble to listen were often puzzled, failing to recognize the *kind* of humor in the music, to perceive that Ellington was, for the most part, indulging in friendly satire with a gentle smile. The Ellington-Strayhorn principle of treating all musical material with respect was as evident in their treatment of pop songs as it was in their own concert pieces. But even jazz enthusiasts who understood Ellington's concert works expected further compositions of the *Such Sweet Thunder* variety and felt that with LPs like *All American In Jazz* or *Midnight In Paris* they were being fobbed off with second best. They failed to realize that Ellington did not repeat himself. A Shakespearian Suite was one problem. That solved, he would find another that made different demands on his imagination and craftsmanship, instead of writing another suite to a similar formula. In this, he differed from all other jazz musicians with the exception of the young Louis Armstrong, whose music of the twenties shows a similar hunger for new horizons.

It is altogether typical of Ellington that, having created *Such Sweet Thunder*, he should react so differently when he next received a commission with a literary flavor, from the Monterey Jazz Festival of 1960. The conception of *Suite Thursday* is totally different from that of *Such Sweet Thunder*. Such constantly new perspectives were puzzling to an audience accustomed to a more stable diet. The reaction of many people to *The Nutcracker Suite* and the *Peer Gynt* selections was equally negative, failing to grasp the nature of the music. In the case of the Tchaikovsky suite, it was obviously helpful that Ellington was dealing with material which, like much of his own music, was written for the dance. Here again the Ellington-Strayhorn principle of respect can be perceived. Never is the essential character of Tchaikovsky's music violated. As was the case with the *At The Bal Masque* selections, the humor of these arrangements seems to have been missed by many people and the work was given short shrift by many influential writers, as if it were some sort of cheap trick or gimmick. Yet in terms of style, there is no more characteristic Ellington LP than *The Nutcracker Suite*, with its colorful and witty arrangements, its totally unmalicious humor, and its great swing and zest. Unfortunately, the influence of critics who continued to praise soloists who had not played a new phrase in years was pervasive. Many enthusiasts are surprised when they find so much great music on Ellington records these critics had advised them to disregard. Yet an approach to Ellington is not always easy. He is in some respects a difficult artist for those unfamiliar with his ways, as musicians as well as listeners have discovered over the years. He is an artist who demands above all to be listened to on his own terms. He fits no pigeonhole, and for variety and continual and prodigious creativity he stands alone in jazz. The true nature of this creativity can be discerned from a study of the very remarkable series of records he made from 1956 to 1962.

Sidemen

Ozzie Bailey

One of Ellington's better ballad singers, Bailey had a pleasantly unaffected style and notably good enunciation. He was able to sing on swinging medium-tempo numbers without sounding grotesque, a rare attribute among Ellington balladeers.

Representative Recordings: What Else Can You Do With A Drum? and *You Better Know It* (from *A Drum Is A Woman*, Columbia, 1956), *Multicolored Blue* (Columbia, 1958), *Hand Me Down Love* (Columbia, 1958)

Aaron Bell

Bell was already an established name in the jazz world when he came into the band to take over the bass chair from Jimmy Woode. His reputation was certainly enhanced during his stay of two and a half years with the band. He had a big, powerful tone which really filled out the bottom of the music, and, like Jimmy Woode, he was able to strike up an excellent musical understanding with both Ellington and Sam Woodyard. His alertness to the needs of the band was enhanced by his creative responses to the many challenges and new situations which it presented. His grasp of Ellington's new works, for which the bass part would often be an empty sheet of manuscript paper and a grin of encouragement from the composer, was equaled by the way he handled traditional items in the band's repertoire.

Representative Recordings: Lay-By (from *Suite Thursday*, Columbia, 1960), *Blues For Jerry* (Columbia, 1961), *Satin Doll* (Goodyear, 1962), *Wanderlust* (*Duke Ellington Meets Coleman Hawkins*, Impulse, 1962)

Chuck Connors

Bass trombone players are rare in jazz, but Ellington employed one of the very best in Connors. Apart from an occasional functional passage or an even rarer theme statement, Connors was not heard in solo, but from the time he joined the band in 1961 to Ellington's death thirteen years later, he gave the Ellington trombone section a rare depth and sonority. Connors was a member of a very distinguished group of Ellington sidemen whose contribution was far greater than the casual observer could imagine.

Representative Recordings: Chant Of The Weed (Reprise, 1962), *It's A Lonesome Old Town* (Reprise, 1962), *Come Sunday* (from *Black, Brown And Beige*, Victor, 1965), *Perdido* (Victor, 1966)

Buster Cooper

During the seven years he was in the Ellington band, Cooper occupied the seat in the trombone section which had traditionally belonged to the plunger-mute specialist. But Cooper did not use the plunger at all as a soloist, preferring an aggressive, almost violently declamatory style on open horn. He was a fiery and vigorous soloist, though his melodic limitations gave his work a certain monotony. He was a first-class section player.

Representative Recordings: One O'Clock Jump (Reprise, 1962), *Bonga* (Reprise, 1963), *The Twitch* (Victor, 1966), *El Busto* (Verve, 1966), *Chico Cuadradino* (from the *Latin American Suite*, Fantasy, 1968)

Milt Grayson

A competent singer whose work lacked any jazz qualities, Milt Grayson was used mainly at Ellington concerts to please those in the audience whom Duke imagined came to his concerts to hear popular ballad singing. Grayson failed to find much favor with Ellington connoisseurs, despite a stint lasting over three years.

Representative Recordings: The Blues (from *Black, Brown And Beige*, Reprise, 1963), *Do Nothin' Til You Hear From Me* (Reprise, 1963)

Jimmy Johnson

Johnson substituted for Woodyard from March 1959 to March 1960. He was a rather heavy drummer, lacking in subtlety and with only a moderate ability to swing.

Representative Recordings: The concert recordings made during Ellington's European tour of September and October 1959

Eddie Mullins

A competent jazz trumpeter with a wealth of experience in top-class bands, Mullins took only occasional solos during his several short spells with Ellington and cannot be said to have made any particular impact.

Representative Recording: Jam With Sam (Goodyear, 1962—Mullins takes the penultimate trumpet solo)

Booty Wood

Among the plunger trombone specialists whose playing came closest in sound to that of the great Tricky Sam Nanton, Wood was not in the band long enough to develop what was clearly a considerable potential as an Ellingtonian. Perhaps his playing lacked the finesse and personality of the greatest Ellington musicians—his solos on the Ellington records are certainly uneven in quality. But the best are clearly by a trombonist of no ordinary abilities. In addition to his skills with the plunger mute, Wood was also a distinctive soloist on open trombone, where his style was that of a disciple of Trummy Young.

Representative Recordings: Sweet And Pungent (Columbia, 1959), *Black And Tan Fantasy-Creole Love Call-The Mooche* medley (Mather Air Force Base dance, 1960)

Jimmy Woode

Woode had what sounded like a small tone, yet it was clearly audible even when the Ellington Orchestra was in full cry. Woode was a very subtle player who seemed, in the best Ducal tradition, to have complete empathy with the piano player. His choice of notes was always impeccable, and his use of rhythmic figures against the band's melodic lines was informed with great taste. Harmonically, he is one of the most interesting of Ellington bassists; at no time were the bass parts more worthy of the listener's attention than when Woode was in the band. He was a complete musician with an easy command of his instrument, which could obscure his skills to the casual listener. These skills were never paraded in the ostentatious fashion of some jazz bass virtuosi (not Duke's, though), but were always directed to purely musical ends. His partnership with Sam Woodyard, a very different kind of artist, was an outstanding feature of the Ellington band of the late fifties.

Representative Recordings: Sonnet In Search Of A Moor (from *Such Sweet Thunder*, Columbia 1957), *Montage* (from *Black, Brown And Beige*, Columbia, 1958), *Satin Doll* (Columbia, 1958), *Bass-ment* (Columbia, 1958), *Just Scratchin' The Surface* (Columbia, 1958), *Mr. Gentle And Mr. Cool* (Roulette, 1958)

Sam Woodyard

Unlike almost every other drummer who played with big bands from the fifties onward, Woodyard never aimed for virtuoso effects or finely wrought precision. Instead he relied on a simple drumming technique and concentrated on playing within the band. With Ellington, he could be an erratic player who at his worst either plodded heavily or hammered away relentlessly in an irritating offbeat style. At his best, however, Woodyard proved himself not only one of the finest big band drummers but also a great Ellingtonian. He was able to inspire the band in a unique fashion, creating a vital, surging swing even in complex scores like *Harlem*. With Woodyard at his best, the band would play with more fire than with any other drummer, and his rapport with Ellington was remarkable. He was also a fine percussion colorist. Owing to the "primitive" nature of his art, Woodyard was much maligned by many critics during his Ellington years, but the musicians in the band held him in high esteem. Many jazz lovers prefer drumming of the Louis Bellson kind, and this is a matter of personal taste. But that is no excuse for failure to appreciate the contribution Woodyard made to the Ellington band. Apart from Sonny Greer, he was the longest-serving Ellington drummer, and as with Greer, his best work can be considered the epitome of Ellingtonian drumming.

Representative Recordings: Half The Fun (from *Such Sweet Thunder,* Columbia, 1956), *Just Scratchin' The Surface* (Columbia, 1958), *Night Creature* (third movement) (Duke Ellington Orchestra and Paris Symphony Orchestra, Reprise, 1963), *Harlem* (Paris concert version, Reprise, 1963), *Step In Time* (Reprise, 1964), *La Plus Belle Africaine* (Verve, 1966)

Chapter 26

The Records—November 1962 to December 1965

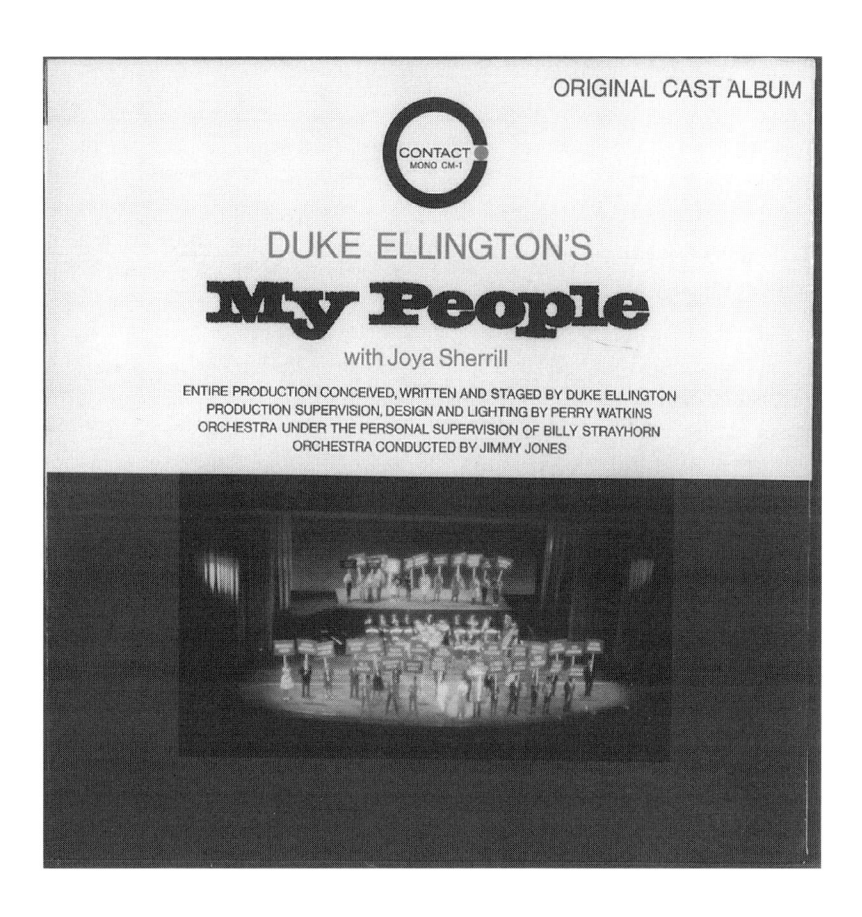

IN NOVEMBER 1962, DUKE ELLINGTON made his first recordings under a new contract with Frank Sinatra's Reprise label. Sinatra had invited Ellington not just to record for Reprise but also to take charge of the company's jazz catalog. Duke was given a free hand in recording his own music and this resulted in changes in his recording policy. He was now at last able to record some of the scores which called for a symphony orchestra, and there were other projects, such as the *Violin Session* of 1963, which would clearly have been difficult to bring off if Duke had not had total freedom in arranging record dates. To the seasoned Ellington follower the Reprise publicity about this new freedom sounded familiar, reminiscent of the ballyhoo at the start of the Capitol contract ten years earlier. Oddly enough, much of the Reprise output was received by the jazz public in much the same way as the Capitol records—with indifference, or even laced with regrets that Duke had not recorded something else. Ellington was a jazz composer, so the average jazz enthusiast expected to hear Ellington compositions on Ellington LPs. When the Reprise catalog sprouted such strange growths as LPs of the Ellington band playing current popular songs, or instrumentals of the swing era, or a set of variations on themes from a popular musical film, many concluded that Duke was giving less than his best and dismissed the music as commercial. In fact the Reprise output was wide and varied and boasted several collections of new Ellingtonia such as *Afro Bossa* and *Concert In The Virgin Islands*.

At the start of the Reprise recordings in December 1962 the personnel of the Duke Ellington Orchestra was:

Trumpets: Cat Anderson, Cootie Williams, Roy Burrowes, Ray Nance (cornet, violin, and vocal).

Trombones: Lawrence Brown, Buster Cooper, Chuck Connors (bass trombone).

Reeds: Russell Procope (alto sax, clarinet); Johnny Hodges (alto sax); Paul Gonsalves (tenor sax); Jimmy Hamilton (clarinet, tenor sax); Harry Carney (baritone sax, clarinet, bass clarinet).

Rhythm: Duke Ellington (piano); Ernie Shepard (bass); Sam Woodyard (drums); Billy Strayhorn (deputy pianist).

Vocal: Milt Grayson.

The most striking feature of this lineup is the return of Cootie Williams to the trumpet section after a 21-year absence. During most of those years Cootie had been leading his own big band which, while it did not achieve any marked degree of critical acclaim, was very popular with dancers. It was the last house band at the famous Savoy ballroom in Harlem, although by the end of that long engagement, Cootie had been forced to reduce the band to small-group dimensions. The basic qualities of Cootie's playing were unchanged, but he was older now, and, even though time had taken a lesser toll than might be expected on a musician who blew the trumpet with such enormous physical commitment, his playing had slowed down. Cootie had never been a particularly fast player, but now he made every effort to avoid rapid phrasing, and his interest in the variety of tone colors he could draw from the trumpet when playing muted also seems to have declined. To compensate for this simplification of style, the sheer strength and authority of his playing had increased, as had the power of expression he could draw from a simple phrase. The other new trumpet man was a West Indian musician, Roy Burrowes, heard occasionally in solos in a pleasant modern style but of no great originality. His main duty was that of section man.

The trombone section was now settled again. The newcomer was Buster Cooper, a player with a volatile, laconic solo style. Cooper was a limited soloist in melodic terms and for this reason Ellington did not use him often. With bass trombonist Chuck Connors a virtual nonsoloist, a lot of work fell on the shoulders of Lawrence Brown, who took the vast majority of the solos as well as playing most of the section lead.

Brown's solos not only encompassed the wide range, from ballads to swingers, which he had covered since he first joined the band, but now also included the plunger-muted specialties. The plunger style imposes additional strain on a brass player's lip and, as the wear of a lifetime as a professional player was already becoming evident, the acceptance of these extra responsibilities was a real sacrifice on Brown's part. They seemed certain to shorten his career, and when he left the Ellington band in 1970 Brown indeed gave up playing altogether. Some of the solos he played in his last years with the band were obvious struggles with a failing, reluctant lip, but he remained a magnificent section leader and a very positive musical personality.

The return of Williams did little to stem the decline in solo strength in the trumpet section, and when Ray Nance left the band in September 1963, the entire brass section became dependent on three men for the bulk of its solos: Cootie and Lawrence, whose playing was increasingly limited by age, and Cat Anderson, whom Ellington seemed reluctant to use other than as a high-note trumpet specialist and purveyor of exotica. As a consequence, the saxes took on a heavier solo task. Fortunately this collection of outstanding reed virtuosi remained intact and was widely recognized as one of the glories of jazz.

The new bassist, Ernie Shepard, was a swinger with a big powerful sound whose work epitomized the basic virtues of jazz bass playing. Duke himself was now much more inclined to feature his solo piano, perhaps as a consequence of having indulged in its delights on the sessions with Hodges, Armstrong, and Mingus, but also in response to the declining solo strength of the band. So far as their writing was concerned, both Ellington and Strayhorn were eager to meet the new musical challenges which the band's changing environment and personnel created. Although weakened in terms of numbers of soloists, the band was still a jazz ensemble of the highest class, a group with unique and widely varied skills, every chair held by a first-class bandsman. Even on the studio recordings the exciting surge of the band's playing sweeps the listener along, Reprise providing a recording quality which does full justice to Duke's rich and colorful music.

* * *

Between late November 1962 and early January 1963, Ellington and his musicians were in the studios on no less than nine occasions. They were working on two projects: a two-record album of famous big band numbers from the swing era and a single disc of Ellington-Strayhorn compositions, made up of mostly new material and a couple of revivals. Reprise was not particularly brisk in issuing Ellington records, and while well engineered their products often left much to be desired in terms of liner information and notes. Although Duke recorded enough material for the two-LP big band project, only one disc was issued by Reprise—and that only after a three-year wait. Titled *Will The Big Bands Ever Come Back?*, it was packaged in pop style and written off by some jazz critics as an essay in nostalgia. The remainder of this project remained unissued until 1974, when it was rescued from the archives and put out by Atlantic under the title *Recollections Of The Big Band Era*. The response of Ellington and Strayhorn to the material on these two discs was typically imaginative and varied. Some numbers, like *One O'Clock Jump, Let's Get Together,* and *Christopher Columbus,* receive conventional scores (and enthusiastic readings by the band), while others change character in astonishing ways: *Artistry In Rhythm* becomes an essay for violin and bass clarinet, *The Waltz You Saved For Me* a medium-tempo 4/4 swinger, and *Ciribiribin* an essay for four trumpet soloists in the manner of *Trumpet No End*.

In looking back on famous big bands of another era, Ellington did not just use the swing repertoire but also took material from the popular nonjazz dance bands. The wide range covered can be seen from the list of titles (the bands with which they were associated are given in brackets):

Will The Big Bands Ever Come Back?:
Tuxedo Junction (Erskine Hawkins), *Smoke Rings* (Casa Loma Orchestra), *Artistry In Rhythm* (Stan Kenton), *The Waltz You Saved For Me* (Wayne King), *Woodchopper's Ball* (Woody Herman), *Sentimental Journey* (Les Brown), *When It's Sleepy Time Down South* (Louis Armstrong), *One O'Clock Jump* (Count Basie), *Goodbye* (Benny Goodman), *Sleep, Sleep, Sleep* (Fred Waring), *Rhapsody In Blue* (Paul Whiteman), *Don't Get Around Much Any More* (Duke Ellington).

Recollections Of The Big Band Era:
Minnie The Moocher (Cab Calloway), *For Dancers Only* (Jimmie Lunceford), *It's A Lonesome Old Town (When You're Not Around)* (Ben Bernie), *Cherokee* (Charlie Barnet), *The Midnight Sun Will Never Set* (Quincy Jones), *Let's Get Together* (Chick Webb), *I'm Gettin' Sentimental Over You* (Tommy Dorsey), *Chant Of The Weed* (Don Redman), *Ciribiribin* (Harry James), *Contrasts* (Jimmy Dorsey), *Christopher Columbus* (Fletcher Henderson), *Auld Lang Syne* (Guy Lombardo).

The Quincy Jones number suggests that it was not simply the old bands which were being saluted. Gershwin's *Rhapsody In Blue* and Don Redman's *Chant Of The Weed* are very definite compositions, and their inclusion adds body to what might otherwise be a collection of popular songs and simple jazz arrangements. The Ellington musicians were well used to the interpretive demands of scores of greater compositional depth than is common in the jazz repertoire, and their handling of Gershwin's and Redman's works is of considerable interest. But perhaps these are best considered in the context of the complete series.

* * *

The very first track of *Will The Big Bands Ever Come Back?* finds Cootie Williams announcing his return with some pungent plunger work on a version of *Tuxedo Junction* which also has a brief Hodges solo. The overriding impression is of the deeply swinging ensemble, different from preceding Ellington bands with perhaps an even more basic jazz sound than before. The brass is very impressive with fine ringing trumpets and deep, rich trombones. The incomparable saxophone team is to the fore, and an important agent of swing is clearly the new bassist, Ernie Shepard. *Smoke Rings* is a Hodges feature and reminds us that no one else (apart from Louis Armstrong) has made so much of simply playing the melody of a popular song. Hamilton contributes a dash of clarinet color, and again the brass is magnificent. Something of Ellington's attitude to Stan Kenton's music may be gleaned from the highly unusual arrangement of *Artistry In Rhythm*.

Nance's violin is responsible for the theme statement, and then Carney's bass clarinet, some unusual piano from Duke, and Cootie's growl trumpet are each introduced in turn to the tonal palette. Throughout the performance, Woodyard plays an oddly syncopated rhythm, using hand drumming. A description of the piece would suggest that satire is the name of the game, but the arrangement is quite serious, and Kenton's powerhouse monochrome is transformed into a rather delicately shaded piece of Ellington tone painting. From Ellington always the unexpected!

The arrangement of *The Waltz You Saved For Me* is similar to that of *Got A Date With An Angel* on *At The Bal Masque*, though the bandleader celebrated here is Wayne King rather than Hal Kemp. The soloists are Hamilton, over delicious low trombones, and Cootie, clearly reinstated as a major soloist from the moment of his return. Although the tempo and the actual notes are retained, the theme of *Woodchopper's Ball* is subjected to a number of rhythmic indignities in the opening and closing ensembles, which are furnished with a rather odd shuffle rhythm from Woodyard. In the middle there is a string of first-class solos of the kind Duke would often invite his players to contribute to an up-tempo blues; Nance (on violin), Hodges, Williams, Brown, Gonsalves, and Hamilton are heard, Nance and Brown making particularly distinguished contributions.

Sentimental Journey, translated into the Ellington language in a totally different way, is given a rather sinister and decidedly theatrical cast. The arrangement features complex voicings; at one point, the theme is played by plunger-muted trumpet and trombone with clarinet, plus a bass clarinet countermelody and a Hodges obbligato. One of the reasons for the success of these performances is the choice of tempo, and the gutsy medium pace of *Sentimental Journey* pays off exceptionally well when the arrangement reverts to more orthodox patterns in the bridge. *When It's Sleepy Time Down South* has lots of Procope's low-register clarinet, but the main responsibility is carried by Nance on cornet. To play the role of Louis Armstrong is really impossible, but Nance brings to the part tremendous authority and sympathy. The scoring offers delights here, too, especially towards the end of Nance's solo, when low trombones and Carney's baritone make some quite glorious sounds.

For *One O'Clock Jump,* the familiar Buck Clayton arrangement is used, with an extension in the form of a Cat Anderson solo. Cat was given so few opportunities to show his abilities as a straightforward jazz soloist in the Ellington band that this passage is especially valuable; one regrets that it fades out during the fourth chorus. This performance of *One O'Clock Jump* is particularly welcome as it is the only one by the band recorded in stereo. As always on this number, Ellington's piano is understated and swinging, and the solos by Gonsalves, Cooper, Hamilton (on tenor), and Williams (growl) are all excellent. Hodges once more weaves his melodic spells on *Goodbye,* which sounds like a Strayhorn arrangement, with Hamilton's clarinet used in an obbligato role. More Hodges thematic playing delights the ear at the strolling medium tempo selected for *Sleep, Sleep, Sleep,* but the highlight is a warm, caressing cornet solo by Nance. In a typically Ellingtonian piece of imaginative manipulation, as Ray's cornet approaches a climax it is suddenly replaced by Cat Anderson's searing trumpet which denies the song's title as it soars into piercing high register—only to be replaced again by Nance as the music settles back into its original mood.

Duke Ellington's previous recordings of Gershwin numbers has varied from the conventional 1953 *Liza* to the bitter, gnarled *Summertime* of 1961. *Rhapsody In Blue*—Gershwin's most famous contribution to the annals of "symphonic jazz"—might seem an odd choice for the Ellington band, but Duke reduces the length of the piece and skillfully translates it into his own musical language without losing its essential character. This is a purely orchestral conception with no attempt to retain the piano and orchestra format of the original. Ellington's piano is just one of the several solo voices used: the famous opening clarinet cadenza is given to Carney's baritone sax, while Nance (on cornet) and a delicate, subtle Gonsalves are chief among the other soloists. There is a perfect balance in Ellington's scoring between orchestra and soloist, and the climax is brilliant, the band in full cry topped off by an Anderson upward glissando giving way suddenly to the stilled, quiet tones of Hodges's alto. This must be considered one of the finest Ellingtonian arrangements. The LP ends with a swinging *Don't Get Around Much Any More,* played over a compelling Woodyard shuffle rhythm. The short solos are by Williams, Hodges, Brown, Ellington, Carney, Gonsalves, and Hamilton.

* * *

The first two scores on *Recollections Of The Big Band Era* are by outside arrangers. Eddie Barefield, a long-serving associate of Cab Calloway, was invited to contribute the arrangement for *Minnie The Moocher* and was also given the responsibility of directing the band in the recording studio. Rather surprisingly there is no vocal, and the featured soloist is Brown on plunger-muted trombone. The performance is a little confused; the band might have done better to run the arrangement down at concerts or dances before recording it. In the case of *For Dancers Only,* Ellington obtained the original arrangement from Sy Oliver and showed excellent taste by *not* adapting it to the Ellington style. As with many of Oliver's scores for the Lunceford band, *For Dancers Only* is wholly self-contained; altering it could only have led to a weakening of its effect. The Ellington musicians obviously relished playing this Lunceford score and respond with flair and drive. The Lunceford saxophone section was legendary, but Ellington's quintet of stars show *their* team spirit and rise to the challenge in magnificent style. Hodges declined to play the Willie Smith fill-ins, so they were given to Hamilton on clarinet. Sy Oliver liked his trombones, and the section is given some meaty work, and for Paul Webster's high-note trumpet part, who better than Cat to top off this tribute from one great band to another? It is unfortunate that the drums were overrecorded.

The amount of care Ellington was prepared to put into some of his recordings is shown by the fact, mentioned by Stanley Dance in his liner notes, that ten takes were made of *It's A Lonesome Old Town When You're Not Around* before the leader was satisfied. The manipulation of extra percussion by brass section members was a feature of the Ellington band at this period, and Anderson's contribution to such goings on was the rubbing together of two derby mutes, a seemingly unpromising idea which in actuality proved very effective. This device was usually reserved for Latin American exotica, but it is used in *It's A Lonesome Old Town* in the context of a somber arrangement. This is primarily a band score, but two trombonists make vital statements—Connors in one of his rare bass trombone solos at the start, and Brown, depicting the loneliness indicated by the title, at the end.

For all its versatility, the Ellington saxophone team could not produce a member who played in the jump style favored by Charlie Barnet on his famous 1939 recording of *Cherokee.* Here Ellington deploys four saxophone soloists, Carney, Hamilton, and Hodges in the first part, Gonsalves after the drum break which divides the two sections of the arrangement. Paul's quiet, subtle playing in the course of a long solo contrasts with the extroverted orchestral backing.

Versions of Quincy Jones's beautiful ballad *The Midnight Sun Will Never Set* had been recorded as alto saxophone features by Marshall Royal with Basie's band and by Benny Carter leading a studio group. The definitive version was certain to be Ellington's from the moment he decided it should be a Hodges showcase. Chick Webb had one of the best swinging dance bands, a unit which used direct and functional arrangements. One of these was *Let's Get Together,* written by Webb himself. Ellington's recording uses a routine similar to that on the original record, with Cootie Williams and Harry Carney as soloists.

One of the problems confronting Ellington when using this sort of material is that his versions might be taken as constituting some kind of challenge to the originals. Few trombonists would care to invite comparison with Tommy Dorsey's high-register melody playing on *I'm Getting Sentimental Over You,* and wisely none of the Ellington team do so. Instead, we have an orchestral score with an emphasis on the saxophone section and on the beauties of Nance's mellow cornet style. In terms of artistic value, such performances by Nance are worth several hours of the extravagant solo blowing by the fashionable jazz brassmen of the sixties.

By the early sixties no other band was properly equipped to play *Chant Of The Weed,* a 1931 Don Redman piece for which Duke Ellington had often expressed his admiration. Re-creation by other bands had either been period pastiches or exercises in "cool," inhibited playing. But the playing of music of this complexity in uninhibited fashion was nothing new to the Ellington musicians, who were also masters of the art of reinterpreting scores from the twenties and thirties into current jazz styles. They play Redman's masterpiece in truly magnificent fashion which must have won approval from its composer, one of the most exacting of musicians. He would, one fancies, have particularly enjoyed the imaginative use of the bass trombone. The playing of the soloists in their brief insets is perfectly judged, and Carney, Nance, Hodges, and Gonsalves are all heard to excellent effect.

It would be difficult to imagine a greater contrast than that provided by the next number, *Ciribiribin,* a sentimental trifle used as a two-tempo trumpet showcase by Harry James. Ellington devises a swinging score, which his four trumpeters use as the basis for solo and duet statements. Roy Burrowes makes one of his rare solo appearances but sounds rather ordinary next to Williams, whose work is full of drive and power, Nance, whose solo is melodic and warmly expressive, and Anderson, whose final extravaganza provides an exciting climax.

Jimmy Dorsey's *Contrasts* becomes Gonsalves's feature and his playing here must be rated with his best on record. *Christopher Colombus* affords an interesting comparison with the adaptation recorded as *Waiting for Duke* under Hodges's name in 1957. The 1962 band gives a vivid performance of this old Fletcher Henderson favorite. There are solos by Nance and Gonsalves, the latter invoking the spirit and style of Chu Berry, composer of the piece and tenor soloist on the popular original Henderson recording.

Recollections Of The Big Band Era ends with *Auld Lang Syne,* done in the style of Guy Lombardo. This is a masterpiece of quiet humor and subtle musical skills. The folk melody and the Lombardo beat are given prominence, while behind them various Ellington voices and voicings are introduced. Carney, Hamilton, Williams, Nance, Brown, and Hodges are among those who emerge from behind the Lombardo curtain.

Although *Will The Big Bands Ever Come Back?* and *Recollections Of The Big Band Era* were made before the recording industry started to exploit the nostalgia market, they have been criticized as commercial manifestations of this exploitation. Here, as on so many other occasions, Ellington was ahead of his time. Some ten years later, the re-creations for live performance of masterpieces by Jelly Roll Morton and King Oliver, Jimmie Lunceford and Chick Webb, Fletcher Henderson and Duke himself became a regular feature of the jazz scene through the agency of musicians such as Bob Wilber and Dick Hyman and the playing of groups like the New York Jazz Repertory Orchestra. In recording such numbers as *Chant Of The Weed* and *For Dancers Only,* Ellington was doing a similar thing, with the important difference that he used a band mostly of musicians who had worked through the eras concerned and who still kept alive many of their musical values. Most importantly, this music is more than a revival of past musical successes—it is an imaginative, creative and often humorous look at the past from a sixties vantage point.

* * *

The third disc derived from these sessions was the first Ellington Reprise LP to be issued. It contains ten new pieces by Ellington and Strayhorn plus two revivals and is known as *Afro-Bossa.* The knowledgeable sleeve notes by Stanley Dance, the first of many to appear on Ellington LPs, were greatly superior to the show-business blurbs on some later Reprise issues. The title indicates the musical content—a development of Ellington's interest in African and Latin American rhythms. His wish to cash in on the then-current craze for the bossa nova is reflected more in the title than in the music. At concerts the title piece, *Afro-Bossa,* was introduced as *Bula.* The piece follows Ravel's famous *Bolero* formula in a dynamic development from *ppp* to *fff.* Much use is made of pedal points and there is some brilliant playing, especially by the brass. The scoring behind the soloists—Hodges against three clarinets, for example—is brilliantly judged and the soloists themselves—Gonsalves and Nance as well as Hodges—know exactly what is required. The second track, *Purple Gazelle,* is the same theme as *Angelica* on the LP with John Coltrane. Hamilton, Williams, Nance, and Gonsalves solo, and Duke has a sprightly dialogue with the reeds before Anderson and Shepard top off a lively climax. *Absinthe* is a Strayhorn piece with echoes of *Chelsea Bridge;* here Anderson is employed rubbing together his two derby mutes, and the bass trombone is brilliantly utilized. Gonsalves has the opening and closing statements with Carney, Nance (outstanding, as so often at this time), Strayhorn himself, and Hamilton as the other soloists.

The nocturnal equivalent of a rainbow is celebrated in *Moonbow,* in which the old Cotton Club combination of growl trumpet (Nance) over three clarinets is deployed against the Latin percussion in a brilliant tone painting. Hodges and Gonsalves have the solo roles here. On *Sempre Amore,* a showcase for Nance's violin, Anderson, Burrowes, and Williams make up a percussion section and Woodyard beats his snare drum with maracas. This piece uses the bossa nova rhythm, and the overall effect is reminiscent of *Bakiff*. The other showcase on the LP is also rather lightweight, albeit in a manner appropriate to its subject—this is *Silk Lace*, or *Caliné*, as Ellington called it at concerts. Jimmy Hamilton is featured in a performance of cool melodic quality. The second new Strayhorn item is *Tigress*, with Latin percussion at once establishing a mood over which Gonsalves sketches the outlines of a sultry theme. Williams and Hamilton duet before Carney gives more substance to the melodic shapes; then Gonsalves returns and the music reverts to the diffuse, subtle mood of the opening. *Angu* was introduced by Ellington at public performances as "not quite a tango, but almost blue"; he would then hold up a sheet of music while Hodges delivered a highly sensuous alto solo—it is doubtful if there was ever any musical notation on the paper used for this charade. Nance is the other soloist in this multicolored score, but the concert performances lacked the most exotic aspect of this studio one—a piano duet between Strayhorn on a mandolin piano and Ellington on an orthodox instrument. *Volupté*, "the essence of voluptuousness," according to Ellington, perhaps reflects best in both its title and its performance the dominant mood of this collection. Ellington solos over the exotic rhythm, and Nance is heard with the saxophones in the middle section.

Bonga (or *Empty Town Blues*) is a musical picture of the ghost towns that succeeded the mining booms on the American continent. The "pep section" of two trumpets and trombone using plungers is a major contributor to one of Ellington's most evocative tone paintings. Hamilton, Brown, and Cooper are among the ghostly voices which evoke the eerie locale so vividly. Ellington's use of Cooper's distinctive trombone style is masterly here. The bass trombone again adds depth to the score and one should also note the brilliance and imagination of both the conception and the execution of Hamilton's clarinet obbligato. The other two titles are revivals, one from the thirties and one from the forties. This new version of *Pyramid* was ultimately turned into a Carney showcase for concert use, but in its original form here it has solos by Brown, Williams, Gonsalves, and Hamilton as well as Carney. This is a typical Ellington re-creation in that it retains the beautiful melodic contours of the original while offering totally new ideas in terms of orchestration. Not a great deal is new in the other revival, *The Eighth Veil*, with Anderson in the solo role. It is difficult to imagine why this number was revived so frequently; perhaps either Ellington or Anderson had a particular affection for it, or maybe it was because its title allowed Ellington to make a witty introduction at concerts. *The Eighth Veil*, however, is the one mediocre track in a collection which otherwise finds Ellington and his team in top form and which can be placed alongside the great Ellington LPs from any era.

* * *

From January until early March 1963, the Ellington band toured Great Britain and Europe. Despite the time-consuming and exhausting travel, Duke worked hard in his capacity as head of the Reprise Records jazz division. During the tour he supervised sessions by Bud Powell, Dollar Brand and his wife, singer Bea Benjamin; he himself recorded with singer Alice Babs and with a trio of violinists, and directed studio sessions at which his band was augmented by symphony orchestras in Paris, Hamburg, Stockholm, and Milan. In addition to this, the band was recorded at length at concerts in Paris. The series of LPs resulting from all this activity give an unusual insight into Ellington's musical versatility over an eight-week period. The contrast between the Ellington of the concert platform and the Ellington of the recording studio is particularly evident. Each of the studio recordings has a different emphasis: the session with Alice Babs was designed to demonstrate the singer's talents; that with the violinists was an adaptation of Ellington musical values and practices to a trio of string players plus rhythm; and the sessions with the various orchestras were used to record both a version of *Harlem* in its original scoring and one of the previously unrecorded *Night Creature* of 1955, also written for the band with a symphony orchestra. The live recordings on the other hand feature the old and tried Ellington concert routines with a handful of recent compositions such as *Suite Thursday* and *Bula*. There is also a performance of *Harlem* by the band alone, which makes an interesting comparison with the contemporary studio recording with the Paris Symphony Orchestra.

* * *

The concerts from which the LPs on Reprise and Atlantic were taken were given in Paris on February 1 and 23, 1963. The first release from these concerts did not appear until four years later, when Reprise issued an LP called *Duke Ellington's Greatest Hits*, which gave no indication of its origins. After a further six years a double album of material from these concerts, entitled *Duke Ellington: The Great Paris Concert*, came out on Atlantic. As may well be anticipated from its title, the *Greatest Hits* LP is made up of very familiar numbers and, rather surprisingly considering the amount of material available from the concerts, includes two studio recordings with applause dubbed in. These are *Don't Get Around Much Anymore* from *Will The Big Bands Ever Come Back?* and *Satin Doll* from the later *Ellington '66* LP.

Among the actual concert recordings is a version of *Do Nothin' Til You Hear From Me* featuring a vocal by Milt Grayson, the band's current "romantic baritone," and Lawrence Brown's trombone. First the singer gives a straight rendition (with piano accompaniment of Duke's best vintage), then Brown takes over in a solo which develops from a poised melodic statement at the start to a barrelhouse conclusion (also backed by superb piano). Grayson returns, and with Brown and Ellington in support drives the number to its second and final climax. The routine was a regular feature of Ellington concerts on this tour. There is a version of another standby of some years' standing, the familiar medley of what Duke calls his "vintage oldies"—*Black And Tan Fantasy*,

Creole Love Call, and *The Mooche.* The soloists are Nance, Procope, and Brown, and it is interesting to note that although Williams was back in the band, Nance was still allocated the plunger-style trumpet parts on these numbers. Brown has a long plunger solo in *The Mooche,* while Procope is heard in his usual routines, on alto in *Black And Tan Fantasy,* and on clarinet in the other two numbers.

The tempo of *Things Ain't What They Used To Be* had shown a tendency to increase ever since the piece had arrived in the repertoire, a tendency which became even more marked when it began to be used as a Hodges showcase. The 1963 Paris version moves along at a fair pace for a number which had started life as a slow blues; Hodges is backed by excellent playing from the trombones and some easy, swinging bass work from Shepard. Hodges plays with immense authority and presence. The recording of *Pyramid* uses the same arrangement as that on *Afro-Bossa* except that the final eight bars are taken by Carney rather than Brown, and a baritone saxophone cadenza is added. As usual in concerts of this period, Grayson is featured in *The Blues* from *Black, Brown And Beige.* Rather surprisingly, Ellington did not bother to use the orchestral score for this and provides instead a trio accompaniment with piano playing of outstanding sensitivity. As on *Do Nothin' Til You Hear From Me,* Grayson is competent rather than distinguished, and his singing lacks any jazz or blues characteristics. Even so, this version of *The Blues* is invaluable for the insight it gives into Ellington's art as an accompanist.

It is followed by what sounds like an impromptu performance of *Echoes Of Harlem,* Williams's trumpet being accompanied by the rhythm section only until the last chord. The central part, which had featured the saxophone section and Cootie's open trumpet in the 1936 original, is omitted. Cootie is recorded very close to the mike and one can hear the intense concentration he puts into tone production and into obtaining the correct tension in the melodic line. The immense power and majesty of Cootie's playing are fully captured here. This is one of the best examples of his work from his second period with the band.

The Atlantic *Great Paris Concert* album opens with another standby of Ellington concerts—the combination of *Kinda Dukish* and *Rockin' In Rhythm.* Duke is in a lively, playful mood during the first number, while *Rockin' In Rhythm* is among the better recordings of the piece from the sixties. Woodyard's drumming is more than a trifle relentless in places, but he provides a solid foundation and the band plays with great energy. Brown not only makes a fine job of the traditional plunger trombone solo but also plays his earlier solo part within the ensemble with great vigor; Carney handles the clarinet passages with his usual skill, and toward the end Anderson piles on the excitement.

Three Hodges showcases follow: *On The Sunny Side Of The Street, Star-Crossed Lovers* (from *Such Sweet Thunder*), and *All Of Me.* Hodges's tone and phrasing throughout are those of a master; no one new to this music could imagine that these were routines followed by Hodges on a nightly basis, so fresh and full of vigor is his playing. The full beauty of *Star-Crossed Lovers* is brought out in this performance; hearing the piece away from the Shakespearean suite, one becomes even more aware how fine both composition and arrangement are. Ellington does away with the ensemble climax, but the beauty of the section with Gonsalves leading the saxophones is fully realized. The still, quiet phrasing of the alto on its reentry is perfect, and, as so often on Ellington records, one is astounded by the sheer quality of Carney's tone as he plays his band parts.

After these Hodges features, we hear an example of Ellington's writing for the band, a brief, functional piano passage being the only solo in the *Theme From "Asphalt Jungle."* By any standards other than Ellington's own the scoring is exceptional, and the piece is given a wonderfully spirited performance. The nonchalant ease with which the saxophones cruise through their cruelly difficult parts is astonishing, and the leader's verbal responses show how much he enjoys their interpretation.

Next come two showcases for Williams, a pairing used to reintroduce him to the Ellington public after his long absence. *Concerto For Cootie* is really a cut-down, slowed-down variation of the melody of *Do Nothin' Til You Hear From Me,* the pop tune which grew out of the original *Concerto For Cootie* of 1940. This rejigged and simplified version in fact provides a perfect vehicle for the Cootie Williams of the sixties. Playing muted throughout, Cootie vividly communicates immense musical power and authority. His second feature, a piece written by Hamilton, *Tutti For Cootie,* was destined to become *the* Williams feature for the next eight or nine years. It is a blues which appears here in its original form, at a more brisk tempo than later, and with less open trumpet. As well as featuring Cootie the piece offers an opportunity for some very basic jazz playing by the band and some nice Ellington piano. It is a good example of a jazz arrangement which has no marked melodic or harmonic qualities yet is so laid out as to give the band an opportunity to swing in a free and uninhibited way. It also performs brilliantly its most obvious function, that of providing a Williams showcase. Cootie is superb here, the brief open trumpet solo offering a particularly choice example of his playing. The strength and depth of his tone and the emotional richness of his phrasing are most impressive.

Ever the band for contrasts, the orchestra follows these numbers with a full-scale performance of *Suite Thursday.* Reference has been made earlier to the qualities of this version in discussing the various recordings of the work. Here *Suite Thursday* fits into the concert program perfectly, and coming after a performance like *Tutti For Cootie* its fundamental jazz characteristics are obvious. *Perdido,* which follows, uses the arrangement heard on the *Piano In The Background* LP of 1960—that is to say, Gerald Wilson's score with additions. Hamilton and Gonsalves take care of the solo responsibilities, and in the trumpet chase, Burrowes is rather outclassed by the vastly more experienced Nance. After Anderson has been featured on *The Eighth Veil,* Ellington announces a request for a "collector's item," and Brown comes forward to play his famous showpiece from the late thirties, *Rose Of The Rio Grande*. His tone is rather rough here and the usual finesse lacking. But his work is not deficient in swing, and the backing by the rhythm section is excellent, as is Duke's unexpected piano solo.

As always in latter-day Ellington concerts, showcases are the standard diet. Next it is Gonsalves's turn with five minutes of *Cop Out*. A swinging tempo, almost too comfortable for a tenor marathon, is set here. It inspires one of the best of the extended Gonsalves solos, but Woodyard's drumming is heard in its least attractive aspect. Then Duke introduces *Bula,* the number which had masqueraded as *Afro-Bossa* on the LP of that title. It is, Duke tells us, "a sort of gutbucket bolero in a primitive rhythm executed in a pre-primitive manner." The interpretation, with the exception of Nance's cornet solo, is superior to the studio version, owing to the greater fire and drive of the band's playing. Certainly the triple-forte ending with Anderson on top is superior to the drum fade out on the studio recording.

From the new and unfamiliar the band moves on to the old and overfamiliar with *Jam With Sam*. Here Carney leads off into a solo routine in which Duke's introduction of each soloist by name is rather unnecessarily padded out with an announcement of his town or city of origin. The soloists concerned are Carney, Gonsalves, Brown, Procope, Burrowes, Cooper, Nance, and finally, to provide the high-note climax, Anderson. Next comes an excellent short version of *Happy-Go-Lucky Local* which also has an Anderson climax, this time representing the escaping steam as the reluctant locomotive is brought to a halt. Further signs of age can be detected in the engine's performance here, but the propulsive swing and the boogie-woogie rhythms are splendidly vigorous. Only two choruses of piano are retained from the first part, but the second half is played complete. This is not a very tidy performance, but it has tremendous guts and drive and an excellent contribution from the trombone section. The performance of *Harlem* which closes this double album has already been discussed—suffice it to say here that it is the only recording of the work on which the band had the benefit of Woodyard's drumming in a concert situation. Sam certainly enhances the energy and vitality of the performance.

* * *

The recordings with the symphony orchestras are on an LP called *The Symphonic Ellington*. The music was recorded as the 1963 tour wound its way through Europe: *Harlem* and the last movement of *Night Creature* with members of the Paris Symphony Orchestra in January; the first and second movements of *Night Creature* with the Stockholm Symphony Orchestra; *Non-Violent Integration* with the Hamburg Symphony Orchestra; and *La Scala, She Too Pretty To Be Blue* with the La Scala Opera Orchestra in Milan, all in February. Of the four works only the last was a new composition, written for this LP, and only the orchestral parts were recorded in Milan. The solos were dubbed in at a later date, after the Ellington musicians had returned home. *Non-Violent Integration* was written for the band and the Philadelphia Orchestra as far back as 1949; *Harlem* was the result of a 1950 commission from the NBC Symphony Orchestra; and *Night Creature* was another commission, this time from Don Gillis, for the Symphony of the Air in 1955.

Many years earlier, Ellington had responded bluntly to a question about adding strings to his orchestra, which seemed to be the fashion among bandleaders at the time. "Strings! Positively no! What on earth would I want with strings? What can anybody do with strings which hasn't been done wonderfully for hundreds of years?" (in a *Down Beat* interview with Leonard Feather, vol. 18, no. 2, January 26, 1951). Yet, from the late forties on, Ellington did write music for strings. This music was usually performed when the Ellington band appeared with symphony orchestras, and gradually a small repertoire of compositions for use on such occasions was built up. *New World A-Comin'* and the *Medley Of Popular Hits* joined *Harlem* as the basis of this "symphonic book." *Non-Violent Integration* was an early example of a work written specifically for one of these events.

Apart from *Harlem,* the most substantial of these works is *Night Creature,* also the most important piece on *The Symphonic Ellington* LP. This version is slightly extended to provide openings for the soloists, whose role in the original appears to have been negligible. It is obvious from the start that *Night Creature* is dance music and Ellington's avowed intention was to show that a symphony orchestra can swing. There is nothing new in dance music for symphony orchestra; the vast repertoire of ballet music is the most obvious indication of this. But *Night Creature* is also uncompromising Ellington music, a *jazz* composition written for symphony orchestra. The band is the dominant element most of the way, with the full ensemble used as additional *tutti* strengthening, and in dialogue with, the soloists. When he writes for the symphony orchestra alone, Ellington scores for strings in the way he normally writes for his saxophone section. The woodwinds are used for coloristic decoration and the brass have traditional Ellington functions.

Night Creature, in three movements, has a distinctly nocturnal mood—especially the second movement. Ellington appended a particularly fanciful program to this work. He said that the first movement portrays a blind bug which comes out at night to dance. The second movement depicts "that imaginary monster we all fear we shall have to meet some midnight, but when we meet him I'm sure that we shall find that he too does the boogie woogie." The musical dangers of such a Disney-like program are largely avoided. The second movement finds Ellington transforming his basic concept into a blues on which he displays a roster of solo talent: first his own string specialist, Nance, is heard in dialogue with the piano; then Williams, in growl style, against the trombones; then Hodges works his magic as surely here as when playing some familiar showcase; and finally Brown, who gets very effective backing from strings and woodwinds. In the passage after these solos, Ellington's writing for strings is particularly impressive. At the beginning and end of the movement there are solos by Ellington in which the pattern of boogie woogie piano is reversed, with an ostinato figure in the very highest register, while the melodic matter is dealt with by the left hand in the bottom range of the keyboard.

The finale is concerned with "that dazzling woman, the queen of the night creatures," who leads her subjects into a final dance which culminates in "the most over-indulged form of up-and-outness." Again there is a very attractive theme, and the development leads to a magnificent climax, the whole massive ensemble topped by Anderson's trumpet. This music certainly dances and swings, and much of the success of this performance of *Night Creature* is due to the wonderfully spirited drumming of Woodyard, who provides a basis of great rhythmic strength. He is certainly not daunted by the need to swing the huge ensemble. In *Night Creature* Ellington shows how he can adapt the combination of his own band and full symphony orchestra to his compositional needs, and it is the best of his works for this combination. Earlier recordings of *Night Creature*—none of them issued—show that most of the solos in *The Symphonic Ellington* version are added to an already self-sufficient orchestral score. They enhance the warmth of the music, and its Ellington flavor, but the purely compositional virtues of the piece are more evident in the earlier performances. Certainly the use of the symphony orchestra here seems a good deal more central to the musical argument than is the case in *Harlem*. (The *Symphonic Ellington* version of *Harlem* has been covered in the discussion of the various recordings of the piece.)

Non-Violent Integration takes the Hamburg Symphony Orchestra on a tour of Ellington territory in which not-very-distant echoes of *Happy-Go-Lucky Local* are heard at one point. The first two solos are by the orchestra's anonymous first oboe and Hodges, who demonstrates what a difference a lifetime's experience makes to the business of jazz phrasing. Hamilton's contribution sounds a little cold, a trifle bloodless even, but Cooper produces a blistering solo of the best vintage. Gonsalves's two choruses combine humor, originality, and great swing, and for the ending Cat Anderson again takes over the lead of a giant ensemble with authority and power. *La Scala, She Too Pretty To Be Blue* is a beautiful Ellington composition in which he uses the strings in masterly fashion. The score is enhanced by the solos of Procope (clarinet), Gonsalves, Brown, and Williams. Procope's warm tone fits perfectly into the string texture, and Gonsalves gives one of those performances which can so easily be taken for granted, his casual manner concealing profound originality. Lawrence Brown's solo is skillfully decorated by the violins—another instance of how well Duke could write for strings when he really applied himself. Cootie's solo is one of his best from this period, played plunger style, and again marvelously placed in context.

* * *

In *The Symphonic Ellington* Duke had again produced a completely original collection. On February 22, 1963, he was at the center of a recording session in Paris, and once more the music was totally original in conception. *Duke Ellington's Violin Session* is perhaps the most impressive illustration from this period of his continuing creativity and zest. The music is built around three notable string players, Stephane Grappelli and Ray Nance on violins and Svend Asmussen on viola, combined with Ellington's own rhythm section. Duke had Billy Strayhorn along to play piano on a couple of tracks, and no doubt to assist in running the session. Procope, Gonsalves, and Cooper provide a discreet background on half the performances.

The tapes from *Duke Ellington's Violin Session* lay on the shelves for thirteen years with only skeleton details known to collectors. When Atlantic issued them in 1976 we were in for a surprise, for here was not simply a set of jam session routines featuring three fine string players, but wonderfully spirited ensemble performances with lots of zest and humor exuding an unmistakable and very basic Ellington flavor. The signs of a hastily arranged and underprepared session can be detected from time to time, but spontaneity and fresh creative response were more important to Ellington than surface polish. The violinists are beautifully contrasted, with Nance's warmth and blues feeling paired with Grappelli's resourceful virtuosity and subtle humor. Asmussen brings a more knockabout brand of humor to the music, while Ellington obviously relishes the dark tone of the viola. Duke's command of the situation, the fact that he created the platform for this wonderful music making, is obvious not only from the musical climate but also from the way in which affairs are directed from the keyboard. *Duke Ellington's Violin Session* affords another opportunity for hearing Duke's ensemble piano at its very best. Ernie Shepard and Sam Woodyard are ideal for this music, providing an object lesson in an accompaniment light enough for the three strings without sounding in any way prissy or characterless. This is one of the very best of Woodyard's sessions with Ellington. No other drummer could have improved on his intelligent, alert and deeply musical playing here. Certainly few drummers of the virtuoso school could have combined sensitivity and swing to this degree.

The first track is *Take The "A" Train,* opening with Ellington's only solo chorus from the session, in which he creates a totally new solo on a theme to which he had already added a veritable library of variations. The three string soloists are then introduced—Asmussen with his dark tone and flippant phrasing, Grappelli with bright, clear virtuosity, and Nance with a more basic, gutty sound and markedly swinging phrasing. Shepard takes a solo, humming in octaves with his bass, before the brief reprise which has Nance decorating the theme played by Grappelli and Asmussen. Each string player is then featured on a ballad from the Ellington repertoire. Grappelli plays *In A Sentimental Mood,* a beautiful song whose chord sequence causes most musicians to shy away from anything more than a straight melodic statement. It is an ideal choice here, with Grappelli the master of the situation in a tasteful and creative interpretation. Asmussen chooses *Don't Get Around Much Anymore* and enters in a manner that sets a humorous mood for a performance which approaches the knockabout in places. This is obviously to Duke's taste and the rhythm section responds perfectly, but only a foolish listener would allow Asmussen's humor to mask his musicianship and jazz craft. Although he sounds like the most basic jazz player on the other tracks, Nance opts for the most stilled and emotional of the ballad interpretations in *Day Dream*, the Strayhorn piece written for Johnny Hodges in 1940. Nance's melodic sensitivity and warmth enhance a beautiful interpretation of Strayhorn's melody.

With *Cotton Tail* we return to jazz making of unrestrained vigor. Grappelli shows his virtuosity; note his use of dynamics, especially in his second solo. The Stuff Smith influence on Asmussen is to the fore in his work, while Nance once more swings superbly. This music is so fresh and unhackneyed, so full of an enthusiasm which some professional musicians might consider unbecoming, that one wonders at Ellington's ability to create such a climate. Grappelli and Asmussen both recorded through the sixties and seventies, but nowhere else do they sound as excited as they do here. The untidy ending to *Cotton Tail* proves the spontaneity of the proceedings. Strayhorn takes over on piano for *Pretty Little One*, and the three string players create a Strayhorn mood on what is indeed a very pretty tune. (From this track on, the three Ellington horn-men are used discreetly.)

Tricky's Licks is a slow-medium blues with Woodyard's hand drumming. *Blues In C*, at fast medium tempo, has notably fine solos from Grappelli and Nance. Next in this group of blues performances comes *String Along With Strings*, an outstanding track in a set where the overall standard is unusually high. There is another great solo sequence, superbly backed by Shepard, Woodyard, and the pianists—Ellington, for the most part, although Strayhorn opens the performance. After the solos the ensemble builds to an exciting, rocking climax of a kind no one but Duke could have conceived. In many ways this performance is the quintessence of Ellington's music—exciting without being in any way frenetic, full of the spirit of the blues but totally new, and warmly emotional while remaining skilled and inventive at the same time. A contrast in mood was now needed, and it is provided by the West Indian number recorded at the session with Coleman Hawkins, *Limbo Jazz*. More use is made of pizzicati here than elsewhere on the date, and though lighter in mood than the exuberant version on the Hawkins LP, the musical vivacity here is in no way inferior. When the West Indian rhythms are abandoned the engineer makes his one error of an otherwise beautifully recorded session by overemphasizing Shepard's bass. The final track, *The Feeling Of Jazz*, has a rather untidy theme statement, and the solos include a brusque, almost brutal contribution from Asmussen. The ending is not far from chaos, but Ellington let it stand.

"What can anybody do with strings that hasn't been done wonderfully for hundreds of years?" Duke had asked in the forties. On *The Symphonic Ellington* and *Duke Ellington's Violin Session* he answers his own question most effectively. On the *Violin Session*, Grappelli, Nance, and Asmussen play with virtuosity and imagination, with enthusiasm and humor, all on a level which Ellington clearly found inspiring.

* * *

The last of the 1963 European Ellington recordings was done with Swedish singer Alice Babs. She had appeared with the Ellington Orchestra on Swedish TV a few weeks before, and, perceiving her remarkable qualities, Duke decided to include her in his Reprise recording plans. Although not very well known internationally, she was a singer of great accomplishment and had made quite an impression in the United States during a 1962 tour by a group called the Swe-Danes, which also included Svend Asmussen. Alice Babs, who began her career as a child star in Sweden, later preferred domestic life and her talent had not been exposed often enough outside her native country. Babs is perhaps the most skilled singer ever heard in jazz: not the best jazz singer, or even the finest artist, but most certainly the most fully equipped vocalist yet to be heard in a jazz context. The most remarkable aspect of her singing is her pitching, although she has denied that she has perfect pitch. The reservations a listener normally brings to Ellington vocalists do not apply here, and even the art of wordless singing becomes enhanced in the hands of an artist of such taste and skill.

Ellington invited Babs to Paris in 1963 to record for Reprise, and they did two sessions together, Ellington choosing to use musicians from outside the band except for Strayhorn and himself. Four French-horn players from the Paris Symphony Orchestra provide an exotic touch on some of the tracks, while a French bassist and drummer were used on the first date, the latter replaced by Kenny Clarke on the second. A clarinetist and tenor saxophonist were added for *C Jam Blues*, but like all other instrumentalists on these sessions, they appear in a subsidiary role. This applies even to Ellington himself. He does not solo on either session and plays in a very restrained manner, in marked contrast to the violin session of the previous week. The music is totally dominated by the singer's personality, which is no doubt just how Ellington wanted it.

Serenade To Sweden was a natural revival for this occasion: it is sung without words, and Babs reveals the full beauty of Ellington's melodic line. Similar qualities are heard on *Azure, Come Sunday* (on which she does use lyrics), and an untitled lullaby by Ellington. She also sings wordlessly on *Satin Doll, C Jam Blues,* and *Stoona,* the last a new number on which Babs's pitching of the blue notes and slurs is really outstanding. The lively *La De Doody Do* is, like *Serenade To Sweden,* a revival from the late thirties. The other Ellington songs on which the lyrics are used are *The Boy In*

My Dreams, Something To Live For, I Didn't Know About You, Take Love Easy (from *Beggar's Holiday*), and *I'm Beginning To See The Light*. The LP is rounded off with a couple of pieces by Babs herself, *Babsie* and *Strange Visitor;* on the second, she accompanies herself on piano. The extensive range of her voice is used to wholly artistic ends at all times, and this must be counted as one of the best vocal records of the decade. Titled *Serenade To Sweden,* it was issued in Europe, but nowhere else, by the Reprise company.

* * *

A number of "live" performances included in the MF Productions Ellington collection derive from this 1963 tour, including good band performances of *Pyramid, Guitar Amour, Star-Crossed Lovers, C Jam Blues,* and *Stompy Jones*. In addition to these, the set includes a lively piano solo of *Dancers In Love* with Duke coaxing some very accurate finger-snapping from his Swedish audience.

* * *

On his return from this very busy tour, Duke immediately became involved with yet another new project. Nineteen sixty-three was the centenary of the Emancipation Proclamation, and a *Century of Negro Progress* exhibition was held in Chicago. Ellington's contribution to this event was a full-length stage show entitled *My People*. In contrast to *Jump For Joy,* his previous stage spectacular, Duke did not use his own band for *My People*. The music was provided by a sixteen-piece band known as the Billy Strayhorn Orchestra. It contained two current Ellingtonians on loan for the occasion, Ray Nance and Russell Procope, plus several alumni and bassist Joe Benjamin, who was destined to play an important Ellington role in the future. On the "Original Cast Album" the following musicians and singers are heard:

Trumpets:	Ray Nance, Bill Berry, Ziggy Harrell, Nat Woodard.
Trombones:	Britt Woodman, Booty Wood, John Sanders (valve trombone).
Reeds:	Russell Procope; Rudy Powell (alto sax, clarinet); Harold Ashby, Pete Clarke (tenor sax); Bob Freedman (baritone sax).
Rhythm:	Jimmy Jones (piano); Billy Strayhorn (celeste); Joe Benjamin (bass); Louis Bellson (drums); Juan Amalbert (conga).
Vocal:	Joya Sherrill, Lil Greenwood, Jimmy McPhail, Jimmy Grissom, The Irving Brunton Singers.
Tap Dancing:	Bunny Briggs.

My People anticipates the *Sacred Concerts* which Ellington produced in the sixties and seventies; indeed it shares a good deal of material with the first of them, the *Concert Of Sacred Music* of 1965. Much of this material is taken from *Black, Brown And Beige,* and it is a mystery why Ellington should have chosen to recast this music. It is not that he no longer considered it valid in its original form, for he used long selections from *Black, Brown And Beige* in his concert programs in the late sixties. Possibly he thought that presenting parts of the work in a fresh context might attract some belated attention to what he still believed to be one of his most important creations.

The first part of the *My People* LP is devoted to sacred music, and Ellington's attempts to create simple and direct religious poetry fail in the opening *Ain't But The One*—a piece of deliberately naive doggerel sung by Jimmy McPhail and the choir and redeemed only by some beautiful drumming by Louis Bellson. *Will You Be There?* is sung by the choir a capella, and, like the first number, it shows that, while Duke could write competently for a choir, such writing is weak both in individual character and musical interest when compared with his instrumental work. In *99% Won't Do,* the orchestra accompanies the singers, and again brilliant drumming steals the day. McPhail then returns to sing *Come Sunday,* and as in the Mahalia Jackson and Alice Babs versions, the piece does not gain by the use of lyrics. Then comes a transformation of the main *Come Sunday* theme into fast tempo as an accompaniment to tap dancer Bunny Briggs in *David Danced*. The biblical reference here is 2 Samuel 6:14, and Ellington uses it to illustrate his belief that each man should worship God through his own special talents. In the first chorus, Briggs is backed by the choir which sings a new set of words to the *Come Sunday* theme; in the second chorus, he is backed by muted trumpet (Bill Berry) and the rhythm section with the choir in the background; this is a very effective and rhythmically potent passage.

David Danced is followed by *My Mother And My Father,* sung by McPhail, in which Ellington pays tribute to his parents in terms which suggest that they were peerless, faultless beings. Despite some Ellingtonian sounds in the orchestral accompaniment, this hodgepodge of sentimental fantasies and pompous doggerel is a failure. The *Montage* segment from *Black, Brown And Beige* follows, in a version that muddies the texture of the scoring by adding a gratuitous choral part. At one point, the choir's rendition of the *Come Sunday* theme sounds like a kind of "sing-along-with-Duke"—a far cry from Carnegie Hall, 1943. A final posing of the question *Will You Be There?* brings the first part of the *My People* LP to a close.

The second part opens with a scene even more incredible than anything heard thus far: Duke Ellington himself in the role of tub-thumping orator, delivering a patriotic and platitudinous narration called *My People*. From the participation of African Americans in all aspects of American life Ellington gradually moves on to the blues, and by way of a stanza of blues verse leads into the next musical part—*The Blues* from *Black, Brown And Beige*. The accompaniment to Milt Grayson's singing of *The Blues* on the concert tour earlier this year had been by the rhythm section alone, but for *My People*, a slightly modified version of the original orchestration was used. The traditional tenor sax solo is taken by Harold Ashby. The sensitivity of his reading is marked by attention to melodic detail, and it makes an interesting comparison with earlier versions by Ben Webster and Al Sears. Joya Sherrill handles the vocal; her interpretation is as sensitive to both words and music as it had been nineteen years earlier. She is followed by two of the singers who succeeded her with the Ellington band—Jimmy Grissom and Lil Greenwood. They alternate in a sequence of short blues vignettes—Grissom singing *Workin' Blues* and *Jail Blues*, with some effective work by Harold Ashby and Booty Wood and with Jimmy Jones on tack piano also prominent. Lil Greenwood sings *My Man Sends Me* and a brief *Lovin' Lover*. The lyrics of these four songs are clever; perhaps a little too clever for the blues, but a blues artist of the caliber of Joe Turner or Jimmy Rushing would have put them over better than the singers heard here.

The two final numbers move on to the civil rights front. Ellington usually maintained that direct civil rights statements were for politicians and that the artist had something else to do, another part to play in the struggle. *King Fit The Battle Of Alabam*, however, is a very direct statement with its reference to freedom riders, sit-ins, and Bull Connor, his hoses and police dogs. This piece is sung by the Irving Bunton Singers over a calypso beat, but the lyrics, for all their praiseworthy content, are undistinguished in style and the choral writing is commonplace. (The lyrics of *King Fit The Battle Of Alabam* were narrated by Ellington at the Newport Jazz Festival in 1963, but no recording of this performance has ever been issued.)

The finale of *My People, What Color Is Virtue?* features more poor verse—"how brave you are" rhyming with "behavior" is a choice example—and though this might have passed muster as accompaniment to a spectacular stage finale, on record it falls flat on its face. It does not have very far to fall from the level established by much of the preceding music. (A previously unissued instrumental from these sessions, *Jungle Triangle*, is included in the five-LP set of Ellington recordings issued by MF Records.)

* * *

As a stage spectacular, *My People* was a great success; reports from all quarters indicate that it was a vivid and enjoyable presentation. The music heard on the "Original Cast Album" was simply one component, albeit an important one, in that presentation. That the music fails to stand up as a unified whole on its own is not necessarily a condemnation of its effectiveness. The disappointing features of *My People* are Ellington's apparent need to borrow so extensively from *Black, Brown and Beige* and the mediocrity of his lyrics and vocal writing. American show business had been an environment in which Ellington's music flowered, and he could create vivid poetic images, as *A Drum Is A Woman* and the *Pedestrian Minstrel* section of his autobiography reveal. He seems to have been less self-critical with his verbal creations than with his music, and consequently his output of lyrics, narrations, and poems is very uneven in quality. At the time of *My People*, Ellington's experience in writing for concerted voices was very limited, and his compositional techniques were ill adapted for the task. With the concentration on vocal writing the Billy Strayhorn Orchestra is given little opportunity to show its abilities in interpreting Ellington's music—and with so many experienced Ellingtonians in the personnel these were clearly considerable.

It is typical of Ellington that for all the boasting and tub-thumping, the main message of *My People* is one of universal love. For all its admirable sentiments, however, the work cannot be regarded as one of Ellington's important creations, at least not on purely musical grounds. To Ellington himself, the enterprise must have been satisfactory; two years later, when he produced the first of his *Concerts Of Sacred Music*, it was to *My People* that he turned for much of his material.

* * *

From September to November of 1963, the Ellington band toured the Far East for the U.S. State Department, and in the early months of 1984 it made a further European tour. By this time there were a couple of changes in the trumpet section, Rolf Ericson and Herbie Jones having replaced Ray Nance and Roy Burrowes. Some of the live recordings in the MF set stem from this European tour, including a new arrangement of *Caravan* featuring Williams and Ellington. An LP has been issued from an Italian TV program of March 22, 1964, by a contingent from the band—Ericson, Brown, Hodges, Gonsalves, Carney, Ellington, French bassist Gilbert Rovere (subbing for Ernie Shepard), and Woodyard. It is one of the paradoxes of Ellington's musical policy that while he would constantly try out new things in the recording studio, at concerts he would stick to tried routines even when, as here, a reduced ensemble would seem to offer an opportunity for experiment and variation. The bulk of the LP is given over to showcases for Hodges (*Sunny Side Of The Street, I Got It Bad, Don't Get Around Much Anymore*), Carney (*Sophisticated Lady, I Let A Song Go Out Of My Heart*), Brown (*Solitude*), and Ellington himself (*Caravan*). All contain admirable playing, but very little that had not been heard many times before. Carney uses the held note trick, long a feature of his performances of *Sophisticated Lady;* he had mastered the circular breathing technique and thus could hold a note almost indefinitely. The brief opening of *"A" Train* is a new head arrangement, but only three-quarters of a chorus is heard. This "Jazz Group" as the LP has it, or "Giants Group," as Ellington introduces it, is heard as a unit on *C Jam Blues* and *Rockin' In Rhythm* only, both rather hastily adapted for the small band. Hodges and Carney, unusually, take solos in *C Jam Blues,* the last two choruses of which come very close to chaos. On *Rockin' In Rhythm,* preceded by a lively version of *Kinda Dukish,* Carney plays his solo on baritone instead of the customary clarinet, and Brown ignores the plunger for his trombone solo. The five musicians in the front line seem to relish the big band impersonation they are called upon to execute here, although the performance is very untidy.

* * *

On their return home the Ellingtonians soon found themselves in the Reprise studios. They made nine sessions for the label during the next nine months. The result was a trio of LPs which have come to typify the Ellington Reprise output in the mind of the average jazz enthusiast. The first two, *Ellington '65* and *Ellington '66,* consist mainly of arrangements of popular hits of the day, while the third presents Ellington's variations on a suite of songs from the film *Mary Poppins.* The attitude of jazz critics, and to an extent of the jazz audience, to these LPs has been one of distrust. As previously noted, records of popular songs by big bands have always been regarded with suspicion by jazz enthusiasts. This trio of Ellington LPs received short shrift from most critics; indeed Ellington's entire Reprise output received very little favorable comment in the jazz press. There were comparisons with the Capitol recordings of a decade earlier, a time when much was also made of Duke having a free choice of material. Once more masterpieces were overlooked.

Once more it was argued that Duke Ellington was a great composer and should be recording Ellington compositions rather than collections of other people's ephemeral pop songs. Such criticism reveals ignorance of Ellington's great contribution to jazz as an *arranger* pure and simple—a contribution which goes back to the very start of his recording career. From the twenties Ellington had recorded popular songs and to suggest that the Reprise LPs represent a lowering of his standards is absurd. No doubt Ellington hoped that such collections of popular songs would sell; at all times he had to be concerned with economic viability. But there is no indication on any of the three Reprise LPs of any condescension by Ellington or his musicians. On the contrary, the typical qualities of Ellington's music—warmth, taste, humor, zest, imagination—are all to the fore in these collections.

* * *

Ellington '65 is devoted to Ellington versions of popular songs of the early sixties, many of them treated as showcases for the soloists. Had these solos been presented in a "Jazz At The Philharmonic" context, they would probably have found greater favor with jazz writers than they did here, with the immeasurable advantage of Ellington's orchestral accompaniments. The opening selection, *Hello, Dolly!,* is treated as a swinger, over a rocking Woodyard beat; Hamilton's rough-toned tenor sax is the only solo voice. *Call Me Irresponsible* is a showcase for Brown; his beautiful playing of the theme is decorated with the most apt embellishments. Cootie Williams's open horn makes a welcome appearance on *Fly Me To The Moon,* and his magnificent tone and pertinent note-placing obviously inspire the rhythm section in this medium-tempo performance. In some respects an LP like this must have been easy to make—musicians such as these need only be given a good melody to guarantee the quality of the solo part. A sketch for the reeds, a few figures for the trombones, and the scoring of a brief orchestral middle part would then suffice for an excellent jazz performance from musicians of this caliber. The importance of Ellington's discreetly judged accompaniments can be heard on the next ballad, *So Little Time,* handed over to Gonsalves. Here again we have a miniature masterpiece with a ravishing theme statement followed by some highly original variations, the whole set in a discreet orchestral framework. Gonsalves leads into the swinger that follows, *Danke Schoen;* the Ellingtonians' humor is to the fore here in the way they treat the theme, while Gonsalves and Cootie Williams (again on open horn) contribute the musical meat. The clarinet in the closing ensemble is by Hamilton. Duke's other clarinet soloist, Russell Procope, is featured in *More,* another track on which solo playing is backed by a perfectly judged orchestral part; trombones are used to excellent effect.

With the kind of program found on *Ellington '65,* one of the strongest soloists was bound to be Johnny Hodges. He makes his first appearance in a lyrical, passionate version of *The Second Time Around.* Jazz musicians of the pre-bop era were usually fine melody players, and the Ellington sidemen were melody masters to a man; yet even in their company Hodges stood out. The alto playing on *The Second Time Around* is a perfect illustration. He is backed by nice work from the trombones and skillful bass playing by Major Holley (the personnel for *Ellington '65,* was as for the European tour earlier that year except that Holley replaced Ernie Shepard). The Hodges ballad is followed by a witty and imaginative arrangement of *Never On A Sunday.* Passages played over a march rhythm from Woodyard's snares are contrasted with swinging sections by the band. The march parts feature Hamilton's clarinet in whimsical vein along with trombones and ingeniously voiced saxophones; the swinging segments are given the full gutbucket treatment with a plunger trombone solo part for Brown and some inspiring drumming.

Brown reappears in his role of master melody player in the opening of *I Left My Heart In San Francisco;* his dialogue with the saxophone section is the epitome of style and grace. Hodges joins in this riot of melody, and he and Brown, greatly assisted by the warmth of the ensemble playing and the beauty of the arrangement, make a masterpiece of jazz ballad playing from a rather ordinary popular song. The last word here is given to the bass trombone. Bob Dylan's *Blowin' In The Wind* opens with the "pep" section of two trumpets and trombone with plungers stating the theme to excellent effect. Ellington ingeniously works Hamilton's clarinet in with the three brass here, never audible as a separate voice, but adding the touch of color and harmony that makes the passage so distinctive. Hodges is employed in the role of swinger and brings a rather unexpected down-home gospel feeling to the song. The use of West Indian rhythms, ingenious mixtures in the voicings, and a touch of Anderson's high-note trumpet all add to the flavor of *Blowin' In The Wind*. The final track is a showcase for Carney's baritone on Acker Bilk's *Stranger On The Shore,* another great ballad performance by another Ellington master.

* * *

Ellington '66 follows a similar pattern. It opens with three ballads—*Red Roses For A Blue Lady* featuring Brown and Hodges, a medium-tempo *Charade* for Cootie's growl trumpet, and a Hodges showcase on *People*. *Red Roses* is a particularly graceful interpretation. There are Ellington versions of two Beatles songs in this collection—*All My Lovin',* which mixes a Latin beat with passages of straight four-to-the-bar, and *I Want To Hold Your Hand,* which is treated as a Cotton Club pastiche with plunger brass and clarinet trios evoking the Ellington sound of almost 40 years earlier. The reed section members are all heard in solo on *All My Lovin'*—Procope and Hamilton on clarinets, Carney, Hodges, and Gonsalves on saxes—while the soloists featured on *I Want To Hold Your Hand* are Brown, who is rather awkward, and Hodges. Lawrence fully redeems himself on *A Beautiful Friendship,* which recalls his very best playing in its unforced lyricism. Much excellent use is made of the saxophone section—and of the bass trombone—in this arrangement. Gonsalves's solo on *Days Of Wine And Roses* is only slightly less impressive than the superb *So Little Time* in *Ellington '65*.

The Ray Charles hit *I Can't Stop Loving You* receives an electrifying performance on *Ellington '66*. A surging medium tempo is established, and the whole performance rests on an infectious Woodyard shuffle rhythm. Hodges provides the introduction; Brown states the theme with fellow trombonist Cooper providing a biting commentary; Williams and Hodges are heard in solo and, after a reprise of the trombone duet, in the coda. The band plays with enormous swing and vitality, and this is one of its great performances of the sixties. While the originality and balance of the arrangement are impressive, the outstanding aspect of the performance is the wonderful swing of the band, inspired once again by Sam Woodyard. By contrast, we return to a ballad mood for *The Good Life* with gentle, tender playing from Carney, Hodges

and Brown before a powerful climax and a brief, telling Hodges coda. *Moon River* is given over to Hamilton's clarinet for one of his most graceful performances on record. The orchestration in the closing passages is brilliantly conceived.

Most of the titles for this LP were made with Nance back on cornet and John Lamb in on bass for Holley. Nance has a short solo in a new version of *Satin Doll,* disguised as a concert recording with applause added in the Reprise LP *Duke Ellington's Greatest Hits*. Duke also introduces a new composition, *Ellington '66,* an unassuming little swinger of delightful quality. Ellington and Woodyard duet at the beginning and end, and there are short solos by Gonsalves and Hodges, but the highlight is the warm, lifting swing of the band. John Lamb establishes himself as another master bassist, and the peerless saxophone section is heard to advantage.

* * *

The *Mary Poppins* LP has a less casual air about it than the previous two collections. Ellington and Strayhorn obviously gave this material considerable thought, and the result is a delightful and imaginative suite, full of lively humor. The opening, *A Spoonful Of Sugar,* features Hodges in his best sixties form, making every note count rhythmically and generating a powerful momentum at a swinging fast medium tempo. *Chim Chim Cheree* opens with Ellington's blithe piano in 3/4 time playing the whimsical theme happily until Cootie's vehement growl trumpet abruptly alters the mood. Gonsalves leads the reeds in a thematic passage which epitomizes the sadness never very far from his playing. There is effective use of clarinets in the ensemble before the tempo increases and the band and Gonsalves are up and away. The casual-sounding piano player, again in 3/4 time, has the last word. *Feed The Birds* provides one of the most illuminating examples of how Ellington uses the contrasting personalities in the band. The arrangement opens with an unaccompanied clarinet extravaganza by Hamilton, followed at once by the theme presented in the very different clarinet style of Procope. This sequence is repeated in the coda except that Procope simply plays one long note, the reference being so vivid that there is no need to recapitulate the theme. The center part of *Feed The Birds* features a rather somber orchestration in which many familiar Ellington devices are heard—Gonsalves and Carney are prominent in the reeds, the trombones lead the trumpets, and there is a Latin beat from the drummer. The only solo voice is Brown's plaintive plunger trombone. For *Let's Go Fly A Kite,* a medium swinging tempo of the kind associated with the Jimmie Lunceford Orchestra is set. The theme is presented on low muted trumpet over characteristic reed voicings. Brown and Williams are heard with plungers, Procope is on clarinet, and the performance ends with Hodges playing obbligato to a gloriously rich ensemble.

The only ballad feature on *Mary Poppins* is by Carney, who interprets *Stay Awake* with such skill and sensitivity one is tempted to conclude his jazz craft has never been better displayed on record. The extraordinary beauty of Carney's tone is perfectly caught by the recording, and his delicate handling of the baritone is as amazing as ever. The final bars, with Carney playing over the band in full cry—brass section, Cat Anderson and all—are truly magnificent. *I Love To Laugh* is transformed into a medium-tempo swinger without solos but with impressive writing for and playing by both the "pep" section and the saxes. Lamb is heard to advantage, Woodyard comes on with an infectious shuffle rhythm, and bass trombone is used effectively.

The next two tracks are notable for their easy, comfortable tempos and natural, unforced swing. The ease and authority of the ensemble phrasing shows the involvement of all the musicians and indicates why master jazzmen loved to play in this band. *Jolly Holiday* has moderate solos by Williams and Brown, and the clarinet in the ensemble is by Procope; an untidy ending rather dissipates the effect of the excellent opening passages. Hodges has a minor role on *Sister Suffragette* which also features Williams in a long plunger solo. The trumpet section is in particularly fine voice here, and one realizes clearly how much Anderson contributes to these three LPs even though he does not play one bar of solo trumpet. (The *Mary Poppins* recordings were done before Nance rejoined; apart from Lamb on bass the only change is in the trumpet section, where Nat Woodard has replaced Rolf Ericson.) *The Perfect Nanny* is a hymnlike tune given over in the main to Hamilton's sculptured phrasing and pure tone. A brief, sensuous solo by Gonsalves provides ideal contrast. The orchestral writing is full of interest—note the use of ensemble clarinet and bass clarinet behind Hamilton's solo, and the reed section voicing in the final statement. *Step In Time* is in mock-martial style, with most unusual use of Woodyard's drums and Lamb's bass as solo instruments. Another easy, swinging tempo is conjured up for *The Life I Lead*. The saxophone section takes care of the theme statement. Williams (on growl trumpet) and Hodges give a demonstration of just how to repeat a theme without the slightest suggestion of monotony before Buster Cooper enters for a forthright solo. The *Mary Poppins* collection ends with an uptempo, swinging excursion by Gonsalves on the theme of *Supercalifragilisticexpialidocious*. This is good, but closer to the Gonsalves of the marathons than to his best work. The clarinet in the ensemble is by Russell Procope. The very effective coda by Gonsalves brings this delightful LP to a close.

* * *

On May 20, 1964, Ellington gave one of his rare public piano recitals. The venue was Columbia University, and in the second half of the concert he was joined by bassist Peck Morrison and Sam Woodyard, and also by Billy Strayhorn, who played both solo and in duet with Duke, and sang his own *Lush Life*. Parts of the concert have been issued on the Foxy and Flutegroove labels (the same collection on both) in rather moderate sound. Included is the only known Ellington recording of his 1934 composition *Bird Of Paradise*, previously known only in a 1935 recording by the Jimmie Lunceford Orchestra; a medley of *New York City Blues, Melancholia,* and *Reflections in D; Little Flower Of Africa; Single Petal Of A Rose;* and *New World A-Comin'*. With the rhythm section, Duke is heard in *"A" Train, Satin Doll, Skillipoop,* and the *Medley Of Popular Hits*. Perhaps the most interesting group performed at the concert was a blues medley of *Happy-Go-Lucky Local, C Jam Blues,* and *John Sanders Blues,* but this has not yet been issued on LP.

In August 1964 the orchestra recorded the soundtrack for an American Airlines documentary, *Cargo By Air*. This has been issued on LP as *Suite For Swinging* and provides a most interesting thirteen minutes of Ellington music. As is often the case with soundtracks, there are some quite sudden and musically illogical changes in mood. The recorded sound is less than ideal. Some of the music in *Suite For Swinging* anticipates the first part of *Ad Lib On Nippon,* a work premiered in January 1965. The use of this material, code-named Igoo by Ellington, is frequently very different from that found on *Ad Lib On Nippon*. In *Suite For Swinging* most of the big guns of the Ellington solo roster are heard—Gonsalves, Hodges, Carney, Williams, Hamilton, and Ellington himself—and the vigorous performance certainly lives up to its title. The various segments seem to be put together arbitrarily, no doubt because of the specific demands of the film, but the music is superb. One wishes that Ellington had chosen to develop the whole of this material, not just the part used in *Ad Lib On Nippon,* into a concert suite.

* * *

In his 1964 concerts Ellington began to introduce movements from his *Impressions Of The Far East* or *Far East Suite* to his audiences. This suite was based on impressions picked up by Ellington and Strayhorn during the State Department tour of 1963. Some of these movements were recorded for Reprise, but have not been issued. The work had to wait until 1966 for a full recording, but a few movements do exist on unofficial issues from this period. Two of them are in the MF Records set in versions from European TV performances, while Canadian TV is the source of three movements in performances dating from September 1964. The MF recordings are from concerts which produced an unusual version of *Caravan,* featuring Ellington and Williams, heard in the same set. The MF *Happy Re-Union,* also from this period, features Gonsalves in a very involved and intricate interpretation of the solo part, full of the most beautiful inventions.

The Canadian recordings also include two movements from the incidental music to Shakespeare's *Timon Of Athens,* written for the Stratford, Ontario, festival of 1963. Of the remaining twelve movements, only the *March* has been issued on record, on the LP by Ellington with the Boston Pops Orchestra made in 1965.

The Canadian TV recordings issued on the Rarities label commence with Ellington reciting the "My Mother And My Father" lyrics from *My People* under the title *My Heritage;* he is accompanied by piano and drums only. This is followed by a new, fast version of *Happy-Go-Lucky Local.* As in the 1963 Paris recording, only two piano choruses survive from the first part. At the point in the second part where Hamilton usually appears as clarinet soloist, Gonsalves enters instead, and the performance then becomes an extended tenor solo over shuffle rhythm without further reference to *Happy-Go-Lucky Local.*

On the Rarities LP, this is followed by a half-chorus of Ellington's first composition, *Soda Fountain Rag,* but Duke comments that he now finds it too hard to play. He goes on instead to his second composition, *What You Gonna Do When The Bed Breaks Down?,* to which he appends a commentary on dancing styles prevalent in Washington in the early twenties. This is *real* parlor social music, Duke tells us. Then he starts to talk about *My People,* noting that he really belongs to several groups of people—the piano players, the listeners, the general appreciators of music, those who aspire to be dilettantes, those who "attempt to produce something fit for the plateau," and those who appreciate Beaujolais. Then, after a few reflections on the music of "my people" and "the people," he takes up the declamation from *My People.* As in that production, it leads to a performance of *The Blues* from *Black, Brown And Beige.* The vocal is sung by Joya Sherrill, once again with great sensitivity; it is interesting to note how much more authoritative the backing is here when compared with that of the alumni group of the *My People* LP. A highlight is the tenor solo by Gonsalves, who gives an interpretation of ravishing beauty. This must be among Paul's finest solos, and it is unfortunate that the extension used in Ashby's version on the *My People* LP is not employed here. *The Blues* is followed by a piano vamp which leads into the standard performance of *Rockin' In Rhythm.* The only fresh feature here is that Brown's first chorus is different from his usual one. The side closes with the same piece with which it opened, *My Mother And My Father,* this time sung by Sherrill over orchestral backing.

The second side opens with three movements from the *Far East Suite—Bluebird Of Delhi,* featuring Hamilton; *Agra,* featuring Carney; and *Amad,* an uptempo romp for piano and band in a very swinging performance during which Brown can be heard in the role of the muezzin calling the faithful to prayer. Dancer Bunny Briggs is featured in another excerpt from *My People,* the *David Danced* segment. Here a solo singer, Emme Kemp, takes on the part scored for full choir and finds the task something of a strain. Hodges has a solo backing the tap dancing, swinging in his most casual and relaxed manner. He then goes on to do full justice to the melody of the first of the *Timon Of Athens* pieces, the *Banquet Theme,* a very beautiful melody. The second of these *Timon* numbers is *Skillipoop*—Duke defined skillipooping as "the art of making what you're doing look better than what you are supposed to be doing." At concerts this piece was usually the prelude to a Woodyard drum solo, but here we have an extended version featuring Hamilton on clarinet and Nat Woodard on trumpet. (The latter was with the band for only a short period; his solo on *Skillipoop* reveals a musician with a good tone and a rather anonymous solo style in the then "modern" manner.) Both Woodard and Herbie Jones have trumpet solos on the version of *Jam With Sam* which follows, Jones essaying a little high-note trumpet before Cat Anderson sweeps in to build a massive climax. Ellington then recites a poem, *When All Our Pulses,* which has some similarities to the *Pedestrian Minstrel* section of his autobiography. The LP ends with a piano solo on *"A" Train* which reveals more fresh Ellington thoughts on this much-played theme before it is faded out. Despite the limitations of the recording quality, this is a valuable collection for the Ellington specialist, containing much otherwise unavailable music.

* * *

Within a few days of completing the last session for the *Ellington '66* LP in January 1965 the band were off on another European tour. The personnel for this tour was:

Trumpets:	Cat Anderson, Cootie Williams, Mercer Ellington, Herbie Jones, Ray Nance (cornet, violin and vocal).
Trombones:	Lawrence Brown, Buster Cooper, Chuck Connors (bass trombone).
Reeds:	Russell Procope (alto sax, clarinet); Johnny Hodges (alto sax); Paul Gonsalves (tenor sax); Jimmy Hamilton (clarinet, tenor sax); Harry Carney (baritone sax, clarinet, bass clarinet).
Rhythm:	Duke Ellington (piano); John Lamb (bass); Sam Woodyard (drums); Billy Strayhorn (deputy pianist).

Ray Nance had rejoined the band for this tour; shortly after its conclusion he left again, and this time his departure was final.

Duke does not seem to have done any recording for Reprise on either his 1964 or 1965 visits to Europe; the contrast with the frantic recording activity of 1963 is most marked. It would appear that Ellington had quickly exhausted the funds placed at his disposal by the company. From this time forward Ellington's work for Reprise diminished, his recordings for them being done on a more casual basis.

* * *

Although none of the 1965 concerts was officially recorded, some items have been issued deriving from TV shows, and there were plenty of unofficial concert recordings. An LP from a Paris concert on this 1965 tour has been issued on the Jazz Club and Jazz Anthology labels. The sound quality is moderate, but the band is in good form, and Duke's announcements have been retained in full, which certainly adds to the atmosphere. The program is typical of those presented on this tour. *Satin Doll* is cut down to one chorus and is linked to the Carney feature version of *Sophisticated Lady*. Anderson is heard in *Miaow,* a new "concerto" featuring aspects of Cat's talents different from those heard on the Latin American–style showcases he was usually given. (*Miaow* later became the final movement of the *Virgin Islands Suite,* where it was retitled *Jungle Kitty*.) There are three Hodges features— a revival of the 1938 *Harmony In Harlem,* scaled down to Hodges jump-band size, plus the more usual *I Got It Bad* and *Things Ain't What They Used To Be*. *Perdido* is heard in the Gerald Wilson arrangement but without the Jimmy Hamilton additions used on the previous tour and with the trumpet chase replaced by a Nance solo. The *Tutti For Cootie* is a fine performance, but the open trumpet solo is off-mike, while *Rockin' In Rhythm* is distinguished by Duke using not *Kinda Dukish* but James P. Johnson's *Carolina Shout* as the piano prelude. He had grown fond of playing versions—some short, some complete—of this stride piano classic at concerts, and here he gives a pretty full rendition before leading the band into *Rockin' In Rhythm*. His revival at the age of 66 of a number he learned from a piano roll during adolescence is a typical Ellington surprise, resulting in an excellent piece of stride piano playing.

* * *

On their return to the United States the band recorded a further LP for Reprise. Entitled *Concert In The Virgin Islands,* it celebrates an Ellington tour there in April 1965. It opens with the four-movement *Virgin Islands Suite,* a lightweight affair full of charming and lively music. The first movement is *Island Virgin,* an Ellington calypso played with considerable grace and with apposite decorations from Hamilton's clarinet. The tempo moves up, Sam Woodyard recalls the "jungle drums" of the swing era, and Hamilton takes over as featured soloist in *Virgin Jungle,* which provides an ideal showcase for his talents. The easygoing, relaxed nature of this music is typified by *Fiddler On The Diddle,* which has Nance's violin in dialogue with the saxes at an easy, swinging tempo. The final movement is *Jungle Kitty,* the showcase for Anderson which had been performed on the European tour as *Miaow*. It is a brilliant, witty concerto out of the same stable as the 1938 *Boy Meets Horn,* with Anderson showing a full understanding of Ellington's intentions and providing a really remarkable coda which gives the suite an unusual ending.

The *Suite* is followed by a couple of Hodges features. The first, yet another recording of *Things Ain't What They Used To Be,* is a fine version which has an atmosphere of spontaneity despite the fact that *Things Ain't* had been a nightly— often twice nightly—feature for Hodges for many years. One secret of great jazz playing is the illusion of spontaneity. Very few jazz soloists have been able (or even wanted to) improvise constantly, and most stick to more or less set patterns in their solos. Much of their success has depended on making these solos sound as if the phrases were newly minted, in just the same way that a good actor will enunciate familiar lines and convince an audience that they are the natural and impromptu speech of the character he is portraying. Hodges was a master of this art, and the Reprise version of *Things Ain't What They Used To Be* provides a perfect illustration. It also shows that age was starting to have an effect on the playing of this 58-year-old musician. The tone is a shade less opulent, with a dryness which had not been heard in his work since the thirties. He had long known the art of making each note work, and now he deploys it in the manner of one who knows that he has to conserve his energies. As on the Paris *Things Ain't What They Used To Be* of three months earlier, the trumpets play the *Blues For Blanton* riff behind Hodges as part of a vigorous band backing. A new Hodges blues follows this familiar example of the genre. On *Big Fat Alice's Blues* Johnny sings the blues with characteristic authority. The saxophone section has an important role in a discreet accompaniment which is judged to perfection and also includes some pungent Ellington piano interjections. The title of this particular piece is wordplay on the Broadway production *Tiny Alice* and several other titles on the LP also reflect Duke's interest in the Broadway season of 1965—*Fiddler On The Diddle* refers to *Fiddler On The Roof, Fade Up* to *Fade In, Fade Out;* and *Barefoot Stomper* to *Barefoot In The Park*.

Another of the band's standards appears in a new guise— Billy Strayhorn's *Chelsea Bridge* as a showcase for Gonsalves. Here Paul gives one of his most masterly displays, digging deeply into the harmonic structure while retaining a high melodic content. His beautifully judged note selection means that the melodic outline is always present, and his lines, no matter how rhythmically or harmonically complex, never clash with the still, static mood of this very distinctive tone painting. *Chelsea Bridge* is followed by a conventional big band score by Cootie Williams, *The Opener,* which was used by Ellington at concerts for some years—always in the middle of a program, despite the title! Gonsalves at his most loquacious, Cooper in his most searing vein, and Anderson are the soloists. Anderson enters in the low register of the trumpet and indulges in a few half-valve effects before soaring off into a high-note ending. The energy of this performance is impressive.

Ellington used the blues structure in a number of ways, but in this collection he treats it very traditionally. In *Mysterious Chick* we return to a time-honored Ellington pattern, a blues in which two soloists alternate chorus by chorus. The prototype for this kind of performance was *Sweet Chariot* of 1930, in which Nanton's plunger trombone alternated with Williams's open trumpet. On *Mysterious Chick* the conversation is conducted by Brown on open trombone and Nance on plunger-muted trumpet. Ellington and the saxophone section have crucial roles, but it is the dialogue between the two contrasting soloists which holds the stage here. *Barefoot Stomper* certainly lives up to its title, with Woodyard driving the band along; Nance has some incisive phrases and Gonsalves evokes a mood near to that which Lester Young used to create with the Basie band. The concluding *Fade Up* is a retitling of *Tutti For Cootie*. This performance is exceptionally fine and is taken at a really telling, rocking medium tempo. But halfway through the open trumpet solo (which is about halfway through the piece) the recording suddenly fades away. There is no apparent reason for this (unless it is to live up to its new title), and one hopes that a complete version will be issued some day.

Concert In The Virgin Islands is a representative collection of mid-sixties Ellingtonia and shows the creative health of both Ellington and his ensemble. It is the last Ellington LP on which Ray Nance is a member of the band. He left quietly and there was no fuss made in the musical press as there had been from time to time when other major Ellingtonians had departed. Yet few players contributed as much to Ellington's music as Nance had done over the years. This really superb artist—a great jazz violinist and a swinging and entertaining singer as well as one of the best jazz trumpeters—never seems to have been rated highly by the writers who set jazz fashion. Which is a reflection on them, for Nance proved his outstanding abilities on hundreds of Ellington recordings, while other less talented players received the plaudits and the top placings in the polls.

* * *

At the Pittsburgh Jazz Festival of June 1965, a "Piano Workshop" concert was held at which jazz pianists of different generations and stylistic persuasions were brought together. Ellington was one of the participants; this was indeed a sign of the times, for in the past Duke would not have been thought sufficiently important as a pianist to justify his inclusion in a parade of important keyboard artists. This concert was recorded by RCA Victor and Ellington is heard on three tracks on the resulting LP, *The Jazz Piano*. On *Sweet Lorraine* he is heard along with Earl Hines and Billy Taylor but does not make any significant contribution, while the blues duet with Hines, *House Of Lords*, is rather disappointing. Duke opens the performance but, after setting the mood in the opening chorus, he settles into a secondary role. Although a good performance by any reasonable standard, neither of the two great artists involved really strikes his best form. Much the best recording from this "Piano Workshop" is a new composition by Ellington, *The Second Portrait Of The Lion*, a tribute to Willie "The Lion" Smith who also was featured at the concert. The piece is one of Ellington's two-tempo constructions, with a stride piano uptempo section alternating with slow, reflective passages. Duke plays brilliantly, toying with several characteristic Smith devices with wry humor. *The Second Portrait Of The Lion* is a piece of considerable charm and certainly would be included in any short list of Ellington's best compositions for solo piano.

* * *

The following month, July 1965, again found Ellington recording at a live event without his band. This was the result of an invitation to join the Boston Pops Orchestra under its famous conductor Arthur Fiedler in the annual concert for the Boston Symphony Orchestra Benefit Fund at Tanglewood. (The Boston Pops Orchestra is the Boston Symphony minus the first desk players; it performs light music rather than the classical repertoire.) The word "pop" had begun to acquire a different meaning by 1965, but the Boston Pops policy remained unchanged: light music played by a first-class symphonic ensemble.

It would be foolish to look for music of great substance on such an occasion, and the true success of the venture with Ellington can be gauged from the fact that over 14,000 people attended the concert. Their contribution to the orchestra's benefit fund was over $48,000. The day before the concert Louis Bellson had rejoined the Ellington Orchestra, and he and bassist John Lamb are present with Duke at the Tanglewood concert. The arrangements by Richard Hayman (not to be confused with Dick Hyman) follow the time-honored Boston Pops formula: lots of melody, a rich sound, plenty of decorative percussion tinkles and bumps, and a lack of concern about sounding too hammy or overdoing the sentiment. In these circumstances, it is surprising that the twelve titles on the RCA LP from the concert include two new Ellington themes. One is a pop song called *Love Scene* which does not seem to have been otherwise recorded by Ellington. In the course of a rather coy and gauche liner note, Ellington observes that this is his latest "words and music effort." It is pleasantly tuneful, and the performance is mainly notable for the drumming of Bellson. The other new theme is the *Timon Of Athens March*, an excerpt from the Shakespearian incidental music of a couple of years earlier. Ellington does not play on this number, which is very obviously a piece of functional incidental music.

To hear Ellington's compositions played by a symphony orchestra can be interesting, but for the most part here the selection concentrates on his popular songs. An exception is *The Mooche*, but the eerie atmosphere of the piece as played by the Ellington band is lost and the effect is of a silky, dressed-up piece of showy light orchestral tinsel. The other numbers are *Caravan, Mood Indigo, I Let A Song Go Out Of My Heart, I'm Beginning To See The Light, Do Nothin' Til You Hear From Me, Sophisticated Lady, Solitude, I Got It Bad,* and *Satin Doll*. In his liner note, Ellington adopts one of his poses—that of the humble jazz piano player overwhelmed at the honor of the invitation to play with the symphony, and oh!, by the way, the program is all of his own songs. The final sentence sums up his stance: "Ah, but it was a wonderful night for the piano player."

***

It is unfortunate that the Ellington band did not record more purely instrumental material at the time of Bellson's second stay, but during this time their "official" recording activities were confined to an LP with Ella Fitzgerald and the first *Concert Of Sacred Music*. An air check has been issued from this period of a number entitled *Flashback From The Future,* but this turns out to be no more than a condensed version of Cootie Williams's rather commonplace *The Opener.*

Of greater importance is the 1965 Monterey Jazz Festival performance of *Ad Lib On Nippon,* which predates the Victor recording by over a year. This has been released in Italy on the I Giganti del Jazz label with an incorrect recording date. The performance is a fine one, and Bellson's drumming is superior to that of Rufus Jones on the Victor, but the playing suggests that Bellson was a less potent drummer for the Ellington Orchestra than Woodyard and that the definitive *Ad Lib On Nippon* will only emerge when a well-recorded version with Woodyard is issued.

***

The LP with Ella Fitzgerald was recorded for Verve and issued as *Ella At Duke's Place.* It is of less interest from the viewpoint of the Ellington band than the previous collaboration with Ella, for here Norman Granz was obviously determined that his star singer should not be upset by the casual ways of the Ellingtonians as she had been in 1957 at the sessions for *Ella Fitzgerald Sings The Duke Ellington Song Book.* (The personnel is unchanged from January 1965, but with Bellson replacing Woodyard.) The band sounds very well drilled, and the careful way in which this music was recorded can be gauged from the high take numbers for some of the items—*Passion Flower* actually reached take-17.

Jimmy Jones had been associated with the Ellingtonians in a variety of capacities, including that of directing "The Billy Strayhorn Orchestra" on the *My People* LP. Here Jones is brought in as assistant pianist and arranger. No doubt having Jones prepare half of the scores in advance was one way of avoiding last minute arranging and part writing in the studio, factors which had upset the singer in 1957. As the Ellington musicians were liable to play with more precision with Bellson on drums, the total effect here is to give the band an unusually conventional sound. The LP is divided into two parts, each covering one side of the disc. The first comprises ballads and the second swinging numbers. Or, in the words of the liner note, the first is *"the pretty, the lovely, the tender, the hold-me-close side"* and the second *"the finger-snapping, head-shaking, toe-tapping, go-for-yourself side."*

The opening number is a version of the first of the Ellington-Strayhorn collaborations, *Something To Live For,* with piano and arrangement by Jimmy Jones. Fitzgerald sings with restraint here, giving an airing to the rarely heard verse, while Gonsalves adds a gentle touch of tone coloring at one point. The lyrics to *A Flower Is A Lovesome Thing* are somewhat effusive, but Ella is at her most professional and Gonsalves again makes a contribution, here in the form of a most beautiful solo. Strayhorn's *Passion Flower* follows, in a Jones arrangement, with Ella singing the unfamiliar lyrics and Hodges in ravishing form. As both this number and the preceding one are credited wholly to Strayhorn, one must assume that the lyrics are by him. Another unexpected vehicle for the singer's talents is the vocal movement from the 1947 *Liberian Suite, I Like The Sunrise*. This is not a very convincing interpretation, although a high level of professional competence is maintained. Jones's arrangement suffers in comparison with Ellington's original, while Fitzgerald handles the lyrics less well than Al Hibbler had done on the earlier recording. *Azure* is one of Ellington's most beautiful songs, yet one for which he never seems to have created an ideal arrangement. Duke is at the piano for this version and takes the major honors in a performance which finds Ella at her least attractive, mangling the words and having recourse to a "little girl" voice in her duet with the piano.

The second, *"finger-snapping, head-shaking"* side opens with a new Ellington song which enjoyed a brief spell of popularity when this version was issued as a single, *Imagine My Frustration*. This combines the talents of Ellington as composer, Strayhorn as lyric writer, and Gerald Wilson as arranger. The theme has one or two familiar twists but the performance is a vigorous one and Ella, who can certainly swing a number at this tempo, keeps the vocal pyrotechnics down to a minimum. Hodges has a very effective solo here, and Anderson's lead in the brass section adds extra bite. The vocal version of *C Jam Blues, Duke's Place,* follows, and here the solos of Williams, Hodges, Hamilton, and especially Gonsalves rather outshine an occasionally uneasy vocalist. Ella regains her best form at the start of *The Brownskin Gal In The Calico Gown,* but after one chorus the tempo goes up, the singer varying the melody in a less-than-engaging way before Hamilton provides a tenor saxophone solo. *What Am I Here For?* is one of the Ellington themes which seems least to require a lyric, but Frankie Laine provided one and Ella presents it in a manner which is much more satisfying than her wordless singing in duet with Paul Gonsalves later in the performance. The band sounds in such fine form here that one rather ungraciously wishes the piece had been given instrumental treatment. The final track, *Cotton Tail,* finds the singer indulging in an extended feast of scat singing which includes chase choruses with Gonsalves and Hamilton on tenors, and a fair amount of excitement is engendered.

Taken overall, *Ella At Duke's Place* is probably more rewarding for connoisseurs of Ella Fitzgerald's singing than for those of the Ellington band. Ella is in good voice throughout, and those who enjoy her scat singing and her taste in melodic decoration will find this collection most rewarding. From an Ellington point of view, the most interesting aspect of *Ella At Duke's Place* is the demonstration of how conventional the band can sound when subjected to long rehearsals of commonplace scores. Duke normally avoided such careful preparation. He believed that it acted against spontaneity, and there is indeed precious little of that quality in *Ella At Duke's Place*. There are some good solos, especially by Gonsalves, and Bellson's playing is a continuous delight, but this is not an important Ellington LP.

* * *

The earlier *Duke At Tanglewood* LP had signaled a new, apparently nonexclusive, tie with the Victor label. The last LP the band made in 1965 was again for Victor, a recording of *Duke Ellington's Concert Of Sacred Music* done in the Fifth Avenue Presbyterian Church, New York, on December 26, 1965. The work had been given its premiere at the Grace Cathedral, San Francisco, on September 16 of that year. Ellington attached the greatest importance to his sacred concerts, and their performance became a regular part of his schedule for the rest of his career. He considered them his most significant works and treated them with the utmost seriousness. Those jazz writers who have condescended to consider them have been inclined to suspend judgment, and one doubts if many people other than Ellington himself would look upon them as the peak of his achievement. For Duke they represented an affirmation of his Christian faith, a faith which had been a constant factor throughout his life but which had never before been proclaimed so strongly in public. Some who attended the sacred concerts have said that Ellington's music brought a new dimension to worship, and the success of the music in this regard cannot be wholly ignored in any overall assessment. Yet we do not today judge the music of the Bach cantatas by its functional value, nor indeed the records of the bands which played the old Savoy Ballroom in Harlem only by their suitability for dancing—if we did, we might find the Savoy Sultans superior to Ellington. Ultimately the merits of Ellington's sacred works must be considered on musical grounds alone and must be evaluated by the same criteria as the rest of his output. It is quite impossible to compare them with anything outside Duke's music because no other major jazz figure has attempted sacred works of this kind.

The most obvious fact about the first *Concert Of Sacred Music* is that so little of it is new. Of the nine tracks on the LP only three contain new material: the opening *In The Beginning God, Tell Me It's The Truth* (which had in fact been heard at concerts in an instrumental version but never recorded), and *The Lord's Prayer*. It does seem curious that for such an act of devotion Ellington should have used so much material taken from earlier works. The first *Concert Of Sacred Music* consists of a potpourri of pieces from *Black, Brown And Beige* (1943) and *My People* (1963), plus a revival of *New World A-Comin'* (1945) and the three new items noted above. The band personnel is the same as that on the previous LPs except that Quentin Jackson was added as fourth trombone just for the recording. Three solo singers—Brock Peters, Esther Morrow and Jimmy McPhail—were used, plus the Herman McCoy Choir and tap dancer Bunny Briggs.

The long opening *In The Beginning God* is preceded by a short introductory piano solo complete with grunts, bass, and drums, which indicate that the event is going to be a wholly Ellingtonian one. The six-note theme of *In The Beginning God* is stated by Carney in a stark fashion quite appropriate for music intended to depict the beginning of the world. Carney plays with great majesty and presence, at first unaccompanied, then in tempo with a rich orchestral backing. After an orchestral climax, Hamilton enters on clarinet, like Carney opening with an unaccompanied passage. Up to this point the music has been of the best Ellington quality with superior melodic content, rich harmonic voicings and fine solo-playing. But then the vocalist enters and the musical interest declines. This is not the fault of Brock Peters, an academic baritone with a good voice. After cries of "In The Beginning—God!" Peters moves into an uptempo passage in which he sings of Ellington's concept of the beginning of things—"no heaven, no earth, no nothin'." Subsequently Peters reverts to speech as he proclaims a list of things which were absent in the beginning of the world. There are a few jokes here, but this segment is no masterpiece of humor or of ecclesiastical music. The return to the original tempo, and to singing rather than shouting, is accompanied by some good work from the rhythm section.

The next section is an uptempo tenor solo by Paul Gonsalves accompanied by the band and also by the choir who shout out the names of the books of the Old Testament. This does nothing to enhance an otherwise very fine example of Gonsalves's work. Then, after a fanfare, Anderson plays the *In The Beginning God* theme before ascending to a high-note climax: "That's as high as we go," says Duke. An out-of-tempo piano passage then leads to the choir shouting the names of the books of the New Testament. The shouts are succeeded by Bellson playing the theme on drums at the start of a drum solo. This solo is presented as an example of Ellington's concept of worship, in which each man offers to his god what he does best. After this solo Bellson brings the tempo down again and makes the final statement of the main theme before the movement ends with some fat chords from the ensemble with Anderson up top. *In The Beginning God* is clearly an uneven composition with the introductory instrumental part outweighing the rest, although on a more conventional level of music making, Gonsalves's tenor solo is an exceptionally fine one.

The remainder of the first side is taken up by a group of three Ellington songs with a gospel flavor. They are sung by Esther Morrow, a gospel singer from Detroit who is described on the sleeve as an Ellington discovery. *Tell Me It's*

The Truth suffers from comparison with the unissued instrumental version, but there is plenty of spirit in this performance with excellent work from Brown and Hodges. A vocal version of *Come Sunday* follows; this is of considerable mediocrity. Finally Morrow sings *The Lord's Prayer* with jumpy, spirited gospel accompaniment from the band.

The second side of the disc consists entirely of old material. First Hodges is featured in his famous reading of *Come Sunday*, here in its original form as an extract from *Black, Brown And Beige;* the passage which used to be played by Nance on violin is taken by Hamilton on clarinet. After this, Jimmy McPhail and the choir do a couple of highly theatrical excerpts from *My People—Will You Be There* and *Ain't But The One*—which in their turn are followed by a piano solo version of *New World A-Comin'*. The orchestral part is not missed here, for even in the earlier version the core of the musical argument was always with the piano. This performance is one of exceptional sensitivity and commitment by Ellington. Finally comes the best of the three versions issued on record of *David Danced Before The Lord With All His Might*. As on the other two recordings, Bunny Briggs is the tap dancer, and he contributes to a lively and affirmative climax. In the middle of *David Danced*, there is a very swinging passage accompanied by the rhythm section alone. It is a pity that Anderson's trumpet obbligato towards the end of this performance is so underrecorded as to be virtually inaudible.

One of the most positive aspects of this first *Concert Of Sacred Music* is the fact that the Ellington musicians are not in any way inhibited by their unusual surroundings. It was clearly Ellington's intention that the band should play in its usual style and totally without inhibition, and in this regard the *Concert* is a total success. But the material itself is too disparate a mixture of old and new, of differing musical styles, for the music to have any overall coherence. The impression is of a very loose and diffuse collection of pieces. Much of the vocal writing is mediocre, and the real successes of the LP are the instrumental parts of *In The Beginning God, New World A-Comin'*, and the revival of *Come Sunday* in the original version. But it would be a mistaken observer who considered the *Concert Of Sacred Music* as the herald of Ellington's decline. At 66, when most men would be thinking of retirement, he was gathering his strength for a huge creative effort which would include, importantly for their creator, two more *Concerts Of Sacred Music*.

* * *

Outstanding Records

1. Reprise Recordings

AFRO BOSSA
WILL THE BIG BANDS EVER COME BACK?
RECOLLECTIONS OF THE BIG BAND ERA (released on Atlantic)
PARIS CONCERT RECORDINGS OF FEBRUARY 1963 (released on Reprise and Atlantic): *Pyramid, Echoes of Harlem, Do Nothin' Til You Hear From Me, The Star-Crossed Lovers, Kinda Dukish,* and *Rockin' In Rhythm, Theme From "The Asphalt Jungle," Concerto For Cootie, Tutti For Cootie, Suite Thursday, Bula, Happy-Go-Lucky Local,* and *Harlem*
THE SYMPHONIC ELLINGTON
DUKE ELLINGTON'S VIOLIN SESSION (released on Atlantic)
SERENADE TO SWEDEN (with Alice Babs)
ELLINGTON '65
ELLINGTON '66
MARY POPPINS
CONCERT IN THE VIRGIN ISLES

2. Other Recordings

CONCERT RECORDINGS ISSUED ON MF RECORDS: *Pyramid, Dancers In Love* (1963), *Caravan* (1964)
"MY PEOPLE" ORIGINAL CAST ALBUM (Contact) especially *The Blues* (from *Black, Brown And Beige*), *David Danced, King Fit De Battle of Alabam*
FROM THE SOUNDTRACK OF "CARGO BY AIR" (Extreme Rarities): *Suite For Swinging*
CANADIAN TV RECORDINGS 1964 (Rarities): *Soda Fountain Rag, What You Gonna Do When The Bed Breaks Down?, The Blues* (from *Black, Brown And Beige*), *Banquet Theme,* and *Skillipoop* (from *Timon Of Athens*)
PARIS CONCERT RECORDINGS OF JANUARY 1965 (Jazz Club; Jazz Anthology): *Tutti For Cootie, Carolina Shout,* and *Rockin' In Rhythm*
THE JAZZ PIANO (RCA): *Second Portrait Of The Lion*
ELLA AT DUKE'S PLACE (Verve)
DUKE ELLINGTON'S CONCERT OF SACRED MUSIC (RCA)

Chapter 27

World Tourist

THE OUTBURST OF CREATIVE ACTIVITY which marked the last decade of Duke Ellington's life would have been astounding even had he not also continued to lead the life of a touring bandleader. That he intensified his touring activities and subjected himself and the band to an even more rigorous life on the road during these years makes his achievement all but incredible. The death of Billy Strayhorn on May 31, 1967, threw a lot more weight on Ellington's shoulders, but, until his own final illness, additional work and hard touring seemed to act as stimulants to him. The effects of this pace on the aging members of the orchestra were less beneficial. During the years covered in the following chapters, age began to take its toll and there was a slow but steady decline in the quality of the band.

The routine of heavy international touring was really established in 1963, when the band visited the Middle and Far East on a State Department tour, suddenly cut short by the assassination of President John F. Kennedy. During this year another European tour was also completed and the band visited Japan for the first time. In 1964 the Virgin Islands were included in the itinerary in addition to the now annual European trip. Other Ellington enterprises in 1964 included playing at the White House in a Festival of the Arts, his date with the Boston Pops Orchestra, and the creation of a new concert work, *The Golden Broom And The Green Apple,* which was premiered by the New York Philharmonic Orchestra at the Lincoln Center in New York City. In 1965 Duke was recommended for a special citation by the music jury of the Pulitzer Prize Committee, but this was rejected by the Advisory Board, to Ellington's very considerable disappointment. His comment on their decision — "Fate doesn't want me to be too famous too young" — became one of his most famous witticisms. During the following year's tour of Europe, Duke presented his *Concert Of Sacred Music* in Coventry Cathedral, then went on to open the restored wing of the Chateau de Goutelas in France and to attend the World Festival of Negro Arts in Dakar, Senegal, for which he wrote *La Plus Belle Africaine.* Also in 1966 he was presented with the President's Gold Medal by the American Ambassador to Spain on behalf of President Lyndon B. Johnson, and still found time to write the music for a stage production of T. S. Eliot's *Murder In The Cathedral* and for the film *Assault On A Queen;* he also directed the recording of the latter.

* * *

So far as the Duke Ellington Orchestra was concerned, its greatest asset during these years was its saxophone section, generally accepted as the best that the music had ever known. Each chair was occupied by a musician of the highest caliber, each a skilled soloist and a strong musical personality. The fruits of Ellington's practice of encouraging the individuality of his musicians, of cultivating their idiosyncrasies even in ensemble playing, can be heard throughout the work of this great reed section. Through the scoring of Ellington and Strayhorn one can hear constantly the voices of such strong individuals as Johnny Hodges, Paul Gonsalves, and Harry Carney. One of the qualities of this section's playing is the strength of the inner parts, which gives a strong harmonic coloring to the music it plays. This flavor is a consequence of Ellington's encouraging these highly personal styles rather than demanding the uniform ensemble playing most bandleaders desired.

One of the qualities Ellington looked for in a musician was the ability to carry a harmony line strongly and with distinction. If one listens to the late thirties records of the John Kirby Orchestra (a sextet), one can hear how strongly Russell Procope does this in the front line of trumpet, clarinet, and alto. This may have been one of the reasons why Ellington approached Procope when Otto Hardwick left the band in 1945. In the section of the sixties, Procope played alto and clarinet; his alto solos were rare — as one might expect with Hodges also in the band — but when he did take a chorus on this instrument it was always of a distinctive character in a pleasant, thirties-oriented style. Procope's alto work in the section was invaluable, owing to both his rich and ample tone and his great understanding of Ellington's requirements. Procope's main solo contribution was on clarinet, where he maintained the New Orleans tradition on this instrument within the band and acted as a foil to Jimmy Hamilton's more academic use of the instrument.

Hodges was, as we have noted, starting to conserve his musical energies, and he was no longer an innovator in his solos.

But he was now an artist of great maturity, who played alto saxophone with a tone and an authority no other musician has equaled. The alto can sound thin and watery when contrasted with the big tone produced by tenor players of the Coleman Hawkins school. When Hodges was around, it was the tenor players who were in danger of sounding weak by comparison with his rich, thick, full-blooded tone. In the section he would coast along at times, but when he chose to deploy his ensemble skills the effect could be felt through the entire band.

Another musician with a sound full of quality and individuality was Gonsalves, now at the peak of his powers, a tenor saxophone virtuoso whose mastery of the instrument was complete. He said that he always cultivated a tone which would fit the Ellington band even in the years before he joined, and his devotion to Ellington music was total. He was able to produce rousing tenor marathons at Ellington's request, but his preference was for solos in slower tempos, where he made his most valuable contributions. He was a master ensemble player whose distinctive tone was often used by Ellington as a lead voice in the section or as the instrument taking an important thread in the harmonic weave.

Jimmy Hamilton also played tenor saxophone and was a better player on this instrument than is generally realized, certainly not the kind of player to lower the standard of this quintet of masters. His tenor solos had a rough-and-tumble sound with a fine quality of swing. Hamilton's main instrument, however, was the clarinet, and he was one of the most comprehensive artists on this instrument ever to be heard in the jazz idiom. He is at his best in situations like those found on *The Nutcracker Suite* or *Mary Poppins* where his role, although at times free-ranging, was essentially an interpretative one.

The key man in the reed section was still Carney, who gave the Ellington band just the same kind of foundation as that given to a New Orleans ensemble by a master tailgate trombone player. The depth and richness of Carney's tone were unique and his continuing consistency was one of the wonders of jazz, while his understanding of Ellington's requirements was based on almost 40 years' service with the band. His work on bass clarinet added a rich timbre to Ellington's array of sounds.

With five such musicians working as a dedicated team it was inevitable that they would attain a high level of musical achievement. This section surpassed any heard with other bands; the only comparable unit was that of the Ellington band of 1940 to 1942. In that section the contributions of the light-toned, creamy alto of Otto Harwick, the direct tenor style of Ben Webster, and the unique big band clarinet style of Barney Bigard make for interesting and rewarding comparison with their counterparts in the band of the sixties. Such comparisons are barren if made simply to decide which section is the better, but, when used to note how each section differs in balance and how they deal with the problems of interpreting Ellington's music, they can lead to greater understanding and enjoyment of the music.

The trombone section of the early sixties worked very differently to the saxophones in that the majority of the important functions were handled by one man, Lawrence Brown. As well as taking solos on ballads, uptempo swingers, slow blues, concert works, and a considerable variety of plunger specialties, Brown also played most of the section lead parts. And if a theme statement *à la* Tizol was required in one of the more exotic numbers such as *Pyramid,* then this task too was given to Lawrence. In other words he was not only coping with the wide range of solo responsibility which he had carried since joining the band in 1932, but also adding to it the solo roles of Tricky Sam Nanton and Juan Tizol. Only an occasional blistering chorus from Buster Cooper challenged Brown's solo monopoly, a monopoly which he certainly had not invited. But in his own way, with every show of reluctance and deference, he was a devoted Ellingtonian, and he literally wore out his lip in his last years of service with the band. The third trombone, Chuck Connors, was a bass trombone specialist and to all practical purposes a nonsoloist. But Brown's vast experience, Cooper's drive, and the depth offered by Connors made up a section of a quality, if not of a variety, to equal any from the Ellington past, and one which the leader certainly worked hard.

There is no doubt that beneath the air of studied nonchalance the veterans of the Ellington band were feeling the strain of constant touring. During the band's tour of 1966 both Brown and Hodges told anyone interested enough to listen that they were tired of travel and on the point of leaving the band for this reason. Ray Nance came through Britain a few months later on a solo tour, and, when this was reported to him, he observed that they had been saying exactly the same thing when he first joined the band in 1941.

The trumpet section was also an accomplished one and had the vast experience of both Cootie Williams and Cat Anderson to call on. Cat was a brilliant lead trumpet in every way, and if Ellington's concentration on his abilities as a high-note player and purveyor of Latin American specialties seemingly ignored other valuable aspects of his solo potential, then at least Cat did not suffer from the kind of overwork which was Lawrence Brown's lot. This enabled him to devote more of his energies to section playing. But with Herbie Jones and Mercer Ellington, to all intents and purposes nonsoloists, this threw a tremendous load onto the shoulders of Williams. Cootie was a trumpet player of immense authority, but his work no longer had either the mobility or the variety it had shown in the thirties and forties. Here the quintet of soloists in the reed section saved the day, eliminating constant demands on the veterans in Ellington's brass team. Yet it is undeniable that the presence of a trumpet soloist of Ray Nance's or Clark Terry's abilities would have been a great advantage at this time. Indeed Nance's departure had left a gap which Ellington could never fill.

The rhythm section of Ellington, Ernie Shepard, and Sam Woodyard was ideal for the band. Ellington remained a peerless band pianist, and in Shepard he had a powerful bassist who filled his demanding chair with distinction. Ellington's bands always had superb bass players; Shepard's qualities were a big sound, fine musicianship and a seemingly innate ability to find the right notes and rhythmic patterns for any given Ellington situation. His successor, John Lamb, was a more studious character who brought a very high level of musical skill to the chair and who contributed in an imaginative way to the musical structures.

The controversial Woodyard is heard to great advantage on many of the recordings from this period. In situations as different as accompanying a violin solo, swinging the band through *One O'Clock Jump,* or hurling the combined forces of the Ellington band and a symphony orchestra into a swinging blues, Woodyard proves himself an Ellingtonian for all seasons. It is fascinating to hear Louis Bellson playing with this same band, and indeed he drums superbly on the recordings which were made during the six months or so that he was back with them. He is a much more precise drummer than Woodyard, yet for all Bellson's great skills Woodyard scores with the looseness and relaxation of his beat and the emotional ferocity of his phrasing. Several members of the band considered that they played better when Woodyard was at the drums.

* * *

One of the factors which had enabled Ellington to avoid the usual pitfalls of a jazz musician writing concert music was his deep concern for the traditions of jazz. As Teddy Wilson observed, "He used advanced techniques *within the jazz framework*." For all his success with concert music, moving into the field of sacred music posed new problems, not least the emphasis on choral writing. In the view of many observers, Ellington had long shown suspect taste when selecting singers for the band, while the recent score for *My People* had suggested that the almost unerring touch with which he wrote for instrumental forces could not be relied upon when he came to deal with voices. There is nothing in the *Sacred Concerts* to cause any major modification of this view, and this is the main reason why musicians and students of Ellington's music have not been able to agree with Duke's own assessment of the importance of these works.

The years 1962 to 1966 also saw the last of the series of recorded collaborations between Ellington and other important jazz artists. Of these one is inclined to regard the session with Coleman Hawkins as the most successful. This was a typical Ellington small-band date with Hawkins added, all the other musicians working in very familiar territory. The session is clearly underprepared by normal standards, but Ellington once again turns this into a virtue by emphasizing the spontaneous nature of the music. The LP with the Basie band contains some very good things but is uneven; this certainly is a date which would have benefited from more careful preparation. It is unfortunate that no one commissioned an Ellington suite for the two orchestras. The discs with Louis Armstrong are also uneven and came just too late in Louis's career for the sparks to fly at such a meeting of giants, but they, too, contain much excellent music. The recordings with Mingus and Coltrane are less satisfactory; Duke plays well on the former, but the session suffers from drumming which is unsympathetic. The Coltrane date is another which was in need of longer preparation. As on all these collaborations, the resolution of problems of compatibility was left largely to chance. In all cases the economic considerations of recording-session time and the fact of Ellington's crowded schedule limited the time available for rehearsal. Despite these factors this series is important and throws a unique light on Ellington's resource and creativity when dealing with unusual musical situations.

* * *

Another aspect of this period is the generally low rating given by reviewers and critics to the Reprise output. There is certainly a wide variety of music here. Two LPs are filled with new material for the band, *Afro-Bossa* and *Concert In The Virgin Isles;* there are three LPs from the 1963 Paris concerts; there is the unique *Violin Session;* the equally unique *The Symphonic Ellington;* the set with Alice Babs; two LPs of Ellington-Strayhorn arrangements of big band themes mainly from the thirties and forties; a couple which give Ellingtonian views of current popular songs; and a set of variations on the *Mary Poppins* music. But, as so often, the critics were busy attending to the latest fads rather than listening to the truly creative endeavors in the jazz field. Certainly the Reprise output is a valuable part of the Ellington heritage, full of superb and original music. And one suspects that the archives of this company may yet reveal more unknown treasures.

Sidemen

Alice Babs

Although Ivie Anderson was a great stylist and Ray Nance an incomparable swinger, there can be little doubt that the most gifted vocalist to record with the Ellington band was Alice Babs. Unfortunately she was never a regular member of the organization, being featured only on special occasions. Her continued presence with the band would undoubtedly have inspired Ellington to write fresh material for her. In the event, we have only a handful of recordings to remind us of the important contribution of this fine artist to Ellington music.

Representative Recordings: La De Doody Do (Reprise, 1963), *Serenade To Sweden* (Reprise, 1963), *Heaven* (from the *Second Sacred Concert,* United Artists, 1968), *T.G.T.T.* (from the *Second Sacred Concert,* United Artists, 1968), *Spacemen* (Phontastic, 1973)

Mercer Ellington

Duke Ellington's son had occasionally written for the band and occasionally deputized for absent musicians, but it was not until January 1965 that he joined on a permanent basis. A multiinstrumentalist, Mercer concentrated on the trumpet from the time he joined the band. He acted purely as a section man and never took a solo. For this reason, there is no list of representative recordings. Mercer's greatest value to Duke was as band manager, taking a good deal of responsibility off the older man's shoulders. After his father's death, Mercer took over the band, but the personnel changes were so extensive that he was soon fronting what was in effect a totally different orchestra. To get an impression of Mercer Ellington's talents and abilities it is necessary to hear the recordings he made before and after his spell with Duke, these talents being more in the directions of bandleading and arranging than as a soloist.

Herbie Jones

Like Mercer Ellington, Herbie Jones served as a player in the Ellington trumpet section. He was a negligible soloist, but a fine section man. He also served as band librarian during his five-year stay.

Representative Recording: Jam With Sam (Verve, 1966—Herbie Jones plays the penultimate trumpet solo)

John Lamb

After the sequence of Jimmy Woode, Aaron Bell, and Ernie Shepard, the quality of the Ellington bass line was maintained with the arrival of John Lamb. Lacking Shepard's drive and verve, Lamb fulfilled the requirements of an Ellington bass player in a quieter manner. But it was a manner which was wholly effective, not least in the skilled harmonic judgment which was so essential a part of the Ellington bassist's function. The taste and vigor of his bass lines and the modest way in which Lamb placed his virtuosity at the service of the band were equally admirable.

Representative Recordings: Step In Time (Reprise, 1964), *West Indian Pancake* (Verve, 1966), *La Plus Belle Africaine* (Verve, 1966), *Bluebird Of Delhi* (from *The Far East Suite*, Victor, 1966)

Ernie Shepard

Duke Ellington was more than usually enthusiastic about the bass and drum team of Ernie Shepard and Sam Woodyard. He likened the bassist to Jimmy Blanton "with an added bop flair" and responded warmly to the humor inherent in Shepard's playing. Not many of the strong bass solos with vocal effects which Shepard liked to play have survived on record, but there is a good one in *Take The "A" Train* on the *Violin Session* and another on the Paul Gonsalves *Tell It The Way It Is* LP on the Impulse label, in the course of a performance of *Duke's Place* (alias *C Jam Blues*). His powerful work in support of the band can be heard on a great variety of LPs, and one suspects that the attitude shown by Shepard in placing his skills at the service of the music rather than courting the favor of the jazz public by virtuoso displays will be recognized more in the long term than it was during his lifetime. Shepard's health was a source of great concern to Ellington, and the bassist was forced to leave the band midway through the 1964 European tour. He died in Germany shortly afterwards.

Representative Recordings: Lay By (from *Suite Thursday*, Reprise, 1963), *String Along With Strings* (Reprise, 1963), *Duke's Place* (Paul Gonsalves group, Impulse, 1963)

Cootie Williams

When Cootie Williams returned to the Ellington band in 1962, he was greatly changed from the musician who had left some twenty years earlier. As an artist he was recognizably the same, the musical personality being wholly consistent, but gone was the youthful, thrusting style of the early years. In its place we found a trumpet style of controlled passion, one which turned the technical problems of advancing age to advantage with a commanding majesty of tone and phrasing. And the emotional content, now matured with the years, was if anything even more compelling than in the past. Cootie's muted playing now lacked the endless variety of tone coloring found in his early work, but its effectiveness can be judged by the short solo he takes on the 1963 recording of *Pyramid,* a powerful passage which crucially affects the climate of the performance. The richness and depth of tone and the rhythmic potency heard in Cootie's solos from his second period with Duke give some idea of the effect he had on the Ellington trumpet section. The discipline of this section was greatly improved with the return of this veteran musician. Williams's contribution to the last years of the Ellington Orchestra could be said to be a "pure" form of artistry, full of innate and powerful musicianship.

Representative Recordings: New Concerto For Cootie (Reprise, 1963), *Tutti For Cootie* (Reprise, 1963, and United Artists, 1969), *Echoes Of Harlem* (Reprise, 1963), *Fly Me To The Moon* (Reprise, 1964), *Take The "A" Train* (Victor, 1966, and United Artists, 1969)

Chapter 28

The Records—1966 to 1967

DUKE ELLINGTON HIMSELF WOULD HAVE regarded his three *Concerts Of Sacred Music* as the most important works of his last years. Many Ellington connoisseurs, however, would nominate instead his three major concert suites from the period—*The Far East Suite,* written in collaboration with Billy Strayhorn in 1964 (although not recorded until 1966); the *New Orleans Suite* of 1970; and the *Afro Eurasian Eclipse* recorded in 1971 (but not released until 1975). There were, of course, other late works of importance, ranging from full suites like the *Latin American Suite* and shorter concert works like *La Plus Belle Africaine* and *Pretty Little Purple Flower* to pieces of three or four minutes duration such as *4.30 Blues* and *Intimate Interlude.* During these years, Ellington's creativity was in full flow, but the standard of the Ellington Orchestra showed a slow, sad decline. As an ensemble it was so far ahead of any competition that it remained the best big band in the jazz field until almost the end. But in these final years the descent from the heights of the marvelous 1965 band was one of increasing momentum.

Ellington's first recording of 1966 was the soundtrack for the Frank Sinatra film *Assault On A Queen,* but this has never been issued on LP. It was Norman Granz who obtained this commission for Ellington, and the score was recorded by a mixture of Ellington musicians and West Coast studio men, including such well-known jazz musicians as Conte Candoli, Buddy Collette, and Bud Shank. Duke was not pleased with the final result, and what both he and Sinatra considered the climax of the score was never used. Ellington kept a tape of this part, so perhaps it (along with the rest of the soundtrack) may be issued at some future time.

* * *

In February 1966 Ellington was invited to open the second wing of the restored Chateau Goutelas in France. This medieval building had been rebuilt by an assorted group of devotees, ranging from local peasants to world-famous artists, as a permanent home of the arts. The effort had been wholly humanitarian, and the way in which artists and artisans, Catholics, and communists had been involved was to Ellington a wholly admirable example of fruitful and selfless cooperation. He was greatly moved by the invitation and hugely delighted by the piano provided for his inaugural recital—a nine-foot Steinway. For the inauguration he dedicated his 1945 composition *New World A-Comin'* to Goutelas, and during the course of his speech he described the composition as referring to "a future place, on earth, at sea or in the air, where there will be no war, no greed, no categorization, and where love is unconditional, and where there is no pronoun good enough for God." Five years later, Ellington premiered *The Goutelas Suite* in New York, a further tribute to an enterprise which had embodied so many of the qualities he valued most.

A recording of the Goutelas performance of *New World A-Comin'* has been issued on the obscure President label, and Ellington's commitment to what he understood the situation and the music to stand for is obvious. No less obvious is his love of this Steinway piano, which he described at the time as the best on which he had ever played. This is the finest recorded performance of *New World A-Comin'*, one in which Duke's gentle tonal world indeed seems quite visionary. The performance takes up one side of the LP, the reverse containing the remainder of the Goutelas recital, the *Medley of Popular Hits,* slightly revised for solo performance. The fact that Ellington chose to perform this *Medley* at Goutelas shows clearly enough that, whatever his critics might think, for him it was anything but a hackneyed and catchpenny commercial offering. Ellington has never been heard to better effect as a ballad player than on this record, and he concludes the *Medley* with a vigorous performance of *Caravan.* The beauty of his touch and the subtlety of his chording are very evident throughout the Goutelas recital, and despite the short playing time this LP must be regarded as one of the best examples of Ellington the pianist on record.

A couple of live concert recordings by the Ellington band come from this time. These are the versions of *Magenta Haze* and *El Viti* which have been released on the MF label. The former reveals a more basic approach by Johnny Hodges when compared with the mid-forties recordings. The second piece is a Cat Anderson vehicle on which the soloist displays his skill and humor against a faintly mocking Spanish background.

* * *

Back in the United States the band recorded the third Ellington LP under the new Victor contract. This was done in May 1966 and entitled *The Popular Duke Ellington.* For this set, which rather disappointingly consists of remakes from the most familiar parts of the Ellington repertoire with only one new piece, the personnel consisted of:

Trumpets: Cootie Williams, Cat Anderson, Mercer Ellington, Herbie Jones.

Trombones: Lawrence Brown, Buster Cooper; Chuck Connors (bass trombone).

Reeds: Russell Procope (alto sax, clarinet); Johnny Hodges (alto sax); Paul Gonsalves (tenor sax); Jimmy Hamilton (clarinet, tenor sax); Harry Carney (baritone sax, clarinet, bass clarinet).

Rhythm: Duke Ellington (piano); John Lamb (bass); Sam Woodyard (drums).

The opening track on *The Popular Duke Ellington* is *Take The "A" Train* with a long and excellent piano solo, which starts in 3/4 time and leads into the standard arrangement with Cootie Williams featured in the solo previously played by Ray Nance. This is the best opportunity on record to hear Cootie's open trumpet at length since his return to the band, and the immense power and majesty of his playing are very impressive. Although Duke and Harry Carney have important parts in the usual Hodges feature version of *I Got It Bad And That Ain't Good,* one's attention is, as ever, seduced by the sensual beauty of Hodges's tone and phrasing. Something approaching the original medium tempo is used for *Perdido* here, and it is played over an insinuating rock rhythm from Sam Woodyard. The first eight bars are taken as a solo by Chuck Connors, a very rare event, while Duke takes the middle eight in this theme chorus in the absence of Nance, whose special province this had been almost from the start. Carney and Hamilton are also heard briefly, but Anderson and Hodges handle the principal solos. Cat, no doubt in deference to Rex Stewart's original solo, plays in the half-valve style with great skill and effectiveness, while Hodges simply reveals a different aspect of his genius from that heard on *I Got It Bad.* The bass trombone is used to fine effect in the ensembles here, while Hamilton is taking a solo over a richly scored passage when the engineer's final fade-out takes place. This is a new and highly effective *Perdido* to place alongside the many versions of this simple Juan Tizol theme which grace the Ellington discography. In the new version of *Mood Indigo,* Paul Gonsalves and Hamilton have short solos while Russell Procope, with his broad low-register clarinet tone, and Duke, with some fresh piano variations on the old theme, have the principal statements. There are some beautiful, if rather studious, effects in the orchestration here. On *Black And Tan Fantasy,* the second theme is given to Carney's baritone as it had been in the middle forties, but there is really not much new in this version. Instead of the traditional two choruses based on Bubber Miley's original solo, Cootie plays one chorus which turns out to be a variation on Miley's solo from *Creole Love Call.* After Duke's version of his *Black And Tan Fantasy* piano solo, Lawrence Brown has a couple of choruses with plunger, the second a version of Tricky Sam's old chorus; then Procope takes one on clarinet before Cootie returns with a very emphatic version of Bubber's coda.

The Twitch is the blues at a swinging medium tempo with Buster Cooper in emphatic mood and he, Williams (with plunger), and Gonsalves have important parts, but the short solo by Hodges is *the* authoritative statement here, a surpassing display of casual jazz mastery. Both *Solitude* and *Do Nothin' Til You Hear From Me* feature Brown on open horn, the first being a new arrangement with some pleasant Ellington piano, the second simply a studio recording of the version which was being used as a Brown showcase at concerts. *The Mooche* is given some slight changes in voicings, but the substance is the same as before, very close to the 1952 Columbia version. Paul Gonsalves provides a touch of breathy tenor in support of the brass statement of the second theme, and Williams takes over the role of growl trumpeter against the opening and closing ensembles. The main soloists are Procope (in duet with Hamilton in his first chorus) and Brown (with plunger), both receiving fine piano backing from Ellington. The coda is a long and drawn out piece of highly theatrical hokum calling for Cotton Club decor and dancing girls, at the very least.

Sophisticated Lady is presented in a rather arch rendering with lots of Ellington piano, some rather self-conscious variations for the band, and brief, overstylized solos from Hodges and Brown. On *Creole Love Call* the first chorus responses are beautifully played by Anderson, but the plunger solo is taken by Williams. Having already played the traditional one-chorus solo from *Creole Love Call* on *Black And Tan Fantasy,* Cootie here contributes an original two-chorus solo of some power. Procope then plays his traditional solo before the ensemble, and Anderson take us through to the coda.

One imagines that the motive for recording an LP of such well-worn Ellington themes—all except *The Twitch* at least a quarter of a century old—was to get stereo versions into the catalog. Overall, the set is fairly successful musically, but there are occasions where Ellington sounds as if even he is trying to eke out one variation too many from some of the themes. Yet much of the music is of interest and distinction, and, in the case of the three uptempo items, *Take The "A" Train, Perdido,* and *The Twitch,* of a powerful, compelling swing.

* * *

The Ellington Orchestra appeared at the 1966 Newport Jazz Festival; a full LP plus two tracks on a second disc have appeared on the Italian I Giganti Del Jazz label, although the origin of the music is not stated on the sleeves, and the dates of recording given are false. The repertoire is dominated by extremely familiar Ellington warhorses, *Wings And Things* being the only title new to LP, although Hodges had recorded it away from Ellington the previous year.

* * *

A couple of weeks after the Newport Festival, Duke recorded a set of piano solos accompanied by Lamb and Woodyard. These were not released until 1974 when they came out on the Fantasy label as the main part of an LP called *Duke Ellington—The Pianist.* (The LP was to have been entitled *Duke Ellington—The Piano Player*—the phrase which Duke employed to refer to himself on stage, but through a misunderstanding it came out as *The Pianist.*) Each of the previous LPs featuring Duke as a soloist—*The Duke Plays Ellington, Piano In The Foreground,* and *Money Jungle*—had a distinctive musical climate of its own, and this set is no exception. *Don Juan* sets the mood, providing an extroverted, zestful opening. This is one of Ellington's theme-and-variation pieces in which he carefully exploits the full rhythmic, melodic, and harmonic possibilities of a seemingly innocent little tune. Here the examination is carried out at the beginning and end, while the middle section is built on looser, more improvisatory passages. The *Slow Blues* which follows is not of the "low down," "funky" kind Duke could play so well but rather an essay in the twelve-bar form, with rich and very consonant harmonies. It is really a sixties parallel to the orchestral works of Ellington's thirties "blue period" such as *Blue Tune* and *Blue Ramble.* The next piece, *Looking Glass,* is one which also occasions a look into the Ellington past. Connoisseurs of Ellingtonia will recall the piano introduction to the 1942 Victor recording of *I Don't Mind.* This was not only played with a striking rhythmic authority but was also based on a very distinctive phrase. This phrase must have stayed in Ellington's mind to suddenly reappear in 1966 as the thematic basis of *Looking Glass.* It is transformed into a typical Ellington ballad, and his piano exploration is concerned with the melodic and harmonic contours of the piece. This is an excellent example of Duke's piano playing.

The next item, *The Shepherd,* looks forward to the *Second Concert Of Sacred Music,* where it is used as a feature for Williams's trumpet. Here it is presented (in two takes) as a piano solo, and so far as the musical climate is concerned we are on familiar Ellington territory indeed—the blues with a touch of gospel flavor, in this case at a rocking medium tempo. A study of the variations in the two takes reveals once more Ellington's fertile melodic imagination. Comparison with the orchestral version in the *Second Sacred Concert* also reveals a good deal about the kind of orchestral thinking which lay instinctively behind much of Ellington's solo piano playing. *Tap Dancer's Blues* has Woodyard doing a soft-shoe routine on wire brushes in another distinctive Ellington composition, in which bassist Lamb has an important solo role. The long *Sam Woodyard's Blues* is Ellington at his loosest on the blues, improvising chorus after chorus with that seemingly endless fund of melodic and rhythmic invention at his beck and call. To the listener who understands jazz improvisation, Ellington creates an impression of boundless riches. The blues dominate the repertoire of this session and many of the tempos are similar, yet the music does not create a feeling of monotony, but rather one of great variety and richness. Perhaps only Sidney Bechet has explored this idiom with such inexhaustible creativity as that shown by Duke Ellington.

* * *

The later part of 1966 found the Duke Ellington Orchestra in the south of France for the Antibes Jazz Festival, where they accompanied Ella Fitzgerald as well as playing their own sets. The following year Ellington's European concerts were again shared with Ella Fitzgerald. Many critics and Ellington devotees were horrified at this situation, and they made no secret of the fact that they would have preferred 100 percent Ellington concerts. Some of the musicians found this puzzling, and I well remember Harry Carney's astonishment at what he considered an ungrateful reaction to the presentation of what he considered the best band *and* the best singer in the business.

After its early tribulations the Fitzgerald-Ellington partnership had settled into a steady, if musically rather sterile, affair. Ella and Duke frequently toured together now. The routine would often be that Fitzgerald would sing most of her set with her own pianist and rhythm section, plus the Ellington band playing arrangements commissioned for her. Duke would sit in on piano for a final number, usually *Cotton Tail*. From an Ellington point of view, such performances were usually of minimal interest, and that is certainly the case with the recordings made at Antibes in 1966. Much of the music was recorded for Norman Granz's Verve label, and selections by both Ella and Duke have received wide circulation.

Two other guests were presented with the band at this Festival, ex-Ellingtonians Ben Webster and Ray Nance. Ellington's attitude to presenting former associates and alumni at concerts had become rather mixed—his prime consideration seems to have been to ensure that they did not outshine current members of his band. If the idea of the guest appearances was not his own, he could be downright obstructive, as when Barney Bigard, Sonny Greer, and Ray Nance were scheduled to appear with the band at the Newport In New York Jazz Festival of 1972. On that occasion, Bigard played one number (*Rose Room*), Greer accompanied the piano for one chorus—plus an encore which Ellington seemed to resent—and Nance did not even get onto the stage. On other occasions, he seems to have gone out of his way to present old associates in a glowing light; the guest appearances of Wellman Braud in the autumn of 1961 and Lonnie Johnson (a man with real but slight Ellington connections) in 1963 were conducted in Ellington's most graceful manner. His attitude to Webster and Nance at Antibes seems to have been somewhere between the two extremes, and there was some hassling about money which did not exactly enhance the rapport between leader and guests. Webster complained afterwards that Ellington would not explain anything about the numbers he expected him to play but just kept reassuring him, saying, "Don't worry baby, you've got it." This has been interpreted as an example of Ellington giving an old associate the cold shoulder, but, knowing his almost obsessive concern with spontaneity, it seems more likely that he was confident of Ben's ability to produce a first-class performance without preparation.

Perhaps the most successful track recorded at Antibes with Webster and Nance is a version—"totally unprepared," Ellington assures his audience—of *All Too Soon*, with a theme statement by Lawrence Brown, a solo of mixed virtues by Nance on violin, and a totally ravishing chorus by Ben at the peak of his form as a ballad player. A cornet passage by Nance leads to a very untidy and manifestly unprepared ending.

* * *

The tracks by the Ellington band alone from this period are a mixed bag. They find the ensemble in excellent form—not particularly tidy but playing with great fire, emotional power, and swing. The weakest recordings are on one side of the Verve LP, *Soul Call*. The title piece is a short Louis Bellson score which succeeds, as Bellson's pieces usually did, in making the band sound like anyone's but Ellington's. This rather anonymous bit of swing band fare has solos by Paul Gonsalves and Cat Anderson. It is followed by a long version of another, more famous Bellson creation—*Skin Deep*, with Sam Woodyard featured. Who the thousands are who receive such drum solos with rapture at concerts is a mystery, for no one will ever admit to liking them either in conversation or in print. As one might expect, this *Skin Deep* (which lasts 12½ minutes) is received with great enthusiasm and is followed at once by another crowd pleaser from the Ellington book, *Jam With Sam*. The soloists are Anderson, Gonsalves, Brown, Procope, Hamilton, Cooper, Jones, and finally Anderson again, this time at the very top of his range.

Next in order of quality are the titles collected on the other Verve LP, *Duke Ellington At The Cote D'Azur*. Among the showcases here are two unusual ones for the trombonists. Buster Cooper is heard in a score provided for him by Anderson, *Trombonio-Bustoso-Issimo*. This provides an ideal framework for Cooper's driving trombone style. (The only other version of this ever issued was recorded in France by a mixture of Ellingtonians and French musicians under the direction of Anderson in 1965.) The other is what Ellington describes as a "Lawrence Brown collector's item"—*Rose Of*

The Rio Grande. It shows all too well how the ravages of time were affecting the trombonist's lip; this version lacks the piano solo which had given the 1963 Paris recording its distinction.

Cat Anderson is featured in a new concoction of Ellington's entitled *The Matador* or *El Viti*, a piece we have already noted in connection with the recording issued on MF records. Here Cat does his Spanish routine with hints of other aspects of his talent before the high-note climax. A rather perfunctory, if swinging, performance of *Diminuendo In Blue* moves into the Gonsalves interlude, but *Crescendo in Blue* never emerges from it on this occasion and the solo becomes the Gonsalves marathon known as *Blow By Blow*. This is a rather superior example of Paul's extended uptempo blues solos, but there seems no good reason why a fine piece of music like *Crescendo In Blue* should be put aside to make room for it. Ellington, notorious for his lack of concern with what had gone before, maybe did not care that his old masterpiece was torn asunder for the sake of a display of instrumental virtuosity.

Perhaps the most intriguing item on the *Duke Ellington At The Cote D'Azur* set is a long track called *The Old Circus Train Turn-Around Blues,* a piece in the twelve-bar format featuring Hodges with lots of very gutty band work, urged on by Woodyard's driving and insistent drumming. This is one of the most elemental solos from the later part of Hodges's recording career. Ellington plays some very basic blues piano, and at times there seems to be a competition between Duke and Woodyard as to who will issue the loudest grunts and shouts of approval at the way the music is developing. This is an instance of this highly sophisticated ensemble playing rough-hewn jazz of the most basic type. (There is in existence a recording of a lengthy rehearsal for this item which will doubtless be issued on disc some day.) Both the rehearsal and much of the music from the concerts at this festival were also filmed.

* * *

The delights of *Duke Ellington At The Cote D'Azur* are considerable, but the finest of the recordings from this festival are to be found on the reverse side of the *Soul Call* LP. There are only two pieces here: the first, *La Plus Belle Africaine*, was written for the first International Festival Of Negro Arts, held in Dakar, Senegal, in January of 1966. By the following winter, the band had become familiar with the piece and their performances were masterly, having reached the point of perfection without any hint of staleness. The Antibes performance of July is not yet of this quality, being rather less perfect in balance and detail, but is nonetheless full of fire and inspiration. The mood set up by the basic motif is reminiscent in many ways of the dark emotional climate of such early Ellington masterpieces as *Black And Tan Fantasy* and *The Mooche*. The techniques used in *La Plus Belle Africaine* are, however, anything but backward looking; the use of the primary motif as the means of generating melodic material for the three major improvisations by bowed bass (Lamb), baritone saxophone (Carney), and clarinet (Hamilton) is very much of the sixties. The structure is built around three massive ensemble climaxes with shouting brass and clamorous percussion, the whole knitted together on the framework of the perfect understanding in the rhythm section between Ellington, Lamb and Woodyard. The recording balance favors the drums; this is never a happy state of affairs with Duke's band, as the big sound he liked from the drums must be heard as part of the ensemble. Despite the unbalanced recording, the peerless contribution of Woodyard is clear for all to hear; this is one of the performances which shows perfectly the empathy between drummer and pianist.

The texture of *La Plus Belle Africaine* is very sparse; only Carney's improvisation, which introduces new material, is accompanied by the band. The recording issued on the MF label would appear to predate that on Verve. It is a more cautious reading, and Carney's solo is without the final cadenza. But Hamilton's playing is of rare melodic grace and beauty, and this alone makes this interpretation essential listening. The concerts of the following winter found an improvement in the performances of the massive ensembles, particularly in the contributions of Hamilton and Anderson, a superior version of Carney's solo, and a general tightening up of the structure. Should one of these be issued on record, it would become the definitive version of an Ellington classic. Until then, the Antibes recording must retain this honor. It is vastly superior to the recordings from October 1971, for by this time Hamilton, Lamb, Anderson, and most importantly Woodyard had left the band. These performances are distinguished by Joe Benjamin's bass playing and Harry Carney's solo work, but Procope here lacks Hamilton's melodic sensitivity and Rufus Jones's drumming simply does not start to contribute in the way that Woodyard's had done. The 1971 recordings are also much shorter—eight minutes against fourteen—and end rather sadly with Ellington leading the audiences in finger-snapping: by this time, the masterpiece was five years old and Ellington's mind was on newer things. This is obvious from the piano work which, though fine, lacks the involvement and the primitive fire of the earlier versions.

On the *Soul Call* LP, *La Plus Belle Africaine* is followed by the five-minute *West Indian Pancake* and indeed may be said to overshadow the shorter piece in a way which is rather typical of later Ellington. We should never cease to be aware that while in these later years he produced a series of outstanding concert works Ellington also continued to write shorter, more conventional pieces and that these were in their own way just as masterly. *West Indian Pancake* is a singularly happy piece of work with a chirpy, bouncing theme and some driving tenor from Gonsalves, the featured soloist. It may be noted here that, while others were shouting about black power and black art, Ellington simply wrote two masterpieces which reflect different aspects of black culture.

* * *

In December of 1966, the Ellington Orchestra recorded the complete *Far East Suite* for Victor. This was issued on an LP which also contained another new work, *Ad Lib On Nippon*. The personnel was as before, with the important exception that Woodyard is replaced by Rufus Jones. Jones ultimately took over permanently in 1968, but at this time the replacement was temporary. In late March 1967, Jones was succeeded by Bobby Durham, who stayed only until early June; then Chris Columbus took over until late July, to be followed by Steve Little, who stayed until Woodyard returned at the end of September. Jones was a skilled and colorful percussionist on the more exotic type of number but never a swinger in the way Woodyard had been. On all but the pieces with "exotic" rhythms Jones's monochromatic and stolid drumming was a rather unhappy feature of the Ellington band's recordings of this period.

* * *

In many respects *The Far East Suite* is Ellington's most important work since *Such Sweet Thunder*. This is not to overlook the fact that he had created music of this quality since the time of the Shakespearian suite, but rather to emphasize that this was his most consistent extended work since that time. (Only *Suite Thursday* could seriously challenge this assertion, and that is a shorter and different kind of composition, as unsuitable for such a comparison as *The Tattooed Bride* would be with *Black, Brown And Beige*.) Ellington's delay in writing *The Far East Suite* was deliberate, to enable him and Strayhorn to absorb their impressions and thus avoid a mock-oriental pastiche. But it would be impossible to create a work about the orient without some reflection of its music.

The opening title indicates Ellington's stance—*Tourist Point Of View*. Low trombone chords, a figure on the string bass, and much shimmering of cymbals suggest the clatter of an Eastern market or bazaar as Carney enters with a full-blown mock-oriental theme. This is quickly taken up by Gonsalves who acts as guide for the rest of this first movement. This is a wonderful example of Paul's melodic ability, while the richness of the scene is painted by the orchestra in a vivid and evocative manner. John Lamb makes a valuable contribution to the whole suite, and in this movement in particular he plays a crucial role. Anderson leads the climax, which is placed in the middle of the piece, and appropriately it is Lamb's bass which has the last word as the engineer fades the music away. The second movement, *Bluebird Of Delhi*, or *Mynah*, recalls a particular and loquacious creature. Hamilton's clarinet contributes the distinctive bird song and leads the musical development; there is a characteristic plenty of thematic material here, from the somber motif on the trombones at the start to the soaring, expansive theme in the middle part. Williams contributes a hint of the blues in a brief solo, but the ensemble climax is less successful than in some concert versions at which Woodyard was present. *Isfahan* is the most traditionally Ellingtonian of these sketches, a ballad feature for Hodges with a strikingly beautiful theme. In *Depk* we find an example of the kind of Ellington bop phrase heard when Clark Terry was in the band, subjected to a harmonic treatment more typical of the jazz of the sixties. There are some unusual saxophone voicings, some highly spiced chords from the piano, and an ending in which the theme is stripped to its essentials by clarinet and baritone sax.

Subsequent events in Lebanon make Ellington's *Mount Harissa*, with its dedication to the statue of Our Lady of the Lebanon, seem ironic, which it most certainly was not intended to be. This music surges in a typical Ellington way with a fine melody over an exotic rhythmic pattern and a great solo by Gonsalves. There is some rhythmically adroit and highly imaginative piano from Duke, plus a hint of the hammiest tango ever heard lurking just out of earshot. *Blue Pepper* has a rock-and-roll beat, strange scale-based melodies in the ensemble, an elemental Hodges blues solo in the middle, and a recapitulation garnished by Anderson's high-note trumpet. Ellington blends these disparate elements together with characteristic mastery. His portrait of the *Taj Mahal* takes into account, Ellington tells us, the fate of its builder who was imprisoned by his son in a room from which he was able to look out on his creation. It is called *Agra* and is given to the baritone saxophone of Carney, whose massive sound and beautiful musicianship do full justice to the subject. The final movement is *Amad*, a lively, pushing, uptempo piece with incisive piano from Duke, who uses the full resources of his harmonic imagination, both at the keyboard and in his writing for the saxophone team. Lawrence Brown calls the faithful to prayer in perhaps the most unexpected of all his roles with Ellington, that of the muezzin. The second of Lawrence's calls brings the vigorous life of the movement and of the suite to an end.

The contrast between this Ellington Orchestra and that of 1957 which recorded *Such Sweet Thunder* can be seen by the fact that while in the latter all but two of the twelve movements are solo showcases, in *The Far East Suite* this ratio is reversed: two showcases out of eight, although Hamilton's role in *Bluebird Of Delhi* is so crucial that it might almost be considered a third. The increased emphasis on the ensemble is very marked, even though Ellington does employ all his major soloists in *The Far East Suite*. The dominance of the reed soloists is also very noticeable.

The Far East Suite is typical of Ellington music from his last period in many ways. As there could never be the slightest chance of his orchestra performing authentic Eastern music, the question of pastiche is solved by presenting the mock-orientalisms with humor. Note for example the way in which the opening theme of the suite is presented initially in a grandiose, almost pompous, statement by Carney's baritone, followed immediately by a satirical echo from Gonsalves's relaxed tenor. The structure of the suite is loose, and, as was the case with *Such Sweet Thunder*, Ellington often performed isolated movements at concerts. The content of the suite varies widely, from the use of modal structures, which were very much the fashion in jazz in the early sixties, to the twelve-bar blues with rock-and-roll drumming. Of the major soloists Carney, Gonsalves, and Hodges are the most prominent, with Anderson, Williams, and Brown heard briefly. On the tracks on which Ellington plays piano, his contribution is inevitably of crucial importance, but fundamentally *The Far East Suite* is an example of Ellington using the ensemble as the basic mode of expression. This is a suite of great musical richness and one which must rank with the greatest achievements of Ellington's career.

* * *

Although included on the *Far East Suite* LP, *Ad Lib On Nippon* is not part of that work, but a quite separate composition, musically closely related to *La Plus Belle Africaine.* The use of a short piano figure as the fulcrum of the composition is similar to *La Plus Belle,* but the structure and development are quite different. *Ad Lib On Nippon* is divided into two distinct sections, the first being written by Ellington and the second by Jimmy Hamilton. Much of the material in the first part is taken from a composition used for the soundtrack of *Cargo By Air* in 1964 and issued on record as *Suite For Swinging.* The Ellington part of *Ad Lib On Nippon* uses three themes which are developed by the piano with occasional and subsidiary use of the orchestra. Ellington reveals fresh aspects of his piano style; his playing here is of the highest quality. The Hamilton segment of *Ad Lib* is more conventional and is to some extent an anticlimax, although, like everything to which Hamilton turned his hand, it is very well constructed and his performance on clarinet is immaculate. But the outstanding feature of this Ellington dedication to Japan is his own piano work in the first part.

An intriguing item from the 1967 European tour is a version of *Sentimental Lady* (or *I Didn't Know About You*) by just Hodges, Ellington, and the rhythm section. The melodic mastery of Hodges has rarely been better captured than on this apparently off-the-cuff encore, which can be heard on one of the MF LPs.

* * *

Ellington's arrangements with RCA Victor must have been on a nonexclusive basis, as the Juan-les-Pins LPs for Norman Granz indicated. Ellington's relationship with Granz is one of the most interesting aspects of this period. Granz served for some time as Ellington's unpaid manager and asserted that he regarded Ellington as the greatest of all jazz musicians, while holding the view that by the mid-sixties the band was many years past its peak. From his recording policy over the years, it is pretty obvious that Granz's taste in jazz is largely for virtuoso improvisations, often in a jam session context. One fancies that he had little taste for the casual and often sloppy attitudes of the Ellington entourage. It is probable that Granz's greatest contribution to music was the massive recording project he set up for Art Tatum in the fifties, without which the world's knowledge of the great pianist would be so much the less. In our present context the recordings of Johnny Hodges which Granz supervised are of the greatest interest, and many of these throw an interesting light on the Ellington band and its soloists, as we have already seen. With the *Back To Back* and *Side By Side* collections Norman Granz captured one of *the* Ellington peaks in a session which was, so far as Duke's contribution is concerned, unique. Granz never seems to have been fortunate enough to have captured the Ellington band at its finest in the studio, although, in the purchase of the 1959 recording of the *Queen's Suite* after Ellington's death, he did acquire for his catalog an Ellington band performance of the highest class.

Granz's action of enticing Hodges, Brown, and Greer away from Duke in 1951 had ensured that he would not always be in Ellington's good books. According to many sources there was a very serious disagreement between the two men at the time of the Juan-les-Pins recordings in the summer of 1966, which resulted in a distinct cooling off in their relationship.

* * *

Whatever the truth of this somewhat confused affair, Ellington was back working for Granz again in the following year when he and the band took part in a nationwide tour under Granz's famous "Jazz At The Philharmonic" banner. Recordings were made for Granz's Pablo label at these concerts and material from the Carnegie Hall concert of March 26, 1967, and that at the Hollywood Bowl on July 1, 1967, were used as parts of the four-LP Pablo set called *The Greatest Jazz Concert In The World.*

Other artists on the set include the Oscar Peterson Trio, Clark Terry, Benny Carter, Zoot Sims, Coleman Hawkins, T-Bone Walker, and Ella Fitzgerald. Again Ella sings a number of songs with the Ellington band; again the band contributions are of an anonymous nature. Hodges and Gonsalves sit in with the Peterson Trio with a typical Jazz At The Philharmonic sequence and, more tellingly, with T-Bone Walker in a couple of extended blues performances. In their turn some of the other artists join with Duke's band for an odd number. In the manner of Ellington's own concerts, there is a strong emphasis on showcases for the various soloists. Procope has a new blues, *Swamp Goo,* which also has some very characteristic Ellington piano, while Hamilton's clarinet is featured on *Hurdle Girdle* (or, as Ellington announces it, *Girdle Hurdle*). Williams is heard in the band version of *The Shepherd* (here entitled *Night Flock*), Brown has the highly melodic *Rue Bleu,* Anderson produces yet another piece of exotica in *Salome,* Carney is featured on *Chromatic Love Affair,* and Gonsalves does his uptempo act on *Up Jump.* The

Carney and Brown features are excellent Ellington compositions, while *Salome* was contributed by French pianist Raymond Fol and features Anderson on both flugelhorn and trumpet. Gonsalves plays with great virtuosity on *Up Jump*, but the most impressive of these new pieces is *The Shepherd* with commanding playing by Williams over a finely judged orchestral backing. This slow, gospel-flavored music is ideal for the Cootie of the sixties, and he and the band lay down a powerful performance.

Of the more familiar material *The Greatest Jazz Concert In The World* includes a version of *Rockin' In Rhythm* in the standard arrangement, played very fast, with stiff drumming and a very short piano introduction. We hear *Mount Harissa* from *The Far East Suite* in a performance with solos from Gonsalves and Ellington which make for a fascinating comparison with those on the RCA LP. Hodges is featured on what turned out to be Billy Strayhorn's last composition, *Blood Count,* which does not seem to have been given a title at the time of this concert and is referred to simply as *Manuscript* as Duke calls to the band to advise them of the next piece. Hodges plays this piece with great concentration and later obliges with versions of *I Got It Bad* and *Things Ain't What They Used To Be*. Williams has a second feature in the familiar *Tutti For Cootie,* a deeply swinging performance, despite heavy drumming from Rufus Jones. Zoot Sims, Gonsalves and Hamilton are featured in a three-way tenor battle called *Very Tenor,* a medium blues which finds Gonsalves a clear victor with Hamilton a perhaps surprising second. Sam Woodyard is much missed in this type of number. Clark Terry is paired with Cat Anderson on an uptempo Ellington romp called *Wild Onions,* while Oscar Peterson joins the band for *Take The "A" Train,* taking the solo usually allocated to Ray Nance or Cootie Williams, but first Duke offers yet another new variation on his opening solo. Peterson's improvisation is quite striking and clearly wins Ducal approval. *Satin Doll* features no less than four saxophone soloists—Benny Carter and Hodges on alto and Gonsalves and Hamilton on tenor. Carter takes the honors here, although all four play well and the brass is positively stinging in the middle eight in the first chorus. Carter and Hodges share a version of *Prelude To A Kiss* in which the competition inspires Hodges to a quite brilliant interpretation. On *Mood Indigo* Procope and Brown (with plunger) play their standard solos. The final guest is Ella Fitzgerald, who is joined by the band at the end of a long vocal set for a version of *Cotton Tail* which will appeal only to devotees of Ella's scat singing.

Ellington, as we know, does not always seem to have liked guests appearing with the band, but there is no strain here as Carter, Peterson, and the others join the ensemble. It is fascinating to hear Carter in an Ellington context, and it is disappointing that there was never any attempt to record him at length with the Ellington ensemble. (He did on one occasion sit in Procope's chair for a couple of weeks while Russell was substituting for an ailing Harry Carney on baritone, but so far no recordings with this personnel have been issued.)

As a chronicle of the Ellington band, *The Greatest Jazz Concert In The World* is an interesting rather than a vital document. The items from the Hollywood Bowl concert are the only issued Ellington recordings with Chris Columbus on drums. There is some excellent music, most notably in the Ellington band items, but most of these last can be heard in superior performances elsewhere. Woodyard is greatly missed here and it is ironic that he can be heard in the non-Ellington part of the set as a member of the trio accompanying Ella Fitzgerald. (Errors abound in the booklet information: the dates are wrong, *Mount Harissa* is shown as *Maharissa, Wild Onions* is shown as *Onions,* and Chris Columbus is omitted from the Ellington band personnel.)

* * *

Ellington's next recording project was yet another step into new territory. He was approached on behalf of the Composers, Authors and Publishers Association of Canada and the Canadian Association of Broadcasters to see if he would mind being "exploited," as he puts it, on behalf of some little-known Canadian composers. He readily agreed, and the result was a couple of recording sessions in July 1967 with groups of Canadian musicians. They played music by three Canadian composers with Duke present as guest piano soloist. The results were issued on an MCA LP entitled *North Of The Border—Duke Ellington In Canada,* which features the music of Ron Collier (who acts as musical director), Norman Symons, and Gordon Delamont. By giving his name to this project Ellington allowed his fame to be used on behalf of these fellow artists—a characteristic gesture. His presence on the sessions was no token affair, and each of the six tracks finds Ellington deeply involved.

Each composer contributes two pieces, one long and one short. Four of these, including Delamont's extended *Song And Dance,* are by a medium-sized group consisting of six brass, two reeds and four rhythm. Collier's extended composition *Aurora Borealis* is performed by a large band of eight brass, six reeds, twelve strings and five rhythm. Ellington has two solos in this performance and at once seems thoroughly at home with its "third stream" idiom. In particular the slow-tempo piano passage is beautifully effective, with characteristic Ellington harmonies. Perhaps the most unusual track, certainly a unique one in the Ellington discography, is Symons's *Nameless Hour,* performed by a string orchestra of sixteen pieces and Ellington's piano. The idiom is a kind of watered-down Bartók: at first isolated string chords are sustained with bare harmonies, then Ellington enters this bleak landscape with detached rhythmic, melodic, and harmonic figures which relate obliquely to the string playing. The music gradually thaws a little in the middle section, and dance-like motifs are heard on the strings; the piano part also expands, but finally both piano and strings return to the stark mood of the opening. Throughout this work, which creates a musical situation different from any previously associated with Ellington, the piano part is of the most perfect rightness; the deep musical knowledge which always lay behind Ellington's debonair manner can be clearly perceived.

The pieces for smaller ensemble also provide musical situations of a kind which Ellington, a man used to creating his own musical problems, rarely encountered, but his response throughout is that of a master. His work on the extended *Song And Dance,* including an excellent unaccompanied solo, is particularly noteworthy. Quite apart from Ellington, this is an LP of considerable interest, but Ellington's contribution transforms it into a unique musical experience. Duke places his immense talent in the service of the composers in a wholehearted way, and the nature of his musical resources which are revealed will be surprising, even to the most knowledgeable Ellington student.

* * *

In August 1967 Duke Ellington played the first of what was to become an annual residence at the Rainbow Grill in New York City. These engagements were unusual in that Duke fronted an Octet, the 1967 version of which featured the following personnel:

Trumpet: Cat Anderson.

Trombone: Lawrence Brown.

Reeds: Johnny Hodges (alto sax); Paul Gonsalves (tenor sax); Harry Carney (baritone sax, clarinet, bass clarinet).

Rhythm: Duke Ellington (piano); John Lamb (bass); Steve Little (drums).

This group made a large number of location broadcasts from the Rainbow Grill. From these an LP has been issued on the Unique Jazz label. For much of their time at the Rainbow Grill the Octet featured the expected tunes with the expected soloists and these make up the bulk of the LP: *Passion Flower, Things Ain't What They Used To Be,* and *Day Dream* for Hodges; *Sophisticated Lady* for Carney; and *Solitude* for Brown. Anderson is the expected soloist in *Take The "A" Train,* but he surprises the listener by playing his solo with plunger mute, while *Mood Indigo* includes a chorus by Carney on bass clarinet. The less familiar numbers are *Tricky's Lick* in a rock-beat version which bears scant resemblance to that on the 1963 *Violin Session; Blues,* which turns out to be the Strayhorn number which was later recorded for Victor as *The Intimacy Of The Blues;* and a snatch of a third new blues called *First Bass.*

* * *

The death of Billy Strayhorn on the last day of May 1967 was a severe blow to Ellington. Their friendship had been deep, sustained by great love and respect. As a memorial to Strayhorn the band recorded an LP of his compositions under the title *". . . And His Mother Called Him Bill,"* which proved to be their last recording for the Victor label. John Lamb and Rufus Jones had left the band by this time; for the sessions done for this LP in New York in August and September 1967, Aaron Bell was on bass and Steve Little on drums. Ex-Ellingtonians Clark Terry, on flugelhorn, and John Sanders, on valve trombone, also appear. The last three titles were done in San Francisco in November; by this time bassist Jeff Castleman had joined and Sam Woodyard was back on drums. For all the playing of the band on the eleven Strayhorn pieces they perform—no sloppy work here—it is Ellington's solo playing of Strayhorn's *Lotus Blossom* which is the most moving tribute. This was recorded as Ellington sat at the piano at the end of a session and started to play as the band was packing up. The extraneous noises add to the atmosphere, especially as the musicians quiet down when they hear the way Duke is playing. The intense emotionalism of the performance can be disturbing to some listeners; it is certainly a most eloquent tribute.

The band numbers include the Hodges feature *Blood Count* (which we have already noted in the *Greatest Jazz Concert* LP), played here with a gripping intensity, and a couple of new numbers in *Charpoy* for Anderson's growl and open horn and *The Intimacy Of The Blues.* This last had been written by Strayhorn for the Octet, and, apart from the backing to Hamilton's clarinet solo, the performance here is by the small group. Anderson has a particularly vehement growl solo, and Brown and Hodges play with typical eloquence, but not the least delightful aspect of the performance is Ellington's ensemble piano contribution.

For the rest *". . . And His Mother Called Him Bill"* consists of remakes of earlier Strayhorn compositions. On the original recording of *Snibor,* Harold Baker had led the ensemble and Ray Nance had played a lyrical, emotional solo; here the bulk of the solo work, much of the lead, and a fair amount of obbligato playing is given to Hodges, whose sound is ideal for Strayhorn's sensuous score. Williams and Hamilton are also heard, and the leader's piano is again very effective. *Boo-Dah* is revived as a vehicle for Clark Terry's flugelhorn in a slightly revised version. Unlike most trumpet players who turn to the flugelhorn, Terry really fills the instrument and both here and on *U.M.M.G. (Upper Manhattan Medical Group)* takes brilliant solos. This last is in an arrangement very close to the 1956 original, with Terry taking over the solos originally played by Willie Cook. *After All* and *Raincheck* are revivals from 1941. The former is a rather simplified arrangement compared with the original and is presented in the form of a showcase for Hodges, whose relaxed and luxurious, lushly toned and highly melodic playing seems here to reflect so many of Strayhorn's musical values. *Raincheck,* another revised version, reminds us that this is *the* band for tone colors; here John Sanders is featured in Tizol's old part and Gonsalves in Webster's, and there is a lot of superlative Ellington piano, including an ending of supreme nonchalance. From 1940 comes *Day Dream,* a Strayhorn ballad which was never really out of the Ellington performing repertoire; here Hodges delivers yet another stunning interpretation.

The remaining two numbers are revivals of fifties Strayhorn tunes. This *Rock Skippin' At The Blue Note* is superior to the original and features Sanders and Williams as well as Ellington and Aaron Bell, while *All Day Long* has a spot of Anderson growl trumpet and some outstanding playing from the saxophone section.

In 1983 French RCA issued a version of *". . . And His Mother Called Him Bill"* with two additional tracks. *My Little Brown Book* is treated as a ballad for orchestra with Brown, Hodges, Hamilton, and Gonsalves—the soloists. Hamilton is featured in *Smada,* which receives a rather unpolished performance by the band. The recording balance on this last item is unsatisfactory, which may have been why it was not used on the earlier editions of the LP.

* * *

One of the surprising aspects of the considerable Ellington output for Frank Sinatra's Reprise label from 1962 to 1965 was that no recording had been made combining the talents of Ellington and Sinatra. After all, Duke had recorded with most of the leading popular singers down the years, and this seemed the logical time for an Ellington-Sinatra LP. Yet it was not until December 1967 that the two artists got together in the Reprise studios. The musical circumstances were, for the Ellingtonians, unusual. The lineup was the expected one—Sinatra plus the Ellington band—but Sinatra also hired Billy May as arranger. With Duke Ellington on hand this does seem more than a little odd. We may conjecture that Sinatra was well aware of Ellington's attitude to such sessions: arriving without any arrangements, hastily remembering songs and rewriting scores in the studio amid an air of inspired chaos. It seems probable that Sinatra knew all about this approach and wanted no part of it. Billy May was the sort of professional who would produce the arrangements on the dot and be on hand to direct as the band ran through the scores. All would then be ready for the singer. This was clearly the pattern followed, and the Ellington band sound uncommonly well rehearsed. May acted as musical director on this session and was in charge of the normal Ellington band personnel, except that Al Porcino was added on trumpet and the drummer was William Miller. The sleeve note writer's descriptions of the recording sessions as having Sam Woodyard on drums are clearly erroneous. May obviously knew his Ellington musicians; his choice of soloists and of lead voices in the reed section is made with real understanding.

In essence this is a Sinatra collection with the Ellington band in a secondary, accompanying role. Only one Ellington song is included, which is rather surprising; even more surprising is the fact that this is *I Like The Sunrise* from *The Liberian Suite.* May's arrangement, perhaps inevitably, lacks the rightness of the old 1947 score, and Harry Carney's solo baritone, which had been so perfect in the theme statement on the original recording, is not used. There are touches of Ellington color from Williams and Brown and some excellent work from Gonsalves. Sinatra handles the vocal line with professionalism, sounding indeed like the kind of romantic baritone which Ellington had always tried to hire for the band.

The other songs are a typical Sinatra selection—*Follow Me, Sunny, All I Need Is The Girl, Indian Summer, Yellow Days, Poor Butterfly,* and *Come Back To Me.* Most of the leading Ellingtonians are heard in short solos or in important ensemble parts, but nowhere is there any music of a distinctly Ellington stamp. There is a certain droll humor in being able to hear the band on such good behavior, playing in so neat and tidy a manner, but it tells us very little about them other than the rather obvious fact that they could play the precision game with the best when this was required. No doubt Billy May greatly enjoyed his assignment; he indulges in some Ellington saxophone mixtures in places, for example in the middle part of *Yellow Days.* The introduction to *Poor Butterfly* by Hamilton and Ellington is taken from the *At The Bal Masque* version of 1958, but there is no repeat of the wonderful Gonsalves solo which made that recording so unforgettable. The coy sleeve design with photos of the two protagonists as children under the title *Francis A. And Edward K.* suggests, rightly, that the LP consists of the kind of sentimental popular music associated with Frank Sinatra throughout his career. The Ellington pickings, though present, are very meager.

Earlier in 1967 Duke Ellington had contributed a suite of incidental music to a production of T. S. Eliot's play *Murder In The Cathedral.* This is one of the truly obscure pieces of Ellingtonia and there is no evidence that Duke ever recorded any of the six movements.

Outstanding Recordings

1. Goutelas Recordings

New World A-Comin', Medley Of Popular Hits

2. RCA Recordings

THE POPULAR DUKE ELLINGTON
THE FAR EAST SUITE
". . . AND HIS MOTHER CALLED HIM BILL" (The 1983 French RCA edition has two additional tracks)

3. Fantasy Issues

THE PIANIST

4. Verve Recordings, Antibes Festival 1966

Old Circus Train Turn Around Blues, La Plus Belle Africaine, West Indian Pancake

5. Newport Jazz Festival Recordings 1966

Wings And Things

6. Pablo Issues—from The Greatest Jazz Concert in the World

The Shepherd (Night Flock), Mount Harissa (Maharissa), Take The "A" Train (with Oscar Peterson), Prelude To A Kiss (with Benny Carter)

7. MCA Recordings

NORTH OF THE BORDER (with the Ralph Colier Orchestra)

8. Duke Ellington Octet Recordings 1967

Take The "A" Train, Tricky's Lick, The Intimacy Of The Blues (Blues)

9. Concert Recordings Issued on MF Records

La Plus Belle Africaine (1966), Sentimental Lady (1967)

Chapter 29

Billy Strayhorn

OF ALL MAJOR JAZZ MUSICIANS, Billy Strayhorn was the one least concerned with popular acclaim. Although a fine pianist, he rarely appeared in public and was quite content to play a back room role in the Ellington organization. He was Ellington's closest musical associate, and his composition *Take The "A" Train* was used by Ellington as his signature tune for over 30 years. Strayhorn contributed many compositions and arrangements to the band, working as cocomposer and coarranger on countless more, including many of the concert suites. Only in rare instances, an example being *The Perfume Suite,* do we know which parts of a collaboration are by Strayhorn and which by Ellington. The fact that musicians and knowledgeable Ellington specialists often cannot tell which parts were written by Billy and which by Duke is the most eloquent testimony to the quality of Strayhorn's contribution.

Although he was a major Ellingtonian (and in some respects a controversial one), Strayhorn's arrival in 1939 did not cause the public outcry heard when other important musicians joined the band. But in 1939, hardly anyone outside the Ellington organization was aware of Strayhorn, and the public began to notice his presence only when the band started to perform his compositions a couple of years later. This quiet way of entering the Ellington fold and becoming an important force in the music was wholly characteristic. Strayhorn was a quiet, retiring man, and his music often reflected his unruffled modesty.

* * *

Ellington referred to Strayhorn as "my writing and arranging companion." Billy's function in the organization was not simply to produce a given number of compositions or arrangements. He acted as resident consultant to whom Ellington could refer his problems. The pattern of cooperation was described by Strayhorn in a 1958 interview with Sinclair Traill:

> we don't have any set routine at all. It can more or less happen in any number of ways. Sometimes Duke will say or play something, or maybe while playing between sets at a dance he'll play something at the piano, and if I ask what is that, he'll say that's my new tune. We'll discuss it briefly and then probably do nothing more about it for six months—until one day he'll say all of a sudden that he'd like to do the tune, or tell me to do it, or even sometimes he'll just do the whole thing himself without saying anything to anyone. Sometimes I write a tune I know will be better if Duke did the arrangement. So I just say, I think you should do this, the tune fits you better than it does me; and he does it. (*Billy Strayhorn—An Interview* by Sinclair Traill, *Just Jazz 3,* edited by Sinclair Traill and Gerald Lascelles, pp. 45–46)

When Strayhorn was first engaged, Ellington looked on him primarily as a lyricist. Soon after he had joined, Billy found himself alone in New York while the band was on a European tour. He used the time to study Ellington's scoring and observed Ellington's working methods closely both before and after the tour. By the time Ellington began to use him as arranger for contingent dates, Billy already had a firm grasp of Ellington's way of working. The scores clearly met with Duke's approval, as he was soon writing for the full band. In the early forties, his arranging and compositional output was boosted by the ASCAP dispute with the radio industry. This dispute made it impossible for Duke to use his own compositions on the air, and new material was needed to fill the gap—material which was quickly provided by Strayhorn.

Another useful aspect of Billy's talents was his availability as deputy pianist. These varied skills made him an ideal person to act as assistant to Ellington, and his disdain for fame stilled any fears Duke might have had about setting up a future rival. The Ellington-Strayhorn partnership developed into one of deep respect and affection as well as a unique musical collaboration. Strayhorn also quickly gained the respect and the liking of most of the Ellington bandsmen, in itself a very considerable feat.

In being able to delegate responsibility to Strayhorn in various ways, Duke was able to take some of the weight off his own shoulders, although there is nothing to indicate that his activities in music diminished as a result of Billy's arrival. Most other bandleaders employed what was known as a "straw boss," a senior musician who could handle the musical side of things, taking rehearsals and generally doing the routine musical tasks which the leader was happy to leave behind. For example, Earle Warren performed those duties for Count Basie, and Budd Johnson for Earl Hines. For an artist of Ellington's seriousness and methods, this kind of delegation would have been unthinkable. While other leaders disciplined their bands to put on a show of flashy playing and to concentrate on precision, Duke's musicians often played in a seemingly sloppy, overly casual fashion. This could give the impression of anarchy, but in musical matters Ellington was leader in fact as well as in name. He held the reins lightly, and indeed it is said that at different times each of the Ellington star sidemen felt that he was *the* key man in the band. A musician was allowed to indulge this feeling until it was seen to conflict with what Ellington saw as the vital interests of his band; then the musician quickly learned the error of his ways. It is no coincidence that the one musician who acted as deputy leader of the Duke Ellington Orchestra was a modest man, quite free from any such delusions.

No man, no matter how self-effacing, could perform Strayhorn's role and be a second-rate artist, a pale reflection of Duke Ellington. Billy's artistic personality was different from Duke's. They had some things in common: a great zest for life and a love of the kind of music which reflected this zest; a pervasive sensualism and a liking for rich and many-layered orchestral color; a total mastery of writing for jazz orchestra; and a way of making musical statements of powerful import in an indirect, unsensational manner. On the other hand, Strayhorn did not share Ellington's love of the primitive. He was not a blues musician in the traditional sense, although he could make fine music on the twelve-bar sequence. Emotionally he was less wide-ranging than Ellington, an altogether more polite sort of artist without Duke's ferocious lack of inhibition. Strayhorn's world was very much that of sophisticated show business and of the top-class nightclub; his piano playing often hints at the sounds of the cocktail lounge. Much of his writing has a soft, feminine quality which is very different from Ellington's rugged masculinity. An Ellington composition such as *Didjeridoo* from *The Afro Eurasian Eclipse* is of a kind wholly foreign to Strayhorn's muse.

* * *

While most jazz commentators pay tribute to Strayhorn's skills, a minority consider that his presence in the Ellington organization had a debilitating effect, that he diverted Ellington from his "natural" path. It was, of course, inevitable that Strayhorn should have a strong influence on Ellington, working as they did in so close an association. But there are too many "primitive" Ellington blues and stomps written in the decades he worked with Strayhorn to suggest that he had been diverted from the directions he had followed in the pre-Strayhorn years. It is interesting to note, however, that the soft, pastel side of Ellington, so prominent since the early forties, became less important in the years after Strayhorn's death in 1967. The fact is that the Ellington-Strayhorn partnership was so long-standing and at so deep a level of artistic collaboration that it is impossible to say how Ellington's own art would have developed if Strayhorn had not come upon the scene.

That Strayhorn learned from a study of Ellington's own scores and by observing the orchestra at work meant that by the time he started to compose for the band he was doing so from an Ellington viewpoint. His use of Ellington techniques inevitably brought his music very close to that of Duke in many important respects, and this, allied to the fact that even the composer credits are an uncertain guide to which pieces Strayhorn worked on, has caused a good deal of confusion among listeners. Even the presence of Strayhorn's name along with Ellington's in the credits did not necessarily mean that he had any hand at all in the music, for sometimes he would only act as lyricist. In such instances his name might appear on the record label even if the recorded version of the song did not have a vocal. By contrast, a piece might appear with Ellington credited as sole composer though he had done no more than sketch the melody, leaving the rest of the work—including the orchestration—to Strayhorn. In some of the suites, all the movements are attributed to the Ellington-Strayhorn partnership because this is the way the whole work was copyrighted. It must be said that much of this chaos is due to Ellington's easygoing ways in the matter of copyrighting. Such an instance occurs with *The Perfume Suite*. Although written in 1944, the work was not copyrighted until 1963, when the entire suite was registered as by Duke Ellington. Yet it is common knowledge that the whole of the first movement, *Balcony Serenade,* and the lyrics of the second, *Strange Feeling,* are by Strayhorn.

The close interlocking of Ellington's and Strayhorn's work often makes identification impossible. The evidence of the music itself is inconclusive; the two musicians became adept at writing in each other's style, one often finishing off a score which the other had started, while on occasions one would deliberately employ the other's favorite devices. The main characteristics of Strayhorn as an arranger when compared with Ellington are his preferences for a smoother, less grainy texture in the voicings, a love of pastel shadings, fuller harmonization, and less counterpoint. The overall effect is more conventional and, generally speaking, tends to make the strong characters in the band like Harry Carney less obvious in the ensemble textures. Strayhorn's long, sinuous melodies are more chromatic, less folklike than Ellington's, and he liked to score these for the saxophone section with the sensuous tone of Johnny Hodges's alto in the lead part. Uptempo numbers of the *Take The "A" Train* variety tend to be scored in an ultraconventional manner with a light and sophisticated feeling. By contrast, when Ellington writes in a deliberately conventional manner, as in the 1938 *Harmony In Harlem* or the 1958 *Just Scratchin' The Surface,* he goes for a more rough-hewn sort of effect with a deeper, heavier swing.

* * *

The very first Strayhorn arrangements to be recorded were functional, simple scores for the Johnny Hodges unit—a pop tune, *Like A Ship In The Night,* recorded in February 1939, and an Ellington-Hodges jump number, *Savoy Strut,* recorded the following month. A score more characteristic of the mature Strayhorn is the Barney Bigard contingent's recording of *Barney Goin' Easy,* which dates from June 1939. This is an adaptation of *I'm Checkin' Out, Goombye* and it transforms the stomping, rumbustious mood of the full band version into a quiet, smooth and rather introspective piece of chamber jazz—an altogether typical Strayhorn transformation. It is significant that Billy's first scores were written for the Hodges and Bigard units rather than for the more extroverted contingents led by Rex Stewart and Cootie Williams. Most of Strayhorn's subsequent contingent work was with the Bigard unit, which was responsible for three of the earliest Strayhorn compositions to be recorded. The most ambitious of these is *Minuet In Blues* in which the use of canonic devices and eighteenth-century keyboard idioms have a somewhat halfhearted air. Its best moments are in the Stewart cornet solo, and much the same can be said of the other two performances, *Lost In Two Flats* and *Tapioca,* both of which are rather ordinary jump numbers.

The music Strayhorn arranged for the Bigard contingent's 1940 and 1941 Bluebird dates is soft and dreamy in mood. His composition *Noir Bleu* is typical, although *Brown Suede, June,* and *Lament For Javanette* are in similar vein. Strayhorn's arrangement of Bigard's medium-tempo *Ready Eddy* from the 1940 session is rather undistinguished, although the performance has some nice Strayhorn piano work.

* * *

The first score which Strayhorn wrote for the full Ellington Orchestra was *Grievin',* recorded in August 1939. This is a "string-of-solos" arrangement of a blues-flavored Ellington song; the solo routine is effective and Strayhorn's orchestral backings are concise and to the point. A couple of months later the Ellington band recorded two more Strayhorn arrangements—*Killin' Myself* and *Your Love Has Faded*. These are more ambitious scores than *Grievin'* and show touches of Strayhorn's love of rich textures and his tendency towards overelaboration. *Your Love Has Faded* uses the individual sounds of several of the band's leading characters with perfect aptness, while *Killin' Myself* has some delectable orchestral touches which offset the now very dated lyrics. Ivie Anderson sings on both titles, and on *Killin' Myself* she is joined by Strayhorn himself in his only recorded vocal. Despite its positive aspects, *Killin' Myself* is a curiously unbalanced score, indicating that Strayhorn was not yet fully in command of his blossoming talents.

By the time the 1940 Victor contract was under way, Strayhorn had become highly skilled in every aspect of writing for the band. His most famous arrangements from this year are *Chloe* and *Flamingo,* neither song being of the type to commend itself to the jazz lover. *Chloe* is a study in contrasting colors and textures and is a masterly achievement; the way in which such diverse solo voices as those of Nanton, Bigard, and Webster are integrated into the orchestral scoring is very impressive. *Flamingo* became a best seller, *the* best seller among the recordings which Ellington made of songs by other writers. Strayhorn's arrangement is distinctive and imaginative, but its overall effect is rather insipid. It is an example of the kind of writing which has caused some observers to regard Strayhorn's art as hollow, or at best soft, at the core. On an emotional level, *Flamingo* is a piece of floundering sentimentality, and its musical density is much lower than is the case with Ellington's popular song scores.

The strong grasp of Ellington's methods continued to be a feature of Strayhorn's writing, but his tendencies toward overelaboration and a soggy sentimentality were also sometimes manifest. This last became a permanent characteristic of his work and was a prime factor in causing his art to be less consistent than Ellington's. There was also a tendency in Strayhorn's early scores toward a rather self-conscious modishness, a deliberate courting of modernity. In a jazz world where fashions and taste are often dictated by a pathetic wish to be up-to-date at all costs, this could be a dangerous attitude. The coda to the 1945 *Esquire Swank* is a good example of this. The number is an Ellington-Hodges composition in the AABA form, but the melodic line is very much of the blues. Strayhorn's arrangement is uncluttered but adds little to the piece, and the discordant coda, which no doubt sounded very modern in 1945, now seems something of an affectation.

Although such tendencies in Strayhorn's arranging had a debilitating effect on the music of the Ellington band, this was never more than marginal. And we should not forget that they were simply aspects of a talent which at its peak could rival Ellington's in its ability to create a concise jazz arrangement or to transform a popular song into a significant work of art. For Strayhorn as an arranger at the very peak of his powers, we can turn to the 1956 recording of *My Funny Valentine*. Here three highly contrasting soloists are used: Jimmy Hamilton on clarinet, Quentin Jackson on plunger-muted trombone, and Ray Nance on open trumpet. In addition to these principal characters Johnny Hodges, Britt Woodman, and Harry Carney are also heard within the ensemble textures. The arrangement is a miracle of light and shade and provides each of the soloists with an ideal backing in just the same way that Ellington was always able to do. The use of the plunger trombone as a major voice in a ballad performance is a bold one, and the introduction of Nance's warm, lyrical open trumpet in the middle of Jackson's chorus is a master stroke. And the orchestral colors glow with that peculiarly Ellingtonian warmth.

***

Turning from Strayhorn's work as an arranger to his contribution as a composer we find a similar balance of qualities and a parallel lack of consistency, at least of the kind of consistency we had come to expect in the music of the Ellington Orchestra. Although Strayhorn would, like Ellington himself, utilize devices created by other musicians, he was a real composer, not just an arranger patching together clichés from the storehouse of jazz fashion and then claiming the result as an original work. His most famous composition, *Take The "A" Train,* was one of the very first he wrote for the Ellington band. For all its conventional sounds—and we should be aware that for Strayhorn it was a deliberate essay in the then-popular Fletcher Henderson style of big band writing—it achieves a musical standard appropriate to the Ellington band of 1941, in itself a very considerable accomplishment. Although recorded by the Ellingtonians in a multitude of guises over the years, the original 1941 Victor version of *Take The "A" Train* provides a perfect realization of Strayhorn's score in a performance full of punch and vivacity.

Strayhorn's uptempo swing numbers were the most obviously vigorous aspect of his writing, and in this category he produced work of considerable variety in terms of both content and quality. The great success of *Take The "A" Train,* a success not limited to Ellington's performances but also including recordings by bands as diverse as Cab Calloway's and Glenn Miller's, naturally led Strayhorn to compose other pieces in similar vein. The most obvious successors of *Take The "A" Train* are two numbers written in the fifties which came to be used mainly at the Ellington Orchestra's dance dates—*Smada* and *Boo-Dah.* Both have their melodies played by low saxophones against punching trombone and trumpet figurations as the basic ensemble sound. *Smada* is a feature for Jimmy Hamilton's clarinet, and on the 1951 recording the band is clearly lifted by Louis Bellson's spirited drumming. *Boo-Dah* was recorded three years later by a rather less inspired band, but it is the more varied of the two scores. Hamilton's clarinet and Ray Nance's open trumpet have solos, and there is an amusing incursion by Cat Anderson's high-note trumpet just before the reprise of the main theme.

The fact that he waited ten years before writing another piece in the style of *Take The "A" Train* indicates that Strayhorn was not interested in turning out pieces to an established pattern, although *Smada* and *Boo-Dah* show him to be well capable of doing this. In September of 1941 the band recorded *Clementine,* an uptempo Strayhorn composition of somewhat more individual cast. The main theme is supple and sprightly and has a nicely contrasting middle eight. The reed voicings used here are typical of Strayhorn, as is the scoring for the trumpet section behind Hodges's solo. Nance is given a four-bar lead-in to Rex Stewart's cornet solo, a most effective device. The band is swinging powerfully as Rex's solo develops, and Sonny Greer's drumming is at its most inspired and inspiring. This recording of *Clementine,* with its fine arrangement and swinging performance, is among several which completely refute the assertion, made by uninformed commentators, that Strayhorn was incapable of creating work which was both original and in the jazz tradition.

One of Strayhorn's most complex scores at fast tempo is *Raincheck,* which dates from 1942. Here he investigates a number of Ellington's favorite textures as well as creating a few of his own. The theme statement is given to Tizol, and there is some fine writing for the saxophone section, with Ben Webster used as a lead voice; Carney can be heard in the section playing with a soft, Websterish tone. As is usual with Strayhorn, the use of the trombones is impressive. This must have greatly pleased Ellington, himself very partial to the sound of this section. Strayhorn's sensitivity to the styles of the individual musicians is well displayed here in the way his saxophone writing so perfectly sets up Nance's entry. Indeed, Strayhorn's total mastery of reed section writing is notable throughout a score which is packed with vivid incident.

The understanding of the Ellington musicians which Strayhorn developed during his first years with the band is heard in the way he places and accompanies the contrasting trombone solos of Lawrence Brown and Tricky Sam Nanton in *Johnny Come Lately* (1942). This is a vigorous, punching score, but when it was presented at the January 1943 Carnegie Hall concert (as *Stomp*) it was given a much less successful companion piece entitled *Dirge.* Although beautifully scored, *Dirge* is very undistinguished melodically. It is a funeral march for jazz orchestra and has a curiously unfinished, workshop quality. Unlike *Johnny Come Lately* it failed to survive in the repertoire.

The most interesting of Strayhorn's later uptempo stomps are *Midriff* (1945), *All Day Long* (1951), *Rock Skippin' At The Blue Note* (1951), and *Upper Manhattan Medical Group* (1956). Neither *All Day Long* nor *Rock Skippin' At The Blue Note* are among Strayhorn's most successful scores, the former finding him almost losing the theme in the busy accompaniment, in contrast to the usual lucidity of his writing. *Rock Skippin' At The Blue Note* is a rather unconvincing piece despite its jaunty theme and punching trombone figures. Ellington's brief piano solo at the end of the 1967 recording of *Rock Skippin'* suggests that the potential of the piece might have been better realized in solo piano terms; certainly the recorded versions are less than wholly convincing, and the choice of Nance's plunger-muted trumpet as the solo voice in the original 1951 recording seems a particularly unhappy stroke.

By contrast, *Midriff* has enjoyed several good recordings which highlight the clear and distinctive scoring, with the trombones in the kind of rhythmic role which was fast becoming a Strayhorn trademark. The clarinet is used imaginatively in the ensemble, and the chorus for five saxophones—a justly celebrated passage—is a quite brilliant conception. The best recording of *Midriff* is that of February 1956, on which the saxophone section plays with great drive, skill, and warmth throughout the performance. Brown's trombone solo on the earlier and later recordings of *Midriff* is not one of his happiest creations, and the 1956 version gains from having the main solo role taken over by Nance.

Upper Manhattan Medical Group (or *U.M.M.G.* as it is sometimes called) was first recorded at the February 1956 sessions which produced the definitive *Midriff,* and in many ways it is the epitome of the Strayhorn jump number. On the 1956 recording the unusual harmonic pattern is handled with great ease by the band. The trumpets and trombones punch out characteristic Strayhorn figures, and the soloists, Willie Cook and Harry Carney, are provided with perfect orchestral support. Duke Ellington considered that the dancelike nature of this particular piece was a perfect reflection of an important aspect of Billy Strayhorn's personality. It is certainly a beautiful piece of writing for jazz orchestra; the original 1956 recording remains the best, although those done in 1959 with Dizzy Gillespie and 1967 with Clark Terry are also first class.

* * *

There is a group of Billy Strayhorn pieces which lie, in both tempo and mood, somewhere between the uptempo jump numbers and the slow, sensuous tone poems. Two of the most characteristic of these appeared in 1947—*Progressive Gavotte* and *Snibor*. The former is not very gavottelike despite its melodic construction, nor is it very "progressive" in the sense that the word was used in jazz circles in 1947. It is, however, one of Strayhorn's most graceful scores, and it receives a perfect interpretation from the soloists, most notably Harold Baker, but also Hamilton, Carney and Hodges. The integration of the rich and luscious harmonies with the graceful melodic line is superb. *Snibor* is scored in a more straightforward way, and its melodic contours are enhanced by the use of Baker's trumpet as the lead voice in a thickly harmonized ensemble. This 1949 Columbia recording also boasts a very pretty trumpet solo by Nance. The piece was premiered at the December 1947 Carnegie Hall concert under the title *The New Look,* but a recording ban caused a delay of two years before it was recorded commercially.

* * *

Although *Take The "A" Train* is Billy Strayhorn's most famous composition, he was associated in most listeners' minds with a slower, more sensual kind of music. *Day Dream,* on which he collaborated with Duke Ellington for the 1940 Hodges Bluebird date, was the first of many of the richly melodic pieces which Strayhorn was to write for Hodges over the years. *Day Dream* remained one of the most popular of the Hodges showcases, and although the soloist himself never gave a finer interpretation than on the 1940 recording, the later versions, for example that from 1956, have the advantage of full orchestral backing.

Soon after the initial recording of *Day Dream* Strayhorn started to exploit this manner of writing in his full band scores. One of the first and most successful of these is *After All,* recorded in February 1941. The soloists are Brown and Hodges, and the performance is notable for the perfect control and warm lyricism of Brown's trombone playing. A comparison with Ellington's tone poems in a similar vein— *Dusk, Blue Serge*—shows Strayhorn's preference for more nebulous harmonies, for lighter textures and softer colors. The 1967 remake of *After All* treats the piece as a Hodges showcase and uses a different arrangement. It is played at a slower tempo, but Hodges and the band have no difficulty in sustaining the soaring melodic lines.

Among the best known of Strayhorn's tone poems is *Chelsea Bridge,* the first recordings of which also date from 1941. There are in all three 1941 records, two for Victor and one for Standard Transcriptions. The composition was inspired by a painting by Whistler, which Billy discovered to have been of *Battersea* bridge only after his tone poem had been written, titled, copyrighted, and issued on record. On the early versions of the piece, the initial statement of the melody is given to Tizol's valve trombone. His perfect musicianship and unobtrusive personality allowed it to be viewed in an objective light. The changes detailed in Chapter 14, in describing three 1941 recordings, suggest that Strayhorn was undecided about the best layout for this score. In later years *Chelsea Bridge* became a tenor saxophone feature for Paul Gonsalves, one of the few musicians capable of doing justice to this beautifully shaded tone poem.

Among the more controversial of Strayhorn's works are those he wrote for Johnny Hodges following the success of *Day Dream*. These were often considered by the jazz critics to be overly scented confections, and there can be no disputing that in them the composer pushed his art to the very limits of sensualism and, at times, sentimentality. The voluptuous *Passion Flower* is typical of a series which includes such compositions as *Violet Blue* (the original version of *Multicolored Blue*), *A Flower Is A Lovesome Thing* (also known as *Passion*), *Charlotte Russe* (the original version of *Lotus Blossom*), *Pretty Little Girl* (the original version of *The Star-Crossed Lovers*), and *Ballad For Very Tired And Very Sad Lotus Eaters*. Although all these works contain beautiful, soaring melodic lines they lack both the musical rigor and the capacity for development revealed in such Hodges showcases as *Magenta Haze* and *Sultry Sunset*. Much the same can be said of the rather rambling showcase which Strayhorn wrote for Carney's baritone in the late forties, *Paradise*. Here the comparatively austere playing of the featured soloist precludes that sensation of wallowing in sentimentality which sometimes emanates from Strayhorn's pieces for Johnny Hodges.

* * *

It is ironic that although Ellington hired Strayhorn originally as a lyric writer, Billy did not provide the words for any of Duke's big popular song hits. The first song for which Ellington wrote the music and Strayhorn the lyrics was *Something To Live For,* recorded in 1939. This was a lifelong favorite of Ellington's, sure to be cited whenever he was asked about his favorites among his own recordings. Perhaps it was the memory of the pleasure afforded by this first collaboration with Strayhorn which caused him to value the record so highly. *Something To Live For* has a distinctive, rather sad Ellington melody, while Strayhorn's lyric is a skilled piece of writing. The song never became truly popular, no doubt because of the subtle qualities of both melody and lyric. The combination of Ellington as composer and Strayhorn as lyricist also produced *I Don't Mind.* This was recorded in 1942 at one of the last sessions in which Ivie Anderson participated, and it features one of her most sensitive vocals. Here the lyric is of a more conventional kind than that of *Something To Live For,* although very well written, and the melody and the arrangement of the piece are most attractive. Strayhorn's name is also on *Kissin' Bug,* a 1945 pop tune written in collaboration with Rex Stewart and Joya Sherrill. Apparently Billy's main contribution here was the middle eight, Rex having supplied the main melodic motif and Sherrill the rest of the theme. The overall effect is pleasant but commonplace, but the quality of Sherrill's singing, the lively band playing, and the professionalism of what sounds like a Strayhorn arrangement combine to give it some distinction.

The most famous of Strayhorn's songs is *Lush Life,* for which he wrote both words and music, a song which was never recorded by the Ellington band. Its most famous recording is that by Nat "King" Cole, its best probably that by Ella Fitzgerald in the *Ella Fitzgerald Sings The Duke Ellington Song Book* set. *Lush Life* has always been held in high regard by musicians and by connoisseurs of the American popular ballad. It is a highly sophisticated song, its lyrics redolent of the nightclub and high living. By the standards of the sturdy black American musical tradition, it is a decadent product, its chromaticism being a rather pale reflection of European art music of a previous era. It has been compared with the songs of Noel Coward, and perhaps this best indicates the style of the piece and the level of Strayhorn's achievement. *Lush Life* is precious, self-pitying, and morbid, but it is clearly the work of an artist of uncommon skills. It stands alone in Strayhorn's output, a celebrated, slightly pretentious attempt to raise the popular ballad to something closer to the level of art song.

* * *

During the 28 years that Billy Strayhorn was with the Duke Ellington Orchestra he collaborated with Ellington on many, although not all, of the latter's large-scale projects. On the first of these collaborations, *The Perfume Suite,* Strayhorn contributed the first movement, *Balcony Serenade,* and the rather uneasy lyrics for the second, *Strange Feeling. Balcony Serenade* is a very beautiful piece and finds Strayhorn concentrating on melodic statements to the exclusion of any development, the principal melody being repeated over and over by the Hodges-led saxophone section, colored by subtle harmonies and by very discreet brass figures. On the Victor studio recording—the best version—this feast of melody is preceded by a varied and brilliantly conceived introduction which opens with a few telling bars of Nance's expressive open trumpet. There is an orchestral climax leading to a musing passage by Duke at the piano, which in turn leads into the first statement of the principal melody. Duke here concentrates on harmonic probing, ending with a pungent little phrase which leads perfectly into the smooth-textured saxophone writing, a typical Ellington touch.

The exact details of Strayhorn's contributions to the suites on which he worked are rarely specified. It is probable that he had the major role in creating the opening movement of the *Deep South Suite, Magnolias Dripping With Molasses.*

Among the most distinguished of Strayhorn's known contributions to the concert suites is *Northern Lights* from *The Queen's Suite,* one of the most brilliant tone poems ever written for the Ellington Orchestra. This movement can be ascribed to Strayhorn as a result of a remark which Ellington makes in his autobiography. He tells us that the movement was inspired by an experience which befell Harry Carney and himself and which he related to Strayhorn, after which Billy wrote the score. Had Ellington not written this, it is doubtful whether we would have been able to ascribe *Northern Lights* to Strayhorn with any degree of certainty. This would have been unfortunate, for the orchestral writing is of a quality quite unsurpassed in the jazz field. There are no solos, but the use of such distinctive voices as those of Baker, Gonsalves, and Carney is of a sensitivity worthy of Ellington himself. The divided reeds, the clarinet choir, and an assortment of brass textures are handled with a mastery which is equalled by the subtle harmonic usage.

One could speculate at length on Strayhorn's contribution to further concert works, but, lacking any firm evidence, it is perhaps more useful to turn to the one concert piece known to be entirely his own creation, the *Overture To A Jam Session* of 1946. Considered in the abstract, there seems no reason why this should not be a total success. The melodic material is well varied, and the primary theme is particularly distinctive; the functional solos are well integrated into the musical argument, and the scoring displays the usual Strayhorn expertise, especially that for the saxophone section which is characteristically rich. The band plays the work with skill and understanding, particularly on the Capitol Transcription recording of 1947. Yet in performance, *Overture To A Jam Session* is an unconvincing whole, giving the impression of a rambling and poorly integrated creation—a diffuse structure with some outstanding passages. The title is singularly inappropriate, as the composition in no way resembles an overture and the spirit of the jam session is totally absent. The work remains of interest because of the excellence of its parts rather than for its total success as a composition.

Chorus 1	Chorus 2	Chorus 3	Chorus 4	Chorus 5	Chorus 6	Chorus 7	Chorus 8	Coda
8 bars	12 bars	12 bars	8 bars	12 bars	8 bars	12 bars	8 bars	2 bars
Hodges	Hodges	Bailey	Hodges	Hodges	Hodges	Bailey	Hodges	Hodges
alto	alto	vocal	alto	alto	alto	vocal	alto	alto
with	with	with	with	with	with	with	with	with
band	band	band	band	rhythm section	band	band	band	band
ballad	ballad	ballad	blues	blues	blues	ballad	ballad	ballad
style	style	style	style	style	style	style	style	style

* * *

While Ellington worked regularly in the blues idiom, Strayhorn gave this basic jazz form comparatively little attention. His sequence of Hodges feature numbers from the forties included a piece called *Violet Blue,* a soft, dreamy ballad built on the twelve-bar pattern. It was not recorded commercially by the band at this time, although air shots exist and Hodges recorded it for Mercer in 1947. But in 1958 the piece was extended and retitled *Multicolored Blue.* Lyrics were added, presumably also the work of Strayhorn; they are in the sad, self-pitying vein of much of his verse. These lyrics were sung by Ozzie Bailey and placed in a most intriguing and successful setting, again featuring Hodges (see above). The eight-bar choruses are shortened variants and do not indicate a secondary theme. The band accompaniment is of burnished, subtle colors behind Hodges on the ballad sections; of darker, more somber cast behind Bailey's singing; and of a shouting and affirmative nature in the accompaniment to Hodges's blues playing. On the standard recording of *Multicolored Blue*—from the 1958 Newport Jazz Festival LP—Hodges's central solo chorus is accompanied by notably fine bass playing by Jimmy Woode. Harold Baker can be heard playing quietly in the Ozzie Bailey choruses; in later performances he assumed a more prominent role. *Multicolored Blue* represents an unusual use of the blues idiom, and the piece is, except perhaps for its lyric, a Strayhorn triumph.

Although Strayhorn used the kind of growl and muted brass techniques developed by Ellington, he used them purely as coloristic devices and lacked Ellington's interest in their exotic potential. A partial exception is *Swamp Drum,* a rare piece of Strayhorn exotica from 1951. This piece was recorded by The Coronets for the Mercer label, and air-shot versions by the full band also exist. There is little difference between these, however, as The Coronets' personnel contains Strayhorn's principal ingredients: the three trombones and Willie Smith on alto sax. *Swamp Drum* is cast in the conventional 32-bar AABA pattern and contrasts the trombone section, led by Quentin Jackson playing in the muted wa-wa style, with a passage for open trombones with a very prominent lead part by Juan Tizol. Willie Smith provides the decoration *à la* Hodges, and Louis Bellson the mock-primitive sounds suggested by the title. The piece is no more than a pleasant trifle, but it is interesting to hear Strayhorn working in what was for him unusual territory.

The air-shot version issued on LP is notable for some extremely fine Ellington piano.

In 1959, Strayhorn returned to the blues in a piece which sounds as if it may have been written off-the-cuff in the recording studio. This is *Sweet And Pungent,* the bulk of which is taken up by a plunger-muted trombone solo by Booty Wood accompanied by just the Ellington-led rhythm section: this is the "pungent" part of the performance. The "sweet" part is provided in the first and last choruses, which consist of pretty harmonic writing for four saxophones, Hodges in the lead part, garnished by Hamilton's clarinet; in the final chorus Booty Wood joins Hamilton in the ad-ib countermelodies. This may be a rather hastily prepared musical sandwich, but the quality of the ingredients makes it a very attractive one. A later and excellent example of Strayhorn working in the blues idiom is the number called *The Intimacy Of The Blues,* recorded by the band after Billy's death in the "... *And His Mother Called Him Bill*" memorial LP. The gentle nature and acute sensitivity of Strayhorn's artistry are fully apparent in this beautiful piece, which is played with appropriate delicacy by the band. The pain Ellington felt at his companion's death is strongly expressed in his eloquent piano commentary.

The Intimacy Of The Blues is clear enough proof that Strayhorn's creative powers were undimmed by the passing of the years. He had continued to contribute scores of high quality, including the brilliantly evocative nocturnal study *A Midnight In Paris* (1961); the exotic *Absinthe,* with its sinuous melody so wonderfully interpreted by Paul Gonsalves; and the equally colorful *Tigress* (both from the *Afro Bossa* LP of 1961). His final composition was *Blood Count,* played by Johnny Hodges and the band with unearthly devotion on the "... *And His Mother Called Him Bill*" collection. The final track on that LP is a piano solo by Ellington of Strayhorn's *Lotus Blossom.* This Strayhorn composition was first recorded by Hodges for Mercer records in 1947 under the title *Charlotte Russe,* and it was a piece Billy liked to hear Duke play at the piano. All Ellington's grief can be heard in a performance of extraordinary emotional power.

* * *

As a pianist, Strayhorn was an even more elusive figure than as an arranger. He plays on a number of the Ellington

Victors from the early forties, but from then on his appearances on record are few indeed. Among the Victor recordings on which his piano can be heard to advantage is *After All* in which he plays an elaborate decorative part in the ensemble; a comparison with the Standard Transcription recording on which Duke plays is most interesting. Among the best recordings from this period which have Strayhorn piano solos are the two takes of *Linger Awhile* by the Rex Stewart unit, for which Strayhorn also did the arrangement. Both solos show a strong Ellington influence, and that on take-1 has hints of stride piano. Recordings such as this reveal that Strayhorn's touch is lighter than Ellington's, his concept of ensemble piano more decorative, and his individuality less marked. His performances in the style of *After All* inevitably bring Art Tatum to mind, and Art was indeed a great influence on Billy. Duke was also a Tatum admirer, and both men were on close terms with the great pianist. None of this seems to have rubbed off on Duke directly, but Strayhorn can at times sound uncannily like Tatum for a few bars—which is, incidentally, just about as much as anyone has ever managed.

The two LPs which Strayhorn made under his own name offer a very good opportunity to study different aspects of his keyboard work. The later of the two in chronological terms finds Strayhorn in total control of the music. The disc, *The Peaceful Side Of Jazz*, was issued in the United States on United Artists and in Great Britain on World Records. It has never been fashionable among jazz buffs, which is hardly surprising as it contains little of the kind of music which normally appeals to them. It was recorded in Paris in 1961 and consists of Strayhorn piano solos, accompanied on most tracks by a string bass and on some by either a small vocal group, which sings wordlessly, or by the Paris String Quartet. Even numbers like *Just A-Settin' And A-Rockin'* and *Take The "A" Train* are done in a dreamy, rhapsodic fashion; quietude reigns and the atmosphere is more than a little enervated.

All the compositions on *The Peaceful Side Of Jazz* are either by Strayhorn or by him and Ellington. Apart from the two pieces already mentioned, the emphasis is on the rhapsodic ballad: *Lush Life, Passion Flower, Strange Feeling, Day Dream, Chelsea Bridge, Multicolored Blue, Something To Live For, A Flower Is A Lovesome Thing*—even a list of the titles sounds like the reverie of a drowsy, depressed sophisticate. The version of *Lush Life* is most interesting in that it shows that this deceptively recitative-like song can stand up without its celebrated lyrics. Although quiet and introspective, the piano playing is of a very high order, sensitive and thoughtful; the interjections by the vocal group are, however, totally redundant. *Passion Flower* is too enervated to capture the erotic flavor of the Ellington recordings, and even the dissonant harmonies of *Strange Feeling* are played in a gentle manner which suggests no more than a vague, diffuse gloom. *Multicolored Blue* is divested of its blues qualities and sounds insipid. The Paris String Quartet must have been as bored as they sound as they repeat the germ motif of *A Flower Is A Lovesome Thing*. Throughout the LP the piano playing is clearly of a high class and the use of texture and tone color most delicate, although without Ellington's range or vigor. There are Ellington touches, but these are clearly in the employ of a musical personality totally different from Duke's. It is interesting to note that although Strayhorn is an accomplished melodist as a writer, as a soloist he is primarily a harmonic thinker, with little in the way of melodic development in his playing. The overall effect of *The Peaceful Side Of Jazz* is of a highly talented musician without quite the creative drive to bring his work to full fruition. It epitomizes his dreamy, sentimental side.

The second LP recorded under Strayhorn's name, *Cue For Saxophone*, was part of a series for Felsted supervised by Stanley Dance in 1959. The session has many of the attributes of a Hodges small-band date and, although Johnny is present, he uses a pseudonym for contractual reasons. The Billy Strayhorn Septet is a somewhat less stereotyped body than those usually found recording under Hodges's name, and the organizing abilities of the leader make for a well-structured collection of informal small-band jazz performances. One suspects that Strayhorn's name was used as leader only because the disc could not have been put out as by the Johnny Hodges Septet. Certainly this music reflects other personalities as strongly as it does Billy's, and because of this it tells us less about him than *The Peaceful Side Of Jazz*, even though—or perhaps because—it contains a more vigorous and a more varied selection of music. Here Strayhorn is working to a formula—that of creating an LP of "mainstream" jazz—rather than acting as a completely free agent. It is also interesting to note that in this jazz-oriented context the Ellington influence is much more to the fore in Strayhorn's keyboard work.

The disc opens with a long slow blues. Strayhorn plays the first chorus in a very Ellingtonian style and goes on to accompany the soloists in a manner very reminiscent of Duke. Even in his ballad solo on *Gone With The Wind* the Ellington influence predominates. On *Rose Room*, Strayhorn's band piano, especially behind Baker's poised trumpet solo, is an outstanding feature of a great performance. On the fast *Watch Your Cue*, the piano chorus grows out of the bass solo which precedes it, quite taking the listener by surprise. It is a sprightly, discordant little essay, fleet and lively in a style not much like Ellington's. Although Strayhorn is, typically, very retiring, *Cue For Saxophone* contains some of his best piano work on record.

* * *

In previous chapters we have seen that no other pianist could bring the kind of inspiration to the full Ellington band which the leader provided, how the whole ensemble was vitalized by Duke's presence at the keyboard. The recordings by the full band under Johnny Hodges's direction in the fifties are a measure of Strayhorn's abilities as a band pianist, for the ensemble plays far better with him than with any pianist apart from Ellington himself. If Strayhorn fails to galvanize the bands in the Ellington fashion, they do at least play with panache and style; with other pianists they tend to sound either anonymous or like an unblended collection of wayward virtuosos. Such Hodges collections as *Ellingtonia '56* and *The Big Sound,* along with a selection of the earlier Victors and the two fifties Strayhorn LPs discussed above, provide a suitable basis for those wishing to study Billy Strayhorn's piano playing.

* * *

Mercer Ellington has pointed out that Duke Ellington's collaboration with members of his band tended to lessen with the arrival of Strayhorn. Such collaboration had always been an important factor in Ellington's music, and it continued to be so right until the end. But from the middle thirties onward its importance diminished from the status of being *the* vital ingredient to that of being an important aspect of the Ellington method. Its sharpest fall in importance occurred when Strayhorn joined the band, although the musicians themselves quickly accepted Strayhorn and never seem to have resented his effect on their methods of music making.

The Strayhorn tendency towards a rather vapid, soft-centered lyricism may not have been the healthiest of influences on Ellington, but other aspects of his taste must always have been a positive force. An instance of this good taste was Strayhorn's opposition to the nightly presentation of the *Medley Of Popular Hits,* although his influence did not, alas, prevail in this instance. Strayhorn was valued by the Ellingtonians not only for his musical abilities but also for his gentle personality, his sharp wit, and his sense of humor.

As Strayhorn's compositions for the Ellington band number only about 40 pieces written over a period of 28 years we could conclude that he was not a very prolific writer. But we should not forget that much of his time was taken up in arranging and in collaborating with Ellington on a variety of projects, including such major triumphs as *Such Sweet Thunder* and *The Nutcracker Suite.* Among the recollections of Strayhorn's associates there are suggestions that his love of the good life sometimes kept him away from the band and from musical activities, but he was certainly always available to Duke for consultation, even if only by long-distance phone. The lack of vigor in a good deal of Strayhorn's work—that aspect of it typified by *The Peaceful Side Of Jazz*—is paralleled by a lack of creative drive which made him happy to play second fiddle to Ellington for the whole of his career. But even allowing for these factors, and for the unevenness of his output, it is undeniable that his finest work marks him as a major jazz figure.

* * *

For reference purposes, here is a listing of the major Strayhorn compositions mentioned in this chapter along with recommendations as to the best recorded versions. These compositions are by Strayhorn alone; the recordings are under Ellington's name unless otherwise stated:

Something To Live For (Ellington-Strayhorn) (1939), *Barney Goin' Easy* (Strayhorn-Ellington) (Bigard unit, 1939), *Minuet In Blues* (Bigard unit, 1939), *Lost In Two Flats* (Bigard unit, 1939), *Tapioca* (Bigard unit, 1940), *Day Dream* (Ellington-Strayhorn) (Hodges unit, 1940), *Lament For Javanette* (Bigard-Strayhorn) (Bigard unit, 1940), *Take The "A" Train* (Victor, 1941), *After All* (Victor, 1941), *Just A-Settin' And A-Rockin'* (Ellington-Strayhorn) (Victor 1941; vocal version, Carnegie Hall, 1949), *Clementine* (Victor, 1941), *Passion Flower* (Hodges unit, 1941), *Noir Blue* (Bigard unit, 1941), *Chelsea Bridge* (Victor, 1941), *Raincheck* (Victor, 1941), *I Don't Mind* (Ellington-Strayhorn) (Victor, 1942), *My Little Brown Book* (Victor, 1942), *Johnny Come Lately* (Victor, 1942), *Dirge* (Carnegie Hall, 1943), *Midriff* (Bethlehem, 1956), *Kissing Bug* (Sherrill-Stewart-Strayhorn) (Victor, 1945), *Balcony Serenade* (Victor, 1945), *A Flower Is A Lonesome (Lovesome) Thing* (Capitol Transcription, 1946), *Overture To A Jam Session* (Capitol Transcription, 1947), *Lush Life* (Ella Fitzgerald, 1957), *Progressive Gavotte* (Columbia, 1947), *Snibor* (Columbia, 1949), *Violet Blue* (original version) (Johnny Hodges, 1947), *All Day Long* (Capitol, 1954), *Rock-Skippin' At The Blue Note* (Columbia, 1951), *Smada* (Columbia, 1951), *Swamp Drum* (broadcast, 1951), *Boo-Dah* (Capitol, 1953), *Upper Manhattan Medical Group* (Bethlehem, 1956), *Multicolored Blue* (Columbia, 1958), *Northern Lights* (Pablo, 1959), *Sweet And Pungent* (Columbia, 1959), *Midnight In Paris* (Columbia, 1962), *Lotus Blossom* (Victor, 1967), *Absinthe* (Reprise, 1963), *Tigress* (Reprise, 1963), *Pretty Little One* (Violin Session, 1963), *Blood Count* (Victor, 1967).

For those requiring a one-volume collection of Strayhorn compositions, the 1967 LP *". . . And His Mother Called Him Bill"* contains eleven representative pieces played by the Ellington Orchestra plus the Ellington solo recording of *Lotus Blossom;* the 1983 reissue on French RCA has two extra tracks.

Chapter 30

The Records—1968 to 1974

TOWARD THE END OF JANUARY 1968, the Duke Ellington Orchestra played a concert at Yale University, and seven years later an LP was released on the Fantasy label called *Yale Concert*. For all but the trio item *Boola Boola*, the recordings used by Fantasy come from a studio session done a month after the concert. The Ellington personnel is unchanged, and the LP finds the rhythm team of Jeff Castleman and Sam Woodyard in exceptional form. The repertoire is unhackneyed, although some of the newer items were subsequently released in earlier versions in the Pablo album *The Greatest Jazz Concert In The World*, recorded the previous year. Of these, *A Chromatic Love Affair*, *Salome*, *Swamp Goo*, and *Up Jump* all appear here in performances which either equal or surpass those on Pablo. *Up Jump* gains much from Woodyard's presence and *Swamp Goo* receives a notably fine performance. The highlight of this LP is unquestionably *The Pretty Little Purple Flower*, an otherwise unrecorded Ellington composition in two movements. (Originally only the slow first part of this work was known as *The Pretty Little Purple Flower*, the second part having only the code name *Eggo*.) Although Carney's distinctive voice is used as an individual element in the ensembles there are no improvised solos in either part, the main role being taken by Ellington at the piano. The slow opening movement is divided from the uptempo second part by a speech in which Ellington tells the audience the story of *The Pretty*

Little Purple Flower from her origins by the roadside, via the medical school, to the company of "the pleasure seeking set." The chat ends with a dreadful Ellington pun quickly followed by the opening of the second movement. Ellington's playing is brilliant in both sections; few individual performances give such a clear idea of the range of his keyboard mastery. Sam Woodyard swings the band mightily in the second section and delivers the percussive effects with a Greer-like sense of color throughout both movements. Apart from the *Second Sacred Concert,* this is Woodyard's last recording with the band and it is doubtful whether he has ever been heard to better effect on record.

Another highlight of this LP is a version of the Yale fraternity song *Boola Boola* played as a piano solo by Ellington with bass and drums. The piece receives a characteristically humorous rendition, and Ellington's piano swings with great power. *Put-tin* for Cootie Williams and *Drag* for Johnny Hodges are new compositions. They are both swingers, powered by Woodyard's drumming, with the soloists at the peak of their late sixties form. Hodges also plays a sensitive version of *Warm Valley*. Williams closes the LP with a version of *Take The "A" Train* which must be just about the slowest interpretation on record of the standard arrangement. *Yale Concert* is a collection which shows just what a healthy state the Ellington band was in at this time. It is one of the most happy and successful of the last years.

Duke Ellington's first *Concert Of Sacred Music* seems to have been rather hastily thrown together. His third such concert, premiered in the last weeks of his active career, also sounds hastily written and underprepared. Much more time—including rehearsal time—was clearly given to the *Second Sacred Concert* before it was recorded as a two-LP set by United Artists in January 1968. Unlike the first such concert, this work consists entirely of new material. For the recording the band is augmented by extra brass—Money Johnson (trumpet) and Benny Green (trombone)—and percussion—both Steve Little and Sam Woodyard are present. Also featured are the A.M.E. Mother Zion Church Choir, the Choirs of St. Hilda's and St. Hugh's School, the Central Connecticut State College Singers, and the Frank Parker Singers. Five solo vocalists are cited on the sleeve, but only two of these have important roles—Alice Babs and Tony Watkins. Alice Babs visited the United States especially to take part in this recording and in a group of live performances of the *Second Sacred Concert*. Watkins was a new and regular member of the Ellington entourage, having moved by mysterious ways from band boy to principal singer. For this recording no fewer than seven "assistants" are acknowledged, including choir and vocal trainers who had rehearsed the choirs at length while the band was on tour.

The pattern of the *Second Sacred Concert* is loose, and the sequence clearly designed to serve as an informal church service. This work contains Ellington's most successful writing for a choir. Although he was unable to stress particular individuals as he could when writing for the band, Duke's distinctive harmonic sense is clearly at work, and the choral writing sounds more Ellingtonian than is the case with earlier works; it would appear that more care was taken with the writing here than with either *A Drum Is A Woman* or the first *Concert Of Sacred Music*. The lyric writing remains uneven, and this second concert suffers, as almost all Ellington's verse does, from some naive, sentimental passages unrelieved by the cutting edge of his sardonic humor.

The *Second Sacred Concert* opens with a short instrumental piece, *Praise God;* after a fast introduction the tempo cuts to slow and Ellington's very beautiful and original theme is played by Carney on baritone sax, his majestic sound enhancing even this strong melody. The second section, *Supreme Being,* opens with Ellington depicting, via the orchestra, the biblical concept of pre-creation chaos. This is a very effective passage, using a kind of slowed-down *Madness In Great Ones* style of writing, enhanced by some adventurous harmonic devices. It is followed by one of the less successful passages, which forms the middle part of *Supreme Being*. In it the choir chants a long and naive Ellington poem on the subject of creation. The rhythm, pitch, and dynamics of this mass chanting are scored, and the result can seem to some listeners like someone shouting aloud to reassure himself about his faith, although this was clearly not Ellington's intention. In the middle there is a poem for one voice called *Sonnet Of The Apple*. That this is not a sonnet matters less than the dreadful style in which it is written. It is supposedly spoken by the apple from the tree of knowledge. The last two lines epitomize the coy style:

That cute little old snake made that pretty lady bite me,
And things ain't really been the same since.

It is almost a relief to get back to the choir chanting about the "Immortal Creator and Ruler of the Universe" after this. *Supreme Being* ends with a second instrumental passage which is in a sweeter and more cohesive style than the opening and includes a prominent role for Jimmy Hamilton on clarinet.

Alice Babs is introduced in a song called *Heaven,* the full melodic qualities of which are expounded by that supreme melodist Johnny Hodges before Babs returns, singing over a Latin beat in contrast to the recitative-like quality of her first vocal. Even when heard alongside Hodges, the melodic qualities of Babs's singing stand out as does her perfect pitching of the notes of this beautiful Ellington theme.

Next comes a long choral movement, *Something About Believing,* which has some fine writing for the band, mainly in a supporting role. Duke takes the introduction on electric piano, and Paul Gonsalves and Benny Green are heard in support of the singing at different points. A particularly swinging tempo is set for this movement and a notable feature of the performance is the excellent bass playing of Castleman. The choral writing is effective here; the choir in no way inhibits the swing, although the lyrics are naive in both construction and sentiment. The passages in which the choir speaks the words are an encumbrance musically and serve also to highlight the awkward primitivism of the verse. Naive lyrics again affect the next section, *Almighty God Has Those Angels,* but Ellington's melody is quite sublime, and the interpretation by Alice Babs and Russell Procope recalls the use of the wordless voice with clarinet in the 1927 *Creole Love Call.* The rich woody sound of Procope's New Orleans-style clarinet and the pure, high voice of Babs provide a typical Ellington blend. After this, Williams is featured in *The Shepherd,* the arrangement virtually identical with that on the *Greatest Jazz Concert* album. This, however, is superior both in performance and recording and must be regarded as the definitive version. The crucial part played by Ellington's piano is very evident in this performance. Some time after Williams had left the band he was asked to return for a concert which was to feature a selection of Ellington's sacred music, including *The Shepherd.* This was at a time when Ellington's ill health was causing him to miss quite a lot of performances. Cootie's reaction to the request was to agree on condition that Duke were fit enough to be there and play the piano on this piece.

The Shepherd is followed by *It's Freedom,* the longest movement in the work which lasts for almost thirteen minutes. It includes the chanting of the word "Freedom" in different languages and the appearance of Ellington as narrator delivering a speech about the four freedoms by which Billy Strayhorn lived. One part of this movement is called *Sweet Fat And That.* Based on what Ellington calls "an old lick of Willie 'The Lion' Smith's," it is performed by the choir, Hodges, Ellington, Castleman, and Woodyard. Duke certainly gets the choir swinging, and this music, in which Woodyard's brushwork plays such an important part, reflects among other things Ellington's unfailing ability to get down to jazz basics. Here, as in a number of the other movements, Ellington plays electric piano with total success, adapting the instrument perfectly to his requirements. Hodges is in very fine form during this section.

The next two parts are instrumental. The unaccompanied piano solo called *Meditation,* whose title is self-explanatory, apparently originated as an improvisation when a meeting between Ellington and the painter Joan Miró was filmed during the 1966 French tour. *The Biggest And Busiest Intersection* has its theological implications detailed in the program notes and is an Ellington uptempo romp for the band of the type which usually featured Gonsalves but here has a passage by the two drummers. Babs returns in a wordless song called *T.G.T.T. (Too Good To Title).* This has a very tricky melodic line, which the singer delivers with perfect poise and grace.

The gospel song which was a natural part of Ellington sacred concerts comes next; *Don't Get Down On Your Knees To Pray Until You Have Forgiven Everyone* is delivered with zest and some individuality by Tony Watkins, with the band effortlessly establishing and maintaining the appropriate musical climate. Next Watkins narrates *Father Forgive,* an Ellington prayer, over a hushed choir; in the later stages Ellington's handling of the voices is impressive. The finale—*Praise God And Dance*—is a recapitulation of the melody of the first movement, *Praise God,* here with lyrics and given a long development. Babs, Hodges, Buster Cooper and Gonsalves are featured as well as the choir and orchestra. There is a final outburst from Cat Anderson's trumpet—a kind of metaphysical *Jam With Sam* ending.

In terms of duration, the *Second Sacred Concert* is Ellington's most ambitious work. Although the musical content is superior to the first concert in that the material is fresh and better organized, the work is again uneven in quality. The handling of words and the naive sentimentalism of much of the verse are the weaknesses here. Some of the music is drawn out to great length without any significant development, although it could be argued that this is excusable in a work intended more as a devotional than an aesthetic exercise. For all its limitations the *Second Sacred Concert* includes much music of Ellington's best late sixties vintage. *Praise God,* the instrumental parts of *Supreme Being, Heaven, Almighty God Has Those Angels, The Shepherd, Sweet Fat And That, T.G.T.T.,* and *Praise God And Dance* are all Ellington works worthy of their creator.

* * *

When Ellington headed a small group from the band in later years he did not usually do what people expected and give a looser, more improvised type of presentation. He seemed rather to delight in performing his usual repertoire with reduced forces. The 1964 San Remo recordings provide a good and typical instance of this. From August 1968 comes a series of recordings by the Octet which include one or two unusual items. These are issued on the Tetco label as from "the famous Fieldcup Concert," but this is a conceit of the record producer. The source of the recordings is a private party or concert hosted in Woodbridge, New Jersey, by the Fieldcrest Company—a well-known American manufacturer of household textiles. The event appears to have taken place on an afternoon during Duke's 1968 Rainbow Grill stand. The Octet had two changes: with Jeff Castleman and Rufus Jones replacing Lamb and Little. Vocalists Tony Watkins and Trish Turner were added. (Sam Woodyard had left for the last time and Rufus Jones was now the regular drummer.)

The unexpected aspect of these recordings is that several of the routines are new. Familiar versions of *Passion Flower* and *Body And Soul* feature Hodges and Gonsalves respectively, and *Take The "A" Train* is in the form heard on the 1967 Octet recordings with Anderson playing the trumpet solo with plunger mute. Cat also uses the plunger in a driving, impassioned solo on *I'm Beginning To See The Light,* a song which was being used by Ellington at concerts as an audience sing-along (one certainly got everything at Ellington concerts!) but which turns up here in the more rewarding guise of an Anderson feature. The vehement expression and great drive of these solos remind us what an excellent jazz soloist Cat was. On an apparently impromptu version of *Me And You,* with vocal by Trish Turner, he turns in an open solo which ends in his best Armstrong manner. *Mood Indigo* here rejoices in a trio of Hodges on alto, Brown on muted trombone, and Carney on bass clarinet and has solos by the last two and Ellington; the bass clarinet solo is a gem. There is a brief, hectic *It Don't Mean A Thing* which features both singers and proves that Ellington had not changed much in his selection of vocalists. *Acht O'Clock Rock* is a somewhat disorganized performance, apparently used as a backing to the dancing of Watkins and Turner, but there is more good work from Hodges and Anderson. *Satin Doll* is extended to include tenor and piano choruses (both superb), and there is a new blues which the producer has called *Contrapuntal Riposte*. It is a typical Ellington medium-tempo blues with much riffing by the saxophones and a fine Hodges solo. Despite the new routines and the fine solos by the sidemen, the outstanding feature of these performances is Ellington's piano work. He was in an unusually lively mood, his playing full of fresh ideas as well as new twists to familiar patterns.

* * *

During a residence in Reno earlier in 1968 when Harry Carney was hospitalized, Russell Procope switched to baritone sax, and his temporary replacement on alto was Benny Carter. No recordings featuring this exceptionally interesting saxophone section have yet come to light, but Carter has stated that he was given no solos.

In September of that year the Ellington band paid its first visit to South America. The most significant result of this tour was the *Latin American Suite,* most of which was recorded a couple of months after the band had returned to the United States. The only issued recording from the tour itself is an LP taken from a TV show in São Paulo on the first night of the tour, September 2. The recording, which appears to have been taken from a TV set, is poor with a good deal of hum. The program is mostly from the standard Ellington concert routine, the disc featuring the *Medley Of Popular Hits* and the piano solo *Meditation,* a drum solo, a couple of Hodges features, a pop song and *C Jam Blues*. The *Medley* includes a magnificent version of *In A Sentimental Mood* featuring Gonsalves, but Paul is far from the recording mike and there are other technical flaws, which is a great pity. Hodges plays *Passion Flower* and *Things Ain't What They Used To Be,* after which Trish Turner sings *Sunny* with a short solo by Lawrence Brown. *C Jam Blues* is taken at a moderate tempo and has solos by Duke, Cootie, Paul, Buster Cooper (excellent), and Procope. This is the best performance on the LP.

* * *

Not the least unusual feature of this last LP is that Procope takes the clarinet solo at the end of *C Jam Blues,* the reason being that Jimmy Hamilton had left the band. His replacement was Harold Ashby, who was not a clarinet soloist at all but a tenor saxophone specialist of the Ben Webster school. Ashby subsequently took up clarinet but never played jazz choruses on the instrument; his only solo responsibility on it was taking Hamilton's part in *Harlem*. Thus, for the first time since the brief period between Barney Bigard's departure and Hamilton's arrival, the band was without a clarinet soloist of the front rank. Hamilton had made many major contributions to Ellington's music over the years, and his departure, following so soon after that of Woodyard, was a reminder that Ellington's supply of high-powered musical personalities and virtuoso specialists was not inexhaustible. The major clarinet responsibilities were now passed on to Procope, who had never had pretensions to the virtuosity practiced by Bigard and Hamilton. Procope was a first-class lead alto saxophonist who doubled clarinet. He could handle section parts with distinction on the instrument and he was also a good soloist in a manner based on that of the New Orleans clarinetists. He was most effective in the low register at slow tempo, although he could turn his hand to a piping obbligato when needed. Anything beyond these not inconsiderable duties was inclined to highlight his limitations.

Harold Ashby had been a first-choice reserve for Ellington's saxophone section over a considerable period, but it was a surprise when he was chosen to succeed Hamilton. The acquisition of a second and contrasting tenor soloist to Gonsalves was hardly a genuine replacement for a clarinet specialist of Hamilton's skills. It is not known whether Ellington made any efforts to replace Hamilton with another clarinetist, but the number of jazz clarinet players capable of holding down this position was by the late sixties exceedingly small. Indeed, musicians capable of performing any but section playing duties in the Ellington band were by this time alarmingly thin on the ground. Many older musicians refused to spend more of their lives on the road, even when their medical advisers would permit it. Brass players of the generation which understood Ellington's music had to nurse their lips to keep alive in the profession, and knew that a lengthy stay in Ellington's brass section could easily spell the end of a career. The younger players were almost all artists with stylistic roots in bop and postbop forms which called for speed of execution, improvisation based on harmony, and a tight, nervous rhythmic style. Ellington needed men with big sounds, melody-based solo styles, and the ability to swing in a loose, relaxed fashion. Most younger musicians did not have such qualities, least of all tonally, and also lacked big band experience. Fashions in jazz had long ago moved away from the big, rich sounds of the Hodges and Carney kind, which were such a basic element in Ellington music.

Such was the situation at the time of the first change in the Ellington reed section for well over a decade. The number of brass soloists had already decreased over the past few years, and with Ashby largely duplicating Gonsalves's role the variety of soloists so long available to Duke was now depleted to a degree which was seriously affecting the music. And the outlook was bleak. In the future, when sidemen left they would be replaced by sound musicians rather than by individualistic artists of the kind on which Ellington had built his musical kingdom. Times had changed and the world simply did not produce that kind of musician any more.

* * *

Although he is not in evidence as a soloist on the São Paulo LP, Willie Cook had rejoined the band for the Latin American tour bringing the trumpets up to five. The section was back to its usual four pieces two months later in November 1968 when Ellington's *Latin American Suite* was recorded. During the tour a film had been made in Mexico of an Ellington concert at which one of the main items had been a performance of *The Mexican Suite;* this was the basis of the *Latin American Suite* but with solos not yet allocated to the sidemen and most of the solo space filled by Duke's piano. By the time the suite was recorded, Herbie Jones had departed after a five-year spell as a section trumpet player, librarian, and copyist. Despite the presence of Cook, Williams, and Anderson none of the trumpets has a single solo note in the *Latin American Suite*. Ellington retained many of the solo spots for his own piano and allocated most others to Gonsalves. The only exceptions are an extended trombone solo for Cooper, a shorter one for Brown and, in one movement, a series of brief Hodges passages. The suite is nonetheless one of Ellington's happiest creations and reflects a tour during which the band was greeted by almost overwhelming hospitality and warmth. The music glows with a sense of happiness and well-being. There is not even time for a slow movement as Ellington and his musicians reflect on the joys of their South American tour. (A chapter in *The World Of Duke Ellington* by Stanley Dance gives a full account of this tour.)

The *Latin American Suite* opens with *Oclupaca*, which any self-respecting code breaker will quickly recognize as Acapulco spelled backwards. Over a festive and insistent drum rhythm a beautiful melody is unfolded by the reeds with the Ellington piano adding a most appropriate commentary. The transition to a straight swinging 4/4 is effected via some stabbing brass chords, and the core of the movement is an inventive tenor solo by Gonsalves played against sustained notes on high muted trumpets. The recapitulation of the original theme is accompanied by some delightful Ellington piano comments. There is more outstanding piano work on *Chico Cuadridino;* indeed the pianist really struts during his opening solo. The first theme is in Duke's Latin American vein, but the introduction of a second riff melody brings in Buster Cooper for a brusque, shouting solo. The first theme is reintroduced, and the climax of the movement is a dialogue between Gonsalves and the brass section. Mercer Ellington is joint composer of this movement, the rest of the *Latin American Suite* being credited wholly to Duke. *Eque* celebrates Ellington's first crossing of the equator and is a study in dialogues. After the introduction Hodges is heard with three clarinets, followed by Gonsalves and the trombone section, and these two conversations between a soloist and a section of the orchestra alternate throughout the piece, until Duke's piano (with more than a hint of those hammy dance hall tangos) takes us out on an unresolved chord. Hodges's playing lacks the suppleness of his best work and is in great contrast to that of Gonsalves, who is here (indeed throughout the suite) on the very top of his form: melodic, sinuous, and fitting Ellington's conception in a way which is really perfect. The fifth movement is for piano, two basses, and drums only and was recorded some time after the rest of the suite, the bassists being Paul Kondziela and Victor Gaskin—in the other movements the bassist is Jeff Castleman. This piece is called *Tina* and is dedicated to the Argentine. Although there are no keyboard gymnastics, the touch revealed in the chording is of great subtlety. This is piano playing of the highest class. At one point, Ellington reduces the role of the piano to that of a percussion instrument in a performance in which his rhythmic mastery is paramount.

The next two movements are the longest in the *Latin American Suite,* lasting seven and a half and seven minutes respectively, but there are no solos other than functional ones by Ellington. The first of these long movements is *The Sleeping Lady And The Giant Who Watches Over Her,* referring to the two mountains which overlook Mexico City. Here melodic aspects of the material receive copious and fascinating development by the ensemble. This is a fine example of Ellington's creative writing in the late sixties, as inventive and resourceful as ever. The voices of the individual sidemen can be heard in the ensemble, while a particular Gonsalves phrase is scored for the orchestra in *The Sleeping Lady . . . ,* reminding us that Ellington was alive to all aspects of his sidemen's musical contributions. The seven-minute *Latin American Sunshine* is a riot of happy melody and vivid orchestral colors. The theme is introduced by Ellington—note again the rhythmic freedom and mastery—before a veritable explosion of orchestral color. Gonsalves and Carney are very prominent in the reed voicings here. *Latin American Sunshine* is a kind of jazz rondo, and in the central episode the trumpet section shows its paces. The final appearance of the main theme is spiced by a brief solo from Brown, and there is much excellent Ellington piano as the piece develops; as in so many of these movements Duke has the last say. In this performance, indeed in much of the suite, Rufus Jones's drumming is solid but with distinct inclinations toward the stolid. The final *Brasilliance* forms a perfect climax to the work with a rich melodic tapestry into which a Latin Americanized version of the Ellington band call is woven; the solos are by Gonsalves and Ellington.

As a whole the *Latin American Suite* is perhaps a little too lightweight to be considered among Ellington's most important works, but it is certainly one of his most happy creations. Apart from the drumming the band sounds in good shape, although the short solos of Hodges and Brown indicate that these two were no longer the virtuosi of earlier years. The outstanding soloists here are Ellington himself and Gonsalves, whose playing is of the very highest standard and whose work in the ensemble is of a Carney-like quality.

* * *

The orchestral items for the *Latin American Suite* were recorded on November 5, 1968, the piano solo *Tina* on January 7, 1970. This latter session also produced the final three tracks for the *Duke Ellington—The Pianist* Fantasy LP. None of these equals *Tina* but all are excellent examples of jazz piano playing. *Duck Amok* is a fast medium Ellington blues of a kind which he often recorded as a soloist; each chorus is treated as a separate entity, and the music progresses by a series of contrasts rather than by development in the usual jazz solo sense. There is some very remarkable chording in the last two choruses and in the coda, and the entire performance swings powerfully. *Never Stop Remembering Bill* is a slow ballad which starts off with a reminiscence of the introduction to *Day Dream*. This piece has a beautiful melody and would have made an excellent showcase for Hodges, but the range of Ellington's skills as a pianist is such that neither alto sax nor colorful orchestration is missed. The final *Fat Mess* is based on a phrase which bears a strong resemblance to Thelonious Monk's *52nd Street Theme,* and the performance is in Ellington's brusque, percussive manner which had so strong an influence on Monk's playing. *Fat Mess* is fully flavored Ellington music with some brilliant bass playing by Victor Gaskin (who is the only bassist present on this track) and a final descending phrase which could be an oblique reference to one of Monk's trademarks.

* * *

During the first few days of September 1969, the Orchestra recorded three sessions for Reader's Digest. The repertoire was of popular tunes; eleven were used in an assortment of Reader's Digest boxed sets, including *Happiness Is . . .* (nine LPs, two Ellington tracks only), *Great Songs, Great Bands* (seven LPs, ten Ellington tracks), *All Star Jazz Festival* (eight LPs, seven Ellington tracks of which five are from these sessions, the others being Victor recordings from 1940 and 1942), and *The Big Bands Are Back Swinging Today's Hits* (six LPs, nine Ellington tracks). The titles are pretty dull—*La Dolce Vita, Spanish Flea,* and *One Note Samba* are typical—and owing to this and to the even more uninteresting overall contents of the LP boxes they have not circulated much among Ellington collectors. Certainly an issue collecting them on a single disc would be welcome. The arrangements used here are by Luther Henderson, Ron Collier, and Wild Bill Davis. The scores have little Ellington flavor although the playing is that of an accomplished jazz orchestra; the solos by Williams, Cook, Hodges, Gonsalves, and Davis are excellent and make a major contribution to an interesting but not essential batch of Ellington recordings. *Moon Maiden* was the only Ellington composition recorded at these Reader's Digest sessions, but though both vocal and nonvocal versions were made neither has been issued to date.

* * *

Nineteen sixty-nine was the year of Ellington's last film score. He recorded the soundtrack for a controversial film, *Change Of Mind,* in which the brain of a white lawyer is transplanted into a black man. The score was recorded by an assortment of musicians with experience in the Ellington, Basie, and Earl Hines bands and has not been issued on disc. For this task Ellington dug far back into his repertoire bringing forward *What Good Am I Without You?* (by Milton Ager) from 1930, part of *Creole Rhapsody* (retitled *Neo-Creole*) from 1931, and *Wanderlust* (originally recorded by the Hodges unit) from 1938. Versions of *Neo-Creole* and *Wanderlust* were recorded by the Ellington band in 1969 and have been released on Pablo.

* * *

Although Ellington continued to hold studio recording sessions at his own expense in the United States, the next recordings by the band to be issued were made in England at concerts in Manchester and Bristol on November 25 and 26, 1969, respectively. The cost of recording had become so high in the United States that major American companies were resorting more and more to recording large units overseas. On April 29, 1969, Duke had celebrated his 70th birthday, and the two-LP United Artists set from the Manchester and Bristol recordings was issued as *Duke Ellington's 70th Birthday Concert.*

The old stability of personnel was no more. In the year which had elapsed since the recording of the *Latin American Suite* there had been further changes. The most important of these was the addition to the Ellington entourage of Wild Bill Davis. Although primarily an organist, Davis was also a fine arranger and could, if needed, act as pianist. Perhaps Ellington hoped that Davis would take over some of Strayhorn's functions in the organization. Davis stayed less than two years. He added a few arrangements to the book but failed to make a major impact on the band. One of his functions at concerts seems to have been to play his arrangement of *April In Paris,* made famous by Basie, while Ellington stood at the mike snapping his fingers and shouting "one more time" in the course of the famous coda. That Davis's organ might swamp the delicate textures of Ellington's scoring was a real danger and a source of concern both in the band and outside it, but the organ was used on only a limited selection of numbers.

Meanwhile, Willie Cook had left again and was replaced by the Swedish trumpeter Rolf Ericson, a fine soloist heard only in the version of *Perdido* first showcasing Clark Terry. Buster Cooper had left the trombone section; his first replacement was Benny Green, but he did not go on the European tour. Norris Turney was added to the band and sat with the trombones, playing trombone parts on alto sax for the duration of the tour. This somewhat makeshift arrangement brought into the band a man who played alto and tenor saxophones, clarinet, and flute and was heard in a solo capacity on all four instruments during his stay. The use of the flute was an innovation in the Ellington band although the instrument had become quite commonplace in jazz. Jimmy Hamilton had become proficient on the flute during his last years with Ellington, but Duke would not let him use it with the band. Presumably he felt that as long as he had a top clarinet specialist of Hamilton's caliber he had no need for a flute. The situation was different after Hamilton's departure, and the new instrumental voice, with its distinctive tone color, was now welcome. (The cool sound of the flute could have seemed out of place in the warmth of the Ellington reed section, but in the event Duke used the instrument sparingly in ensemble.) What Hamilton thought of this development has not been revealed.

The full personnel of the Ellington band on the 1969 European tour was:

Trumpets:	Cat Anderson, Cootie Williams, Mercer Ellington, Rolf Ericson.
Trombones:	Lawrence Brown, Chuck Connors (bass trombone).
Reeds:	Russell Procope (alto sax, clarinet); Johnny Hodges (alto sax); Norris Turney (alto and tenor saxes, clarinet, flute); Paul Gonsalves (tenor sax); Harold Ashby (tenor sax, clarinet); Harry Carney (baritone sax, clarinet, bass clarinet).
Rhythm:	Duke Ellington (piano); Wild Bill Davis (organ, deputy pianist); Victor Gaskin (bass); Rufus Jones (drums).
Vocal:	Tony Watkins.

The program of the *70th Birthday Concert* album is typical of Ellington concerts of this period. It opens with the *Kinda Dukish-Rockin' In Rhythm* combination, with some very gutsy piano on the former; the drumming is loud and relentless during *Rockin' In Rhythm* but fails to inhibit the joy in the performance of this 39-year-old composition. Brown plays his "tailgate" part in the ensemble and the plunger trombone solo with considerable vigor, while Anderson makes sure that the climax *is* a climax. Ashby is the first of the featured soloists, in a number labeled *B.P.*—Ellington's code for its full title, *Black Power Blues*. Duke's piano announces at the outset that this is a medium-tempo blues in the best Ellington tradition, and the band swings in a way which seems timeless. Ashby plays a fine solo; he had by now acquired that poise and indefinable "class" which was characteristic of the established Ellington musician. The remainder of the first side is taken up by two familiar Williams features, *Take the "A" Train* and *Tutti for Cootie* (the latter title shown as *Tootie For Cootie* on sleeve and label, reflecting the way Ellington pronounced it). Williams is in fine form here despite the odd fluffed note, playing with a huge tone, immense power, and great majesty. This *"A" Train* is probably the best of the versions featuring Cootie, but *Tutti,* taken at a slowish tempo, is performed in rather tired fashion by the band, though Williams himself plays superbly and features a lot of open trumpet work.

On the second side Procope is heard in a new feature, *4.30 Blues,* while Anderson revives an old one, *El Gato*. The Procope number is one of the best Ellington wrote for him, a blues of the most basic kind. It opens with richly chorded piano before a theme statement by three clarinets. Procope's clarinet solo, played in the low register with a thick, rich tone, is given quite magnificent backing, including a chorus in which the soaring muted trumpets bring back memories of the first great Ellington trumpet section, that of the early to middle thirties. This performance makes it obvious that Ellington has struck gold again in the person of his new bass player, Victor Gaskin.

Anderson wrote *El Gato* for the Ellington trumpet section of 1958, and on its previous recordings it was a showcase for four trumpet soloists. Here Cat is featured alone, and well though he plays, this is less satisfying than the more varied routine of the earlier recordings. In the long introduction there is some half-valve trumpet *à la* Rex Stewart, reminding us that Cat was using *Boy Meets Horn* as a second feature at this time, although Duke seemed reluctant to call the number. After Anderson, Hodges appears for his three showcases, of which only *Things Ain't What They Used To Be* comes into the hackneyed category. *Black Butterfly* is brought forward from 1936, this being its first appearance as a Hodges feature. Johnny does full justice to one of Ellington's most beautiful melodies and a touch of supplementary color is provided by Turney's clarinet solo. The third Hodges number, *Laying On Mellow,* in its easy swing and relaxation celebrates another traditional Ellington mood, that of the casual medium-tempo swinger.

The third side of this double album introduces Wild Bill Davis, who first appears in *Satin Doll*. The band plays a chorus and a half of the usual arrangement, with a short trumpet solo, then Ellington shouts "Wild Bill Davis" and the organist takes over. He is a swinger, and to the accompaniment of cries from Ellington of "Wild Bill Davis—one more time" he proceeds to take *Satin Doll* for a very vigorous ride. Duke seemed never to be able to forget Davis's *April In Paris;* perhaps his continual references to it via cries of "one more time" were meant to make sure that his audiences knew that this was the man responsible for that famous arrangement. The closing section of *Satin Doll,* with Anderson playing the theme in the highest register in duet with the organ, is certainly very exciting. Ellington clearly announces that the next item is a Wild Bill Davis composition called *Azure Te* and repeats the title a couple of times for good measure. Despite this, the label, the listing on the sleeve, and the sleeve note all wrongly identify the piece as the 1937 Ellington song *Azure*. Wild Bill Davis's *Azure Te* had been recorded previously on one of the LPs by Hodges and Davis for Norman Granz's Verve label, and Hodges also appears with Davis on this version. It is followed by *In Triplicate,* a development of the Gonsalves solo from *Diminuendo and Crescendo In Blue,* featuring the tenors of Gonsalves, Ashby, and Turney. Jones is quite unable to swing this kind of number in the way Sam Woodyard could, but there is some good playing from the tenors, with Gonsalves outstanding. In some performances *In Triplicate* was played with an extended Ellington piano introduction, but here Wild Bill Davis, after a preliminary duet with the piano, provides the bulk of the introduction in his most robust fashion. The final two showcases are *Perdido* for Rolf Ericson's flugelhorn and *Fife* for Norris Turney's flute, both pleasant if inconsequential.

The *Medley Of Popular Hits* takes up the bulk of the final side of the album and in addition to the short snippets of *In A Sentimental Mood* and *Prelude To A Kiss* and piano choruses on *I Let A Song Go Out Of My Heart* and *Don't Get Around Much Anymore,* there are full-length versions of *Do Nothin' Til You Hear From Me* (featuring Brown), *Just Squeeze Me* (Ashby), *Mood Indigo* (Procope on clarinet), *Sophisticated Lady* (Carney), and *Caravan* (Ellington). The finale is a very strange affair, a quintet of organ, flute, piano, bass, and drums playing a piece called *Black Swan* in which everyone, including the drummer, takes a solo. The piece is in a Latin American cocktail-music style and is notable for the very un-Ellingtonian textures produced by what is basically a very un-Ellingtonian instrumentation. As an encore, Duke combines his finger-snapping and "Love you madly" routines over a quiet background of *Satin Doll*. This album is a very fine one overall, well recorded and giving a vivid impression of what it was like to attend an Ellington concert of the late sixties. As was the case with most of his concerts, Ellington could have presented a much more interesting program; but as usual he balanced his selections in favor of the old established pieces he believed his audiences expected.

* * *

A further live version of *Black Butterfly,* issued on MF Records and recorded in Sweden during this tour, finds Hodges in even more ravishing form. An encore version of the 1939 *Serenade To Sweden* is played by Brown and the rhythm section; a typical unprepared, off-the-cuff Ellington vignette.

Also from this tour come LPs taken from a Paris concert, issued initially on Japanese BYG and then on Affinity, the former giving a more generous selection. They add little to the United Artists recordings, though a version of *C Jam Blues* taken from this Paris concert (issued on the Italian I Giganti Del Jazz label) finds avant-garde tenor saxophonist Archie Shepp sitting in with the band. The rest of this LP consists of a version of *The Mooche* (taken from a medley performed at the 1966 Newport Jazz Festival) and non-Ellington recordings.

* * *

In the first week of April 1970, the Ellington band was engaged to open a new club in Vancouver, The Cave, and a couple of LPs have been issued on the TOM label of recordings made at the event. The sound quality is poor, the information on the liners inadequate, and that on the labels inaccurate. For example, *4.30 Blues* is said to be *Creole Love Call* and neither *C Jam Blues* nor *Kinda Dukish* is mentioned. The correct sequence of the two LPs is as follows: Side one: *C Jam Blues, Kinda Dukish-Rockin' In Rhythm* (end of coda missing), *4.30 Blues* (incomplete version; first half missing), *Fife, B.P. Blues, Take The "A" Train;* side two: *Tenorsaxophonic Callisthenics* (a.k.a. *Up Jump*), *Birth Of The Blues, Passion Flower, Things Ain't What They Used To Be,* drum solo, *Medley Of Popular Hits* (*In A Sentimental Mood, Prelude To A Kiss, Do Nothin' Til You Hear From Me, Don't Get Around Much Any More*); side three: *Medley* continued (*Mood Indigo, I'm Beginning To See The Light, It Don't Mean A Thing, I Got It Bad, Just Be Cool, Sophisticated Lady,* and *Caravan*—the last incomplete); side four: *Happy Birthday, Take The "A" Train, I Can't Get Started, Be Cool And Groovy For Me, April In Paris,* and a second drum solo. Lawrence Brown had left the band by this time and Booty Wood had rejoined as his replacement.

The two recordings of *Take The "A" Train* are both of the standard arrangement featuring Williams and the differences are slight. *Birth Of The Blues* is an Anderson feature with an amusing introductory announcement by Ellington; this seems to be the only Ellington version on record of this Anderson arrangement. The Hodges *Passion Flower* is a very evocative reading. The two Jones drum solos are just that—there is no pretense of surrounding them with music, and the only contributions from the band are the stabbing chords which bring each version of the bash to an end. In the *Medley,* both Procope and Wood have solos in *Mood Indigo,* and Ellington leads a bout of community singing on *I'm Beginning To See The Light*. Tony Watkins brings his vocal talents to *It Don't Mean A Thing* and *Be Cool And Groovy,* the latter a piece of Ellington "rock and roll" in which he briefly joins Watkins at the vocal mike. With Brown absent, *Do Nothin' Til You Hear From Me* is turned over to Wild Bill Davis. Davis is also responsible for the new arrangement of *I Got It Bad,* which features Hodges. The *Happy Birthday* is a one-chorus affair celebrating the birthday of a lady in the audience. *I Can't Get Started* is a ballad feature for Ashby, who plays quite magnificently. Both *Don't Be Cool,* another rock and roll number, and *April In Paris* are features for Davis, with Ellington at the microphone enjoying himself with shouts of "Wild Bill Davis—one more time." The few new and revised items made this set of some interest, but it is regrettable that the sound quality is so poor.

* * *

In 1970 Ellington was commissioned by the New Orleans Jazz Festival to write a suite. The *New Orleans Suite* was premiered at the Festival on April 25, 1970, in five-movement form. Two days later, the band was in the studio in New York to record these five movements for Atlantic, and on May 13 they completed the project by recording a further four movements. Between these two sessions Johnny Hodges died suddenly of a heart attack in his dentist's waiting room. The blues solo he took on *Blues For New Orleans* at the first of these sessions thus is the last he played on an Ellington recording date. Lawrence Brown had already left, and the band's elite of experienced Ellingtonians was shrinking at an alarming rate. For the first of the two *New Orleans Suite* sessions the personnel was:

Trumpets:	Cootie Williams, Money Johnson, Mercer Ellington, Al Rubin, Fred Stone (the last four doubling flugelhorn).
Trombones:	Booty Wood, Julian Priester, Dave Taylor (bass trombone).
Reeds:	Russell Procope (alto sax, clarinet); Johnny Hodges (alto sax); Norris Turney (alto and tenor saxes, clarinet, flute); Paul Gonsalves (tenor sax); Harold Ashby (tenor sax, clarinet); Harry Carney (baritone sax, clarinet, bass clarinet).
Rhythm:	Duke Ellington (piano); Wild Bill Davis (organ); Joe Benjamin (bass); Rufus Jones (drums).

Davis plays on *Blues For New Orleans* only. Johnson and Taylor were deputizing for the temporarily absent Cat Anderson and Chuck Connors. And Tony Watkins was a regular member of the entourage, although not featured on this recording.

All titles except the four *Portraits* were recorded on this date; these were done on the second session which had Anderson and Connors returning and was of course without Hodges.

The *New Orleans Suite* is not perhaps the most musically concentrated of Ellington's concert suites, but it is a singularly satisfying one. It includes several movements comparable with his greatest achievements. In the format used on the Atlantic LP it starts with the blues, ends with gospel music, and has as its central climax a celebration of the famous New Orleans street parades. Hodges's solo in the opening *Blues For New Orleans* is long and excellent, proving that he remained a blues master to the last. There is more than a hint of modern, gospel-flavored blues here, notably in the opening dialogues between organ and piano and in Davis's later organ solo work. But this movement belongs to Hodges, and the scoring for the saxophones behind his solo, with a very basic blues sound, reminds us that Ellington had a deep understanding of the great alto player's music and knew precisely the kind of accompaniment needed to set off his playing. *Bourbon Street Jingling Jollies* is the first important feature number which Ellington wrote for Norris Turney's flute, an evocation of the New Orleans scene in which the rich backing, which utilizes the flugelhorns, contrasts with the cool melodic lines of the solo instrument.

The first of the *Portraits,* dedicated to Louis Armstrong, is a major disappointment. It is an offhand, overly casual affair—and this is especially regrettable when we consider the importance of its subject. The soloist featured in *Portrait Of Louis Armstrong* is naturally enough Cootie Williams who, although his failing technique is evident here, plays with great beauty and feeling. Yet the piece sounds underrehearsed, and the trumpet playing lacks the majesty, the fire, and the poise of Cootie's best work. We are reminded that no one ever played jazz music with Armstrong's authority, not even Williams. This was really an impossible assignment for any trumpet player, although it is interesting to conjecture what Cootie might have made of it in his prime.

Thanks For The Beautiful Land On The Delta is a feature for Ashby in which melodic delights are lovingly cultivated, one of the richest passages occurring at the point where the three alto saxophones appear in the accompanying orchestral texture. The fifth movement, *Portrait Of Wellman Braud,* is an Ellington concerto for bass and orchestra of a very original kind, the featured soloist being the band's new bassist, Joe Benjamin. Best known as a virtuoso bass player in the modern jazz field, Benjamin had in fact worked for the Ellington organization in a nonplaying capacity on and off since 1943. He was a major jazz bassist, and his long experience of Ellington's methods resulted in his playing like a veteran Ellingtonian from the day he joined the band. The quality of his playing is at once evident in this suite, not least in his work on *Portrait Of Louis Armstrong*. On *Portrait Of Wellman Braud* he plays the awkward, insistent descending scale patterns in brilliant fashion. The authority of his playing, considering that he was a musician interpreting an unfamiliar score of so unusual a nature, is outstanding. Ellington's use of Williams's growl trumpet, Procope's clarinet, and Carney's bass clarinet is most imaginative here.

As its title suggests, *Second Line* is an evocation of a New Orleans street parade. The melodic essence of the movement is outlined at the outset by Procope's clarinet. It is then developed in a big band score of astonishing vigor and freshness. The ensemble is embellished by Procope's clarinet and by the unusual device of a trombone duet—almost a trombone duel—between Booty Wood (with plunger) and Julian Priester (on open horn). Williams and Procope have solos in *Second Line,* but the success of the piece is due to the wonderful conception of the orchestral part.

Sidney Bechet had always been one of Ellington's favorite musicians; for the *Portrait Of Sidney Bechet* in this *New Orleans Suite,* Duke had planned to persuade Johnny Hodges to bring his soprano saxophone out of its 30-year retirement. Other people had tried this without success, but Ellington was a very persuasive man, and of course Bechet was one of Johnny's heroes too. The death of Hodges prevented the world from knowing whether Duke would have succeeded or not and, if he had, what the Hodges soprano would have sounded like in the seventies. Ellington now assigned the solo part to Paul Gonsalves. Thus the piece became a kind of Hodges memorial as well as a portrait of his mentor. The main section consists of a rather slight melody played over a Latin American rhythm. In his theme statements and his variations Gonsalves plays with an austere concentration of melodic line, every note seeming to carry a heavy emotional load. This is a very moving, very tender, tragically beautiful performance in which Paul pays a very personal tribute to his friend and colleague. In terms of musical style, there are no clear connections with Bechet's music, although the emotional intensity is a common factor. But we should remember that Duke conceived the piece as a showcase for soprano sax.

Ellington's interest in the jazz waltz has a new flowering in *Aristocracy à la Jean Lafitte.* Lafitte was a New Orleans character of the early nineteenth century who doubled the roles of aristocrat and pirate. In Ellington's portrait the dignified aristocratic theme statement is in the capable hands of Carney and the wild, piratical flugelhorn solo is by Fred Stone. Stone, a Canadian musician, had impressed Ellington during the *North Of The Border* recording sessions in 1967. He plays in a manner somewhat anonymous by Ellington standards, but this solo is highly skilled and makes its point musically, if without any great subtlety. (A superior version of this solo was played by Johnny Coles on later concert tours by the band.)

The *New Orleans Suite* ends with the fourth of the *Portraits,* the beautiful *Portrait Of Mahalia Jackson.* After a "gospel" piano introduction, Turney's flute states a very beautiful theme over the reeds. The flute is the only voice which stands out from the ensemble, the individual contributions of Williams, Procope, Gonsalves, and Julian Priester being really a part of the extraordinarily rich orchestral fabric. The deliberately coarse-grained reed writing evokes, in a remarkable fashion, the sound of a harmonium in some old wooden southern chapel. Both here and on *Second Line,* trombonist Priester seems to understand the needs of Ellington's music to a degree unusual for one new to the band, and it seems unfortunate that his stay was so short. *Portrait Of Mahalia Jackson* ends with Turney's flute floating melodic arabesques over thick ensemble harmonies to which the clarinets give a distinctive tonecoloring.

* * *

Although the band was beginning to show the effects of losing so many key sidemen, Ellington was still able to score more than half the movements of the *New Orleans Suite* as concertos for the soloists: *Bourbon Street Jingling Jollies* for Turney, *Portrait Of Louis Armstrong* for Williams, *Thanks For The Beautiful Land On The Delta* for Ashby, *Portrait Of Wellman Braud* for Benjamin, and *Portrait of Sidney Bechet* for Gonsalves. Indeed the solo strength of the band is deployed much more freely here than on the slightly earlier *Latin American Suite.* The reed section is clearly still the core of the band, with Turney's flute doing much of the work previously allocated to Hamilton's clarinet.

The arrival of Joe Benjamin meant that this most vital of Ellington roles was in the hands of a man ideally equipped for its demands. But the death of Hodges was a body blow to the orchestra. Ellington had lost the musician who was *the* supreme master on alto sax and an artist whose understanding of Ellington music was profound. A soloist of Hodges's genius could never be replaced, while his loss as a bandsman was beyond measure. Certainly the Ellington ensemble sound never had quite the same glow after the loss of Johnny Hodges.

* * *

Such reminders of his own mortality as the death or retirement of leading bandsmen seemed simply to spur Ellington on to new endeavors. His next recordings, done later in May 1970, found him again breaking new ground when he recorded three of his concert works with the Cincinnati Symphony Orchestra under Erich Kunzel. On two of these, the piano player's contribution is negligible, but he is featured on a version of *New World A-Comin',* which here reverts to the original format of a concerto for piano and orchestra.

The arrangements for the orchestra used on this LP were by Luther Henderson and Joe Benjamin (the latter presumably functioning mainly as copyist), and as always when Ellington's music is played by a symphony orchestra it sounds depersonalized by comparison with the interpretations by his own band. And the sound of "light music" *à la* Kostelanetz often seems dangerously near. Nonetheless, Ellington reveals a new aspect of his versatility in this *New World A-Comin',* that of piano soloist with symphony orchestra. The version of *Harlem,* which has an unnecessary bit of piano playing tagged on to justify Ellington's billing on the sleeve, has already been discussed. This would certainly not be a first choice among recordings of the work, but the orchestra does play it with understanding and conviction; the percussion work is stiff enough to make one suspect that Rufus Jones is present. It is particularly interesting to hear one of the symphony clarinetists playing in a precise, academic fashion the solo which was usually played by Gonsalves in band performances of *Harlem.*

New World a-Comin' and *Harlem* occupy one side of the LP; the reverse is taken up by an important three-movement Ellington work, *The Golden Broom And The Green Apple*. Again Ellington's piano makes a brief and rather unnecessary appearance. This work was originally conceived for symphony orchestra and was written for a Franco-American Festival in 1965. It was premiered at the festival by the New York Philharmonic in a concert at which Ellington also acted as narrator in a performance of Aaron Copland's *Preamble For A Solemn Occasion,* which was performed as a memorial to Adlai Stevenson.

The five-year gap between the writing of *The Golden Broom* and its recording is short for Ellington works written for symphony orchestra. In noting this, one realizes that his statements about the value of having his own orchestra on hand to play his new compositions were more than idle interview chatter. The first movement (or *Stanza I,* as Ellington styles it) opens with a very beautiful theme—throughout the work Duke's melodic genius flows without inhibition. After a set of variations a second theme is introduced. This depicts the "Beautiful Rich City Witch" as she dashes through space on her golden broom, although the mood is plush and easy and there is little sense of anyone dashing anywhere. The music becomes more somber with some good writing for cellos as it develops and there is a hint of melancholy towards the end. The second movement, or *Stanza II,* deals with the "Poverty Strick' Country Chick" and her Green Apple and has an appropriately blithe and innocent air. There is some beautiful woodwind writing with double bassoon and vibraphone adding unusual tone colors, while the ultrainnocent melodies are supported by rock rhythms! At one point, the first trumpet of the orchestra plays the main melody of this movement so beautifully that one wonders that Duke did not hire him on the spot for his own band. Towards the end, the solo voices of violin and contrabassoon are juxtaposed in a way which reminds us that Duke always had his own personal way with instrumentation. In the final movement (or *Stanza III*), we meet the "Handsome Traffic Policeman" who has to decide to whom to give his last ticket—the "Beautiful Rich City Witch" or the "Poverty Strick' Country Chick." The rhythm in the lower strings at the start recalls the middle movement of *Night Creature:* this is obviously Ellington's favorite boogie bass for symphony orchestra. The writing is very blues-inflected and there is some effective string scoring. The climax is built up gradually and includes drum breaks; it concludes the work in a wholly satisfactory fashion.

These recordings were made for Decca, and the LP was issued in their prestigious classical *Gold Seal* series—a rare instance of recognition of Ellington's importance as a composer outside the jazz world.

The Golden Broom And The Green Apple shows how well Ellington's music can be adapted for symphony orchestra. Yet in *Harlem,* a work familiar in the versions by the Ellington Orchestra, one feels that neither the instrumentation nor the idiom is *quite* right for the music. We may have felt the same way about *The Golden Broom* had Ellington ever rescored the work for the band. By symphonic standards, this music has a curiously dated sound, hardly more "modern" than the writing of the New Orleans-born composer Gottschalk, a musician of the mid-nineteenth century.

The superbly recorded Decca 12-inch LP is accompanied by a 7-inch disc on which Ellington explains the three pieces to the accompaniment of selections from the music. The full program of *The Golden Broom And The Green Apple* is also included on the sleeve. This Ellington LP with the Cincinnati Symphony Orchestra is the kind of record jazz enthusiasts are inclined to ignore, and it is true to say that the reasons why the American companies were so reluctant to record and issue such music was not always ignorance or prejudice; often it was a sure knowledge that the resulting LPs would not sell. This is regrettable, for not only are his recordings with symphony orchestra full of imaginative music and Ellington humor, but they also contain major works not otherwise available.

* * *

Nineteen seventy also saw the composition of Ellington's ballet *The River,* commissioned by the American Ballet Theater. The work was premiered at Lincoln Center in New York City on June 25, 1970, and was a considerable critical success. A slightly augmented Ellington Orchestra recorded the twelve sections of Duke's score, but these have never been issued. A posthumous performance under the direction of Mercer Ellington by The Duke Ellington Orchestra and the Warsaw Philharmonic has been released on a two-LP set on the Frog Box label (along with versions of *New World A-Comin'* and *Three Black Kings* by the same forces).

* * *

Apart from some odd sides recorded privately and later put out on Pablo, the next issued Ellington recordings date from almost a year after the Cincinnati sessions. In February 1971, the band recorded another important Ellington suite, *The Afro-Eurasian Eclipse*. At this time the personnel was:

Trumpets: Cootie Williams, Money Johnson, Mercer Ellington, Eddie Preston.

Trombones: Booty Wood, Malcolm Taylor, Chuck Connors (bass trombone).

Reeds: Russell Procope (alto sax, clarinet); Norris Turney (alto and tenor saxes, clarinet, flute); Paul Gonsalves (tenor sax); Harold Ashby (tenor sax, clarinet); Harry Carney (baritone sax, clarinet, bass clarinet).

Rhythm: Duke Ellington (piano); Joe Benjamin (bass); Rufus Jones (drums).

Though it was recorded in 1971, *The Afro-Eurasian Eclipse* was not issued until 1975 when it appeared on the Fantasy label. It is not known what the exact sequence of the suite would have been had Ellington supervised this issue, for the work was never performed in its entirety in public, although a seven-movement version was given at the 1970 Monterey Jazz Festival. The Fantasy LP contains eight movements including *Acht O'Clock Rock,* already familiar to Ellington concertgoers, three movements which had been fully titled by Duke—*Chinoiserie, Didjeridoo,* and *Afrique*—three known only by their four-letter code words—*Gong, Tang,* and *True*—and one—*Hard Way*—which seems to have only a tenuous connection with the program of the suite. Of these eight movements only *Chinoiserie* and *Acht O'Clock Rock* were performed regularly in public.

At concerts, the connection between *Acht O'Clock Rock* and *Afro-Eurasian Eclipse* was rarely if ever mentioned, but *Chinoiserie* was given a witty introduction in which Duke explained the origin of the suite as his reaction to a statement by Marshall McLuhan that the whole world was going oriental. A recording of Ellington reciting this introduction opens the LP of *Afro-Eurasian Eclipse*. After Ellington has completed his piano introduction to *Chinoiserie* (or as he used to call it with an oriental bow, his "riki-tiki"), the two altos introduce a mock-oriental theme of *Mikado*-like cast. This is given a full-sounding arrangement in the best Ellington manner with scoring designed to inspire the maximum swing. Turney's alto makes its presence felt in the ensemble. The soloist is Harold Ashby, who enters as the band changes gear into a steady 4/4 beat. He plays a well-constructed solo, but this studio version is not as inspired as several concert performances which were, incidentally, always accompanied by an Ellington ritual dance.

The second movement is Ellington's tribute to the Australian aborigine and his primitive instrument the *Didjeridoo*. Rufus Jones sets the mood with a suitably primitive rhythm before Carney introduces the basic motif with harsh decorations from the pianist. Duke is brilliant here in that percussive style he first exploited fully in *La Plus Belle Africaine*. Carney provides the main solo and a brilliant coda for *Didjeridoo,* a superb example of Ellington's late "exotic" manner. The same style is indicated in the title of the next number, *Afrique*. Over drumming which would do full justice to a Hollywood jungle movie, a thematic fragment is thrown around between Procope, Carney, Ashby, Turney, and Gonsalves (note how Gonsalves, by his tone and the way he varies the rhythm of the phrase, enhances the musical climate established by the others) followed by an ultraprimitive dialogue between the trombone section and the piano. All the while Jones's drums are a menacing presence and then, after more understated band music with piano commentaries, he emerges as the main soloist. This must be the most imaginative lead-up to a drum solo in jazz history; if the solo itself is musically an anticlimax, it at least upholds a long-standing jazz tradition.

A more contemporary kind of primitivism is reflected in *Acht O'Clock Rock,* a rock and roll outing which had often been used at concerts for accompaniment to dance routines by Tony Watkins and Trish Turner. The soloists varied, and in this version Ashby and Turney are featured, the latter's alto chanting the timeless message of the blues. *Gong* opens with a brief uptempo passage with wa-wa brass and a fleeting appearance by Gonsalves before a gong sounds and we settle down to a slow medium tempo as Duke introduces the main section of the movement. His piano uses rich harmonies here, and the playing of Joe Benjamin is a perfect complement. The reed voicings are of particular interest with much use being made of the new combination of flute and clarinet. The leader's piano provides the closing bars, which lead to a final sounding of the gong. This gong is retained for use at the end of *Tang,* a ferocious tango with a typical late Ellington theme and copious use of Carney's baritone sax. The band plays with great abandon here; at one point Benjamin can be heard slapping the bass. From the wonderful opening reed harmonies to the concluding gong after the reprise of the same chords, *Tang* is full of fresh and original music.

True is a waltz which finds Gonsalves in a fierce mood both in the theme statement and in the course of some highly idiosyncratic variations. There is an unaccompanied coda after the usual pattern of Gonsalves features, but on this one the excitement is wholly musical, being a perfectly logical conclusion to what has gone before. The final movement, *Hard Way,* features Turney on alto, playing in the style of Hodges. The title does not exaggerate the difficulties of following Hodges, but Turney's work is clearly that of an accomplished artist paying tribute to the great man rather than that of a mere imitator. His own musical personality comes over clearly, while the trombones and the bassist remind us of the kind of accompaniment which Hodges had enjoyed. The saxophone section also gives a demonstration of its continuing qualities.

The "primitivism" of *The Afro-Eurasian Eclipse* is really no more authentic than that of a Hollywood jungle film or of the Cotton Club decor which adorned Ellington's music both literally and metaphorically in the twenties. It reflects Ellington's *impressions* of people and places while at the same time reasserting an aspect of his musical character which had been dormant for much of the time he had worked with Strayhorn. The music of *La Plus Belle Africaine* and *The Afro-Eurasian Eclipse* relates to the menacing music of Ellington's first period such as *Black And Tan Fantasy* and *The Mooche*. The demands that audiences made on popular musicians in post-depression America, the stance of the big band leader in the swing era, and the influence of the gentle personality of Billy Strayhorn all combined to bury this vein of Ellington's music. Then, rather surprisingly, at the opposite end of his career there is a resurgence of violent, menacing, "primitive" music of a kind which would have seemed out of character for the smooth sophisticated Ellington of the forties and fifties. In this new music the techniques were still the traditional Ellington ones and the musical language still of a basic, earthy nature. It cannot be stressed too strongly that just below the surface this "primitive" music is essentially Ellingtonian and never remotely African (or Aboriginal). Had Ellington been a time traveler *Afrique* would have been a wholly acceptable substitute for *Jungle Nights In Harlem* as a background for a Cotton Club dance routine.

The Afro-Eurasian Eclipse is Ellington's most important work since the *Far East Suite*, more weighty than the *Latin American Suite* and more consistent in quality than the *New Orleans Suite*. For all the band's reduced solo strength and the decline in the number of strong individual voices, and despite some mediocre drumming, this still is a great ensemble well attuned to the task of interpreting Ellington's scores. It is sad that this was probably the last major recorded achievement of the Ellington band.

* * *

Four months after *The Afro-Eurasian Eclipse,* in April 1971, the band recorded *The Goutelas Suite*. When Ellington had been invited to reopen restored Chateau Goutelas in 1966 he had considered the invitation a great honor. We have already noted the outstanding quality of the solo piano recordings made on that occasion; some five years later, this short suite was premiered at Lincoln Center in New York, and the studio recording was made a fortnight later. Harold Minerve is in the band on alto, deputizing for the temporarily absent Procope.

A special fanfare is played at the beginning and the end of the piece, and this encloses a suite of four movements. The opening *Goutelas* reflects Ellington's awe as he approached the chateau through a corridor of 50 children holding torches. This and the following *Get-With-Itness* are both short pieces. The diverse reed styles of Minerve, Turney (clarinet), Ashby, and Carney are heard in the breaks in the fast, 3/4 time *Get-With-Itness,* reflecting the diversity of people involved in the Goutelas project.

The centerpiece of the suite is the long, slow movement entitled *Something,* which is designed to evoke the age and traditions of Goutelas. Ellington's piano has an important role both in the ensemble and in short solos. The ensemble scoring is full of the most delicious details with divided reeds, changes of lead, skilled deployment of Carney's massive sound, and the use of the two tenor saxophones as a kind of minisection. The harmonies used in *Something* are of great beauty in themselves. The finale is *Having At It,* an uptempo Gonsalves outing which gives the impression of having been hastily thrown together as a makeweight by the hard-working 72-year-old composer. To deduce a decline in Ellington's powers from this would be as foolish as to do so from the equally perfunctory *Circle Of Fourths,* which closes the 1956 *Such Sweet Thunder*. *The Goutelas Suite* consists of some rather lightweight music clustered around a sublime central slow movement, a movement most clearly *not* the work of an artist in decline.

* * *

It was not until 1976 that *The Goutelas Suite* was issued on an LP on Norman Granz's Pablo label, *The Ellington Suites*. This also contained *The Queen's Suite* of 1959 and *The UWIS Suite* of 1972. Subsequently, Pablo issued two further Ellington LPs containing an assortment of material from 1969 to 1972. The first was called *The Intimate Ellington,* the second *Up In Duke's Workshop*. The earliest recordings date from April 1969 and include an uptempo piano improvisation with bass (Paul Kondziela) and drums (Rufus Jones) which finds Duke in his brusque, no nonsense manner—this is called *Edward The First*. From the same session comes a slow performance of *Wanderlust,* played over a double-time shuffle beat, scored for a reduced ensemble of eight horns and three rhythm. Williams has a powerful statement, aided by Ashby, but the outstanding feature is Ellington's fine blues piano. The extended piano and bass solos which end the performance are supremely inventive and full of character. From the following month, May 1969, comes a full band version of *Black Butterfly,* which uses the same arrangement as that for the *70th Birthday Concert* album. Hodges and Turney, the latter on clarinet, take solos, and the scoring for reeds is exquisite. From June 1969 comes a recording of *Neo-Creole,* an extract from the incidental music for the film *Change Of Mind*. This is unfortunately the only part of the original score which has been issued on record, although *Wanderlust* was also used in the film. *Neo-Creole* is based on the blues theme from the 1931 *Creole Rhapsody,* given a "boogaloo beat" and featuring Ashby in the main solo role, although Turney's alto is also heard.

In July 1969 Ellington recorded a solo track, doubling on vocal and celeste, of a song he calls *Moon Maiden*. It is wholly in character that when Ellington reflected on the possibilities of space flight his mind should turn at once to the opposite sex. *Moon Maiden* indicates how Duke would have gone about chatting up the ladies had such been found on the moon during his lifetime. He talks rather than sings, and the main interest in this slight Ellington curio is Duke's solo, the only one he ever recorded on celeste. Also from the summer of 1969 comes a version of *Layin' On Mellow* played by one trumpet, one trombone, and the saxophone and rhythm sections. Hodges is featured in a very mellow performance of a piece which was clearly less familiar to the band at this stage than it was on the later *70th Birthday* album recording. Ellington's wry, sparse piano at the close inspires him to call out "Count Basie" as the performance ends.

From the summer of 1970 comes a recording called *Some Summer Fun* by the full band; this is an uptempo, twelve-bar theme utilized for a *C Jam Blues*–type of routine in which Williams, Gonsalves, Priester, Davis, and Ashby are all heard as soloists. Each solo is preceded by a four-bar break and consists of two twelve-bar choruses. Gonsalves is perhaps the pick of a fine bunch of soloists, while Davis makes some important ensemble contributions and the piano player sets the scene with a solo of characteristic excellence.

Mendoza (from the same session) appears to have escaped from the *Latin American Suite,* being named after an Argentine city to which the band paid an apparently riotous visit. The Latin beat is obligatory under these circumstances; over it Davis indulges in some witty dialogues with Ellington's piano and the band as well as contributing a fine solo. The other soloists are Procope with his woody tone on low-register clarinet, Wood on plunger-muted trombone, Gonsalves in a typically adventurous display, and Fred Stone, who is fast, accurate, and academic.

New versions of *I Got It Bad* and *Sophisticated Lady* date from December 1970. The former is in a new arrangement by Davis and features Williams on trumpet; though intended as a vocal showcase this instrumental version of the arrangement is very effective. Cootie's lip lets him down occasionally, but there are some beautiful melodic touches in his solo. The version of *Sophisticated Lady* is less successful; it is played over a mambo beat and features a duet between Turney on flute and Carney on baritone sax. Another Davis arrangement is heard in *Bateau,* a new Ellington theme. This is a highly effective score played over a Latin beat and with more brilliant band piano from Ellington.

The two finest tracks on *The Intimate Ellington* are both slow blues dating from February 1971. The first is a piano solo accompanied by Benjamin and Jones and issued as *Edward The Second*. This was improvised over bass figures by Benjamin in a kind of modified habanera rhythm. Ellington's invention and his mastery of the blues have never been better illustrated, and he certainly sounds very inspired here. The bass playing is also outstanding in what is a masterpiece of piano jazz. The second blues has Carney on bass clarinet and Turney on flute added to the participants on *Edward The Second*. The bass part is so important that what we really hear is a series of trios between piano, bass, and one of the wind instruments culminating in a quartet for all four, the whole played over the basic rhythms laid down by Jones. Again Ellington is utterly original, while Carney plays one of the best bass clarinet solos he ever recorded, and Turney once more proves himself to be perfectly in accord with Ellington's conception. The title given to this wonderful performance is *Intimate Interlude*.

From the same February 1971 sessions the full band is heard in a casual *Love Is Just Around The Corner* with Williams featured on open trumpet. The session the day after this produced *Hick* (mistitled *Dick* on sleeve and label), which sounds like another fugitive from the *Latin American Suite*. Davis is featured on organ to excellent effect.

The track titled *Symphonette* on *The Intimate Ellington* is actually part of *Beige* from *Black, Brown And Beige,* with Carney on baritone in a solo part he had played on clarinet in 1943; this extract ends with the *Sugar Hill Penthouse* segment for the reed section. Coming as it does in the middle of a miscellany of late sixties and early seventies compositions this revival does not sound at all out of place; it reminds us of the unity and consistency of Ellington's music down the years. It is a beautiful performance which does full justice to the inimitable reed voicings. If this trumpet section sounds a little ordinary compared with earlier editions, one must also observe that they play well enough to project the full flavor of Ellington's writing.

Two items from June of 1971 bear the four-letter Ellington codes *Eulb* and *Tenz*. Both are shortish studies for the band with copious Ellington piano of the highest quality and many delightful details of scoring and playing in the ensemble parts. This date also produced a prototype version of *Goof,* later to be used as a feature for trumpeter Johnny Coles. Here the piano takes the solo role. The last title, chronologically speaking, on these Pablo LPs is *Blem,* a blues dating from December 1972. The solos here are by Ashby, Turney (on alto), Money Johnson, Gonsalves, Tyree Glenn (making a welcome if brief return to the band; heard here on plunger trombone), and Minerve (on piccolo). Both the Pablo collections have been described as sweepings from the cutting room floor, but all this music comes from previously unknown sessions sponsored by Duke himself; one wonders what delights still remain from these and other so far unpublicized recording dates.

* * *

In October 1971 the band was in the middle of another tour of Britain and Europe, and once again United Artists decided to record them in Britain. The concerts at Bristol and Birmingham were taped and used as the source for a two-LP album which has sometimes been issued as *The English Concert* and sometimes under the name of the longest of the works it contains, the *Togo Brava Suite*. Wild Bill Davis had left, and Ellington was sporting a slightly enlarged band with five trumpets and six saxophones. The full personnel for the tour was:

Trumpets:	Cootie Williams, Mercer Ellington, Johnny Coles, Eddie Preston, Money Johnson (also vocal).
Trombones:	Booty Wood, Malcolm Taylor, Chuck Connors (bass trombone).
Reeds:	Russell Procope (alto, clarinet); Norris Turney (alto and tenor saxes, clarinet, flute); Harold Minerve (alto sax, flute, piccolo); Paul Gonsalves (tenor sax); Harold Ashby (tenor sax, clarinet); Harry Carney (baritone sax, clarinet, bass clarinet).
Rhythm:	Duke Ellington (piano); Joe Benjamin (bass); Rufus Jones (drums).
Vocal:	Nell Brookshire (or Bobbie Gordon, as she sometimes preferred to be called), Tony Watkins.

Tony Watkins is not heard on the United Artists album, which opens with a superb version of *C Jam Blues,* marred only by the audience applause for the previous solo drowning out the four-bar breaks which open each new one. This is extremely annoying and particularly so in the case of Gonsalves, whose opening break is a classic of rhythmic subtlety. At the outset Ellington sets a very sober tempo, while the audience applauds itself for being clever enough to recognize this highly distinctive number. The thick, gutty sound of the saxophone section here is wholly of the jazz tradition and sheer delight to the jazz lover's ear. The solos are by Williams's driving open horn, the richly intricate tenor saxophone of Gonsalves, the plunger-muted trombone of Wood, and Procope's clarinet.

Ellington's tribute to Togoland, a nation on the west coast of Africa, is entitled the *Togo Brava Suite*. It received its premiere at the Newport Jazz Festival of 1971 and is a typical Ellington short suite in four movements. Duke's ultrarelaxed piano indicates the nature of his musings on the *Soul Soothing Beach*. This is played over a cha-cha beat and leads into a melodic statement by the saxophones with an appropriately soothing lead alto. The only soloist, Turney on flute, expands the mood. "And now into the jungle," says Ellington, introducing his second movement, called *Naturellement*. This example of late-period Ellington jungle music is taken at a fast tempo and has some impressionistic orchestral effects before the main soloist, Harold Ashby, enters and builds to a ferocious climax. It is interesting to note Ashby's development of the rough-toned, growling aspect of Ben Webster's style here. This Ashby solo is followed by an orchestral climax of rather stagey "jungleism" and much zest in which Carney's baritone makes a powerful contribution and Jones's drumming is very prominent. The last two movements, *Amour Amour* and *Right On Togo,* are played without a break, the former starting with a delicately poised solo by Duke over a bass figure with variations from Joe Benjamin. A strutting theme is stated by the band, followed by a flute solo over more soul-soothing saxophones. This leads to a big climax with drum breaks, and the movement ends with a brief piano coda. *Right On Togo* has a gospel-like theme which is developed into another climax with drums breaks; this brief movement is really more in the nature of an extended closing fanfare.

After the *Suite,* Ellington introduces Gonsalves for a revival of *Happy Reunion*. This finds Gonsalves in his most lyrical ballad style, and he gives us a more elaborate improvisation than on the 1958 original. The lyricism is maintained in a most delicate fashion throughout the intricate and involved tracery of the melodic line.

Addi features the alto of Harold "Geezil" Minerve, who certainly obtains some audience response. He plays post-Parker phrases in the approved seventies style with an attack reminiscent of Earl Bostic or Pete Brown. It would have been interesting to have known how the Ellington of ten or fifteen years earlier would have treated Minerve's alto; but by 1971 Duke was no longer absorbing the styles of his new musicians in depth but simply using them as section men and devising simple numbers, such as *Addi* and *Goof,* for their showcases. Ashby was the last man to join the band whose personality Duke used in the old way as a specific element within his compositions. Even Turney was given flute solos which could just as easily have been played by Jimmy Hamilton on clarinet were he to return to the band, while Johnny Coles, an outstanding trumpeter and a sensitive artist, was used primarily as a section man. (Coles's usual feature was a highly perfunctory version of *How High The Moon.*) Being unable to find soloists with a melodic style he could use, Ellington concentrated on musicians with the kind of big sound he required for the ensemble. In his new compositions of the seventies Ellington would use short solos by Williams, Wood, Turney, and Procope, but the lion's share of the solo work was handled by Gonsalves, Carney, and Duke himself, with Ashby also used quite extensively.

The somewhat confused programming of the *Togo Brava Suite* album presents *Lotus Blossom* at its halfway point, although Ellington always used this piano solo to close the concerts. Shorter and less obviously emotional than the performance on "*. . . And His Mother Called Him Bill,"* this is nonetheless a very beautiful example of Ellington's piano playing. Both the Gonsalves features on this set are revivals, the second being *Cotton Tail* from 1940. This is taken at a sprightly tempo, although not so fast as the frenetic Bethlehem recording of 1956. Gonsalves is in excellent form, while Duke, as ever, devises a new solo for his eight bars. Hodges is missed as the lead voice in the saxes here, as indeed is Anderson in the famous trumpet passage which he used to lead with so much fire and punch. The drumming by Jones is solid enough although lacking in swing. But Paul is in fine form; his coda is of the very best vintage.

In addition to playing alto, tenor, clarinet, and flute, Turney also did some writing while he was with Ellington, his most memorable contribution in this field being his tribute to Johnny Hodges, *Checkered Hat,* a ballad for alto saxophone. Just as in *Hard Way* we heard Turney swinging in a style which was an individual interpretation of Hodges's innovations; in *Checkered Hat* he offers an essay in the Hodges ballad manner which is full of his own personality. His scoring too is perfectly apt. The version of *La Plus Belle Africaine* which follows is, as has already been pointed out, much inferior to the 1966 recording. Woodyard is badly missed, while Procope's work sounds crude by comparison with Hamilton's interpretation of the clarinet solo on the original. Much the best things about this version are Benjamin's tasty and melodic bass playing and the solo by the ever reliable Harry Carney. *In A Mellotone* is taken at a very easy medium tempo, but Jones does not play with the degree of relaxation called for, and indeed achieved, by the rest of the band. Williams plays an imperious solo and the saxophones deliver the intricate accompanying passage, but the two do not blend as they had in the 1940 or 1956 versions. An excellent and unusual aspect of this performance is the presence of a Procope alto solo. Another revival from the early forties follows in *I Got It Bad* in the new Davis arrangement. We have heard an instrumental version of this in the *Intimate Ellington* set, but here it is used as originally intended—as a vocal showcase. The singer is Nell Brookshire, and she does little to improve Ellington's poor reputation in the matter of selecting vocalists. Williams plays a trumpet solo, and at one point he briefly joins in the singing.

The label and the sleeve then lead us to expect a performance of *Goof* featuring Johnny Coles. Instead we hear an Ellington piano solo of the composition called *Melancholia* in the 1953 Capitol collection of Ellington piano solos. After this quiet interlude the *Togo Brava Suite* album ends on a rather ordinary note with a slight Ellington composition featuring Turney, *Soul Flute*.

* * *

An interesting supplement to the *Togo Brava Suite* collection is an LP recorded at a Warsaw concert on October 30, 1971, and issued on the Poljazz label. Only *Addi, La Plus Belle Africaine*, and *Lotus Blossom* are heard on both issues. *La Plus Belle Africaine* is a better performance than the English one, with Procope making a much more effective contribution, although in quality this is still some way behind the interpretations with Hamilton, Lamb, and Woodyard. The way in which Ellington uses the piano in the manner of an African percussion instrument is very evident here. *Things Ain't What They Used To Be* appears as a feature for Malcolm Taylor's raw plunger-muted trombone, with an evocation of Hodges by the three altos at the end. *Goof* does actually appear here; it is a feature for Johnny Coles taken at a slower tempo than the prototype version on Pablo; Coles contributes a beautifully played solo in the postbop idiom. Money Johnson sings *Hello Dolly* in the style of Louis Armstrong and plays some Louis-styled trumpet. *Satin Doll* has a new chorus of piano improvisations, and there are short versions of three Ellington songs, clearly extracted from a performance of the *Medley Of Popular Hits*. As an encore to one of these Nell Brookshire sings an uptempo blues. The Polish producers obviously do not know the titles of *Addi* or *Goof*, while *Hello Dolly* is labeled as *Unknown No 2*(!), perhaps to avoid publisher's royalties.

Also apparently from this tour is the live version of *Chinoiserie* found in the MF records set. This has a very fiery solo by Ashby in the featured role along with some characteristically heavy drumming from Rufus Jones.

* * *

Although a full year elapsed before any further Ellington records were made for public issue—an alarming gap caused by the economic situation of the American record industry—there were no important changes of personnel during this time. Eddie Preston had left the trumpet section and Vince Prudente had replaced Malcolm Taylor in the trombones. For the recording of *The UWIS Suite*, Russ Andrews substituted for Paul Gonsalves in the saxophone section. This suite was recorded on October 5, 1972, and issued as part of the posthumous Pablo collection *The Ellington Suites*. It would prove to be the last of the Ellington suites recorded by the band. The work celebrates an Ellington Festival, with the band in residence, at the University of Wisconsin during a week in July 1972. The premiere of *The UWIS Suite* was the climax of this unique festival, and the three orchestral movements were preceded by a piano solo which was not repeated for the recording. We have, therefore, a three-movement orchestral suite with the titles of the movements reduced to the increasingly habitual four-letter code words. *UWIS* is the opening movement and much the most substantial. The entry of the orchestra after the leader's short piano prelude sets a typical Ellington mood, the harmonies and the voicings mysteriously cloudy but the emotional commitment and communication direct and open. There is much fine Benjamin bass in this movement. Carney presents the theme on baritone and there are short solos for Ashby, Turney, and Procope in the course of this basically orchestral conception. The tempo is an easy walking gait and the mood expansive. It is an astonishing revelation of how freely creative Ellington was at the age of 73, before his fatal illness started to erode his strength. In some ways this movement is reminiscent of Ellington middle-period music with the absence of exotic effects and primitive rhythms common in his late work. At the end the instrumentation is unusual but the mood characteristic, as piccolo and flute combine in whimsical pronouncements.

The other two movements are much slighter. *Klop* is yet another Ellington first—the band's first official recording of a polka, the title manufactured by reducing the word to four letters and reversing them. This short movement is manifestly enjoyed by the band; the humor is very Ellingtonian. By contrast the last movement introduces a very traditional Ellington form—the train blues. The piece is entitled *Loco Madi* and an electric bass is added; over a fast rhythm provided by this instrument, the band rolls along easily with solos by Ashby, Johnson, and Turney, the latter on alto. Turney is still wailing the blues when the train and the band fade away into silence.

* * *

Although there were key Ellingtonians still in the orchestra, it was by this time far removed from the great Ellington ensembles of the previous four decades. Only Gonsalves, Carney, and Benjamin could be said to be contributing work of the highest Ellington class. Cootie Williams was still there, but his abilities on the most physically demanding of all jazz instruments were much reduced by age. Booty Wood, Chuck Connors, Russell Procope, Norris Turney, and Harold Ashby were also capable of making telling contributions in both solo and ensemble, but the old finesse was frequently lacking in the band work. Yet, despite the failings of the ensemble, Ellington's outstanding creativity as both pianist and composer made him able to triumph despite his band's decline. But at this time the first signs of Ellington's debilitating fatal illness, cancer of the lung, were beginning to show. With the leader weakening and further personnel changes taking place soon after the *UWIS Suite* recordings, the band continued to deteriorate. By the time they next recorded for public release a year later, Williams, Wood, Turney, and Jones had all departed and Gonsalves was often absent.

* * *

Meanwhile Ellington did a couple of recording dates which marked his swan song as a solo pianist. The sessions were organized by Norman Granz, who after a break of several years was back in the record business full time, building up an impressive catalog for his Pablo label. While also issuing older Ellington recordings which Duke had made at his own expense, Granz had recorded the band back in 1967 for the Pablo album called *The Greatest Jazz Concert In The World*. Then, in December 1972, he set up a session for Ellington on piano and Ray Brown on bass. Brown had been for decades a regular Granz associate and, along with Charlie Mingus and Oscar Pettiford, one of the most skilled of that remarkable generation of bass players which burst on to the jazz scene in the years immediately after the Second World War. Granz had long been an admirer of the duets recorded by Ellington and Jimmy Blanton in 1940 and badly wanted to do a similar date with Ellington and Brown, the bass star of his jazz repertory company. For his part, Brown had always acknowledged Blanton's work with Ellington as his first inspiration. So the situation seemed to be right for a set of duets by two masters. What happened has not been revealed but the music is anything but easygoing, and the session, at which musical sparks fly throughout, has an atmosphere of tension, as if each musician were out to make the meeting into a cutting contest. Certainly Brown is fully extended, and there is none of that complacent air that recorded encounters between star jazz musicians often engender. Knowing that it took Granz many years of persuasion to set up the session we may deduce that Duke was not very keen on the idea, and indeed may have wished to use his own bass player even if really persuaded that such a session was desirable. His dislike of looking backwards and his ambivalent attitude toward recording with people outside the Ellington organization probably affected his approach to the music here. He may even have felt maneuvered by Granz and been resentful. Or perhaps tension and conflict reflect Ellington's internal fight against his wasting disease.

Whatever the reason, Ellington gives Brown a very lively time indeed and rarely lets the bassist settle into a comfortable pattern. On some of the numbers, especially the first and last movements of the *Fragmented Suite For Piano And Bass*, there seems to be some kind of contest concerning rhythmic complexity going on; Ellington wins, but not without some sterling efforts on Brown's part. Of the four numbers recorded by Ellington and Blanton in 1940 only two appear on the Ellington-Brown Pablo set, *Pitter Panther Patter* and *Sophisticated Lady*. Brown does not play a single note with the bow, in contrast to Blanton who had made great use of it in his duets with Duke.

The Ellington-Brown LP, *This One's For Blanton*, opens with a version of *Do Nothin' Til You Hear From Me* which sets the climate. At the outset Duke simply hammers the rhythm of the melody out on the very highest keys of the piano while Brown makes melodic responses. Then Duke plays the melody in a manner which hints at his cocktail style and employs very rich harmonies, especially on the bridge. In this opening duet the two musicians explore the possibilities of their situation in a rigorous manner. At times, the music is an equal-voiced duet, at others, simply a solo by the bass with only the most sketchy piano accompaniment. Ellington's playing commands attention for much of the time and varies from delicate chording and whimsical decoration to a most violent percussive manner.

On *Pitter Panther Patter* the wide range of Ellington's stylistic references is again obvious, as indeed is the great virtuosity of Brown's bass playing. The bassist includes a few direct Blanton quotations here. The Hodges unit recording of *Things Ain't What They Used To Be* is mentioned by Brown in an album note as being one of the Blanton/Ellington records which had made so strong an impression on him as a young man, presumably the reason for its inclusion here. On this version Brown's apparent determination to display his virtuosity in every bar of the music throughout the session results in a restless quality which seems quite wrong in this context.

Sophisticated Lady has 32 bars of Ellington piano sandwiched between two unaccompanied bass solos. The composition of this solo is odd, as Ellington comes in at the middle eight and plays to the end of the first chorus accompanied by the bass and then proceeds to play the first sixteen bars of the next chorus unaccompanied before handing back to Brown. Ellington's deployment of harmony and his keyboard command are masterly here, and this solo gives an impression of great musical richness. It could no doubt have been extended with rich dividends. After four numbers associated with Blanton, the old traditional blues *See See Rider*, with its Ma Rainey associations, seems an odd choice. Ellington's discordant piano at the start would have one suspect that the theme was by Thelonious Monk, and indeed the most direct references to the melody of the old folk blues are in Brown's part in the middle of the performance. Those expecting an Ellingtonian development of the melody in the manner of his blues on the 1959 *Back To Back* LP will be disappointed, for this is one of Ellington's violent, discordant blues improvisations.

The whole second side of the disc is taken up by what is described as *Fragmented Suite For Piano And Bass*. Ellington's suites were frequently rather loosely strung together, but little effort seems to have been made to unite these four movements in any way: *Fragmented* this suite certainly is, even by Ellington standards. The first and last movements are rhythmic studies of an advanced order, Ellington punctuating the bass line with a succession of highly percussive chords and ingenious rhythmic patterns. Both these outer movements have a Spanish flavor as if Ellington were casting Brown in the role of some kind of Americanized and modernized flamenco guitarist. Ellington's melodic line in the fourth movement is one of austere strength, and one can sense the problems this poses to Brown in creating a suitable second part. This is a very original Ellington conception. The two inner movements are at medium and fast medium tempo respectively, and the second of them uses the theme which was titled *Pleading For Love* in the 1961 *Piano In The Foreground* collection, while the third contains a particularly brilliant piano improvisation. Ellington deploys an unusually wide range of stylistic reference throughout this collection; it is really remarkable how his piano can adopt so many different guises, perform so many different functions, and still retain so distinct a stylistic identity.

The string bass was an important voice in Duke Ellington's music right from the day Wellman Braud joined his orchestra in 1927 up to the time that this Pablo LP was recorded, when Joe Benjamin was the regular bassist. It is therefore particularly interesting to hear how a master bass player without an extended and intimate experience of Ellington's music will cope with an Ellingtonian situation. Brown always chooses the right notes, but he sometimes surrounds them with so many others than one wonders if a spell with Duke's band might have caused him to reflect on the merits of musical economy. In *This One's For Blanton,* we are presented with one of the most astonishing displays of string bass virtuosity in the history of recorded jazz, a display which is geared, quite spontaneously, to the musical situation in a brilliant and imaginative way. More importantly, it contains Duke Ellington's brilliant swan song as a solo pianist.

* * *

Only a calendar month less a day separates *This One's For Blanton* and Ellington's other Pablo piano LP, *Duke's Big Four,* but in musical terms the difference is immense. For the first time, Duke's physical decline is apparent in the music. While by the none-too-demanding standard of the ordinary jazz LP *Duke's Big Four* gets by well enough, by Ellington standards it is a mediocre record. Norman Granz surrounds Ellington with three of the Granz circus of virtuosi; two of these are long-serving Granz-men, Ray Brown and Louis Bellson, the other a then relatively new member of the troupe, guitarist Joe Pass. As is made clear in Derek Jewell's biography of Ellington, Duke's relationship with Granz was often stormy, and it could just be that Duke coasts his way through this session because he didn't really want to be on it in the first place. The piano playing sounds very tired throughout and lacks the punch, drive, and zest which Ellington had displayed on the duet recordings with Brown. Some of the strength seems to have gone out of his fingers; at no time does the piano assert the expected Ellingtonian authority. Confusion in voice leading between piano and guitar is common, and the whole set lacks the cohesion of an Ellington session. To hear Duke playing like this is a shattering experience. On the evidence of this record, it seems astonishing that he still had the stamina to carry on his exacting bandleading and touring duties for another year. By January 1973 it is painfully obvious to anyone who knows his playing that Duke was a very sick man indeed. The unexpected yet perfectly placed notes and the beautiful chords are there, but the strength has gone and it is almost unbearably sad to anyone who knows Duke's earlier playing. Yet even in this state Ellington was a sufficient musician to make things sound good superficially, so the LP is a superior example of the Norman Granz studio jazz session. It has been suggested that Pass hogs the limelight unduly here, but it could be that he was taking as much weight as possible off the shoulders of the pianist. The themes chosen are *Cotton Tail, The Hawk Talks, Prelude To A Kiss, Love You Madly, Just Squeeze Me, Everything But You,* plus an Ellington *Blues*. There is much less of the Ellington flavor in this performance of *Just Squeeze Me* than there was in the version with Armstrong's All Stars in 1961, and it would be difficult for anyone lacking personnel information to recognize these as Ellington performances. The other three musicians are skilled professionals of a very high order and they ensure that the surface veneer is bright and fully finished. But close listening reveals that Pass's crippling lack of swing and Brown's restless virtuosity are weakening factors; the overall effect is of very bland music making. It is useless to speculate how this session would have turned out had Ellington been in full vigor; certainly it would have been *very* different. *Duke's Big Four* is an average enough record of small-group jazz making from any other aspect, but from the viewpoint of its greatest participant it is a rather sad document.

* * *

In July 1973 the Ellington band recorded four titles in New York with Alice Babs. The personnel was:

Trumpets: Money Johnson, Johnny Coles, Barry Lee Hall, Willie Cook, Mercer Ellington.

Trombones: Vince Prudente, Art Baron, Chuck Connors (bass trombone).

Reeds: Russell Procope (alto sax, clarinet); Harold Minerve (alto sax, flute, piccolo); Harold Ashby (tenor sax, clarinet); Percy Marion (tenor sax); Harry Carney (baritone sax, clarinet, bass clarinet).

Rhythm: Duke Ellington (piano); Joe Benjamin (bass); Rocky White (drums).

Vocal: Alice Babs.

Cook's return was only of brief duration; Gonsalves was temporarily missing; but the change on drums was permanent, Rocky White being a young musician with a lively if conventional manner. The regular vocalists at this time were Tony Watkins and Anita Moore.

The four titles with Alice Babs have been released on the Phontastic label. It is interesting to hear her with the full band in a secular part of the repertoire. On these performances the singing is heavily featured; for the most part the band is heard in a supporting role. *Far Away Star* is a composition and arrangement by Nils Lindberg, with Babs singing both with lyrics and wordlessly. On Ellington's 1939 *Serenade To Sweden* she features wordless soprano singing of great melodic sensitivity and perfect musicianship. An unexpected revival for this session is *Spacemen* from 1958, and on this uptempo performance Babs is heard along with Willie Cook and Johnny Coles. She gives an astonishing display of vocal technique. *Jeep's Blues* presents different problems; although the singing is of great beauty, it is not in the blues idiom, a quite serious flaw in this number.

* * *

Two months later the Ellington band recorded an LP with a very different singer, Teresa Brewer. Having made her name with some rather adolescent pop singing in the forties, she considerably extended her range in the sixties and seventies. She was married to Bob Thiele, a noted jazz record producer who had done much sterling work for the Impulse label and was now running his own Flying Dutchman company. The Ellington-Brewer LP was first released on that label and later reissued on Columbia.

There are two newly recorded Ellington songs in this set, *Poco Mucho*, a trivial piece, and *It's Kind Of Lonesome Out Tonight*, a pleasant ballad dating from 1947. Three titles are accompanied by Ellington and a studio rhythm section, the rest by the band. Ray Nance and Tyree Glenn reinforce the brass section and their presence raises the quality of the solos. On *I Ain't Got Nothin' But The Blues*, Nance and Glenn play a plunger-muted duet and they, along with Procope, Ashby, and Carney make notable solo contributions throughout the LP.

On two tracks, five additional trumpet players bring the section up to nine and are used very effectively on a revival of *I've Got To Be A Rug Cutter*. Here Teresa Brewer and Bunny Briggs indulge in a spot of tap dancing as well as doing a lively vocal duet. Instrumentally this is a good LP with the Ellington band in lively form. The arrangements, by Duke and Ernie Wilkins, are solid jazz scores, if lacking in the touches of genius found in most of Duke's output. On three tracks, Miss Brewer is joined in vocal duets by Briggs, a quite ordinary singer. Brewer brings plenty of verve and enthusiasm to her singing, but she is no jazz stylist and often sounds affected to jazz-oriented ears. But this is a rewarding LP for the Ellington enthusiast, one which finds the band in better than average form so far as its seventies recordings are concerned.

* * *

The last issued LPs by Duke Ellington and his Orchestra— and there are later live recordings—were both made in England during Duke's final European tour in late 1973. The first was recorded at the premiere of Ellington's *Third Sacred Concert—The Majesty Of God* at Westminster Abbey, London, on October 24, 1973, United Nations Day. The second is from recordings made at an ordinary concert by the band at Eastbourne on December 1, 1973. The personnel is that of the July recordings with Alice Babs except that Willie Cook is absent. The band had been greatly weakened during this tour by the frequent absences of Gonsalves. The vocalists were still Tony Watkins and Anita Moore; for the *Sacred Concert*, they were joined by Alice Babs and the John Aldis Choir.

With so few experienced Ellington men on hand it is perhaps not surprising that Duke used fewer solos than ever before in the *Third Sacred Concert*. A list of the players the band had lost since the first two *Sacred Concerts* makes very sad reading: Cootie Williams, Cat Anderson, Lawrence Brown, Johnny Hodges, Jimmy Hamilton, Norris Turney, John Lamb, Louis Bellson, Sam Woodyard—a grievous loss of talent. By the time of the *Third Sacred Concert*, Ellington was himself very ill, but with the extra devotion which he always put into his sacred works he sounds much more authoritative at the piano than was the case at the *Duke's Big Four* recording session. But his old strength is clearly not there.

After speeches by Sir Colin Crow, chairman of the United Nations Association, and Ellington himself, who sounds exhausted, the concert opens with *The Lord's Prayer*, a solemn and majestic piano solo by Duke. Alice Babs sings beautifully on *My Love*, which also contains a solo by that most devoted Ellingtonian, Harry Carney. Here the band scoring is quiet and the ensemble does not sound very distinctive. But the rhythm section functions well, and the drumming seems more apt for Ellington than had been the case for some time. The acoustics of the famous location are, however, less than ideal. The band was only moderately familiar with this music, having run through it a few times after-hours in a Chicago night club the previous week. Apart from this they had only one day's rehearsal with the choir. Alice Babs too had only the one day's rehearsal, but she sounds more familiar with the material than the bandsmen; her singing is full of brilliant musicianship. In *Is God A Three Letter Word For Love?* she is accompanied by some beautiful Ellington piano as well as by a wordless choir. In the middle section of this segment, Tony Watkins appears in the guise of preacher and delivers a sermon in that exaggerated manner which Ellington seemed to admire but which to many ears seems to border on parody. One of the few uptempo pieces in the concert is *The Brotherhood,* a tribute to the United Nations Association. Here the choir sings brilliantly; indeed throughout the concert they give a display of musical professionalism at its finest. With Gonsalves in the hospital his parts had been handed over to Ashby, but the only Ashby solo on the issued portions of the *Third Sacred Concert* is an extended one in *The Brotherhood,* during which he is accompanied variously by the band, the choir, and the rhythm section alone. Although he sounds very close to Ben Webster here, Ashby is basically his own man and this is one of his best solos on record.

There is further admirable if restrained Ellington piano on *Hallelujah* and his accompaniment to the choir is a model of taste and discretion, as is the diminuendo ending. This is perhaps not the most impressive *Hallelujah* ever written for a choir, but it certainly has a most brilliant piano part. The long *Every Man Prays In His Own Language* is a series of separate segments by the band, the choir, the saxophone section (some beautiful writing here), Alice Babs, Art Baron (playing recorder), Babs with the choir, and finally Ellington as narrator with the choir. Duke sounds like a very sick man here, and the music glows only intermittently. The inevitable Watkins gospel song is *Ain't Nobody Nowhere Nothin' Without God.* It is delivered in the familiar melodramatic manner and is less convincing than the gospel song from the *Second Sacred Concert.* Finally, the movement which is used as the subtitle of the entire work—*The Majesty Of God*—opens with a superb Ellington piano solo at a slow medium walking tempo. There are beautiful passages for the band with piano, for Carney in solo, for brass and piano, for Babs, and even one in 3/4 time for choir and orchestra. This movement is the best organized in the concert and provides a suitable climax for the last extended work which Ellington was able to perform in public. (He later composed *Three Black Kings,* an orchestral piece, but this was not performed until after his death.) The musical value of the *Third Sacred Concert* is not so great as that of the *Second,* but it has many highlights. The number of these which are provided by Ellington as an executant is amazing, considering the circumstances.

* * *

The *Eastbourne Performance,* as the final RCA LP is called, is something quite different, although apart from the absence of Alice Babs and choir the personnel is the same as for *The Third Sacred Concert.* The selections used by RCA from the Eastbourne concert do not feature Tony Watkins, while the singer who was left out of the issued part of the *Third Sacred Concert,* Anita Moore, is heard on one number. The acoustics of the hall allow for a much better recording quality, and one can certainly better appreciate the superb playing of Joe Benjamin, as well as the drumming of young Rocky White. The ensemble, however, is clearly not of the standard associated with Ellington. He covers this up by making every track either a solo feature or a number which calls for little band playing. He even presents a "Dixieland" version of *Tiger Rag,* and three of the eleven tracks are piano solos.

One of these solos opens the program—*The Piano Player,* an Ellington medium-tempo improvisation. Despite his failing physical state, Duke is clearly as fully alert mentally and as inventive as ever. The piano introduction to *Creole Love Call* lacks the old authority, but for all that, Duke plays some beautiful piano on this old composition. The opening ensemble consists of three clarinets and Money Johnson's muted trumpet, while the solos are by Carney on bass clarinet, playing Rudy Jackson's old chorus, and Procope on clarinet in a two-chorus improvisation. Harold Minerve's alto is featured in the 1944 *Don't You Know I Care?,* a pleasantly melodic performance over a Latin beat with the band's playing sounding more in the Ellington tradition than anywhere else on the set. The version of *I Can't Get Started* which follows is one of the best examples of Harold Ashby's art to be heard on record; his solo here is a really matured piece of musical thinking. This number had been used as a feature for Ashby virtually since he joined the band in 1968. The bizarre, discordant piano introduction and accompaniment we had heard from Duke on previous tours are toned down here, but the piano still adds greatly to the performance. Ellington then gives a very warm introduction to Anita Moore, who proceeds to sing and shout a not very distinguished creation of his, *New York, New York.* Duke wrote both words and music for this item, and the lyrics can be found in his autobiography, the reading of them being a tempting alternative to listening to this performance.

Pitter Panther Patter (wrongly titled *Pitter Patter Panther* on sleeve and label) reveals, by comparison with the version on *This One's For Blanton,* just how much Ellington's piano work was now affected by his deteriorating health. But he husbands his resources superbly, and Joe Benjamin provides an ideal bass part. A perfunctory *How High The Moon* does little to indicate the talents of the featured soloist, Johnny Coles. Another member of the trumpet section is given a showcase as Ellington introduces Money Johnson and the music of "the future . . . one hundred years from today." After some discordant hokum from the band, Johnson settles into a not very distinguished *Basin Street Blues* in the style of Louis Armstrong. The music sinks even lower with a wild and thoroughly mediocre Dixieland *Tiger Rag* played by Johnson, Vince Prudente on trombone, Procope on clarinet, and the rhythm section. These two performances are of very low quality for an Ellington concert. The musicians in his bands of the thirties, forties, fifties, or sixties could have covered up for the leader's illness, but by this time the stars had almost all departed. Things recover somewhat with a rather sketchy new

Ellington piece called *Woods*, which features the tenors of Ashby and Percy Marion in solos, duets, and chases. The concert ends with the *Meditation* solo from the *Second Sacred Concert*—hushed reflective piano over bowed bass.

And there, for the moment, the Ellington discography ends. Pending issue of later recordings, the *Eastbourne Performance* LP stands at the end of Duke Ellington's long recording career, a career which had begun almost exactly 50 years earlier with *Jig Walk, Choo Choo,* and *Rainy Nights.*

* * *

Outstanding Recordings

1. Fantasy Issues

YALE CONCERT
LATIN AMERICAN SUITE
THE AFRO-EURASIAN ECLIPSE

2. United Artists Recordings

from THE SECOND CONCERT OF SACRED MUSIC: *Supreme Being, Heaven, Almighty God Has Those Angels, The Shepherd, Sweet Fat And That, T.G.T.T.,* parts of *Praise God And Dance*
from *TOGO Brava* SUITE/THE ENGLISH CONCERT: *Togo Brava-Brava Togo Suite, C Jam Blues, Happy Reunion*

3. Duke Ellington Octet Recordings 1968

Take The "A" Train, Contrapuntal Riposte, I'm Beginning To See The Light

4. Atlantic Issues

THE NEW ORLEANS SUITE

5. Decca Recordings

LP with the Cincinnati Symphony Orchestra

6. Pablo Issues

THE GOUTELAS SUITE
from THE INTIMATE ELLINGTON: *Edward The First, Edward The Second, Intimate Interlude, Symphonette* (the last a selection from the final part of *Black, Brown And Beige*)
from UP IN DUKE'S WORKSHOP: *Wanderlust, Mendoza, Blem*
THE UWIS SUITE
THIS ONE'S FOR BLANTON (with Ray Brown)

7. 1973 Recordings with Alice Babs

Spacemen, Jeep's Blues

8. 1973 Recordings with Teresa Brewer

I've Got To Be A Rug Cutter

9. Miscellaneous Concert Recordings

from the MF label: *Black Butterfly* (1969), *Chinoiserie, Happy Reunion* (1971)
October 1971, Warsaw: *Goof*

Chapter 31

The Final Years

THE DEATH OF STRAYHORN IN 1967 was a great blow to Ellington. The two had been the closest of friends for over a quarter of a century, and Billy's death robbed Duke of his principal musical assistant, his right hand both as writer and as bandleader. Their musical collaboration was unique: sometimes one would arrange the other's music from rough drafts; sometimes they would work together by writing different parts of the same arrangement. If Duke arrived at an impasse in a particular score, then he would pass it to Billy for completion, a pattern which also operated in reverse. They were constantly available to each other for consultation on musical matters, often at odd hours and in unusual places. Ellington had the greatest possible respect for his "writing and arranging companion," and this is reflected in the famous eulogy in which he enumerated the four freedoms by which Billy Strayhorn had lived.

Strayhorn died after a long and debilitating illness. He continued to write for the band while in the hospital, and his last composition, *Blood Count*—a feature for Johnny Hodges—was played with a moving intensity by the orchestra in the months after his death. From this time onwards Ellington included in his concerts, usually as the closing item, a piano solo version of Strayhorn's *Lotus Blossom* in tribute to his late partner. "That is what he most liked to hear me play," Duke would explain. Whether Strayhorn's death at the early age of 51 reminded Duke, then 68, of his own mortality we do not know, but from this time on his rate of work as composer increased dramatically.

At different times after Strayhorn's death, Jimmy Jones and Wild Bill Davis acted as deputy pianists and arrangers with the Ellington band, but no one could really take Billy's place; no other musician had his particular combination of talents and his deep understanding of how Ellington's mind worked musically. The additional responsibilities which fell on Ellington's shoulders after Strayhorn's death were delegated to others as far as was possible, in other words not very far at all. The remainder were shouldered by Ellington without apparent effort, and he threw himself more furiously than ever before into the business of composing.

* * *

In this period, the costs of recording in America, like everything else, had increased, pricing large—and to a degree even small—jazz groups out of the recording studios, since jazz sales had never approached those of popular artists. Fees per musician, set by union rules, were high, and the hours allowed before overtime scale came into operation were limited. Regulations concerning the number of tracks which could be produced per session were also restrictive. These were among the reasons for the reduction in the number of studio recordings done by the Ellington Orchestra for the larger companies, but the band continued to record privately for Duke and some of this material has found its way onto record.

Economic factors also served to restrict the number of venues at which a big band could be successfully presented for either a one-nighter or a residency. The auditorium had to be large enough but not too massive, the audience for a big band had to be available in the locality, and the staging needed to be right. This last was important, since a big band presented a totally different problem from those posed by the rock bands with their amplified instruments and garish lighting. The lack of relevant experience of younger sound engineers and lighting specialists could present problems at larger venues for the Ellington Orchestra and its audience. These problems could also be present at a club engagement, but the main problem here was the shrinking number of clubs willing and able to employ a big band. So Ellington turned increasingly to concert tours, especially abroad.

The band played in Europe, Africa, and Japan in 1966 (the year of the Chateau Goutelas opening); they toured Europe in 1967 and South America in 1968, the West Indies and Europe in 1969, the Far East and Australia in 1970, Russia and Europe in 1971, the Far East in 1972, and Europe and Africa in 1973. Between the premiere of the *Third Sacred Concert* on October 24, 1973, in London and the Royal Command performance at the London Palladium on November 26, the band visited Sweden, Denmark, Germany, Austria, Yugoslavia, Spain, France, Belgium, Ethiopia, and Zambia! This kind of routine was the main reason why many veteran Ellingtonians were no longer touring with the band. But

Ellington himself seemed to take it all in his stride, and what exhausted many musicians half his age—musicians who had no responsibilities other than getting up on the stand each night and playing a fairly settled repertoire—seemed simply invigorating to the pianist-composer-arranger-bandleader.

One thing he found continually stimulating in these last years was the warmth with which he and his musicians were received throughout the world. The South American and Russian tours were new experiences for the Ellingtonians; each was in its different way a total success. The fact that his music was known and loved in countries with cultures as diverse as these was a source of great pleasure to Ellington. He knew that he had opened corridors of communication between sections of the human race who normally regarded each other with hostility. The message of love and tolerance which he spelled out in his sacred concerts was not a new development in Ellington music, but rather an element which had always been implicit in it. Prior to the sacred concerts the message was delivered in purely musical terms, but people knew well enough what Duke Ellington stood for, and in his last years he must have known how universally this was understood.

* * *

Quite apart from the continuing creation of short pieces, which were by this time usually in the form of showcases for different members of the band, the Ellington output of concert music is amazing for a 52-weeks-a-year globe-trotting bandleader. His extended compositions from this period included the film scores for *Assault On A Queen* and *Change Of Mind;* the incidental music for a production of T. S. Eliot's *Murder In The Cathedral; La Plus Belle Africaine* for the International Festival of Negro Arts at Dakar, Senegal; the little-known but brilliant *Pretty Little Purple Flower;* the second and third concerts of sacred music; the *Latin American Suite;* the ballet *The River; the New Orleans Suite* for the 1970 New Orleans Jazz Festival; *The Afro-Eurasian Eclipse; The Goutelas Suite; The Togo Brava Suite; The UWIS Suite;* and finally *The Three Black Kings.* This music has the range and the depth of a major artist; its scope is beyond that of any other jazz musician. Some of this music has not yet been issued, but in time it will doubtless appear, probably along with works as yet unknown.

Much of the music that Ellington wrote was never heard away from his recording sessions. One of the reasons for this was the highly conservative nature of his programs at public appearances. Only when involved in a prestigious concert in combination with a symphony orchestra would a full program of his concert music be given, and even then it was highly probable that the *Medley Of Popular Hits* would be dragged in at some point during the evening. The sheer frustration felt by Ellington devotees when the introductory fanfare to this *Medley* rang out was almost physically painful. It is true that it always included some outstanding solos and new arrangements of old standards and that Duke's genius as a melody player was always strongly in evidence. But the appearance of the *Medley* meant that much of the concert would be taken up by familiar items and often by the questionable delights of Ellington's vocalists, rather than by the new music which so many in the audience wanted to hear. Yet when the English writer Benny Green asked Ellington why he did not present programs made up of three or four of his major concert works, he replied that he doubted that his audiences would really want that. One wonders whether Ellington was aware just how many of his audience winced at the words which heralded the *Medley Of Popular Hits*—"I've been very lucky as a song writer, ladies and gentlemen. . . ."

We should of course remember that Ellington was a very old hand at understanding what his audiences wanted—he had led a very successful professional life because of it—and that he knew exactly what he was doing. Many leaders who had adopted a more uncompromising stance had long since lost their bands. Ellington's band always worked, so if the reiterations of the *Medley Of Popular Hits* and the occasional halting of the music for a drum solo were the price paid for their constant output of new music, then the cost was low indeed, even if a consequence was that much of this new music was confined to the recording studio.

* * *

After the absurd incident in 1965 when the Pulitzer Prize Committee rejected its music advisory board's recommendation of a special citation for Ellington, other honors were bestowed on Duke. Among those he must have valued highly were an honorary Doctorate of Music from Yale University in 1967; the Presidential Medal of Freedom in 1969; and two awards from abroad—the Emperor's Star of Honor from Ethiopia and the Legion of Honor from France, both in 1973. The list of such awards which Ellington chose to include in his autobiography *Music Is My Mistress* makes for interesting if occasionally amusing reading. In these last years Ellington's life seems to have been made up for the most part of the triple functions of graciously accepting honors, keeping his band hard at work for 52 weeks of the year, and writing new music at a prodigious rate. As a combination of activities this is unique; for a man of more than 70 it is simply astounding. In 1969, a special Ellington birthday party was hosted by the President of the United States at the White House, but the following night the band was back on the road doing a routine engagement.

* * *

The sudden death of Johnny Hodges was another blow which Ellington suffered during these years. Their long association had produced music of unique beauty, and, as a member of the Ellington musical repertory company, Hodges was irreplaceable. The departures of Lawrence

Brown and Cat Anderson at around the same time as the death of Hodges combined to deliver a triple blow from which the Ellington band never fully recovered. Before this, Sam Woodyard had departed, and Ellington was never again to find a drummer with the right combination of talent and temperament for his band. By virtue of the experience and devotion of the remaining star soloists and the fine musicianship and imaginative artistry of some of the newer and less celebrated members, the Ellington Orchestra remained a fine ensemble, but neither in solo strength nor in orchestral subtlety was it able to maintain earlier standards.

These were the most serious blows the band had ever suffered. When Hodges, Brown, and Greer had left in 1951, Ellington was able to recruit musicians of the caliber of Willie Smith, Juan Tizol, Britt Woodman, and Louis Bellson. By the early seventies, musicians with that kind of background and ability were either deceased or too old to want to travel. The musicians of the younger generations excelled in the mechanics of music making to a degree which their elders had hardly dreamt possible, but they did not possess the musical style, the individuality of musical character, or the imaginative application which were essential in Ellington's band. So it was that while the leader continued to pour out masterpiece after masterpiece the band slowly but steadily deteriorated before his eyes. To the very end the Ellington Orchestra contained musicians of the stature of Harry Carney, Russell Procope, Joe Benjamin, and Harold Ashby. And in the years after the loss of Hodges, Brown, and Anderson such players as Cootie Williams and Paul Gonsalves continued to make vital contributions. But the decline in the quality of the ensemble was plain for all to hear.

For all its limitations, the Ellington Orchestra continued to interpret its leader's scores with a special understanding. It would be foolish indeed to ignore Ellington's late works because of the limitations of the band which plays them. Only in its recordings in the last year or so of its existence does the decline of the band allied to Ellington's own poor health have a crucial effect on the music. During the years immediately prior to this, Ellington skillfully covered any deficiencies in the band by continuing to do what he had always done—adapt his writing to the band's current strengths. The difference now lay in increasing weaknesses that needed to be kept in the background.

* * *

Ellington's attitude to the aging process was fascinating. That he was deeply concerned is obvious from his endless stream of witticisms denying his chronological age. Of these, the references to certain pieces being written "before I joined the band" and to his being born at the 1956 Newport Jazz Festival were the most common. Throughout his life he had displayed an attitude of rather studied indifference to what people might think of his music in the future—what posterity would make of his work. He had a particular dread of biographies which he had expressed as far back as the thirties. "They are like tombstones," he had said, "nobody wants one." It was, therefore, very surprising to learn in the late sixties that Duke was about to write an autobiography. Would he decide to lift the masks which had obscured his personality and his musical methods all those years? Would the wisdom of the great man be summarized for future generations? Would the humanity of his music be spelled out in philosophical terms? Would he abandon the oblique manner and speak directly to his audience?

One of Ellington's primary motives in writing the book is made plain in Derek Jewell's biography; he needed the money. *Music Is My Mistress* was the result of a hard bargain designed to provide more cash for the endless task of keeping his expensive band going. Maybe by this time Duke, ever conscious of his prestige, thought that a man of his eminence *should* provide the world with an autobiography. He seems to have written the book in a characteristic way, jotting down notes on sheets of paper in a haphazard fashion. The results were gradually assembled into book form by Stanley Dance, with Duke having overall control. The result is at first sight a disappointment in the terms of the kind of book people thought Ellington could and should have written. But these hopes did not really show much understanding of Ellington's personality and methods. *Music Is My Mistress* is a very characteristic Ellington product. It is presented as a mixture of show-biz autobiography and illustrated scrapbook. All Ellington's honors are listed, and the photographic illustrations picture him with the eminent at regular intervals throughout the book. All the important Ellington musical associates are discussed, but always anecdotally and often very briefly. These features are mixed with biographical material and notes and reflections on places visited in the course of his tours as well as with miscellaneous writings including poems and song lyrics. Ellington reflects on the nature of jazz, and there is even a stream-of-consciousness prose poem called *Pedestrian Minstrel*. The book does give the impression of being a jumbled assembly of miscellaneous thoughts and reflections, and it addresses itself to the reader on a rather bewildering number of levels. It is easy to suspect that we have been presented with a book wholly lacking in depth or substance. What we in fact have is a literary version of *the* favorite Ellington trick, that of presenting something of real substance in the guise of a happy little entertainment.

In *Music Is My Mistress* we learn about Ellington's attitudes to life and death; of his views of humanity and the world; and of his opinions on art, religion, music, race, and a myriad of other topics. The book also provides an invaluable guide to his late music. All this is presented in the bland, rather off-putting way of an American show-biz autobiography. In this Ellington remained true to the world which gave him the platform for his life's work. Perhaps we are too close to the Ellington phenomenon to evaluate fully the importance of his autobiography. But one thing is certain: for as long as Ellington's creations are considered to be of importance and worth, so long will *Music Is My Mistress* continue to throw a unique light on both the man and the music.

* * *

From the early seventies, Ellington's health had started to deteriorate. Although something of a hypochondriac, he had always been a very fit man; to cope with his lifestyle and his work schedule he could hardly have been otherwise. But now he started to lose weight, to become moody, to conserve his energies carefully for the vitally important tasks of writing and leading the band. Doctors were consulted, hospital treatment was recommended and refused. Even when lung cancer was diagnosed, this was largely ignored. The work went on. Ellington looked worse and felt worse, but he was sustained by his faith in God. When his doctor and close friend Arthur Logan died suddenly in November 1973, Ellington said that he would not live another six months himself. In January 1974, he collapsed while working but quickly returned to continue leading the band. He entered the hospital for what proved to be the last time in March 1974, and his health continued to deteriorate steadily. He died on May 24, 1974, still in the hospital; on his death bed he had continued working. He had two projects in hand, a stage musical, *Queenie Pie,* and his last work for orchestra, *Three Black Kings.* His courage and endurance in the terrible circumstances were astonishing as was the energy and optimism which went into *Three Black Kings.* Posthumous performances of this work by The Duke Ellington Orchestra, directed by Mercer Ellington, show that there was no falling off in the composer's creative powers despite his age and terminal illness. To the end, his Christian faith was unshaken; he seemed to believe that somehow or other he would be spared to carry on his work. By an almost uncanny coincidence, three major figures of the last phase of the Ellington orchestra died within a few months of Duke—Joe Benjamin in a road accident in January 1974, Paul Gonsalves a few days before Duke in May, and less than five months later, Harry Carney in October.

When the band reconvened, it was under the leadership of Mercer Ellington and with only a few of the old personnel. Harold Ashby and Russell Procope did not continue; Cootie Williams returned but he and Harry Carney stayed only briefly. Mercer continued to lead The Duke Ellington Orchestra. Some years after Duke's death they made the only issued recording of *Three Black Kings.* In this performance they join forces with the Warsaw Philharmonic Orchestra, and the recording was issued on the Frog Box label. The set also includes performances of *The River* and *New World A-Comin'* by the same forces. And there are several LPs by the orchestra under Mercer's direction. But the music, inevitably, is different. The Duke Ellington chapter in the annals of twentieth-century art closed on May 24, 1974.

Sidemen

Harold Ashby

While occupying most of his time playing with bands in the New York area, Harold Ashby had long been the principal reserve to the great Ellington reed team of the fifties and sixties. When Jimmy Hamilton left the band in 1968, Ashby took his place, even though he was a tenor saxophone specialist and Hamilton had been the band's clarinet virtuoso. The presence of Ashby gave Ellington a musician capable of taking over the important tenor chair held by Gonsalves should the dubious health and erratic habits of that worthy lead to his absence. To join what most musicians regarded as the greatest saxophone section in history was a tremendous challenge. Ashby's strength was that he brought to the situation the kind of individual musicianship and imagination essential for success in the Ellington band. Although both Ashby's and Gonsalves's playing shows their admiration for Ben Webster, they had each developed a distinctive style. Gonsalves was also powerfully affected by Coleman Hawkins, and he had noticeably individual ways of treating harmony and rhythm. Ashby had developed the Webster manner along more orthodox lines. Compared with his mentor, his tone is more austere, and he uses the upper register more. Some admirers of Webster have noted that his use of the growling, shouting style which he often favored at fast tempos had a rather superficial, unconvincing air. Ashby, however, took over this aspect of Webster's style to advantage; in this regard the pupil is to be preferred to the master. On ballads Ashby is very much his own man with an emotionally direct lyricism. He is also a fine blues player.

Representative Recordings: B.P. Blues (United Artists, 1969), *Thanks For The Beautiful Land On The Delta* (from the *New Orleans Suite,* Atlantic, 1970), *Chinoiserie* (from *The Afro-Eurasian Eclipse,* Fantasy, 1971), *Naturellement* (from the *Togo Brava Suite,* United Artists, 1971), *I Can't Get Started* (Victor, 1973)

Joe Benjamin

In the *New Orleans Suite,* Joe Benjamin plays the *Portrait Of Wellman Braud,* the last of the great Ellington string bassists thus paying tribute to the first. Ellington's was always *the* band for bass players. No one valued the services of a first-class bassist more than Duke, nor created such meaty parts for them. They were always given ample opportunity for imaginative contributions to the music. While in most bands the bassist would simply play time while making variations on the chord patterns, in Duke's band he would play evolving and varied figures against the band while also contributing to the harmonic/rhythmic framework. Although Benjamin had worked as a copyist for the Ellington organization since the early forties, he was better known for his playing with Lena Horne, Sy Oliver, Dave Brubeck, Gerry Mulligan, and, best of all perhaps, for his long partnership with drummer Roy Haynes as accompanist to Sarah Vaughan. He was also a session man of high standing, experienced in radio, television, and symphonic work. Benjamin therefore brought to the Ellington band both a vast professional experience and a long-standing, inside knowledge of Ellington's methods. His immaculate and imaginative playing on all the records he made with Duke reveal his qualities fully. Note especially his work on *The Afro-Eurasian Eclipse,* which is Ellington bass playing in the great tradition.

Representative Recordings: Portrait Of Wellman Braud (from the *New Orleans Suite,* Atlantic, 1970), *Intimate Interlude* (Pablo, 1970), *Pitter Panther Patter* (Victor, 1973)

Johnny Coles

In his last years, Ellington no longer wrote with the special sounds of all the sidemen in mind. The styles of the newer musicians in particular never seemed to have become a part of Ellington's imaginative process. The individuality of Johnny Coles, a distinguished soloist in the fifties school of modern jazz trumpet, was hardly ever used in the way Duke had used Clark Terry's style a decade or so earlier. The consequence is that while Coles is a distinguished musician, he made little impression as an Ellingtonian. Ellington once said that you needed to know how a musician played poker before you could write for him; by the time Coles came in Ellington had neither the time nor the inclination to play poker with his sidemen. As things stand, the only Coles solos on issued Ellington recordings are conventional jazz choruses on numbers like *Goof* or *How High The Moon;* they do not include numbers calling for interpretive skills. Those fortunate enough to have heard the band play *Aristocracy à la Jean Lafitte* from the *New Orleans Suite* when Coles was featured will recall how brilliantly he took his flugelhorn solo in that composition.

Representative Recordings: Goof (Poljazz, 1971), *How High The Moon* (Victor, 1973)

Wild Bill Davis

Wild Bill Davis stayed with the Ellington band for just under two years. Prior to this he had a most successful career as a solo organist, having begun as pianist and arranger. His recordings include a notable series with Johnny Hodges. Perhaps his best known arrangement is *April In Paris,* featured with such success by the Basie Orchestra of the middle fifties. With the Ellington Orchestra, Wild Bill was heard mainly on organ, used discreetly and never on numbers on which the organ might overpower the delicate Ellington tone colors. His organ solos were in that vigorous, forthright swinging style with which he had become associated. He also functioned as deputy pianist and arranger, his main contribution in the latter capacity being a version of *I Got It Bad* which Duke used quite extensively.

Representative Recordings: Azure Te (United Artists, 1969), *Black Swan* (United Artists, 1969), *April In Paris* (TOM, 1970), *Blues For New Orleans* (from the *New Orleans Suite,* Atlantic, 1970)

Money Johnson

Money Johnson was featured both as trumpeter and vocalist during the last years of the band's existence. It was obvious that he was not a jazz musician of the class of the earlier Ellington trumpet stars, but his contributions were both professional and swinging.

Representative Recordings: Hello Dolly (Poljazz, 1971), *Basin Street Blues* (Victor, 1973)

Rufus Jones

After the departure of Sam Woodyard, a number of drummers occupied the Ellington percussion chair. Of these, Rufus Jones served the longest. He was the kind of heavy drummer which Ellington obviously preferred, but his playing lacked the swing of such predecessors as Greer and Woodyard. Jones's greatest virtue was his ability as a percussion colorist in Duke's more exotic features, especially those of a Latin American rhythmic cast. Certainly his work on this type of number had more vitality than that on the straightforward jazz performances.

Representative Recordings: Chico Cuadradino (from the *Latin American Suite,* Fantasy, 1968), *Eque* (from the *Latin American Suite,* Fantasy, 1968), *Intimate Interlude* (Pablo, 1971), *Afrique* (from *The Afro-Eurasian Eclipse,* Fantasy, 1971), the *Togo Brava Suite* (United Artists, 1971)

Harold Minerve

Harold "Geezil" Minerve was heard on alto sax, flute, and piccolo during the last years of the Duke Ellington Orchestra. He was a forceful player and a fiery soloist, as befits a jazz musician whose experience included a spell in the Buddy Johnson Orchestra. Like so many of the younger musicians whom Ellington brought in to replace the retiring veterans in the seventies, Minerve lacked the strong personality and the sheer musical class of his predecessors.

Representative Recordings: Addi (United Artists, 1971), *Don't You Know I Care* (Victor, 1973)—both on alto sax.

Vince Prudente

Vince Prudente was the trombone soloist in the band for its last three years. He was adept in both open solos and in the plunger style, but his playing lacked the finish and the personality of his predecessors. At the present there are no representative Prudente solos with Ellington on published recordings.

Norris Turney

When he first joined the Ellington band, Norris Turney brought the reeds up to six pieces and quickly revealed his versatility in playing flute, clarinet, alto, and tenor saxes up to the high standard required by the Ellington band. He spent one tour playing alto sax as part of the trombone section! On the death of Johnny Hodges, he took over the chair vacated by that great musician, just about the most demanding position a saxophonist could be called upon to fill. Turney was not a second Hodges, nor did he pretend to be. As a soloist he was featured as often on flute as on alto, while in the section his playing was of a positive nature with a full-blooded alto tone. When he took a solo on alto, he showed a strong debt to Hodges, but he was not a mere imitator. His flute replaced the cool voice of Jimmy Hamilton's clarinet, while on tenor he added a third and very robust solo manner to the more subtle styles of Gonsalves and Ashby. Turney also made contributions as a clarinet soloist and as composer/arranger. His *Checkered Hat,* a personal tribute to Hodges, is a striking musical portrait. During the years he was with the band, Turney's all-round musicianship made a significant contribution to the music. He is a swinging jazz musician, and the skill with which he filled the place of Hodges has rarely been given its due.

Representative Recordings: on flute—*Bourbon Street Jingling Jollies* (from the *New Orleans Suite,* Atlantic, 1970), *Soul Soothing Beach* (from *Togo Brava Suite,* United Artists, 1971); on clarinet—*Black Butterfly* (United Artists, 1969); on alto—*Hard Way* (from *The Afro-Eurasian Eclipse,* Fantasy, 1971), *Checkered Hat* (United Artists, 1971); on tenor—*In Triplicate* (United Artists, 1969—Norris Turney is the third tenor soloist)

Rocky White

When Rocky White came into the Ellington Orchestra to replace Jones, the music started to swing more, and he was probably the most successful of that group of young musicians who joined the band in the seventies. Not a jazz personality of the order of Sonny Greer or Sam Woodyard, Rocky White was a drummer whose qualities were those of a solid craftsman rather than an exciting innovator.

Representative Recordings: Jeep's Blues (Phontastic, 1973), *Don't Get Around Much Anymore* (with Teresa Brewer, Flying Dutchman, 1973), *The Brotherhood* (from the *Third Sacred Concert,* Victor, 1973), *New York, New York* (Victor, 1973)

Chapter 32

Duke Ellington's Music in Perspective

JAZZ MUSIC OCCUPIES A UNIQUE PLACE in the annals of Western art, and it is difficult, even so many years after its appearance, to judge its importance. This music is unusually dependent on recordings—wholly so for the preservation of its great works. In academic music the written score is the medium of preservation, and the essential experience is in the concert hall or in the opera house, with home listening to recorded performances an important but not essential supplement. So far as the masters of jazz are concerned, one simply cannot hear the music of Louis Armstrong, Jelly Roll Morton, Sidney Bechet, or Duke Ellington in undiluted form other than via recordings. The concerts by contemporary jazz musicians in which the compositions and sometimes the solos of the early masters are performed are a valuable activity, yet here it is the music which is heard in the concert hall which acts as a supplement to the phonograph record. In jazz we are faced not only with a new kind of music but also with a change in the medium through which its best works can be heard. This is not to argue that recorded jazz is to be preferred to that heard live, but the choice between hearing Armstrong, Morton, Bechet, or Ellington in actual performance or on record has only ever been possible for that minority of the jazz audience who were, to use one of Ellington's favorite phrases, in the right place at the right time. And that time has, unfortunately, passed.

Contemporary recordings, however, allow us to hear the music of the jazz masters played by them with all the authority, freshness, and immediacy of a creator's own performance. To hear the major jazz soloists on records tells us far more about their art than listening to even the most skilled of re-creations. In the case of the music of Duke Ellington we can hear the interpretations by the great Ellington soloists of the works which Duke wrote specifically for them. Without the recordings, we could know comparatively little about Ellington's music.

In this book we have ignored for the most part the recordings of Ellington's music by other artists. The vast majority of these use his instrumental compositions as the basis for conventional jazz performances or his songs as the basis for conventional popular ballad renderings. In either case the results are hardly of even marginal importance in terms of Ellington's own art. There are also a few recordings by other artists who seek to interpret Ellington's works as compositions. The most ambitious of these to date is the recording of the complete *Black, Brown And Beige* by the Alan Cohen band, which we discussed in the context of that work. It was found to offer a totally different musical experience from that provided by the recordings of the work by Ellington's own orchestra. There is no doubt that Ellington's works will continue to be the basis of jazz performances of many kinds, from freely improvised jam session music to careful re-creations of the Cohen variety. The last can be—and we can cite the Cohen recording as proof—most enjoyable musical experiences. But the gulf between them and the performances of Ellington's own orchestra is a clear illustration of the fact that the record is just as important in the case of the music's greatest composer as it is in those of the great jazz soloists.

* * *

One aspect of Ellington's personality which was of great relevance to his success was his remarkable respect for musicians as people and his encouragement of their individuality. His attitude to his sidemen is well illustrated by his reaction to a set which the band played at a theater date soon after Ben Webster joined. Ellington was so busy enthusing in the wings about Ben's playing in *Cotton Tail* that he did not even notice that Webster had failed to keep up with his section mates in the very fast version of *Daybreak Express* which followed. "If you don't get on that train on time you just have to wait for the next one" was Ben's comment. The disciplinary situation in the Ellington band was unique. Cat Anderson once insisted (in conversation with the author) that discipline of a formal kind did not exist at all in the Ellington Orchestra. The band was based on respect, the mutual respect of the musicians for Duke and his for them. That as a consequence they would sometimes be minus a member or two, or would often play untidily and sometimes with poor intonation, was perhaps inevitable. But their playing was always full of character and never of that dreadful anonymity of so much big band music of the postwar period. Perhaps the temporary absence of members of the band may have turned Ellington's mind in the direction of such unusual instrumental combinations as those found in *On A Turquoise Cloud* or

Blues In Blueprint. And some of the live recordings of the band from dances are so full of spirit and swing that the lack of precision and the patches of poor intonation are hardly noticed. Machinelike precision is hardly ever compatible with perfect relaxation or with jazz playing of real character, and no one was more aware of this than Duke Ellington.

Rex Stewart recalled (in conversation with the author) that Duke had only once directly expressed satisfaction with his playing, the occasion being when Rex had asked for a salary increase after playing really well at a particularly prestigious concert. Duke highly praised Rex's playing, particularly for a specific solo during the evening's performance. Then, scratching his chin, Duke observed that it had not been quite so good as the way Rex had played it thirteen days earlier during an obscure dance hall engagement. Rex was astounded that Duke had even noticed his playing on that night, still less remembered it; and by the time Rex had recovered Ellington had concluded the conversation, successfully evading further discussion of Rex's salary. Such ruses were Ellington's regular response to any attempt on the part of the sidemen to discuss finance.

On other occasions Duke could be generous, and he often showed his approval in unusual ways. The day after he had discovered that Stewart played golf, Rex found a full set of first-class clubs on his hotel room bed. On another occasion, after Rex had complained that his cornet part in a new piece should have been scored for bass clarinet, he found a new one waiting for him at his hotel. Ellington had, Rex surmised, recalled that he had played the instrument during his childhood in Washington.

On other occasions Duke would bring different methods to bear in his handling of musicians. On a journey on which Ellington was traveling with the band an angry Oscar Pettiford tried to insist on talking money matters with him; Duke's reaction was simply to go to sleep under the eyes of the enraged bassist.

Other jazz leaders have been famous for spotting talent, but Ellington was supreme, not only in recognizing musical potential, but also at bringing it to fruition. Many great musicians came to full maturity in his band. Take the case of Jimmy Blanton; Ellington's meeting with the great bassist may of course have been chance, but the way Blanton was so quickly featured in the most perfect settings within Ellington's music was most certainly not. Blanton had not been with Ellington a month before he was in the recording studios making the first of that remarkable series of piano-bass duets, a format devised by Ellington for the occasion. Outstanding among many other instances is that of Paul Gonsalves, whose entry into the band was accompanied by comment from many of Duke's followers to the effect that he should have selected a more robust and more conventional tenor player. Yet in Gonsalves, Ellington chose a man who proved to be not only one of the most important innovators of his period and a musician of the most remarkable flexibility, but also an artist whose influence on Ellington's own concepts, especially in the harmonic field, proved to be most fruitful.

In return for the musical resources and artistic inspiration which the musicians brought to the band, Ellington rewarded them by creating incomparable settings for their solos. It is an amazing fact that none of the many brilliant jazz soloists who played with Ellington ever sounded so good away from the band. Many of these musicians were little known when they joined Duke—Johnny Hodges, Cootie Williams, and Ray Nance, for example—and their music grew to maturity in his band. But even players who were established jazz soloists when they joined the band—such as Rex Stewart, Taft Jordan, and Ben Webster—developed their styles to ultimate perfection with Duke. And, as Stewart astutely observed, those who left never sounded *quite* so good without Ellington's unique sense of musical presentation at their disposal.

* * *

Before embarking on a consideration of the development of the Ellington Orchestra and its composer-leader, it is worth stressing that this development was dictated by the availability of the kind of musician with whom Duke could work in a creative way. He often stressed the need for compatibility and explained in an interview with Jack Cullen of Station CKMW, Vancouver, that this was a key factor in the recruitment of new musicians:

> If we need a musician and somebody's available, we let them play a couple of nights and if we like them we say, "Well, why don't you stay around, and see whether you like us or not?"; and this is very important, whether they like us or not, because if they don't we can't use them. . . . (Quoted from Varese LP VS 81007)

Towards the end of his career, as we have seen, Duke found it difficult to find the kind of musicians with the right combination of skills needed to make a contribution to his music. What Ellington required, in addition to a temperamental affinity with his approach, was a musician with a strong melodic sense, an ability to swing, an awareness of the importance of inner harmony parts, and a strong and preferably individual tone. The musicians who came up after the swing era excelled in fast phrasing and harmonic expertise. They lacked the rhythmic qualities of earlier generations because they rarely played for dancing, and they did not have the big tones and section expertise which stem from big band experience. And many of them lacked interest in melodic presentation. That Duke could use musicians who played in what are still called "modern" styles is shown in the contributions of such musicians as Clark Terry, Willie Cook, Britt Woodman, Paul Gonsalves, and Jimmy Hamilton. But these were men who, in addition to being adept in the "modern" styles, also excelled in the Ellingtonian virtues mentioned above. And they were all musicians with previous big band experience. In later years, when musicians of earlier generations became too old to tour, the supply of suitable players dried up completely. Looked at in retrospect, the breakup of the 1956–1959 band seems to have been the point at which this first became a problem, but it was not until the three-year period of 1968 to 1970 that it caused the band to deteriorate markedly. In these three years, Ellington lost Sam Woodyard, Jimmy Hamilton, Johnny Hodges, Lawrence Brown, and Cat Anderson, and these men were literally irreplaceable in the jazz world of that time.

For the previous 40-odd years, Ellington had been unerring in his selection of musicians who fitted the demanding and somewhat eccentric demands of his band and its music. He always chose men who contrasted strongly with those already in the band, never duplicating a style or a sound. Even the Ellington musicians who were not renowned as soloists—men like Arthur Whetsol, Juan Tizol, and Otto Hardwick—were strong individuals who made important contributions to the ensemble. Indeed it is difficult to imagine any other leader who would have utilized the talents of such musicians in so fruitful a way, or to find another band where they would have been allowed such individual expression. Ellington not only handled jazz musicians better than any other bandleader, but his imaginative grasp of their ensemble potentialities also far outstripped those of any other leader.

* * *

A chronological examination of Ellington's recordings offers a fascinating view of the evolution of his musical style: sometimes one can follow almost day by day the slight modifications in the playing of the band in a working environment. Moving slowly through Ellington's recorded history as we have done in this book, we see clearly its smooth and natural development. If we move the focus of our attention suddenly from one period to another the changes seem, by contrast, quite startling. It is then that we realize how much the music was evolving, although its rate of change was almost imperceptible.

Duke Ellington's music was greatly admired by his fellow jazz musicians, and this admiration also extended to the playing of his orchestra. (A lone dissenting voice was that of Jack Teagarden, who considered that the band never played in tune.) To most jazz musicians the Ellington Orchestra was supreme, and its evolution is a subject as interesting as that of its leader's music. If we were to make comparisons across the years, for example by considering the Ellington Orchestra of 1933 followed by that of 1940, then we would find some very interesting changes. By 1933 the Ellington band had already achieved that degree of ensemble skill, sensitivity, and expertise which, allied to its solo strength, placed it beyond competition. The instrumentation of the 1933 band was identical with that of 1940 (except that Fred Guy had switched from banjo to guitar), and their personnels were surprisingly similar. In the trumpet section there was a specialist lead player who was also used as melodic soloist: in 1933 this was Arthur Whetsol and in 1940 Wallace Jones. The second trumpeter was a mercurial character of eccentric style: Freddie Jenkins in the earlier band and Rex Stewart in the later. The third trumpet was the basic jazz soloist and growl specialist, functions performed by Cootie Williams in both bands. Despite their similarities, the two sections sound quite different, partly due to the changing fashions in brass styles and partly to the different characters of the musicians. For example, Whetsol was a stronger musical personality than Jones, but Jenkins not so strong as Stewart. Some of the change is due to new developments in Ellington's approach to brass and his writing for the section. Although the 1933 team could produce a range of dynamics and tone colors hardly inferior to that of seven years later, it has a poised, almost classical sound through the many moods of the music which it plays. By 1940 Ellington was a more relaxed master of his art, and the trumpet section has a more casual, lazy attack; yet this can suddenly be transformed into a concentrated fury which would have been quite foreign to the 1933 unit.

The trombonists were the same in both bands, and this was without much doubt the greatest trombone section in jazz history. It is characteristic of Ellington that, when most leaders were striving to make their trombone sections play like one man, he should want his to sound like what it was, a combination of three very distinctive individualists: the sophisticated, master-of-all-trades Lawrence Brown; the reticent, exotic Juan Tizol; and the blues-playing, "primitive" Tricky Sam Nanton. Ellington always used his trombones as a distinct section and not as an adjunct to the trumpets in the manner of some jazz arrangers. In 1933, three-piece trombone sections were new, and Duke was delighted to use his in new compositions, most notably in the magnificent *Slippery Horn*. A further brilliant example of his use of the 1933 section can be found in *Jive Stomp*. By 1940 the section had not changed in personnel or nature, but its full potential for variety had been realized. In particular, the sensuous and supple phrasing when Brown had the lead was greatly relished by the leader. As was the case with the trumpets the rather austere, "classical" style of the 1933 section had given way to a much warmer sound by 1940.

In 1933, the Ellington reed section consisted of Otto Hardwick (alto and bass saxes, clarinet), Johnny Hodges (alto and soprano saxes), Barney Bigard (clarinet and tenor sax), and Harry Carney (baritone and alto saxes, clarinet). In 1940, the same four musicians were still in residence, but Hardwick seems to have given up the bass sax, and Carney now played bass clarinet in addition to his other instruments. Most importantly, Ben Webster had been added on tenor. In his 1933 section Ellington had three saxophone masters in Hardwick, Hodges, and Carney, although Hardwick and even Carney were some way behind Hodges in the rhythmic aspects of jazz playing. This section also boasted similar contrasts in musical

	Jan 1928	**May 1928**	**1932**	**1940**	**1946**	**1950**	**1951**	**1956**	**1968**
Altos:	OH	JH	OH JH	OH JH	RP JH	RP JH	RP WS	RP JH	RP JH
Tenors:	BB	BB	BB	BW BB	AS JHtn	PG JHtn	PG JHtn	PG JHtn	PG HA
Baritone:	HC	HC	HC	HC	HC	HC	HC	HC	HC

(AS-Al Sears; BB-Barney Bigard; BW-Ben Webster; HA-Harold Ashby; HC-Harry Carney; JH-Johnny Hodges; JHtn-Jimmy Hamilton; OH-

character to those noted in the trumpet and trombone teams. The 1933 Ellington saxes have a great variety of tone colors at their disposal, ranging from a creamy sound when Hardwick's is the prominent voice to a deep, somber sonority heard when Carney's baritone is given an important role. Barney Bigard's function in all this was to provide a middle-range voice on tenor saxophone but more often and more importantly either to join the section on clarinet or to play a separate clarinet obbligato role in the manner of the New Orleans-style jazz bands. As Ellington's saxophone writing increased in complexity through the thirties, the limitations of Bigard as a saxophone section player—as opposed to his contribution on clarinet, which was always of the highest class—became more and more apparent. In some ways this section was the weakest part of the band, perhaps because of the comparative lack of swing in the section work of Bigard and Hardwick. The arrival of Webster not only gave the orchestra another top class soloist but more significantly added a master ensemble player in the middle range of the saxophone section. It is not to minimize Webster's contribution as a soloist to suggest that his part in the revitalization of the Ellington band in early 1940 was achieved primarily through his work in the section. And he had a considerable influence on the playing of the other saxophonists, most noticeably Carney, whose phrasing takes on a distinctly Webster-like cast and whose section work becomes a good deal more subtle rhythmically.

One might note here the astonishing stability of the Ellington saxophone team over the years, a fact seen clearly from the table above, in which the musicians are designated by their initials.

Although many jazz enthusiasts seem unaware of the fact, the most important part of any jazz group is its rhythm section. Without the right kind of rhythm section no orchestra can swing, no soloist can play in a relaxed and comfortable manner. Without a rhythm section which is skilled and imaginative in the fields of dynamics and harmony as well as rhythm, the finest orchestra will sound monotonous and dull. At first, the Ellington section was a rather disorganized affair, and, when it stabilized in personnel with the arrival of Wellman Braud in 1927, it seems to have become overly dependent on him for its drive and thrust. By 1933 the quartet of Duke Ellington (piano), Fred Guy (banjo), Wellman Braud (bass), and Sonny Greer (drums) had been together more than five years and had settled into a much more integrated way of playing. Braud was still the dynamo, but the work of the other three had increased in rhythmic potency. Whatever subtleties Braud may have lacked harmonically, he made up for by the drive and vitality of his playing.

The rhythm section as a unit is probably the most neglected aspect of the much praised Ellington Orchestra of 1940. The phenomenal Jimmy Blanton had just joined the band on bass, replacing Billy Taylor, a musician more correct in harmonic usage than Braud but less vigorous rhythmically. Blanton not only extended the harmonic and rhythmic language of the string bass but also he brought to the Ellington section a drive which it had lacked in the previous few years. Greer was an ideal partner for the new bassist, a drummer weighty enough to carry the band and a master of light and shade. In the earliest years, Guy's banjo had been the fulcrum of the section owing to his steady time, but since then his importance had slowly but inexorably diminished. With Blanton's arrival, the guitar part became virtually redundant and the rhythm section was now based on a triumvirate of piano, bass and drums.

* * *

If we make a similar leap in our Ellington listening and compare the Ellington band of 1940 with those of 1951 and 1958, we find further fascinating contrasts. In the fifties the only change which had taken place in the instrumentation of the band was the dropping of the rhythm guitar and the addition of a fourth trumpet. It is to the playing of the rhythm section that our ears will be drawn if we listen to the 1951 band with that of 1940 in mind, for it is here, especially in the drumming, that the most obvious differences will be found. The crisp, driving playing of Louis Bellson sets the tone for the whole band, which plays with greater precision and a sharper attack than any other Ellington band before or since. This period in the band's history was unusual in that change was anything but gradual, the sudden departure of Greer, Hodges, and Brown followed by the arrival of Bellson and Willie Smith having a cataclysmic effect. The difference in the playing of the Ellington band with Bellson instead of with Greer is a perfect illustration of the importance of the drummer in a jazz ensemble.

The brass and reed sections of the 1951 band also present interesting contrasts if we compare them to 1940 or 1933. Of the newcomers, only Ray Nance, who had joined in late 1940, and Paul Gonsalves, newly recruited, were major characters to be compared with the Ellington sidemen of the thirties in their impact on the music. Of the thirties sidemen, only Tizol and the ever present Carney were in the 1951 band. The trumpets were a powerful section, but not until Clark Terry and Willie Cook joined towards the end of 1951 were they up to the expected Ellington standard in solo strength. And even when so fine a musician as Terry had settled into the band he never had the same impact that, say, Rex Stewart had made on the ensemble of the late thirties and early forties. This was mainly because Ellington now relied less on individual musicians, in part, at least, a reaction to the instability of the personnel. The trombones continued to be a fine section, but Quentin Jackson was not a soloist of Tricky Sam Nanton's caliber, although he performed the plunger role more than adequately. Nor had Britt Woodman, for all his virtuosity, a range of style comparable with that of Lawrence Brown. The fact was that neither was an individualist or an innovator in the manner of his predecessor. In the saxes, the loss of Johnny Hodges was obvious, but in Willie Smith the band had acquired a section leader of a kind rare in the Duke Ellington story—a strong disciplinarian. The reeds play with unusual precision and blend during Smith's brief stay, but the subtleties of tone colors normally associated with this Ellington section are less varied than was usually the case, despite the addition of Gonsalves, who proved over his years with Ellington to be a great ensemble player.

To move forward to the band of 1958 is to find again a different kind of rhythm section creating a new sound as the basis of the music. Once again the key man is the drummer, Sam Woodyard, a musician as different from Bellson as the latter was from Greer. The new drummer was a stylistic maverick, playing in a manner which is some ways seemed a throwback to earlier jazz drummers yet which also incorporated bop devices. Ellington often claimed that he was a primitive artist, and he certainly liked a very basic jazz sound in his rhythm section. This is what Woodyard provided, and the rapport between drummer and pianist was often astounding, as indeed was the swing Sam could engender when on his best form. Although the 1958 Ellington band was a collection of outstanding virtuoso soloists, the presence of Woodyard at the drums corrected any tendency for it to sound like an overly sophisticated collection of prima donnas. It is an interesting fact that the majority of the band preferred to work with Woodyard, although Bellson was a drummer more highly rated by outside commentators. So far as bassists were concerned, both the 1951 and the 1958 bands had fine players in the Blanton tradition—Wendell Marshall (who was Blanton's cousin) and Jimmy Woode.

* * *

Despite Willie Smith's efficiency and the virtues of his immediate successors on alto, Hilton Jefferson and Rick Henderson, the return of Johnny Hodges in 1955 was an enormous boon. Hodges's great rhythmic strength—quite as basic as Woodyard's—made its mark at once on his return, and of course he brought many other qualities to the band—tone, personality, and an exquisite melodic sense among them. A truly golden period followed his return, and the solo strength of the band *circa* 1958 was the equal of any which Ellington had ever led. Although each individual sideman had a less vital role to play than his counterpart in the Ellington band of the thirties, each player was nonetheless a distinctive individual artist and still functioned as such in the Ellington ensemble as well as in solo.

* * *

The kind of organic evolution which we have observed in the Ellington Orchestra is also to be found in the leader's development as a pianist. Ellington's very earliest records reveal a moderate performer with a style of little or no individuality. From then on we can follow the gradual evolution of a jazz pianist who by the mid-fifties was the master of all situations. One can hear from the records that this development of what became one of the most individual of all jazz piano styles, was dictated wholly by musical demands and never by a wish to impress the audience by displays of pianistic acrobatics. On the solo recordings of October 1928 we find Ellington already using the piano as a medium for his musical thinking in a rather special way. In a sense, this is not so much pianistic music as the musings of a composer at the keyboard. The approach revealed on these records was built upon over the years, but the fundamental approach to the piano which they exhibit was never wholly lost. Ellington never developed digital dexterity in an obviously eye-or ear-catching way, for he simply did not aspire to that kind of pianism. He did not even bother to put a deliberate stylistic gloss over his playing, which remained unvarnished to the last. He probably felt that this would have interfered with what he wanted to express. And of course his prime musical purposes would have been impossible to achieve from the stance of a virtuoso pianist/bandleader. So instead of following a conventional course of development for a jazz pianist, Duke developed a remarkable mastery of touch in an infinity of shadings; he could play a chord in different ways by giving different weight to each constituent note, and this allied to his subtle gradations of rhythmic timing and of dynamics gave his playing a variety and authority not exceeded by even the most dexterous of jazz piano masters.

On the band records from the late twenties onwards, we find piano passages which, played as they are in Ellington's offhand manner, do not sound special yet which on examination prove to have the most perfect relevance to their context. In the great band of the 1933 to 1936 period, Duke's playing had become one of the vital factors in the orchestral balance. By the late thirties, it became obvious that the piano playing of Ellington himself was the basis on which his entire orchestra rested. As recordings of dances and club dates from the early forties have become available, it has become clear how vital Ellington's contribution as an executive musician really was. When playing without piano the band sounds comparatively ordinary, the arrival of Duke at the keyboard seeming to generate some mysterious source of energy within the ensemble, the music acquiring a vitality and a glow which it had not had before.

Duke's playing in the duets with Jimmy Blanton and on the band recordings of the early forties shows an increasing refinement of the rhythmic aspect of his piano work. Strangely enough, the solo piano recordings he made at this time seem, particularly from a rhythmic point of view, a deliberate throwback to an earlier style. All through the forties and early fifties Duke carried on playing the most magnificent piano, although most of this was in an ensemble context. The exceptions, such as the piano solos on *Frankie And Johnny* or those in that remarkable creation *The Clothéd Woman,* showed those who took the trouble to listen that Duke was now as great an instrumental master as any of the stars in his orchestra. It seems to have been in the years leading up to the renaissance of 1956, when the band was short of experienced Ellington hands, that Duke started to feature himself more as a soloist. By the middle fifties his keyboard mastery was at its peak, as is shown by his playing on the 1956 Newport Jazz Festival recordings. The piano playing on *Back To Back* and *Side By Side* sessions with Hodges and on the solo recordings from the fifties onwards constitute a body of work as musically rich and rewarding as any in the history of piano jazz.

* * *

Turning to Ellington's work as a composer, we should perhaps ask first what sort of composer he was. We might, for the purposes of our inquiry, define the jazz composer as being an artist who creates music for jazz ensemble of an organized and structured nature which does not inhibit the natural expression of the musicians. These musicians are subsidiary creative figures in the enterprise rather than simply interpreters, as would be the case in the world of academic music. The main difficulty in testing any such definition is that it really only covers a handful of artists—Ellington and Jelly Roll Morton in the "old" jazz tradition, Charles Mingus, John Lewis, and perhaps Gil Evans in the "new." I would not suggest for one moment that the output of any of these other artists is comparable in overall achievement with that of Ellington, but each of the four does treat the music in a way which is at least superficially similar to Duke's methods.

The resemblances between Duke Ellington's procedures and those of other artists are slight, for Duke was a highly idiosyncratic artist in method as well as in style. No other jazz composer had the kind of abilities as a bandleader which went into the creation and maintenance of the Ellington Orchestra. Other jazz composers can be seen either as codifiers or as innovators, but Ellington took the tools handed down to him by tradition and used them in a way which was not so much a development or a defiance of standard practices as a complete disregard of them. He was also unusual in that he positively needed his band of individualistic jazz musicians on hand for inspiration as well as for interpretation. The most obvious manifestation of this on record is on those end-of-session recordings made when the new material and the revivals were done and Duke could relax with his musicians in an extemporized uptempo blues. The spirit of zest and the sense of enjoyment radiating from the piano on these occasions is plain for all to hear. And it is typical of Ellington that he should take relaxation in music.

* * *

The growth of Ellington the composer is, of course, a parallel development to the growth of the orchestra and of the pianist, and this too can be seen with clarity with the aid of records. The evolution from the early individuality of *East St. Louis Toodle-oo* and *Black And Tan Fantasy* through the mastery of *Mood Indigo* and *Old Man Blues* to the prolific output of the middle thirties is the story of Ellington's first major phase as a composer. The early appearance of a piece of concert music—*Creole Rhapsody* in 1931—suggests that Ellington's basic artistic policy was decided early in his career. It is easy to view his output from the middle thirties onward using concert works as signposts, but this could give them an undue prominence. Although such compositions are an important and a very serious part of the Ellington output, they do not always represent his highest achievement. The aesthetic magnitude of such stomps and blues as *Stompy Jones* and *Across The Track Blues* often exceeds that of contemporary concert pieces, despite the more ambitious nature of the concert works.

Right through the recordings which the Ellington band made in the thirties, one can hear the expansion and enrichment of Duke's art as a composer. When in 1940 his band-leading skills produced an ensemble of near-ideal quality, the composer was fully equipped to take advantage of the situation. This resulted in what is arguably the very finest set of jazz records in existence. The absence of any large-scale concert work from the years 1940, 1941, and 1942 was no doubt due to the gestation of *Black, Brown And Beige,* for all the fact that this score was actually written down on paper during a four-week period. By the time of the premiere of *Black, Brown And Beige* in January 1943, Cootie Williams, Barney Bigard, and Jimmy Blanton had left; it is interesting to speculate what the Ellington band of 1940, with these three worthies in residence, would have made of this score. *Black, Brown And Beige* is in many important respects a turning point in Ellington's career as a composer. To understand the nature of Ellington's work from the forties onwards, one needs to study the growth of his compositional methods in the years leading up to *Black, Brown And Beige*. On the records from the twenties to the early forties, the development of Ellington's techniques and the nature and scope of his artistic ambitions are clearly defined as problem after problem of jazz composition is faced and solved. On the records made after the completion of *Black, Brown And Beige,* he handles the mechanics of composition with the air of an accomplished master, effortlessly expanding and deepening the scope of his art.

Duke Ellington exploited this range in his later years, his masterpieces among the concert works alone being as diverse in subject matter and style as *The Tattooed Bridge, Harlem, Such Sweet Thunder, The Queen's Suite,* and *Suite Thursday*. The shorter pieces cover a similar range of expression, a range which encompasses such extremes as *Lady Of The Lavender Mist* and *H'ya Sue, New York City Blues* and *Three Cent Stomp,* to cite simply four recordings done over a period of five months in 1947. It should not be forgotten that in addition to being the greatest jazz composer Duke Ellington was also the best arranger, and right from his earliest years we can hear brilliant arrangements of pieces by other writers. Often these are popular songs, but there are also arrangements of other composers' instrumental pieces, such as Don Redman's *Paducah* and *Chant Of The Weed,* recorded by Ellington in 1929 and 1962, respectively. In the sixties, compositions by Tchaikovsky and Grieg were arranged by Ellington and Billy Strayhorn in a masterly fashion. Once more the records enable us to trace Ellington's development in this field and to note the close relationship between the style of his arrangements and that of his compositions at any one time.

Ellington's composer's insight enabled him to see deeper into a musical structure and to build from such insight in a way which was not possible for most jazz arrangers, and indeed one can regard many of his arrangements more properly as recompositions. Sometimes these are treated in the same way as the rearrangements of his own older material which appeared as revivals from time to time. But the most amazing aspect of Ellington's revivals was the fact that many of his pieces were presented 20, 30 or 40 years after their composition in arrangements which were virtually unchanged. This is not only unique in jazz music but also a remarkable proof of the durability of works which are sometimes—wrongly—regarded as mere period pieces.

* * *

The reworking of old material as well as the constant adaptation of established Ellington techniques to new problems point to the deep sense of tradition which informed Ellington's music. He was deeply conscious of the traditions of jazz, and many of his works reflect his proud awareness of the contribution of the African American to the world's musical heritage. And of course within his music there were many strands of tradition with which he created for his bandsmen a stylistic basis as valid as that forged by environment in New Orleans or Kansas City. For all his deep regard for tradition, Ellington was by a long, long way the most creative innovator African American music has ever known. This could seem a contradiction in the insulated world of jazz fashion and terminology. Yet it was at root this deep regard for tradition in both jazz as a whole and within his own music which gave Duke Ellington the basis on which to build so wide-ranging and so emotionally positive an output with such sure-footed originality.

* * *

By the criterion of the academy, Duke Ellington was a nonstarter as a composer. To say this is not to denigrate his compositions nor to deny the formal beauty of such works as *Sepia Panorama* or *The Tattooed Bride* or indeed *Across The Track Blues*. But Ellington's virtues, and by the same token his techniques as a composer, are entirely those of jazz. In his career he had many opportunities for turning away from what many would see as the limitations of jazz, but he remained true to his conception of music in the African American tradition. Of his works written for the Ellington band plus symphony orchestra, the most successful, *Night Creature,* is the one where his declared intention was to make the symphony orchestra swing. It is all the more remarkable, therefore, how many distinguished academics have understood that his work was that of an outstanding musician, for as early as the thirties, praise from such quarters was forthcoming. Sometimes the kind of perception shown by Ellington's academic admirers can seem grotesque, as in Constant Lambert's famous comparison of *Hot And Bothered* with Ravel and Stravinsky. Yet men like Lambert and Percy Grainger were among the very first outside the closed world of the jazz musician to realize that Duke Ellington represented something very extraordinary in music. And they realized it at an early stage in his career.

Almost from the outset Ellington's scoring was of a highly individual kind. Quite apart from his masterly use of muted brass and his famous "mixtures" of unusual instrumental combinations, his use of the individual sounds and styles of his musicians within the ensemble is something one hardly ever hears in other jazz scoring, even in a simple form. Yet with Ellington this was a basic compositional technique. The part played by Harry Carney's baritone sax in the band is justly celebrated, but note how the quieter voices like those of Paul Gonsalves or Juan Tizol are used. The times at which the lead is switched to Gonsalves's tenor or an important harmony part is given to Tizol's strong yet curiously unassertive tone are often those at which "the Ellington effect" seems to be at its most enigmatic.

The way in which the sections in Ellington's band assumed a different character when different players were used in the lead part is almost as astonishing as the perfect aptness with which Duke rang such changes. Arthur Whetsol, Cootie Williams, Rex Stewart, Wallace Jones, Harold Baker, Cat Anderson, and Clark Terry would each give the trumpets a different character when playing lead. In the thirties and forties the trombones would sometimes be led by Lawrence Brown, sometimes by Juan Tizol, and occasionally by Tricky Sam Nanton. In the fifties similar contrasts were available when Ellington had a trombone trio consisting of Britt Woodman, John Sanders, and Quentin Jackson. So far as records are concerned, the permutation of leads and voicings seems almost endless, varying from the great contrasts between Otto Harwick on lead alto and Johnny Hodges in the same role (not to mention Hodges leading on soprano sax), to the subtle use of Carney's huge baritone sound in the saxophone voicing. To judge from reading and from conversations, many people hear the theme statement of *Dusk* (1940) as a duet between muted trumpet (Wallace Jones) and clarinet (Barney Bigard), and fail to notice the very soft muted trombone (Lawrence Brown) providing a harmony part above the trumpet lead. Yet it is the subtle touch of color and harmony provided by the muted trombone which gives the passage its distinctive quality. (This is one of the many variations on the *Mood Indigo* voicing heard in Ellington's music down the years.)

In the past, many listeners outside the United States imagined that Ellington's orchestral effects were obtained by clever manipulation of microphones in the recording studio. This understandable illusion was shattered by the band's tours of Europe, notably those of 1933, 1950, and 1958, each of which introduced the band to a large number of people who had previously heard it only via recordings.

* * *

Ellington once described the ear as the most essential instrument, and he was certainly an avid listener. In his early days he was profoundly influenced by Sidney Bechet, by James P. Johnson, and by Willie "The Lion" Smith. There are hints on his early records which suggest that he was familiar with the music of the major pre-Ellington ensemble in jazz, King Oliver's Creole Jazz Band. His most apt usage of the King Oliver-inspired style of Bubber Miley, of the Bechet-influenced playing of the young Johnny Hodges, of Bigard's and Braud's pure New Orleans styles, and of the Louis Armstrong facet of Cootie Williams's work indicate that Duke had acquired the habit of listening and learning early in his career. Ellington's failure to appreciate Jelly Roll Morton's contribution strikes an odd note in this context and has never been properly explained, as Gunther Schuller has pointed out. Perhaps an encounter between the two led to Morton's boastful manner causing such offense as to cloud Ellington's usually clear perception in musical matters.

It is less surprising to find that Morton had a low opinion of Ellington, for Jelly was not always a good judge of musicians from outside his own New Orleans environment:

> He ain't no piano player. He's got a good band and he's made a lot of money but you know who made him? He's got Bigard, a good New Orleans boy, sitting right beside him all the time telling him what to do. Take Bigard away and Ellington ain't nowhere. (*Jelly Roll Morton in Washington* by Kenneth Hulsizer, *Jazz Music*, February/March 1944, p. 112)

Ellington expressed his views on Morton more succinctly:

> He played piano like one of those high school teachers in Washington; as a matter of fact, (the) high school teachers played better jazz. (Quoted in *Duke: A Portrait Of Duke Ellington* by Derek Jewell, p. 141)

A very odd pair of appraisals which are really of no credit to either man.

But with the exception of Morton's music, the pattern of discerning receptivity was carried on throughout Ellington's long career. He continued to listen to what was happening in jazz and beyond, and, for a musician of his strong individuality, he was constantly and to a remarkable degree inspired and influenced by the music of others. The influence of Jimmie Lunceford and Count Basie can be heard in Ellington's music of the swing era, although these are completely absorbed into his own distinctive style. Later, when musicians inspired by the Gillespie-Parker innovations came into the band—men like Clark Terry, Willie Cook, Britt Woodman, Jimmy Hamilton, and Paul Gonsalves—he used bop and postbop techniques in a characteristically individual way. But Duke's use of musical devices usually stood quite apart from the mainstream of the development of jazz. Instead, their use reflected Ellington's own evolution as a composer and, coincidentally, often anticipated musical fashion. Perhaps the most remarkable aspect of Ellington's "creative listening," as we might call it, was his perception of the musical personalities of the men within his own band. It was the deep understanding of their music which enabled him to use their musical styles as elements in his compositions.

The most powerful influence on the music of the young Duke Ellington was that of Sidney Bechet. When we look back on that primary influence with the knowledge of 50 years of Ellington's music, we can see just how profound it was. Forty-one years after he had first heard Bechet in Washington, Ellington described him in an interview as:

> the greatest of all the originators, Bechet, the symbol of jazz. I remember hearing him . . . in 1921—the greatest thing I ever heard in my life. . . . I consider Bechet the foundation. His things were all soul, all from the inside. (*Down Beat*, June 7, 1962, p. 15)

Coming from Ellington, a man who chose words carefully, especially when speaking of his fellow musicians, this is a remarkable statement.

Sidney Bechet was arguably the greatest reed player in

jazz history, and without much doubt he was the greatest exponent of the blues. On his many recordings in the blues idiom, Bechet's prodigious invention and his searing intensity of emotional expression clearly indicate the kind of impression he must have made on young musicians in the twenties. In many ways, his is jazz music *par excellence,* without frills, direct in language, unmannered in style, fiery, passionate, and totally committed. Both Bechet and Ellington liked and played pretty music, but in both cases the blues was at the root. One way in which Ellington differed from Bechet is that he did not come from a blues background—Washington was well away from blues territory. But under Bechet's inspiration Ellington learned the language and encouraged it in his band. From all periods of Ellington's recording career one finds blues performances of the most eloquent kind—for example *The Blues With A Feeling* (1928), *Sweet Chariot* (1930), *Bundle Of Blues* (1933), *Saddest Tale* (1934), *Country Gal* (1939), *Across The Track Blues* (1940), *H'ya Sue* (1947), and *Blues To Be There* (1956). The frequency of such performances on record is a sure reminder that the grounding in jazz basics which Bechet gave to Duke at the outset of his career was never forgotten.

* * *

Ellington often commented on people and events and places which had inspired his music, pointing out that this music was always about something, a reaction to a specific stimulus. The evocative, sometimes highly poetic titles which he gave to his works are evidence of this—*Stevedore Stomp, Misty Mornin', The Gal From Joe's, Moon Mist, On A Turquoise Cloud,* and *Thanks For The Beautiful Land On The Delta* are just a half dozen contrasting examples from different periods in Ellington's life. It is all too easy for Ellington's listeners to be tempted by such titles into thinking of his music in programmatic terms. In fact he hardly ever reacted to the stimuli behind his compositions in such a simple way. We have noted how at one time he intended to present the composition we know as *Harlem Air Shaft* to the public as *Rumpus In Richmond*. This fact did not prevent him from giving a detailed description of the various activities amplified by a Harlem air shaft as though the work portrayed them. The riotous melodic proliferation and the vivid colors of this composition are clearly a reflection of Ellington's reaction to the initial stimulus—be it a Richmond rumpus or a Harlem air shaft—rather than a retrospective painting of a detailed picture. Yet this is a work which has been accepted as a piece of program music by generations of jazz writers.

Perhaps *The Tattooed Bride* best indicates Ellington's attitude to program music. For once, there is a fairly detailed story behind the music, yet Duke considered it to be so unimportant that he often omitted to even mention the tale of the athletic gentleman and his bride to the audience. Instead, he would introduce the work with a chat about the parallel between the shape of a certain tattoo pattern and that of the musical phrase from which the work germinates. He clearly felt that stressing the importance of that motif, albeit in a lighthearted way, was more helpful to his listeners than informing them of the story behind a work which he liked to call, because of this very "program," a "musical striptease." Duke Ellington's titles are a useful guide to the nature of the music, but they only rarely indicate the presence of a detailed story or "program." And one should note that on some occasions when such a program is present as a dominant factor, as in *Black, Brown And Beige,* it can result in a weakening of the musical structure.

* * *

As well as being a composer of instrumental works, Ellington was also a prolific songwriter. Some of his songs started out as instrumental pieces which acquired lyrics (e.g. *Solitude, Sophisticated Lady,* and *In A Sentimental Mood*) or were modified in anything from title to basic structure (e.g. *Dreamy Blues, Never No Lament,* and *Concerto For Cootie,* which became, respectively, *Mood Indigo, Don't Get Around Much Anymore,* and *Do Nothin' Til You Hear From Me*). Although these, and the Ellington songs which actually started life as such, are first-class examples of their kind, they are not as important in Ellington's output as songs might be in the case of an academic composer. This is because of their deliberately popular and therefore unambitious nature, and because of the frequently trite lyrics which were appended to them. Yet Ellington lacked musical snobbishness, and his songs were often given arrangements and performances wholly comparable with his more obviously jazz-oriented instrumentals.

It may seem odd that an artist could invite comparison with Ravel and Stravinsky on the one hand and with Irving Berlin and Richard Rodgers on the other. This indeed is another instance of Ellington's many-sidedness: remember he once said that he should be called "tentacles for short." In another artist, such an approach could lead to a diffusion of energy, to a neglect of the essential aspects of his art. With Ellington this never happened, perhaps because all kinds of artistic activity were so natural to him. He would appear before the public in a multiplicity of guises, but he never ever allowed any of these to interfere with what he clearly saw as his prime vocation—the creation of music for the band. Had he done so, as a man of less tenacity and energy might well have done, then his many-sidedness would have been a handicap, a serious personality flaw. In Ellington's case it produced unexpected and often delightful bonuses to his main work. But basically he was as single-minded about his vocation as a serious artist must be.

* * *

Another facet of Ellington's character was his financial ability. It is an aspect of his personality which is sometimes considered to be unworthy in an artist, yet without the skill as well as the determination to make his band a financial success and to maintain an economically viable supporting organization the survival of the Ellington band over half a century would have been impossible. In later years, the orchestra was subsidized by the royalties from Ellington's many song hits, but if the band itself made a loss Duke would be quick to point out in his oblique way that "a musical profit comes way ahead of a financial loss."

Throughout his life, Duke Ellington dealt with a great variety of people and situations with astonishing success and ease. He handled the sharks of show business as well as he dealt with the nice guys. His band was full of temperamental individuals who had bitter and often prolonged feuds—but Duke handled them all. From the world's finest concert rooms to some dingy dance hall in the backwoods, from San Francisco's Grace Cathedral to the gambling rooms of Las Vegas, Duke Ellington presented Duke Ellington music. He never explained his success with so great a variety of people or in such extremes of environment. Perhaps the nearest he came was in a remark made to Derek Jewell after charming a Las Vegas crowd with selections from his latest concert suite and persuading them into enjoying it: "Well, I'm sure glad I learned social significance in the pool-room."

As with most musicians of his generation, Duke had a deep sense of obligation to his audience. On one occasion, after the band had played a superb *Black And Tan Fantasy* at a Manchester concert, Ellington observed that he had only played the number because he had found a note on the piano requesting it. He surmised that a member of his audience may have traveled miles just to hear this one favorite piece— "Who am I to deny him that pleasure?" asked Duke, adding that he didn't really like playing those old things and would prefer to bring over new material for each tour.

* * *

Like every other artist who achieves something worthwhile, Ellington was willing to take chances in his work. His reliance on the mood of his bandsmen, his casual methods of composition, and his way of barely meeting deadlines were factors which indeed left a good deal to chance. As a consequence, again like most other accomplished artists, he had his failures. He confided to close friends and associates that he was sometimes so dissatisfied with what he wrote that he threw it away without showing it to anyone—"I would prefer that no one catches on to how lousy I can write," he once told Rex Stewart apropos manuscripts which he tore up and flushed down the toilet. Ellington's range and ambition were also factors which forced him to take risks. Yet surprisingly few of his creations give the impression of a man overreaching himself.

Most of Ellington's poor recordings court a deliberate banality in the cause of popular success. There were times when the inspiration of the composer or his band burned low and the music sounded dull, although usually one or other of the musicians—frequently Ellington himself—would provide the spark which set the band alight. In his later years, Duke could sometimes sound like a man imitating himself, particularly when he was trying to write a "hit" song. But apart from the would-be potboilers, the most frequent failures are found in the works where Duke wrote the words as well as the music, either as lyric writer for a song or for one of his stage works. His best narrations—such as the *New Orleans* section of *A Drum Is A Woman*—are fully worthy of his genius, but at the other extreme—the lyrics of *Azalea* or some of the texts from the sacred concerts—his writing can be embarrassing in its banality. Ellington's art had its limitations and it knew failure. But for a man of so prolific an output over so long a period, the wide range and the low failure rate are both deeply impressive.

* * *

Although Ellington was primarily a composer he showed little interest in the majority of his works once they had been written and performed for a month or so; most were forgotten once they had fallen from the performing repertoire of the band. Irving Townsend tells how he, Arthur Logan (Duke's doctor and a very close friend), and Billy Strayhorn collected Ellington's music in manuscript form, using surviving band parts and published scores where possible; where not, they had transcriptions taken from the records. The plan was to present this collection of his works to Duke as a 60th birthday gift. John Sanders was engaged to manage the project, which resulted in what Townsend described as an impressive stack of leather-bound volumes. Townsend wrote:

> I could not be present on the night in Logan's apartment when the presentation was to be made by Arthur and Billy, so I waited anxiously for Arthur's call the following day. "He was impressed," Logan told me on the phone. "He made polite noises and kissed us all," he continued, his words coming more slowly, "but, you know, the son of a bitch didn't even bother to take it home." (*Ellington in Private* by Irving Townsend, *Jazz Journal,* October 1976, p. 8)

Duke Ellington had virtually no interest in his past. Even the revivals of old compositions were produced to please the audience of Ellington faithfuls, or to suit a featured soloist, or in the hope of a popular success in the constant crusade to keep the band on the road. His own artistic interest was directed, unerringly and unwaveringly, at the center of the creative process. The finished, polished final product held little attraction for him—once it had been perfected. For Duke Ellington, the dynamic nature of music as a creative, living flux was the essence of the matter. This gave to his music a warm, living quality which wholly reflected the man. His was among the most human as well as the most imaginative contributions to twentieth-century art.

Appendix 1

Bibliography

Editor's note: Sections 1–5 of this bibliography appear as originally prepared and annotated by G. E. Lambert; where appropriate the names of publishers and later reprintings or subsequent editions have been added. To provide an updated listing of works on Ellington, section 6 lists, without annotation, books that have appeared since 1983.

1. GENERAL WORKS ON DUKE ELLINGTON

Dance, Stanley. *The World of Duke Ellington.* New York and London: Macmillan, 1970, 1971; New York: Da Capo, 1981. This important book contains interviews with Duke Ellington, Billy Strayhorn, and most of the leading Ellington sidemen. These offer valuable insights into life in the Ellington band and into its musical and social environment.

Ellington, Duke. *Music Is My Mistress.* Garden City, New York: Doubleday, 1973. Ellington's autobiography makes little more than a token effort to tell the story of his life. Instead he presents a series of reflections and ruminations on music, people, and places. Although uneven, the book includes many passages of unique perception concerning the world of jazz. These are sometimes couched in casual, off-the-cuff phraseology and sometimes in Ellington's vivid, poetic prose style. The book also contains the composer's comments on most of his major concert works.

Ellington, Mercer (with Stanley Dance). *Duke Ellington in Person.* Boston: Houghton Mifflin, 1978; New York: Da Capo, 1979. Written from the sometimes uncomfortable standpoint of a musical son of a musical genius, this book offers a more rounded portrait of Ellington the man than any other biographical volume. Perhaps it wavers unduly between being a biography of Duke, an autobiography of Mercer, and a series of anecdotes on life with father and father's band, but it makes a vital contribution to our understanding of Duke Ellington and his music.

Gammond, Peter, ed. *Duke Ellington—His Life and Music.* London: Phoenix House, 1958; New York: Da Capo, 1977. A valuable and wide-ranging scrapbook of Ellingtonia. Mostly reprints of magazine articles, including Richard O. Boyer's "The Hot Bach," a classic portrait from *The New Yorker.*

George, Don R. *Sweet Man, the Real Duke Ellington.* New York: Putnam, 1981. (Published also as *The Real Duke Ellington* in London: Robson, 1982.) A volume of anecdotes by a man who was lyric writer for some of Ellington's best songs of the forties. There is not much about Ellington's music here, and what there is includes some obvious errors. The book concentrates on Duke's social life and offers a limited view, illuminated by some amusing anecdotes.

Huon, H. F. *Index to Duke Ellington's Music Is My Mistress.* Melbourne: The Author, c1975; rev. ed., Pewaukee, Wisconsin: QED-CO, c1980. An essential aid for anyone wishing to refer to Ellington's autobiography.

Jewell, Derek. *Duke: A Portrait of Duke Ellington.* New York: Norton, 1977; London: Elm Tree, 1977 (rev. paperback ed., 1978). The best straightforward biography of Duke Ellington to appear to date. Much stronger on the last decades, when the author and Duke were personally acquainted, than on the earlier years.

Lambert, G. E. *Duke Ellington.* London: Cassell, 1959; New York: A. S. Barnes, 1961. Full text included in Stanley Green, ed., *Kings of Jazz,* South Brunswick, New Jersey: A. S. Barnes, 1978. This volume in Cassell's Kings of Jazz series contains a biographical summary and an evaluation of Ellington's recorded output up to the mid-fifties.

Montgomery, Elizabeth Rider. *Duke Ellington, King of Jazz.* Champaign, Illinois: Garrard, 1972. An introduction designed for children and young readers.

[Preston, Denis. *Mood Indigo.*] This volume was mentioned in the jazz press in 1946 and is listed in several bibliographies, but it is probable that it was never published. Neither the British Museum nor any of the large libraries of jazz literature in the United States has copies, nor do the many private collectors approached by the author. Several persons claim to have seen copies but none retained them; perhaps a text circulated in manuscript or proof form, but the author could obtain no record of publication or even a description of its contents.

Ulanov, Barry. *Duke Ellington.* New York: Creative Age, 1946; Da Capo, 1975. Written in a glib, show-business fashion, the style of this book has dated badly and makes for uncomfortable reading. Yet for those willing to dig beneath the surface, it can still yield valuable information and perspectives.

2. DISCOGRAPHICAL WORKS ON DUKE ELLINGTON

Aasland, Benny. *The "Wax Works" of Duke Ellington.* Stockholm: Foliotryck, 1954 (limited ed. for the Duke Ellington Music Society, Danderyd, Sweden: Aasland, 1954). This pocket-size one-volume discography packs a vast amount of information into its pages. In addition to the usual discographical matters of recording dates, location, personnel, and record issues, it includes details of composer credits and soloists.

———. *The "Wax Works" of Duke Ellington: The 6 March 1940–30 July 1942 RCA Victor Period*. Jarfalla, Sweden: Duke Ellington Music Society, 1978. The first of a series of large format "Wax Work" volumes which contain almost all relevant information except for composer credits. It is supplemented by contemporary band photographs plus reproductions of record labels and sleeve notes.

———. *The "Wax Works" of Duke Ellington: The Recording Ban Period, 31 July 1942–11 November 1944*. Jarfalla, Sweden: Duke Ellington Music Society, 1979. The second volume of the new large-format "Wax Works" series. Includes copies of concert programs in addition to previous features.

Bakker, Dick M. *Duke Ellington on Microgroove, 1923–February 1940*. Alphen aan de Rijn, Netherlands: Micrography, 1972. A 26-page pamphlet designed as a supplement to the first three volumes of Massagli, Pusateri, and Volonte's *Duke Ellington's Story on Records* (see below). Contains recording dates, original recording company, titles, and microgroove issues only.

———. *Duke Ellington on Microgroove, 1923–1942*. Alphen aan de Rijn, Netherlands: Micrography, 1974. Greatly expanded version of the above entry, now including personnels, band names, and indexes.

———. *Duke Ellington on Microgroove, Volume One: 1923–1936*. Alphen aan de Rijn, Netherlands: Micrography, 1977. The first of a projected three-volume set, expanding the project to include discussion of outstanding discographical problems, details of soloists, original 78 issues, and composer credits, in addition to previous features.

Jepsen, Jorgen Grunnet. *Discography of Duke Ellington*. 3 vols. Biographical notes by Knud H. Ditlevsen. Copenhagen: Knudsen, 1959. A discography, using the standard format, carrying the Ellington output up to July 1958, now outdated by later publications having the benefit of later research.

Massagli, Luciano, Liborio Pusateri, and Giovanni Volonte. *Duke Ellington's Story on Record*. Milan: Musica Jazz, 1966–1983. This massive discography consists of sixteen volumes: 1925–1931; 1932–1938; 1939–1942; 1943–1944; 1945; 1946; 1947–1950; 1951–1952; 1953–1955; 1956–1957; 1958–1959; 1960–1962; 1963–1965; 1966–1967; 1968–1970; and 1970–1974. This is the definitive Ellington discography. It contains full personnels; recording dates and locations; initial 78 rpm issues; all microgroove issues; full routines of every performance, including soloists and composer credits; and indexes. The volumes are inevitably dated as new information comes to light; a revised edition is in preparation.

Sanfilippo, Luigi. *General Catalogue of Duke Ellington's Recorded Music*. Palermo: Centro Studi di Musica Contemporanea, 1966. A useful brief discography with personnels, recording dates, and original issues. Sections on V-discs and films are included.

Timner, W. E. *Ellingtonia: The Recorded Music of Duke Ellington*. Montreal: The Author, 1976; 4th revised ed., Lanham, Maryland: Scarecrow Press/Rutgers Institute of Jazz Studies, 1996. A most valuable "short" discography, though still a large book. The main discography gives band name; date (and location after the first edition); personnel; titles; indication of whether the music derives from a studio, public performance, or sound track; and first label of issue, if any. There are copious and very useful indexes. An innovation is the inclusion of recordings by the foremost sidemen even when Ellington is not present, a controversial but undeniably useful addition which adds considerably to the bulk of the discography.

3. GENERAL WORKS WHICH CONTAIN IMPORTANT ELLINGTON MATERIAL

Charters, Samuel, and Leonard Kunstadt. *Jazz: A History of the New York Scene*. Garden City: Doubleday, 1962; New York: Da Capo, 1984. Contains an interesting chapter on Ellington's early years in New York City.

Chilton, John. *Who's Who of Jazz: Storyville to Swing Street*. London: Bloomsbury Book Shop, 1972; Philadelphia: Chilton, 1972; revised eds., Alexandria, Virginia: Time-Life Books, 1978 and 1979; 4th revised ed., London: Macmillan, 1985; New York, Da Capo, 1985. This basic reference contains biographical entries on all the Ellington sidemen born before 1920.

Dance, Stanley. *The World of Swing*. New York: Scribner's, 1974; New York: Da Capo, 1979. The second volume in a series by Dance, which commenced with his *The World of Duke Ellington* (see above). There are chapters on several musicians associated with Ellington—Elmer Snowden, Taft Jordan, Dud Bascomb, and Quentin Jackson—and these are of special value to the Ellington student. There are other Ellington references, and the book gives a vivid picture of the environment in which the Ellington band worked. Dance's *The World of Earl Hines* and *The World of Count Basie*—the third and fourth of his series—are less concerned with Ellingtonian topics, but there are many interesting references and, as is the case with *The World of Swing*, the books are of great value in their own right.

de Toledano, Ralph, ed. *The Frontiers of Jazz*. New York: Durrell, 1947; Gretna, Louisiana: Pelican, 1994. The very first magazine article attempting a serious assessment of Ellington, "Black Beauty" by R. D. Darrell, published in *Disques* in 1932. This has now been reprinted; see Tucker (1993). Wilder Hobson's "Duke Ellington," which appeared in *Fortune* the following year, was the second, and its reprint here makes this admirable anthology important for the Ellington student.

Gleason, Ralph J. *Celebrating the Duke and Louis, Bessie, Billie, Bird, Carmen, Miles, Dizzy and Other Heroes*. Boston: Little, Brown, 1975; New York: Da Capo, 1995. Despite its rather ridiculous title, this is a volume of serious jazz criticism. The Ellington section, over one hundred pages, is taken from Gleason's columns for the *San Francisco Chronicle* from 1952 to 1964. The bulk of this section is taken up by "A Ducal Calendar," which reports happenings in the world of Ellington as well as accounts of local appearances by the band over twenty-two years.

Hodeir, André. *Jazz: Its Evolution and Essence*. London, 1956; New York: Grove, 1980. Includes Hodeir's celebrated analysis of "Concerto for Cootie" plus other material of interest to the Ellington specialist.

James, Burnett. *Essays on Jazz*. London: Sidgwick and Jackson, 1961; New York: Da Capo, 1990. Includes a chapter in which James relates the movements in *Such Sweet Thunder* to the passages in Shakespeare which inspired them and establishes a stronger connection than most jazz writers have perceived. Also contains excellent essays on "Johnny Hodges" and "The Impressionism of Duke Ellington."

Lyttelton, Humphrey. *The Best of Jazz*. London: Robson, 1978. A series of essays on early jazz recordings by a musician who is also a brilliant writer and perceptive critic. The chapter on Ellington takes the form of an excellent short introduction to his work, followed by analysis and evaluation of the 1927 Victor recording of "Black and Tan Fantasy."

McCarthy, Albert. *Big Band Jazz*. New York: Putnam, 1974; London: Peerage, 1983. The standard work on its subject, this large volume not only contains an excellent chapter on Ellington but also covers thoroughly the musical setting for Ellington's achievements throughout his long career.

McCarthy, Albert, and Nat Hentoff, eds. *Jazz: New Perspective on the History of Jazz*. New York: Rinehart, c1959. An anthology which includes the first version of Gunther Schuller's important "The Ellington Style: Its Origins and Early Development."

McCarthy, Albert, Alun Morgan, et al. *Jazz on Record*. New York: Oak, 1958; London: Hanover, 1958. Includes a lengthy section on Ellington and his sidemen by the present author.

Panassié, Hugues. *The Real Jazz*. Revised ed., London, 1960; New York: Barnes, c1960; Westport, Connecticut: Greenwood, 1973. The sections on Ellington are examples of Panassié's writing at its very best—lucid, informative, and showing great sympathy with the music.

Panassié, Hugues, and Madeleine Gautier. *Dictionary of Jazz*. London: Jazz Book Club, 1956, 1959. Entries on Ellington and the most important of his sidemen. Some biographical material is included, but the book is most valuable for its pithy and perceptive critical evaluations.

Schuller, Gunther. *Early Jazz*. New York: Oxford, 1968, 1986. Contains the second version of his "The Ellington Style: Its Origins and Early Development," as well as other references. A scholarly study only slightly marred by occasional errors of historical fact.

Shapiro, Nat, and Nat Hentoff, eds. *Hear Me Talkin' to Ya*. New York and London: Rinehart, 1955; New York: Dover, 1966. This famous anthology of jazz musicians talking about their lives and their music contains many references to Ellington.

———. *The Jazz Makers*. New York: Rinehart, 1957. A book of essays on famous jazz musicians which includes "Duke Ellington" by Leonard Feather. Feather was associated with Ellington in a variety of capacities, and his various books also contain informative writing about Duke.

Stewart, Rex. *Jazz Masters of the Thirties*. New York: Macmillan, 1972; New York: Da Capo, 1982. Includes several chapters in which Stewart reminisces on his days in the Ellington Orchestra and on the personalities of Duke and his leading sidemen. Essential reading.

4. DISCOGRAPHICAL WORKS WHICH CONTAIN IMPORTANT ELLINGTON MATERIAL

It has not been considered necessary to refer in detail to the several important early discographies, such as Hilton R. Schleman's *Rhythm on Record* (1936), the several editions of Charles Delaunay's *Hot Discography* (1936 to 1952), Orin Blackstone's *Index to Jazz* (1947), and Carey and McCarthy's *Jazz Directory* (1949 to 1958). Although vital works in their day, these volumes have been superseded by later general discographies.

Evensmo, Jan. *Ben Webster*. Jazz Solography Series, No. 6. Hosle, Norway. The Author, 1978. This discography with critical comments contains much interesting information as well as stimulating evaluations.

Jepsen, Jorgen Grunnet. *Jazz Records, 1942–1962*. 11 vols. Copenhagen: Knudsen, 1962–1971. The standard post-1942 jazz discography. Volume 3 contains the large Ellington section, but other volumes include recordings Duke made with other artists and the recordings of the important Ellington sidemen under their own names.

Panassié, Hugues. *Discographie Critique des Meilleurs Disques de Jazz*. Paris: Laffont, 1958. The only important critical discography yet published, this major work includes an admirable section on the recordings of Ellington.

Rust, Brian. *Jazz Records, 1902–1942*. 2 vols. 5th ed., Chigwell: Storyville, 1983. The definitive discography of the period includes complete coverage of Ellington and his associates.

5. MAGAZINES AND JOURNALS

To attempt even a partial listing of the thousands of articles on Ellington is beyond the scope of this bibliography. Mention should be made, however, of one publication which is essential for anyone wishing to keep up-to-date with details of new Ellington record issues. This is the *Bulletin of the Duke Ellington Music Society*, obtainable by subscription from Sjef Hoefsmit, Voort 18b, 2328 Hoogstraten, Belgium.

6. AN UPDATED BIBLIOGRAPHY OF WORKS FIRST PUBLISHED AFTER 1983

Bigard, Barney. *With Louis and the Duke*. London: Macmillan, 1985.
Bushell, Garvin. *Jazz from the Beginning*. Ann Arbor: University of Michigan, 1988.
Collier, James L. *Duke Ellington*. New York: Oxford, 1987.
Dietrich, Kurt. *Duke's Bones: Ellington's Great Trombones*. Rottenburg: Advance Music, 1995.
Gammond, Peter. *Duke Ellington*. London: Apollo, 1987.
Hajdu, David. *Lush Life: A Biography of Billy Strayhorn*. New York: Farrar, Straus, Giroux, 1996.
Hasse, John E. *Beyond Category: The Life and Genius of Duke Ellington*. New York: Simon and Schuster, 1993.
Hoefsmit, Sjef. *Comments on Timner's Ellingtonia (Third Edition)*. Jarfalla: Duke Ellington Music Society, 1991.
Lotz, Rainer, and Ulrich Neuert. *The A.F.R.S. "Jubilee" Transcription Programme*. Frankfurt: Norbert Ruecker, 1985.
Moule, Francois X. *The Duke Ellington Recorded Legacy on L.P.s and CD.s, Volume 1*. Le Mans: The Author, 1992.
Nielsen, Ole. *Jazz Records 1942–80: A Discography, Volume 6: Duke Ellington*. Copenhagen: Stainless Wintermoon, 1991.

Rattenbury, Kenneth. *Duke Ellington, Jazz Composer.* London and New Haven: Yale, 1990.

Ruland, Hans. *Duke Ellington: Sein Leben, Seine Musik, Seine Schallplaten.* Gauting-Buchendorf: Oreos, 1985.

Schuller, Gunther. *The Swing Era.* New York: Oxford, 1989.

Stewart, Rex, and Claire Gordon. *Boy Meets Horn.* Ann Arbor: University of Michigan Press, 1991.

Stratemann, Klaus. *Duke Ellington on Film.* P.O., Germany: The Author, 1985.

———. *Duke Ellington: Day by Day and Film by Film.* Copenhagen: Jazz Media, 1992.

Tucker, Mark. *Ellington: The Early Years.* Urbana: University of Illinois, 1991; Oxford: Bayou, 1991.

———. ed. *The Duke Ellington Reader.* New York: Oxford, 1993.

Valburn, Jerry. *The Directory of Duke Ellington's Recordings.* Hicksville, New York: The Author, 1986.

———. *Duke Ellington on Compact Disc.* Hicksville, New York: The Author, 1993.

Volonté, Giovanni M., and Antonio Berini. *Duke Ellington: un gino, un mito.* Florence: Ponte alle Grazie, 1994.

Appendix 2

Discography

Contents

General Introduction	330
The Labels: Countries of Origin	331
Part One—The 78 Era	
Introduction	332
Collected Editions	332
Selected Editions	333
Other Issues of Interest	333
1924–1932	333
Collected Editions	333
Selected Editions	333
Other Issues of Interest	333
1933–February 1940	334
Collected Editions	334
Selected Editions	334
Other Issues of Interest	334
Contingent Recordings	334
March 1940–1946	335
Collected Editions	335
Selected Editions	335
Other Issues of Interest	335
Contingent Recordings	335
Part Two—The Transitional Period	
Introduction	336
1947–1955	336
Collected Editions	336
Selected Editions	336
LP Issues	336
Other Issues of Interest	336
Part Three—The LP Era	
Introduction	337
1956–October 1962	337
November 1962–1965	338
1966–1970	339
1970–1974	339
Part Four—Addendum, by Sjef Hoefsmit	339

GENERAL INTRODUCTION

A fully adequate discographical appendix which would be useful to the specialist Ellington collector as well as to the person with a more casual interest would have to take the form of a complete listing of Duke Ellington's recorded music, or at least that portion of it which has been issued on disc. If personnels and record issues were included, as is standard practice in discographies, then the size of the book would be nearly doubled. Even if such a listing were restricted to the bare bones of recording dates, record companies, and titles the result would still add unduly to the length of the volume.

Authors of general works on jazz musicians, including those on Ellington, have usually presented a brief discographical appendix in the form of a list of currently available LPs. Such a bare listing would clearly be inadequate in a book dealing specifically with Ellington's recorded output, and it is obvious that some form of compromise between the two extremes of a complete discography and a cursory record list is needed. The listing which follows is an attempt at an acceptable compromise.

Any list of available Ellington LPs would certainly be out of date by the time this volume reached the bookshops simply because of the issues and deletions which would have taken place during the time the book was being printed. The major record companies frequently delete a record and then reissue it some time later, often with a different catalog number. The smaller companies usually keep jazz issues in the catalog for a longer period, but they can also often behave in an eccentric fashion. It would be quite wrong to ignore a recording in this appendix because it has not been available for many years, as it could well be reissued a couple of times within twelve months of the book's going to press.

What follows is an attempt to give an indication of the availability of the essential Ellington recordings on LP. For many reasons catalog numbers have been ignored. They are subject to change, their use could mislead readers into ordering discs after they have been deleted, and they take up much space. It must be stressed that this list is only a general guide and that the reader should check carefully on current availability before attempting to obtain any specific LP. Deleted and hard-to-find LPs often crop up in the second-hand section of the specialist dealer's shops and in the lists which many jazz record retailers distribute by post. For those requiring general information on new releases and reissues, the review columns and the advertisements in the specialist jazz magazines *Jazz Journal International* and *Storyville* are useful, but the most detailed and comprehensive information can be found in the periodicals at the end of Appendix One; full discographical information on Ellington's recordings can be found in the discographies listed in Appendix One.

* * *

The listing below is divided into four sections for ease of reference and for clarity. The first of these deals with the era when the 78 rpm record was standard, the second with the transitional period, and the third with the microgroove era. Although 78 rpm collectors still exist today, there is no attempt here to offer a guide to a group of people who are usually well versed in their subject and for whom specialist information is easily obtained. But the general collector will need a guide through the maze of LP reissues of 78 rpm recordings.

No truly collected edition of Ellington recordings exists or has ever been attempted. The British Vintage Jazz Music label has commenced a series of Ellington LPs culled from all the various labels for which Duke recorded, but their total exclusion of the early vocal accompaniments and the limitations they impose on the number of takes used means that this edition is just another selection of Ellington recordings. All the other so-called collected editions—and for the sake of convenience we will continue to refer to them as such here—are even further from the ideal, usually concerning themselves only with the limited number of labels which their company or its predecessors were contracted to in the years of the 78 rpm record. These collected editions will probably form the core of any serious Ellington collection, but in the case of the French CBS edition, *THE COMPLETE DUKE ELLINGTON,* many people will have reservations because of the poor quality of remastering on many of the early albums.

These "complete" editions are detailed in full in the second part of this introduction, and the appropriate volumes are cited in each chronological section within the 78 rpm era. They are followed by a list of selected editions, LPs which give a general coverage of a period, including much of the best music, without attempting to be complete. Many readers will prefer to collect the Ellington music of their choice in this way. On these sections it has been necessary to be very selective, otherwise one would have had a gigantic list of LPs, far too large for its purpose. Readers requiring fuller information are again referred to specialist sources. The final part of each section within the 78 rpm era and the transitional period is headed *Other Issues of Interest* and these include LPs which contain important recordings not found in either the collected or selected editions.

The transitional years are those between 1950 and 1955 when the companies were releasing Ellington material on singles (usually 78 rpm, but also some 45 rpm microgroove issues) or on LPs, the latter both 10-inch and 12-inch. The Capitol recordings of 1953 to 1955 show clearly the problems of collecting this period, for while a number of Capitol LPs have been issued and reissued at regular intervals down the years, many of the Ellington band's recordings for this label have only rarely been published in LP form, some not at all.

Once we move into the microgroove era proper, the number of Ellington singles falls to an insignificant number and disappears altogether after about a decade. As Ellington LPs during this period were made up in a planned and programmed fashion one might have thought that all reissues would follow the original format, but this is not always the case. Taking the American Columbia output as an example, we find that most of their LPs have indeed been reissued in their original form but the music from *THE LIBERIAN SUITE, ELLINGTON UPTOWN IN HI FI, THE NUTCRACKER SUITE,* and *PEER GYNT SUITE/SUITE THURSDAY* has reappeared in a bewildering series of fresh juxtapositions. And the two LPs on the Bethlehem label originally issued as *HISTORICALLY SPEAKING THE DUKE* and *ELLINGTON PRESENTS* have been reissued on a wide variety of labels under a wide variety of titles. Identification of these and other LPs which have been subjected to similar treatment is not difficult when armed with the information contained in the text of this book or in the standard discographies.

As is the case in the preceding sections, the microgroove era listing is a selective one, but it does attempt to cover all the important Ellington releases, those of high musical and/or historical interest. In this sense this appendix is an extension of the *Recommended Records* listings found in the main text of the book. Section four of the discography is a listing of CD and LP issues containing material used for the first time after the completion of the manuscript of this book by Eddie Lambert. It was compiled by Sjef Hoefsmit.

THE LABELS: COUNTRIES OF ORIGIN

In the case of some major record labels which are owned by companies who operate on an international basis, the country of origin is shown against the LPs listed in this appendix.

Ace of Clubs	U.K.
Affinity	U.K.
Aircheck	U.S.A.
Alto	U.S.A.
Atlantic	international distribution
Bethlehem	U.S.A.
Biograph	U.S.A.
Black Lion	U.K.
Blu-Disc	U.S.A. (limited edition)
Capitol	international distribution
Caracol	France
C.B.S.	international distribution
C.B.S./Realm	U.K.
Collectors Classics	Denmark
Columbia	international distribution
Contact	U.S.A.
D.E.S.O.R. Disc	U.S.A.
D.E.T.S.	U.S.A. (limited edition)
Doctor Jazz	U.S.A.
Ember	U.K.
Epic	international distribution
Extreme Rarities	U.S.A.
Fairmont	U.S.A.
Family	Italy
Fanfare	U.S.A.
Fantasy	U.S.A.
F.D.C.	Italy
Flutegrove	U.K.
Flying Dutchman	U.S.A.
Folkways	U.S.A.
Foxy	France
Gaps	Holland
Gardenia	Holland
Giants Of Jazz	U.S.A.
Goodyear	U.K.
Hindsight	U.S.A.
Hot 'n' Sweet	France
Hurricane	Italy
I Giganti del Jazz	Italy
Impulse	U.S.A.
Jazz Archives	U.S.A.
Jazz Club	France
Jazz Connoisseur	Italy
Jazz Guild	U.S.A.
Jazz Legacy	France
Jazz Panorama	Sweden
Jazz Society	Sweden
Jazz Supreme	Italy
Jazzy	Holland
Joyce	U.S.A.
Koala	Australia and U.S.A.
London	international distribution
Max	Sweden
M.C.A.	international distribution
Meritt	U.S.A. (limited edition)
M.F. Records	U.S.A.
Musica Jazz	Italy
Ozone	U.S.A.
Pablo	international distribution
Philips	international distribution
Phontastic	Sweden
Pickwick International	U.S.A.
Poljazz	Poland
President	France
Prestige	U.S.A.
Prima	France
Privateer	France
P.S.P.	Brazil
Queen Disc	Italy
Rare Records	France

Raretone	Italy
Rarities	U.K.
RCA Victor	international distribution
RCA Vintage	international distribution
Reprise	international distribution
Riverside	international distribution
Roulette	international distribution
Session Disc	U.S.A.
Skata	U.S.A.
Smithsonian Collection, The	U.S.A.
Stardust	U.S.A.
Sunburst	U.S.A.
Swaggie	Australia
Swing House	U.K.
Swing Treasury	U.S.A.
Tax	Sweden
Tetco	U.S.A.
T.O.M.	U.S.A.
Unique Jazz	Italy
United Artists	international distribution
Up-To-Date	U.S.A. (limited edition)
Varese	U.S.A.
Verve	international distribution
Victor	international distribution
Vintage Jazz Music	U.K.
Vocalion	U.K.
Vogue	France and U.K.
World Record Club	U.K.
World Records	U.K.

PART ONE—THE 78 ERA

Introduction

COLLECTED EDITIONS

Under this heading LPs from the following editions will be found:

The Works of Duke Integrale, Volumes 1–24 (French RCA)

This edition, issued on single LPs, covers all Victor and Bluebird recordings from the years 1927 to 1951 in chronological order, including the contingent recordings of 1940–1941 which were made under the names of various sidemen. A few alternative takes have been missed but otherwise the edition is complete within its terms of reference. The remastering is uneven, below the highest class overall, but acceptable. See Appendix Three for details of the different versions of Volumes 14 to 17 of this edition.

The Complete Duke Ellington, Volumes 1–15 (French CBS)

This edition consists of fifteen double-LP albums, one volume to an issue, and covers in chronological order all Ellington issues from Pathé, Columbia, OKeh, Harmony, Cameo, Perfect, Velvet Tone, and (American) Oriole; Brunswick from February 1932; Variety, Master, and Vocalion from 1937. Contingent sessions recorded under the names of various sidemen from 1936 to 1940 are included. Taken overall the series covers the period 1925 to March 1940. A few takes have been missed but otherwise the edition is complete within its terms of reference. The remastering is uneven, at its poorest well below that of the RCA set, but overall it is adequate and indeed excellent in some instances.

The Essential Duke Ellington, Volumes 1–... (Vintage Jazz Music)

This edition, which is issued on single LPs, has reached Volume 2 at this writing and so far covers the years 1924–1927. It covers Ellington's band recordings and solos in chronological order irrespective of the label of origin; the first two volumes are drawn from Blu-Disc, Pathé, Gennett, Vocalion, Brunswick, Columbia, Victor, and OKeh. The edition does *not* include the early piano roll or any of the vocal accompaniments. Some takes are missing as a matter of policy, these being thought to be of little interest. The remastering is of a high quality throughout, as are the sleeve notes.

Duke Ellington, Volumes 1–4 (French MCA)

This is a set of single LPs and has not been issued as a complete edition. It does, however, collect in nonchronological order all Ellington's recordings for Vocalion, Brunswick, and Melotone from 1926 to 1931, thus filling in the gaps left by the French RCA and French CBS editions. The individual LPs bear the following titles:

VOLUME ONE—THE BEGINNING
VOLUME TWO—HOT IN HARLEM
VOLUME THREE—ROCKIN' IN RHYTHM
VOLUME FOUR—THE JUNGLE BAND

The remastering, although several years old, is of an acceptable standard.

Duke Ellington Treasury Series (D.E.T.S./Phontastic)

This set of single LPs collects the Duke Ellington Treasury Series broadcasts of 1945 and 1946, each LP containing a one-hour broadcast (later in the series some of the broadcasts ran for one and a quarter hours and these inevitably have had to be accommodated on more than one LP). The sound quality is excellent. The series is issued on a subscription basis by the Meritt Record Society on their D.E.T.S. label; it is intended that the full edition will contain 48 LPs. At this writing, 33 LPs have been issued. The Swedish Phontastic label have started to issue this series publicly, but it seems unlikely at the time of writing that they will issue the complete edition.

Duke Ellington—The Radio Transcriptions, Volumes 1–5 (Hindsight/London)

This set of five single LPs collects the Duke Ellington Capitol Transcriptions of 1946 and 1947, omitting only five performances, four of which are popular ballad recordings. The sound quality is excellent although there is some evidence of "declicking." The five missing items can be found on *DUKE ELLINGTON 1928–1947* (Jazz Supreme) in slightly less good sound.

The Complete Duke Ellington 1947–1952 (French CBS)

A six-LP boxed set containing all Ellington's Columbia recordings from the period stated except those included in the *Masterpieces* and *Ellington Uptown* LPs. The *Controversial Suite* is included, but there are no alternative takes. Overall the sound quality is excellent, but some of the more obscure items are not very well transferred.

SELECTED EDITIONS

These are sets or single LPs which offer a selection of the material found in the collected editions. The following recurrent series require some explanation:

The Indispensable Duke Ellington, Volumes 1–10 (French RCA)

This edition is issued in five double-LP albums, two volumes to an album. It is intended to be an alternative to THE WORKS OF DUKE INTEGRALE, presenting a selection only of the Victor output. This is a later issue than the collected edition and the sound quality is somewhat superior.

RCA Vintage

A group of LPs with well-chosen content and excellent sound quality. The series does, however, omit many of the best Ellington recordings from the forties as these had been issued on four earlier RCA Victor LPs: *AT HIS VERY BEST, IN A MELLOTONE,* and *THE INDISPENSABLE DUKE ELLINGTON, VOLUMES 1 AND 2* (not to be confused with the much later French RCA double albums which use the same title).

The Ellington Era (Columbia [U.S.A.]/CBS [U.K. and Europe])

These are a pair (Volumes 1 and 2) of three-LP boxed sets, each of which offers a roughly chronological selection of the Ellington output for the same labels covered by the French CBS *THE COMPLETE DUKE ELLINGTON*. The contingent recordings are not included. The general standard of remastering is excellent, although there are a few falls from grace. The first box was issued in Britain in single LPs, which were labeled as Volumes 1, 2, and 3, a procedure which has led to some confusion as the three-LP boxes are also called Volumes 1 and 2.

OTHER ISSUES OF INTEREST

These are usually LPs which contain items missing from the "collected" or selected editions, including films, broadcasts, newly issued takes, etc.

1924–1932

COLLECTED EDITIONS

THE WORKS OF DUKE INTEGRALE, VOLUMES 1–8 (French RCA)
THE COMPLETE DUKE ELLINGTON, VOLUMES 1–5 (French CBS)
DUKE ELLINGTON, VOLUMES 1–4 (French MCA)
THE ESSENTIAL DUKE ELLINGTON, VOLUMES 1–... (Vintage Jazz Music)

SELECTED EDITIONS

THE INDISPENSABLE DUKE ELLINGTON, VOLUMES 1/2 (1927–1929) (French RCA)
FLAMING YOUTH (1927–1929) (RCA Vintage)
DAYBREAK EXPRESS (1931–1934) (RCA Vintage)
DUKE ELLINGTON MASTERPIECES 1928–1930 (French RCA)
THE ELLINGTON ERA, VOLUMES 1 AND 2 (1927–1940) (Columbia/CBS)
TOODLE-OO (1926–1928) (Vocalion)
HOT FROM HARLEM (1927–1930) (World Records) (two-LP set)

OTHER ISSUES OF INTEREST

The early Ellington piano roll is not on any of the above issues; it can be found on *DUKE ELLINGTON'S RARE AND UNISSUED MASTERS* (F.D.C.) (Volume 1 of a series but not shown as such on sleeve or label), a rather mixed anthology covering the years 1924 to 1939, and on *DUKE ELLINGTON 1924–1929* (*Hot 'N' Sweet*) which contains a useful selection of early Ellington recordings. It includes several of the vocal accompaniments which Ellington did in the early years of his recording career. These are for the most part omitted from the "collected editions." Along with much band work which is included in these editions, they can also be found on the following LPs: *THE DUKE 1924* (Riverside/London), an old 10-inch LP; *'28–'31, EARLY DUKE,* and *IN HARLEM* (all on the Jazz Panorama label); and *THE*

UNHEARD AND RARELY HEARD DUKE ELLINGTON (Blu-Disc) (a limited edition available only to members of the Meritt Record Society and not duplicating any previous microgroove issues).

The complete soundtrack of the 1929 film *Black and Tan* can be found on *DUKE ELLINGTON'S BAND SHORTS (1929–1935)* (Biograph). The Ellington performances from the film *Check And Double Check* are on *ELLINGTON AT THE MOVIES* (Privateer) in rather poor sound.

The following LPs from this period also contain recordings of interest, although since their issue much of the music has been included in the collected editions: *A STUDY IN ELLINGTONIA 1926–1931, A STUDY IN ELLINGTONIA 1932–1937* (both on Raretone); *DUKE ELLINGTON 1932–1933* (Gaps); *DUKE ELLINGTON 1932–1936* (Gardenia); and *DUKE ELLINGTON 1928–1947* (Jazz Supreme).

1933–February 1940

COLLECTED EDITIONS

THE WORKS OF DUKE INTEGRALE, VOLUMES 8–9 (French RCA)
THE COMPLETE DUKE ELLINGTON, VOLUMES 5–15 (French CBS)

SELECTED EDITIONS

THE INDISPENSABLE DUKE ELLINGTON, VOLUMES 3/4 (1930–1934) (French RCA)
DAYBREAK EXPRESS (1931–1934) (RCA Vintage)
THE ELLINGTON ERA, VOLUMES 1 AND 2 (1927–1940) (Columbia/CBS)
AT THE COTTON CLUB (1931–1939) (Tax)
BRAGGIN' IN BRASS (1936–1939) (Tax)
COTTON CLUB STOMP (1937–1939) (Tax)
DUKE ELLINGTON 1938 *(two-LP Set)* (The Smithsonian Collection)
DUKE ELLINGTON 1939 *(two-LP Set)* (The Smithsonian Collection)

OTHER ISSUES OF INTEREST

The four 1933 recordings for English Columbia are part of *RIDIN' IN RHYTHM* (World Records) a two-LP anthology from which these are the only Ellington items. The 1933 English Decca recordings are not on any of the above issues. They can be found on *DUKE ELLINGTON 1928–1947* (Jazz Supreme) (the only edition with both standard and alternative takes), *THE MUSIC OF DUKE ELLINGTON, BENNY CARTER, JIMMY DORSEY AND UNA MAE CARLISLE* (Ace of Clubs), and *HARLEM SPEAKS* (Family) (an Ellington anthology, 1932–1933).

The Ellington films from this period can be found on *DUKE ELLINGTON AT THE MOVIES* (1929–1934) (Privateer) (poor sound quality), *DUKE ELLINGTON'S BAND SHORTS* (1929–1935) (Biograph), and *IN HOLLYWOOD/ON THE AIR* (1933–1940) (Max).

The important broadcasts from the late thirties can be found on *IN HOLLYWOOD/ON THE AIR* (1933–1940) (Max), *ON THE AIR 38/39* (Max), *ON THE AIR 1940* (Max), *AT THE COTTON CLUB 1938, VOLUMES 1 AND 2* (Jazz Archives), *AT THE COTTON CLUB* (1937–1938) (Jazz Panorama—this includes the privately recorded piano/vocal version of *I've Got To Be A Rug Cutter*) and *AT THE SOUTHLAND/AT THE COTTON CLUB* (1937–1940) (Collectors Classics).

The following LPs also contain music of interest from this period, although most of it is included in the collected editions: *LEW LESLIE'S BLACKBIRDS OF 1928* (Columbia), *A STUDY IN ELLINGTONIA 1932–1937, A STUDY IN ELLINGTONIA 1937, A STUDY IN ELLINGTONIA 1938, A STUDY IN ELLINGTONIA 1939* (all on Raretone), *DUKE ELLINGTON 1932–1933* (Gaps), *DUKE ELLINGTON 1932–1936, DUKE ELLINGTON 1936–1940* (both Gardenia), and *THE UNHEARD AND SELDOM HEARD ELLINGTON, VOLUMES 1 AND 2* (Blu-Disc—the majority of the tracks not duplicated on other issues). The Raretone, Gaps, and Gardenia LPs were intended as "gap fillers" for earlier issues.

CONTINGENT RECORDINGS, 1936 TO FEBRUARY 1940

These are included in *THE COMPLETE DUKE ELLINGTON VOLUMES 7–15* (French CBS). Many LPs containing selections from this group of recordings have been issued, including the following:

ANTHOLOGIES
THE ELLINGTON SIDEMEN (Epic and Philips)
THE DUKE'S MEN (Epic)

BARNEY BIGARD
BARNEY GOIN' EASY (Tax)
A STUDY IN ELLINGTONIA—BARNEY BIGARD (Raretone)

JOHNNY HODGES
HODGE PODGE (Epic and CBS/Realm)
LOVE IN SWINGTIME (Tax)
A STUDY IN ELLINGTONIA—JOHNNY HODGES (Raretone)

REX STEWART
REX STEWART MEMORIAL (Epic and CBS/Realm)

COOTIE WILLIAMS
  COOTIE AND THE BOYS FROM HARLEM (Tax and Swaggie)
  COOTIE AND HIS RUG CUTTERS (Tax and Swaggie)

March 1940–1946

COLLECTED EDITIONS

THE WORKS OF DUKE INTEGRALE VOLUMES 9–23 (French RCA)
(note: see Appendix Three regarding the different versions of Volumes 14 to 17 of this edition.)
DUKE ELLINGTON TREASURY SERIES, VOLUMES 1 TO 33 (D.E.T.S.)
DUKE ELLINGTON–THE RADIO TRANSCRIPTIONS, VOLUMES 1 TO 3 (London and Hindsight)

SELECTED EDITIONS

THE INDISPENSABLE DUKE ELLINGTON, VOLUMES 5/6 (1940) (French RCA)
THE INDISPENSABLE DUKE ELLINGTON, VOLUMES 7/8 (1941–1942) (French RCA)
THE INDISPENSABLE DUKE ELLINGTON–VOLUMES 9/10 (1944–1946) (French RCA)
AT HIS VERY BEST (1927 [1 title], the balance 1940–1946) (RCA)
IN A MELLOTONE (1940–1942) (RCA)
THE INDISPENSABLE DUKE ELLINGTON–VOLUMES 1/2 (1940–1946) (RCA)
JUMPIN' PUNKINS (1940–1941) (RCA Vintage)
JOHNNY COME LATELY (1942–1945) (RCA Vintage)
PRETTY WOMAN (1945–1946) (RCA Vintage) (Includes the two titles recorded for French Swing in 1946, which are not included in the French RCA editions.)
THE GOLDEN DUKE (1946–1951) (Prestige two-LP set) (Contains the bulk of Ellington's 1946 Musicraft output, plus some material from Mercer Records recorded later.)

OTHER ISSUES OF INTEREST

Studio Recordings

Meritt 1 (an anthology by various artists) includes two unissued takes from the 1940 Victor sessions, one of which, *Bojangles*, subsequently appeared on *THE INDISPENSABLE DUKE ELLINGTON, Volumes 5/6 (1940)* (French RCA).

BLUE SKIES (1943–1945) (Swing Treasury) (A selection of World Transcriptions.)
THE TRANSCRIPTION YEARS, VOLUME ONE (1941–1945) (Tax and Swaggie) (A Selection of Standard and World Transcriptions. No subsequent volumes have appeared.)

Concert Recordings

CARNEGIE HALL CONCERT JANUARY 1943 (Prestige three-LP set)
CARNEGIE HALL CONCERT DECEMBER 1943 (Ember two-LP set)
CARNEGIE HALL CONCERT DECEMBER 1944 (Prestige two-LP set)
CARNEGIE HALL CONCERT JANUARY 1946 (Prestige two-LP set)
CARNEGIE HALL CONCERT NOVEMBER 1946 (Queen Disc, one-LP)
CHICAGO CIVIC OPERA HOUSE CONCERT NOVEMBER 1946 (Prima two-LP set)

Broadcasts and Other Live Recordings

DUKE ELLINGTON LIVE FROM THE HOTEL SHERMAN, CHICAGO, VOLUMES 1 AND 2 (Jazz Supreme) (Collects many of the 1940 broadcasts from this venue.)
THE JIMMY BLANTON YEARS (1940–1941) (Queen Disc) (Contains the *America Dances* broadcast of June 1940 plus other air shots.)
THE DUKE 1940 (Jazz Society two-LP set) (Recordings from the Fargo dance date of November 7, 1940.)
FARGO ENCORES (1940) (Jazz Guild and Phontastic) (The rest of the Fargo material, plus air shots from September 1940.)
DUKE ELLINGTON AT THE HURRICANE, VOLUMES 1 AND 2 (1943) (Hurricane) (Each volume contains two of the *Pastel Hour* broadcasts.)
A DATE WITH THE DUKE, VOLUMES 1 TO 8 (1945) (Fairmont) (Selections from the D.E.T.S. transcriptions)
DUKE ELLINGTON AND HIS ORCHESTRA–11 OCTOBER 1946–25 OCTOBER 1946 BROADCAST RECORDINGS (Fanfare).
DUKE ELLINGTON 1943–1946 (Jazz Society), THE FABULOUS FORTIES VOLUME 1 (1940–1943), VOLUME 2 (1944–1947) and VOLUME 3 (1940–1944) (Rarities) are all Ellington anthologies containing interesting broadcast material.

CONTINGENT RECORDINGS, 1940–1941

These are included in the French RCA collected edition but the following include all the titles but without alternative takes:

THING'S AIN'T WHAT THEY USED TO BE–JOHNNY HODGES AND REX STEWART: (1940–1941) (RCA Vintage)
BARNEY BIGARD AND ALBERT NICHOLAS (includes the Bigard unit recordings 1940–1941; the Albert Nicholas sides have no connection with Duke Ellington.) (RCA Vintage)

PART TWO—THE TRANSITIONAL PERIOD

Introduction

In August 1947 Duke Ellington started recording under a new contract with Columbia. This contract was to run until August 1952 and during this period the public issue of microgroove recordings commenced. As a consequence we are here dealing with Ellington recordings which were initially issued on LP records in addition to the categories we have covered previously. Many such Columbia and Capitol LPs have been the subject of straightforward reissues down the years. Here they are listed under *LP ISSUES*. The LPs listed under other categories which are from Columbia or Capitol recordings derive from 78 or 45 singles or are a mixture of these plus tracks taken from previously issued LPs and from unissued vault material.

1947–1955

COLLECTED EDITIONS

THE COMPLETE DUKE ELLINGTON 1947–1952 (French CBS) (six-LP set)
DUKE ELLINGTON—THE RADIO TRANSCRIPTIONS, VOLUMES 4 AND 5 (London and Hindsight)
THE WORKS OF DUKE INTEGRALE, VOLUME 24 (French RCA) (This recording from the Seattle Concert of March 25, 1952, has also been issued as a separate LP outside the *INTEGRALE* series.)

SELECTED EDITIONS

THE DUKE 1899–1974 (Columbia/CBS two-LP set)
THE WORLD OF DUKE ELLINGTON (1947–1951) (Columbia/CBS two-LP set).
THE WORLD OF DUKE ELLINGTON, VOLUME 2 (1951–1957) (Columbia/CBS two-LP set).
DUKE ELLINGTON AND THE ELLINGTONIANS (1950–1951) (French Vogue two-LP set) (Mercer recordings, including the Ellington-Strayhorn duets, *New Piano Roll Blues,* and the Coronets titles.)
BAND CALL (1953–1954) (World Record Club) (A long deleted selection taken from Capitol 78s. Other LPs which include material from Capitol 78 issues usually also contain recordings from Capitol LPs which they duplicate unnecessarily.)
DUKE ELLINGTON, WE LOVE YOU MADLY (1953–1954) (Pickwick International) (An assorted selection of Capitol recordings including some previously unissued items.)

LP ISSUES

THE LIBERIAN SUITE (10 inch) (1947) (Columbia)
MASTERPIECES BY ELLINGTON (1950) (Columbia)
ELLINGTON UPTOWN (1951–1952) (Columbia) (The version of this LP entitled *ELLINGTON UPTOWN IN HI FI* substitutes *The Controversial Suite* for *Harlem* but is otherwise identical. These two suites and *The Liberian Suite* have been subjected to various combinations in their presentation on later LPs, while both versions of *ELLINGTON UPTOWN* have also been returned to the catalog from time to time.)
PREMIERED BY ELLINGTON (10 inch) (1953) (Capitol)
THE DUKE PLAYS ELLINGTON (1953) (Capitol)
DANCE TO THE DUKE (1953–1954) (Capitol)
ELLINGTON '55 (1953–1955) (Capitol)
ELLINGTON SHOWCASE (1953–1955) (Capitol)

OTHER ISSUES OF INTEREST

Studio Recordings
THE STUDIO RECORDINGS, VOLUME 1 (1937–1947) (Up-To-Date)
THE STUDIO RECORDINGS, VOLUME 2 (1947–1949) (Up-To-Date)
THE STUDIO RECORDINGS, VOLUME 3 (1926–1952) (Up-To-Date)
THE STUDIO RECORDINGS, VOLUME 4 (1947–1949) (Up-To-Date)
THE STUDIO RECORDINGS, VOLUME 5 (1929–1956) (Up-To-Date)
THE STUDIO RECORDINGS, VOLUME 6 (1930–1958) (Up-To-Date)

(Up-To-Date LPs are limited editions, available only to members of The Meritt Record Society. Apart from one item from 1926 and five alternative takes from 1937–1939, this series consists of unissued takes of Columbia recordings, 1947–1952. Volume 4 includes *The Liberian Suite, Harlem,* and *The Controversial Suite* in alternative take form.)

Concert Recordings
DUKE ELLINGTON, VOLUME 4—APRIL 30, 1947 (Cornell Concert) (Stardust)
DUKE ELLINGTON, THE HOLLYWOOD BOWL CONCERT—AUGUST 31, 1947, VOLUMES 1 AND 2 (Unique Jazz)
CARNEGIE HALL CONCERT DECEMBER 1947 (Prestige two-LP set)
CARNEGIE HALL CONCERT NOVEMBER 1948 (Caracol two-LP set)
CARNEGIE HALL CONCERT NOVEMBER 1952 (F.D.C. two-LP set)
ELLINGTON IN CONCERT (World Record Club)

ELLINGTON IN CONCERT, VOLUME 2 (World Record Club)
THE DUKE AT CORNELL, VOLUME 1 (D.E.S.O.R. DISC)
(The three LPs above were recorded at concerts at Cornell University in December 1948.)
METROPOLITAN OPERA HOUSE CONCERT JANUARY 1951 (Rare Records, two LPs) (This set also includes some D.E.T.S. material.)

Broadcasts and Other Live Recordings
THE UNDOCUMENTED ELLINGTON, VOLUME 1 (1946–1949) (Up-To-Date)
DUKE ELLINGTON; BEN WEBSTER; BILLY (sic) HOLIDAY (Ozone) (Includes eight Ellington tracks from 1949)
LIVE AT THE CLICK RESTAURANT, PHILADELPHIA 1948, VOLUME 1 (Raretone)
LIVE AT THE CLICK RESTAURANT, PHILADELPHIA 1948, VOLUME 2 (Raretone)
LIVE AT THE EMPIRE HOTEL, HOLLYWOOD, FEBRUARY 1949, VOLUME 3 (Raretone)
LIVE AT THE CLICK RESTAURANT, PHILADELPHIA 1949, VOLUME 4 (Raretone)
THE WINNERS (Giants Of Jazz) (contains the broadcast of January 2, 1951, plus non-Ellington recordings.)
HOORAY FOR DUKE ELLINGTON (1951) (Session Disc)
DUKE ELLINGTON, VOLUME 2—JUNE 1951 (Stardust)
HE'S MR. EDWARD KENNEDY DUKE ELLINGTON (May 1951) (Alto)
THE DUKE IS ON THE AIR (1952) (Aircheck)
FIRST ANNUAL TOUR OF THE PACIFIC NORTHWEST, SPRING 1952 (Folkways two-LP set)
DUKE ELLINGTON, VOLUME 1—JANUARY–APRIL 1952 (Stardust)
DUKE ELLINGTON—RAREST STYLE 1952 (Sunburst)
DON'T WORRY 'BOUT ME . . . —DUKE ELLINGTON 1952 (Skata)
THE UNUSUAL ELLINGTON (1952–1955) (Jazz Guild and Phontastic)
DUKE ELLINGTON, VOLUME 3—APRIL 1953 (Stardust)
DUKE ELLINGTON: THE WASHINGTON ARMORY CONCERT—APRIL 30, 1955 (Jazz Guild and Phontastic)

PART THREE—THE LP ERA

Introduction

From the middle fifties onwards the vast majority of Duke Ellington's recordings were issued on LPs, although occasional singles continued to be issued for a further decade. From this point onwards, therefore, the standard Ellington record is the 12-inch LP. All the items listed below are either 12-inch LPs or parts of 12-inch LPs, and only the original company of issue is cited. The obvious inferences may be made regarding later issues, for example that American Columbia releases would be issued in Britain and Europe initially on Philips and later on CBS. Such companies as Verve, Reprise, and Pablo are international in scope, and it can be assumed that the record has been distributed throughout the label's range unless otherwise indicated.

In the listing below LPs are designated by CAPITAL LETTERS and items which simply form part of an LP issue are in lower case.

1956–October 1962

BLUE ROSE (with Rosemary Clooney) (1956) (Columbia)
HISTORICALLY SPEAKING THE DUKE (1956) (Bethlehem)
DUKE ELLINGTON PRESENTS (1956) (Bethlehem)
ELLINGTON AT NEWPORT (1956) (Columbia)
DUKE ELLINGTON AND BUCK CLAYTON AT NEWPORT (1956) (Columbia)
Black And Tan Fantasy from the 1956 Newport concerts is on *LIVE UNRELEASED HIGHLIGHTS FROM NEWPORT* (Columbia two-LP set)
ELLINGTON AT TANGLEWOOD, VOLUMES 1 AND 2 (1956) (Queen Disc two-LPs) *Diminuendo And Crescendo In Blue) (July 28, 1956)* from the Connecticut Jazz Festival is on *JAZZ FESTIVAL JAZZ* (Queen Disc)
A DRUM IS A WOMAN (1956) (Columbia) (See Chapter 22 for discussion of the different pressings of this LP.)
Improvisation In Three Parts (1957) (Columbia) (Included in the two-LP set *THE WORLD OF DUKE ELLINGTON, VOLUME 2*. Five of the piano improvisations were recorded and the other two can be found on *DUKE ELLINGTON: THE STUDIO SESSIONS, VOLUME 6* [1930–1958] [Up-To-Date].)
SUCH SWEET THUNDER (1956–1957) (Columbia)
DUKE ELLINGTON: THE STUDIO SERIES, VOLUME 5 (1926–1956) (Up-To-Date)
Carrolltown Dance Date June 1957 (selections from the recordings made during this engagement have been issued on Doctor Jazz (a fine two-LP set), Jazzy and Koala).
ELLA FITZGERALD SINGS THE DUKE ELLINGTON SONG BOOK (1957) (Verve, four LPs, two of which contain performances by the Duke Ellington Orchestra.)
ELLINGTON INDIGOS (1957) (Columbia; old releases on the British Philips label were entitled *SOLITUDE*. The mono and stereo versions of this LP have different takes of three of the recordings.)
ONE NIGHT STAND WITH DUKE ELLINGTON (1957) (Joyce)

BLACK, BROWN AND BEIGE (1958) (Columbia)
Travis Air Force Base Dance Dates, March 1958 (selections from the recordings made during these engagements have been issued on Jazz Connoisseur, Koala, and Unique Jazz.)
AT THE BAL MASQUE (1958) (Columbia)
THE COSMIC SCENE (1958) (Columbia)
NEWPORT 1958 (1958) (Columbia)
JAZZ AT THE PLAZA, VOLUME 2 (1958) (Columbia) (Volume 1 does not contain any Ellington recordings.)
DUKE ELLINGTON LIVE 1958 (1958) (Musica Jazz)
DUKE ELLINGTON: THE STUDIO SERIES, VOLUME 6 (1930–1958) (Up-To-Date)
DUKE ELLINGTON 1899–1974 (1958–1971) (M.F. Records five-LP set) (This album contains recordings made both in the studio and at live performances. These discs have also been issued as five separate LPs on the Black Lion label and these are superior pressings.)
BILLY STRAYHORN LIVE (1958) (Roulette) (Actually this LP is by the Duke Ellington Orchestra with Duke, not Billy Strayhorn, at the piano; it has been reissued under different titles on different labels; some of these LPs state, correctly, that the music is by Duke Ellington and his Orchestra.)
ELLINGTON JAZZ PARTY (1959) (Columbia)
BACK TO BACK (1959) (Verve—Duke Ellington and Johnny Hodges)
SIDE BY SIDE (1959) (Verve—Duke Ellington and Johnny Hodges)
(These two LPs have frequently been reissued as a two-LP set.)
The Queen's Suite (1959) (issued as part of the Pablo LP *THE ELLINGTON SUITES*)
ELLINGTON MOODS (1959) (Jazz Legacy; the SESAC recordings, also available in other issues.)
ANATOMY OF A MURDER (1959) (Columbia)
NEWPORT JAZZ FESTIVAL 1959 (Foxy two-LP set)
FESTIVAL SESSION (1959) (Columbia)
DUKE ELLINGTON LIVE (1959) (Affinity two-LP set)
THE ELEGANT MISTER ELLINGTON (1959) (Swing House)
"VIP" (1959) (Swing House)
BLUES IN ORBIT (1959) (Columbia)
The Nutcracker Suite (1960) (Columbia; originally issued as a complete LP but combined with the *Peer Gynt Suite* on reissues)
PIANO IN THE BACKGROUND (1960) (Columbia)
Peer Gynt Suite (1960) (Columbia; originally combined with *Suite Thursday* but coupled with *The Nutcracker Suite* on reissues.)
THE UNKNOWN SESSION (1960) (Columbia)
Mather Air Force Base Dance Date—July 1960 (selections from the recording made during this engagement have been issued on Unique Jazz and Koala.)
Suite Thursday (1960) (Columbia; originally issued with the *Peer Gynt Suite* but reissued combined with other material)
PIANO IN THE FOREGROUND (1961) (Columbia)
LOUIS ARMSTRONG AND DUKE ELLINGTON—THE BEAUTIFUL AMERICANS (1961) (Roulette two-LP set)
PARIS BLUES—ORIGINAL SOUNDTRACK (1961) (United Artists)
BATTLE ROYAL—DUKE ELLINGTON AND COUNT BASIE (1961) (Columbia)
ALL AMERICAN IN JAZZ (1962) (Columbia)
GOODYEAR JAZZ CONCERT, VOLUME 1—DUKE ELLINGTON AND BOBBY HACKETT (1962) (Goodyear)
A MIDNIGHT IN PARIS (1962) (Columbia)
DUKE ELLINGTON MEETS COLEMAN HAWKINS (1962) (Impulse)
MONEY JUNGLE—DUKE ELLINGTON, CHARLIE MINGUS, MAX ROACH (1962) (United Artists)
DUKE ELLINGTON AND JOHN COLTRANE (1962) (Impulse)
DUKE (1962) (Varese; interview with Jack Cullen)
(Note: Most of the Columbia LPs 1950–1962 have been reissued on French CBS in the early 1980s.)

November 1962–1965

WILL THE BIG BANDS EVER COME BACK? (1962–1963) (Reprise)
RECOLLECTIONS OF THE BIG BAND ERA (1962–1963) (Atlantic)
AFRO-BOSSA (1962–1963) (Reprise)
DUKE ELLINGTON—THE GREAT PARIS CONCERT (1963) (Reprise)
DUKE ELLINGTON'S GREATEST HITS (1963) (Reprise)
THE SYMPHONIC ELLINGTON (1963) (Reprise)
DUKE ELLINGTON'S JAZZ VIOLIN SESSION (1963) (Atlantic)
ALICE BABS AND DUKE ELLINGTON—SERENADE TO SWEDEN (1963) (Reprise)
MY PEOPLE—ORIGINAL CAST ALBUM (1963) (Contact)
DUKE ELLINGTON AND HIS JAZZ GROUP (1964) (Caracol)
Suite For Swinging (1964) (Extreme Rarities; included in the LP *HOT JAZZ ON FILM, VOLUME 4*.)
ELLINGTON '65 (1964) (Reprise)
ELLINGTON '66 (1964–1965) (Reprise)
DUKE ELLINGTON—1964 PIANO SOLOS (Flutegrove)
DUKE ELLINGTON AND HIS FAMOUS ORCHESTRA (1964—Canadian TV recordings) (Rarities)
DUKE ELLINGTON—MARY POPPINS (1964) (Reprise)
DUKE ELLINGTON IN EUROPE, VOLUME 1 (1965—Paris Concert) (Jazz Club)

CONCERT IN THE VIRGIN ISLANDS (1965) (Reprise)
(A Reprise boxed set of five LPs entitled *DUKE ELLINGTON—SOUVENIRS* contains the following: *AFRO-BOSSA* (all but three tracks), *MARY POPPINS* (complete), *THE SYMPHONIC ELLINGTON* (complete), *ELLINGTON '65* (complete), *ELLINGTON '66* (four tracks only), *WILL THE BIG BANDS EVER COME BACK?* (all but one track), *DUKE ELLINGTON'S GREATEST HITS* (all but four tracks), and one track from *CONCERT IN THE VIRGIN ISLANDS* included in error and not mentioned in the album notes. These notes and the labels contain a number of errors.)
Second Portrait Of The Lion (1965) (Victor; included on the LP *THE JAZZ PIANO*.)
THE DUKE AT TANGLEWOOD (1965) (Victor; with the Boston Pops Orchestra.)
ELLA AT DUKE'S PLACE (1965) (Verve; with Ella Fitzgerald.)
DUKE ELLINGTON'S CONCERT OF SACRED MUSIC (1965) (Victor)

1966–1970

DUKE "SOLO" (1966—Goutelas recordings) (President)
THE POPULAR DUKE ELLINGTON (1966) (Victor)
ANTIBES CONCERT, VOLUME 1 (1966) (Verve)
ANTIBES CONCERT, VOLUME 2 (1966) (Verve)
(These two LPs were previously issued as *DUKE ELLINGTON AT THE COTE D'AZUR* and *SOUL CALL*.)
DUKE ELLINGTON, JOHNNY HODGES, COOTIE WILLIAMS, CAT ANDERSON (Newport 1966 recordings) (I Giganti del Jazz)
THE PIANIST (1966–1970) (Fantasy)
THE FAR EAST SUITE (1966) (Victor)
THE GREATEST JAZZ CONCERT IN THE WORLD (1967) (Pablo; a four-LP set which also features non-Ellington material.)
NORTH OF THE BORDER—DUKE ELLINGTON IN CANADA (1967) (MCA; with the Ron Collier Orchestra.)
THE DUKE ELLINGTON OCTET—RAINBOW ROOM BROADCASTS 1967 (Unique Jazz)
". . . AND HIS MOTHER CALLED HIM BILL" (1967) (Victor; the 1983 French RCA edition has two additional tracks.)
DUKE ELLINGTON—FRANK SINATRA (1967) (Reprise)
YALE CONCERT (1968) (Fantasy)
SECOND SACRED CONCERT (1968) (United Artists two-LP set)
"FAMED FIELDCUP CONCERT"—THE DUKE ELLINGTON OCTET (1968) (Tetco)
THE DUKE IN SÃO PAULO (1968) (PSP)
LATIN AMERICAN SUITE (1968–1970) (Fantasy)
THE INTIMATE ELLINGTON (1969–1971) (Pablo)
UP IN DUKE'S WORKSHOP (1969–1972) (Pablo)

PARIS JAZZ PARTY (1969) (Affinity)
70th BIRTHDAY CONCERT (1969) (United Artists two-LP set)

1970–1974

DUKE ELLINGTON OPENS THE CAVE (1970) (TOM, two LPs)
NEW ORLEANS SUITE (1970) (Atlantic)
DUKE ELLINGTON WITH THE CINCINNATI SYMPHONY ORCHESTRA (1970) (Decca)
THE AFRO-EURASIAN ECLIPSE (1971) (Fantasy)
Goutelas Suite (1971) (Issued as part of the Pablo LP *THE ELLINGTON SUITES*)
THE ENGLISH CONCERT/TOGO BRAVA SUITE (1971) (United Artists two-LP set)
THE LAST TIME (1971) (Poljazz; Warsaw concert)
UWIS Suite (1972) (Issued as part of the Pablo LP *THE ELLINGTON SUITES*)
THIS ONE'S FOR BLANTON! (1972) (Pablo; Duke Ellington and Ray Brown)
DUKE'S BIG FOUR (1973) (Pablo)
FAR AWAY STAR (1973) (Phontastic; with Alice Babs; the Duke Ellington orchestra is featured on four tracks only.)
DUKE ELLINGTON AND TERESA BREWER (1973) (Flying Dutchman and Columbia)
THIRD SACRED CONCERT—THE MAJESTY OF GOD (1973) (RCA Victor)
EASTBOURNE PERFORMANCE (1973) (RCA Victor)

PART FOUR—ADDENDUM OF NEW ELLINGTON ISSUES (*COMPILED BY SJEF HOEFSMIT*)

This listing is of CD and LP issues containing material issued for the first time after the completion of the manuscript of this book by Eddie Lambert. It is alphabetical by CD or LP title, with cross references to identical issues under different titles. The numbers in the righthand column indicate the number of tracks issued for the first time since 1983; these include newly discovered or alternate takes, as well as previously unissued live performances.

A CONCERT OF SACRED MUSIC FROM GRACE CATHEDRAL
   CD   Status(E)DSTS 1015   11
ALHAMBRA 29 OCTOBRE 1958
   2CD   RTE/UNE Musique/Europe 1(F)710707   21
ALL STAR JAZZ SHOW #4
   LP   Sounds Great Live(US)SG-8017   7
ALL STAR ROAD BAND
   2LP   Doctor Jazz(E)ASLD-850   15
   2LP   Doctor Jazz(J)K18P 6276-7   15
   2LP   Doctor Jazz(US&F)W2X-39137   15
   CD   Doctor Jazz WGK-39137-2   15

CD	Doctor Jazz WK-39137E	15
CD	Doctor Jazz(F)FDC-5000	15
CD	Zillion/Sony(Eur)2610482	15

ALL STAR ROAD BAND #2
2LP	Doctor Jazz W2X-40012	18
CD	Doctor Jazz(F)FDC-5011	15
CD	Zillion/Sony(Eur)2610492	15

A MORNING IN PARIS
CD	ENJA Records(G) ENJ-CD-9309-2	2

AN EVENING WITH THE DUKE
LP	Giants Of Jazz GOJ-1003	10

AND HIS MOTHER CALLED HIM BILL
LP	RCA(F)NL-89166	2
CD	RCA Bluebird 6287-2-RB	4
CD	RCA Bluebird(Eur)ND-86287	4
CD	RCA(J)BVCJ-5010	4
CD	RCA(J)R32J-1072	4

APRIL IN PARIS
CD	West Wind(G)WW 2406	14

AT THE BLUE NOTE, CHICAGO
CD	Vogue(Roulette)VG 651-600 062	4

AT THE PLEYEL, PARIS
2CD	Magic DAWE-39&40	22

BEN WEBSTER—COTTON TAIL
CD	RCA Victor 07863-66790-2	1

BEN WEBSTER—PERDIDO
CD	Moon Records(It)MCD049-2	1

BERLIN '65—PARIS '67
CD	Pablo PACD-5304-2	10

BEST OF DUKE ELLINGTON
LP	Pablo 2310.845	12

BILLY STRAYHORN
LP	Musica Jazz(It)2MJP-1055	12

BILLY STRAYHORN—LUSH LIFE
CD	Red Baron(US)AK 52760	18

BIRDLAND—1952
CD	Jazz Unlimited(Sw)JUCD 2036	20

BLANTON-WEBSTER BAND
4LP	RCA Bluebird(US)5659-1-RB29	0
3CD	Bluebird(J)BVCJ-7009/10/11	?
3CD	RCA Bluebird(Eur)7432-13181-2	0
3CD	RCA Bluebird(US)5659-2-RB	1
3CD	RCA(J)B18D-4008/-10	?
3CD	RCA(J)R30J-1003/-5	?

BLUE NOTE BROADCASTS
LP	DETS 47	18

BLUE NOTE BROADCASTS
LP	DETS 48	16

BLUE ROSE
CD	CBS 466444-2	1

BLUES IN ORBIT
CD	CBS(Eur)460823 2	3
CD	Columbia CK-44051	3

BROADCASTS 14 APRIL 1945 & 1 AUGUST 1953
LP	DETS Bonus	8

BRUNSWICK-VOCALION RARITIES
LP	MCA-1374	2

CABIN IN THE SKY
CD	Rhino(US) R2 72245	1

CALIFORNIA CONCERTS
CD	GNP(J)240E-6849	9
CD	GNP(J)K28Y-6258	9

CANADA, LIVE PERFORMANCES 1956–1973
LP	Marlor Productions Ellington '87	15

CARNEGIE HALL 1948
2CD	VJC(US)VJC-1024/25-2	8

COMPLETE CAPITOL RECORDINGS
5CD	Mosaic Records(US) MD5-160	9
8LP	Mosaic Records(US)	9

COMPLETE DUKE ELLINGTON 1947–1952
3LP	CBS 66607	3
5CD	CBS 462985-2/89-2	3
5CD	CBS(F)463465-2	3

COOL ROCK
CD	Laser Light(US)15 782	12

COSMIC SCENE
CD	CBS 467179-2	1

COUNT BASIE—DUKE ELLINGTON—JOE WILLIAMS
LP	I Giganti Del Jazz GJ-79	2

DELLA REESE WITH DUKE ELLINGTON
CD	Jazz Band(It) EBCD2110-2	21

DES COMPOSITIONS DE BILLY STRAYHORN
CD	RCA Bluebird(F)ND-90330	4
	same as And His Mother Called Him Bill	

DON BYAS
CD	Musica Jazz(It)MJCD1088	1

DUKE & ELLA IN CONCERTO
CD	Jazz Blues Soul(It)JBS 93B02b	18

DUKE ELLINGTON
CD	Jazz Archives(H)90.105-2	5

DUKE ELLINGTON
CD	Jazz Plus(It)JP-001	17

DUKE ELLINGTON
CD	Jazz Time(Sp)JT-004	10
	same as In the Uncommon Market	

DUKE ELLINGTON 1928–1947
LP	Jazz Supreme JS-102	4

DUKE ELLINGTON & ELLA FITZGERALD AT GREEK THEATRE
CD	Status Records(E)DSTS 1013	10

DUKE ELLINGTON & HIS ORCHESTRA
LP	Circle CLP-101 Volume #1	12
LP	Circle CLP-102 Volume #2	10
LP	Circle CLP-103 Volume #3	7
LP	Circle CLP-104 Volume #4	9
LP	Circle CLP-105 Volume #5	9
LP	Circle CLP-106 Volume #6	13
LP	Circle CLP-107 Volume #7	18
LP	Circle CLP-108 Volume #8	13
LP	Circle CLP-109 Volume #9	10

Discography

DUKE ELLINGTON & HIS ORCHESTRA
- CD Circle CCD-101 Volume #1 18
- CD Circle CCD-102 Volume #2 18
- CD Circle CCD-103 Volume #3 23
- CD Circle CCD-104 Volume #4 25
- CD Circle CCD-105 Volume #5 20?

DUKE ELLINGTON & HIS ORCHESTRA 1965–1972
- CD Musicmasters(J)PHCE 5036 15
- CD Musicmasters(US)5041-2-C 15

DUKE ELLINGTON–'65 REVISITED
- CD Affinity(E)CD AFRS 1000 15

DUKE ELLINGTON–1951–1958
- CD Giants Of Jazz(It)53066 6

DUKE ELLINGTON–MEL LEWIS BIG BAND–THAD JONES
- LP I Giganti Del Jazz GJ-64 3

DUKE ELLINGTON A PARIGI/LIVE
- CD Blu Jazz(It)BJ-003 5

DUKE ELLINGTON AND HIS ORCHESTRA "V.I.P."
- LP Swing House SWH-28 7

DUKE ELLINGTON IN CONCERT
- LP Century(J)20EL-5503 4

DUKE ELLINGTON IN HAMILTON
- 2CD Radiex Music(Can)RDX-1000 25

DUKE ELLINGTON IN SWEDEN
- LP Jazz Information(Sd)CAH-4001 10

DUKE ELLINGTON OCTET LIVE AT THE RAINBOW GRILL
- CD Moon Records(It)MCD070-2 15

DUKE ELLINGTON ORCHESTRA
- LP EchoJazz(E)EJLP 04 2
- CD EchoJazz(E)EJCD 04 2

DUKE ELLINGTON (1)
- CD Sarpe Top Jazz(Sp)S-1002 6
- CD Top Jazz(It)DJ-002 6

DUKE ELLINGTON (2)
- CD Sarpe Top Jazz(Sp)S-1013 5

DUKE ELLINGTON (3)
- CD Sarpe Top Jazz(Sp)S-1018 14

DUKE ELLINGTON (4)
- CD Sarpe Top Jazz(Sp)S-1024 12

DUKE ELLINGTON–PASSION FLOWER
- CD Moon Records MCD 074-2 12

DUKE 56/62 #1
- 2LP CBS 88653 15

DUKE 56/62 #2
- 2LP CBS 88654 18

DUKE 56/62 #3
- LP CBS 26306 10

DUKE IN SÃO PAULO
- LP ESP 001 9

DUKE IS ON THE AIR
- LP Queen Q-071 17

DUKE'S BIG 4
- LP Pablo 2310.703 7
- LP Pablo(J)MTF-1001 7
- LP Pablo(J)MW-2090 7
- CD Pablo(J)J33J-20009 7
- CD Pablo(J)VDJ-28041 7

EARLY ELLINGTON BRUNSWICK/VOCALION
- 3CD Decca(US)GRD-3-640 7

ECHOES OF HARLEM
- CD Musica Jazz(It)MJCD1101 1

ELLA FITZGERALD SONGBOOK
- CD Verve 314519639 5

ELLINGTON AT BASIN STREET
- CD Music & Arts(US)CD 908 17

ELLINGTON SUITES
- LP Pablo 2310.762 15
- LP Pablo(E)2335.743 15
- LP Pablo(J)MTF-1043 15
- LP Pablo(Sp)27 521 LM 15
- CD Pablo(F)98.830 15
- CD Pablo(J)J33J-20008 15
- CD Pablo(J)VDJ-28006 15
- CD Pablo(J)VICJ 23579 15

ELLINGTON THE PIANIST–PIANO IN THE FOREGROUND
- CD CBS(F)465638 2 1

EUROPEAN TOUR
- LP Bandstand BDLP-1509 4
- CD Bandstand BDCD-1509 4
- CD Black Lion(J)TKCB-30025 4

FAR EAST SUITE–SPECIAL MIX
- CD RCA Bluebird 7863/66551-2 4

FARGO
- 2CD VJC(US)VJC-1019/20-2 7

FEATURING PAUL GONSALVES
- LP Fantasy(Arg)3645 8
- LP Fantasy(J)VIJ-6449 8
- LP Fantasy(US)F-9636 8

1ST ANNUAL CONNECTICUT JAZZ FESTIVAL
- LP IAJRC-45 7
- CD IAJRC CD 1005 9

GIRL'S SUITE–PERFUME SUITE
- LP CBS 85933 14
- LP CBS Sony 25AP-2776 14
- LP Columbia FC-38028 14

GREAT CHICAGO CONCERTS
- 2LP Jazz Heritage(US)923584F 11
- 2CD Jazz Heritage(US)523584W 11
- 2CD Limelight(EEC)844 401-2 11
- 2CD Musicmasters (US)65110-2 11
- 2CD Polygram 844 401-2 11

GREAT DUKE ELLINGTON
- CD Musica Jazz(It)MJCD1091 13

GREAT LONDON CONCERTS
- LP Jazz Heritage(US)913583Y 14
- CD Jazz Heritage(US)513583L 14
- CD Musicmasters(UK)518 446-2 14

    CD   Musicmasters(US)65106-2 — 14

GREATEST JAZZ CONCERT IN THE WORLD
- 4LP   Pablo 2625.704 — 20
- 4LP   Pablo(E)2660.109(2335.721/-724) — 20
- 4LP   Pablo(J)MW-9057/-9060 — 20
- 3CD   Pablo(US)PACD 2625-704-2 — 20
- 7 tracks are different from LP box

HAPPY BIRTHDAY DUKE!
- 5CD   Laser Light 15783/84/85/86/87 — 39
- 5CD   Laser Light(G)15 965 — 39

HAPPY REUNION
- LP   Doctor Jazz FW-40030 — 5
- CD   Zillion/Sony(Eur)2610642 — 5

HAPPY REUNION—NEW MOOD INDIGO
- CD   Doctor Jazz(F)FDC-5007 — 13

HARLEM
- LP   Pablo Live(J)28MJ-3523 — 10
- LP   Pablo Live(US)2308-245 — 10
- CD   Pablo(F)98.817 — 10
- CD   Pablo(G)CD-2308-245 — 10

IL CONTRABASSO NEL JAZZ
- CD   Musica Jazz(It)MJCD1089 — 1

IN CONCERT NEW YORK 1964
- CD   i Maestri Del Jazz(It)1004-1 — 12

IN LONDON 1958
- LP   Marlor Productions Ellington '88 — 29

IN THE UNCOMMON MARKET
- LP   Pablo 2308-247 — 10
- LP   Pablo Live(J)28MJ-3547 — 10
- CD   Pablo(F)98.818 — 10
- CD   Pablo(J)J33J-20125 — 10
- CD   Pablo(US)2308-247-2 — 10

INCOMPARABLE DUKE ELLINGTON & HIS ORCHESTRA
- LP   Dance Band Days (GB)DBD-11 — 2

INTIMACY OF THE BLUES
- LP   Fantasy(US)F-9640 — 11
- CD   Fantasy(F)98.558 — 11
- CD   Fantasy(J)VDJ-1065 — 11

INTIMATE ELLINGTON
- LP   Pablo 2310.787 — 10
- LP   Pablo(J)MTF-1067 — 10
- CD   Pablo(US)OJCDD-730-2 — 10

JAM A DITTY
- CD   Jazz & Jazz(It)JJ-602 — 15

JAZZ COLLECTOR EDITION
- CD   Laser Light(US)15 753 — 2

JAZZ PARTY
- CD   CBS 460059 2 — 2
- CD   Columbia(US)CK-40712 — 2

JAZZ POTPOURRI #2 1925–1933
- LP   Merritt 24 — 1

JIVE RHAPSODY
- CD   Moon Records MCD084-2 — 8

JOHNNY HODGES
    LP   Musica Jazz(It)2MJP-1082 — 6

LA NUOVA MUSICA #2
- CD   Stradivarius CD STR 10009 — 6

LAMPLIGHTER'S ALL STAR JAZZ
- CD   Chess/Vogue(F)655.004 — 1

LE SUITES "SINFONICHE"
- LP   Musica Jazz(It)2MJP-1021 — 5

LIVE 1958, GÖTEBORG
- LP   Musica Jazz(It)2MJP-1005 — 11

LIVE AT MONTEREY PART 1
- CD   Status Records(E)DSTS 1008 — 13

LIVE AT MONTEREY PART 2
- CD   Status Records(E)DSTS 1009 — 5

LIVE AT NEWPORT '58
- 2CD   Columbia C2K 53584 — 16

LIVE AT NEWPORT '59
- CD   Emarcy(G&US)842 071-2 — 3
- CD   Emarcy(J)EJD-6 — 3

LIVE AT STUTTGART—VOL. 1
- LP   Jazz Band(F)EB-411 — 9

LIVE AT THE 1957 STRATFORD FESTIVAL
- CD   Music & Arts(J)CD-616 — 11

LIVE AT THE APOLLO 1944–1947
- LP   Everybodys 3003 — 1

LIVE AT THE BLUE NOTE
- 2CD   Roulette(UK)8 28637 2 — 20

LIVE AT THE CARNEGIE HALL—VOL. 1
- CD   Jazz Up(It)JU-322 — 13
- CD   Moon Records MCD061-2 — 13

LIVE AT THE CARNEGIE HALL—VOL. 2
- CD   Jazz Up(It)JU-323 — 14
- CD   Moon Records MCD062?-2 — 14

LIVE AT THE SALLE PLEYEL
- CD   JMY-1011-2 — 12

LIVE AT THE WHITNEY MUSEUM
- CD   Impulse(Eur)IMP 11732 — 12

LIVE CONCERTS IN PARIS—1958
- CD   Magnetic(F)MRCD-119 — 17

LIVE FROM HOTEL SHERMAN, CHICAGO #1
- LP   Jazz Supreme JS-704 — 16

LIVE FROM HOTEL SHERMAN, CHICAGO #2
- LP   Jazz Supreme JS-705 — 18

LIVE IN EUROPE, GUEST STAR: ELLA FITZGERALD
- CD   Musica Jazz(It)MJCD1099 — 15

LIVE IN ITALY—VOL. 1
- CD   Jazz Up(It)JU-305 — 15
- CD   Polydor(J)POCJ-1877 — 15

LIVE IN ITALY—VOL. 2
- CD   Jazz Up(It)JU-306 — 11

LIVE IN MEXICO
- CD   Tring JHD0-16 — 15
- 2CD   Gentle Price(H)GP20052 680928 — 15

LIVE IN PARIS
- LP   Magic AWE-19 — 9

LIVE IN SANTA MONICA #1

Discography 343

LP   Queen Q-069   11
LIVE IN SANTA MONICA #2
LP   Queen Q-070   10
LIVE PERFORMANCES 1953–1973
LP   Marlor Productions Ellington '86   12
LOS ANGELES CONCERT 1954
LP   GNP Crescendo(US)GNPS-9049   11
LP   Jazz Legacy/Vogue(F)500.207   11
CD   Vogue VG 651-600142   11
MEXICAN CONCERT
2CD   Gentle Price(H)GP 20052   15
MONEY JUNGLE
LP   Blue Note BT-85129   4
CD   Blue Note CDP 7 46398 2   6
CD   Liberty(J)CP32-5186   6
CD   Liberty(J)TOCJ-5347   6
MPS VARIATION 76
LP   MPS 0666 719   1
NAT KING COLE TRIOS
CD   VJC(US)VJC-1011-2   1
NEW MOOD INDIGO
LP   Doctor Jazz FW-40359   10
LP   Signature AK-40359   10
CD   Doctor Jazz(F)FDD-5002   10
CD   Zillion/Sony(Eur)1610682   10
NEWPORT JAZZ FESTIVAL(S): LIVE
2LP   CBS C2-38262   1
2LP   CBS Sony 40AP-2771-2   1
2LP   Columbia C2-38262   1
1949 BAND SALUTES ELLINGTON '90
LP   Marlor Productions Ellington '90   6
PARIS JAZZ CONCERT
2CD   RTE/UNE Musique/Europe 1(F)50 317   2
PASADENA CONCERT 1953
LP   GNP Crescendo(US)GNPS-9045   12
CD   Vogue VG 651-600105   12
PASSION FLOWER
CD   Moon Records(It)MCD074-2   12
PIANO SOLO AND ORCHESTRA
CD   Jazz Collection(It)JCD 05   12
PRIVATE COLLECTION 1-STUDIO SESSIONS,
  CHICAGO, 1956
LP   WEA(G)255.398-1   15
CD   LMR 83000   15
CD   WEA(G)255.398-2   15
PRIVATE COLLECTION 2-DANCE CONCERTS,
  CALIFORNIA, 1958
2LP   WEA(G)255.399-1   16
CD   LMR 83001   16
CD   WEA(G)255.399-2   16
PRIVATE COLLECTION 3-STUDIO SESSIONS,
  NEW YORK, 1962
LP   WEA(G)255.400-1   16
CD   LMR 83002   16
CD   WEA(G)255.400-2   16

PRIVATE COLLECTION 4-STUDIO SESSIONS,
  NEW YORK, 1963
LP   WEA(G)255.401-1   16
CD   LMR 83003   16
CD   WEA(G)255.401-2   16
PRIVATE COLLECTION 5-THE SUITES, NEW YORK,
  1968 & 1970
2LP   WEA(G)255.402-1   22
CD   LMR 83004   22
CD   WEA(G)255.402-2   22
PRIVATE COLLECTION 6-DANCE DATES—
  CALIFORNIA 1958
CD   SAJA Records 7 91230-2   5
CD   WEA(G)255.922-2   5
CD   WEA(J)27P2-2816   5
PRIVATE COLLECTION 7-STUDIO SESSIONS
  1957 & 1962
CD   SAJA Records 7 91231-2   20
CD   WEA(G)255.923-2   20
CD   WEA(J)27P2-2817   20
PRIVATE COLLECTION 8-STUDIO SESSIONS
  '57, '65, '66, '67
CD   SAJA Records 7 91232-2   17
CD   WEA(G)255.924-2   17
CD   WEA(J)27P2-2818   17
PRIVATE COLLECTION 9-STUDIO SESSIONS 1968
CD   SAJA Records 7 91233-2   15
CD   WEA(G)255.925-2   15
CD   WEA(J)27P2-2819   15
PRIVATE COLLECTION 10-STUDIO SESSIONS
  '65, '66,' 71
CD   SAJA Records 7 91234-2   11
CD   WEA(G)255.926-2   11
CD   WEA(J)27P2-2820   11
RED HOT SUMMER DANCE
CD   Red Baron RED 469285 2   7
CD   Red Baron(US)AK 48631   7
CD   Sony(J)SRCS 5932   7
RED WHITE & BLUES
LP   Rosetta Records RR-1302   1
REFLECTIONS IN ELLINGTON
LP   Everybodys 3005   11
REX STEWART—HOLLYWOOD JAM
LP   Duke 1017   1
S.R.O. DUKE ELLINGTON
LP   LRC(J)YX-7361-SL   3
CD   Denon DC-8540   4
CD   Denon(J)33C38-7680   4
SARAH VAUGHAN MEMORIAL ALBUM
CD   Milan(F)CH-311   3
CD   VJC(US)VJC-1015-2   3
SATIN DOLL
LP   Koala AW-14284   3
SATIN DOLL
CD   ZETA(F)ZET-722   12

SHOWCASE
 3LP Pathé-Marconi-Capitol(F)1551893 2
SOLOS, DUETS AND TRIOS
 CD Bluebird(J)BVCJ-5113 1
 CD RCA Bluebird 2178-2-RB 1
SOPHISTICATED LADY
 CD Crescendo/Vogue VG 671 670502 5
 CD Jazz Society VG 671 670502 5
SOUVENIR ELLINGTON CONFERENCE 1984
 EP DETS 6
STAN GETZ
 LP Raretone 5012-FC 1
 LP Musica Jazz(I)1061 1
STEREO AIR FORCE DANCE DATE 1958 #2
 LP Unique Jazz UJ-34 8
STEREO REFLECTIONS IN ELLINGTON
 CD Natasha Imports(US)IN-4016 6
STOCKHOLM CONCERT, 1966
 LP Pablo Live(J)28MJ-3464 1
 LP Pablo Live(US)2308-242 1
 CD Pablo(F)98.819 1
 CD Pablo(J)VDJ-28028 1
STUDIO SERIES, #5—1929–1956
 LP Up-To-Date UTD-2006 13
STUDIO SERIES, #6—1930-1958
 LP Up-To-Date UTD-2007 11
STUDIO SERIES, #7—1929-1962
 LP Up-To-Date UTD-2008 10
STUDIO SERIES, #8—1933-1967
 LP Up-To-Date UTD-2009 15
TAKE THE "A" TRAIN
 CD Four Star(US)FS40063 4
 same as S.R.O. Duke Ellington
TENDER LEAF TEA SHOW
 LP Joyce(US)1212 2
THEATRE DES CHAMPS ELYSEES
 2CD RTE/UNE Musique/Europe 1(F)710433/434 24
THE BRITISH CONNEXION
 CD Ellington '97 Conference Souvenir CD 12
THE POPULAR DUKE ELLINGTON
 CD RCA/BMG 68705-2 CD 1
THINGS AIN'T WHAT THEY USED TO BE
 CD LRC(US)CDC9061 9?
 CD Laserlight Digital 17 097 9?
THIS ONE'S FOR BLANTON
 LP Pablo 2310.721 9
 LP Pablo(E)2335.728 9
 LP Pablo(J)MTF-1002 9
 LP Pablo(J)MW-2136 9
 CD Pablo(J)J33J-20010 9
 CD Pablo(J)VDJ-28032 9
TRANSBLUCENCY
 CD Jazz & Jazz(It)JJ-612 8

TREASURY BROADCASTS
 LP DETS 13-7 July 1945 7
 LP DETS 14-14 July 1945 10
 LP DETS 15-21 July 1945 15
 LP DETS 16-28 July 1945 12
 LP DETS 17-4 August 1945 11
 LP DETS 18-11 August 1945 11
 LP DETS 19-18 August 1945 8
 LP DETS 20-25 August 1945 13
 LP DETS 21-1 September 1945 14
 LP DETS 22-8 September 1945 11
 LP DETS 23-15 September 1945 9
 LP DETS 24-22 September 1945 10
 LP DETS 25-6 October 1945 13
 LP DETS 26-13 October 1945 4
 LP DETS 27-13&20 October 1945 5
 LP DETS 28-20&27 October 1945 8
 LP DETS 29-27 October & 3 November 1945 14
 LP DETS 30-3&10 November 1945 15
 LP DETS 31-10&17 November 1945 11
 LP DETS 32-17&24 November 1945 14
 LP DETS 33-20 January 1946 14
 LP DETS 34-13&20 April 1946 11
 LP DETS 35-27 April 1946 13
 LP DETS 36-4 May 1946 7
 LP DETS 37-18&25 May 1946 11
 LP DETS 38-1 June 1946 8
 LP DETS 39-8 June 1946 9
 LP DETS 40-6 July 1946 9
 LP DETS 41-27 July 1946 9
 LP DETS 42-3 August 1946 12
 LP DETS 43-17 August 1946 13
 LP DETS 44-24 August 1946 17
 LP DETS 45-31 August 1946 17
 LP DETS 46-5 October 1946 & June 1943 21
29TH DEATH ANNIVERSARY
 CD Jazz Portraits(EEC) CD 14564 10
UNKNOWN ALBUM TITLE
 LP Retrival(E)FJ-123 2
UNUSUAL ELLINGTON
 LP Jazz Guild 1004 11
UP IN DUKE'S WORKSHOP
 LP Pablo 2310.815 8
 LP Pablo(J)MTF-1116 8
WASHINGTON, D.C. ARMORY CONCERT
 LP Jazz Guild 1002 8
WAY LOW
 LP Duke 1015 14
WISE WOMAN—DINAH WASHINGTON
 LP Rosetta Records RR-1313 1
WOODY HERMAN THE V-DISC YEARS #2
 ? Hep(E)35 1

Appendix 3

French RCA Integrale, Volumes 14 to 17: A Guide

When French RCA reached Volume 17 of their *THE WORKS OF DUKE INTEGRALE* series, they received complaints from the Duke Ellington estate about the use, from Volume 14 onwards, of material which had not been recorded for RCA Victor and to which, according to the complainants, they had no legal right. The recordings in question were two complete sessions out of the three which Ellington had recorded for Standard Transcriptions in the Victor studios in 1941 and a number of off-the-air recordings.

French RCA decided to delete these volumes and to reissue them without the offending material. Unfortunately they chose to do so without any publicity, and they used identical sleeve designs and catalog numbers for the revised volumes. As a result, without close examination it is impossible to tell one edition from the other. As the original issues were widely distributed before the switch, LPs of both editions are in circulation and the following listing is included to enable the reader to identify the LPs.

The original editions are of considerable value as the Standard Transcription items are heard in much better sound here than on other issues. (The third Ellington Standard Transcription session, that of December 3, 1941, was not issued on French RCA but can be heard in good sound quality on the Tax LP *DUKE ELLINGTON—THE TRANSCRIPTION YEARS, VOLUME 1,* which has also been issued on Australian Swaggie.

* * *

NOTES

1. All sessions from which disc issues have been released are included in this listing from the start of both versions of Volume 14 to the end of Volume 17 New. These are given for the sake of completeness even if the material has not appeared in the French RCA Integrale series. The Victor session of January 12, 1942, is shown complete, even though Volume 17 New uses only two titles. All sessions are by Duke Ellington and his Orchestra unless otherwise stated.

2. From the listing, the "concertina" effect of the changes can be seen clearly: the period previously covered by four LPs is now covered by just less than three. Once this principle is grasped the other facts fall easily into place.

3. Those wishing to obtain all Ellington music issued in the series will need to buy the old edition up to Volume 17 and the new edition from Volume 16, the last named for two tracks only, *Five O'Clock Drag* and *Rocks In My Bed*. This is because of a very thoughtless piece of planning by the company, as Volume 17 New has only twelve tracks and could have easily accommodated these, thus saving the people who required the complete series the expense of buying one LP for two tracks only.

4. The film recordings of *Bli-Blip* and *Flamingo* are listed here in the sequence given on the French RCA sleeves although later research indicates that they actually date from early December 1941.

December 28, 1940 (Victor)
    The Sidewalks Of New York   Vol 14 Old   Vol 14 New
    Flamingo   Vol 14 Old   Vol 14 New
-1 The Girl In My Dreams   Vol 14 Old   Vol 14 New
-2 The Girl In My Dreams   Vol 14 Old   Vol 14 New

January 15, 1941 (Standard Transcriptions)
    Take The "A" Train   Vol 14 Old   Not on New
    I Hear A Rhapsody   Vol 14 Old   Not on New
    Bounce   Vol 14 Old   Not on New
    It's Sad But True   Vol 14 Old   Not on New
    Madame Will Drop Her Shawl   Vol 14 Old   Not on New
    Frenesi   Vol 14 Old   Not on New
    Until Tonight   Vol 14 Old   Not on New

West Indian Stomp	Vol 14 Old	Not on New
Love and I	Vol 14 Old	Not on New
John Hardy's Wife	Vol 14 Old	Not on New

January 16, 1941 (broadcast; Duke Ellington and Jimmy Blanton with the John Scott-Trotter Orchestra)

Jive Rhapsody	Vol 14 Old	Not on New
Jumpin' Punkins	Vol 14 Old	Not on New

February 15, 1941 (Victor)

	Take The "A" Train	Vol 15 Old	Vol 14 New
-1	Jumpin' Punkins	Vol 15 Old	Vol 14 New
-2	Jumpin' Punkins	Vol 15 Old	Vol 14 New
	John Hardy's Wife	Vol 15 Old	Vol 14 New
	Blue Serge	Vol 15 Old	Vol 14 New
	After All	Vol 15 Old	Vol 14 New

May 14, 1941 (Victor; solos)

-1	Dear Old Southland	Vol 15 Old	Vol 14 New
-2	Dear Old Southland	Vol 15 Old	Vol 14 New
-1	Solitude	Vol 15 Old	Vol 14 New
-2	Solitude	Vol 15 Old	Vol 15 New

June 2, 1941 (broadcast; Duke Ellington and Jimmy Blanton with the John Scott-Trotter Orchestra and Chorus)

Frankie And Johnny	Vol 15 Old	Not on New

June 5, 1941 (Victor)

	Bakiff	Vol 15 Old	Vol 15 New
-1	Are You Sticking?	Vol 15 Old	Vol 15 New
-2	Are You Sticking?	Vol 15 Old	Vol 15 New
	Just a-Settin' And a-Rockin'	Vol 16 Old	Vol 15 New
	The Giddybug Gallop	Vol 16 Old	Vol 15 New

June 26, 1941 (Victor)

	Chocolate Shake	Vol 16 Old	Vol 15 New
-1	I Got It Bad	Vol 16 Old	Vol 15 New
-2	I Got It Bad	Vol 16 Old	Vol 15 New

July 2, 1941 (Victor)

	Clementine	Vol 16 Old	Vol 15 New
	The Brown Skin Gal	Vol 16 Old	Vol 15 New
-1	Jump For Joy	Vol 16 Old	Vol 15 New
-2	Jump For Joy	Vol 16 Old	Vol 16 New
	Moon Over Cuba	Vol 16 Old	Vol 16 New

July 3, 1941 (Bluebird; Rex Stewart Orchestra)

	Some Saturday	Vol 16 Old	Vol 16 New
	Subtle Slough	Vol 16 Old	Vol 16 New
-1	Menelik	Vol 16 Old	Vol 16 New
-2	Menelik	(alleged on Blu-Disc T-1003 and Fr RCA PM 42359 but aurally these are -1)	
	Poor Bubber	Vol 16 Old	Vol 16 New

same session (Johnny Hodges Orchestra)

Squatty Roo	Vol 17 Old	Vol 16 New
Passion Flower	Vol 17 Old	Vol 16 New
Things Ain't What They Used To Be	Vol 17 Old	Vol 16 New
Goin' Out The Back Way	Vol 17 Old	Vol 16 New

summer 1941 (films)

Bli-Blip	Vol 17 Old	Not on New
Flamingo	Vol 17 Old	Not on New

July 5, 1941 (broadcast)
    Raincheck | Vol 17 Old | Not on New
    Just A-Settin' And A-Rockin' | Not on Fr RCA | Rarities RAR-56

September 17, 1941 (Standard Transcriptions)

Clementine	Vol 17 Old	Not on New
Chelsea Bridge	Vol 17 Old	Not on New
Love Like This Can't Last	Vol 17 Old	Not on New
After All	Vol 17 Old	Not on New
The Girl In My Dreams	Vol 17 Old	Not on New
Jumpin' Punkins	Vol 17 Old	Not on New
Frankie And Johnny	Vol 17 Old	Not on New
Flamingo	Vol 17 Old	Not on New
Bakiff	Vol 17 Old	Not on New

September 29, 1941 (Victor)

Five O'Clock Drag	Not on Old	Vol 16 New
Rocks In My Bed	Not on Old	Vol 16 New
Bli-Blip	Not on Old	Vol 17 New
-1 Chelsea Bridge	Not on Old	Vol 17 New

same session (Bluebird; Barney Bigard Orchestra)

Brown Suede	Not on Old	Vol 17 New
Noir Bleu	Not on Old	Vol 17 New
"C" Blues	Not on Old	Vol 17 New
June	Not on Old	Vol 17 New

October 9, 1941 (broadcast; Duke Ellington with the John Scott-Trotter Orchestra)
    Take The "A" Train | Not on Fr RCA | Queen Disc Q-007

December 2, 1941 (Victor)

-2 Chelsea Bridge	Not on Old	Vol 17 New
Raincheck	Not on Old	Vol 17 New
What Good Would It Do?	Not on Old	Vol 17 New
I Don't Know What Kind Of Blues I Got	Not on Old	Vol 17 New

December 3, 1941 (Standard Transcriptions)

Stomp Caprice	Not on Fr RCA	Tax m-8037
Bugle Breaks	Not on Fr RCA	Tax m-8037
You And I	Not on Fr RCA	Tax m-8037
Have You Changed? (Blue Tears)	Not on Fr RCA	Tax m-8037
Raincheck	Not on Fr RCA	Tax m-8037
Blue Serge	Not on Fr RCA	Tax m-8037
Moon Mist	Not on Fr RCA	Tax m-8037
I Don't Want To Set The World On Fire	Not on Fr RCA	Tax m-8037
Easy Street	Not on Fr RCA	Tax m-8037
Perdido	Not on Fr RCA	Tax m-8037

    (all titles from this session also on Swaggie S-1388)

Early December 1941 (film)
    C Jam Blues (Jam Session) | Not on Fr RCA | Extreme Rarities ER-1002
    Cotton Tail (Hot Chocolate) | Not on Fr RCA | Extreme Rarities ER-1002

January 21, 1942 (Victor)

Perdido	Not on Old	Vol 17 New
C Jam Blues	Not on Old	Vol 17 New
-1 Moon Mist		—Vol 18—
-2 Moon Mist	Not on Fr RCA	RCA(E) and (US) and most other issues

Appendix 4

The Ellington Musicians and the Dates They Were with the Band

The following list does not include details of periods in (or out) of the band of less than one calendar month, or guest appearances with the band.

A

Charlie Allen (trumpet)	Jan 1935–Apr 1935
Hayes Alvis (bass)	early 1935–Feb 1938
Ivie Anderson (vocal)	Feb 1931–Aug 1942
William "Cat" Anderson (trumpet)	Sep 1944–Feb 1947
	Dec 1950–Jul 1951
	Dec 1951–Nov 1959
	Apr 1961–Mar 1962
	Apr 1962–Mar 1963
	Jul 1963–Jun 1969
	Aug 1969–Jan 1971
Russ Andrews (tenor sax)	Sep 1972–Nov 1972
Harold Ashby (tenor sax)	Jul 1968–Apr 1974

B

Louis Bacon (trumpet)	Sep 1933–Jan 1934
Ozzie Bailey (vocal)	Apr 1957–Sep 1959
Harold "Shorty" Baker (trumpet)	Feb 1938–Apr 1938
	Autumn 1942–Apr 1944
	May 1946–Dec 1946
	Mar 1947–Dec 1951
	May 1957–Sep 1959
	Dec 1961–Mar 1962
Butch Ballard (drums)	Mar 1950–Jul 1950
	Mar 1953–Jul 1953
Eddie Barefield (reeds)	Mar 1947–May 1947
Art Baron (trombone)	Aug 1973–Apr 1974
Dud Bascomb (trumpet)	May 1947–Dec 1947
Sidney Bechet (clarinet, soprano sax)	Summer 1925
as band coach c.	May 1932
Aaron Bell (bass)	Apr 1960–Oct 1962
Louis Bellson (drums)	Mar 1951–Mar 1953
	Jul 1965–Jan 1966
Joe Benjamin (bass)	Jan 1970–Mar 1970
	Mar 1970–Aug 1971
	Sep 1971–Jul 1973
	Aug 1973–Jan 1974
Bill Berry (trumpet)	Dec 1961–Sep 1962
Barney Bigard (clarinet, tenor sax)	Jan 1928–Jul 1942
Dave Black (drums)	Jul 1953–Jul 1955
Louis Blackburn (trombone)	Jan 1961–Dec 1961
Jimmy Blanton (bass)	Oct 1939–Oct 1941
Wellman Braud (bass)	Sep 1927–late 1935
Jimmy Britton (vocal)	Autumn 1942–Jan 1943
Nell Brookshire (vocal)	Dec 1970–Feb 1972
Hillard Brown (drums)	Oct 1944–Mar 1945
Lawrence Brown (trombone)	Spring 1932–Jun 1943
	Aug 1943–Feb 1951
	May 1960–Jan 1970
Dave Burns (trumpet)	Jul 1949–Mar 1950
Roy Burrowes (trumpet)	Mar 1962–Apr 1963
Don Byas (tenor sax)	Apr 1950–Jun 1950

C

Harry Carney (baritone and alto saxes, clarinet, bass clarinet)	Jun 1927–Mar 1974
Jeff Castleman (bass)	Oct 1967–Mar 1969
Bill Clarke (drums)	Jan 1951–Feb 1951
Johnny Coles (trumpet, flugelhorn)	Sep 1971–Apr 1974
Chris Columbus (drums)	Jun 1967–Jul 1967
Chuck Connors (bass trombone)	Jul 1961–Apr 1974
Willie Cook (trumpet)	Nov 1951–Mar 1956
	Apr 1956–Jan 1958
	Mar 1958–Jun 1958
	Dec 1959–Nov 1961
	Sep 1968–Oct 1969
	Dec 1969–Jan 1970
	Feb 1970–Mar 1970
Buster Cooper (trombone)	Jun 1962–Jun 1969
Leon Cox (trombone)	Dec 1961–Jun 1962
Marion Cox (vocal)	May 1946–Feb 1947
Chester Crumpler (vocal)	Jun 1947–Jul 1947

349

D

Kay Davis (vocal)	Autumn 1944–Jul 1950
Wild Bill Davis (organ, piano)	Sep 1969–Jul 1971
Wilbur De Paris (trombone)	Nov 1945–Jun 1947
Frank Dunlop (drums)	Mar 1960–Apr 1960
Bobby Durham (drums)	Mar 1967–Jun 1967

E

Bass Edwards (tuba)	late 1925–spring 1926
Jean Eldridge (vocal)	winter 1938–Mar 1939
Marie Ellington (vocal)	autumn 1944–Sep 1945
Mercer Ellington (trumpet)	Jan 1965–Apr 1974
Lu Elliot (vocal)	Aug 1949–Mar 1950
Ralph Ericson (trumpet, flugelhorn)	Apr 1963–May 1964

F

Bernard Flood (trumpet)	Jan 1946–Apr 1946
Fats Ford (trumpet)	Jul 1950–May 1951
	Nov 1959–Apr 1961
Jimmy Forrest (tenor sax)	Jun 1949–Feb 1950
George Francis (banjo)	Jan (?) 1924–Apr 1925
Wulf Freedman (bass)	Jan 1974–Apr 1974

G

Victor Gaskin (bass)	Sep 1969–Jan 1970
Matthew Gee (trombone, baritone horn)	Nov 1959–Mar 1960
	Sep 1960–Jan 1961
Dizzy Gillespie (trumpet)	Oct 1943–Nov 1943
Tyree Glenn (trombone, vibraphone)	May 1947–Apr 1950
	Jun 1972–Jul 1972
Paul Gonsalves (tenor sax)	Sep 1950–Feb 1953
	Mar 1953–Sep 1972
	Dec 1972–Apr 1974
Bobbie Gordon (see Nell Brookshire)	
Bill Graham (alto sax)	Jan 1958–Mar 1958
Milt Grayson (vocal)	Mar 1960–May 1963
Benny Green (trombone)	Jun 1969–Jul 1969
	Aug 1969–Oct 1969
Lil Greenwood (vocal)	Jun 1958–Sep 1958
	Nov 1958–Sep 1960
Sonny Greer (drums	1923–Oct 1944
	Mar 1945–Feb 1951
Jimmy Grissom (vocal)	Dec 1951–Jan 1958
Fred Guy (banjo, guitar)	Spring 1925–May 1949

H

Barry Lee Hall (trumpet)	Jun 1973–Apr 1974
Jimmy Hamilton (clarinet, tenor sax)	Jun 1943–Jul 1968
Otto Hardwick (alto, baritone and bass saxes)	1923–Spring 1928
	Apr 1932–Jun 1943
	Autumn 1943–Apr 1946
Chauncey Haughton (clarinet, tenor sax)	Jul 1942–Jun 1943
Shelton Hemphill (trumpet)	Feb 1944–Jul 1949
Rick Henderson (alto sax)	Mar 1953–Jul 1955
Gregory Herbert (alto sax)	Jul 1964–Aug 1964
Al Hibbler (vocal)	Aug 1943–May 1947
	Aug 1947–Mar 1950
	Sep 1950–Dec 1951
Johnny Hodges (alto and soprano saxes)	May 1928–Feb 1951
	Aug 1955–Dec 1957
	Mar 1958–Sep 1960
	Oct 1960–May 1970
Major Holley (bass)	Mar 1964–May 1964

I

Charlie Irvis (trombone)	early 1924–summer 1926

J

Quentin Jackson (trombone)	Oct 1948–Oct 1959
Rudy Jackson (clarinet, tenor sax)	Jun 1927–Dec 1927
George Jean (trombone)	Jan 1954–Apr 1954
Hilton Jefferson (alto sax)	Apr 1952–Mar 1953
Herb Jeffries (vocal)	Jan 1940–Autumn 1942
Freddie Jenkins (trumpet)	Oct 1928–Dec 1934
Jimmy Johnson (drums)	Mar 1959–Mar 1960
Money Johnson (trumpet)	Jun 1969–Jul 1969
	Sep 1970–Apr 1974
Claude Jones (valve trombone)	Apr 1944–Oct 1948
Herbie Jones (trumpet)	Oct 1963–Oct 1968
Nat Jones (clarinet, alto sax)	Jun 1943–Autumn 1943
Reunald Jones (trumpet)	Nov 1961–Dec 1961
Rufus Jones (drums)	Dec 1966–Mar 1967
	Mar 1968–Jul 1973
Wallace Jones (trumpet)	Autumn 1936–Feb 1944
	Jan 1947–Mar 1947
Taft Jordan (trumpet)	Jun 1943–Jun 1947

K

Ted Kelly (trombone)	Mar 1950–Jun 1950
Chubby Kemp (vocal)	Mar 1950–Sep 1950
Al Killian (trumpet)	Dec 1947–Jul 1950
Paul Kondziela (bass)	Mar 1969–Sep 1969
	Dec 1969–Jan 1970

L

John Lamb (bass)	Aug 1964–Aug 1967
Yvonne Lanauze (vocal)	Oct 1950–Feb 1951
Steve Little (drums)	Jul 1967–Sep 1967

M

Alva Beau McCain (tenor sax)	Feb 1950–Sep 1950
Murray McEachern (trombone, alto sax)	Apr 1973–Aug 1973
Howard McGhee (trumpet)	Nov 1961–Dec 1961
John Malcolm (trumpet)	Dec 1969–Feb 1970
Percy Marion (tenor sax)	Oct 1973–Apr 1974
Wendell Marshall (bass)	Sep 1948–Jan 1953
Andres Meringuito (see Fats Ford)	Mar 1953–Sep 1954
Louis Metcalf (trumpet)	Autumn 1926–Jun 1928
Bubber Miley (trumpet)	Autumn 1924–Feb 1929
Harold Minerve (alto sax, flute, piccolo)	Sep 1971–Apr 1974
Charlie Mingus (bass)	Jan 1953–Feb 1953
Anita Moore (vocal)	Jul 1972–Sep 1972
	Apr 1973–Apr 1974
Peck Morrison (bass)	Oct 1954–Jan 1955
	May 1964–Aug 1964
Eddie Mullins (trumpet)	Dec 1959–Dec 1961
	Mar 1962–Apr 1962

N

Ray Nance (trumpet, violin, vocal)	Nov 1940–Sep 1945
	Apr 1946–Nov 1961
	Jan 1962–Sep 1963
	Jan 1965–Jun 1965
Joe Nanton (trombone)	Summer 1926–Jul 1946

O

Norma Oldham (vocal)	Jun 1951–Jul 1951

P

Dolores Parker (vocal)	Sep 1947–Spring 1948
Buddy Pearson (alto sax)	May 1971–Jun 1971
Oscar Pettiford (bass)	Nov 1945–Spring 1948
	Feb 1953–Mar 1953
	Sep 1954–Oct 1954
Eddie Preston (trumpet)	Apr 1963–Jun 1963
	Jan 1971–Dec 1971
Julian Priester (trombone)	Jan 1970–Jun 1970
Russell Procope (alto sax, clarinet)	Apr 1946–Apr 1971
	Jun 1971–Apr 1974
Vince Prudente (trombone)	Mar 1972–Apr 1974

R

Alvin Raglin (bass)	Nov 1941–Oct 1945
Prince Robinson (tenor sax, clarinet)	Intermittently 1925–1927
Betty Roché (vocal)	Aug 1942–Apr 1944
	Dec 1951–Feb 1953
Charlie Rouse (tenor sax)	May 1949–Mar 1950
Ernie Royal (trumpet)	Mar 1950–Jul 1950

S

John Sanders (valve trombone)	Apr 1954–Sep 1959
Tony Scott (tenor sax, clarinet, flute)	Feb 1953–Mar 1953
Al Sears (tenor sax)	May 1944–May 1949
Mack Shaw (tuba)	Jun 1926–Apr 1927
Ernie Shepard (bass, vocal)	Oct 1962–Mar 1964
Joya Sherrill (vocal)	Autumn 1944–Jan 1946
Hal Singer (tenor sax)	May 1948–Nov 1948
Willie Smith (alto sax)	Mar 1951–Mar 1952
Rex Stewart (cornet)	Dec 1934–Jun 1943
	Sep 1943–Dec 1945
Fred Stone (trumpet, flugelhorn)	Apr 1970–Aug 1970
Billy Strayhorn (arranger, piano)	Mar 1939–May 1967

T

Billy Taylor (bass)	Jan 1935–Oct 1939
Dave Malcolm Taylor (trombone)	Jun 1970–Mar 1972
Clark Terry (trumpet, flugelhorn)	Nov 1951–Oct 1959
Juan Tizol (valve trombone)	Sep 1929–Apr 1944
	Mar 1951–Dec 1953
	Mar 1960–May 1960
	May 1961–Jul 1961

Nelson Trottman (bass)	Oct 1945–Nov 1945	Elbert "Skippy" Williams (tenor sax)	Aug 1943–May 1944
Norris Turney (alto and tenor saxes, clarinet, flute)	May 1969–Jul 1969 Oct 1969–Feb 1973	Francis Williams (trumpet)	Jan 1946–Jun 1949 Nov 1951–Dec 1951
		Nelson Williams (trumpet)	Jun 1949–Nov 1951
		Sandy Williams (trombone)	Jun 1943–Aug 1943
		Booty Wood (trombone)	Sep 1959–Dec 1960
V			Aug 1963–Sep 1963
Dick Vance (trumpet)	Aug 1951–Dec 1951		Dec 1969–Apr 1972
			Aug 1972–Oct 1972
W		Nat Woodard (trumpet)	May 1964–Jan 1965
		Jimmy Woode (bass)	Jan 1955–Apr 1960
		Britt Woodman (trombone)	Feb 1951–Sep 1960
Tony Watkins (vocal)	Nov 1966–Apr 1974	Sam Woodyard (drums)	Aug 1955–Mar 1959
Ben Webster (tenor sax)	Feb 1940–Aug 1943		Jul 1959–Sep 1959
	Nov 1948–Jun 1949		Apr 1960–Jun 1965
Arthur Whetsol (trumpet)	1923–Summer 1924		Feb 1966–Nov 1966
	Mar 1928–Autumn 1936		Sep 1967–Mar 1968
			Mar 1973–Apr 1973
Rocky White (drums)	Jul 1973–Apr 1974		
Cootie Williams (trumpet)	Feb 1929–Nov 1940		
	Sep 1962–May 1973		
	Feb 1974–Apr 1974		

INDEX

1. Titles (of tunes, songs, films, etc.) have all been indexed when reasonably useful information is revealed; casual references have been omitted.

2. Titles of individual items are given in *italics*. Titles of LPs are given in *ITALIC CAPITALS*.

3. Since Ellington's sidemen are mentioned extremely frequently, entries for them have been made sparingly and have been limited to: a) reasonably substantial references, and b) lists of orchestra personnel at particular dates. See also Appendix 4.

4. Material appearing in the 4 appendices has not been indexed.

A-flat Minor, 197
Absinthe, 230, 243, 283
Accent On Youth, 59
Accordian Joe, 38
Ace Of Spades, 55
Acht O'Clock Rock, 290, 298
acoustic recordings
   quality, 46–47
Across The Track Blues, 66, 91, 95, 99
Ad Lib On Nippon, 147, 253, 257, 270, 271

Addi, 301
Admiration, 59
Affinity label, 216
Afrique, 298
Afro-Bossa, 243–44, 246
Afro-Eurasian Eclipse, The, 297–99
AFRS (Armed Forces Radio Service), 122
After All, 101, 102, 108, 125, 273, 281, 284
Agra, 270
Ain't But The One, 249
Ain't Misbehavin', 56, 117
Ain't Nobody Nowhere Nothin' Without God, 306
Ain't The Gravy Good, 81
Air Conditioned Jungle, 120, 121, 123, 124, 143, 146
Alabamy Home, 71
ALL AMERICAN IN JAZZ, 226–27
All Day Long, 173, 273, 280
All God's Chillun Got Rhythm, 70, 71
All Heart, 196
All My Lovin', 252
All Of Me, 203, 245
All Too Soon, 90, 171, 221, 268
Allen, Charlie
   1932–36, 59
Allen, Henry "Red", 6, 34
Almighty God Has Those Angels, 289
Alternate, 164
Alvis, Hayes, 66
Amad, 270
American Airlines, 253
American Ballet Theatre, 297
American Federation of Musicians, 109, 149

American Society of Composers, Authors and Publishers, 108
Amour Amour, 301
ANATOMY OF A MURDER, 215
... AND HIS MOTHER CALLED HIM BILL, 273, 274
Anderson, Cat, 133, 136–37, 173, 209, 262
   1943–46, 121, 127, 128
   1946–50, 141, 154
   1951–56, 163, 169, 176
   1959–62, 226
   1962–65, 240, 254
   1966–67, 266
   1968–74, 293
   outstanding recordings, 211
Anderson, Ivie, 52, 59, 66, 70, 88, 107
Angelica, 230, 243
Angu, 244
Animal Crackers, 8
Anitra's Dance, 220
Antibes Jazz Festival
   concerts, 268
Antidisestablishmentarianismist, 148
Any Time, Any Day, Anywhere, 55
Apes And Peacocks, 215
April In Paris, 91, 292
Aquacades, 182
Arabesque Cookie, 219
Arabian Lover, 36
Are You Sticking?, 101, 116
Aristocracy à la Jean Lafitte, 296
Armed Forces Radio Service, 122
Armstrong, Louis, 3, 45, 129, 223–24
arrangers
   Ellington, 251
   for songs, 126–27, 135
Artistry In Rhythm, 241
Ase's Death, 220
Ashby, Harold, 293, 295, 297, 300, 304, 312
Asmussen, Svend, 247–48
Asphalt Jungle Theme, 225, 245
Assault On A Queen, 265
At A Dixie Roadside Diner, 90, 95
AT THE BAL MASQUE, 200
At Your Beck And Call, 73

353

Atlantic label, 245, 295, 307
Auld Lang Syne, 243
Aurora Borealis, 272
Autumn Leaves, 196
Awful Sad, 23, 28
Azalea, 145, 165, 223
Azure, 71, 257
Azure Te, 294

B-sharp Blues, 171
B-Sharp Boston, 152
Babs, Alice, 244, 248–49, 263, 288, 305
Baby, 55
Baby Please Stop And Think About Me, 117
Baby When You Ain't There, 52
Back Room Romp, 78
BACK TO BACK, 207
Back To School, 226
Bailey, Ozzie, 193, 217, 236
Baker, Harold "Shorty", 107, 137
    1943–46, 113
    1946–50, 141, 149, 154
    1951–56, 163
    1959–62, 226
Bakiff, 101, 103, 116, 173
Balcony Serenade, 119, 198, 282
Ballard, Butch, 169, 184–85
ballet music, 297
Ballet Of The Flying Saucers, 193
Ballin' The Blues, 170
Band Call, 173
Bandana Babies, 24
bands
    1930s, 83, 84–85
    1940s, 93, 109, 157
    1950s, 183–84
    See also names of band leaders
Bang Up Blues, 153
Banner label, 41
Barefoot Stomper, 256
Barnet, Charlie, 39
Barney Goin' Easy, 79, 279
Barney's Concerto, 61
Baron, Art, 304
Barzillai Lew, 118
Bascomb, Doug, 159
Basie, Count, 94–95, 109, 175
    collaboration with Ellington, 224–25
    influence on Ellington, 84
    One O'Clock Jump, 127
    problems of big bands, 183–84
    quoted, 163
Basin Street Blues, 168, 306
Bass-ment, 174
Basso Profundo, 149
Bateau, 300
Battle Of Swing, The, 74, 142
BATTLE ROYAL, 224–25
B.B.C. *See* British Broadcasting Corporation
B.D.B., 225

Beale Street Blues, 130, 143
Beautiful American, The, 224
Beautiful Friendship, A, 252
Beautiful Indians, The, 142, 143
Beautiful Romance, 81
Bechet, Sidney, 14, 15, 31, 53, 322–23
Beer Barrel Polka, The, 199
Before My Time, 162, 167
Beggar's Blues, 36
Beggar's Holiday (show), 147–48
Bell, Aaron, 226, 236
Belle Of The Nineties (film), 57, 64
Bellson, Louis, 163, 181, 182, 185
Benjamin, Joe, 295, 297, 300, 305, 312–13
Benny Goodman Orchestra, 82
Bensonality, 165
Berkshire Music Barn
    concerts, 192
Berlin
    1961 visit, 208
Berry, Bill, 226
    quoted, 235
Best Wishes, 54
Bethlehem label, 177–78, 179
Beyond Category, 196
BIG BAND SOUND OF JOHNNY HODGES, THE, 206
Big City Blues, 58
Big Drag, The, 172
Big Fat Alice's Blues, 255
Big House Blues, 40
Big Nick, 230
BIG SOUND, THE, 206
Bigard, Barney, 107
    1924–27, 9, 30
    1927–29, 21, 24
    1929–31, 34
    1932–36, 51, 59
    1936–40, 70
    1940, 88
    and his band, 79, 99, 103
    quoted, 28
Biggest And Busiest Intersection, The, 289
BILLY STRAYHORN LIVE!, 203
Billy Strayhorn Orchestra, 249
Bird Of Paradise, 253
Birdland (New York), 182
Birmingham Breakdown, 9, 10, 48, 58, 73
Birmingham Breakdown, New, 70
Birth Of The Blues, 294
Black, Dave, 185
Black And Tan (film), 32, 33
Black And Tan Fantasy, 3, 4
    1924–27, 11
    1927–29, 19, 20
    1929–31, 33, 39
    1932–36, 53, 64
    1943–46, 116, 119, 124
    1951–56, 172–73
    1966–67, 267
Black And Tan Fantasy, New, 72

Black And Tan Fantasy, Prologue To, 72
Black Beauty, 22, 28, 33, 81, 91, 116, 119, 124, 221
Black Bottom Stomp, 28
Black, Brown And Beige, 315, 320–321
    1943–46, 111–15, 118, 120, 129
    1956–59, 196–97
BLACK, BROWN AND BEIGE, 196–97
Black Butterfly, 70, 81, 293, 294, 299
Black Giants, 225
Black Power Blues, 293
Black Swan, 294
Blackbirds Medley, 55
Blackbirds of 1928 (musical), 54
Blackout, 61
Blanton, Jimmy, 77, 85–86, 107, 316
    1940, 88
  piano-bass duets, 91
Blem, 300
Bli-Blip, 103
Blood Count, 272, 273, 283, 309
Bloom, Rube, 11
Blow By Blow, 269
Blowin' In The Wind, 252
Blu-Disc label, 6, 7
Blue Abandon, 131
Blue Again, 41
Blue Belles of Harlem, 18, 115, 123
Blue Bubbles, 21
Blue Cellophane, 118, 119, 120, 121, 124
Blue Feeling, 57
Blue Goose, 88, 89, 91, 95
Blue Harlem, 53
Blue Is The Evening, 80
Blue Is The Night, 130
Blue Light, 74
Blue Lou, 144
Blue Mood, 54
Blue Moon, 172
Blue Pepper, 270
Blue Ramble, 53
Blue Reverie, 80
Blue Rose, 177
BLUE ROSE, 177
Blue Serge, 101, 104, 126
Blue Skies, 117, 120, 127, 142
Blue Tears, 104
Blue Tune, 4, 52, 64
Bluebird label, 92, 102, 103
Bluebird Of Delhi, 270
Bluejean Beguine, 170
Blues, 77, 165, 179
Blues, The, 245, 250, 254
    1943–46, 114, 118, 123, 129
    1962–65, 245, 250, 254
BLUES A-PLENTY, 207
Blues A-Poppin', 81
Blues At Sundown, 165
Blues Cluster, 123, 129
Blues For Blanton, 152, 171, 255
Blues For Jerry, 223

Blues For New Orleans, 295
Blues I Love To Sing, The, 19, 20
Blues In Blueprint, 217
Blues In C, 248
Blues In Hoss' Flat, 225
BLUES IN ORBIT, 217
Blues Of The Vagabond, 37, 43
Blues On The Double, 122, 127
Blues Serenade, A, 74
Blues To Be There, 153, 191
Blues With A Feeling, 23, 28
Blutopia, 120, 121, 123
Body And Soul, 91, 126, 165, 201, 222
Bojangles, 88, 89, 91, 95, 98
Bolling, Claude, 209–10
Bonga, 244
Boo-Dah, 171, 228, 273, 280
Boogie Bop Blues, 146
Boola, 111
Boola Boola, 288
bop music, 158
Boston
  concerts, 115
Boston Pops Orchestra
  concerts, 256
Boudoir Benny, 81
Bounce, 100
Bouncing Buoyancy, 76
Bourbon Street Jingling Jollies, 295
Boy Meets Horn, 74, 89, 98, 116, 117, 125, 168
Boys From Harlem, The, 81
Braggin' In Brass, 73
Brasilliance, 291
brass instruments
  growl and wa-wa, 6–7, 17
brass section
  Duke Ellington Orchestra, 133, 317, 319
Brassiere, 90
Braud, Wellman, 31, 48
    1927–29, 20, 24
    1929–31, 34
    1932–36, 52, 59
Breakfast Dance, 34, 37, 46
Brewer, Teresa, 305
Bristol, Florence, 6
Britain
    1933 visit, 56, 63–64
    1948 visit, 149
    1958 visit, 214, 233
    1963 visit, 244
    1969 visit, 292
    1971 visit, 300
    1973 visit, 305
British Broadcasting Corporation, 89
Britt And Butter Blues, 164
Britton, Jimmy, 113
broadcasts
    1936–40, 70–71, 73, 75, 76, 77, 85
    1940, 89, 91
    1942, 105

broadcasts (*continued*)
   1943–46, 118, 122–29
   1946–50, 142, 145, 151
   1956–59, 192, 198
   1959–62, 221
   1962–65, 250, 253
   1968–74, 290
   outstanding recordings, 132, 156, 179, 231
Brookshire, Nell, 300
Brotherhood, The, 306
Brown Berries, 20
Brown Betty, 151, 164
Brown, Lawrence, 63, 66, 162, 181, 240, 262
   1932–36, 51, 59
   1936–40, 70
   1940, 87
   1943–46, 113, 121, 128
   1946–50, 141, 149, 154
   1959–62, 226
   1962–65, 240, 254
   1966–67, 266
   1968–74, 293
Brown Penny, 148
Brown, Ray, 303
Brown Suede, 103, 108
Brownskin Gal In Calico, The, 102
Brownskin Gal In The Calico Gown, The, 257
Brunswick label
   1924–27, 10
   1927–29, 24
   1929–31, 34, 36, 37, 38, 40, 42
   1932–36, 52, 53, 54, 58, 59, 60, 61, 65
   1936–40, 75–76
Buffet Flat, 74
Bugle Breaks, 104, 126
Bugle Call Rag, 21, 53, 55, 64, 84, 104
Build That Railroad, 153
Bula, 246
Bullock, Chick, 41
Bundle Of Blues, 55
Bundle Of Blues (film), 55
Bunn, Teddy, 36
Bunny Hop Mambo, 173
Burris, Dick, 97
Burrowes, Roy, 240

C Blues, 103
C Jam Blues
   1940–42, 103, 104
   1943–46, 117, 126, 129
   1946–50, 142, 153
   1951–56, 174
   1959–62, 217, 223
   1962–65, 257
   1968–74, 300–301
Cabin In The Sky, 118
Café Au Lait, 197
Caliné, 244
Call Me Irresponsible, 251
Call Of The Canyon, 98

Cameo label
   1927–29, 24
   1929–31, 35, 36
Canadian TV, 253–54
Candy, 128
Capitol label
   1951–56, 169–75
   outstanding recordings, 179
Capitol Transcriptions, 130–31, 144
   outstanding recordings, 132, 155
Caravan, 49
   1936–40, 70, 71, 79
   1940–42, 98
   1943–46, 117, 119, 125
   1951–56, 164
   1956–59, 199
   1959–62, 230
Cargo By Air (documentary), 253, 271
Carnegie Blues, 114, 118, 123, 124
Carnegie Hall
   concerts
      1943–46, 111, 114, 115, 116, 129
      1946–50, 144, 149
      1966–67, 271
Carney, Harry, 31, 262
   1924–27, 9
   1927–29, 20, 24
   1929–31, 34
   1932–36, 51, 59
   1936–40, 70
   1940, 88
   1943–46, 113, 121, 128
   1946–50, 141, 149, 154
   1951–56, 163, 169, 177
   1959–62, 217, 226
   1962–65, 240, 254
   1966–67, 266
   1968–74, 293, 295, 297, 300, 304
Carnival In Caroline, 73, 80
Carrolltown dance date, 198
Carter, Benny, 54
CAT ANDERSON, CLAUDE BOLLING AND CO., 210
CAT ANDERSON PLAYS AT 4 A.M., 209
Cat Walk, 164
Catlett, Sid, 120, 125, 128
celeste solos, 299
Change My Ways, 148
Change Of Mind (film), 292
Chant For F. D. Roosevelt, 123
Chant Of The Weed, 243
Charlie The Chulo, 99, 103
Charlotte Russe, 283
Charpoy, 273
Chasin' Chippies, 80
Chat With Cat, A, 209
Chatterbox, 71, 98
Chaugogagog Maushaugagog Chaubunagungamaug, 143
Check And Double Check (film), 29, 39
Checkered Hat, 301
Chelsea Bridge, 102, 103, 103–4, 125, 255, 281

Cherokee, 242
Chew Chew Chew, 79
Chicago, 56
Chicago
   concerts, 142–43
Chicago Stomp Down, 20
Chico Cuadridino, 291
Chile Bowl, 173
Chim Chim Cheree, 252
Chimes Blues, 28
Chinoiserie, 219, 302
Chloe, 91, 98, 279
Chocolate Dandies, 48
Chocolate Kiddies, 6, 13
Chocolate Shake, 101
Choo-Choo, 7
Chopsticks, 117
Christopher Columbus, 207, 243
Cincinnati Daddy, 37
Cincinnati Symphony Orchestra, 296
Circle Of Fourths, 194
Ciribiribin, 243
City Called Heaven, A, 123
Clarinet Lament, 61, 98
Clarinet Melodrama, 174
Clarke, Buddy, 81
Clayton, Buck, 127
Clementine, 102, 125, 152, 280
Clooney, Rosemary, 177
Clothéd Woman, The, 147
Clouds In My Heart, 54, 58, 79
Cocktails For Two, 57, 170
Cohen, Alan, 113, 114, 315
Coles, Johnny, 300, 304, 313
Collier, Ron, 272
Coloratura, 120, 198
COLORS IN RHYTHM, 210
Coltrane, John, 230, 263
Columbia label
   1924–27, 10
   1929–31, 35, 36
   1946–50, 145–48, 152, 153
   1951–56, 163–64
   1956–59, 189–91, 192–94, 196–98, 203
   1959–62, 216, 217, 218–21, 222, 224
   outstanding recordings, 155, 179, 203, 231
Columbia University, 253
Come On Home, 165
Come Rain Or Come Shine, 131
Come Sunday, 113, 114, 118, 123, 129, 197, 249
Come To Baby Do, 120
Comme Ci, Comme Ca, 227
CONCERT IN THE VIRGIN ISLANDS, 255–56
Concerto For Cootie, 88, 89, 91, 95, 117, 245
concerts
   Antibes Jazz Festival, 268
   Berkshire Music Barn, 192
   Boston, 115
   Boston Pops Orchestra, 256
   Britain, 292, 300

   Carnegie Hall. *See* Carnegie Hall: concerts
   Chicago, 142–44
   Connecticut Jazz Festival, 192
   Cornell University, 144
   Los Angeles, 120, 148, 271
   Monterey Jazz Festival, 221–22
   N.A.A.C.P., 161–62
   outstanding recordings, 132, 155, 179, 204, 231
   Paris, 244–45, 254–55
   piano, 253
   Pittsburgh Jazz Festival, 256
   sacred, 249, 258–59, 263, 288–89, 305–6
   standard format, 184, 201
   tours increasingly frequent, 309
   Warsaw, 302
   Washington, 176
   Yale University, 287
Cong-go, 223
Congo Brava, 88, 95, 99
Connecticut Jazz Festival
   concerts, 192
Connors, Chuck, 236, 262
   1959–62, 226
   1962–65, 240, 254
   1966–67, 266
   1968–74, 293, 297, 300, 304
contingent groups
   Duke Ellington Orchestra
      1936–40, 69, 78–82, 92
      1940–42, 99, 102, 103
      1951–56, 164
      1962–65, 250–51
      outstanding recordings, 82, 92, 106
      post-1961, 205–9
      Strayhorn arrangements, 279
Contrapuntal Riposte, 290
Contrasts, 243
Controversial Suite, 161–66
Cook, Willie, 169, 176, 185, 217, 304
Cooper, Al, 84
Cooper, Buster, 236, 240, 254, 266
Cooper, Harry, 7
Cootie's Concerto, 61
Cop Out, 197, 206, 246
Copout Extension, 216
Coquette, 172
Coral label, 210
Cornell, Joe, 38
Cornell University
   concerts, 144
Coronets, The, 164–66
COSMIC SCENE, THE, 201
Cotton, 60
Cotton Club, 13, 27, 29, 45
Cotton Club Parade of 1938, 72–77
Cotton Club Shim Sham, 55
Cotton Club Stomp, 33, 35, 38, 75
Cotton Tail
   1940, 88, 89, 91
   1940–42, 98

Cotton Tail (continued)
   1943–46, 125
   1946–50, 151, 153
   1951–56, 168, 178
   1962–65, 248, 257
   1968–74, 301
Country Gal, 77
Cowboy Rhumba, 145
Cox, Baby, 22
Cox, Leon, 226
Creeper, The, 10
Creole Love Call
   1927–29, 19, 20
   1932–36, 53, 65
   1943–46, 117, 120, 123, 124
   1946–50, 151, 152
   1968–74, 306
Creole Rhapsody, 41, 42–44
Crescendo In Blue, 71
Crosby, Bing, 53
Crosstown, 130
CUE FOR SAXOPHONE, 208, 284
Cullen, Jack, 230

Daddy's Blues, 174
Dallas Doings, 56
dance date recordings, 97–99
   outstanding recordings, 204, 231
Dance No. 1, 147
Dance No. 2, 147, 162
Dance No. 4, 147
Dance No. 5, 147
DANCE TO THE DUKE, 175
Dancers In Love, 120, 151, 171, 198
Dancing In The Dark, 196
Danke Schoen, 251
Dankworth Castle, 214
Date With The Duke, A (broadcast show), 122
David Danced, 249, 254, 259
Davis, Kay, 137
   1943–46, 121, 128
   1946–50, 141, 149
Davis, Pike
   1924–27, 7
Davis, Wild Bill, 208–9, 292, 293, 295, 313
Day At The Races, A (film), 70
Day Dream, 92, 125, 248, 273, 281
Day In Day Out, 77
Daybreak Express, 57, 59
Days Of Wine And Roses, 252
De Paris, Wilbur, 128, 137, 141
Deacon Jazz, 7
Dear Old Southland, 56–57, 101
Decca label, 56, 297, 307
Deep Night, 165
Deep Purple, 178
Deep South Suite, 142, 143–44
Delamont, Gordon, 272
Delta Mood, 80
Delta Serenade, 57

Demi-Tasse, 79
Depk, 270
Design For Jivin', 118
D.E.T.S. *See* Duke Ellington Treasury Series label
Diane, 226
Dicty Glide, The, 34, 35, 45
Didjeridoo, 298
Diga Diga Do, 24, 55, 80
Diminuendo And Crescendo In Blue, 71–72, 123, 129, 168, 190–91, 200
Diminuendo In Blue, 142, 269
Dinah, 53, 73
Dinah Lou, 60
Dinah's In A Jam, 73, 118
Dirge, 116, 280
Discontented Blues, 174
Dixie, 55
Do Nothin' Till You Hear From Me, 88, 95, 117, 148, 244, 267, 303
Doctor Jazz, 28
Doctor Jazz label, 198
Doggin' Around, 94
Doin' The Frog, 21
Doin' The New Low Down, 24
Doin' The Voom Voom, 24, 28, 36, 75
Don Juan, 267
Don't Call Me, I'll Call You, 206
Don't Ever Say Goodbye, 172
Don't Get Around Much Any More, 88, 95, 116, 125, 148, 228, 242, 248
Don't Get Down On Your Knees To Pray . . . , 289
Don't You Know I Care?, 118, 121, 127, 221, 306
Dooji Wooji, 82
Double Check Stomp, 38, 39, 48
Double Ruff, 131
Down A Carolina Lane, 55
Down Beat Shuffle, 121
Down In Our Alley Blues, 10
Downtown Uproar, 80, 82
Drag, 288
Dragon's Blues, 56
Drawing Room Blues, 129
Dreamy Blues, 40
Drop Me Off At Harlem, 55, 66
DRUM IS A WOMAN, A, 192–93, 233
Drummer's Delight, 79
Dry Long So, 81
Dual Highway, 221
Duck Amok, 292
Ducky Wucky, 54, 64
Duel Fuel, 216
Duet, 162, 165
DUKE AT TANGLEWOOD, 258
DUKE ELLINGTON: THE GREAT PARIS CONCERT, 244
DUKE ELLINGTON: THE PIANIST, 267–68, 292
DUKE ELLINGTON: THE UNKNOWN SESSION, 211, 221
Duke Ellington and his Kentucky Club Orchestra, 9
DUKE ELLINGTON AT THE COTE D'AZUR, 268
DUKE ELLINGTON JAZZ PARTY, 203
DUKE ELLINGTON MEETS COLEMAN HAWKINS, 229

Duke Ellington Orchestra
  broadcasts. *See* broadcasts
  concerts. *See* concerts
  contingent groups. *See* contingent groups
  dance date recordings, 97–99
  development and comparisons, 317–19
    1927–29, 28
    1929–31, 45–46, 47
    1932–36, 63
    1936–40, 84, 85, 93–96
    1940–42, 109
    1943–46, 128, 133–34
    1946–50, 157–59
    1951–56, 181
    1956–59, 234
    1968–74, 311
  ensemble groups, 46
  flute introduced, 293
  name changes, 6, 8, 9, 30, 51
  Octet, 273, 289
  origins, 1
  personnel
    1924–27, 6, 9
    1927–29, 19–20, 24, 27
    1929–31, 34
    1932–36, 51–52, 59
    1936–40, 70, 83
    1940, 87–88, 94–95
    1940–42, 107–10
    1943–46, 113, 116, 120–21, 128–29
    1946–50, 141, 149, 154
    1951 resignations, 162, 181
    1951–56, 163, 169, 176–77, 181
    1956–59, 189, 234, 235
    1959–62, 216–17, 226
    1962–65, 240, 254
    1966–67, 266
    1968–74, 290, 293, 295, 297, 300, 302–3, 304
    frequent changes, 134–35, 158, 184
    long service, 83
    management by Ellington, 46, 65, 96, 108, 182–83, 278, 315–16
    qualities, 46, 96, 133, 134, 155, 157–58, 311
    See also under individual names
  reed section, 317–18
  rhythm section, 48–49, 318
  saxophone section, 318
  signature tune, 100
  transcriptions. *See* transcriptions
  trombone section, 317
  trumpet section, 133, 158
DUKE ELLINGTON PRESENTS, 178
Duke Ellington Sextet, 78
Duke Ellington Treasury Series label, 122–29
  outstanding recordings, 132
Duke Ellington Trio, 75
DUKE ELLINGTON'S CONCERT OF SACRED MUSIC, 249, 258–59
DUKE ELLINGTON'S GREATEST HITS, 244
Duke Ellington's Hot Five, 23

DUKE ELLINGTON'S 70TH BIRTHDAY CONCERT, 292–94
DUKE ELLINGTON'S VIOLIN SESSION, 247–48
DUKE PLAYS ELLINGTON, THE, 171, 175
Duke Steps Out, The, 33, 34, 36, 64
DUKE'S BIG FOUR, 304
DUKE'S IN BED, 206, 211
Duke's Jam, 206
Duke's Place, 198, 223, 257
Dusk, 89, 95
Dusk In The Desert, 72
Dust Bowl, 207

E And D Blues, The, 195
Each Day, 79
Early Mornin', 79
East St. Louis Toodle-oo, 3
  1924–27, 9–10
  1927–29, 21, 28
  1929–31, 37–38
  1932–36, 53
  1936–40, 76, 77
  1951–56, 177
East St. Louis Toodle-oo, New, 70
EASTBOURNE PERFORMANCE, THE, 306
Easy Street, 104
Ebony Rhapsody, 57
Echo Tango, The, 169, 173
Echoes Of Harlem, 54, 61, 73, 80, 91, 245
Echoes Of The Jungle, 29, 43, 46, 64
Edison, Harry, 208
Edward The First, 299
Edward The Second, 300
Edwards, Bass, 15
  1924–27, 7
Eerie Moan, 55
Eggo, 287
Eighth Veil, The, 131, 143, 164, 244
Elizabeth II, Queen, 214, 233
ELLA AT DUKE'S PLACE, 257–58
ELLA FITZGERALD SINGS THE DUKE ELLINGTON SONG BOOK, 194–96
ELLINGTON '55, 175
ELLINGTON '65, 251–52
ELLINGTON '66, 252
ELLINGTON AT NEWPORT, 190–91
Ellington, Duke [Edward Kennedy]
  as arranger, 251, 321
  as bandleader, 182–83, 278
  as composer, 3–4, 28–29, 95, 320–22, 323
  as narrator, 249, 289, 306
  attitudes to
    academic music, 93
    entertainment and show business, 45
    finance and money, 1, 2, 316, 323–24
    former associates' appearances, 268
    his age, 233, 311
    program music, 323
    race, 233
    records and recording, 1–4
    royalty, 233

Ellington, Duke [Edward Kennedy] (*continued*)
   biography, 14
      autobiography, 311–12
      death of mother, 60
      illness and death, 312
   celeste solo, 299
   fear of sailing, 63
   honours bestowed, 310
   inimitable style, 210–11
   interviews recorded, 56, 230–31
   orchestra. *See* Duke Ellington Orchestra
   piano solos
      recorded, 101, 171, 253, 267–68, 292, 303–4, 306
      technique, 7, 22, 48–49, 79, 84, 319–20
   quoted
      on Bechet, 322
      on *Black, Brown Beige*, 112
      on commercialism, 63
      on compatibility with colleagues, 316
      on *East St. Louis Toodle-oo*, 9
      on European Tour, 64
      on *Happy-Go-Lucky Local*, 143
      on *Harlem Air Shaft*, 89
      on Henderson, 47
      on Irvis, 6
      on jive, 56
      on Miley, 14
      on Morton, 322
      on string instruments, 246
   works
      earliest recorded, 5
      publishing, 84
      recording by other artists, 315
      See also under individual titles
   See also Contents List
Ellington Inc., 30
ELLINGTON INDIGOS, 196
Ellington, Marie, 118, 121
Ellington, Mercer (son), 210, 263–64
   1962–65, 254
   1966–67, 266
   1968–74, 293, 295, 297, 300, 304
   outstanding recordings, 211
Ellington, Ruth (sister), 84
ELLINGTON SHOWCASE, 176
ELLINGTON SUITES, THE, 299
ELLINGTON UPTOWN, 165–66
ELLINGTONIA '56, 206
ELLINGTONIA: MOODS AND BLUES, 209
Emancipation Celebration, 113, 114, 118, 123, 148
Embraceable You, 131
Empty Ballroom Blues, 81
Empty Town Blues, 244
ENGLISH CONCERT, THE, 300–302
ensemble groups
   Duke Ellington Orchestra, 46
Eque, 291
Ericson, Rolf, 293
Esquire Jump, 120
Esquire magazine jazz awards, 120, 129

Esquire Swank, 121, 129, 130, 279
Eulb, 300
Every Hour On The Hour, 119, 122, 127
Every Man Prays In His Own Language, 306
Every Tub, 56, 94
EVERYBODY KNOWS JOHNNY HODGES, 209
Everything But You, 119, 122, 127, 221
Everything Goes, 131
Everything Is Hotsy Totsy Now, 7
Ev'ry Day, 79, 82
Exposition Swing, 61

Fade Up, 256
Fallin' Like A Raindrop, 173
Fancy Dan, 124, 163, 164, 168
Fanfare label, 142
Fantasy label, 267, 287, 298
   outstanding recordings, 274, 307
Fantazzm, 151
Far Away Blues, 144
Far Away Star, 305
Far East Suite, 253, 254, 270
Farewell Blues, 59
Fargo dance date, 97–99
Fast And Furious, 53, 54, 65
Fat Mess, 292
Fat Mouth, 214
Fat Stuff Serenade, 79
Father Forgive, 289
Feed The Birds, 252
Feeling Of Jazz, The, 228, 230, 248
Felanges, 168
Felsted label, 208
Ferryboat Serenade, 98
Festival Junction, 191
FESTIVAL SESSION, 216
Fickle Fling, 118, 124, 131
Fiddler On The Diddle, 255
Fieldcrest Company, 289
Fields, Dorothy, 20, 24
Finesse, 75, 142
FIRST TIME, 224–25
Fitzgerald, Ella, 194–96, 257–58, 268
Five O'Clock Drag, 103, 118
Five O'Clock Whistle, 90, 98
Flaming Sword, The, 91, 98
Flaming Youth, 24, 25, 36
Flamingo, 84, 101, 103, 153, 170, 279
Flashback From The Future, 257
Fleurs Africaines, Les, 230
Flippant Flurry, 142
Flirtibird, 215, 228
Flood, Bernard, 128
Flower Is A Lovesome Thing, A, 131, 221, 257
flute
   in Orchestra, 293
Fly Me To The Moon, 251
Flying Home, 172, 175
Follow Me, 165
Fontainebleau Forest, 223

Foolin' Myself, 81
For Dancers Only, 242
Ford, Fats, 154, 163, 217
Four And One Half Street, 79
4.30 Blues, 293
Foxy label, 216
Fragmented Suite For Piano And Bass, 303
Francis, George, 6
Franco-American Festival, 297
Frankie And Johnny, 101, 102, 119, 120, 121, 126, 148
Franklin D. Roosevelt Memorial Broadcast, 123
Frantic Fantasy, 121, 124
Freeze And Melt, 35
Frenesi, 100
Frisky, 144
Frivolous Banta, 173
Frolic Sam, 79, 82
Frou Frou, 214
Frustration, 122, 123, 124
Fugue-a-ditty, 129

Gal Avantin', 81
Gal From Joe's, The, 72, 73, 77
Garry, Sid, 41
Gaskin, Victor, 293
Gathering In A Clearing, A, 130, 210
Gato, El, 202, 293
Gee, Matthew, 217
Gennett label, 8
Georgia Grind, 7
Get Happy, 164
Get It Southern Style, 79
Get Yourself A New Broom, 55
Get-With-Itness, 299
Ghost Of A Chance, 130
G.I. Jive, 118
Giants Group, 251
Giddybug Gallop, The, 101
Giganti Del Jazz label, 267
Gillespie, Dizzy, 203, 207
Girl In My Dreams Tries To Look Like You, The, 102
Girls, The, 225–26
Give It Up, 81
Give Me The Right, 172
Glenn, Tyree, 145, 149, 154, 159
Go Away Blues, 117, 127
God Bless America, 99
Goin' Nuts, 36
Goin' Out The Back Way, 102
Goin' To Town, 23, 35
Golden Broom And The Green Apple, The, 261, 297
Golden Cress, 61, 143, 145
Golden Feather, 142
Gong, 298
Gonna Tan Your Hide, 173
Gonsalves, Paul, 185–86, 191, 209, 262, 316
    1946–50, 154
    1951–56, 163, 169, 177
    1959–62, 217, 226
    1962–65, 240, 254
    1966–67, 266
    1968–74, 293, 295, 297, 300
Good Gal Blues, 82
Good Life, The, 252
Good Queen Bess, 92
Good Woman Blues, 152
Goodbye, 242
Goodman, Benny, 83
Goodyear Tires, 227, 231
Goof, 300, 302
Gordon, Bobbie, 300
Got Everything But You, 24
Goutelas Suite, The, 266, 299
Grace Valse, 215
Grainger, Percy, 63
gramophone. *See* records and recording
Grandpa's Spells, 28
Granz, Norman, 271, 303
Grappelli, Stéphane, 247–48
Grayson, Milt, 226, 236, 240
GREAT TIMES, 153
GREATEST JAZZ CONCERT IN THE WORLD, THE, 271–72, 287
Greenwood, Lil, 217
Greer, Sonny, 15, 48, 95, 162, 181
    1924–27, 6, 7, 9
    1927–29, 20, 24
    1929–31, 34
    1932–36, 52, 59
    1936–40, 70
    1940, 88
    1943–46, 113, 121, 128
    1946–50, 141, 149, 154
Grieg, E., 220
Grievin', 76, 77, 177, 279
Grissom, Jimmy, 169, 177, 186
growl
    brass technique, 6–7
Guitar Amour, 228
Guy, Fred, 15–16
    1924–27, 7, 9
    1927–29, 20, 24
    1929–31, 34
    1932–36, 52, 59
    1936–40, 70
    1940, 88
    1943–46, 113, 121, 128
    1946–50, 141, 149
Gypsy Without A Song, A, 74

Half Past Midnight Tempo, 127
Half The Fun, 194
Hall, Adelaide, 20, 55
Hall, Barry Lee, 304
Hallelujah, 306
Hamilton, Jimmy, 107, 137, 262, 290
    1943–46, 121, 128
    1946–50, 141, 149, 154
    1951–56, 163, 169, 177
    1959–62, 217, 226

Hamilton, Jimmy (*continued*)
1962–65, 240, 254
 1966–67, 266
Hand Me Down Love, 198
Handy, W. C., 23, 130
Happening, The, 164
Happy Anatomy, 215
Happy As The Day Is Long, 55
Happy-Go-Lucky Local, 142, 143, 173, 246, 254
Happy One, The, 206
Happy Re-Union, 201, 301
Hard Way, 298
Hardwick, Otto, 16
 1924–27, 6, 7, 9, 10, 11
 1927–29, 19
 1932–36, 51, 59
 1936–40, 70
 1940, 88
 1943–46, 113, 121, 128
Harlem, 161, 166–67, 246, 296
Harlem Air Shaft, 323
 1940, 89–90, 91, 94, 95
 1940–42, 98
 1943–46, 117, 125
 1951–56, 168, 174
Harlem Flat Blues, 24, 36
Harlem Footwarmers, The, 37, 40
Harlem River Quiver, 20
Harlem Speaks, 56, 65, 70–71
Harlem Suite, 161
Harlem Twist, 21
Harlemania, 34, 38
Harmony In Harlem, 72, 73, 84
Harmony label, 21
Harrison, Jimmy, 8
Haughton, Chauncy, 105, 109, 113
Haunted Nights, 36
Have A Heart, 80, 81
Have You Changed?, 104
Having At It, 299
Hawk Talks, The, 164, 168
Hawkins, Coleman, 3, 229, 263
Hayes, Edgar, 54
Hayfoot, Strawfoot, 105
He Makes Me Believe He's Mine, 148
Hearsay, 143
Heaven, 288
Heaven Can Wait, 98
Hello, Dolly!, 251, 302
Hello Little Girl, 203
Hemphill, Shelton, 121, 128, 137, 141, 149
Henderson, Fletcher, 28, 47, 84, 109
Henderson, Rick, 169, 186
Herman, Woody, 183
Hero To Zero, 215
He's The Greatest Thing There Is, 152
Hesitating Blues, 57
Hey! Baby, 130
Hiawatha, 142
Hibbler, Al, 138

 1943–46, 121, 128
 1946–50, 141, 149, 154
 1951–56, 163
Hick, 300
High Life, 24, 25
Hines, Earl, 48
Hip Chic, 74
HISTORICALLY SPEAKING: THE DUKE, 177
Hit Me In The Nose Blues, 24
Hit Me With A Hot Note And Watch Me Bounce, 121
Hit Parade of 1937 (film), 70
Hittin' The Bottle, 40
Hodge Podge, 82
Hodges, Johnny, 31–32, 162, 181, 208, 255, 261–62, 296
 1927–29, 22, 24
 1929–31, 34
 1932–36, 51, 59
 1936–40, 70
 1940, 88
 1943–46, 113, 121, 128
 1946–50, 141, 149, 154
 1951–56, 177
 1959–62, 217, 226
 1962–65, 240, 254
 1966–67, 266
 1968–74, 293, 295
 and his band, 81–82, 92, 102, 205–9
 outstanding recordings, 211
Hodges Medley, 149
Holiday, Billie, 58
Hollywood Bowl
 concerts, 148, 271
Hollywood Hangover, 122, 127
Home Again Blues, 40
Home Town Blues, 82
Honey Hush, 75, 79
Honeysuckle Rose, 94, 99, 117, 120, 126, 128, 172
Hop Head, 10
Hop, Skip and Jump, 117, 124
Hoppin' John, 164
Hot And Bothered, 22–23, 28, 52
Hot Feet, 33, 34, 35, 48
Hotsy Totsy Boys, 7
Hottentot, 24
How Blue Can You Get?, 124
How Can You Do A Thing Like That To Me?, 146
How Come You Do Me Like You Do?, 6
How High The Moon, 144, 146, 151, 306
How You Sound, 151
Hughes, Spike, 63, 64
Humoresque, 151
Hundred Dreams Ago, A, 223
H'ya Sue, 145, 151
Hyde Park, 56
Hymn Of Sorrow, A, 58

I Ain't Got Nothin' But The Blues, 118, 121, 123, 127, 305
I Can't Believe That You're In Love With Me, 80, 120, 131, 146
I Can't Get Started, 178, 222, 306
I Can't Give You Anything But Love, 24, 40, 80, 170

I Can't Realize You Love Me, 41
I Can't Stop Loving You, 252
I Could Get A Man, 148
I Couldn't Have Done It Alone, 227
I Didn't Know About You, 105, 118, 121
I Don't Know What Kind Of Blues I Got, 104
I Don't Know Why I Love You So, 60
I Don't Mind, 105, 127, 282
I Don't Want Anybody At All, 117
I Don't Want To Set The World On Fire, 104
I Fell And Broke My Heart, 148
I Got It Bad, 102, 123, 124, 191, 266, 300, 302
I Hear A Rhapsody, 100
I Left My Heart In San Francisco, 251
I Let A Song Go Out Of My Heart, 72, 73, 81, 119, 228
I Like The Sunrise, 146, 257, 274
I Love My Lovin' Lover, 165
I Love To Laugh, 253
I Met My Waterloo, 57
I Must Have That Man, 24, 55
I Never Felt This Way Before, 77, 92, 99
I Want To Hold Your Hand, 252
I Wish You Love, 227
I Wonder Why, 117
Idiom '59, 216
If Dreams Come True, 73
If I Gave My Heart To You, 173
If I Thought You Cared, 79
If I Were You, 226
If You Can't Hold The Man You Love, 8, 10
If You Were In My Place, 72, 73, 81
If You're Ever In My Arms Again, 79
I'll Come Back For More, 79
I'm Afraid of Lovin' You Too Much, 152
I'm Beginning To See The Light, 118, 121, 123, 127, 289
I'm Checkin' Out, Goombye, 76, 77, 79, 177, 279
I'm Getting Sentimental Over You, 243
I'm Gonna Go Fishin', 228
I'm Gonna Hang Around My Sugar, 7
I'm Gonna Sit Right Down And Write Myself A Letter, 206
I'm Just A Lucky So And So, 120, 224
I'm Satisfied, 56
I'm Slappin' 7th Avenue With The Sole Of My Shoe, 73
I'm So In Love With You, 41
Imagine My Frustration, 257
Immigration Blues, 10
Impressions Of The Far East, 253
Improvisation In Three Parts, 197
Impulse label, 229
   outstanding recordings, 231
In A Blue Summer Garden, 153
In A Jam, 61, 122, 125, 131
In A Little Red Cottage By The Sea, 75
In A Mellotone
   1940, 90, 91
   1943–46, 125, 129
   1946–50, 142
   1951–56, 178
   1959–62, 218
   1968–74, 301

In A Mizz, 76
In A Sentimental Mood, 59, 71, 119, 124, 171, 230, 247
In The Beginning God, 258
In The Hall Of The Mountain King, 220
In The Mood, 173
In The Shade Of The Old Apple Tree, 56, 122, 126
In Triplicate, 294
Indian Summer, 164, 178
Indiana, 130
Indigo Echoes, 59
Informal Blues, 75
International Festival of Negro Arts, 269
interviews
   recorded by Ellington, 56, 230–31
Intimacy Of The Blues, The, 273, 283
INTIMATE ELLINGTON, THE, 299–300
Intimate Interlude, 300
Irresistible You, 118
Irvis, Charlie, 6, 7, 8, 16
Is God A Three Letter Word For Love?, 305
Is It A Sin?, 172
Is That Religion?, 34, 42
Isfahan, 270
Island Virgin, 255
Isle Of Capri, 173
Isn't Love The Strangest Thing, 61
It Don't Mean A Thing
   1932–36, 52
   1936–40, 70
   1943–46, 117, 119, 120, 124
   1946–50, 145, 152
   1951–56, 174
   1968–74, 290
It Shouldn't Happen To A Dream, 142
It Was A Sad Night In Harlem, 61
It's A Glory, 43, 98
It's A Lonesome Old Town When You're Not Around, 242
It's All Coming Home To You, 24
It's Bad To Be Forgotten, 223
It's Been So Long, 118
It's Freedom, 289
It's Gonna Be A Cold, Cold Winter, 7
It's Kind Of Lonesome Out Tonight, 305
It's Love I'm In, 148
It's Mad Mad Mad, 148
It's Monday Every Day, 148
It's Sad But True, 100
It's Swell Of You, 71
It's The Dreamer In Me, 73
I've Got The World On A String, 55
I've Got To Be A Rug Cutter, 70, 305
I've Just Seen Her, 226

Jack The Bear, 88, 89, 95, 117, 125, 178
Jackass Blues, 10
Jackson, Quentin, 186
   1946–50, 149, 154
   1951–56, 163, 169, 176
Jackson, Rudy, 9, 16, 20
Jail Blues, 250

Jam With Sam, 162, 163, 168, 246, 254
Jam-a-ditty, 129, 142
Jamaica Tomboy, 214
Janet, 171, 172
Japanese Dream, 34
Javapacha, 225, 228
jazz
   and "swing," 83, 135
   beginnings, 45
   decline of big bands, 157
   evolution, 135–36, 158
   importance of recordings, 2, 315
   quality of early recordings, 46–47
   standard of playing, 47, 93
Jazz A La Carte, 79
JAZZ AT THE PLAZA, VOL. TWO, 202
Jazz Club label, 255
Jazz Cocktail, 54
Jazz Convulsions, 36
Jazz Festival Jazz, 202
Jazz Hot, Le, 74
Jazz Lips, 34, 37, 46
JAZZ PIANO, THE, 256
Jazz Pot-pourri, 74, 76
Jazz Supreme label, 91
Jazzopators (Bigard), 79
Jeep Is Jumpin', The, 82, 125, 131, 178, 229
Jeep's Blues, 81, 191, 305
Jefferson, Hilton, 186
Jeffries, Herb, 77, 88, 96
Jenkins, Freddie, 4, 24, 32, 34, 51
   quoted, 28
Jenny, 127, 131
Jig Walk, 5–6
Jitterbug's Lullaby, 82
Jive Rhapsody, 101
Jive Stomp, 4, 56, 64
John Hardy's Wife, 100, 101
John Sanders Blues, 175
Johnny Come Lately, 105, 116, 117, 125, 153, 206, 280
JOHNNY HODGES AND THE ELLINGTON ALL STARS, 206
JOHNNY HODGES AT THE SPORTSPALAST, BERLIN, 208
JOHNNY HODGES WITH BILLY STRAYHORN, 209
Johnson, Charlie, 8
Johnson, James P., 14
Johnson, Jimmy, 217, 237
Johnson, Lonnie, 22
Johnson, Money, 295, 297, 300, 304, 313
Jolly Holiday, 253
Jolly Wog, 36
Jones, 201, 202
Jones, Alberta, 8
Jones, Claude, 121, 128, 138, 141
Jones, Herbie, 254, 264, 266
Jones, Jimmy, 257
Jones, Jo, 208
Jones, Rufus, 313
   1966–67, 270
   1968–74, 293, 295, 297, 300

Jones, Wallace, 86
   1936–40, 70, 72
   1940, 87
   1943–46, 113
Joog, Joog, 152
Jordan, Taft, 121, 128, 138, 141
Jubilee Stomp, 21
Jubilesta, 71, 80
Jump For Joy, 102, 126, 144, 228
Jump For Joy (show), 101–2, 108, 118
Jumpin' At The Woodside, 225
Jumpin' Frog Jump, 118
Jumpin' Punkins, 16, 101, 102, 143, 144
Jumpin' Room Only, 119
Jumpin' With Symphony Sid, 164
June, 103, 108
Jungle Band, The, 42
Jungle Blues, 29, 37
Jungle Jamboree, 29, 36
Jungle Kitty, 255
jungle music, 29
Jungle Nights in Harlem, 29, 38
Jungle Triangle, 250
Juniflip, 199, 202
Junior Hop, 92
Just Another Dream, 79
Just A-Settin' And A-Rockin', 101, 102, 126, 151, 168, 172
Just Good Fun, 75
Just One More Chance, 225
Just Scratchin' The Surface, 199, 201
Just Squeeze Me, 102, 121, 125, 130, 142, 151
Just You, Just Me, 130

Keep A Song In Your Soul, 41
Keep Your Temper, 38
Kenton, Stan, 183
Kentucky Club, 13
Kickapoo Joy Juice, 149
Killian, Al, 149, 159
Killin' Myself, 77, 279
Kinda Dukish, 172
King Fit The Battle Of Alabam, 250
Kirby, John, 84
Kirk, Andy, 48
Kissin' My Baby Good Night, 61
Kissing Bug, The, 119, 122, 127, 282
Kitty, 148
Ko-Ko
   1940, 88, 89, 91, 95
   1940–42, 98
   1943–46, 111, 125
   1951–56, 178
Koala label, 221
Kruger, Jerry, 80
Krum Elbow Blues, 82

La Di Doody Do, 74
La Scala, She Too Pretty To Be Blue, 247
Lady Be Good, 172
Lady In Blue, 75

Lady Mac, 193–94
Lady Of The Lavender Mist, 151
Lady Who Couldn't Be Kissed, The, 71
Lamb, John, 254, 264, 266
Lambert, Constant, 23, 63, 64, 321
Lambeth Walk, The, 74
Lament For Javanette, 99
Lanauze, Yvonne, 154
Last Legs Blues, 205
Later, 162, 167, 168
Latin American Suite, 290, 291–92
Latin American Sunshine, 291
Launching Pad, 216
Laura, 178
Laying On Mellow, 293, 299
Lazy Duke, 37, 46
Lazy Man's Shuffle, 78
Lazy Rhapsody, 4, 52, 54, 58
Lenox (Mass.)
   concerts, 192
Lesson In C, A, 80
Let The Zoomers Drool, 121, 124, 205
Let's Get Together, 242
Let's Go Blues, 147
Let's Go Fly A Kite, 252
Let's Have a Jubilee, 59
Liberian Suite, The, 146–47
Life I Lead, The, 253
Light, 113, 123
Lighter Attitude, The, 113
Lightnin', 54, 55, 64
Lightning Bugs And Frogs, 215
Li'l Farina, 8
Limbo Jazz, 229, 248
Limehouse Blues, 43, 151
Linger Awhile, 92, 284
Little John's Tune, 214
Little Posey, 76, 77
Live And Love Tonight, 57
Liza, 176
London
   1933 visit, 56, 64
   1948 visit, 149
   1973 visit, 305
Lonely Co-ed, A, 76
Lonesome Lullaby, 178
Long, Long Journey, 129
Long, Strong and Consecutive, 120
Look And Listen, 124
Looking Glass, 105, 267
Lord's Prayer, The, 305
Los Angeles
   concerts, 120, 148, 271
Lost In Loveliness, 225
Lost In Meditation, 72, 80, 81
Lost In The Night, 214
Lost In Two Flats, 79, 279
Lots O' Fingers, 53, 65
Lotus Blossom, 273, 283, 301, 309
Louisiana, 24

Love And I, 100
Love In My Heart, 78
Love In Swingtime, 74
Love Is Just Around The Corner, 300
Love Is Like A Cigarette, 61
Love Like This Can't Last, 102
Love Scene, 256
Love You Madly, 153
Lover Man, 130
Lovin' Lover, 250
Low Key Lightly, 215
Lull At Dawn, A, 99, 103
Lullaby For Dreamers, 214
Lunceford Orchestra, 65, 84, 93
Lush Life, 151, 282, 284

McHugh, Jimmy, 20, 24
McHugh, Mary, 81
McKinney's Cotton Pickers, 28, 47–48
Madame Will Drop Her Shawl, 100
Mademoiselle De Paris, 227
Madness In Great Ones, 194
Magazine Suite, 121, 123
Magenta Haze, 129, 131, 142, 266
Magnolias Dripping With Molasses, 143
Main Stem, 105, 116, 117, 126, 152, 199
Majesty Of God, The, 306
Malatoba Spank, 203
Malneck, Matty, 23
Man With Four Sides, The (play), 182
Manhattan Murals, 151, 162
Maori, 37, 54
March Of The Hoodlums, 34, 36
Mardi Gras Madness, 79
Margie, 59
Marion, Percy, 304
Marshall, Wendell, 149, 154, 159, 163, 169
MARY POPPINS, 252–53
Master label
   1936–40, 69, 70, 71
MASTERPIECES BY ELLINGTON, 154–155
Matador, The, 269
Mather Air Force Base dance date, 221
Matthieu, Bill, 220
May, Billy, 274
Me And You, 77, 88, 290
Meditation, 289
Medley Of Popular Hits, 116, 144, 184, 266, 294, 310
Meet Mr. Rabbit, 206
Melancholia, 171, 302
Mella Brave, 149
Mello-ditty, 129
Memories Of You, 39
Memphis Blues, 57, 130, 143
Mendoza, 300
Menelik The Lion Of Judah, 102
Mercer label, 152–53, 164
   outstanding recordings, 155, 179
Merry-Go-Round, 55, 59, 65, 77
Metcalf, Louis, 9, 16, 19

Metronome All Out, 103, 121, 129
Mexicali Rose, 70
Mexican Suite, The, 291
MF Productions label, 199, 249
   outstanding recordings, 275
Miaow, 255
Midnight In Paris, 227–28, 283
Midnight Indigo, 215
Midnight Sun Will Never Set, The, 242
Midriff, 121, 123, 126, 130, 178, 280–81
Mighty Like The Blues, 74, 221
Miley, James "Bubber", 16–17
   1924–27, 6, 7, 8, 9, 10, 11
   1927–29, 19, 23, 24, 27
   Black And Tan Fantasy, 11, 20
   Diga Diga Do, 24
   East St. Louis Toodle-oo, 9
   excellence acknowledged, 8–9
   Flaming Youth, 25
   last years, 27
Mills Blue Rhythm Band, 54, 64
Mills, Florence, 21
Mills, Irving
   contract with Ellington, 29–30
   Ellington severs connection, 83–84
   first meets Ellington, 15
   Hotsy Totsy Boys, 7
   importance to Ellington, 45
   Master label, 69
   partnership with Ellington castigated, 233
   recorded as MC, 35
Minerve, Harold, 300, 304, 313
Mingus, Charles, 229–30
Minnehaha, 142
Minnie The Moocher, 64, 242
Minor Goes Muggin', The, 120
Minuet In Blues, 79, 279
Miró, Joan, 289
Mississippi Dry, 36
Misty Mornin', 23, 35
Mitchell, Ray, 54
Mitchell, Sue, 79
Mobile Bay, 92
Mobile Blues, 81
MONEY JUNGLE, 229–30
Monk, Thelonius, 136
Monologue, 162, 163
Montage, 113, 123, 129, 249
Monterey Jazz Festival
   concerts, 221–22, 225, 298
Mooche, The
   1927–29, 22
   1929–31, 37, 38
   1940–42, 98
   1943–46, 131
   1951–56, 166
   1962–65, 256
   1966–67, 267
Mood Indigo, 4
   1929–31, 40, 41, 46

   1932–36, 52
   1936–40, 78
   1940–42, 98
   1943–46, 116, 117, 119, 124
   1946–50, 153, 154
   1951–56, 177
   1956–59, 196
   1959–62, 221, 229
   1966–67, 266
   1968–74, 290
Mood label, 209
Mood To Be Wooed, The, 118, 120, 121, 124
Moon Maiden, 292, 299
Moon Mist, 104, 105, 123, 126, 131
Moon Over Cuba, 102
Moon Over Dixie, 52
Moon River, 252
Moonbow, 243
Moonglow, 52, 58
Moonlight Fiesta, 49, 59, 79, 164
Moonstone, 214
Moore, Anita, 306
More, 251
Morning Glory, 88
Morning Mood, 220
Morton, Jelly Roll, 28, 37, 322
Moten Swing, 172
Mount Harissa, 270, 272
Mournful Serenade, 28
Move Over, 22, 42
Mr. Gentle And Mr. Cool, 201, 228
Mr. Handy's Medley, 130, 148
Mr. J. B. Blues, 91
Mullins, Eddie, 217, 237
Multicolored Blue, 145, 201, 283, 284
Murder At The Vanities (film), 57, 64
Murder In The Cathedral (play), 274
Music Is My Mistress (autobiography), 311–12
Musicraft label, 141–42
   outstanding recordings, 155
mutes
   brass instruments, 6–7, 17
My Day, 81
My Friend, 151
My Funny Valentine, 178, 279
My Greatest Mistake, 90
My Heart, My Mind, My Everything, 197
My Heart Sings, 118, 228
My Heritage, 254
My Honey's Lovin' Arms, 118, 126, 130
My Last Goodbye, 57, 77
My Little Brown Book, 105, 125, 127, 230, 274
My Love, 305
My Man Sends Me, 250
My Mother And My Father, 249, 254
My Old Flame, 57, 170
My People (show), 249, 250
MY PEOPLE, 249–50
My Sunday Gal, 92
Mynah, 270

Myrtle Avenue Stomp, 74
Mysterious Chick, 255
Mystery Song, The, 43, 91

N.A.A.C.P. *See* National Association for the Advancement of Colored People
Naivety, 120
Nameless Hour, 272
Nance, Ray, 97, 109–10, 158, 247–48, 256
   1943–46, 113, 121
   1946–50, 149, 154
   1951–56, 163, 169, 176
   1959–62, 217, 226
   1962–65, 240, 254
Nanton, Joe "Tricky Sam," 17, 94
   1927–29, 19, 24
   1929–31, 34
   1932–36, 51, 59
   1936–40, 70
   1940, 87
   1943–46, 113, 121
   East St. Louis Toodle-oo, 9, 11
   growl technique, 6–7, 8, 9
National Association for the Advancement of Colored People, 161–62
Naturellement, 301
Negro Arts, International Festival of, 269
Neo Creole, 221, 292, 299
Never No Lament, 88, 95, 98, 116, 125
Never On A Sunday, 251
Never Stop Remembering Bill, 292
New Birmingham Breakdown, 10, 70
New Black and Tan Fantasy, 72
New East St. Louis Toodle-oo, 70
New Look, The, 149, 152
New Orleans Jazz Festival, 295
New Orleans Low Down, 10
New Orleans Suite, 295–96
New Piano Roll Blues, The, 153
New World A-Comin', 60, 115, 116, 123, 150, 266, 296
New York
   concerts
      1943, 111, 115, 116
      1946, 129, 144
      1947, 149
      1951, 161–62
      1965, 258, 59
New York City Blues, 147
New York, New York, 306
Newport Jazz Festival
   1956, 182, 183, 190, 233
   1958, 201
   1959, 216
   1966, 267
Newport Jazz Festival Suite, 153, 191
NEWPORT 1958, 201–2
Newport Up, 191
Night At The Cotton Club, A, 35, 233
Night Creature, 175, 246
Night Song, 81

Night Stick, 214
Night Time, 172
Night Walk, 164, 168, 206
Nightlife, 227
Nine Little Miles From Ten-Ten-Tennessee, 34, 41
9:20 Special, 127, 131
99% Won't Do, 249
No Greater Love, 61
No Papa No, 23
No Regrets, 228
Nobody Knows The Trouble I've Seen, 123
Nobody Was Lookin', 143
Noir Bleu, 103, 108
NORTH OF THE BORDER–DUKE ELLINGTON IN CANADA, 272–73
Northern Lights, 215, 282
NOT SO DUKISH, 207
Nothin', Nothin', Baby Without You, 170
NUTCRACKER SUITE, 218–19, 236

Oclupaca, 291
Oh Babe! Maybe Some Day, 61, 70, 73, 98
Oh! How I Love My Darling, 7
OKeh label
   1927–29, 20, 21, 22, 23
   1929–31, 36, 37, 40
Oklahoma Stomp, 36
Ol' Man River, 80
Old Circus Train Turn-Around Blues, The, 269
Old King Dooji, 74, 76, 125
Old Man Blues, 4, 34, 39, 40, 49
Old Plantation, 71
Oliver, King, 7, 28
Oliver, Sy, 65
On A Turquoise Cloud, 146
On Display, 105
On The Air, 98
On The Alamo, 127, 131
On The Sands Of Time, 118
On The Sunny Side Of The Street, 73, 127, 152, 245
Once Upon A Dream, 148
Once Upon A Time, 227
142nd Street and Lenox Avenue, 55
One More Once, 225
One O'Clock Jump, 94, 127, 131, 145, 173, 175, 242
One That Got Away, The, 129
One, Two, Button Your Shoe, 70
Open Mike, 209
Opener, The, 255
orchestra (Ellington's). *See* Duke Ellington Orchestra
Orchids For Madame, 145
Ordinary Thing, An, 207
Original Jelly Roll Blues, 28
Oscalypso, 152
Otto, Make That Riff Staccato, 121
Our Children, 227
Out Of Nowhere, 118
Out The Window, 94
Overture To A Jam Session, 142, 143, 282

Pablo label, 214, 231, 271, 299, 303, 304
   outstanding recordings, 275, 307
Paducah, 34, 48
Paradise, 151, 281
Paramount Pictorial Magazine (film), 70
Paris
   1950 visit, 209
   1958 visit, 209
   1959 visit, 216
   concerts, 244–45, 254–55
Paris Blues, 224, 225, 228
Paris, Wilbur de, 128, 137, 141
Park At 106th, 145
Parker, Charlie "Bird," 3
Parker, Dolores, 148
Parlor Social De Luxe, 7
Parlor Social Stomp, 7
Pass, Joe, 304
Passion Flower, 284
   1940–42, 102
   1943–46, 122, 123, 131
   1951–56, 171
   1962–65, 257
Pastel Period (show), 118
Pathé label, 7
Payne, Benny, 40, 41
PEACEFUL SIDE OF JAZZ, THE, 284
Peanut Vendor, The, 42
Peckin', 41, 81
PEER GYNT SUITE, 220
Pelican Drag, 79
Pennies From Heaven, 70
People Will Say We're In Love, 118
Perdido, 84, 104, 126, 131, 166, 245, 266
Perfect label, 37
Perfect Nanny, The, 253
Perfume Suite, The, 119, 120, 123, 198, 278, 282
personnel. *See* Duke Ellington Orchestra: personnel
Petit Waltz, 228
Pettiford, Oscar, 128, 138, 141
phonograph. *See* records and recording
Phontastic label, 305
piano
   recitals, Ellington, 253
   solos, Ellington
      recorded, 101, 171, 256, 267–68, 292, 303–4, 306
      technique, 7, 22, 48–49, 79, 84, 207–8, 319–20
PIANO IN THE BACKGROUND, 219–20
PIANO IN THE FOREGROUND, 222
PIANO PLAYER, THE, 306
piano rolls, 5–6
Pie Eye's Blues, 217
Pigeons And Peppers, 80
Pitter Panther Patter, 91, 121, 125, 129, 303, 306
Pittsburgh Jazz Festival
   concerts, 256
player piano rolls, 5–6
Pleading For Love, 223, 304
Please Be Kind, 165
Please Forgive Me, 74

Plucked Again, 77
Plus Belle Africaine, La, 147, 269, 301, 302
Poco Mucho, 305
Poinciana, 118
Poor Bubber, 102
POPULAR DUKE ELLINGTON, THE, 266–67
popular songs, 148, 157, 251
   arrangements, 126–28, 135
   See also under individual titles
Porgy, 55
Porto Rican Chaos, 59
Portrait Of A Lion, A, 75
Portrait Of Bert Williams, A, 89, 95, 116
Portrait Of Ella Fitzgerald, 195
Portrait Of Louis Armstrong, 295
Portrait Of Mahalia Jackson, 296
Portrait Of Sidney Bechet, 296
Portrait Of Wellman Braud, 295
Powell, Scat, 80
Praise God, 288
Praise God And Dance, 289
prayer meetings
   jazz associations, 38
Preacher Blues, 207
Preer, Evelyn, 10
Prelude in C Sharp Minor, 73
Prelude To A Kiss, 74, 119, 125, 171, 196
PREMIERED BY ELLINGTON, 170, 175
President label, 265
Preston, Eddie, 300
Pretty Little Girl, 194
Pretty Little One, 248
Pretty Little Purple Flower, The, 287
Pretty Woman, 130
Previn, André, 183
Priester, Julian, 295
Prima Bara Dubla, 201
Prime, Alberta, 7
Primpin' For The Prom, 165
Princess Blue, 202, 214
Procope, Russell, 107, 126, 138, 154, 261
   1946–50, 141, 149, 154
   1951–56, 163, 169, 177
   1959–62, 217, 226
   1962–65, 240, 254
   1966–67, 266
   1968–74, 293, 295, 297, 300, 304
program music
   Ellington's attitude, 323
Progressive Gavotte, 146, 281
Prologue To Black and Tan Fantasy, 72
Prudente, Vincent, 304, 313–14
publishing
   Ellington's works, 84
Pulitzer Prize, 310
Purple Gazelle, 243
Pussy Willow, 75, 76, 98
Put-tin, 288
Put Yourself In My Place, Baby, 148
Pyramid, 74, 81, 244, 245

Queen Disc label, 192
Queenie Pie, 312
QUEEN'S SUITE, THE, 214–15, 234
Quintones, The, 79

Rabbit's Jump, The, 82
radio broadcasts. *See* broadcasts
Raeburn, Boyd, 135
Ragamuffin Romeo, 34, 37
Raglin, Alvin Junior, 103, 107, 110, 113, 121
Rainbow Grill (New York), 273
Raincheck, 102, 103, 104, 273, 280
Rainy Nights, 7
Raisin' The Roof, 34
Raising The Rent, 55
Rarities label, 254
Ray Charles' Place, 229
RCA label, 271, 306
   outstanding recordings, 179, 274
Reader's Digest, 292
Ready Eddy, 99
Ready Go, 202
RECOLLECTIONS OF THE BIG BAND ERA, 241, 242
records and recording
   by artists other than Ellington, 315
   contrast between labels, 65
   different "takes", 65–66
   early quality, 46–47
   effect of increasing costs, 309
   Ellington's attitude, 1–4
   See also Contents List; Individual titles in main sequence; broadcasts; concerts; transcriptions
Red Carpet, 202, 203
Red Garter, 202
Red Hot Band, 21
Red Roses For A Blue Lady, 252
Red Shoes, 202
Redman, Don, 7, 34
reed section
   Duke Ellington Orchestra, 317–18
Reflections In D, 171
Reinhardt, Django, 142
religious music
   concerts, 249, 258–59, 263, 288–89, 305–6
Reminiscing In Tempo, 60, 123, 151
Rendezvous With Rhythm, 81
Rent Party Blues, 24, 37, 82
Reprise label, 239–45, 248, 251, 255, 263, 274
   outstanding records, 259
Retrospection, 171
revival meetings
   jazz associations, 38
Rexatious, 78
Rhapso-ditty, 129
Rhapsody In Blue, 242
rhythm section
   Duke Ellington Orchestra, 48–49, 318
Ricitic, The, 229
Ridin' On A Blue Note, 72, 125
Riff 'n' Drill, 124, 131

Riff Staccato, 119, 127
Right On Togo, 301
Ring Dem Bells
   1929–31, 39, 40
   1932–36, 65
   1940, 91
   1940–42, 100
   1943–46, 116, 117, 124
   1946–50, 143
   1951–56, 162
River And Me, The, 41
River Seine, 228
River, The, 297
Roach, Max, 229–30
Robbins, Jack, 84
Robertson, Dick, 38, 39, 40
Robinson, Prince, 17
   1924–27, 7, 8, 9
Roché, Betty, 108, 110, 113, 118
Rock City Rock, 197
Rock Skippin' At The Blue Note, 165, 274, 280
Rockabye River, 117, 129, 151
Rockin' Chair, 41
Rockin' In Rhythm
   1929–31, 34, 41, 42
   1932–36, 55
   1936–40, 70, 71, 75
   1940–42, 98
   1943–46, 116, 117, 124
   1946–50, 151
   1951–56, 173
   1962–65, 245, 251
   1968–74, 293
Rocks In My Bed, 103, 124
Rocky Mountain Blues, 40, 49
Romp, The, 128
Roosevelt Memorial Broadcast, 123
Rose Of The Rio Grande, 73, 76, 99, 116, 246, 268–69
Rose Room, 53, 56, 73, 90, 117, 284
Roulette label, 203, 223
   outstanding recordings, 204, 231
Royal Ancestry, 196
Royal Garden Blues, 130
Rubin, Al, 295
Rude Interlude, 56
Rug Cutters (Williams), 80–81
Rug Cutter's Swing, 98
Rugged Romeo, 129, 131
Rumpus In Richmond, 90, 98, 323
Runnin' Wild, 40
Russell, Louis, 38, 48
Rutledge, Leroy, 7

sacred music
   concerts, 249, 258–59, 263, 288–289, 305–6
Saddest Tale, 4, 58
Sailboat In The Moonlight, A, 81
St. James Infirmary Blues, 37
St. Louis Blues
   1927–29, 23

St. Louis Blues (continued)
   1932–36, 53, 57
   1940, 91, 99
   1943–46, 130
   1946–50, 143, 144, 152
   1956–59, 201
Sam Woodyard's Blues, 267
Sampson, Edgar, 10
San Juan Hill, 79
San Remo, 289
Sanders, John, 176, 186–87
Saratoga Swing, 35, 46, 103
Satin Doll, 170, 199, 252, 290, 293
Saturday Night Function, 24, 25, 28, 36
saxophone section
   Duke Ellington Orchestra, 318
Scattin' At The Cotton Club, 70
Schwiphti, 222
Sears, Al, 118, 121, 128, 139, 141, 149
Second Line, 295
Second Portrait Of The Lion, 256
SECOND SACRED CONCERT, 288–89
Second Time Around, The, 251
See See Rider, 303
Segue In C, 225
Self-Portrait Of The Bean, 229
Sempre Amore, 243
Sentimental Journey, 241
Sentimental Lady, 105, 117, 126, 271
Sepia Panorama, 90, 91, 94, 95, 96, 98
September Song, 172
Serenade To Sweden, 75, 76, 248–49, 294, 305
Sergeant Was Shy, The, 76, 77, 89, 91
Serious Serenade, 173
SESAC, 213, 231
Sharpie, 80
Shaw, Mack, 8, 9, 15
She, 164
She Was A Thinking Thing, 213
She Wouldn't Be Moved, 151
Sheik Of Araby, The, 53, 61, 98
Shepard, Ernie, 240, 262, 264
Shepherd, The, 267, 272, 289
Sherman Shuffle, 105
Sherrill, Joya, 108, 118, 121, 139
She's Gone, 81
Shoe Shine Boy, 61
Shout 'Em Aunt Tillie, 38
Showboat Shuffle, 59
SIDE BY SIDE, 207
sidemen. *See* Duke Ellington Orchestra: personnel
Sidewalks Of New York, 98, 99–100
signature tune
   Duke Ellington Orchestra, 100
Silk Lace, 244
Silvery Moon And Golden Sands, 81
Sinatra, Frank, 239, 265, 274
Singin' In The Rain, 146
Single Petal Of A Rose, The, 215
Sissle, Noble, 93

Sister Suffragette, 253
Six Or Seven Times, 36
Skillipoop, 254
Skin Deep, 166, 168, 191, 268
Skrontch, The, 73
Skunk Hollow Blues, 82
Sky Fell Down, The, 196
Slap Happy, 74, 91, 98
Sleep, Sleep, Sleep, 242
Sleeping Lady And The Giant Who Watches Over Her, The, 291
Slip Of The Lip, A, 105, 117
Slippery Horn, 53, 55, 65
Sloppy Joe, 35, 103
Slow Blues, 267
Smada, 165, 217, 228, 274, 280
Smile, 173
Smith, Billy, 41
Smith, Jabbo, 20
Smith, Stuff, 195
Smith, Willie, 162–63, 187
Smith, Willie "The Lion", 14
Smoke Rings, 241
SMOOTH ONE, THE, 208
Smorgasbord And Schnapps, 75
Snader Telefocal Transcriptions, 169
Snake Hip Dance, 36
Snibor, 149, 152, 273, 281
Snowden, Elmer, 13
So, 222
So Far, So Good, 88, 89
So Little Time, 251
Society of European Stage Authors and Composers, 213
Soda Fountain Rag, 5, 254
Solace, 79
Solid Old Man, 75, 79, 91, 125, 129, 142
Soliloquy, 11
Solitude
   1932–36, 57, 58, 65
   1936–40, 71, 78
   1940–42, 101
   1943–46, 119, 124
   1946–50, 153, 154
   1959–62, 230
   1966–67, 267
SOLITUDE, 196
Solveig's Song, 220
Some Of These Days, 64
Some Saturday, 102
Some Summer Fun, 299
Somebody Loves Me, 117
Someone, 105, 126, 131, 196
Something, 299
Something About Believing, 288
Something To Live For, 75, 76, 125, 165, 221, 257, 282
Song And Dance, 272, 273
Song Of The Cotton Field, 10
songs, 148, 157
   arrangements 126–28, 135, 251
   Ellington as composer, 323
   See also under individual titles

Sonnet For Caesar, 193
Sonnet For Hank Cinq, 193
Sonnet For Sister Kate, 194
Sonnet In Search Of A Moor, 194
Sonnet Of The Apple, 288
Sono, 129
Sophisticated Lady
   1932–36, 55, 56
   1936–40, 70, 71, 78
   1940, 91, 98
   1943–46, 119, 125
   1946–50, 153, 154
   1966–67, 267
   1968–74, 300, 303
Sophistication, 120
SOUL CALL, 268
Soul Soothing Beach, 301
SPACEMEN, 218, 305
Speak To Me Of Love, 227
Sponge Cake And Spinach, 79
Spoonful Of Sugar, A, 252
S'posin', 151
Springtime In Africa, 222
Squaty Roo, 102
Stack O'Lee Blues, 21
Standard Transcriptions, 100, 102, 104
Stanza I, 297
Stanza II, 297
Stanza III, 297
Star Blues, 218
Star-Crossed Lovers, The, 194, 245
Stardust, 99, 170
Stardust label, 144
Stars, 54
Stay Awake, 252
Step In Time, 253
Steppin' Into Swing Society, 8, 83, 210
Stevedore Stomp, 35, 48
Stevedore's Serenade, The, 74
Stevie, 230
Stewart, Rex, 66–67, 316
   1932–36, 59
   1936–40, 70
   1940, 87
   1943–46, 113, 121
   and his band, 78–79, 92, 102
Still Water, 214
Stockholm
   1939 visit, 75
Stomp Caprice, 104
Stomp For Beginners, 120
Stomp, Look And Glisten, 149
Stomp, Look And Listen, 146, 149, 178
Stompin' At The Savoy, 172
Stompy Jones, 57, 66, 79, 91, 98, 125, 178
Stone, Fred, 295
Stormy Weather, 55, 56, 78, 170
Strange Feeling, 120, 123, 282, 284
Stranger On The Shore, 252

Strayhorn, Billy, 86, 108, 273, 277–85
   1940, 88
   1943–46, 113, 121, 125–26, 128
   1946–50, 141, 149, 154
   1951–56, 163, 169, 177
   1959–62, 217, 226
   1962–65, 240, 254
   death affects Ellington, 309
   and his band, 249
   outstanding recordings, 211
   quoted, on co-operation with Ellington, 277
String Along With Strings, 248
Strollers, The, 105
Subtle Lament, 75, 91
Subtle Slough, 102, 121, 123, 125, 130
Suburban Beauty, 197
Suburbanite, The, 124, 129, 131
Such Sweet Thunder, 193–94, 233, 234
Sucrier Velours, Le, 215
Suddenly It Jumped, 120, 123, 124, 130, 151
Sugar Hill Penthouse, 114, 118, 123, 300
Sugar Hill Shim-Sham, 78
Sugar Rum Cherry, 219
Suite Ditty, 129
Suite For Swinging, 253, 271
Suite Thursday, 221–22, 245
Sultry Serenade, 146, 164, 168
Sultry Sunset, 142, 143
Summertime, 117, 178, 222
Sump'n 'Bout Rhythm, 58
Sunset And The Mocking Bird, 215
Sunswept Saturday, 215
Supercalifragilisticexpialidocious, 253
Supreme Being, 288
Swamp Drum, 164, 283
Swamp Fire, 130
Swampy River, 22, 54
Swannee River Rhapsody, 52
Swannee Shuffle, 36
Sweatman, Wilbur, 13
Sweden
   1939 visit, 75, 200
Sweet Adeline, 226
Sweet And Pungent, 283
Sweet Chariot, 40–41
Sweet Dreams Of Love, 38
Sweet Fat And That, 289
Sweet Jazz O'Mine, 38
Sweet Lorraine, 256
Sweet Mama, 37, 39
"swing"
   and jazz, 83, 135, 157
Swing, Baby, Swing, 78
Swing House label, 216
Swing label, 130
Swing Low, 54
Swing Pan Alley, 80
Swing Session, 71
Swing Shifters Swing, 105
Swingers Get The Blues Too, The, 218

Swinger's Jump, The, 218
Swingin' In The Dell, 82
Swingin' On The Campus, 82
Swinging The Blues, 94
Swingtime in Honolulu, 73, 80
Symons, Norman, 272
Symphomaniac, 151
Symphonette, 114, 300
SYMPHONIC ELLINGTON, THE, 246–47
Symphony In Black (film), 58, 64
Syncopated Shuffle, 37

Taffy Twist, 228
Taj Mahal, 270
Take It Easy, 21
Take Love Easy, 148
Take The "A" Train
    1940–42, 100, 101
    1943–46, 129, 131
    1946–50, 151, 152
    1951–56, 162, 166
    1956–59, 206
    1962–65, 247
    1966–67, 266, 272
    Strayhorn composition, 84, 108, 280
Take The Coltrane, 230
"takes"
    recordings, 65–66
Tang, 298
Tangerine, 105
Tap Dancer's Blues, 267
Tapioca, 79, 279
Tattooed Bride, The, 150, 153, 323
Tatum, Art, 284
Taylor, Billy, 59, 66, 70
Taylor, Dave, 295
Taylor, Malcolm, 297, 300
Tchaikovsky, P. I., 218–19
Tea And Trumpets, 78
Tea For Two, 117, 131
Teagarden, Jack, 317
Teardrops In The Rain, 121, 127
Telecasters, The, *194*
television broadcasts. *See* broadcasts
Tell Me It's The Truth, 258–59
Tell You What I'm Gonna Do, 120
Tempo Music, 84
Tenderly, 168, 196
Tenz, 300
Terry, Clark, 169, 176, 187
    quoted, 182
Tetco label, 289
Texas Blues, 206
Texas Shuffle, 94
T.G.T.T., 289
Thanks For The Beautiful Land On The Delta, 295
That Lindy Hop, 40
That Rhythm Man, 36
That's The Blues, Old Man, 92
Them There eyes, 41, 65

Theme For Trambeam, 174
Theme Medley, 149
There Shall Be No Night, 90, 98
There's A Lull In My Life, 71
Things Ain't What They Used To Be
    1940–42, 102, 105, 110
    1943–46, 117, 120, 126
    1946–50, 144
    1951–56, 168, 171, 173
    1956–59, 200
    1962–65, 245, 255
    1968–74, 302
THIRD SACRED CONCERT – THE MAJESTY OF GOD, 305–6
THIS ONE'S FOR BLANTON, 303–4
Thomas, George, 8
Those Bells, 115
Three Black Kings, 306, 312
Three Blind Mice, 73
Three Cent Stomp, 117, 124, 146, 151
Three J's Blues, 217
Three Little Words, 39, 40 170
Threesome, 162, 163
Tiger Rag, 24, 64, 73, 80, 168, 306
Tigress, 244, 283
Time's A-Wastin', 120, 126
Timon Of Athens, 253, 256
Tina, 291, 292
Ting-A-Ling, 164
Tip Toe Topic, 131
Tired Socks, 82
Tishomingo Blues, 23
Tizol, Juan, 36, 37, 49, 94
    1932–36, 51, 59
    1936–40, 70
    1940, 87
    1943–46, 113
    1951–56, 163, 169
To You, 225
Toasted Pickle, 81
Togo Brava Suite, 300–302
TOM label, 294
Tonal Group, A, 129, 142
Tone Parallel To Harlem, A, 161, 166–67
Tonight I Shall Sleep, 118, 119, 120, 124, 221
Tonk, 129, 153
Too Good To Title, 289
Too Much In Love, 118
Toot Suite, 202
Toot Toot Tootie Toot, 219
Tootin' Through The Roof, 77, 91, 94, 125, 151
Top And Bottom, 81
Total Jazz, 196
Tough Truckin', 59
Tourist Point Of View, 270
Towers, Jack, 97
Transblucency, 123, 124, 129, 130, 131
transcriptions
    1940–42, 100, 102, 104
    1943–46, 117, 121, 122, 130–31
    1946–50, 144

1951–56, 169
1959–62, 213
defined, 85
outstanding recordings, 106, 132
Travis Air Force Base dance dates, 198–99
Trees, 64
Trent, Jo, 7
Triangle, The, 58
Tribal, 152
Tricky's Licks, 248
Triple Play, 149
Trombone Blues, 7
trombone section
    Duke Ellington Orchestra, 317
Trombone Trio, 174
Trombonio-Bustoso-Issimo, 268
Troubled Waters, 57
Truckin', 60
True, 298
Trumpet In Spades, 61, 116, 125
Trumpet No End, 117, 142, 143, 151
trumpet section
    Duke Ellington Orchestra, 133, 158
T. T. On Toast, 74
Tulip Or Turnip, 142
Turcaret (play), 224
Turney, Norris, 293, 295, 297, 300, 314
Tutti For Cootie, 245, 256, 293
Tuxedo Junction, 241
TV broadcasts. *See* broadcasts
Twelfth Street Rag, 42
Twelfth Street Rag Mambo, 173
Twitch, The, 267
Twits And Twerps, 61, 74
Two O'Clock Jump, 127, 145
Tymperturbably Blue, 203
Tyrolean Tango, 173

Ultra Blue, 122, 124, 127
Ultra De Luxe, 172
Ultra Violet, 124
U.M.M.G., 178, 273, 281
Unbooted Character, 124, 131, 143, 177, 178
Under Paris Skies, 227
Under The Balcony, 198
Underneath The Harlem Moon, 66
Unique Jazz label, 273
United Artists label, 229, 231, 288, 300
    outstanding recordings, 307
Until I Met You, 225
Until Tonight, 100
Up And Down, Up And Down, 194
UP IN DUKE'S WORKSHOP, 299
Up-To-Date label, 6
Upper Manhattan Medical Group, 178, 273, 281
Uptown Downbeat, 61
Utt-da-zay, 79
UWIS Suite, The, 302

V-Discs, 117–18

Vagabonds, 165
Valburn, Jerry, 122
Vance, Dick, 187
Vancouver
    1970 visit, 294
Vapor, 216
Varese label, 230
Variety label, 69, 78
Velvet Tone label, 37, 39
Verve label, 194–95, 206–8, 257, 268
    outstanding recordings, 204, 211, 274
Victor label
    1924–27, 9, 10
    1927–29, 20, 20–21, 24
    1929–31, 34, 35, 36, 38, 39, 41, 43
    1932–36, 52, 54, 65
    1940, 85–86, 87–92, 99
    1941–42, 101–5
    1943–46, 118–20, 129–30
    1962–65, 258
    1966–67, 266–67, 270
    outstanding recordings, 105–6, 132
Violet Blue, 144, 201, 205, 283
V.I.P.s Boogie, 162, 163
Virgen De La Macarena, La, 173
Virgin Islands Suite, 255
Virgin Jungle, 255
Viti, El, 266, 269
Vivi, 199
Vocalion label, 9, 10, 21
Volupté, 244

wa-wa brass, 6–7, 17
Wailing Interlude, 199
Wait For Me Mary, 118
Waiting For The Duke, 207, 243
Walkin' And Singin' The Blues, 198
Wall Street Wail, 37, 38
Waltz You Saved For Me, The, 241
Wanderlust, 82, 229, 292, 299
Wang Wang Blues, 40
"Wanna Go Back Again" Blues, 8
Ware, Ozzie, 23, 24
Warm Valley, 91, 98, 99, 126, 168, 171, 230
Warsaw
    concerts, 302
Washington
    concerts, 176
Washington Wobble, 19, 20
Washingtonians, The, 6, 7, 8, 13, 15
Watch The Birdie, 80
Watch Your Cue, 284
Watchin', 80
Watermelon Man, 74
Watkins, Tony, 293, 300
Way Down Yonder In New Orleans, 98
Way Early Subtone, 215
Way Low, 76, 125
We Speak The Same Language, 227
Webb, Chick, 84, 93–94

Webster, Ben, 85–86, 96, 108
   1940, 88
   1943–46, 113
   1946–50, 149
Weely, 76
West Indian Dance, 113, 114, 118, 123
West Indian Pancake, 269
West Indian Stomp, 100
West, Mae, 57
Wham, 99
What A Country!, 227
What Am I Here For?, 105, 116, 126, 228, 257
What Are You Going To Do When The Bed Breaks Down?, 5, 254
What Can A Poor Fellow Do?, 20
What Color Is Virtue?, 250
What Good Am I Without You?, 41, 292
What Good Would It Do?, 104
What More Can I Say?, 172
What You Gonna Do When The Bed Breaks Down?, 5, 254
When A Black Man's Blue, 41
When All Our Pulses, 254
When Cootie Left The Duke, 107
When It's Sleepy Time Down South, 241
When My Sugar Walks Down The Street, 73
When You're Smiling, 37, 65
Where Or When, 196
Whetsol, Arthur, 32
   1927–29, 21, 23, 24, 29
   1929–31, 34
   1932–36, 51
Which Way?, 226
Whispering Grass, 91, 98–99
White, Rocky, 305, 314
Who Knows, 171
Who Said "It's Tight Like That"?, 35
Who Struck John?, 144
Wild Man, 224
WILL THE BIG BANDS EVER COME BACK?, 240, 241
Will You Be There?, 249
Williams, Cootie, 49, 107, 240, 262, 264
   1929–31, 34, 36, 41
   1932–36, 51, 59
   1936–40, 70, 72
   1940, 87
   1962–65, 240, 254
   1966–67, 266
   1968–74, 293, 295, 297, 300
   and Rug Cutters, 80–81
Williams, Elbert, 118, 139
Williams, Francis, 128, 139, 141, 149, 158

Williams, Nelson, 154, 156, 163
Williams, Spencer, 23
Willow Weep For Me, 196
Wilson, Gerald, 220
Without A Song, 92, 170
Woman And A Man, A, 148
Women, Women, Women, 148
Wonder Of You, The, 120
Wood, Booty, 217, 237, 295, 300
Woodchopper's Ball, 241
Woode, Jimmy, 217, 237
Woodman, Britt, 163, 169, 176, 184, 187, 217
Woods, 307
Woods, Jimmy, 177
Woodyard, Sam, 176, 219, 226, 237, 263, 319
   1951–56, 177
   1959–62, 226
   1962–65, 240, 254
   1966–67, 266
Work Song, 113, 118, 123
Workin' Blues, 250
World Is Waiting For The Sunrise, The, 152
WORLD OF DUKE ELLINGTON, THE, VOL. TWO, 197
World Transcriptions, 117, 121, 122
   outstanding recordings, 132

YALE CONCERT, 287–88
Yearning For Love, 61
Yellow Dog Blues, 23
You And I, 104
You Can Count On Me, 76
You Can't Run Away From Love Tonight, 71
You Dirty Dog, 229
You Don't Love Me No More, 130
You Gave Me The Gate, 73
You Got It Coming, 206
You Gotta Crawl Before You Walk, 148
You never Know The Things You Miss, 121
You Of All People, 152
You Oughta, 151
You Took Advantage Of Me, 98
You Walked Out Of The Picture, 81
You Went To My Head, 73
You, You Darlin', 88
You'll Never Go To Heaven, 81
You'll Never Know, 118
Young, Trummy, 223
Your Love Has Faded, 77, 279
You're Lucky To Me, 40
Ysaguirre, Bob, 7